Key to atlas pages 18-143

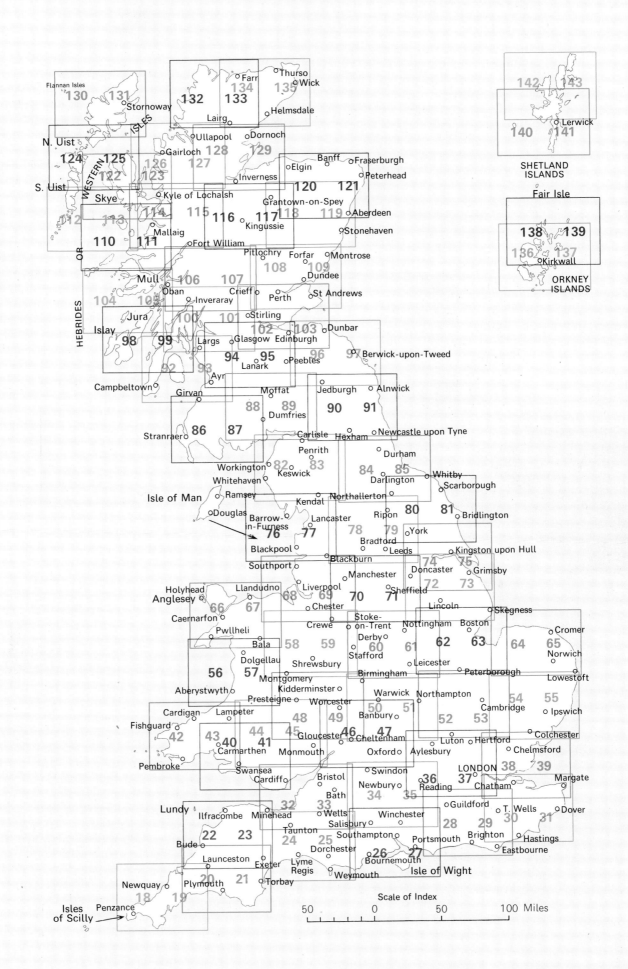

SHETLAND ISLANDS

ORKNEY ISLANDS

Fair Isle

HEBRIDES

Scale of Index

50   0   50   100 Miles

The Ordnance Survey
ATLAS
of Great Britain

The Ordnance Survey
ATLAS
of Great Britain

Book Club Associates

London

1:250 000 maps and index made by the Ordnance Survey, Southampton

Maps on endpapers, pages 14-143, 180-224 © Crown Copyright 1982

Arrangement and all other material
© The Hamlyn Publishing Group Ltd. 1982

This edition published 1983 by Book Club Associates
by arrangement with

Ordnance Survey   and   Country Life Books
an imprint of Newnes Books
Astronaut House, Feltham,
Middlesex, England.

First published 1982

Printed in Great Britain

Contents

Introduction

William Somerville, writing in 1735, described Britain as a 'highly favoured isle'. Today, we may still agree that, while there are many problems of a man-made kind, in most respects Britain is indeed a fortunate country geographically. Its island position near to but separate from Western Europe, its temperate climate, generally plentiful rainfall, great variety of rock types, land forms and soils, its resources of coal and iron, clays and limestones, natural gas and oil, provide a great range of opportunities.

Few areas in the world of similar size offer so great a diversity both of physical and of human characteristics as does Britain. Contrast the remote hamlets of the Scottish Highlands with the thronging streets of Glasgow or London, the open arable lands of East Anglia with the upland grazings of the hills, the industrial landscapes of the Black Country or West Yorkshire with the rural areas that surround them, the New Towns of today with cities, like York, which preserve the fabric of medieval times. The traveller, using this atlas, will be aware, every few miles, of change in the landscape around him. Each observation, each view provokes questions about the evaluations of environment that have been made by people in the past and about the origins of the present use of land. How can we make the best use of the land of Britain today, using it and all its resources fully yet wisely, matching the desire to exploit with the need to conserve?

Diversity of Physical Conditions

Even a swift glance at the relief map shows clear evidence of variety in the contrast between the generally high relief of western and northern Britain and the lower lands of the east and south. Geographers have drawn a broad division between the Highland Zone and the Lowland Zone, separated by an imaginary line drawn across the country from the estuary of the River Tees to that of the Exe. The distinction is not complete for west of the Tees-Exe line there are areas of Lowland, for example in Cheshire and Lancashire and in the Midland Valley of Scotland, while in the Lowland Zone there are uplands and sharp ridges which at points rise to above or near to 305 m (1000 ft). But land over that height dominates in the Highland Zone; there are outstanding mountains such as Ben Nevis (1343 m 4406 ft) and Snowdon (1085 m 3560 ft) and the plains and valleys interrupt or break the generally highland character of the relief.

To a large extent this division reflects geological characteristics. The Highlands are composed mainly of old rocks, primarily of Pre-Cambrian and Palaeozoic ages, which have been folded and fractured in the great Caledonian and Hercynian (Armorican) earth movements and heavily eroded over very long periods of time. The rocks of the Lowland Zone are mainly sedimentary rocks of Mesozoic or Tertiary ages and have been folded into scarplands. The Lowlands have been likened to 'a grained surface' of sawn timber, alternating belts with varied powers to resist denudation—'grained wood, worn with age'. Even in a nearly continuous outcrop there are many differences in the height and form of the scarps; the local geological structures vary as do the soils. A full understanding of the land forms in much of Britain must also embrace a knowledge of events subsequent to the deposition and folding of the rocks, especially the effects of the Ice Age, changes in levels of land and sea and erosional processes. Having been the locations of ice caps during the Ice Age, the Highlands bear the clearest signs of glacial erosion: corries or cwms in the mountains, characteristically U-shaped valleys, *roches moutonnées*, hanging valleys. The effects of deposition of materials by ice may also be seen in the Highlands, but these are still more widely exhibited in the Lowlands, by the widespread glacial drifts of the Midlands and East Anglia where deposits of boulder clay smooth the relief and obscure the underlying rocks. The ice sheets and their deposits also altered patterns of drainage and the present courses of rivers such as the Thames, Severn and Warwickshire Avon are, in part, the products of the Ice Age. Even in the areas south of the Thames which were not covered by ice sheets, the effects of near-glacial conditions may be discerned.

The idea of a division into Highland and Lowland Zones is thus a useful way to begin the study of the geography of Britain. Yet there are great differences within the Highland Zone itself, between areas such as Snowdonia or the Scottish Highlands with summits rising to over 1000 m (3300 ft) where sharp relief is a product of geological fracturing and glaciation, and many other extensive areas of the Zone with smoother relief and high-level plateau-like land forms. We may instance the Southern Uplands of Scotland, many parts of the Pennines or the plateau of mid-Wales. For such areas B. W. Sparks has suggested the term Upland Britain, so giving a threefold regional division: Highland, Upland and Lowland.

Regional Contrasts in Climate

Our climate may be a source of both humour and annoyance but, despite occasional extreme events, it is another aspect of the favourability of Britain's physical geography. It is greatly influenced by Britain's maritime situation just off the western edge of the Eurasian land mass. It has been said that, climatically, 'Britain is a battleground', invaded and conquered by one air mass itself soon to be re-conquered by another. The four chief, but not the only, types of air mass are Tropical Maritime, Tropical Continental, Polar Maritime and Polar Continental. Each brings its own type of weather and the battles join along 'fronts', bringing a sequence of sometimes frequent and possibly stormy changes in the weather. There is much variability of weather from day to day and place to place, providing a constant topic of conversation and, according to one's point of view on particular occasions, delight or frustration.

In terms of a world classification of climates the whole island lies within the cool temperate type. Nevertheless notable differences may be discerned within Britain itself. Regional and local differences derive from many factors, including latitude, proximity to the sea, altitude, the relief of the land, aspect, exposure to wind and degree of urban development. Generalising, in winter the west is warmer than the east, while in summer the south is warmer than the north. Precipitation, though, varies from one place to

another more than temperature. The west has more rainfall than the east, with areas of over 1500 mm (60 in) of annual rainfall on the Highland and Upland areas mostly in winter. The east is much drier, with annual totals of less than 750 mm (30 in) over much of the English Lowlands and with the greater proportion falling in the latter six months and, in some areas, in the summer.

Many attempts have been made to divide Britain into climatic regions and to characterise the differences from place to place. One of the simplest attempts superimposes the isotherms for January which run broadly north-south, and for July, which have an east-west trend, to produce four quadrants. The north-west quadrant has cool summers and mild winters, the south-west quadrant has warm summers and mild winters. The north-east quadrant is epitomised by cool summers and cold winters and the south-east, which shows the greatest contrasts in temperature, by warm summers and cold winters. When the general difference in rainfall between west and east is also recalled, a broad regional picture emerges.

A rather more complex pattern of regional climates has been suggested, by S. Gregory. He employs three sets of indicators, the length of the growing season, the magnitude of rainfall and the seasonality of rainfall (*see map page 11*). The growing season of nine or more months of the south-western coasts falls to eight or seven months in Lowland Britain, to six or five months in the Uplands and to four or less in the Grampians and the Western Highlands of Scotland.

Under the heading of rainfall magnitude, Gregory distinguishes those areas that receive at least 1250 mm (50 in) of rain a year with a high probability of its occurrence each year, from those that receive less than 750 mm (30 in) a year with a much lower probability of regularity, with an area of moderate rainfall lying between the two. In terms of rainfall seasonality, he distinguishes the areas of maximum rainfall in the winter half of the year (western Britain and a part of southern England south of the Thames) from the areas of maximum rainfall in the second half of the year. These comprise most of the rest of the country, except for the area between the Thames and the Wash where there is a weakly developed summer maximum.

But yet another distinction should be introduced. About 80% of the population lives in towns and about 11% of the surface area of England and Wales is built upon. Cities, especially large ones, tend to modify the climate. Buildings interrupt air flow and reduce wind speeds; air pollution is higher. The warm air which, particularly by night, covers cities produces what have been termed 'heat islands'. Most towns with high central building densities average 1°-2°C warmer than surrounding countrysides; and on occasions much higher differences are recorded.

It must also be remembered that, even in a temperate climate, departures from the 'norm' and extreme events do occur. A recent example is that of the great drought of 1975-76 which followed a tendency to low rainfall totals in the early 1970s. And, though we do not fully understand the causes, climates do change over time. There have certainly been notable fluctuations in the climatic record of the last 1000 years and it should not be assumed that present climatic conditions will continue unchanged indefinitely.

Climate is one of the factors that influence soil and, broadly speaking, it is possible to draw a distinction between the acidic podsolic soils of the cooler and wetter north and west where high winter rainfall leaches out the soluble salts to leave an impoverished grey soil beneath a black humus layer, and the less leached brown forest soils of the Lowland Zone. But soils also depend upon the parent material, be that solid rock or glacial drift. As we travel from one part of the country to another we notice the rapidity with which changes in the solid rocks occur, very noticeably for example in the scarplands of the Lowland Zone, and soil types reflect such changes. The distribution of glacial drift has been a particularly important factor. We may distinguish between sandy soils, loamy and usually very fertile soils, clay soils often heavy to work, and calcareous soils derived from limestone. A third factor which influences soil type is vegetation, and some soils have a very high content of organic matter. Such soils include the black, fenland soils and peaty and moorland soils. Local elements of geology and relief influence soil type: some areas of hard rock are bare of soil, and the degree of slope may also be important, particularly influencing drainage. It must also be remembered that many of our soils have been tilled, drained and fertilised for centuries, so that they are no longer in a completely natural state.

Atlantic Britain, Highland Britain and Lowland Britain

The concept of Highland and Lowland Zones has also been employed in interpreting the distribution of early settlements. Pioneers in this work were Sir Cyril Fox and Dr L. F. Chitty who in 1932 published a remarkable book, *The Personality of Britain*. They used detailed mapping of archaeological evidence, to examine the distribution of prehistoric settlements in terms both of the physical conditions and what was known of the organisation and technology of each wave of incoming peoples. They recognised two principal sets of embarkation areas for those moving from Europe to Britain. These were the coasts of northwest Europe from Brittany to the Rhine with routes across the narrow seas and, for those to whom the sea was a highway, the coasts from Spain to Brittany and from the Rhine to the Norwegian fjords.

In Megalithic and early Bronze Age times the Atlantic seaways from Spain were much in use and Britain was in the van of western European progress. But in the middle Bronze Age, land routes across Europe sapped the importance of the Atlantic routes. Britain tended, therefore, to become 'a country on the edge of the known world, the last to receive and absorb cultures moving from east to west'. The Lowland Zone, adjacent to the Continent, was easily invaded and new cultures from the Continent were imposed.

Although later writers have cast doubts upon Fox's ideas, many agree that from about 1000 BC the contrast between Highland and Lowland was very significant. Peoples of the later Bronze and Iron Ages were better equipped than their predecessors to tackle the clearance of the woodlands and to till the heavier soils in the vales. The Romans, it is true, overstepped into the Highland Zone but the boundary

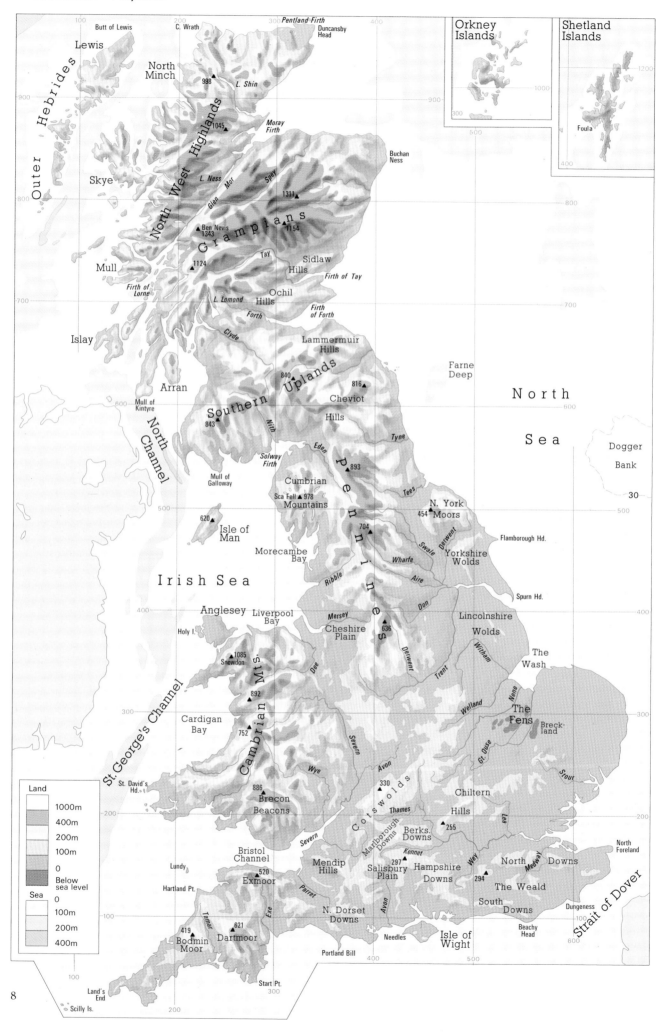

Orkney Islands

Shetland Islands

Lewis
Butt of Lewis
C. Wrath
Pentland Firth
Duncansby Head

Outer Hebrides
North Minch
998
L. Shin
1045
Moray Firth
Buchan Ness

Skye
North West Highlands
L. Ness
Glen Mor
Spey
1311
Grampians
Ben Nevis 1343
1154

Mull
1124
Tay
Sidlaw Hills
Firth of Tay

Firth of Lorne
L. Lomond
Ochil Hills
Firth of Forth

Islay
Forth
Clyde

Arran
Lammermuir Hills
Farne Deep

Mull of Kintyre
Southern Uplands
840
Cheviot Hills
816

North

North Channel
843
Sea

Mull of Galloway
Nith
Eden
Pennines
893
Tyne

Dogger Bank

30

Cumbrian Mountains
Sca Fell 978
Tees

N. York Moors
454
Flamborough Hd.

620
Isle of Man
704
Swale
Derwent
Yorkshire Wolds

Morecambe Bay
Wharfe
Aire
Spurn Hd.

Ribble
Don

Irish Sea
Derwent
Lincolnshire Wolds
The Wash

Anglesey
Liverpool Bay
Mersey
636
Trent

Holy I.
Cheshire Plain
Witham

The Fens
Breckland

1085 Snowdon
Dee
Welland
Nene

892
Gt. Ouse
Stour

Cardigan Bay
Cambrian Mts.
752
Severn

Avon
330
Chiltern Hills
Lee

St. George's Channel
Wye
Cotswolds
255

St. David's Hd.
886
Brecon Beacons
Thames
Berks. Downs

Marlborough Downs
Kennet
297
North Downs
Medway
North Foreland

Bristol Channel
Severn
Mendip Hills
Salisbury Plain
Hampshire Downs
Wey
294
The Weald

Lundy
520
Parret
Avon
South Downs
Dungeness

Hartland Pt.
Exmoor
Exe
N. Dorset Downs
Beachy Head
Strait of Dover

419
621
Tamar
Needles
Isle of Wight
600

Bodmin Moor
Dartmoor
Portland Bill

Land's End
Scilly Is.
Start Pt.

Land
1000m
400m
200m
100m
0
Below sea level
Sea
0
100m
200m
400m

8

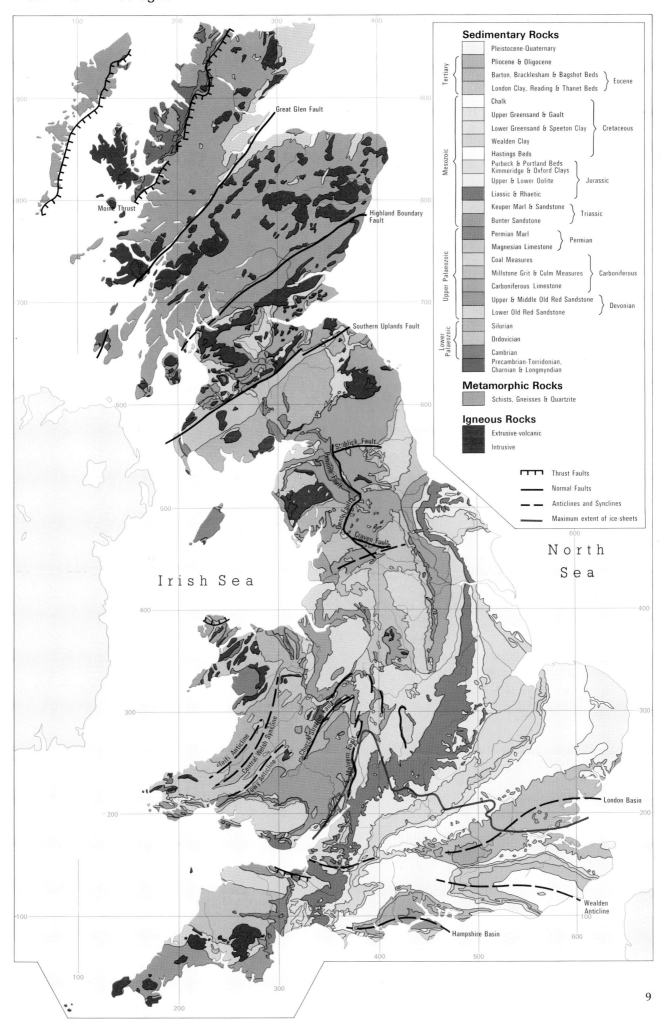

Sedimentary Rocks

Tertiary
- Pleistocene-Quaternary
- Pliocene & Oligocene
- Barton, Bracklesham & Bagshot Beds } Eocene
- London Clay, Reading & Thanet Beds } Eocene

Mesozoic
- Chalk
- Upper Greensand & Gault } Cretaceous
- Lower Greensand & Speeton Clay } Cretaceous
- Wealden Clay
- Hastings Beds
- Purbeck & Portland Beds
- Kimmeridge & Oxford Clays } Jurassic
- Upper & Lower Oolite
- Liassic & Rhaetic
- Keuper Marl & Sandstone } Triassic
- Bunter Sandstone } Triassic

Upper Palaeozoic
- Permian Marl } Permian
- Magnesian Limestone } Permian
- Coal Measures
- Millstone Grit & Culm Measures } Carboniferous
- Carboniferous Limestone
- Upper & Middle Old Red Sandstone } Devonian
- Lower Old Red Sandstone } Devonian

Lower Palaeozoic
- Silurian
- Ordovician
- Cambrian
- Precambrian-Torridonian, Charnian & Longmyndian

Metamorphic Rocks
- Schists, Gneisses & Quartzite

Igneous Rocks
- Extrusive-volcanic
- Intrusive

- Thrust Faults
- Normal Faults
- Anticlines and Synclines
- Maximum extent of ice-sheets

Great Glen Fault

Moine Thrust

Highland Boundary Fault

Southern Uplands Fault

Stublick Fault

Pennine Fault

Dent Fault

Craven Fault

Irish Sea

North Sea

Teifi Anticline

Central Welsh Syncline

Towy Anticline

Church Stretton Fault

Malvern Fault

London Basin

Wealden Anticline

Hampshire Basin

9

between the civil and military zones was approximately that between Highland and Lowland Britain (*see map page 145*). Even in Anglo-Saxon times, the western frontier of their influence at the end of the 6th century was aligned along the outcrop of the Palaeozoic rocks (*see map page 147*).

Such observations led Fox to the proposition that historically the Lowland Zone had nourished 'richer cultures' than the Highland. 'Taking Britain as a whole,' he observed, 'the most important centres of any culture or civilisation are likely to be in the south-east of the islands.' Such circumstances, he went on, had led to the 'tragedy' of the early history of Britain. Fresh invasions from the east had, on the one hand, paralysed older cultures by largely destroying them where they were most flourishing and on the other, had tended to cut off the survivals of those cultures in the west from the stimuli of continued contact with Europe.

But the Highland Zone was not simply a barrier to cultural advance nor a region where outliers of former Lowland cultures might precariously survive. There were subtler and more positive influences. Whereas in the Lowland Zone newer cultures were successively imposed on earlier, in Highland Britain they tended to be absorbed by the older cultures. Historically Lowland Britain was characterised by replacement, Highland Britain by fusion and continuity. The power of absorption of the Highland Zone had indeed provided it with a distinctive cultural character of its own. The survival of Celtic languages and traditions was the clearest example.

Later writers have tended to place increased emphasis on one aspect of the geography of the Highland Zone which Fox noted but did not develop, namely the tendency for the shores of the Irish Sea (and its northern and southern approaches) to form a 'culture pool'. R. H. Kinvig (1958), for example, while accepting the value of the idea of a Highland Zone, argued that a better understanding may be gained by subdividing the Highlands into an 'Atlantic Zone' and a 'Moorland Area' lying inland from it.

His Atlantic Zone included the coastal belt of plains and low plateaux along the western and northern coasts and also the islands of Man, the Hebrides, the Shetlands and the Orkneys. He and others distinguished 'Atlantic Britain' on grounds of both physical and historical geography. Historically, the zone had played an active rather than a passive role in that, open southwards to influences *via* sea routes from France, Iberia and the Mediterranean and northwards to influences from Scandinavia, it had been a receiving zone for peoples and cultures. In prehistoric times there was south-north traffic and the builders of the megalithic tombs came by sea. From the 4th century AD onwards contacts between the various parts of Atlantic Britain, and with Gaul and beyond, intensified. Many of the ideas associated with Celtic Christianity came by these routes. By about AD 800 Norse settlers had begun to penetrate and to settle. Eventually the Isle of Man became the capital of an island realm consisting of all the Hebrides. In the 12th century a separate diocese, the Episcopal See of the Isles, was established based on St Patrick's Isle at Peel (*see map page 150*).

E. Estyn Evans (1958) has carried this argument forward into the present day, suggesting a number of aspects of modern social and folk life in the coastlands of western and northwestern Europe which link what he refers to as the 'Atlantic Ends of Europe'. The thesis is that 'these western lands have a cultural heritage which is rich and varied, and signs are not lacking at the present day that some of these areas are once again going to play a more active part than they have done in the immediate past'. Those words remind us of the rise of national pressures and demands for the devolution of government from London, the route centre of the Lowland Zone.

Thus the simple Highland Zone-Lowland Zone concept requires modification. The case for the existence of an Atlantic Britain is strong and the difference between the true Highlands and the Uplands must also be kept in mind. Such broad divisions as have been indicated form a useful starting-point for more detailed studies of the great variety of regional conditions in Britain.

Land and People

The land of Britain, varied in its landscape and in the resources that it offers, is small in area in relation to the demands of its population of 54,129,000 (1981). The total land area of England, Wales and Scotland is about 22,752,000 hectares (56,200,000 acres), allowing only 0·42 HA (1·04 acres) per head of population, and for England and Wales only about 0·3 HA (0·75 acres) per head. The needs are many and include housing, industry, mineral extraction, transport, agriculture, water supply, recreation and defence. Agriculture accounts in England and Wales for more than three-quarters of land use, with woodland covering about 7% and urban, industrial and associated development about 11%. There is great variation in the quality of agricultural land: about 13% of the land area is under rough grazing and only 3% is truly of first-class quality (*see maps pages 168 and 169*). In 1900 only about 5% of the land surface was in urban uses, but the proportion has increased more rapidly than has population, and land has been much in demand as cities have spread outwards. In the inter-war years losses of farmland to urban uses amounted at times to over 25,000 HA (60,000 acres) a year. The concern aroused led to the improvement of planning control, and since 1945 about 15,700 HA (38,800 acres) a year or about 0·1% of the total land surface of England and Wales has been transferred from agricultural to urban uses. It is not surprising that land use conflicts have arisen over development proposals, for example for the extension of urban land, motorway construction, the creation of reservoirs, the sinking of new coal mines, the building of new power stations, the enlargement of airports or the improvement for agricultural use of heath or wetlands.

Urban and Industrial Britain

The dominant feature of the human geography of Britain is the existence of a great urban system, the product mainly of the rapid industrial and urban growth of the last 200 years. In 1801 some nine million people lived in England and Wales, and one in three lived in towns. By 1851 the population had grown to 18 million and just over a half were urban dwellers. By the beginning of the 20th century, out of 32·5 million people 78% were urban dwellers. Since that

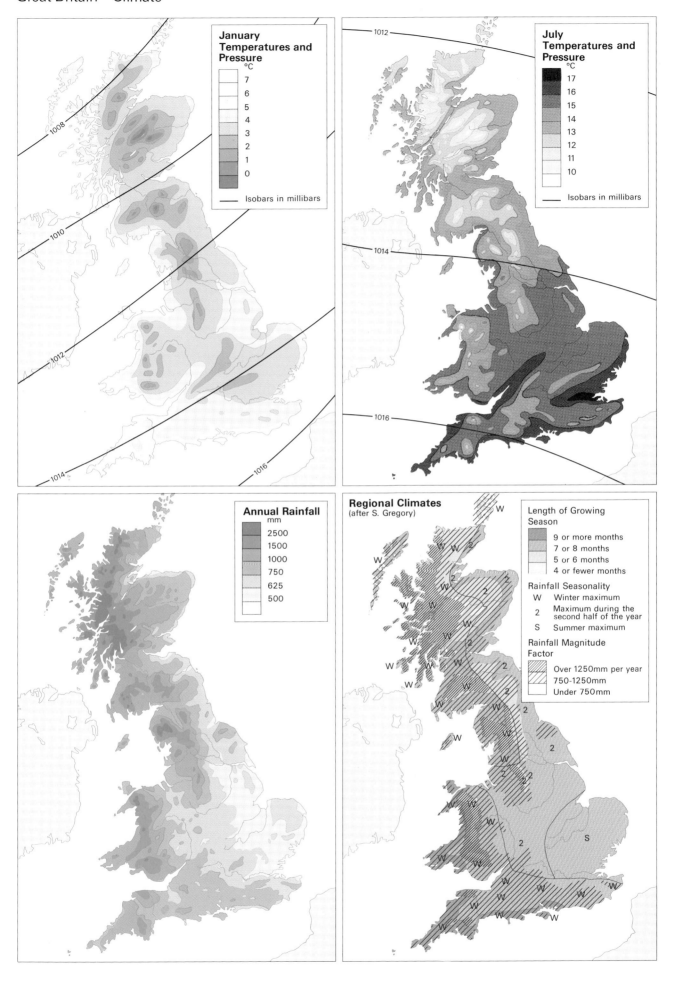

January Temperatures and Pressure
°C
7
6
5
4
3
2
1
0
—— Isobars in millibars

1008
1010
1012
1014
1016

July Temperatures and Pressure
°C
17
16
15
14
13
12
11
10
—— Isobars in millibars

1012
1014
1016

Annual Rainfall
mm
2500
1500
1000
750
625
500

Regional Climates
(after S. Gregory)

Length of Growing Season
9 or more months
7 or 8 months
5 or 6 months
4 or fewer months

Rainfall Seasonality
W   Winter maximum
2   Maximum during the second half of the year
S   Summer maximum

Rainfall Magnitude Factor
Over 1250mm per year
750-1250mm
Under 750mm

11

time, although the proportion living in towns and cities has not grown greatly, the actual number has and the character and shapes of the urban areas have greatly changed.

Look first at what some call the Central Urban Region, others the British megalopolis (*see map page 173*). A band of dense population stretches northwestwards from the English Channel across the Thames, through the Midlands, dividing on each side of the Pennines and continuing into Lancashire and Yorkshire. The southern part of this megalopolis is focused around London, the midland and northern parts contain a number of urban groups around, for example, Birmingham, Manchester and Leeds. The urban areas do not actually join together; there are breaks of green land between them. But the whole area is closely bound together by main railway lines and motorways that reflect the strength of the economic links between the cities and their activities in the zone.

Outside this English megalopolis some other important urban and industrial zones occur. Indeed the eye may take another line, starting with the South Wales industrial region and Bristol, continuing to the northeast through the West and East Midlands and terminating on Humberside. Traversing northwards there is the industrial region of northeast England with Newcastle-upon-Tyne as its main centre. The central industrial belt of Scotland with Glasgow and Edinburgh as the principal cities provides homes for about three-quarters of Scotland's population of 5·25 million.

The appearance, character and prosperity of the cities and industrial districts in these strongly urbanised zones vary widely. Some of the cities, Edinburgh, Durham, York, Coventry, above all London, were important in medieval times. But supreme significance must be given to the Industrial Revolution of the 18th and 19th centuries. For this was also a geographical revolution. As new methods for smelting iron using coke were introduced the coalfields became important, and mining and industrial towns began to spring up where none had existed before. Developments in industry, including the introduction of the factory system in the metal-using and textile industries, brought people into rapidly-growing industrial cities such as Birmingham and Manchester. Commercial activities intensified. Canals and, after 1830, railways linked the industrial districts together. External trade prospered and new ports were required: estuaries were deepened, channels constructed, dock systems developed on the Thames, Mersey and Clyde. The Clyde, Tyne, Wear and, for a time, the Thames also built the ships which imported food and commodities for conversion into manufactured products and carried away the finished products and the export coal for the bunkers of the great merchant fleets. London grew as port, manufacturing region, chief centre of commerce, and as the location of government and as the biggest centre of wholesale and retail trade (*see maps pages 155 and 157*).

These great developments of what has been described as the palaeotechnic phase of industrial development and which underlie present patterns must be seen in terms of Britain's position as the leading industrial power at a time when the world market was expanding. In time it was to be overtaken, but much of the physical fabric constructed at that time remains. Each industrial region developed its own group of specialised activities. The West Midlands was the home of the metal industries, Lancashire of cotton and the West Riding of woollen textiles. South Wales had its iron and steel, coal, tinplate and non-ferrous metal industries. The northeast and Scotland had coal, iron and steel, shipbuilding and marine engineering. Such a system of specialised industrial regions worked well while the market was strong, but in the Great Depression of 1929-31 those areas that had rather narrowly-based industrial structures and were dependent on industries that were declining nationally fared badly. Unemployment soared and poverty struck. South Wales, Clydeside, northeast England, West Cumberland are examples of what for a time were termed Depressed Areas. By contrast, areas such as the West Midlands and Greater London where the industries were more diversified and which possessed strong shares in such industries as electrical engineering and electrical goods, motor vehicles, the food and drink trades and the service industries, which were expanding nationally, remained relatively prosperous.

The contrast in conditions between the regions and the movement of people away from the hard-hit areas to the more prosperous districts raised new questions. To what extent did the nation possess a responsibility towards areas that had contributed greatly to the national wealth but now, for no fault of their own, found themselves in hard straits? If a responsibility existed, how should it be exercised and what methods could be found to rectify the disparities between areas? Preliminary steps to devise remedies were introduced by 1939 but it is since 1945 that 'regional' policies have been developed and more will be said about these in a later section of this atlas.

The 19th-century industrial districts developed their own distinctive landscapes. Mrs Gaskell writing in 1857 described the Yorkshire landscape between Keighley and Haworth: 'what with villas, great worsted factories, with here and there an old fashioned farm-house . . . it can hardly be called "country" any part of the way'. But those who lived there were perhaps more fortunate than those in the slums of inner Manchester or those in the Black Country, 'black by day and red by night' as the flames from the open blast furnaces were reflected from the clouds. The industrial towns threw out branching lines of houses along the roads joining them and by the end of the century a number of great conurbations, areas in which the built-up areas had become contiguous, had been formed. We now find seven major conurbations, each different from the others. London, by far the largest, grew outwards from its central core to engulf land in Middlesex, Hertfordshire, Essex, Kent and Surrey. Its population in 1981 was 6,696,000 (though, like all the major conurbations, population has been declining recently). The other major conurbations are West Midland, Greater Manchester, Merseyside, Tyneside, West Yorkshire and Clydeside. These conurbations hold about 32% of the population of Great Britain. Outside the conurbations there grew railway towns like Crewe and Swindon, ports such as Southampton, fishing ports such as Grimsby, resort towns like Bournemouth and Blackpool. And many smaller manufacturing towns developed.

Problems of Adaptation and Modernisation

The Great Industrial Age thus contributed vastly to the establishment of the basic pattern of modern urban settlement. Much of its physical structure remains with us; some of it is mean, like the slum houses of the inner areas of the big cities which have been the subject of vigorous clearance, especially since 1945. The street patterns of cities built in the Victorian period were not designed for modern traffic conditions and adapting them to the needs of road transport without damage to the environment poses acute problems. The great railway termini such as St Pancras, Liverpool Street or Waverley remind us of the role of the railway. Some at least of the canals are still at work carrying freight. Although much of the derelict land created by the mines, furnaces and brickworks has been cleared, some still remains: indeed now that the Industrial Age has passed into history a number of industrial museums serve as reminders of the need to create new industries and fresh environments of which we can be proud.

Such changes are symptomatic of the modernisation of the geography of Britain which has been proceeding since the end of the 1939-45 war and especially in the last two decades.

Coal is king no longer. Though still important in the economy, coal production is only about two-fifths of the maximum reached in 1913. For power, we now have a choice of coal, oil, natural gas, or electricity (produced from coal, oil, natural gas, nuclear fuels or, mainly in Scotland, from water power). The period 1965-75 has been described as that of 'a revolution in the UK fuel and power industries unmatched since British coalfields were first developed'. Oil is now more important to the economy than coal and this revolution which began on a basis of imported oil and gas can now draw on the resources of the North Sea. The exploitation of the oil and gas fields has itself produced a revolution in the geography of the North Sea.

The transport system has changed equally radically in the 20th century. The railway system has been reduced in length of rail and transformed technically by electrification and diesel haulage. But except for services such as high speed inter-city trains, commuter traffic and specialised freight, rail has given place to road. Some 2400 km (1500 miles) of motorway have been built in twenty years and the number of motor cars in use has multiplied by six since 1951. There is also the choice of travelling between cities by air and the development of international air traffic has had major consequences for ocean shipping. In freight transport, containerisation in turn has had its effect on 19th-century dock systems, while hovercraft and hydrofoil provide additional types of ferries across the English Channel.

Dramatic changes have also befallen our cities. No longer after 1961 did the population of major conurbations (with one exception) continue to grow. Out-migration exceeded growth by natural increase and in-migration. Decentralisation has provided the key-note. Post-war regional plans, such as that prepared for Greater London by Sir Patrick Abercrombie in 1944, recognised the need to re-create the environment of the inner areas of the industrial conurbations and advocated the delineation of Green Belts to prevent continuing outward sprawl and the creation of New Towns to house 'overspill' population. Later, other towns beyond the conurbations were designated as 'expanded' towns for the same purpose. To the decentralisation created by planning policies has been added the movement away from the conurbations by families who prefer to live in medium-sized or small towns. Possession of the motorcar has given more freedom of choice in deciding where to live. Thus a new urban form, the 'city region', has been brought into existence. The London city region, for example, has a radius of up to about 65 km (40 miles) comprising a region of towns functionally linked together. It extends to Ashford, Basingstoke, Swindon, Milton Keynes, Bedford and Chelmsford. Many of the industrial enterprises formerly located in the Victorian inner areas have moved out to the towns expanding beyond the conurbation edge, leaving gaps behind in the employment structure of the inner city. Indeed the trend to decentralisation has brought about a degree of polarisation between the more prosperous conditions of life in the outer parts of the city regions and the unemployment, poor social facilities and dreary environments of some parts of the inner cities. In such areas lies one of the great challenges for an age of modernisation and a central problem for the 1980s.

The other lies in the adaptation of industry and the provision of new forms of employment. Economic recession in the last years of the 1970s accelerated the speed at which the older industries have drastically slimmed down their labour forces. Unemployment in 1981 has a different distribution from that of 1931 and is no longer localised only in the coalfield-based industrial areas of the north and Wales.

But while most of the people live in towns and cities, and urban land uses are encroaching on the countryside, agricultural land still makes up over three-quarters of the land use of Britain. The distinction between cities and countryside is less clear than it was. City regions extend their influence and their connecting roads and power lines stamp an artificial pattern on the countryside. City dwellers look to the countryside for recreation. Agriculture too has become more intensive. In the 1960s and early 1970s its production increased at an average rate of 2·5% per year while manpower fell dramatically. It now takes only 2·7% of the labour force to grow or rear the crops and livestock that supply 65% of the temperate foodstuffs consumed in Britain. City and countryside have become more inter-related. Agriculture supplies milk, meat, cereals, fruit and vegetables for consumption in the cities which, in turn, produce agricultural machinery, farm requisites and fertilisers for the farm. Meanwhile the appearance of the countryside itself changes especially in those areas where hedgerows have been removed in the interests of mechanised farming, where Dutch elm disease has been prevalent, or where farming takes over hillsides and heathlands. Concern for the countryside and its wildlife has recently been loudly expressed on such issues. Despite such changes there is a rich and diverse countryside to be studied, valued and cared for. It is hoped that the maps of the chapters on historical geography and modern Britain—sketchy though they inevitably are on such a scale—will add to the awareness of these changes and this diversity.

A Short History of the Ordnance Survey

The Ordnance Survey is nearly 200 years old and was formally founded in 1791 under the Board of Ordnance, from which its name is derived. By that time the Survey had already fixed scientifically the relative positions of the Greenwich and Paris observatories by means of a triangulation which formed the basis of later maps.

The Ordnance Survey in the 19th Century

The first production of the one inch to one mile map of Southern England was to satisfy military needs during the Napoleonic Wars. However, after the peace of 1815, maps came to be valued for land transfer, civil engineering and the improvements in drainage and sanitation necessitated by urban growth in early Victorian Britain. Geological outcrops and archaeological sites were also recorded and by the mid-19th century the Ordnance Survey provided a national mapping service for scientific, military and governmental needs. The authority for many of its activities is the Ordnance Survey Act of 1841. As a result of growing governmental requirements for more detailed larger scale maps, Ireland was surveyed at six inches to the mile and the same scale was used in 1840 for maps of northern England and Scotland. After a controversy about the largest 'basic' scales at which Britain should be surveyed, it was decided in 1858 to adopt a scale of 1:2500 (or 25 inches to the mile) for cultivated areas and 1:10 560 (or six inches to the mile) with contours for uncultivated areas of mountain and moorland. Towns of more than 4000 population were to be surveyed at 1:500 or 10 feet to the mile.

Smaller scale maps were derived from the large-scale mapping. The one-inch map continued and a quarter-inch to one mile series was completed in 1888. At the end of the century a smaller scale topographical map at ten miles to the inch or 1:625 000 was authorised.

The first 1:2500 large scale survey was finished in 1896 and by 1914 the first revision had been completed. Methods of map production had changed with the introduction of colour printing and photography but the cost of revising them caused town plans at the scale of 1:500 to be abandoned in 1893 except where locally funded.

The Ordnance Survey Between the Wars

Government economies were intensified by the First World War so that in 1922 Ordnance Survey manpower was drastically reduced and only revision of large-scale maps covering areas of rapid change could be continued. However, increased government legislation in the inter-war years required accurate maps for implementation of official action in land registration, town planning and slum clearance. By the early 1930s it was becoming clear that the Ordnance Survey had been left ill-equipped to supply sufficiently accurate maps. A Departmental Committee under the chairmanship of Sir J. C. Davidson was set up in 1935 to consider how to restore the effectiveness of the national survey. Its Report published in 1938 could not be implemented systematically until after the 1939-45 war but it formed the framework upon which the present-day Ordnance Survey has developed.

The Ordnance Survey Since 1945

The major innovation of the Davidson Report was to introduce the metric National Grid as a reference system, and a single projection to cover the whole country. Previous 1:2500 large scale maps had been produced on separate county projections and this led to a loss of accuracy along county boundaries.

Large-scale maps were to be continuously revised so that they should never become so outdated as in pre-war days. A larger scale of 1:1250 (50 inches to the mile) was to be investigated and if suitable used to map more densely populated urban areas. The 1:25 000 ($2\frac{1}{2}$ inches to one mile) medium-scale map was to be tried, and if successful extended to cover the whole country in a national series.

After the war additional staff were recruited and the large-scale survey, metric conversions and revisions proceeded at the basic scales of 1:1250, 1:2500 and 1:10 000. Smaller-scale maps of one inch to one mile, 1:25 000 scale, 1:250 000 scale or a quarter-inch to one mile and the 1:625 000 scale development of the late Victorian ten-mile map were all published after derivation from large-scale surveys. The One-inch National Series was converted to 1:50 000 scale by the early 1970s.

A Retriangulation was completed in 1962 and forms the basis of present mapping, which also uses the results of a third geodetic levelling when the heights of Ordnance Survey Bench Marks were revised.

In the 1960s the compilation of a computer data base began and the first large-scale maps became available on magnetic tape. Demand for quickly available survey revision information also led to the publication of maps on microfilm and the development of the supply of un-published survey information. During this period the Ordnance Survey has been establishing close contact with map users of all kinds in order to keep abreast of modern mapping needs.

The headquarters of the Ordnance Survey are in Southampton, which has been its home since 1841. Here the large-scale maps are drawn and printed using Master Survey documents maintained in field offices scattered all over Great Britain. Retail customers may obtain Ordnance Survey large scales maps through a countrywide Agency Network and small scales maps through a large number of stockists.

As the resurvey task nears completion much greater emphasis is being given to the swift revision and supply of mapping information. The growing computer data base and the development of new survey and production methods have an increasingly important role in the provision of a rapid and comprehensive service which is of great value to the general public and all sectors of industry and commerce for many purposes.

Ordnance Survey Products

The Ordnance Survey produces maps in many forms and for various specialities which are described below, beginning with the large-scale maps from which the more popular small-scale maps are derived.

LARGE-SCALE MAPS
Maps at 1:1250 scale
(1 cm to 12·5 metres or 50 inches to 1 mile)
Maps at 1:2500 scale
(1 cm to 25 metres or 25 inches to 1 mile)
These are the largest-scale maps produced by the Ordnance Survey. The 1:1250 maps cover urban districts in Great Britain where the population is more than 20,000 per 1000 HA (2471 acres). Each one shows (in black and white) an area of 500 m by 500 m. 1:2500 maps cover less densely populated urban land and normally show areas of 2 km east to west by 1 km north to south.

House numbers and street names, administrative boundaries and heights are shown on both scales of map together with 100 m national grid lines. Acreages are shown on 1:2500-scale maps.

These maps may be bought printed on paper, as transparencies, or more cheaply as printouts from microfilm negatives. This microfilm service is known as the Ordnance Survey SIM (Survey Information on Microfilm) service. Maps can also be obtained on magnetic tape from the Southampton Office as a special service. Lists of large-scale maps on tape are available on request.

The maps are regularly updated and copies of updates may be obtained through the SIM service. The most recent large-scale mapping information may be seen at Ordnance Survey local offices (listed in the Telephone Directory) and all offices can supply copies of the latest survey documents under the SUSI (Supply of Unpublished Survey Information) service.

1:10 000 scale maps
(1 cm to 100 m or approximately 6 inches to 1 mile)
These maps cover the whole country and are the largest-scale of map produced for mountain and moorland areas. Each sheet covers an area of 5 km by 5 km and shows contours in brown on a monochrome base which includes most street names. 1:10 560 scale maps will remain available until they are replaced by 1:10 000 scale sheets.
Town and City Maps
Scale 1:10 000
Town and city maps have been published of four cities and it is intended to extend this series. They are colourful street maps with larger-scale insets of the centre with a street index and items of interest conspicuously shown. Another such map is of Central London which folds to a small size and is coloured with highlighted tourist information.

1:25 000 SCALE MAPS
(4 cm to 1 km or 2 inches to 1 mile)
Pathfinders
(1:25 000 Second Series)
These maps are the Ordnance Survey walker and rambler maps showing the countryside in great detail including rights of way in England and Wales and field boundaries. They are coloured and cover areas of 20 km (12½ miles) from east to west by 10 km (6¼ miles) from north to south. Pathfinders are gradually replacing the smaller First Series maps at the same scale showing areas of 10 km square. The whole of Great Britain is covered by Pathfinder or First Series 1:25 000 maps.
Outdoor Leisure Maps
These maps of popular recreational areas generally cover some 200 square miles. They are based on Pathfinders or First Series 1:25 000 scale maps but give much additional information about available leisure activity.

SMALL-SCALE MAPS
Landranger Maps
1:50 000 scale (2 cm to 1 km or about 1¼ inches to 1 mile)
This is the successor of the old 'One-inch' map and it has become the Ordnance Survey's most popular series. At first, one-inch maps were in monochrome with hachuring to indicate relief. Colours with contours appeared at the end of the 19th century.

The Landranger scale of 1:50 000 was introduced in the early 1970s and the maps are readily recognised by their magenta covers. Each sheet depicts an area of about 620 square miles. Many show tourist information and this is being added to the others when revision takes place. Rights-of-way are marked on maps of England and Wales so that the series can be used for walking as well as for exploring by car.

ROUTE MAPS
The history of the Ordnance Survey popular maps of a smaller scale than 1:50 000 shows a tendency to focus on the needs of the motorist. Two are published at present and are described below.
Routemaster Series of Great Britain
1:250 000 scale (1 cm to 2·5 km or approximately 1 inch to 4 miles)
These maps are the modern successors of the late Victorian Quarter-inch (1:253 440 scale) regional sheets, of which two series had been published by 1928. They were then superseded by a third series designed as a map for motorists in 21 sheets. A fourth series was published in the early 1930s with sheetlines redesigned to reduce the number to 19.

After the war, a fifth series was published in 1957 with a new specification which included hill shading and a rationalised metric scale of 1:250 000 to conform with European standards and a national projection. This series was a combination of a regional physical map with motoring

information. During 1978-79 the 1:250 000 series was again redesigned to cover Britain in nine sheets to give prominence to information of use to tourists and all travellers.

Routeplanner of Great Britain
1:625 000 scale (1 cm to 6·25 km or approximately 1 inch to 10 miles)

The ten miles to the inch scale has been used for Ordnance Survey maps since 1820 when it was first engraved as an index to show the sheetlines of the first one-inch maps. A topographical map of Great Britain at this scale was not published until 1904 when it was issued in twelve sheets. By the 1930s edition the sheet lines had been redesigned so that only three and later two sheets were necessary to cover Britain and the needs of motorists were recognised by showing Ministry of Transport Class A and B roads and AA and RAC telephone boxes.

After the war the scale was enlarged slightly to 1:625 000 and when it was published in 1946 it became known as *The Road Map* with a larger-scale inset for the area covered by London.

In 1964 the map was redesigned and an annually revised Route Planning map was published in two sheets with insets of road networks, a mileage chart and information about British Rail motorail services. National Parks, Forest Parks and areas of outstanding natural beauty were also shown. The newly designed map was immediately successful and since then modifications have been added to make it more useful to motorists. It is now published on one sheet printed both sides to show the whole of Great Britain with the title *Routeplanner*.

ARCHAEOLOGICAL MAPS
Notable archaeological sites have long been included in Ordnance Survey large and small scale maps. More comprehensive period or thematic maps are also available and are described below.

Map of Roman London
Scale 1:2500 (1 cm to 25 metres or 25 inches to 1 mile)

This is a coloured large-scale map of part of the City of London which highlights and describes Roman sites. Roman finds are displayed in over 40 attractive pictures and the sheet also includes a brief history of the Roman occupation of England with seven smaller maps and an illustrated chronology of finds.

Hadrian's Wall
Scale 1:31 680 (1 cm to 0·32 km or 2 inches to 1 mile)

This is an attractively coloured strip map and list of features of Hadrian's Wall, one of the best preserved Roman walls in Europe. It also contains a bibliography.

The Antonine Wall
Scale 1:25 000 (4 cm to 1 km or 2½ inches to 1 mile)

This is a companion strip map of the Scottish Roman wall with identifiable remains and sites highlighted and with a brief description of the wall.

Roman Britain
Scale 1:625 000 (1 cm to 6·25 km or 1 inch to 10 miles)

This map is available in two sheets, North and South, separately or folded in a hard cover with an explanatory text. The map shows Britain between AD 43 and 410. The text includes supplementary maps and lists of sites in various categories.

Britain in the Dark Ages
Scale 1:1 000 000 (1 cm to 10 km or 1 inch to 16 miles)

This map is available with or without an explanatory text and depicts Celtic, pagan and Christian Anglo-Saxon features between AD 410 and 871. The Roman road system is also shown and the text includes a bibliography and gazetteer.

Monastic Britain
Scale 1:625 000 (1 cm to 6·25 km or 1 inch to 10 miles)

The North and South sheets are available with or without a bound text. The maps and text show the geographical distribution and historical development of monastic houses between the Norman Conquest and their suppression in the 16th century.

Britain Before the Norman Conquest
Scale 1:625 000 (1 cm to 6·25 km or 1 inch to 10 miles)

This map is published in two sheets which are available separately with or without a bound text. The map shows Anglo-Saxon, Scandinavian and Celtic forces in Britain from the accession of Alfred the Great to the Norman Conquest. The text introduces and summarises the period and includes useful indexes of names and features.

REPRODUCTIONS OF OLD MAPS
The Ordnance Survey publishes three reproductions of old maps from the 14th to 19th centuries. They are a strip map known as the Bodleian Map of Great Britain from 1360, Symonson's 1596 map of Kent and an 1840 edition one-inch map of Southampton.

EDUCATIONAL MAPS
As well as map extracts published especially for schools, the Ordnance Survey has two publications for all students. They are Student Map Packs each of which contains photographs and maps at different scales as well as one map from the early 19th century. Study notes, geological and land use maps are included for detailed study of a particular area of geographical interest. The areas are Maesteg in South Wales and Washington New Town near Sunderland.

ADMINISTRATIVE MAPS
A number of Ordnance Survey Maps are available which feature administrative, parliamentary or judicial boundaries highlighted on a grey base. They include maps of Greater London at 1:63 360 scale, of the Counties of England and Central Lowlands of Scotland at 1:100 000 scale, the Regions of Scotland at 1:250 000 scale, and of the whole of Britain at 1:625 000 scale.

ORDNANCE SURVEY 1:250 000 Maps

Legend

Primary Routes. These form a national network of recommended through routes which complement the motorway system. Selected places of major traffic importance are known as Primary Route Destinations and are shown on this map thus EXETER. Distances and directions to such destinations are repeated on traffic signs which, on primary routes, have a green background or, on motorways, have a blue background.

To continue on a primary route through or past a place which has appeared as a destination on previous signs, follow the directions to the next primary destination shown on the green-backed signs.

ROADS
Not necessarily rights of way

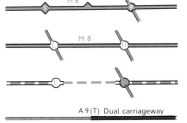 Motorway with service area, service area (limited access) and junction with junction number

Motorway junction with limited interchange

Motorway and junction under construction with proposed opening date where known

 A 9 (T) Dual carriageway — Trunk road

 A 86 — Main road

A 86 — Roundabout or multiple level junction

B 9163 — Secondary road

Road under construction

Toll — Toll   Road tunnel

A 851   B 8056 — Narrow road with passing places

Other tarred road   Other minor road

Gradient 1 in 7 and steeper

 18   23 — Distances in miles between markers

The representation on this map of a road is no evidence of the existence of a right of way

WATER FEATURES

 Canal

 Lake   Marsh

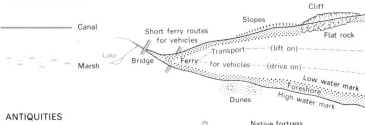

ANTIQUITIES

CANOVIVM · Roman antiquity

Castle · Other antiquities

𝔪 Ancient Monuments and Historic Buildings in the care of the Secretaries of State for the Environment, for Scotland and for Wales and that are open to the public

⁂ Native fortress

⚔ Site of battle (with date)

------ Roman road (course of)

GENERAL FEATURES

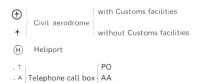

⊕ Civil aerodrome { with Customs facilities
✦ { without Customs facilities

Ⓗ Heliport

. T
. A   Telephone call box { PO / AA / RAC
. R

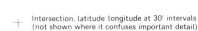 Buildings

Wood

⚓ Light-vessel   ⚲ Windmill

🗼 Lighthouse   Ⓐ Radio or TV mast

▲ Youth hostel

+ Intersection, latitude longitude at 30' intervals (not shown where it confuses important detail)

RAILWAYS

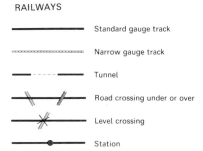

———————— Standard gauge track

·············· Narrow gauge track

Tunnel

Road crossing under or over

Level crossing

Station

RELIEF

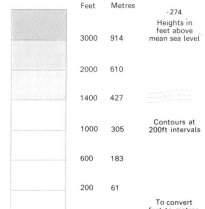

Feet	Metres
3000	914
2000	610
1400	427
1000	305
600	183
200	61
0	0

·274 Heights in feet above mean sea level

Contours at 200ft intervals

To convert feet to metres multiply by 0·3048

BOUNDARIES

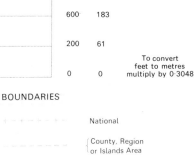

National

County, Region or Islands Area

1:250 000 Scale

| 10 | 5 | 0 | Kilometres 5 | 10 | 15 |

| 5 | 0 | Miles | 5 | 10 |

4 centimetres to 10 kilometres (one grid square)

1 kilometre = 0·6214 mile   1 mile = 1·61 kilometres

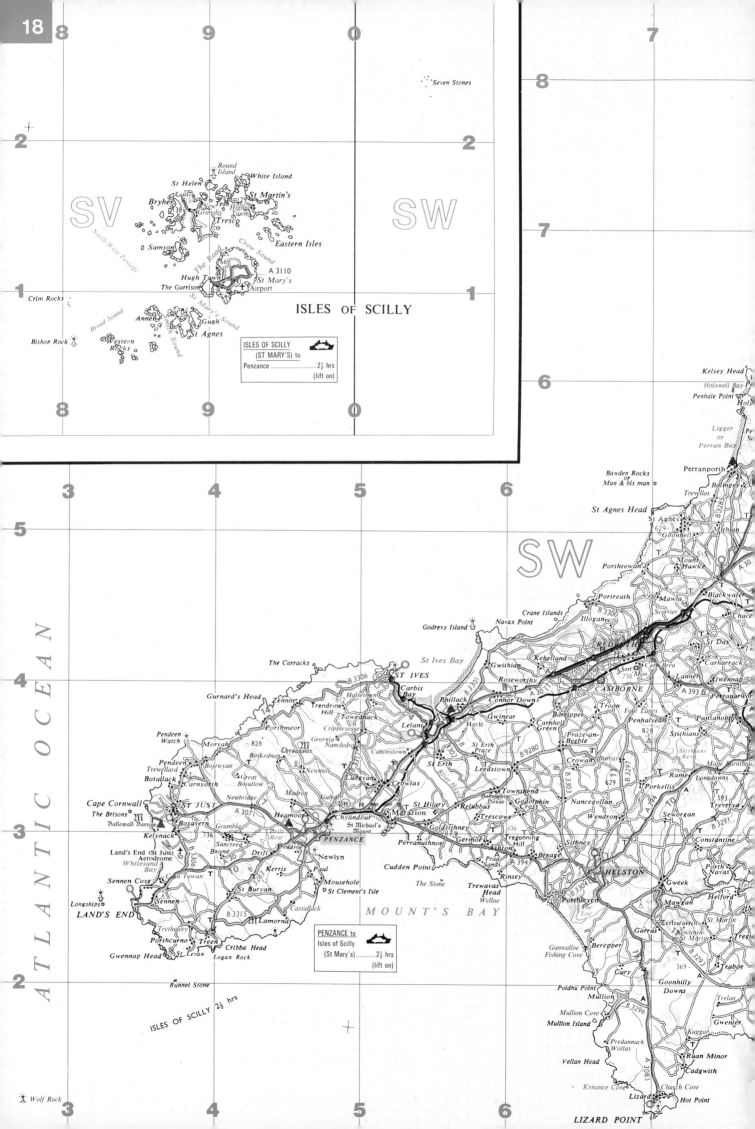

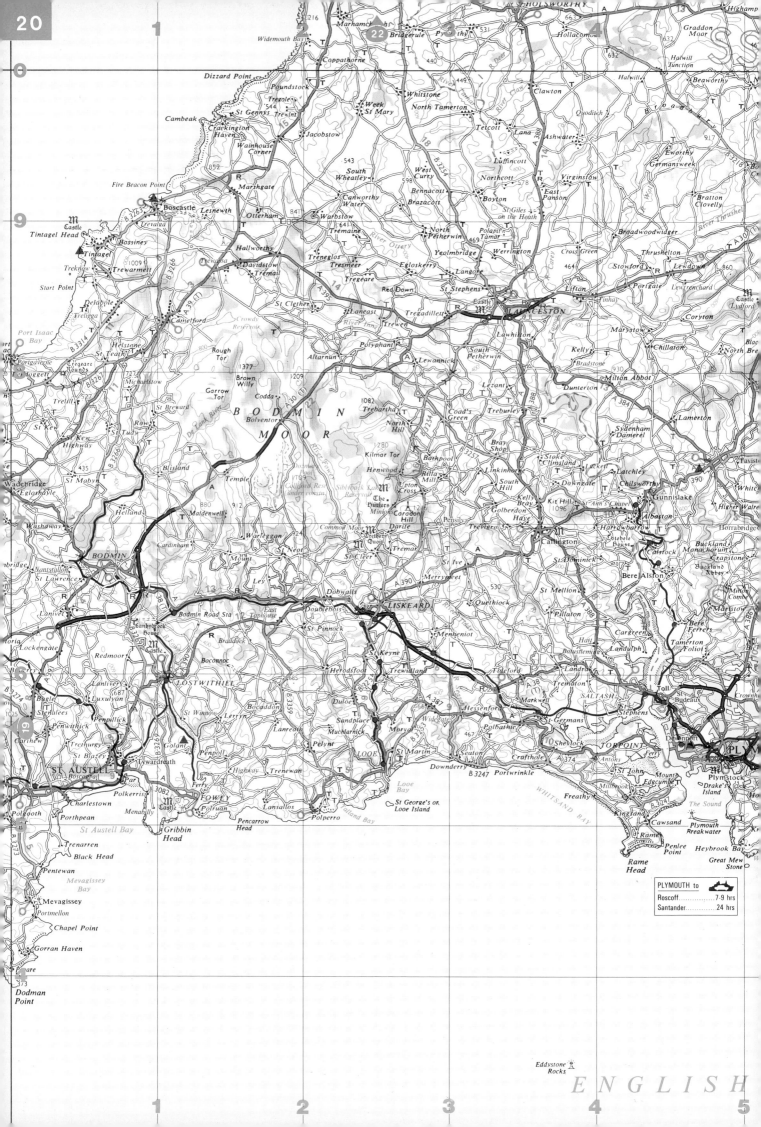

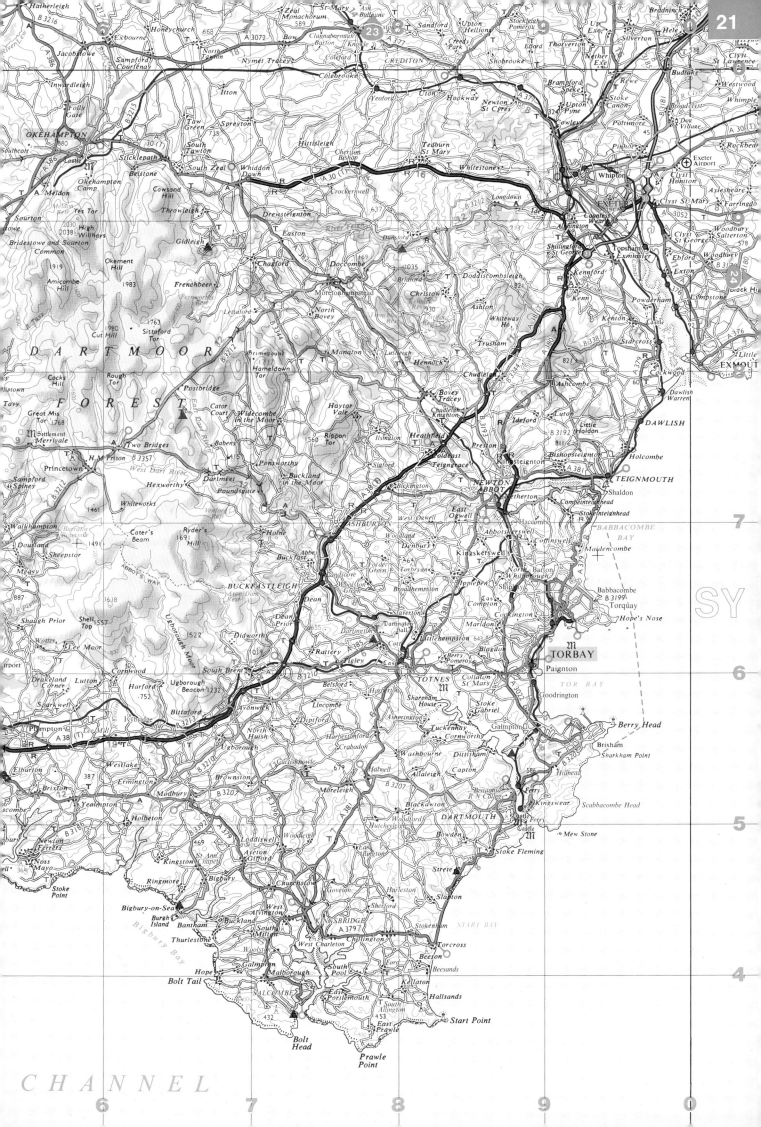

BRISTOL CHANNEL

ILFRACO...

LUNDY

North West Point

466

Great Shutter Rock · Rat Island

Bull Point
Rockham Bay
Morte Point 451 · Mortehoe
Lee 675
Woolacombe
654
Morte Bay
Trin...
688

Baggy Point
Pickwell
North Buckland
George...
Croyde
518
Knowl...
Saunton
Pi...
He...
Pu...

BARNSTAPLE
Braunton
Braunton
Burrows

OR

Bideford
Bar
Fremingto...

BIDEFORD BAY
Appledore
Westward Ho!
NORTHAM
Tapeley
Westleigh
Horw...

HARTLAND POINT
Titchberry
Windbury Point
Abbotsham
BIDEFORD
Woolfow...
Alver...

Hartland Quay
Stoke
Hartland
564
Clovelly
Clovelly Dykes
Buck's Mills
Fairy Cross
547
Landcross
Littleham
Weare
Gifford

Philham
Dyke
710
Buck's Cross
Parkham
Buckland
Brewer
Monkleigh

Elmscott
R
710
Woolfardisworthy
Parkham
Ash
709
Melbury
Frithelstock
G...

South Hole
Welcombe
771
Meddon
Ashmansworthy
East Putford
West Putford
708
Stibb Cross
Langtree
Little
Torring...

Knaps Longpeak
Gooseham
512
Eastcott
Dinworthy
Bulkworthy
Abbots
Bickington
Newton
St Petrock
Peters
Marland...
Wins...

Morwenstow
734
Youlstone
Bradworthy
A 388
616
400

Higher Sharpnose Point
Shop
656
Woodford
Coombe
Upper Tamar
Lake Re.
Sulcombe
Milton Damerel
400

Lower Sharpnose Point
Kilkhampton
Alfardisworthy
Lower Tamar
Lake
Soldon
Cross
R. Tamar
560

Stibb
A 39 (T)
B 3254
Holsworthy
Beacon
635
Thornbury
Shebbear
Buckland
Filleigh

BUDE
Poughill
57
Grimscott
Chilsworthy
Clokbury
Bradford
400

Bude Haven
STRATTON
Launcells
A 3072
10
Pancrasweek
HOLSWORTHY
663
Black
Torrington
574
Sheepwa...

BUDE
BAY
216
Marhamchurch
Bridgerule
Pyworthy
531
Hollacombe
400
13
Higham...

Widemouth Bay
Coppathorne
440
R. Deer
632
Halwill
Junction
632

Dizzard Point
Poundstock
449
Whitstone
R. Tamar
Clawton
Halwill
Beaworthy
46...

Cambeak
Tregole
544
Trewint
St Gennys
Week
St Mary
North Tamerton
R. Claw
Quoditch
917

Crackington Haven
Jacobstow
Tetcott
Lana
Ashwater
Eworthy
Germansweek

Wainhouse Corner
852
543
South
Wheatley
West
Curry
598
Luffincott
Northcott
578
Virginstow
Bratton
Clovelly

Fire Beacon Point
Marshgate
Canworthy
Water
Bennacott
Brazacott
Boyton
East
Panson

Boscastle
Lesnewth
Otterham
Tremaine
841
Warbstow
64
St Giles
on the Heath
Broadwoodwidger
River Thrushel

Castle
Tintagel Head
Trevalga
Treneglos
North
Petherwin
Polapit
Tamar
469
Werrington
Thrushelton

Bossiney
Hallworthy
Tremail
Egloskerry
Langore
Cross Green
Stowford
Lewdown
860

Tintagel
1009
Trewarmett
Trewassa
Davidstow
Tresmeer
Tregeare
Red Down
St Stephens
464
Portgate
Lewtrenchard

Start Point
B 3266
Trengune
St Clether
Tregadillett
LAUNCESTON
Lifton
Tinhay
Coryton
Castle
Lydford

Trekniw
Delabole
Treligga
Camelford
Crowdy
Reservoir
Laneast
Trewen
Lawhitton
Marystow
Chillaton
North Br...

Port Isaac
Bay
B 3314
Helstone
St Teath
Rough
Tor
1377
Altarnun
Polyphant
Lewannick
South
Petherwin
Kelly
Bradstone
930
Milton Abbot

Portgaverne
Doggett
Michaelst...
Brown
Willy
20
Lezant
Dunterton
Garrow
Tor
Codda

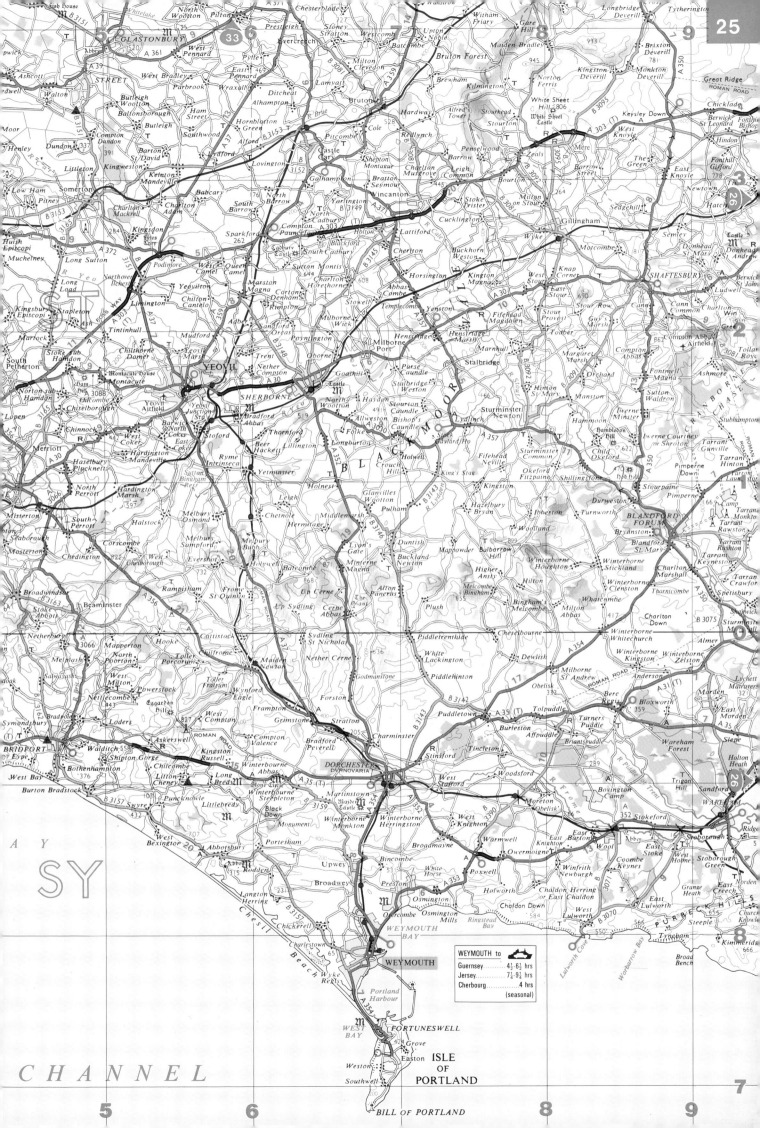

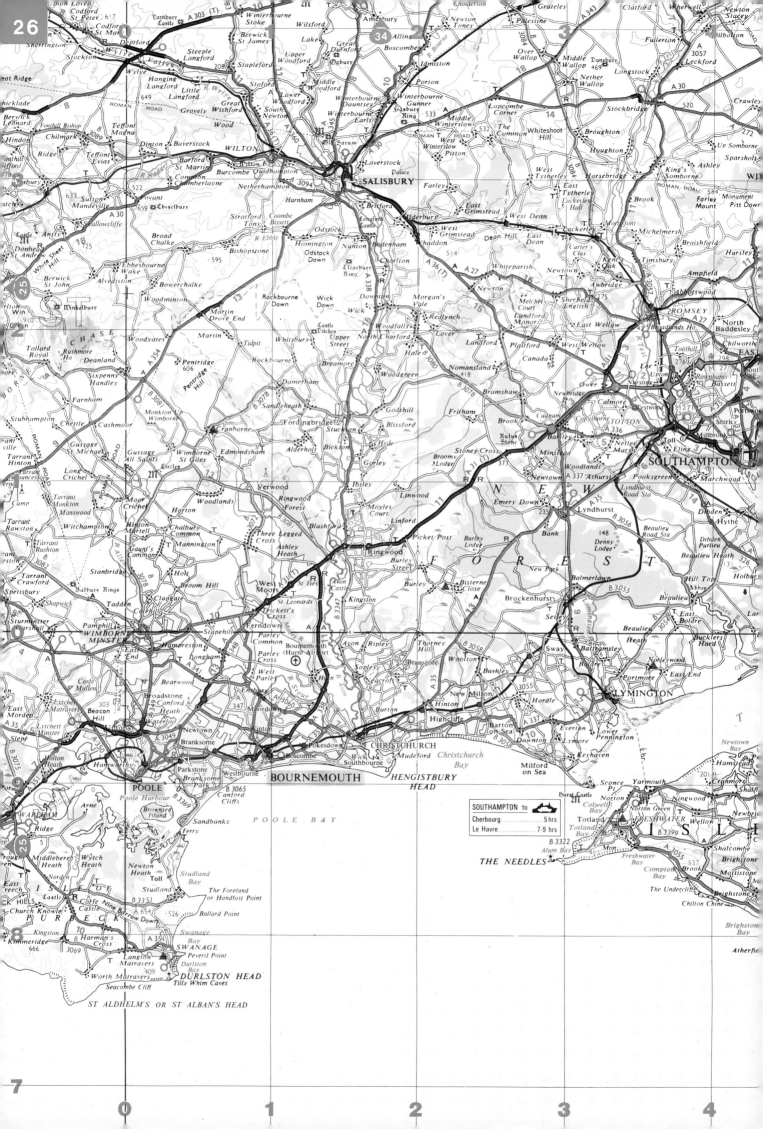

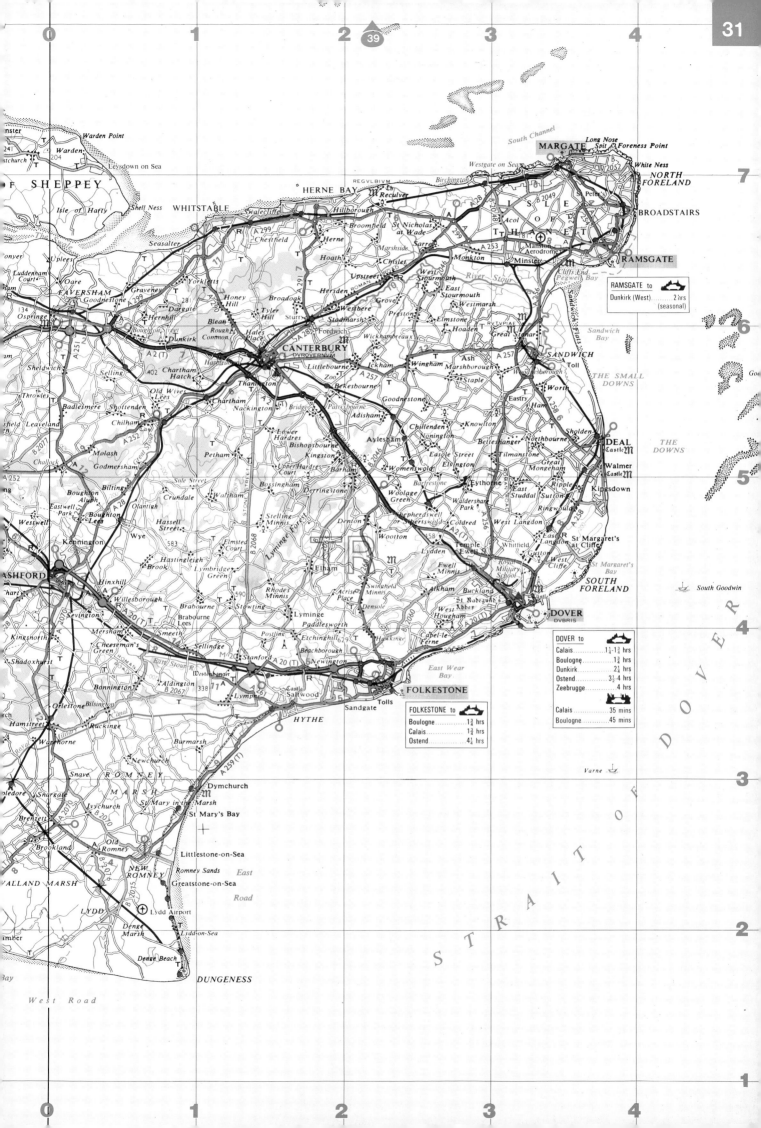

Major map labels

RHONDDA
PONTYPRIDD
CAERPHILLY
NEWPORT
CARDIFF
PENARTH
BARRY
CWMBRAN
CAERLEON
CLEVEDON
WESTON-super-MARE
BRIDGWATER
TAUNTON
MINEHEAD
WATCHET
DUNSTER
BRIDGEND
COWBRIDGE
TONYPANDY

BRIDGWATER BAY
MOUTH OF THE SEVERN
VALE OF TAUNTON DEANE
BRENDON HILLS
QUANTOCK FOREST

SS

Flat Holm
Steep Holm
Breaksea Point
Nash Point
Sully Island
Barry Island
Lavernock Point
Brean Down
Berrow Flats
Stert Flats
Middle Grounds
Usk Patch
Sand Point
Sand Bay
Weston Bay

Grid numbers: 1, 2, 3, 4 (top); 7, 6, 5, 4, 3 (left and right margins)
44, 41, 23, 24 (junction markers)

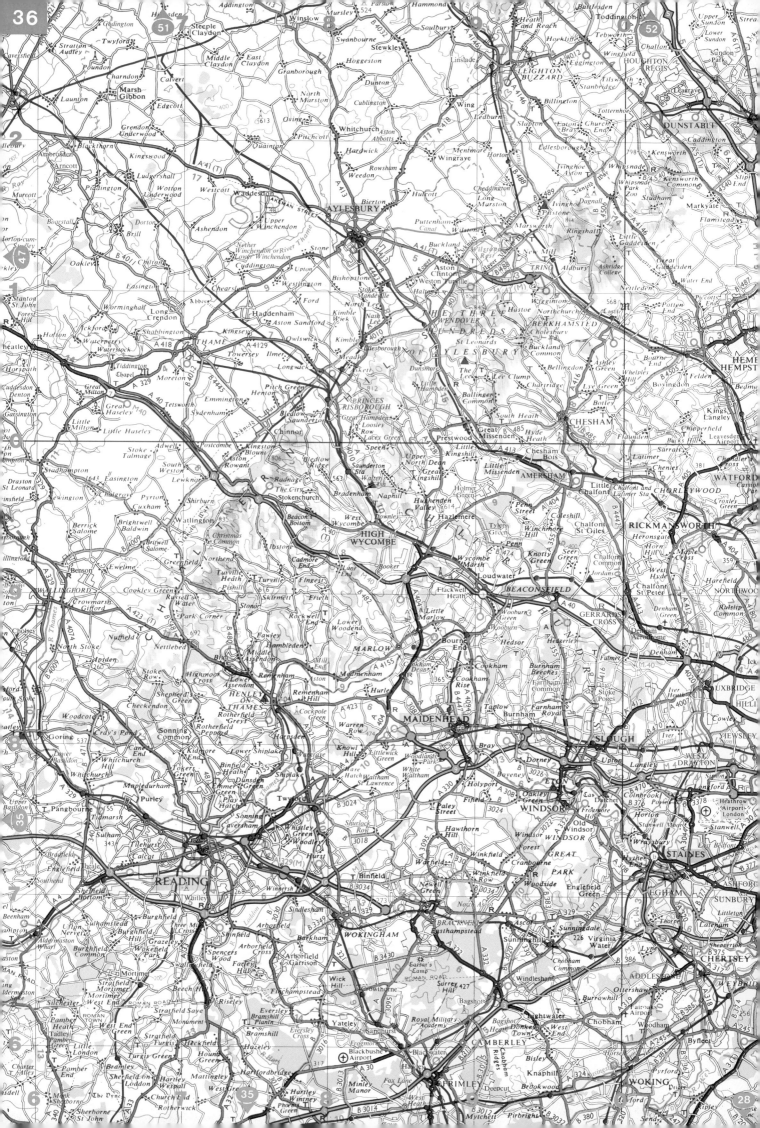

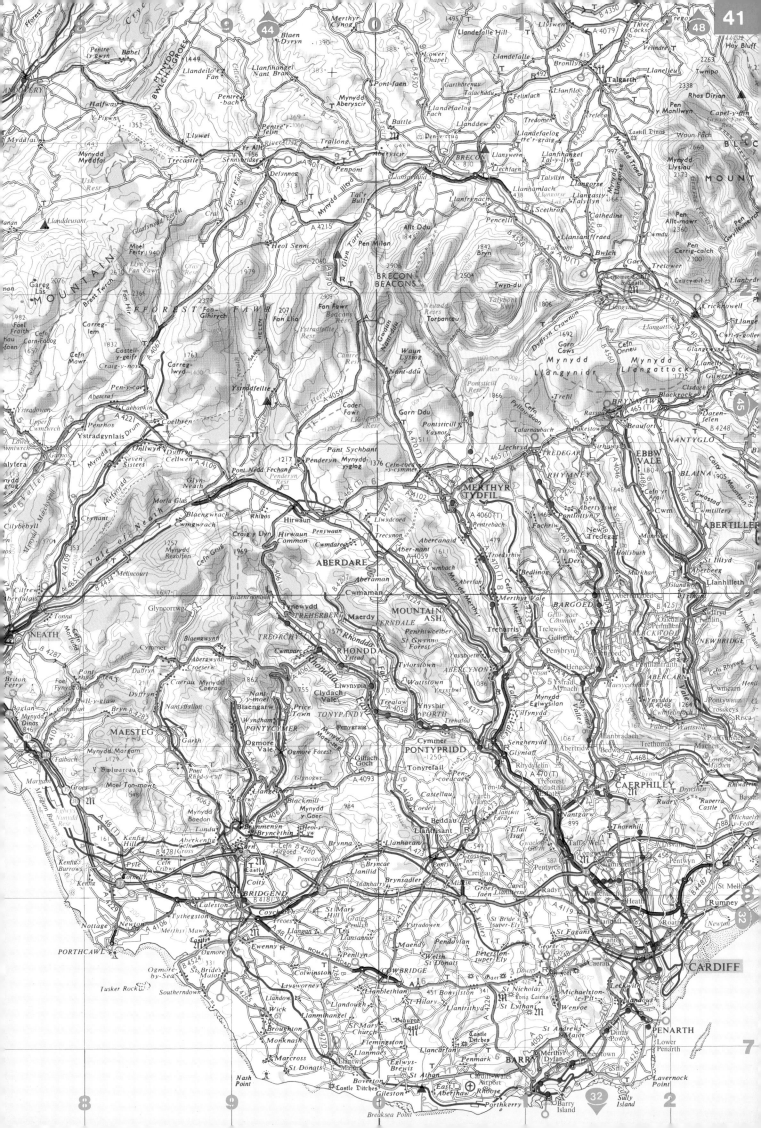

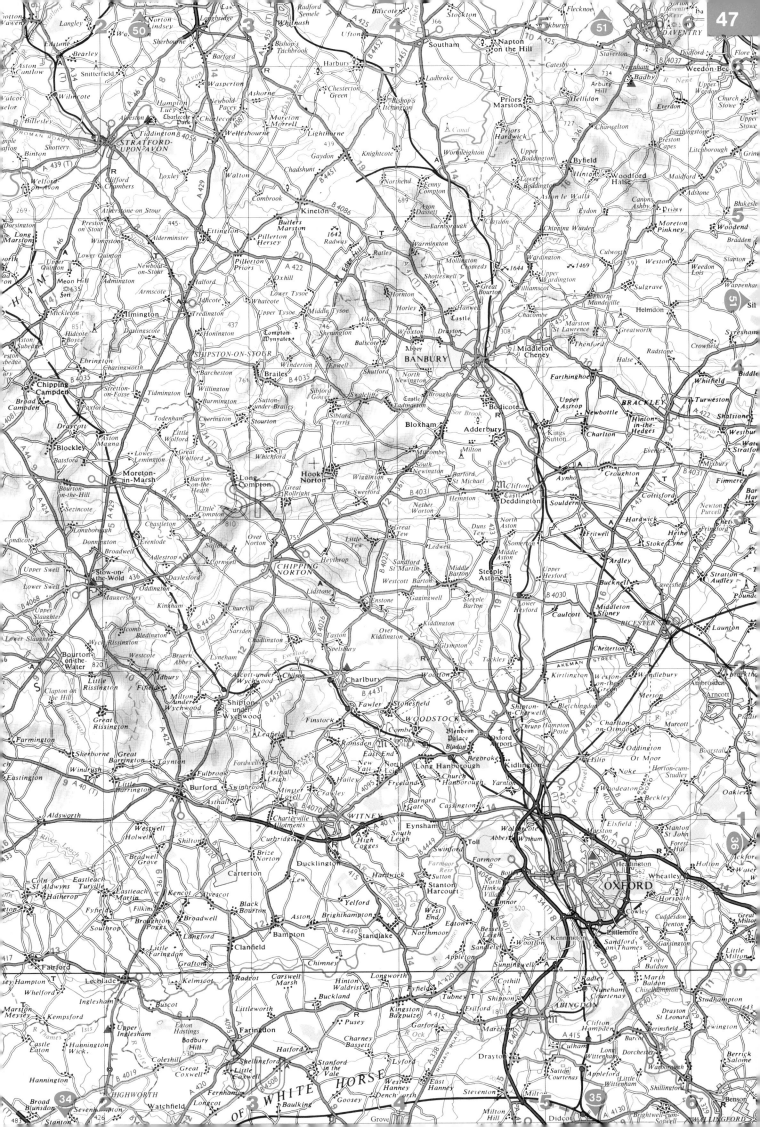

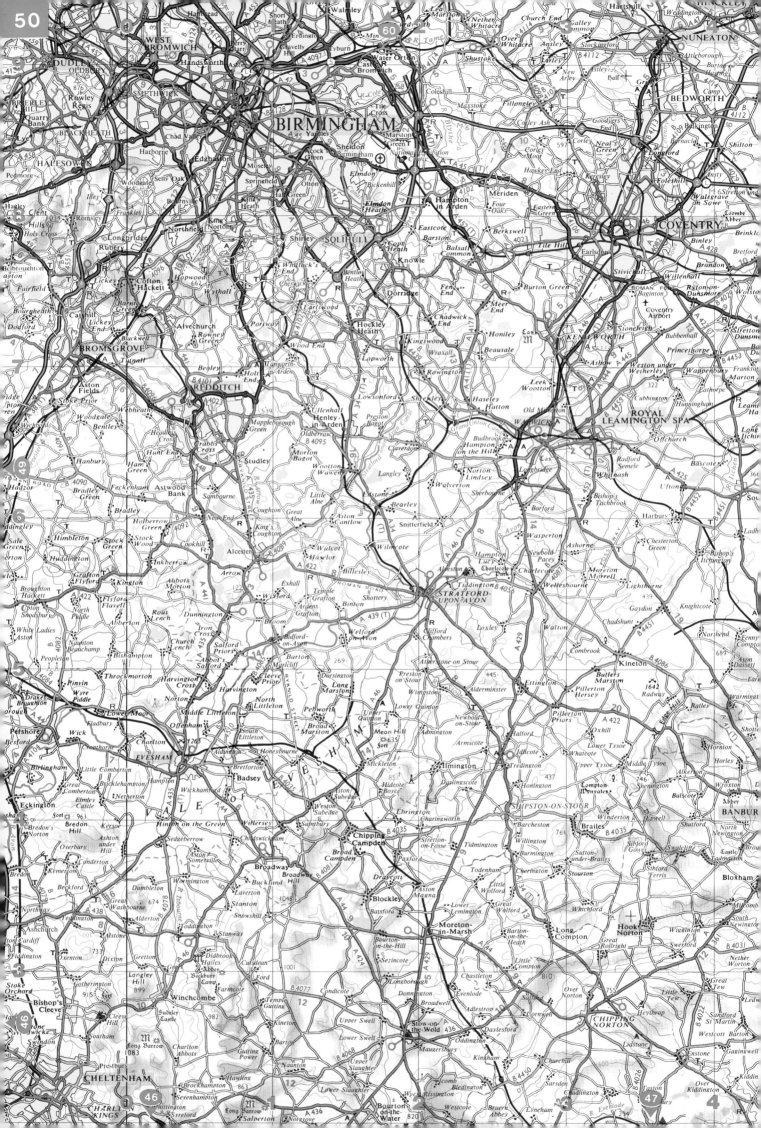

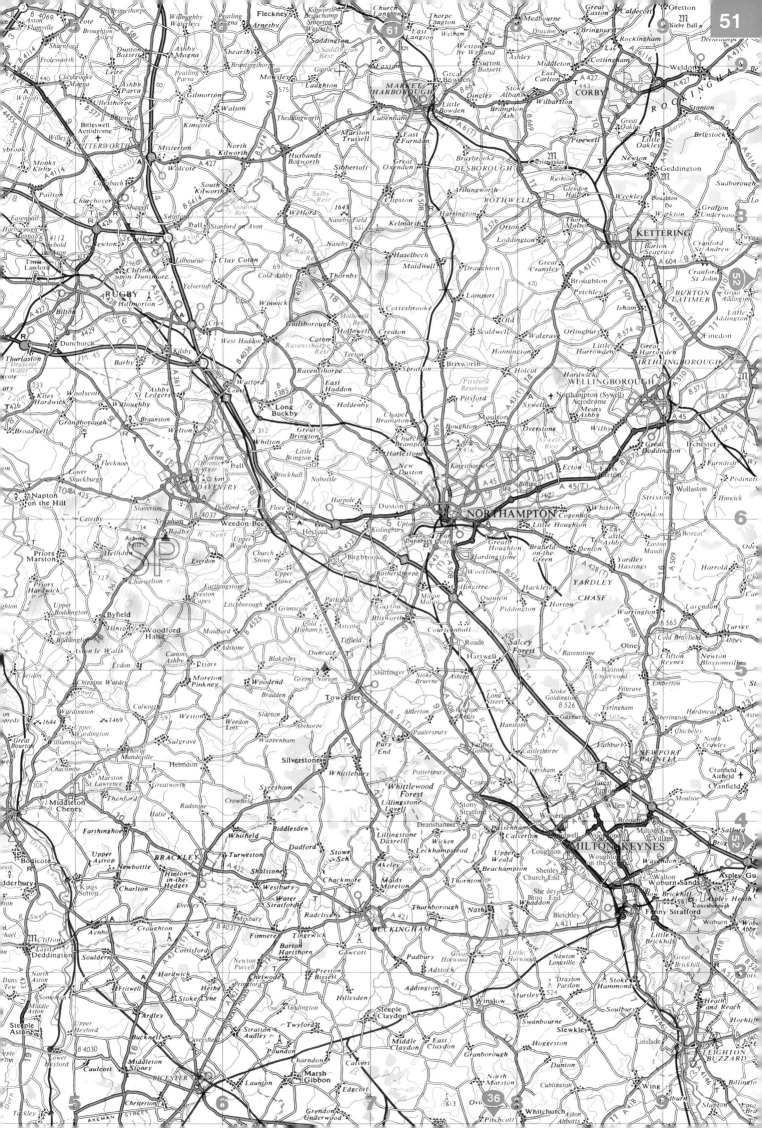

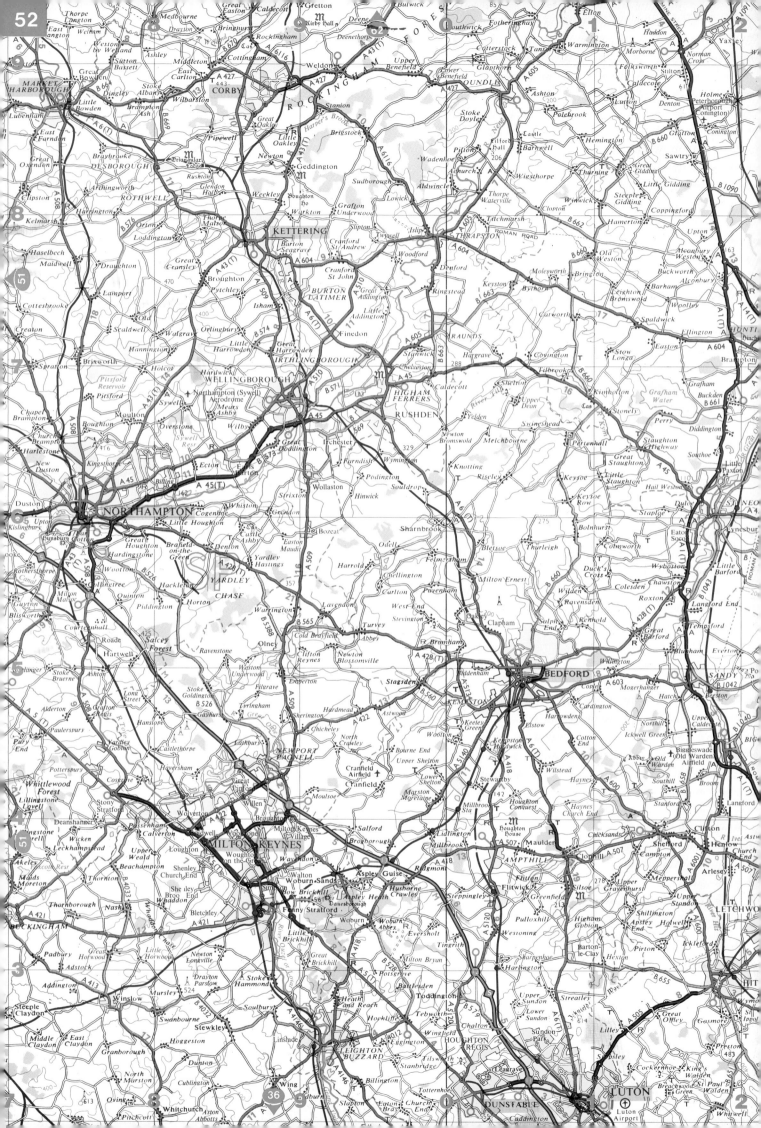

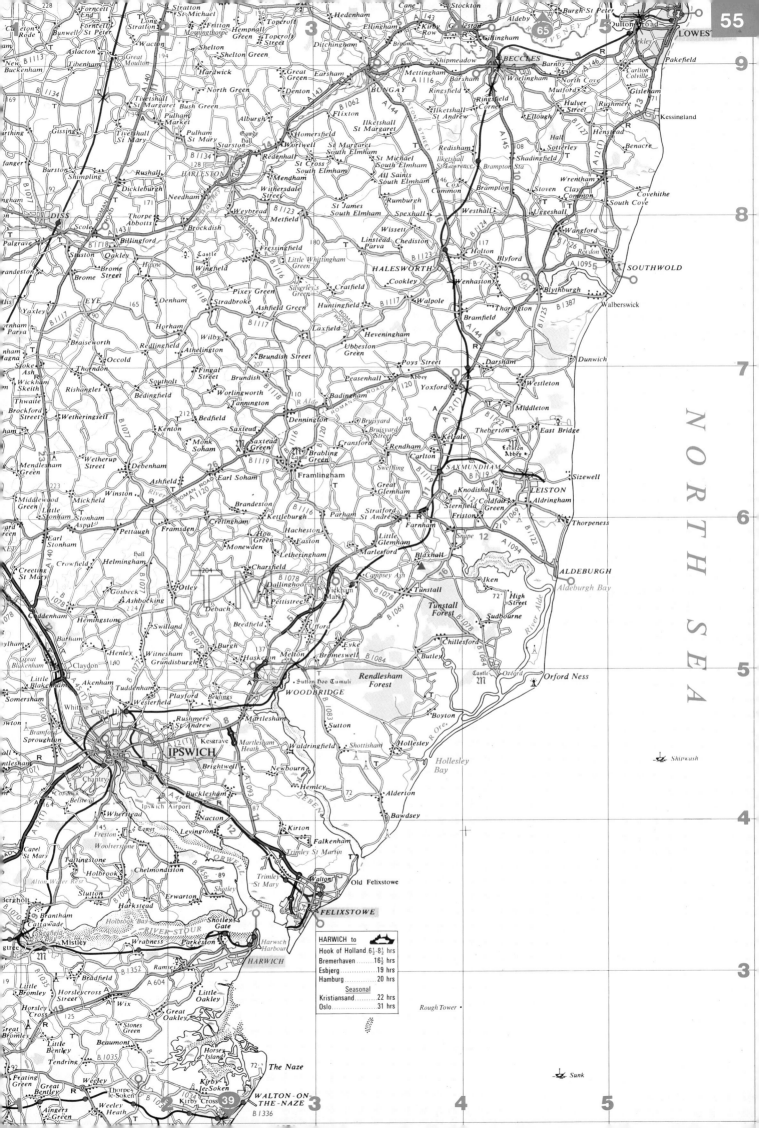

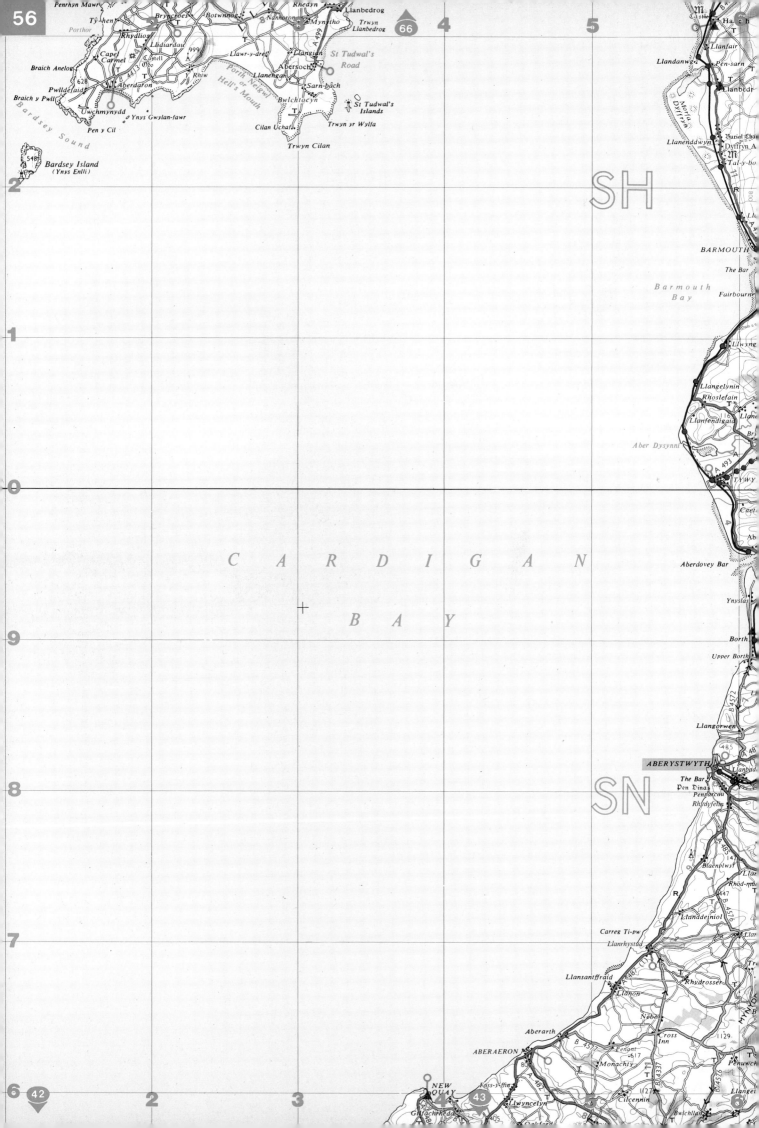

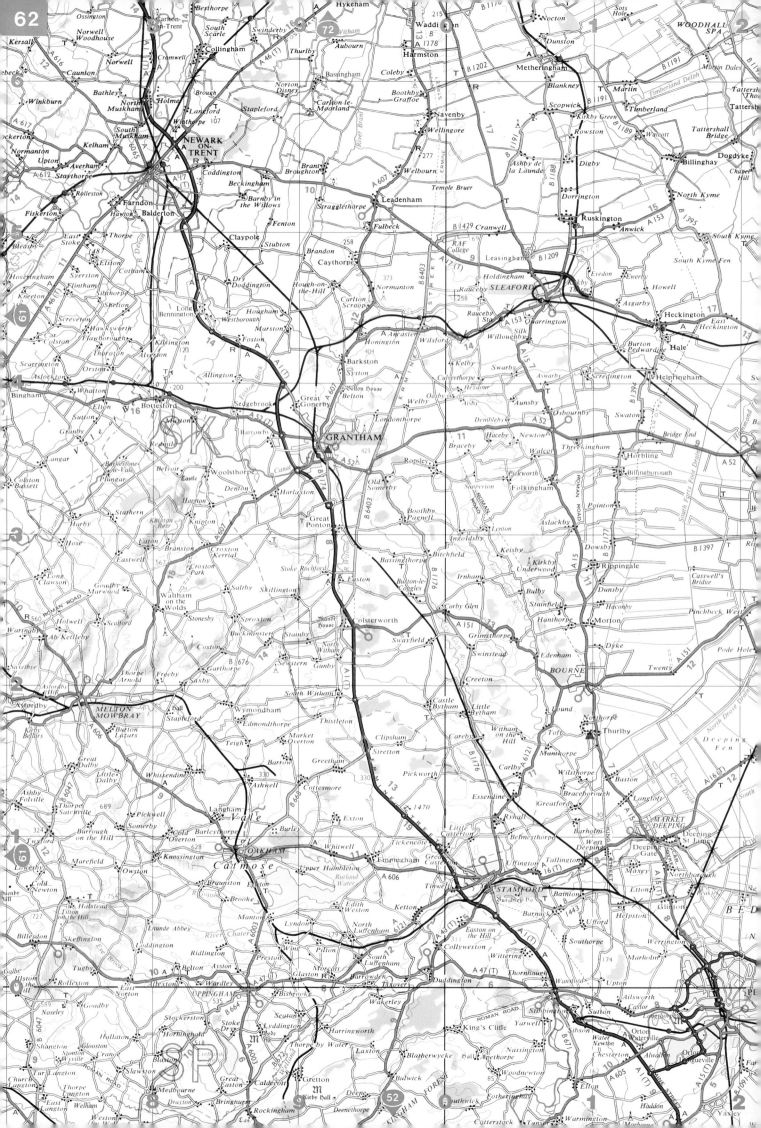

N O R T H   S E A

SHERINGHAM
West-Runton
CROMER
Kelling Weybourne Upper Sheringham Beeston Regis East Runton Overstrand
Bodham East Beckham Aylmerton Felbrigg Sidestrand
West Beckham Gresham Crossdale Street Trimingham
Edgefield Baconsthorpe Sustead Roughton Northrepps Gimingham Mundesley
Bessingham Hanworth Thorpe Market Southrepps Paston
Plumstead Matlaske Thurgarton Alby Hill Gunton Sta Bacton
Little Barningham Aldborough Antingham Bradfield Knapton Keswick Walcott
Saxthorpe Calthorpe Wickmere Suffield Swafield Edingthorpe
Itteringham Erpingham Colby NORTH WALSHAM Witton Happisburgh
Oulton Blickling Banningham Spa Common Crostwight Ridlington Happisburgh Common
Ingworth Felmingham Honing Lessingham Hempstead
Heydon Oulton Street Tuttington Westwick Bengate Worstead East Ruston Sea Palling
Southgate Aylsham Burgh next Aylsham Skeyton Dilham Ingham Waxham
Cawston Marsham Brampton Swanton Abbott Smallburgh Stalham Hickling
Reepham Eastgate Buxton Scottow Tunstead Sutton Hickling Green Horsey
Brandiston Buxton Heath Lamas Little Hautbois Sco Ruston Neatishead Cathield Hickling Heath
Hevingham Stratton Strawless Coltishall Irstead Somerton
Swannington Horstead Belaugh Ludham Potter Heigham Winterton-on-Sea
Alderford Waterloo Hainford Horning Bastwick Martham
Felthorpe St Helena Fretenham Hoveton Upper Street Repps Hemsby Newport
Morton Horsford Wroxham Thurne Rollesby Scratby
Weston Longville Newton St Faith Crostwick Woodbastwick Clippesby Ormesby St Margaret California
Taverham Horsham St Faith Spixworth Rackheath Salhouse Ranworth Burgh St Margaret Ormesby St Michael
Ringland Drayton Norwich Airport New Rackheath Panxworth South Walsham Billockby Thrigby Filby Mautby Caister-on-Sea
Honingham Costessey Catton Sprowston Little Plumstead Hemblington Upton Runham West End West Caister Heliport
Easton Hellesdon Thorpe End Garden Village Burlington Acle Stokesby
Marlingford New Costessey Thorpe St Andrew Great Plumstead Blofield Lingwood Damgate R Bure
Bowthorpe Bawburgh Harlham Colney NORWICH Postwick Brundall Beighton GREAT YARMOUTH
Barford Trowse Newton Kirby Bedon Surlingham Strumpshaw South Burlingham Tunstall Halvergate Marshes Burgh Castle GORLESTON ON SEA
Wramplingham Little Melton Bramerton Buckenham Freethorpe Berney Arms Sta ROMAN FORT Bradwell
High Green Cringleford Keswick Rockland St Mary Hassingham Southwood Cantley Wickhampton Belton
Kimberley Ho Hethersett Caistor St Edmund Claxton Limpenhoe Hopton
Ketteringham Swardeston Dunston Framingham Earl Hellington Ashby St Mary Langley Street Reedham
WYMONDHAM East Carleton Stoke Holy Cross Yelverton Bergh Apton Thurton Hardley Street Norton Fritton
Mulbarton Poringland Langley Marshes Lound Blundeston Corton
Bracon Ash Howe Chedgrave Thurlton Herringfleet
Spooner Row Wreningham Newton Flotman Shotesham Brooke Loddon Norton Subcourse Thorpe Somerleyton
Ashwellthorpe Hapton Saxlingham Nethergate Mundham Hales Haddiscoe OULTON BROAD
Tacolneston Forncett St Mary Tasburgh Kirstead Green Seething Raveningham Maypole Green LOWESTOFT
Forncett End Forncett St Peter Stratton St Michael Tharston Thwaite St Mary Kirby Cane Toft Monks Stockton Burgh St Peter
Bunwell Long Stratton Hempnall Morningthorpe Topcroft Street Woodton Hedenham Kirby Row Aldeby Oulton
Carleton Rode Wacton Shelton Ditchingham Ellingham Gillingham R WAVENEY Kirkley

Haisborough

Whimpwell Green
Halvergate
Breydon Water
YARMOUTH ROADS
R Bure
RIVER YARE
R Chet
R WAVENEY

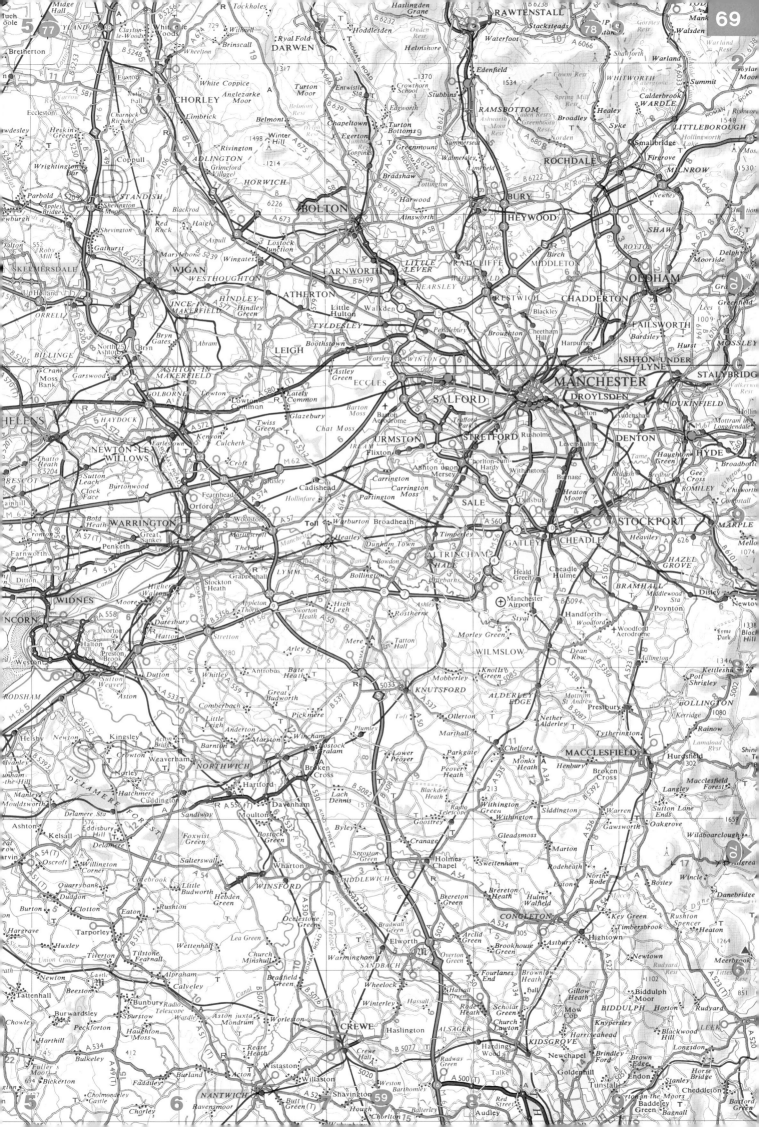

DEWSBURY
WAKEFIELD
OSSETT
HORBURY
NORMANTON
FEATHERSTONE
PONTEFRACT
KNOTTINGLEY
Low Eggborough
Hensall
Snaith
Rawcliffe
Gowdall
Cowick
Pollington
Great Heck
Whitley
Cridling Stubbs
Darrington
East Hardwick
Purston Jaglin
Sharlston
West Hardwick
Crofton
High Ackworth
Wentbridge
Womersley
Little Smeaton
Kirk Smeaton
Walden Stubbs
Fenwick
Sykehouse
Moorends
Thorne Waste or Moors
Thorne
Fishlake
Crigglestone
Walton
Netherton
Hill Top
Wintersett
Ryhill
Kinsley
Ackworth Moor Top
Thorpe Audlin
Badsworth
Upton
Norton
Campsall
Askern
Emley
West Bretton
Woolley
Notton
South Hiendley
HEMSWORTH
South Elmsall
Burghwallis
Thorpe in Balne
Kirk Bramwith
Stainforth
Hatfield
Clayton West
High Hoyland
DARTON
ROYSTON
Shafton
Brierley
Skellow
Carcroft
Dunscroft
Barnby Dun
Kexbrough
Staincross
Carlton
South Kirkby
Grimethorpe
Hampole
DENBY DALE
Cawthorne
Clayton
Hooton Pagnell
CUDWORTH
Great Houghton
Brodsworth
ADWICK LE STREET
Toll Bar
Dunsville
Kirk Sandall
Hatfield Woodhouse
BARNSLEY
Gawber
Ardsley
Arksey
Edenthorpe
Armthorpe
BENTLEY
Hatfield Moor
Silkstone
DARFIELD
Thurnscoe
Hickleton
Marr
DONCASTER
Hoyland Swaine
DODWORTH
Silkstone Common
WORSBROUGH
Goldthorpe
Barnburgh
Sprotbrough
Nutwell
Cantley
Wroot
Wentworth Castle
WOMBWELL
Bolton upon Dearne
Branton
Auckley
Oxspring
Birdwell
Jump
Brampton
High Melton
Bessacarr
Blaxton
Thurgoland
Tankersley
MEXBOROUGH
Adwick upon Dearne
Cadeby
Warmsworth
HOYLAND NETHER
Elsecar
WATH UPON DEARNE
Old Denaby
Wortley
CONISBROUGH
New Edlington
Loversall
New Rossington
Rossington
Finningley
STOCKSBRIDGE
Deepcar
SWINTON
High Green
Wentworth
Nether Haugh
Kilnhurst
Hooton Roberts
Wadworth
Bolsterstone
Ewden Village
Chapeltown
RAWMARSH
Ravenfield
Thorpe Hesley
Greasbrough
Thrybergh
Braithwell
Wharncliffe Side
Grenoside
Dalton
Stainton
Tickhill
Austerfield
Misson
Oughtibridge
Ecclesfield
ROTHERHAM
Bramley
MALTBY
Bawtry
High Bradfield
Harworth
Bircotes
Scaftworth
Everton
Worrall
Hooton Levitt
Scrooby
Low Bradfield
Wickersley
Tinsley
Whiston
Roche Abbey
Oldcotes
Mattersey
Brinsworth
Catcliffe
Firbeck
Ranskill
Stannington
Treeton
Thurcroft
Laughton en le Morthen
Langold
SHEFFIELD
Ulley
Aughton
Dinnington
Letwell
Blyth
Torworth
Aston
Handsworth
Gildingwells
Fulwood
Todwick
Woodhouse
Kiveton Park
Anston
Woodsetts
Carlton in Lindrick
Barnby Moor
Sutton
Beighton
Hackenthorpe
Wales
Thorpe Salvin
Hathersage
Carl Wark
Dore
Gleadless Townend
Mosborough
Harthill
Shireoaks
Ranby
Babworth
EAST RETFORD
Beauchief
Norton
Greenhill
Killamarsh
Netherthorpe Airfield
Rhodesia
WORKSOP
Coal Aston
Eckington
Totley
Dronfield Woodhouse
DRONFIELD
Nether Padley
Renishaw
Eaton
Apperknowle
West Handley
Barlborough
Holmesfield
Unstone
Froggatt
Clowne
Whitwell
Hodthorpe
Gamston
Common Side
Clumber Park
Elkesley
West Drayton
Whittington
Welbeck Abbey
Moorhall
Barlow
Curbar
STAVELEY
Creswell
Bothamsall
Newbold
Brimington
Holbeck
Carburton
Haughton
Bevercotes
Baslow
Cutthorpe
CHESTERFIELD
Elmton
Norton
West Markham
Long Duckmanton
Shuttlewood
Whaley
Pilsley
Chatsworth House
Calow
Nether Langwith
Cuckney
Thoresby
Wadshelf
Old Brampton
BOLSOVER
Walesby
Edensor
Arkwright Town
Meden Vale
Holymoorside
Hasland
Carr Vale
Scarcliffe
Church Warsop
Budby
Kirton
Walton
Temple Normanton
Upper Langwith
Laxton
Beeley
Palterton
Boughton
Wingerworth
WARSOP
Edwinstowe
Ollerton
Wellow
Rowsley
Grassmoor
Glapwell
Shirebrook
New Tupton
Doe Lea
New Houghton
Ompton
Stanton in Peak
Holmewood
Alton
North Wingfield
Pleasley
MANSFIELD WOODHOUSE
Old Clipstone
Ashover
Hardwick Hall
New Clipstone
Kneesall
Two Dales
CLAY CROSS
Forest Town
Kersall
Upper Hackney
Teversal
Eakring
Birchover
Milltown
Pilsley
Tibshelf
MANSFIELD
Skegby
Wensley
Stretton
Bilsthorpe
Maplebeck
Winster
MATLOCK
Morton
Stanton Hill
Brightgate
Matlock Bath
Tansley
Brackenfield
Stonebroom
Higham
Huthwaite
SUTTON IN ASHFIELD
Winkburn
Bonsall
Lea
Shirland
Westhouses
Rainworth
Kirklington
Wessington
Ible
Cromford
Holloway
South Normanton
KIRKBY IN ASHFIELD
Farnsfield
Hockerton
Middleton
South Wingfield
Blidworth
Haywood Oaks
Edingley
Normanton
Upton
Whatstandwell
Crich
Pinxton
Ravenshead
Halam
WIRKSWORTH
ALFRETON
Annesley Woodhouse
Carsington
Alderwasley
Fritchley
Swanwick
Selston
Annesley
Newstead
Southwell
Pentrich
Somercotes
Ironville
Bagthorpe
Linby
Hognaston
Ambergate
Heage
RIPLEY
New Brinsley
Underwood
Papplewick
Oxton
Halloughton
Fiskerton
Kirk Ireton
SHERWOOD FOREST
72
61
79

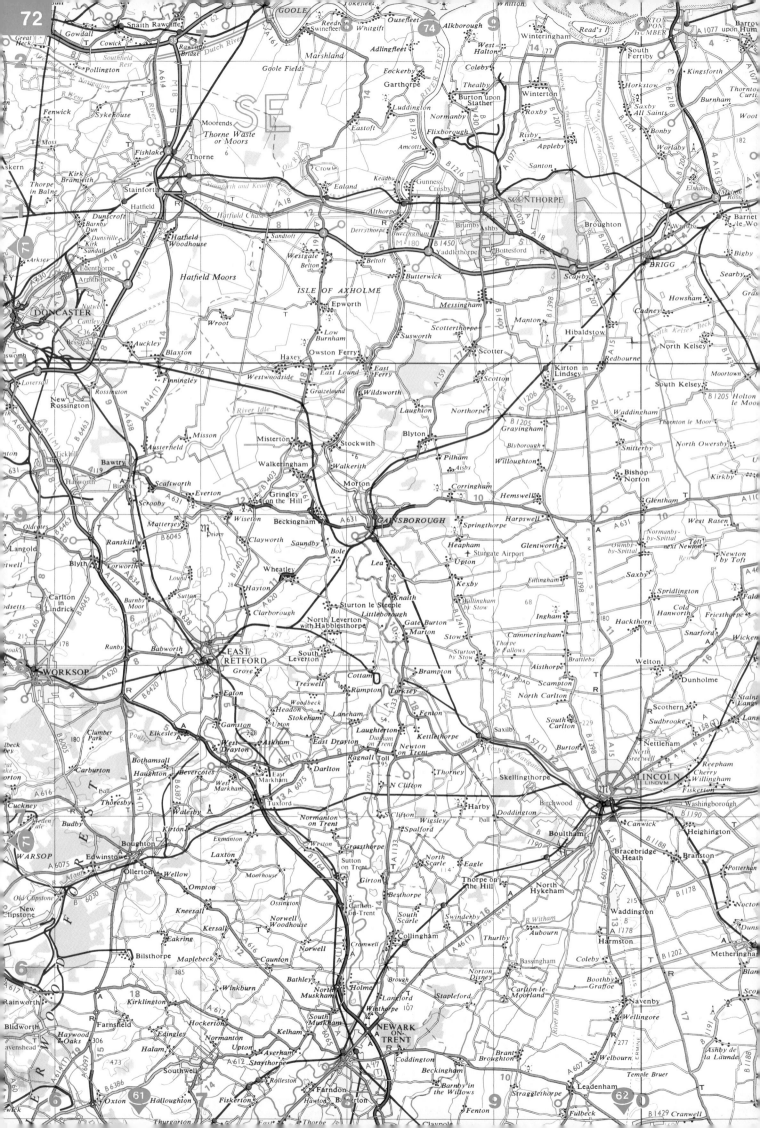

83

Water Yeat · Rusland · Crosthwaite · Grigghall · Oxenholme · New Hutton

Oxen Park · Finsthwaite · Cartmel Fell · The Howe · Row · Brigsteer · Natland · Old Hutton · Killington

Colton · Spark Bridge · Newby Bridge · Lakeside · Staveley-in-Cartmel · Witherslack Hall · Castle · Sedgwick · Gatebeck · Stainton · Middleton · Calf Top 1999 · Gawthrop · Rise Hill 1825 · Lea Yeat

Penny Bridge · Backbarrow · Ayside · High Newton · Witherslack · Mill Side · Town End · Leasgill · Endmoor · Crooklands · Warth Hill · Rigmaden Park · Barbon · Crag Hill · Deepdale · Stone House · Wold

Greenodd · Field Broughton · Meathop · Heversham · Milnthorpe · Hall · Hincaster · Scout Hill 933 · Lupton · Old Town · Bullpot Fm · Gayle

Arrad Foot · Lindale · Storth · Beetham · Holme · Furleton · Kearstwick · Casterton · Whernside 2416 · Blea Moor

Cartmel · Holme Island · Arnside · Yealand Redmayne · Burton-in-Kendal · Hutton Roof 899 · Kirkby Lonsdale · Leck Fell · Scales Moor · Chapel le Dale · Ribblehead

Holker · Cark · Allithwaite · Grange-over-Sands · Silverdale · Yealand Conyers · Priest Hutton · Whittington · Cowan Bridge · Ireby · Westhouse · Roman Road · Simon Fell 2376

Flookburgh · Kents Bank · Warton · Borwick · Yealand · Nether Burrow · Newton · Tunstall · Cantsfield · Ingleborough Hill · Skirwith · Ingleton · Newby Moss · 78

Ravenstown B5277 · Humphrey Head Point · Warton Sands · Carnforth · Capernwray · Arkholme 466 · Melling · Wennington · Low Bentham · Burton in Lonsdale · High Bentham · Newby

MORECAMBE · Cartmel Wharf · Over Kellet · Gressingham · Tatham · Hornby · Clapham · Austwick

Mort Bank · BAY · Yeoman Wharf · Bolton-le-Sands · Nether Kellet · Wray · Keasden · Eldroth

Slyne · Aughton · Claughton · Lowgill · Burn Moor Fell · Gigg · Wham

Hest Bank · Halton · Whit Moor · Goodber Common · Tatham Fells · Burn Moor

MORECAMBE · Torrisholme · A683 Caton · Brookhouse · Caton Moor · Salter · Thrushgill · Botton Head 1595 · Catlow Fell · Black · Rath

HEYSHAM to Douglas ... 3¾ hrs · Heaton · LANCASTER · Crossgill · Little Dale · Haylot Fell · Blanch Fell · Long Gill

Nuclear Power Sta · Middleton · Scotforth · Quernmore · Upper Brow Top · Clougha Pike · Ward's Stone 1839 · Mallowdale Fell · White Hill 1786 · Wolfhole Crag · Wiggle

Heysham Lake · Overton · Lee Fell · Tarnbrook · Lee · FOREST · Croasdale Fell · Tosside · Stocks Res

Sunderland Bank · Glasson B5290 · Galgate · Abbeystead · Marshaw · Wyresdale Tower (ruin) 1296 · Whins Brow 1561 · Slaidburn

FLEETWOOD to Douglas ... 3 hrs (seasonal) · Thurnham Hall · Dolphinholme · Street · Hawthornthwaite Fell · Sykes · Dunsop Bridge · Newton · Hareden · Easington Fell 1300 · Holden

Bernard Wharf · Cockerham · Forton · Fell Top 1572 · Calder Fell · Sykes Fell · BOWLAND · B6478

North Wharf · Braides · Scotton · Oakenclough · Fair Snape Fell 1707 · Whitewell · Browsholme Hall · Grindleton · West Bradford · Sawley Abbey

FLEETWOOD · Rossall Point · Pilling Lane · Pilling · Stake Pool · Winmarleigh · Calder Vale · Chipping · Bashall Eaves · Walker Fold · Waddington · Low Moor · Chatburn · Worston

Knott End-on-Sea · Preesall · Garstang · Nateby · Churchtown · Claughton · Beacon Fell 873 · Hesketh Lane · CLITHEROE · Pendleton

Stalmine · Eagland Hill · Hambleton · Out Rawcliffe · Ratten Row · Catterall · White Chapel · Inglewhite · Knowle Green · Moor Nook · Stonyhurst College · Hurst Green · Great Mitton · Barrow · Wiswell

CLEVELEYS · THORNTON · Toll · Great Eccleston · Bilsborrow · Longridge Fell · Billington · Whalley · Read

Bispham · Carleton · POULTON-LE-FYLDE · St Michael's on Wyre · Crossmoor · Elswick · Inskip · Barton · Goosnargh · LONGRIDGE · Ribchester · Copster Green · Salesbury · Langho · GREAT HARWOOD · Simonstone

BLACKPOOL · Hardhorn · Singleton · Roseacre · Cuddy Hill · Haighton Green · Grimsargh · Balderstone · Wilpshire · CLAYTON LE-MOORS

North Shore · Normoss · Staining · Esprick · Catforth · Broughton · Osbaldeston · Mellor · RISHTON

Great Marton · Weeton · Wharles · Woodplumpton · Sharoe Green · FULWOOD · Samlesbury Aerodrome · Mellor Brook · CHURCH

South Shore · Common Edge · Plumpton · Wesham · Treales · Cottam · Ribbleton · Walton-le-Dale · Samlesbury · Osbaldeston · OSWALDTWISTLE · ACCRINGTON

Blackpool Airport · Higher Ballam · KIRKHAM · Salwick Sta · Lea Town · PRESTON · Higher Walton · Samlesbury Bottoms · Pleasington · Baxen

St Anne's · Moss Side · Warton · Clifton · Newton · Wrea Green · Freckleton · Higher Penwortham · Hoghton · Feniscowles · Lower Darwen · HASLINGDEN

LYTHAM ST ANNE'S · Warton Aerodrome · Lytham · Hutton · New Longton · Bamber Bridge · Gregson Lane · Brindle · Tockholes · Earcroft · Belthorn · Haslingden Grane

Salter Bank · Longton · Walmer Bridge · Midge Hall · Whittle Woods · DARWEN · Oeden Res

Foulnaze · Hesketh Bank · Much Hoole · LEYLAND · Clayton-le-Woods · Wheelton · Wilmill · Ryal Fold · Hoddlesden · Helmshore

Horse Bank · Banks · Becconsall · Hundred End · Tarleton · Bretherton · 69 · Whittle Coppice · Turton Moor · Crowthorn School · Stubbins

Marshside · Churchtown · Mere Brow · Croston · Sollom · Euxton · Anglezarke · Entwistle Res

North Shore · Banks Sands · Crossens

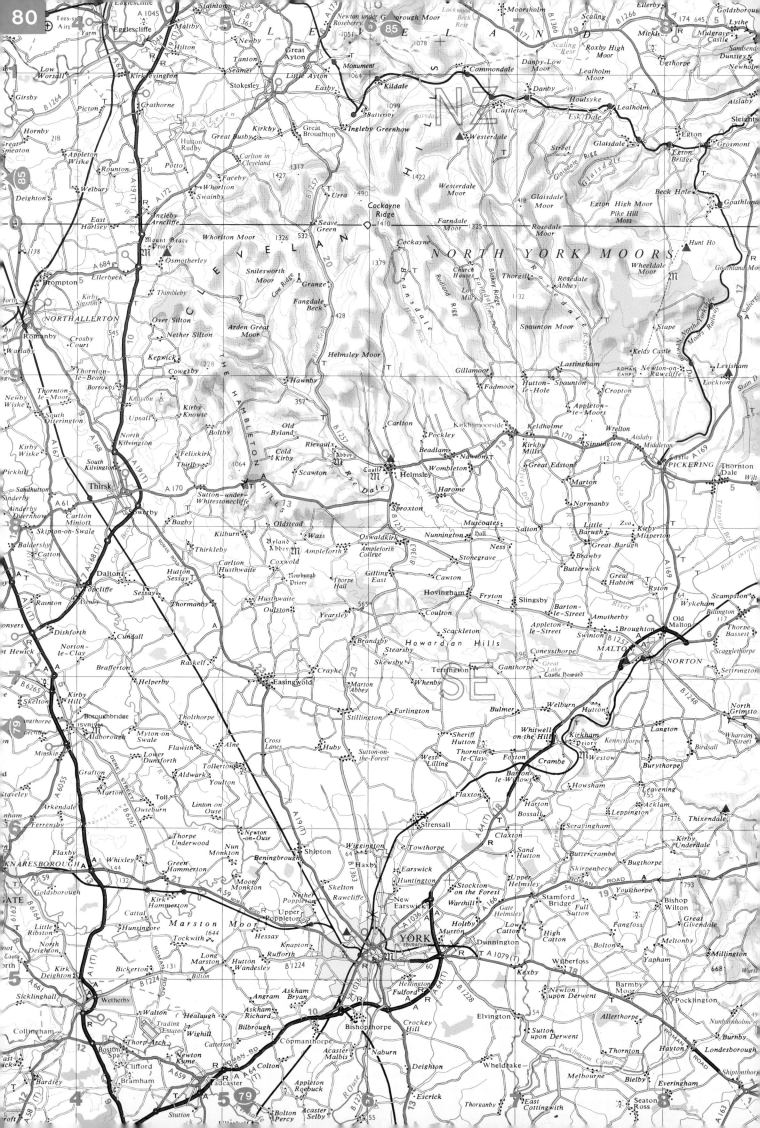

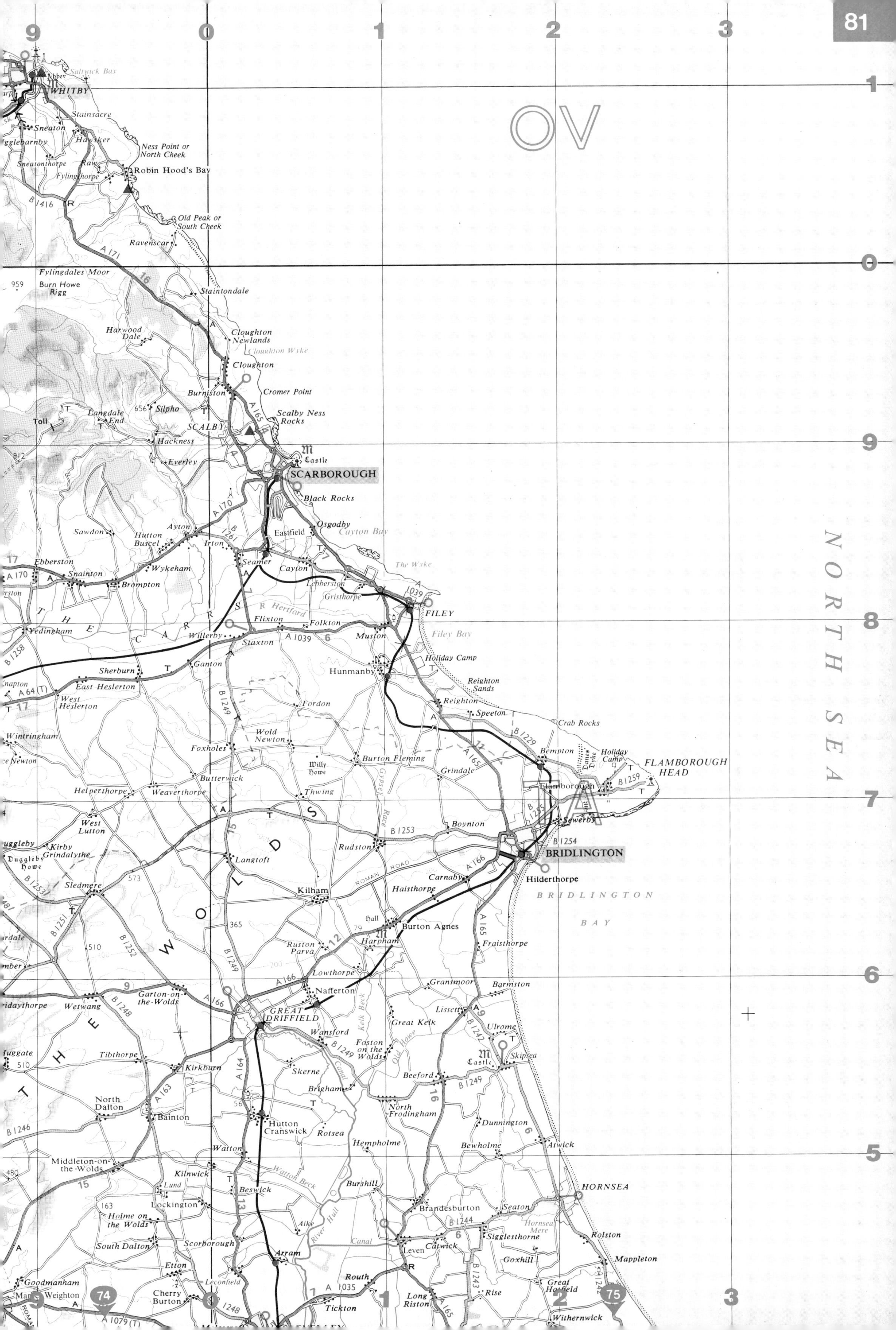

9 0 1 2 3

1

WHITBY
Saltwick Bay
Abbey
Stainsacre
Hawsker
Sneaton
Ness Point or North Cheek
Sneatonthorpe
Raw
Fylingthorpe
Robin Hood's Bay
B 1416
R
Old Peak or South Cheek
Ravenscar

0

A 171

16
Fylingdales Moor
Burn Howe Rigg
959
Staintondale

A

Harwood Dale
Cloughton Newlands
Cloughton Wyke

Cloughton

Burniston
Cromer Point
Scalby Ness Rocks
Langdale End
656 Silpho
SCALBY
Hackness
Everley
Toll
T
B 812

9

Castle
SCARBOROUGH
A 170
Black Rocks
Ayton
Sawdon
Hutton Buscel
Irton
Osgodby
Eastfield
Cayton Bay

B 1261

17 Ebberston
A 170
Snainton
Wykeham
Seamer
Cayton
The Wyke

Brompton
Lebberston
A 1039

Yedingham
Willerby
Flixton
Folkton
Gristhorpe
FILEY

Staxton
A 1039
Muston
Filey Bay

B 1258
Sherburn
Ganton
Hunmanby
Holiday Camp

East Heslerton
Fordon
Reighton Sands
A 64 (T)
West Heslerton
Speeton
Reighton
B 1249
Crab Rocks

Wintringham
Wold Newton
A 165
Bempton
Holiday Camp
Foxholes
Butterwick
Burton Fleming
Grindale
FLAMBOROUGH HEAD
B 1229
Helperthorpe
Weaverthorpe
Thwing
Flamborough
B 1259

7

West Lutton
Boynton
Sewerby
Duggleby
Kirby Grindalythe
Rudston
B 1253
B 1254
Langtoft
BRIDLINGTON
Sledmere
Kilham
Carnaby
Hilderthorpe
A 166
573
Haisthorpe
BRIDLINGTON BAY

365
Hall
Burton Agnes
A 165
Fraisthorpe
B 1251
B 1252
Harpham
510
Ruston Parva
200
Lowthorpe
Gransmoor
Barmston

6

9
Garton-on-the-Wolds
Nafferton
Lissett
A 165
Wetwang
B 1248
GREAT DRIFFIELD
A 166
Ulrome
Tibthorpe
Wansford
Foston on the Wolds
Skipsea
510
Kirkburn
A 164
Skerne
Beeford
Castle
North Dalton
Brigham
North Frodingham
Dunnington
A 163
Bainton
Hutton Cranswick
Rotsea
Hempholme
Bewholme
Atwick
B 1246

5

Middleton-on-the-Wolds
Watton
480
15
Kilnwick
Lund
Beswick
Burshill
HORNSEA
Lockington
163
Brandesburton
Seaton
Hornsea Mere
Rolston
Holme on the Wolds
Scorborough
Aike
B 1244
Sigglesthorne
South Dalton
Arram
Catwick
Goxhill
Mappleton
Etton
Routh
B 1243
Great Hatfield

Goodmanham
Leconfield
Long Riston
Rise
Withernwick
Market Weighton
Cherry Burton
Tickton
74
B 1248
A 1035
75
A 1079 (T)

NORTH SEA

OV

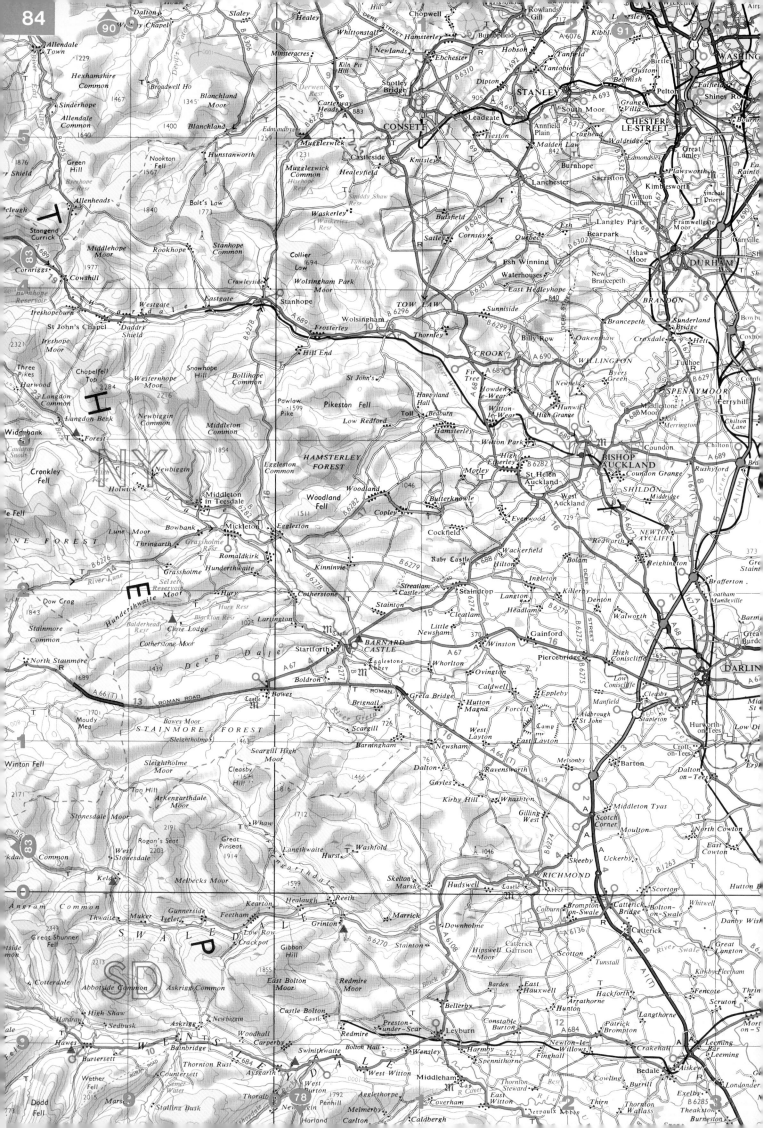

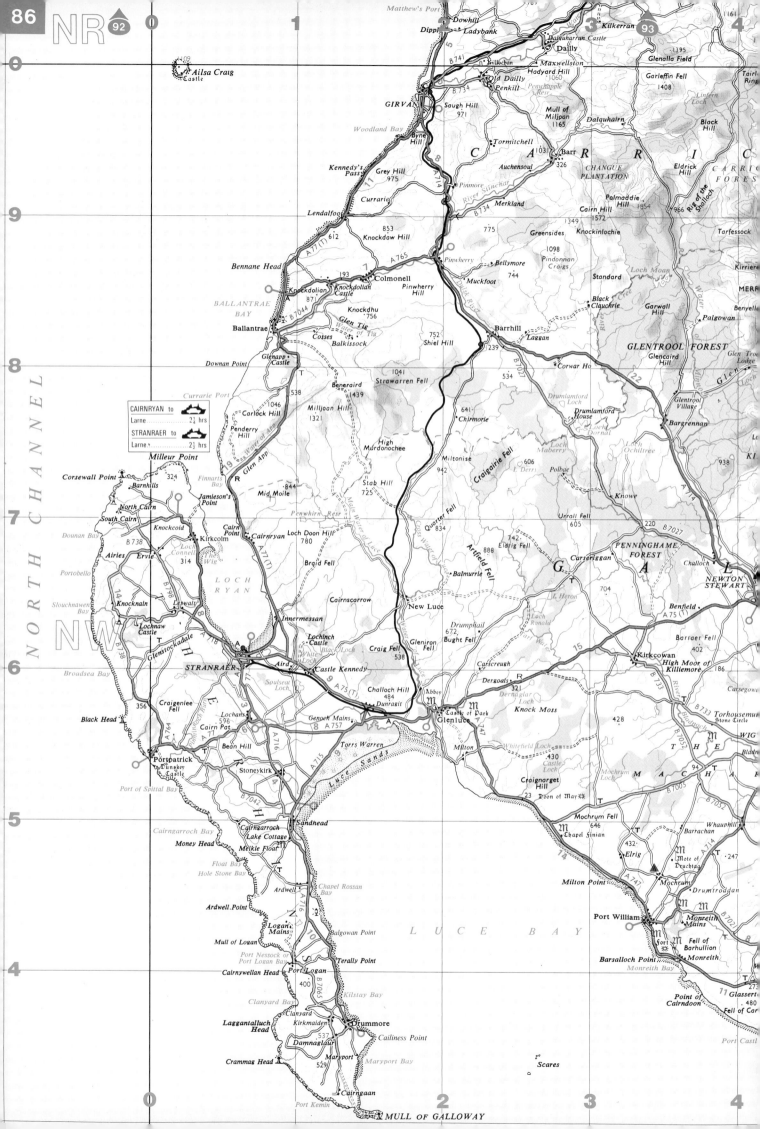

Inchmurrin
Priory
Boquhan
Gartness
Ballikinrain Castle
Loch Walton
Cringate Law
Crosskeys
Arden
Gartocharn
Croftamie
Killearn
Cairnoch Hill
Rhu
Castle
HELENSBURGH
Balloch Castle
Craighat
Dumgoyne
Earl's Seat
CAMPSIE FELLS
Carron Valley Forest
Carron Bridge
DUNIP
Balloch
Craigendoran
Auchencarroch
Strathblane Hills
Rosneath
Darleith Ho
Jamestown
Auchineden Hill
Duntreath Castle
Birkenburn Resr
Tomtain
High Banton
Head of Dennyloanhead
Colgrain
Alexandria
Bonhill
Dumbarton Muir
Burncrooks Resr
Netherton
Clachan of Campsie
Kilsyth Hills
Banton
Ardmore
Gelston
Renton
Blanefield
Strathblane
Balgrochan
KILSYTH
Kilmannan Resr
Lennoxtown
Queenzieburn
Banknock
GREENOCK
Cardross
Bellsmyre
KILPATRICK HILLS
Cochno Loch
Mugdock
Milton of Campsie
Dullatur
Croy
Pillar Bank
PORT GLASGOW
DUMBARTON
Greenside Resr
Mugdock Resr
Birdston
Twechar
CUMBE
Newark Castle
Finlaystone Ho
Milton
MILNGAVIE
Blairskaith
Torrance
KIRKINTILLOCH
Eastfield
Langbank
Old Kilpatrick
Bowling
Duntocher
Faifley
Bardowie
Balmore
Waterside
Luggiebank
Bardrainney
Auchenderes Resr
Erskine Br. Toll
BEARSDEN
Cadder
Lenzie
Condorrat
Mollinsburn
Leperstone Resr
Bishopton
Drumchapel
Antonine Wall
Bridgend
Auchinloch
Annathill
Rossland
Bishopton Sta
Erskine
CLYDEBANK
Temple
Bishopbriggs
Lumloch
Riggend
Kilmacolm
Inchinnan
Yoker
Stepps
Muirhead
Glenboig
Stand
Barochan Ho
Georgetown
Springburn
Garnkirk
Gartcosh
Glenmavis
RENFREW
Glasgow Airport
Airdriehill
Quarrier's Homes
Bridge of Weir
Houston
Partick
Lochwood
Carruth Ho
Govan
COATBRIDGE
Brookfield
Linwood
PAISLEY
GLASGOW
Coatdyke
Ranfurly
Kilbarchan
Elderslie
JOHNSTONE
Pollokshields
Shettleston
Baillieston
Old Monkland
Heathfield
Millikenpark
RUTHERGLEN
Birkenshaw
Calderbank
Mistylaw Muir
Glenburn
Carmyle
Viewpark
Mossend
Howwood
Waterside
Nitshill
Pollokshaws
Cathcart
Newton
Holytown
Ladyland Moor
Lochwinnoch
Uddingston
Bellshill
Burnt Hill
Fort
Hareley Resr
Cambuslang
Flemington
Bothwell
New Stevenston
Nether Kirkton
BARRHEAD
Thornliebank
Clarkston
Carmunnock
Stonefield
Barr Castle
Neilston
Patterton Sta
Busby
Nerston
MOTHERW
Newton Mearns
Rogerton
High Blantyre
Kilbirnie
Uplawmoor
Neilston Pad
Netherplace
Thorntonhall
EAST KILBRIDE
HAMILTON
Beith
Waterfoot
Low Waters
Glengarnock
Gateside
Harelaw Dam
Jackton
Meikle Earnock
Lugton
Long Loch
Halket
Eaglesham
Quarter
Larkhall
The Den
Barrmill
Gabroc Hill
Limekilnburn
Millheugh
Highfield
Burnhouse
Ballageich Hill
Auldhouse
Stutherhill
Dalry
Dunlop
Fullwood
Corsehouse Resr
Dunwan Dam
Melowther Hill
Lochgoin Resr
Ashgi
Auchentiber
Chapelton
Swinhill
STEWARTON
Craigendunton Resr
Corse Hill
Udstonhead
Stonehouse
Glassford
CUNNINGHAME
Burnfoot Resr
Rough Hill
Strathaven
KILWINNING
Fenwick
Waterside
Whitelee Forest
Blackwood
Monkgreenan
Rowallan Castle
Whitelee Hill
Sandford
Cunninghamhead
Caldermill
STEVENSTON
Kilmaurs
Craufurdland Castle
Moscow
Stobieside
Kype Muir
Lesma
IRVINE
Springside
Knockentiber
KILMARNOCK
NEWMILNS
DARVEL
Loudoun Hill
Drumclog
Hawkwood Hill
Irvine Bay
Crosshouse
Dreghorn
Hurlford
GALSTON
GREENHOLM
Stockbrigg
Drybridge
Gatehead
Riccarton
Mill Rig
Auchingilloch
Tod Law
Dundonald
Earlston
Shortlees
Sornhill
Glengavel Resr
Nutberry Hill
Barassie
Middleyard
Loans
Bogend
Craigie
Carnell
Little Hartmidden
Twopenny Knowe
Bibblon Hill
Symington
Hagsh Hill
TROON
Blackside
Middlefield Law
Hareshaw Hill
Meikle Craigs
Millburn
Auchmillan
Glenbuck
Rosemount
Black Hill
Netherwood
Monkton
Mossgiel
Prestwick Scotland Airport
Tarbolton
Mauchline
Limmerhaugh
Smallburn
Muirkirk
Carmacou
PRESTWICK
Catrine
Sorn
River Ayr
Kames
Urit Hill
Failford
New Prestwick
Shawwood
Airds Moss
St Quivox
Annbank Station
Stair
Cairn Table
Whitletts
Annbank
Trabboch
KYLE
AYR
Wallacetown
Trabbochburn
Auchinleck
Ochiltree
Lugar
Cronberry
Glenmuir
Wardlaw Hill
Cairn Kinny
Sundrum
Belston
HOLMHEAD
Logan
Glenmuirshaw
Doonfoot
Coylton
Hillhead
CUMNOCK
Dalblair
Mount Stuart
Burns Cott
Alloway
Drongan
Netherthird
Martnaham Loch
Doonholm
Skares
Auchtitench Hill
Fingland
Newark Castle
Brown Carrick Hill
Sinclairston
Kirkland Hill
Sauchrie
Culroy
Dalrymple
Hollybush
Littlemill
Carsgailoch Hill
Pathhead
Kirkland
Rankinston
New
Mansfield

NORTH SEA

NU

ST ABB'S HEAD

BERWICK-UPON-TWEED

HOLY ISLAND
Lindisfarne

FARNE ISLANDS
Staple Sound

THE CHEVIOT

91

NORTH SEA

FIRTH OF TAY

TAYPORT
SCOTSCRAIG
NEWPORT-ON-TAY
Woodhaven
Wormit
Tay Bridge
Road Bridge
Dundee Airport
TENTSMUIR FOREST
Leuchars
Leuchars Junc Sta
Earlshall
Eden Mouth
Guardbridge
ST ANDREWS BAY
ST ANDREWS
Kinkell Ness
Buddo Ness
Strathkinness
Babbet Ness
Boarhills
North Carr
Kingsbarns
Cambo Ness
Carr Brigs
Tullybothy Craigs
FIFE NESS
Balcomie
CRAIL
West Ness
KILRENNY
ANSTRUTHER
PITTENWEEM
ST MONANCE
Isle of May
Priory
Sauchar Point
ELIE
EARLSFERRY
Chapel Ness
Ruddons Point
LARGO BAY
Lower Largo
Lundin Links
LEVEN
Innerleven
METHIL
BUCKHAVEN
Macduff's Castle
East Wemyss
West Wemyss
Dysart
Pathhead
KIRKCALDY
Linktown
KINGHORN
Pettycur
BURNTISLAND
Inchkeith
Oxcars
Inchmickery
Cramond Island
Granton
Leith
Black Rocks
EDINBURGH
Portobello
Arthur's Seat
Duddingston
Morningside
Craiglockhart
Colinton
Fairmilehead
Craigmillar
Liberton
Gilmerton
Danderhall
Millerhill
Inveresk
MUSSELBURGH
PRESTONPANS
COCKENZIE AND PORT SETON
Wallyford
TRANENT
Gladsmuir
Macmerry
New Winton
New Town
Samuelston
Ormiston
Elphinstone
Whitecraig
Cousland
Pencaitland
Bolton
East Saltoun
West Saltoun
Gilchriston
HADDINGTON
Huntington
Garleton Hills
Athelstaneford
East Linton
Traprain
Pitcox
Stenton
Papple
Garvald
Carfrae
Gifford
Yester Ho
Danskine
Longyester
DALKEITH
Eskbank
Bonnyrigg and Lasswade
Mayfield
Newtongrange
Newtonloan
Gorebridge
Arniston Engine
Pathhead
Crichton
Fala Dam
Fala
Blegbie
Humbie
LOANHEAD
Straiton
Roslin
Rosewell
Bilston
Poltonhall
Auchendinny
PENICUIK
Howgate
Leadburn
Carrington
Temple
North Middleton
Tynehead
Middleton
Fala Moor
Falahill
Gilston
Soutra Mains
Crib Law
Hunt Law
Blythe Edge
NORTH BERWICK
Craigleith
Bass Rock
Fidra
Eyebroughy
Tantallon Castle
St Baldred's Boat
Auldhame
Scoughall
Whitekirk
St Baldred's Cradle
Tyne Mouth
Dirleton
Gullane
N Berwick Law
Kingston
DUNBAR
West Barns
Broxburn
Tyninghame
Gullane Bay
Aberlady Bay
Aberlady
Gosford Bay
Gosford Ho
Spittal
Longniddry
Seton Ho
Ballencrieff
Drem
Elvingston
Dunbar Common
Clints Dod
Lammer Law
Meikle Says Law
Cranshaws Hill
LAMMERMUIR

FIRTH OF FORTH

NEWBURGH
Lindores
Grange of Lindores
Dunbog
Glenduckie
Abdie
Collessie
Monimail
Letham
Cupar
Springfield
Ceres
Bridgend
Pitscottie
Dairsie or Osnaburgh
Kemback
Blebocraigs
Denhead
Prior Muir
Stravithie
Dunino
Kingsmuir
Kellie Law
Carnbee
Arncroach
Colinsburgh
Kilconquhar
Abercrombie
Drumeldrie
Charleton Ho
Kirkton of Largo
Wester Newburn
Largo Law
Montrave
Langdyke
Bonnybank
Kennoway
Windygates
Markinch
Milton of Balgonie
Balcurvie
Coaltown of Balgonie
Thornton
Auchterderran
Cluny
Gallatown
Coaltown of Wemyss
Star
Muirhead
Freuchie
FALKLAND
Kingskettle
Kettlebridge
Balmalcolm
Pitlessie
Kingskettle
LADYBANK
Pitlessie
Priory
Craigrothie
Baldinnie
Radernie
Peat Inn
Lathones
New Gilston
Largoward
Backmuir of New Gilston
Kilmany
Rathillet
Balmullo
Logie
Moonzie
Kilmaron
Foret Hill
Brunton
Luthrie
Creich
Hazelton Walls
Balmerino Abbey
Bottomcraig
Kirkton
Gauldry
Cruivie Castle
Lucklawhill
Carrick
LESLIE
Cadham
GLENROTHES
Kinglassie
Thornton
Auchtertool
Chapel
KINGHORN
Pitkevy
Leslie
Howe of Fife
Kinloch
Dunshelt
Strathmiglo
Falkland
Lomond Hills
Glassie
Pitkeys

TIREE

TIREE to
Coll .... ¾ hr
Oban.................... 4½ hrs

Treshnish Isles

Bac Mór or
Dutchman's Cap
Bac Beag

Staffa
Fingal's Cave

NL

Réidh
Eilean

IONA
Baile
Mór

Abbey
Fionnphort

Stac an Aoineidh

Eilean na h-
Aon Chaorach
Greave

Soa
Island

Fidden

Erraid

Eilean
nam Muc

Eileah
a'Chalmain

Rubha nam
Maol Móra

Eilean
Annraidh

Rubha nan
Cearc

Garbh Phort

Aridhglas

Beinn a'
Ghlinne Mhóir

ROSS

Ardalanish

Beinn a'
Chaol-airigh

Rubh'
Ardalan

West Reef

Torran Rocks

Sgeir Dhoirbh

Dubh
Artach

COLONSAY

Cailleac
Uragais

Kilchattan
An Rubha

Scalas

Eilean a'
Chladaich

Araskenish

Eilean
Leathann

Dubh
Eilean

Priory

ORON

Eilean
nan Ro

Caolas Mór

Ceann
Riobha

NQ

Nave
Island

Ardnave
Point

Eilean Beag

Rubha
Bholsa

Sgairail

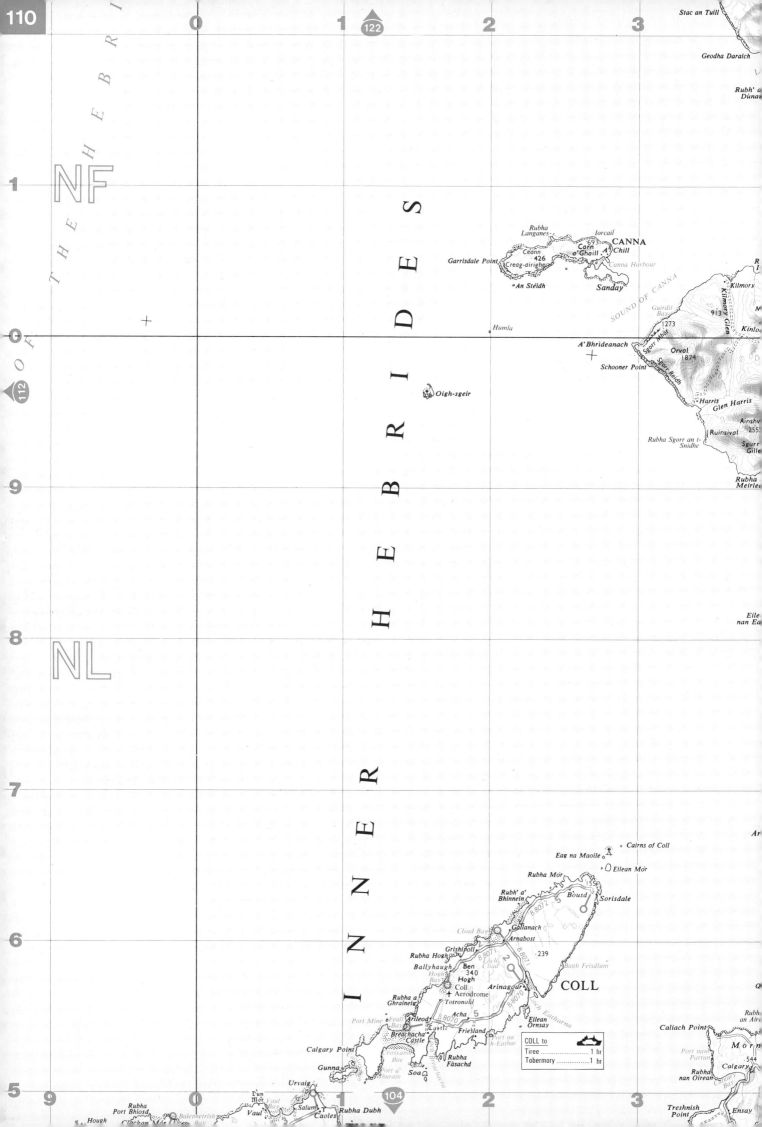

Stac an Tuill

Geodha Daralch

Rubh' a'
Dúnan

NF

THE HEBRIDES

Rubha
Langanes-   Iorcail
Ceann   69   Carn   CANNA
.426   a'Ghaill   Chill
Garrisdale Point   Creag-airighe
An Stéidh   Sanday

Kilmory
Guirdil
Bay   913   M
Kinlo

Humla

A' Bhrideanach   Sgorr Mhòr   Orval   1273
Schooner Point   Sgorr Reidh   1874

Oigh-sgeir   Harris   Glen Harris
Ainshv
Rubha Sgorr an t-   Ruinsival   2555
Snidhe   Sgurr
Gille

Rubha
Meirlee

Eile
nan Ea

H E B R I D E S

NL

I N N E R

Ar

Cairns of Coll
Eag na Maoile   Eilean Mòr

Rubha Mòr

Rubh' a'   Bousd   155   Sorisdale
Bhinnein   B 8072   5
Gallanach
Cliad Bay   Arnabost
Grishipoll   B 8071   B 8071   Bàgh Feisdlum
Rubha Hogh   .239
Ballyhaugh   Ben   Loch
Hogh   340   Cliad
Bay   Hogh   2   B 8071
Coll   Arinagour   COLL
Rubha a'   Aerodrome
Ghrainels   Totronald   B 8070
Acha   5
Port Mine   Feall   Arileod   B 8070   Eilean
Bay   Castle   Ornsay
Breachacha   Friesland   Port na
Castle   h-Eathar

Caliach Point

Rubha
an Aire

Morv

Calgary Point   Rubha
Fàsachd   544
Crossapol   Calgary
Gunna   Bay   Soa

Rubha
nan Oirean

COLL to	
Tiree	1 hr
Tobermory	1 hr

Urvaig   Treshnish
Dun   Point   Ensay
Mòr   Vaul
Rubha   Bay   104
Port Bhiosd   Salum   Rubha Dubh
Hough   Balephetrish   Vaul   Caoles
Bay

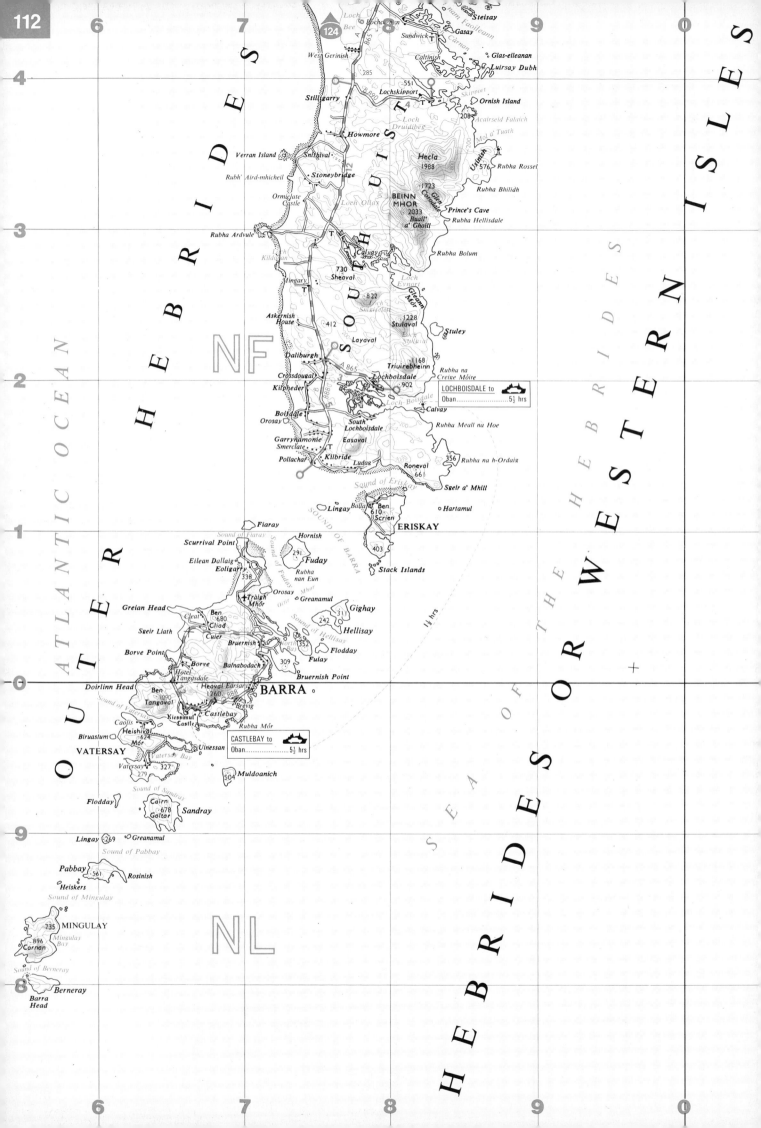

ATLANTIC OCEAN

OUTER HEBRIDES

SEA OF THE HEBRIDES OR WESTERN ISLES

SOUTH UIST

NF

NL

Loch Bee
Loch Druidibeg
Lochskipport
124
West Gerinish
Sandwick
Caltinish
Glas-eileanan
Luirsay Dubh
551
Stilligarry
Ornish Island
208
Acairseid Falaich
Howmore
Loch Druidibeg
Verran Island
Snishival
Hecla
1988
Usinish
Rubha Rossel
Rubh' Aird-mhicheil
Stoneybridge
Usinish 576
Ormiclate Castle
Loch Ollay
1723
Rubha Bhilidh
Beinn Mhor
2033
Glen Corodale
Buall' a' Ghoill
Prince's Cave
Rubha Hellisdale
Rubha Ardvule
Calvay
Rubha Bolum
Loch Kildonan
730
Sheaval
Loch Eynort
Tingary
822
Gleann Mor
Askernish House
412
1228
Stulaval
Stuley
Layaval
Loch Stulaval
Daliburgh
1168
Triuirebheinn
Rubha na Creige Moire
Crossdougal
LOCHBOISDALE to Oban..................5½ hrs
Kilpheder
Lochboisdale
902
Boisdale
Orosay
South Lochboisdale
Calvay
Garrynamonie
Smerclate
Easaval
Rubha Meall na Hoe
Pollachar
Kilbride
Ludag
356 Rubha na h-Ordaig
Roneval
661
Sound of Eriskay
Sgeir a' Mhill
Lingay
Balla
Ben 610 Scrien
Hartamul
Fiaray
ERISKAY
Scurrival Point
Hornish
Eilean Dallaig
291
Fuday
Eoligarry
338
403
Stack Islands
Orosay
Rubha nan Eun
Greian Head
Traigh Mhor
Greanamul
Gighay
Ben 680 Cliad
311
Clett
242
Hellisay
Sgeir Liath
Cuier
Bruernish
352
Borve Point
Floarnish
Floaday
Borve
Balnabodach
309
Fulay
Hotel Tangasdale
Heoval Earsary
Bruernish Point
Doirlinn Head
Ben Tangaval 1090
1260 888
BARRA
Brevig
Castlebay
CASTLEBAY to Oban..................5½ hrs
Caolis
Kiessimul Castle
Rubha Mor
Biruaslum
Heishival Mor 624
Uinessan
VATERSAY
Vatersay Bay
Vatersay 279 327
Muldoanich 504
Sound of Sandray
Floaday
Cairn 678 Goltar
Sandray
Lingay 269
Greanamul
Sound of Pabbay
Pabbay 561
Rosinish
Heiskers
Sound of Mingulay
Mingulas Bay
MINGULAY 735
Carnan 896
Sound of Berneray
Berneray
Barra Head

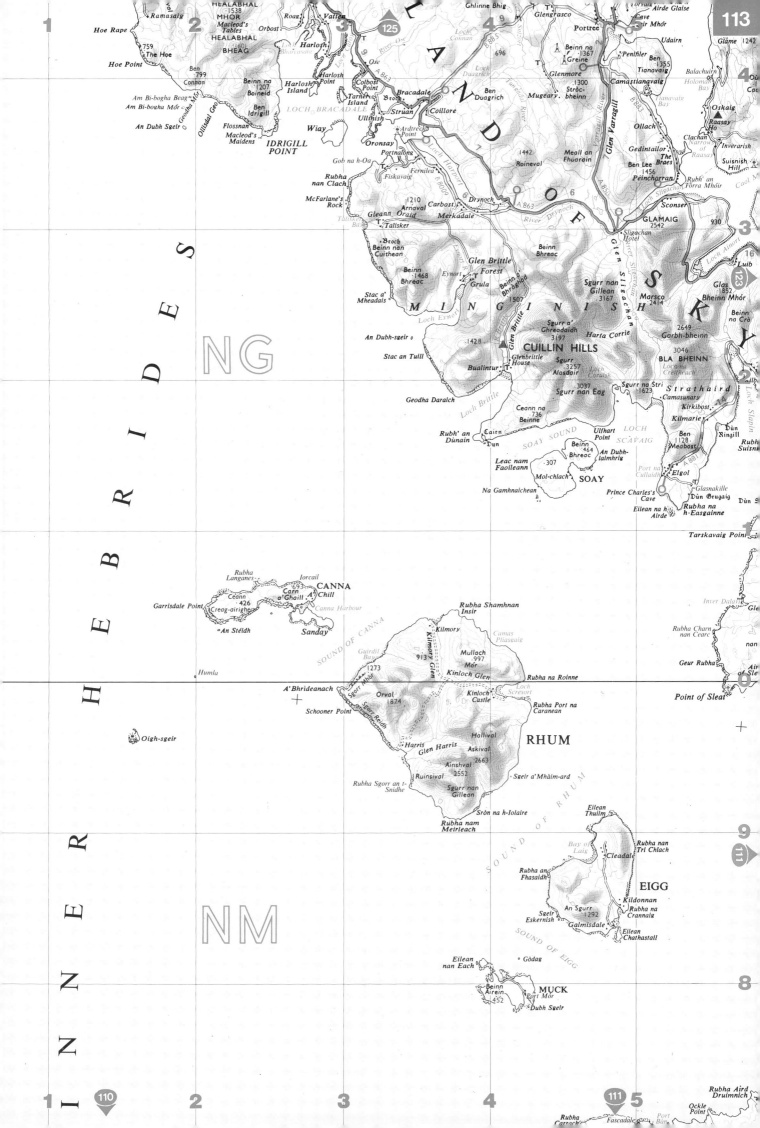

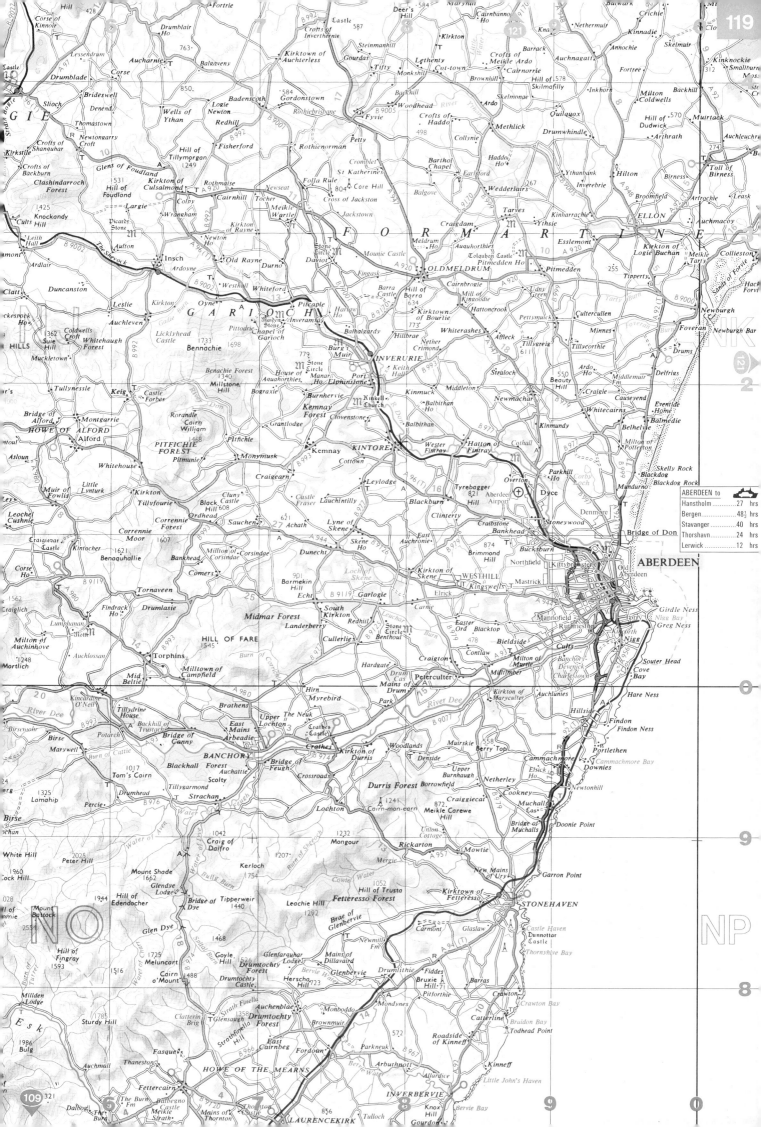

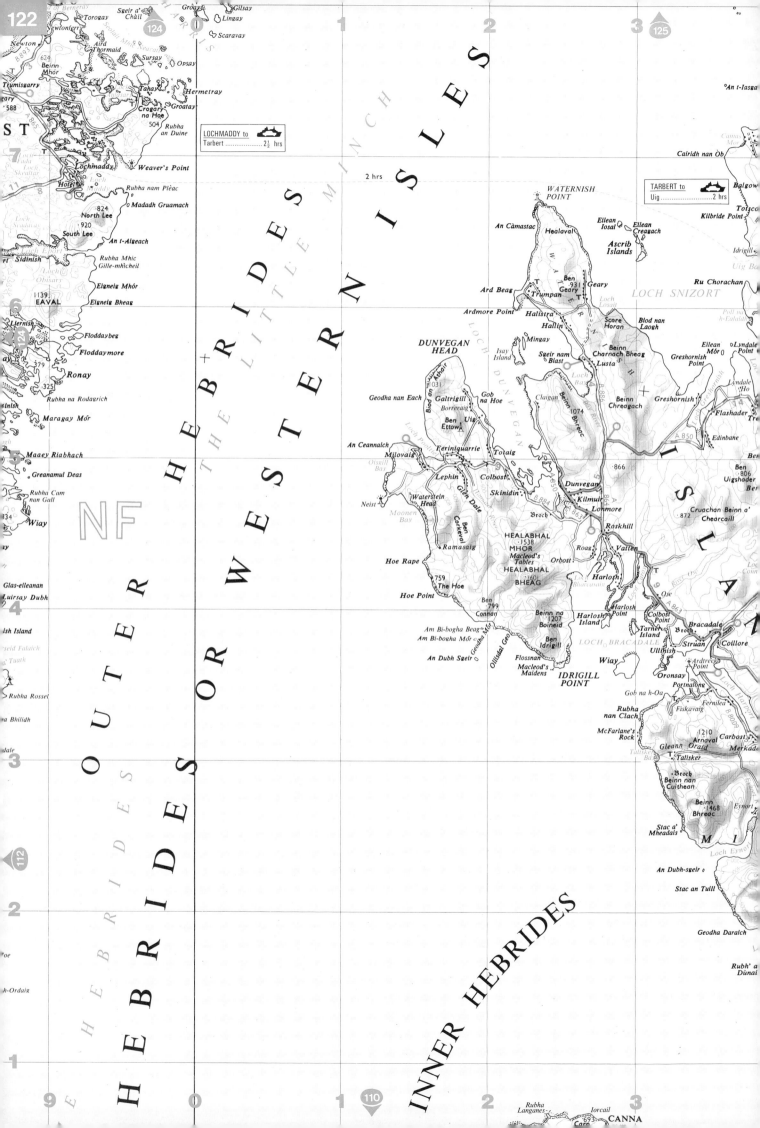

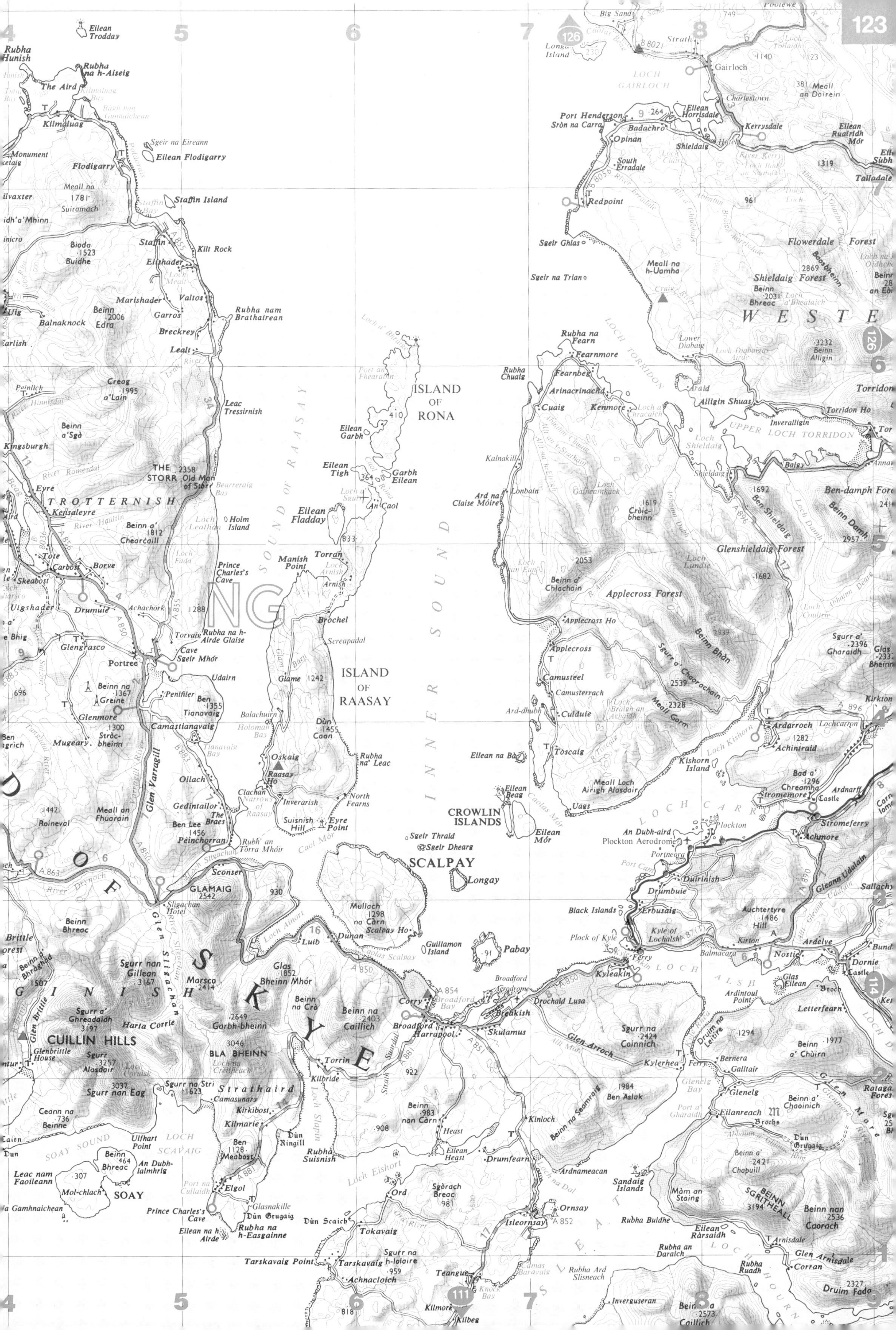

Rubha Hunish
Eilean Trodday
Rubha na h-Aiseig
The Aird
Kilmaluag
Monument
Flodigarry
Eilean Flodigarry
Sgeir na Eireann
Meall na
Suiramach
1781
Staffin Island
Kilt Rock
Bioda Buidhe 1523
Staffin
Elishader
Valtos
Marishader
Garros
Breckrey
Balnaknock
Beinn Edra 2006
Lealt
Creag a' Lain 1995
Leac Tressirnish
Rubha nam Brathairean
Port an Fhearann
ISLAND OF RONA
Garbh Eilean
Eilean Garbh
Eilean Tigh
410
THE STORR 2358
Old Man of Storr
Bearreraig Bay
Holm Island
Loch Leathan
TROTTERNISH
Kensaleyre
Eilean Fladday
Manish Point
Torran
Arnish
SOUND OF RAASAY
Beinn a' Chearcaill 1812
Prince Charles's Cave
Brochel
Screapadal
Tote
Carbost
Borve
Drumuie
Achachork
1288
Torvaig
Rubha na h-Airde Glaise
Cave
Sgeir Mhor
Portree
Udairn
ISLAND OF RAASAY
Glame 1242
Glengrasco
Penifiler
Ben Tianavaig 1355
Balachuirn
Holoman Bay
Dun Caan 1455
Beinn na Greine 1367
Glenmore
Stroc-bheinn 1300
Camastianavaig
Tianavaig Bay
Oskaig
Raasay Ho
Rubha na' Leac
Ollach
Clachan
Narrows of Raasay
Inverarish
North Fearns
Mugeary
Meall an Fhuarain
Gedintailor
The Braes
Ben Lee 1456
Peinchorran
Suishnish Hill
Eyre Point
Rubh' an Torra Mhoir
Sgeir Thrald
Sgeir Dhearg
CROWLIN ISLANDS
Roineval 1442
SCALPAY
Longay
Sconser
GLAMAIG 2542
930
Sligachan Hotel
Mullach na Carn 1298
Scalpay Ho
Beinn Bhreac
Loch Ainort
Luib
Dunan
Guillamon Island
Pabay
Sgurr nan Gillean 3167
Marsca 2414
Glas Bheinn Mhor 1852
Garbh-bheinn 2649
Beinn na Cro
Harta Corrie
CUILLIN HILLS
Sgurr a' Ghreadaidh 3197
Beinn na Caillich 2403
Broadford
Corry
Breakish
Skulamus
Harrapool
Glenbrittle House
Sgurr Alasdair 3257
BLA BHEINN 3046
Torrin
Kilbride
922
Sgurr na Stri 1623
Sgurr nan Eag 3037
Strathaird
Camasunary
Kirkibost
Kilmarie
Beinn nan Carn 983
Heast
Ceann na Beinne 736
Ben Meabost 1281
Dun Ringill
Rubha Suishnish
SOAY
Beinn Bhreac 464
An Dubh-lalmhrig
Port na Cullaidh
Elgol
Glasnakille
Dun Grugaig
Mol-chlach
307
Prince Charles's Cave
Eilean na h-Airde
Rubha na h-Easgainne
Dun Scaich
Tokavaig
Tarskavaig Point
Tarskavaig
Sgurr na h-Iolaire 959
Teangue
Achnacloich
Kilmore
Kilbeg

WESTER
Big Sand
Longa Island
Gairloch
LOCH GAIRLOCH
Charlestown
Port Henderson
Sron na Carra
Kerrysdale
Opinan
Badachro
Shieldaig
Ellean Horrisdale
Ellean Ruairidh Mor
South Erradale
Redpoint
Talladale
1319
Sgeir Ghlas
Flowerdale Forest
Sgeir na Trian
Meall na h-Uamha
Shieldaig Forest
Beinn Bhreac 2031
WESTE
Rubha na Fearn
Fearnmore
Fearnbeg
Arinacrinachd
Cuaig
LOCH TORRIDON
Kenmore
Arald
Torridon
Torridon Ho
Ard na Claise Moire
Lonbain
Kalnakill
UPPER LOCH TORRIDON
Inveralligin
Alligin Shuas
Balgy
Croic-bheinn 1619
Loch Shieldaig
Shieldaig
Ben-damph For
Beinn Damh 2957
Beinn a' Chlachain
2053
Applecross Forest
Glenshieldaig Forest
Loch Lundie 1682
Applecross Ho
Beinn Bhan 2939
Sgurr a' Gharaidh 2396
Applecross
Sgurr a' Chaorachain 2539
Camusteel
Meall Gorm 2328
Culduie
Camusterrach
Ard-dhubh
Ellean na Ba
Toscaig
Kirkton
Ardarroch
Lochcarron
Loch Kishorn 1282
Achintraid
Kishorn Island
Meall Loch Airigh Alasdair
Bad a' Chreamha 1296
Ardnarff
Stromemore
Castle
Uags
Ellean Beag
Stromeferry
Achmore
Ellean Mor
An Dubh-aird
Plockton
Plockton Aerodrome
Portneora
Duirinish
Drumbuie
Auchtertyre
Black Islands
Erbusaig
Hill 1486
Kirton
Plock of Kyle
Ardelve
Kyle of Lochalsh
Balmacara
Nostie
Dornie Castle
Ferry
Kyleakin
ALSH
Glas Eilean
Broadford Aerodrome
Sgurr na Coinnich 2424
Ardintoul Point
Letterfearn
Drochaid Lusa
Beinn a' Chuirn 1977
Glen Arroch
Bernera
Galltair
Kylerhea
Ferry
1984
Ben Aslak
Kinloch
Beinn na Seamraig
Glenelg
Ellean Heast
Glenelg Bay
Beinn a' Chaoinich 2421
Drumfearn
Ardnameacan
Sandaig Islands
Chapuill
Sgorach Breac 981
Ord
Isleornsay
Ornsay
Mam an Staing
Beinn Sgritheall 3194
Beinn nan Caorach 2536
Rubha Buidhe
Ellean Rarsaidh
Tarskavaig
Teangue
Loch Eishort
Camas Daraveile
Rubha Ard Slisneach
Inverguseran
Rubha an Daraich
Rubha Ruadh
Glen Arnisdale
Corran
Druim Fada 2327
2573

ST KILDA OR HIRTA

NA

Boreray 1245

Soay 1225

1234 ST KILDA OR HIRTA

Dun

Levenish

NF

ST KILDA lies about 41 miles or 66 km WNW of Griminish Point NF 7276

NA

NA

130

Gasker 105

Hushinish
Hushinish Point
1603 Husival Mòr

Govig
Arda Mòra
Leosaval 1352
Fore

Horsanish

Rubha Leacach

Taransay Glorigs

Rubha nan Toias
Sythe Harbour

Soay

877
Ben Raah

TARANSAY

Aird Vanish 324

Paible

Rubha Sgeirigin

SOUND OF TA

Aire Nisa

518
Clet Nisal

H E B R I D E S

Toe Head
Rubha Màs a' Chnuic

Coppay

Chaipaval 1207

Rubh' an Teampuill

Northton
922

Rubha Romagi

Sgeir Liath
Borve

Scarastavore

1305
Bleaval

Greabhal

1507
Roineabhi

265 Shillay

Little Shillay
Sound of Shillay

Brenish Point

PABBAY

642 Beinn a' Charnain
Rubh' a' Bhaile Fo Thuath

Quinish

Kyles Lodge

Ensay 161

Leverburgh

Carminish Islands

Carminish Strond

Rodel

RE PO

Sound of Spuir
Sound of Pabbay

Spuir

SOUND OF HARRIS

147 Killegray

Langay

Gilsay
Lingay

Scaravay

9 9

Haskeir Island 123

Haskeir Eagach

H E B R I D E S

Caolas a' Mhòrain

BERNERAY

Boreray

Rubha Bhoisnis

Beinn Shlèibhe
Bruist — Massacamber

281 Borve
Baile

Vatiam

Sgeir a' Chàil

Groatay
Hermetray

Scaravay

E N F

Aird a' Mhòrain

Veilish Point

Oronsay

Newton
Newtonferry
Aird Thormaid

624 Beinn Mhòr

Torogay

Sursay
Opsay

Tahay

O U T E R

Sgeir Orival

Griminish Point

Scolpaig

Vallay

Sollas

Lingay

Trumisgarry

Crogary Mór 588

Crogary na Hoe 504

Rubha an Duine

Manish Point
Rubha Dubh Tighary

Tigharry

Hougharry

Causamul

Aird an Rùnair

Balmartin

Clettraval 435

Vallay Strand

Grenitote

Loch nam Geireann

NORTH UIST

756

Marrival

332

Loch Scadavay

Loch Fada Loch Skealtar

Lochmaddy

Weaver's Point

Hotel
Loch Maddy

Rubha nam Plèac

A T L A N T I C   O C E A N

Balranald

Rubha Port Scolpaig

Deasker

Rubha Raouill

Bayhead
Paible

458

Claddach Kirkibost

Kirkibost Island

Oitir Fhladhaich

Loch Hunn
Loch Langass

296

A 867

Madadh Gruamach

North Lee 824

South Lee 920

An t-Aigeach

Heisker or Monach Islands

Huskeiran

Shillay

Hearnish

Stockay

Ceann Ear

SOUND OF MONACH

Vorogy

Claghan-a-Luib

894

Locheport

Loch Scadavay

Loch Eport

Sidinish

Rubha Mhic Gille-mhìcheil

Samala

Teanamachar

Baleshare

Bail' Uachdraich

224

Loch Caravat

Loch Obisary

Eigneig Mhór

Eigneig Bheag

Eachkamish

Carinish

Llernish

1139 EAVAL

Oitir Mhór

Floddaybeg

Floddaymore

Benbecula Aerodrome

Beul an

Uachdar

Balaglas

Grimsay

Ronay

Balivanich

Gramsdale

Flodda

379

T H E   L I T

Nunton

Griminish

408 Rueval

Rossinish

Rubha na Rodagrich

325

BENBECULA

Maragay Mór

Torlum

73 Loch Heouravay

Maaey Riabhach

Linielate

Creagorry

Greanamul Deas

Hornish Point

Rubha Cam nan Gall

Ardivachar Point

Ardivachar

Eochar

334

Wiay

Loch Bee

Steisay

Gasay

Lochearnan

West Gerinish

Sandwick

Loch Faoileann

Glas-eileanan

Luirsay Dubh

112

Stilligarry

Lochskipport

551

Ornish Island

Skipport

H E B R

9 8 7 6

8

7

6

5

4

OR PAIRC

NB

NORTH HARRIS

2153 Ullaval
Stulaval
2165 Oreval Harris
Meavaig
B 887
Cliasmol
2392 Uisgnaval Mór
Clisham 2622
Clett Ard
Maaruig
Beinn Mhór 1874
1069
1542
Crionaig
1217 Uisenis
1532
1473
Caiteshal
1096

Eishken
Lodge
Lemreway
Gob na Milaid
Srianach
Eilean Iubhard
Camas Alti nam Bearnach

Gob na Milaid

Mol Truisg
Gob Rubh' Uisenis
Rubha Bhrollum
Rubh' a' Bhaird

Shiant Islands
Garbh Eilean
Galtachean
Eilean Mhuire
Cadha na Gaoidhsich
Eilean an Tighe

SOUND OF SHIANT

OR WESTERN ISLES

S O R   W E S T E R N   I S L E S

Gob Aird an Tolmachain
Bunavoneadar
Sgaoth Aird 1829
Ardhasaig 1547
Gillaval Glas 1547
Tarbert
Laxadale Lochs
Beinn Dhubh 661
Ben Luskentyre 1532
Isay
LOCH TARBERT
Luskentyre
A 859
Aird Mheadhonach
Scotasay
Carragreich
Urgha
Ard Chaolais
Geo Dubh
Rheniginadle
Ard Caol
Loch Trollamarig
Toddun 1733
Eilean Mór a' Bháigh
Scalpay
Eilean Glas
Rubha Crago
Aird Riabhach
East Loch Tarbert
Ferry
341
South Harris Forest
Carnach
Rubha Bhocaig

SCALPAY

NG

E MINCH

DES OR

2 hrs

24 hrs

2 hrs

Fladda-chùain 83
Sgeir nam Maol

Eilean Trodday

Rubha Hunish
Rubha na h-Aiseig
The Aird
Kilmaluag Bay
Bàgh nan Gunnaichean
Loch Hunish
Tulm Bay
An t-Iasgair
Lùb Score
Kilmaluag
Monument
Bornesketaig
Camas Mòr
Cairidh nan Òb
Kilvaxter
1781 Suiramach
Meall na
Flodigarry
Sgeir na Eireann
Eilean Flodigarry
Staffin Island
Staffin Bay
Balgown
Suidh 'a' Mhinn
Totscore
Linicro
Bioda Buidhe 1523
Staffin
Kilt Rock
Kilbride Point
Idrigill
Uig
Balnaknock
Beinn Edra 2006
Marishader
Garros
Valtos
Elishader
Loch Mealt
Rubha nam Brathairean
Breckrey
Ru Chorachan
Earlish
Lealt

WATERNISH POINT
An Càmastac
Healaval
Eilean Iosal
Eilean Creagach
Ascrib Islands
Ben Geary 931
Geary
Ard Beag
Trumpan
Halistra
Hallin
Mingay
Score Horan
Biod nan Laogh
Eilean Mòr
Lyndale Point
Greshornish Point
Peinlich
Hinnisdal
Creag a'Lain 1995
Leac Tressirnish
Ardmore Point
Isay Island
Sgeir nam Blast
Beinn Charnach Bheag
Lusta
Greshornish
Kingsburgh
Beinn a'Sgà
Loch Snizort Beag
THE STORR 2358 Old Man of Storr
DUNVEGAN HEAD
Geodha nan Each
Biod an Athair 1031
Galtrigill
Borreraig
Gob na Hoe
Claigan
Beinn Bhreac 1074
Beinn Chreagach
Lyndale Ho
Flashader
Treaslane
The Aird
Eyre
Kensaleyre
River Romesdal
TROTTERNISH
Bearreraig Bay
An Ceannalch
Milovaig
Ferinquarrie
Totaig
Edinbane
Bernisdale
Ben Uigshader 806
Tote
Carbost
Borve
Beinn a' Chearcaill 1812
Holm Island
Eilean Fladday
Manish Point
Lephin
Colbost
Skinidin
Dunvegan
Kilmuir
Lonmore
Roskhill
Cruachan Beinn a' Chearcaill 872
Skeabost
Glen Bernisdale
Ben Uigshader
Uigshader
Achachork
Drumuie
1288
Prince Charles's Cave
Waterstein Head
Glen Dale
Neist
Moonen Bay
Ben Corkeval
Ramasaig
Hoe Rape
759 The Hoe
Hoe Point
HEALABHAL MHOR 1538 Macleod's Tables
HEALABHAL BHEAG
Ben Con 799
Beinn na Boineid 1207
Am Bi-bogha Beag
Roag
Vatten
Orbost
Harlosh
Harlosh Island
Harlosh Point
Colbost
Tarner Island
Broch
Bracadale
Beinn Duagrich
Cruachan
Loch Duagrich
Ose
Beinn na Greine 1367
Glengrasco
Portree
Udairn
Glenmore
Penifiler
Ben Tianavaig 1355
Cave Sgeir Mhór
Rubha na h-Airde Glaise
Torvaig
Beinn na h-Airde
Balachuirn
Mugeary
Stròc-bheinn 1300
Camas a' Ghlinne
Glame 1242
Holoman Bay
Sound of RAASAY

131

126

126

113

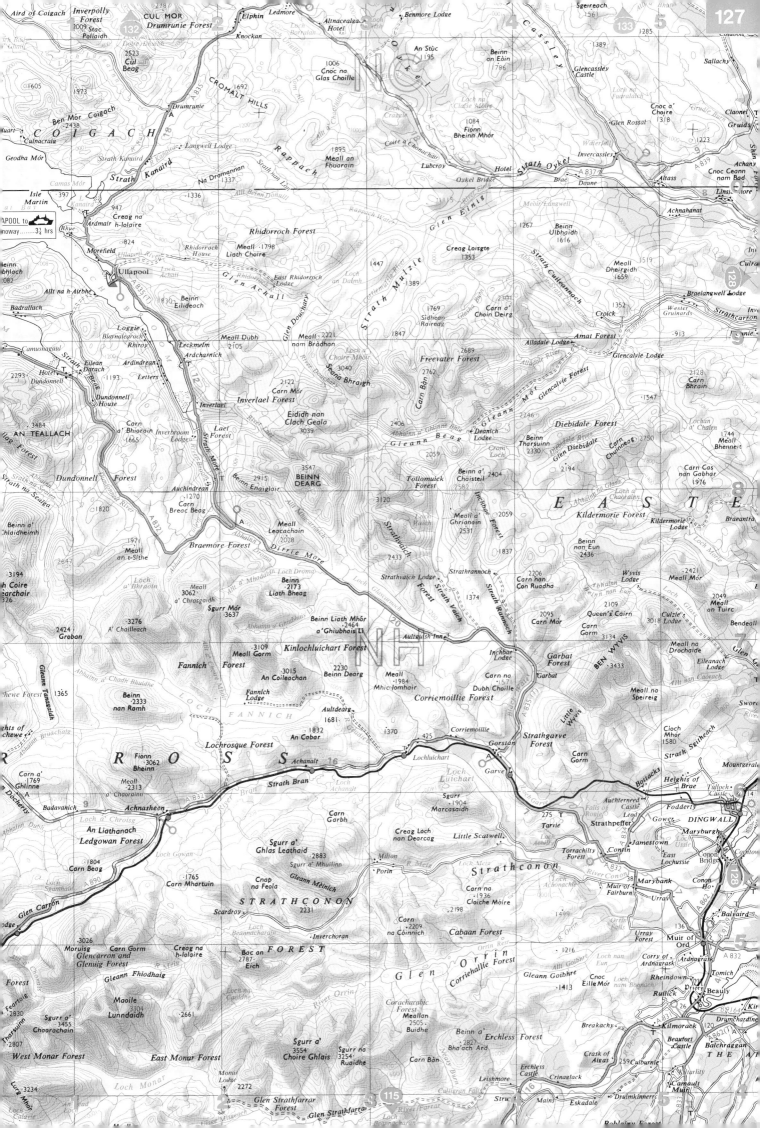

A T L A N T I C   O C E A N

Flannan
Isles

RONA AND
SULA SGEIR

HW

Lisgear Mhór

Rona

Lòba Sgeir

Gealldruig Mhór

Sula
Sgeir

RONA lies about 44 miles or 70 km NNE of the BUTT OF LEWIS NB 5166

H E B B R

Gallan Head

Camas Geodhachan
an Duilisg

Aird
Uig

Geodha Nasavig

Fiavig Bostá

670
Forsnav

Sgeir Fiavig Tarras

Crowlista

Tim

Ard More
Mangersta

Camas
Uig

Ardroil

Mangersta

Aird Fenish

Clette
Leathann

Staca Leathann

Islivig

Tarain

Aird Brenish

Mealisval

Brenish

Camas a' Mhoil

625
Laival a
Tuath

Mealasta
Island

Mealasta

Griomaval

R

E

NA

Kearstay

Gob na h-
Airde Móire

L. Teallasavay

Branch Mór

SCARP

1012
Sron
Romul

994
Taran Mór

Manish

Loch a'
Ghlinne

T

Hushinish

1603
Husival Mór

227
Tirga
Mór

Gasker
105

Hushinish Point

Hushinish
Bay

Gòvig

Arda Móra

Leosavol
1352

Forest of

Horsanish

Amhuinns

U

Rubha Leacach

Taransay Glorigs

Rubha nan Totag

Sythe Harbour

Soay Mór

HST

877
Ben
Raah

TARANSAY

Aird
Vanish
324

Pable

SOUND OF TARANSAY

Rubha
Sgeirigin

Aird
Nisabost

NF

124

Rubha Màs
a' Chnuic

Rubha Romagi

518
Seil

Clett
Nisabost

Toe Head

Sgeir
Liath

Borve

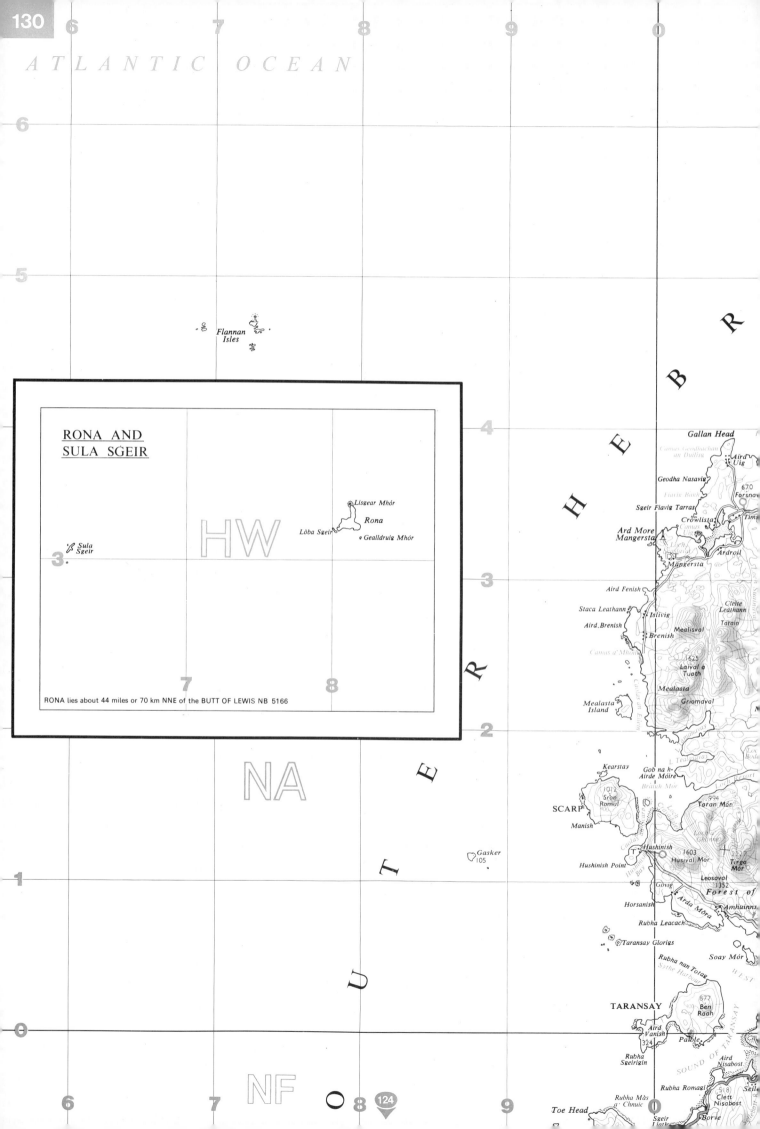

STACK SKERRY & SULE SKERRY

HX

Sule Skerry

2

○ *Stack Skerry*

6

Stack Skerry lies about 32 miles or 50 km N of WHITEN HEAD NC5068

NB

THE MINCH

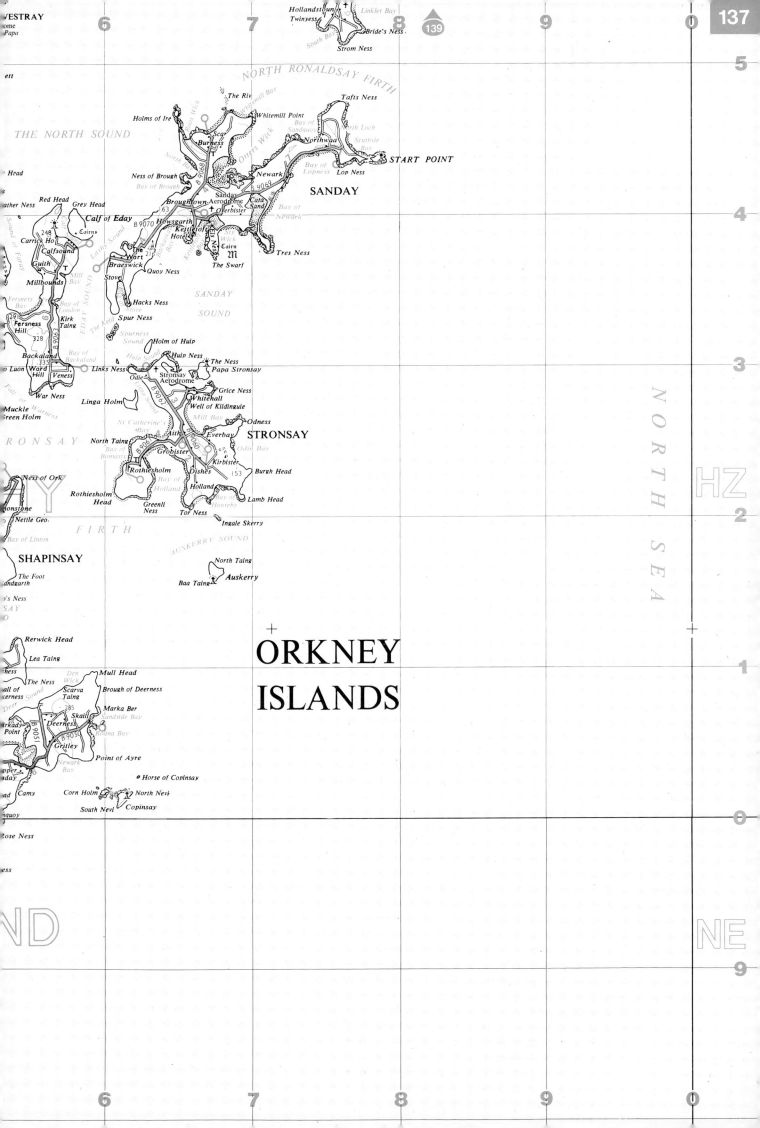

VESTRAY
ome
Papa

Hollandstoun
Twinyess
Linklet Bay
South Bay
Bride's Ness
Strom Ness

139

NORTH RONALDSAY FIRTH

THE NORTH SOUND

Head

Holms of Ire

The Riv
Whitemill Bay
Whitemill Point
Bay of
Sandauov
Tafts Ness
North Loch
Scuthvie
Bay

Sca
Burness
Northwaa
START POINT
Lop Ness

ather Ness
Red Head
Grey Head
Calf of Eday

Ness of Brough
Bay of Brough
Newark
Bay of
Lopness

Carrick Ho
248
Cairns

Calfsound
Guith

Sanday
Broughtown Aerodrome
Oterbister
Cata
Sand
SANDAY

B 9070 Howsgarth
Kettletoft
Hotel
Bay of
Newark

Millhounds

The
Wart
Braeswick
Stove

Cairn
Tres Ness

The Swarf

Quoy Ness

Fersness
Bay
Bay of
London

Kirk
Taing

SANDAY

Fersness
Hill
328

Hacks Ness
SOUND

Backaland
335
Bay of
Backaland

The Keld
Spur Ness

Spurness
Sound

Luon Ward
Hill
Veness

Holm of Huip

Huip Ness
The Ness
Papa Stronsay

War Ness

Links Ness

Odie

Stronsay
Aerodrome

Grice Ness

Muckle
Green Holm

Linga Holm

Whitehall
Well of Kildinguie

RONSAY

St Catherine's
Bay

Mill Bay
Odness

North Taing
Bay of
Bomasty

Aith
Everbay
STRONSAY
Odin Bay

Grobister

Kirbister

Ness of Ork

Rothiesholm
Dishes
153
Burgh Head

AY

Rothiesholm
Head
Bay of
Holland
Holland

nstone
Nettle Geo.

Greenli
Ness
Bay of
Houseby
Lamb Head

FIRTH
Tor Ness

Bay of Linton
Ingale Skerry

AUSKERRY SOUND

SHAPINSAY
North Taing

The Foot
ndgarth
Baa Taing
Auskerry

's Ness
SAY

Rerwick Head
Lea Taing

ORKNEY

ness
The Ness
all of
erness
Den
Wick
Mull Head
Scarva Taing
Brough of Deerness

ISLANDS

rkady
Point
285
Marka Ber
Skaill
Sandside Bay

Deerness
Roana Bay

Gritley
Point of Ayre

er
day
Newark
Bay

Horse of Copinsay

ad Camy
Corn Holm
North Nevi
South Nevi
Copinsay

nquoy

Rose Ness

ess

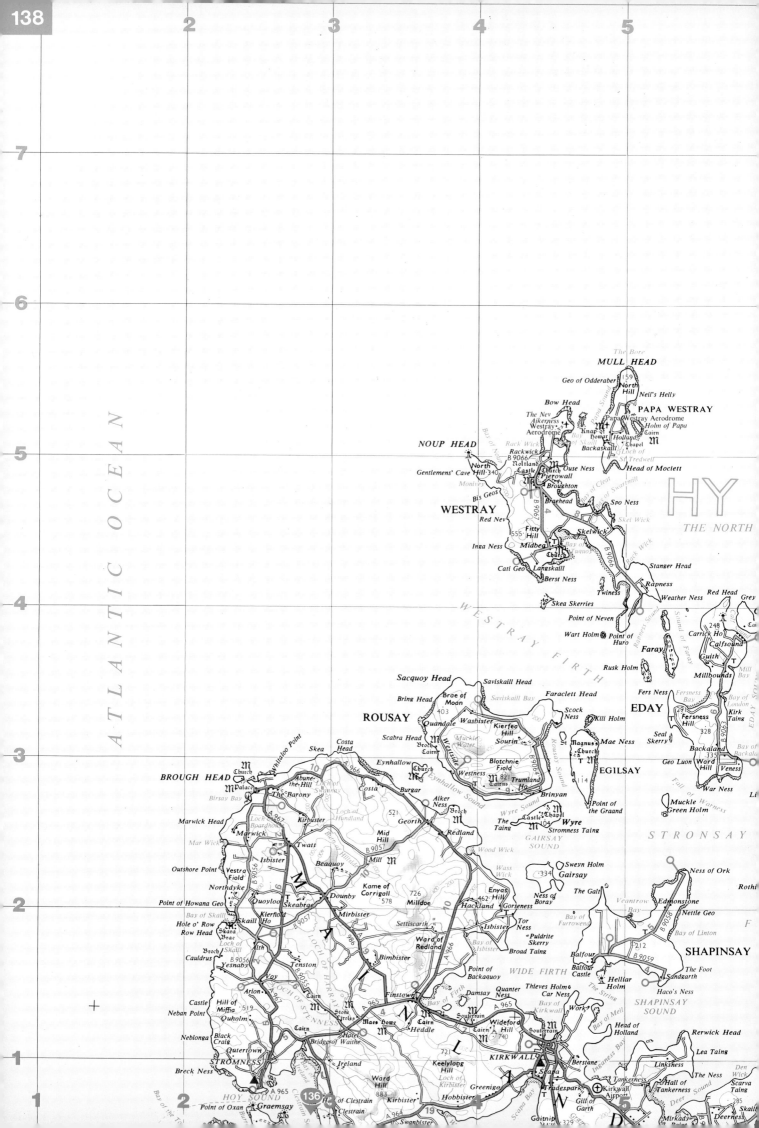

ATLANTIC OCEAN

MULL HEAD

Geo of Odderaber
North Hill 159
Neil's Helly

Bow Head
The Nev
Aikerness
Westray
Aerodrome

PAPA WESTRAY
Papa Westray Aerodrome
Holm of Papa
Knap
Howar
Holland
Chapel

NOUP HEAD
Rack Wick
Backaskaill

Rackwick
B 9066
Noltland
Castle
Church
Pierowall
Broughton
Ouse Ness
Head of Moclett

Gentlemens' Cave
North Hill 340
Monivey
Braehead

WESTRAY
Bis Geos
Red Nev
Fitty Hill 555
Spo Ness
Skel Wick

B 9067
Skelwick
HY
THE NORTH

Inga Ness
Midbea
Church
Bay of Tuquoy
B 9066

Cati Geo
Langskaill
Berst Ness
Stanger Head

Twiness
Rapness

Skea Skerries
Weather Ness
Red Head
Grey

WESTRAY FIRTH
Point of Neven
248
Carrick Ho
Calfsound
Cai

Wart Holm
Point of Huro
Faray
Guith
Millbounds
Mill Bay

Rusk Holm
Fers Ness
Fersness Bay
Bay of London

Sacquoy Head
Saviskaill Head
Faraclett Head
EDAY
Fersness Hill 29
Kirk Taing

Bring Head
Brae of Moan
Saviskaill Bay
Scock Ness
Kili Holm
328
Bay of Backa

ROUSAY
Quandale
403
Washbister
Kierfea Hill 200
Sourin
St Magnus Church
Mae Ness
Seal Skerry

Scabra Head
Broch Cairn
Muckle Water
Blotchnie Field
EGILSAY
Geo Luon
Ward Hill 335
Veness

Whitaloo Point
Costa Head
Eynhallow
Westness
Cairns
Trumland Ho
14
War Ness
Li

BROUGH HEAD
Church
Skea
B 966
Church
Brinyan
Castle
104
Wyre
Point of the Graand
Muckle Green Holm

Palace
Abune-the-Hill
Loch of Swanay
Costa
Burgar
The Taing
Stromness Taing
STRONSAY

Birsay Bay
The Barony
Aiker Ness
Broch
GAIRSAY SOUND

Marwick Head
Kirbuster
521
Georth
Wyre Sound
Wood Wick

Mar Wick
Marwick
Mid Hill
Redland
Wass Wick
Sweyn Holm
Ness of Ork
Rothi

Outshore Point
Isbister
Twatt
B 9057
Mill
334
Gairsay

Vestra Fiold
Beaquoy
Kame of Corrigall 578
726
Milldoe
Ness of Boray
The Galt
Veantrow Bay
Edmonstone

Northdyke
B 9056
Quoyloo
Skeabrae
Dounby
Enyas Hill 462
Hackland
Gorseness
Bay of Furrowend
Nettle Geo
B 9038
Bay of Linton

Point of Howana Geo
Kierfiold
B 9057
Mirbister
Settiscarth
Isbister
Tor Ness
SHAPINSAY
F

Hole o' Row
Row Head
Skaill Ho
986
Ward of Redland
A 966
Puldrite Skerry
Broad Taing
Balfour
212
B 9059

Skara Brae
Loch of Skaill
Aith
Bimbister
Point of Backaquoy
Balfour Castle
Helliar Holm
The Foot
Sandgarth

Broch Cauldrus
Yesnaby
Voy
Tenston
Finstown
Damsay
Quanter Ness
Thieves Holm
Car Ness
Haco's Ness

Arion
Cairn
Stone Circles
Maes Howe
Point of Firth
Bay of Firth
WIDE FIRTH
Work
SHAPINSAY SOUND

Castle
Neban Point
Hill of Miffia 519
Ouholm
Cairn
Heddle
Southtown
Wideford Hill 740
Bay of Kirkwall
Head of Holland

Neblonga
Black Craig
Quterton
Bridge of Waithe
Ireland
721
Cairn
Southtown
A 965
Rerwick Head
Lea Taing

STROMNESS
Breck Ness
Ward Hill 883
Keelylong Hill
Loch of Kirbister
KIRKWALL
Scapa
Berstane
The Ness
Linkshess
Den Wick
Scarva Taing

HOY SOUND
A 965
136
Ho of Clestrain
Point of Oxan
Graemsay
Kirbister
Greenigo
Hobbister
Tradespark
Gill of Garth
Kirkwall Airport
Hall of Tankerness
Deerness

Bay of the Tr
Clestrain
Swanbister
A 964
19
Gaitnip
Deer
Mirkady
Deernes
D

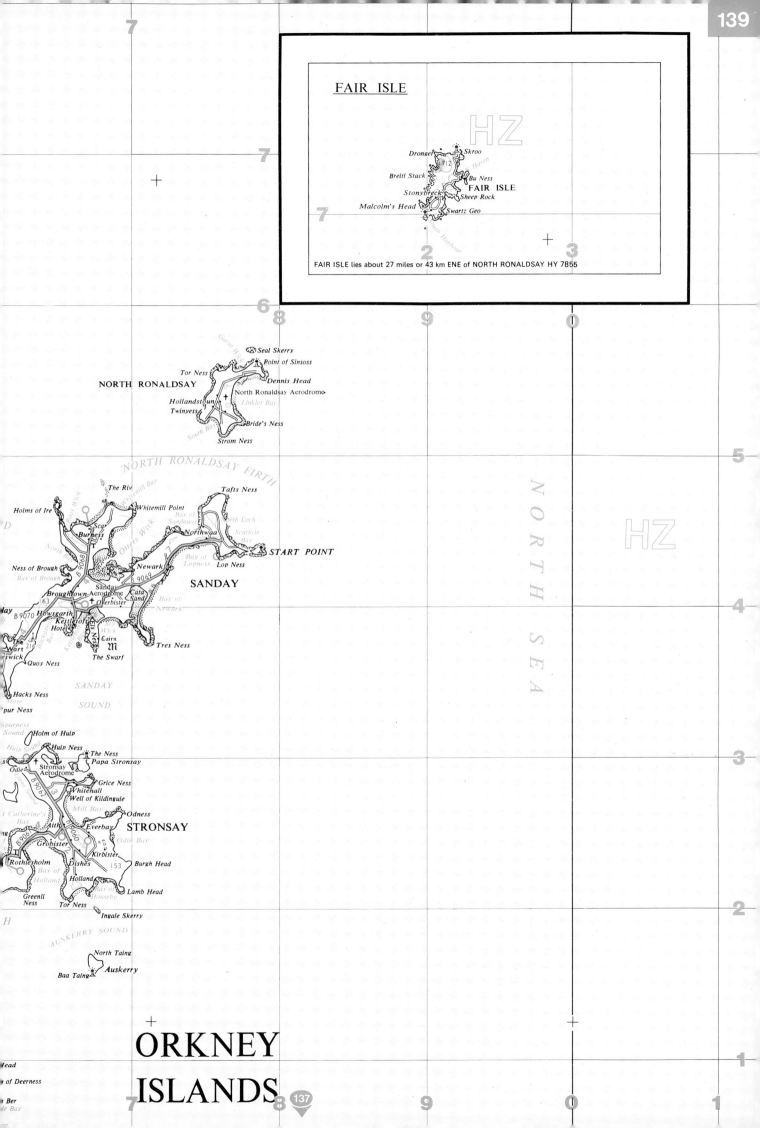

FAIR ISLE

HZ

Dronger • • Skroo
Breiti Stack
Stonybreck • Bu Ness
FAIR ISLE
Sheep Rock
Malcolm's Head
Swartz Geo
712

FAIR ISLE lies about 27 miles or 43 km ENE of NORTH RONALDSAY HY 7855

7
7
7
2
3

6
8
9
0

Seal Skerry
Point of Sinsoss
Tor Ness
Dennis Head
NORTH RONALDSAY
North Ronaldsay Aerodrome
Hollandstoun
Linklet Bay
Twinyess
Bride's Ness
South Bay
Strom Ness

5

NORTH RONALDSAY FIRTH

The Riv
Tafts Ness
Holms of Ire
Whitemill Point
Whitemill Bay
Bay of
Sandauoy
Scar
Northwaa
Scuthvie
Burness
Bay
Otters Wick
START POINT
B 9068
Newark
Lop Ness
Ness of Brough
Bay of
Bay of Brough
Lopness
SANDAY
Broughtown Aerodrome
Cata
Sanday
Sand
Bay of
163
Overbister
Newark
B 9070 Howsgarth
Kettletoft
Hotel
Cairn
The Wart
216
m
Quoy Ness
The Swarf
Tres Ness

4

N O R T H   S E A

HZ

Hacks Ness
SANDAY
pur Ness
SOUND

Spurness
Sound
Holm of Huip
Huip Ness
The Ness
Papa Stronsay
Odie
Stronsay
Aerodrome
Grice Ness
Whitehall
Well of Kildinguie
Mill Bay
Catherine's
Odness
Bay
Aith
Everbay
STRONSAY
Odin Bay
B 9062
Grobister
Kirbister
Rothiesholm
Dishes
Burgh Head
153
Bay of
Holland
Holland
Lamb Head
Greenli
Bay of
Ness
Tor Ness
Houseby
Ingale Skerry

3

2

AUSKERRY SOUND

North Taing
Auskerry
Baa Taing

ORKNEY

1

Head
of Deerness
Ber
e Bay

ISLANDS

142

SHETLAND
ISLANDS

ATLANTIC OCEAN

ST MAGNUS BAY

Grind of the Navir
Holes of Scraada
Ure
Scarfi
ESHA NES
Braehoulland
Sae
Breck Tangwick
Burnside
The Bruddans
Isle of Stenness
Hillswick
Isle of Stenness
Stenness
Skerry of Eshaness
Dore Holm
Ness of Hillswick
The Drongs
Baa Taing

Isle of Nib

Erne
Lang

Strom Ness
Ve Skerries
MUCKLE ROE
Murbie Si

Cribble
North Ness
Swarbacks Head
Fogla Skerry
Virda Field
PAPA STOUR
Vementry
Biggings
Gruna
Isle of
West Burrafirth
Holm of Melby
West
Burrafirth
Melby Ho
Garth
Brindister
Noonsbr
Quilva Taing
Sandness
Unifirth
Summa
Water
Pund Head
Sandness Hill
Burga
Water
Bay of Deepdale
Loch of
Dales
Burn of Dale
Stourbrough Hill
Bridge of Wal
Mu Ness
Voe of Da
Ste
Browland
Wats Ness
Skarpigarth
Walls
Grutin
Burraland
Braga Ness
Vaila
Uskie Geo
Vaila
Hall
Word of
Culswick
Vaila
Broch
Strom Ness
The Nev
Westerwick
Giltarump
Wester Wick
West Moulie

Da Logat
Strem Ness
The Kame
Harrier
Da Scrodhurdins
Ham
Head o'
da Taing
Wester Hævdi
The
Sneug
FOULA
Wick of
Mucklabrek
Hametoun
Hellabrick's Wick
Hesti Geo
South Ness

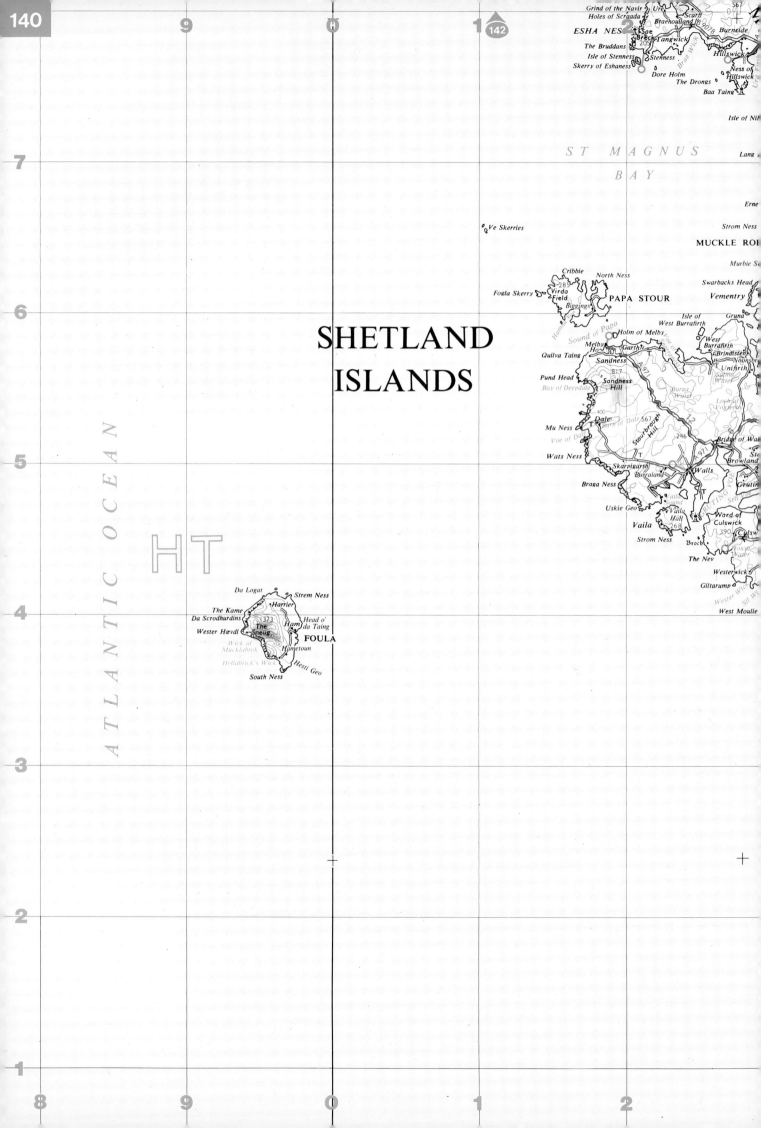

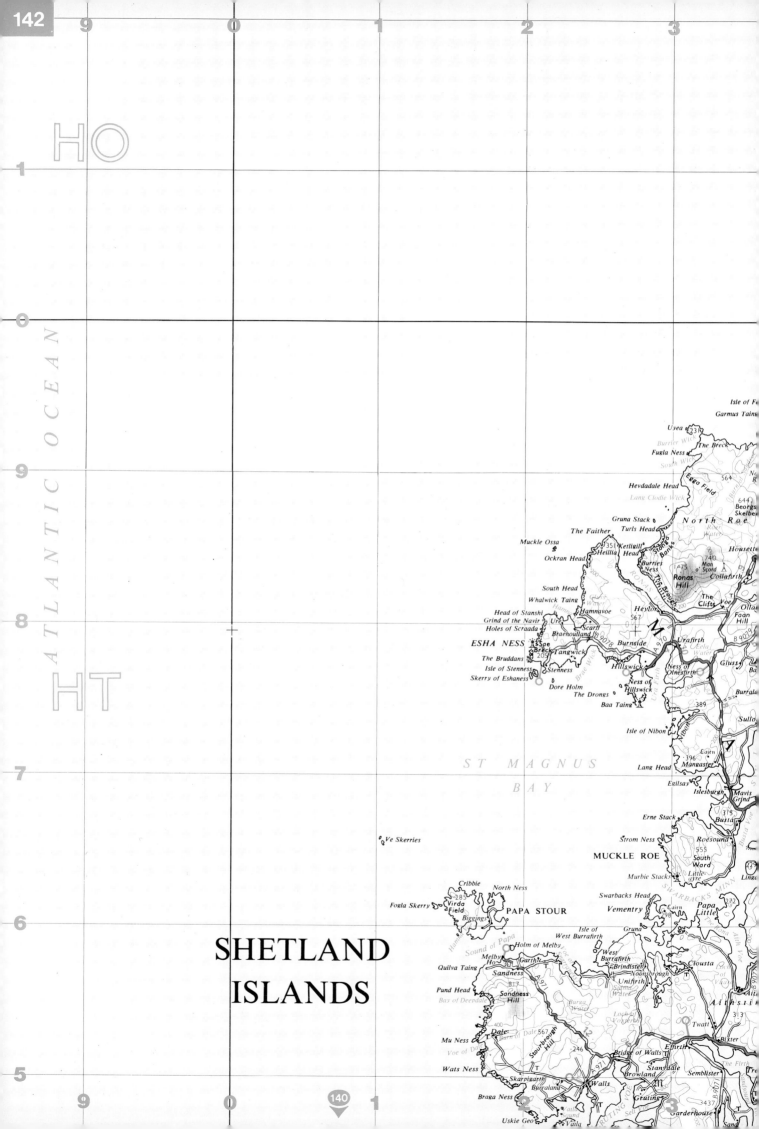

ATLANTIC OCEAN

HO

HT

Isle of F
Garmus Tains

Uyea
Burrier Wick
Fugla Ness
South Wick
The Breck

Esga Field
564
No
R

Hevdadale Head

Lang Clodie Wick
644
Beorgs
Skelber

Gruna Stack
The Faither
Turls Head
North Roe
Roer
Water

Muckle Ossa
351 Kettigill
Heillia Head
Stonga
Banks

Honsett

Ockran Head
Burries
Ness
475
740
Man
Scord
Collafirth

Ronas
Hill

South Head
The
Voe
The
Clifts

Whalwick Taing
Heylor

Head of Stanshi
Hammavoe
567
Ollar
Faan
Hill

Grind of the Navir
Ure

Holes of Scraada
Scarff
Braehoulland
B 9078
Burnside
Urafirth
B 9071

ESHA NESS
Sae
Breck Tangwick
M
A 970
Aela
Water

The Bruddans
205
Hillswick
Ness of
Olnesfirth
Gluss
Ba

Isle of Stenness
Stenness

Skerry of Eshaness
Ness of
Hillswick
Burrafe

Dore Holm
389

The Drongs
Sullo

Baa Taing

Isle of Nibon
Nibon

Cairn

St MAGNUS
396
Mangaster

Lang Head
Egilsay

BAY
Islesburgh
Mavis
Grind

Erne Stack
315
Busta

Ve Skerries
Strom Ness
Roesound

MUCKLE ROE
555
South
Ward

Murbie Stacks
Little-
ayre
225
Linge

Cribbie
North Ness
Swarbacks Head
SWARBACKS MINN
272

Fogla Skerry
285
Virda
Field
Swarbacks Head
Vementry
Cairn
Papa
Little

Biggings
PAPA STOUR
398

SHETLAND
Isle of
West Burrafirth
Gruna

Holm of Melby
West
Burrafirth
Clousta

Melby
Ho
Garth
Brindister

ISLANDS
Quilva Taing
Sandness
Noonsbrough
Unifirth

817
Aithsti

Pund Head
Sandness
Hill
Bursta
Voe

313

400
Twatt

Mu Ness
Dale
Burn of Dale
567
12
Bixter

Voe of Dale
246
Bridge of Walls
Efirth

Stourbrough
Hill
A 971
Standale
Browland

Wats Ness
Walls
Semblister
Tre

Skarpigarth
B 9071

Braga Ness
Burraland
Gruting
9437

Uskie Geo
Vaila
Garderhouse
Sand

The Historical Geography of Britain

Prehistory

The physical environment in which the early cultures of Britain developed at the end of the Ice Age was very different from our contemporary environment, though the principal structure of this island, the disposition of mountain and lowland, remain much the same. The main changes have occurred in the nature and distribution of vegetation types and the extent of woodland and forest cover, in the reduction of undrained land, and in climate.

The early prehistoric cultures of Britain in the Palaeolithic and Mesolithic periods made very little impact on the landscape, although their cave sites and excavated open sites provide an accurate picture of their essential economic character and artefacts. The basis of the economy was the hunting of wild animals and the collecting of wild plants, but this was eventually replaced during the Neolithic (or New Stone) Age by a food-producing economy. The dating of the beginnings of this new culture is only approximate, but it appears that settlement by farmers in Britain occurred before 4400 BC. The Neolithic period terminated about 2000 years later. The initial phase of cultural development, the 'early' Neolithic, took place in the earlier part of the fourth millennium BC, and is associated with stock-breeding, cereal cultivation, flint- and stone-working industries, and distinctive pottery types. The early Neolithic site at Windmill Hill in Wiltshire has revealed a predominance of bones of 'domesticated' animals rather than wild animals, and of the emmer type of wheat – a cultivated crop. The evidence for early Neolithic settlement is not extensive, but it has been inferred that isolated farmsteads predominated.

Flint was extensively used for axes and other implements, including leaf-shaped arrowheads, and there were important flint mines in Sussex, at Findon, for example. Flint-mining also occurred in Cornwall and in Westmorland, and at a later date the famous mine at Grimes Graves in Norfolk came into operation. Distinctive pottery types included the Grimston type, mainly found in Yorkshire and the North, and the more southern Hembury type. In the later Neolithic, material evidence changes: new forms of pottery appear, with decorations and round bases, such as Peterborough ware and grooved ware, and the use of the older, harder rocks for axes intensifies. The economy seems to have to become more pastoral.

A distinctive and notable feature of the Neolithic is the wide range of burial monuments. The main categories of burial monument are the ubiquitous chambered and unchambered tombs, sometimes covered with earth (such as earthen long barrows), sometimes with stones (cairns). The best-known sites are the 'henge' monuments with large standing stones, the most spectacular of which are sites such as Stonehenge and Avebury in Wiltshire. The dominant relic feature of the Neolithic in Scotland is the chambered tomb and long mound, found extensively in the Clyde region and in the extreme north, and the Orkney and Shetland Islands.

The succeeding culture – the Bronze Age – lasted from 2500 to 900 BC, and whereas there is evidence that the Neolithic culture was strong, spontaneous and regional, the initiation of the Bronze Age apparently occurred through colonisation. The evidence for this occurs in the form of the material culture of a group of people known as the Beaker folk (named for the type of pottery with which they are associated), who began the change from Neolithic to Bronze culture. There was no overall and sharp break between these two phases of British prehistory, for change was rapid in the Lowland Zone of the south and east and slower in the Highland Zone of the north and west. The Bronze Age also brought a change to a warmer and drier climate although a marked deterioration began again about 1100 BC.

The most important innovation of the Bronze Age was the introduction of metal tools – initially in the form of thin copper blades of knives and daggers. The early Bronze Age witnessed a series of stages of copper-working, with main production centres in northwest England, Renfrewshire in Scotland, Wessex, Wales and the Welsh border. Flint exploitation continued in the early Bronze Age, but then declined. Settlements seem to have been small clusters of dwellings; barley became a more important crop than wheat. With the climatic deterioration of the end of the early Bronze Age there was more intensive use of river valleys and watery lowlands – an indication, too, of a changing religious focus. The upper (altitudinal) margins of cultivation declined and new regions of power developed, including north Wales and the Thames valley. The settlements of the middle and later Bronze Age included enclosed farmsteads with associated enclosed fields, and so-called 'Celtic' field systems, and large numbers of stone settlements on the uplands of the southwest. Some hilltop forts and enclosures date from this period, but the most characteristic feature is the round burial barrow or cairn, of which very large numbers survive. Other important features of the Bronze Age are the extensive trade in copper products, the decorative personal bronze ornaments, the continued construction and reconstruction of henge monuments (including work at Stonehenge), and the remarkable settlements at Skara Brae in the Orkneys.

The Iron Age culture was first seen about 900 BC, lasting to the Roman invasion of AD 43, and left its mark extensively in the landscape. Initiated by small groups of continental settlers, the first phase of the Iron Age in Britain continued the traditions of the Bronze Age, using small settlements and the first enclosures of old tribal centres with ramparts. Major innovations began in the 8th century BC, including hillforts, new metallurgy and pottery. The period immediately before the Roman invasion saw strong continental influence from Belgic invaders in the south and east (the north and west undergoing very little change), the emergence of strong regional tribal cultures (such as the Thames region, Arras culture in Yorkshire, Cornwall) and widespread trade with the Roman Empire. The Iron Age invaders were Celtic-speaking; they introduced new crops

Prehistory to the Romans The distribution and types of chambered cairns, chambered tombs and long barrows reflect the diversity of Neolithic Britain, very different from the settlement patterns of Roman Britain.

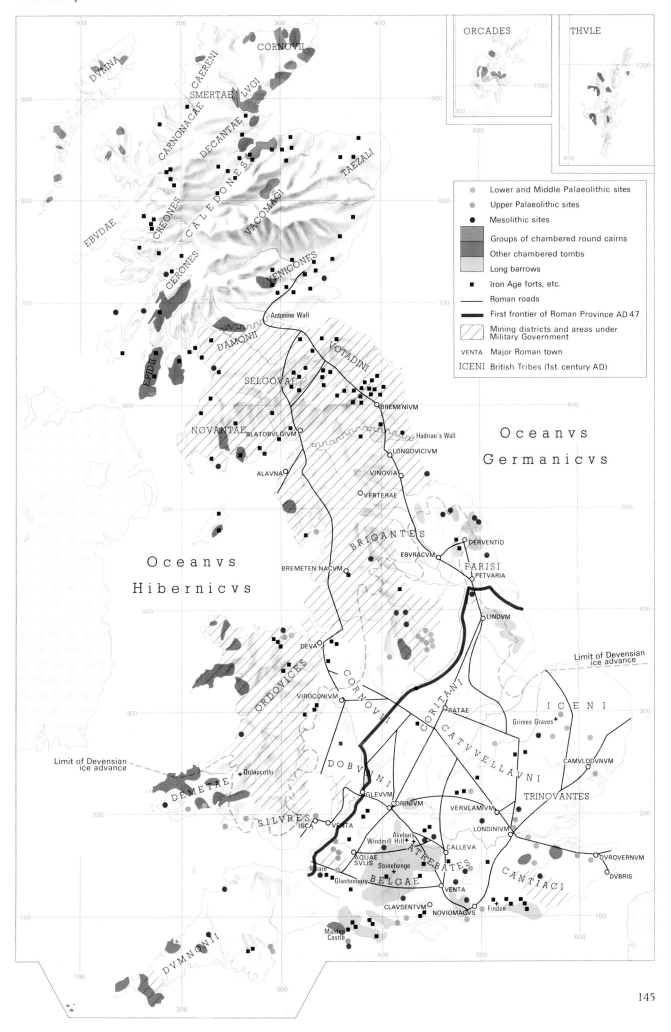

ORCADES

THVLE

Oceanvs
Germanicvs

Oceanvs
Hibernicvs

CORNOVII

DVMNA

CAERENI

SMERTAE

CARNONACAE

DECANTAE

LVGI

CREONES

EBVDAE

CALEDONES

CERONES

VACOMAGI

TAEZALI

VENICONES

Antonine Wall

DAMONII

VOTADINI

SELGOVAE

EPIDII

BREMENIVM

NOVANTAE

BLATOBVLGIVM

Hadrian's Wall

LONGOVICIVM

ALAVNA

VINOVIA

VERTERAE

BRIGANTES

DERVENTIO

EBVRACVM

PARISI

BREMETEN NACVM

PETVARIA

LINDVM

Limit of Devensian
ice advance

DEVA

ORDOVICES

VIROCONIVM

CORNOVII

CORITANI

RATAE

ICENI

Grimes Graves

CAMVLODVNVM

CATVVELLAVNI

Limit of Devensian
ice advance

Dolaucothi

DEMETAE

DOBVNI

TRINOVANTES

GLEVVM

CORINIVM

VERVLAMIVM

SILVRES

ISCA

VENTA

LONDINIVM

DVROVERNVM

Avebury
Windmill Hill

CALLEVA

AQUAE
SVLIS

ATREBATES

Stonehenge

CANTIACI

DVBRIS

Meare

BELGAE

VENTA

Glastonbury

CLAVSENTVM

NOVIOMAGVS

Findon

Maiden
Castle

DVMNONII

Legend:

- Lower and Middle Palaeolithic sites
- Upper Palaeolithic sites
- Mesolithic sites
- Groups of chambered round cairns
- Other chambered tombs
- Long barrows
- Iron Age forts, etc.
- Roman roads
- First frontier of Roman Province AD 47
- Mining districts and areas under Military Government
- VENTA   Major Roman town
- ICENI   British Tribes (1st. century AD)

such as rye and oats, and used horse-drawn chariots. The major evidence of the Iron Age in the landscape are the hillfort settlements of England (such as Maiden Castle in Dorset), Wales and Scotland. In addition to the walled hillforts are the lake-villages of the southwest, notably Glastonbury and Meare in Somerset. In the late Iron Age tribal capitals or *oppida* developed, such as St Albans and Colchester, and the heavier soils of the Lowland areas were cultivated by use of the new heavy ploughs. Coinage was introduced, as were new processes for corn-grinding and pottery production.

The Claudian invasion of Britain in AD 43 did not end the Iron Age, nor did it completely 'Romanise' Britain. The Roman cultural influence is mainly to be found in the south and east, partly because of the existence there of indigenous political groups, and was least in the north and west which were primarily zones of military occupation. The whole of Britain was, however, only a frontier province of the Roman Empire and one occupied at a very late stage of that Empire's development; it did not reach the same cultural levels as the more central regions of the continental Empire. Christianity reached Britain in the 4th century, and perhaps helped to accelerate the change away from Celtic Iron Age culture, for Christianity had Roman characteristics. There was therefore both continuity and change between Iron Age and Early Christian-Roman culture. The cultural continuity is best seen at the peasant level in the Highland Zone of the north and west. The cultural provinces of Scotland (Atlantic, Western Isles, Southwest and South) remained much the same, to judge by the distinctive types of settlement, pottery and burial monument. Change was more obvious in the south and east of Britain, but it was rarely total and all-embracing, for 'native' settlements continued to exist, even in the Lowland Zone.

The political map of Roman Britain shortly after the conquest (c. AD 47), indicates a frontier zone which includes most of north England, Wales and Scotland. The construction of Hadrian's Wall in c. AD 123-128 and the Antonine Wall in AD 142 are further testimony to the status of these regions, which remained under military rule.

The major landscape features associated with Roman Britain are towns, roads, mining, and various types of agricultural and rural settlement, notably villas, though there was also continuity of settlement in addition to the more obvious Roman innovations.

Under the Roman system of civic administration, each unit or *civitas* had a capital – in the southeast this was usually a pre-Roman site or *oppidum*, elsewhere a *colonia* or colony town, initially populated by Roman citizens and soldiers. At a lower level in the 'urban' hierarchy were small settlements called *vici*, some of which were walled and built on the site of earlier fortified settlements. The total population of Roman Britain was probably under one million, and there were about 60 towns, which varied considerably in size, though none compared with the larger towns and cities of 20th-century Britain. The dimensions of Roman London, for example, were about 1600 metres by 800 metres (1 mile by ½ mile); this was also about the size of the larger towns such as Verulamium (St Albans), Corinium (Cirencester) and Viriconium (Wroxeter). The other Roman towns were very

much smaller. The larger towns had a planned layout, with the forum at the centre, surrounded by a grid-iron street plan. The public buildings included baths, temples and basilicas, hotels (*mansio*), theatres and amphitheatres. Town defences were constructed in some of the towns at the end of the 2nd century AD.

One of the attractions of Britain to the Romans was its mineral resources – silver, gold and other metals were described as the 'price of victory'. Expectations of gold were high, but the only known Roman mine was at Dolaucothi in Carmarthenshire, where advanced mining techniques were used and an eleven-kilometre (seven-mile) aqueduct channel constructed to convey water to the site. Copper resources were exploited in North Wales and Anglesey, but the most extensively-worked mineral was lead, principally in the Mendips, and also in the Matlock area of Derbyshire, Shropshire, Cheshire, Flintshire, Yorkshire and Cumberland. Lead was a major export. Iron was worked in Sussex and the Forest of Dean.

The network of Roman roads in Britain is impressive and extensive, both in terms of its density and the technological achievement that it represents. Some of the major Roman roads remain as trunk roads to the present day, though others have lost their former status. The Fosse Way and Watling Street are two well-known surviving examples of this network. The best-known farm buildings of Roman Britain are the villas (although this term really refers to a whole rural estate). Villas have been described as 'farms with Romanised buildings'; they were most common in Lowland Britain and parts of South Wales. They were less numerous, however, than non-Roman native settlements in the countryside of Roman Britain. Some were built on the sites of Iron Age farms. The villas themselves changed during the period of the Roman occupation. Most Romanised villas had principal farmsteads constructed to a regular (usually rectangular) plan, but this dates from a rebuilding period of the 2nd century. The largest and most luxurious of the villas are quite late in date, and in a minority.

There were some improvements in agricultural techniques in the Roman period, including corn-drying and threshing and perhaps ploughing, though we know little of the size and shape of fields or of the systems of cultivation.

Britain in the Dark Ages

There was no sharp discontinuity between the Roman and Saxon phases of colonisation of Britain: we know, for example, that Anglo-Saxons were used as mercenaries by the Romans in Britain to assist with town defences at the time of the withdrawal of the Roman administration around AD 400. The period of most intense settlement by the Anglo-Saxons was c.400-800. These people were of Germanic origin and their culture was very different from the Roman; they took control of parts of eastern England in the period 400-450, when it seems that Kent and Sussex may have been settled by these rebellious mercenaries. Other pockets of

The Dark Ages The earliest Saxon settlement is denoted by areas in which pagan burials have been found, followed by places with names ending in *-ingas*. The burhs are of later date. Place-names in *-by* indicate Scandinavian settlements, and 'maerdref' sites named *llys-* are sites of royal courts in Wales.

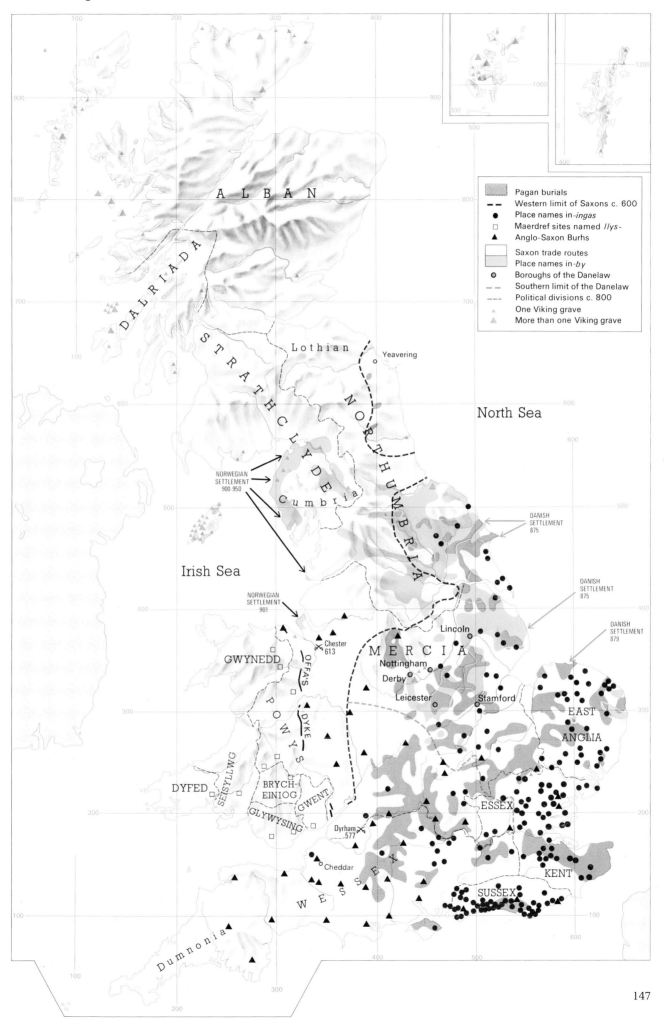

ALBAN

DALRIADA

STRATHCLYDE

Lothian

○ Yeavering

NORTHUMBRIA

North Sea

NORWEGIAN
SETTLEMENT
900-950

Cumbria

DANISH
SETTLEMENT
875

Irish Sea

NORWEGIAN
SETTLEMENT
901

DANISH
SETTLEMENT
875

Lincoln ◉

DANISH
SETTLEMENT
879

GWYNEDD

OFFA'S

Chester
613

M E R C I A

Nottingham ◉
Derby ○

Leicester ○   Stamford ○

EAST
ANGLIA

POWYS

DYKE

SEISYLLWG

DYFED

BRYCH-
EINIOG

GWENT

ESSEX

GLYWYSING

Dyrham
577

KENT

○ Cheddar

W E S S E X

SUSSEX

Dumnonia

Legend:

- ▨ Pagan burials
- – – Western limit of Saxons c. 600
- ● Place names in-*ingas*
- □ Maerdref sites named *llys-*
- ▲ Anglo-Saxon Burhs
- ▢ Saxon trade routes
-   Place names in-*by*
- ◉ Boroughs of the Danelaw
- – – Southern limit of the Danelaw
- - - - Political divisions c. 800
- ▲ One Viking grave
- ▲ More than one Viking grave

settlement were established along the east and south coasts, and, in spite of resistance from the Britons to the Anglo-Saxons, by the mid-6th century the earliest kingdoms had emerged in the south and east. The more powerful kingdoms were those which emerged in the southwest (Wessex), midlands (Mercia) and north (Northumbria). These were involved in struggles not only with each other but also the Britons of the Highland Zone. The early Anglo-Saxon period was one of pagan belief – the distribution of pagan burials is a good indicator of early settlement patterns, as is the distribution of place-names ending in *-ingas* – but the mission of St Augustine in 597 led to the conversion of the Saxons to Christianity by 670. Evidence of territorial struggle, particularly against the Welsh, survives in the dramatic form of Offa's Dyke, a 192-kilometre (120-mile) earthwork, built in the late 8th century. The general trend of territorial control towards the 10th century involved a reduction in the number and the control of the English kingdoms as Wessex became dominant, the emergence of a major territory – Gwynedd, centred in Snowdonia – in Wales, and the beginnings of a national identity for Scotland.

The effect of the Anglo-Saxon colonisation on the economy and life of Britain, especially Lowland Britain, was profound. A new language was introduced and a new colonisation initiated which changed the intensity of settlement. Much of our evidence for these activities comes from the place-names of the period and from archaeology. The Saxon settlements were not all in virgin territory, for in southern England there was already a fairly dense pattern of Roman-British settlement. There is evidence of Saxon settlement being influenced by pre-existing patterns. The earliest evidence (in the 'mercenary' phase before the Roman withdrawal) is of settlement in Roman towns, villas and forts, but the evidence for later periods also reflects the class structure of society. Two royal palaces have been identified, one at Yeavering in Northumberland, dating from the 7th century, the other at Cheddar in Somerset – a rural palace of the kings of Wessex. At the other end of the scale were the dwellings and farmsteads of yeomen and peasant farmers. It has been suggested that the poorer peasants lived in villages with large numbers of small huts with sunken floors, the best example of which is at Mucking in Essex. The German long-house seems not to have been used widely.

The agricultural mix obviously varied from region to region. Generally the commonest cereals were oats, barley and wheat. Ploughing of the possibly 'open' fields may have been done with a heavy plough pulled by oxen or horses. Animal husbandry was more important in the Highland Zone, and associated with migration to summer pastures.

The early Saxons were not accustomed to town life and it is difficult to assess the degree of continuity of occupation of the Roman towns. Some Roman towns were immediately deserted on the Roman withdrawal, and it is clear that the urban system as a whole declined and decayed. The question of the continued occupation of Roman British town sites is complex, but there is evidence to suggest that life continued in many of these towns, albeit under changed circumstances, and, as Martin Biddle says, 'far from there being a complete break between Roman Britain and Anglo-Saxon England, the new evidence shows that the roots of the English settlements were planted while Britain was still part of the empire and were strengthened for as long as the *civitates* remained in being' *(Archaeology of Anglo-Saxon England*, ed D M Wilson). Roman defence lines were followed by the walls of some medieval towns – London, Lincoln, Canterbury and Chichester, for example. In towns such as Colchester and Winchester continuity was initially preserved by the construction of Saxon royal palaces on the Roman sites. From the late 7th century, however, there were signs of a new town growth, and these early Anglo-Saxon towns were mainly trading and industrial centres, frequently coastal or riverine in location, such as Hamwih (Southampton), Dover, Sandwich, Ipswich. The major commercial centres were London and York. By 880 there were about ten English towns, but by the early 10th century there were about 50, with some of the newer towns built for military rather than commercial reasons. By the end of the Anglo-Saxon period it is thought that there were about 100 places that might be described as towns, in which lived about 10% of the population. Much of this later urban growth came in the form of *burhs*, fortified against the Danish invaders.

During the course of the 9th century a new element entered Britain's social, cultural and political mix in the form of Scandinavian attacks and settlements. The first recorded raid on England took place in 793 – on the monastery at Lindisfarne; the raids intensified in the 9th century, and in 851 the Vikings first wintered in England. In midland and eastern England the primary influence was that of the Danes, who had previously attacked the coastal lowlands of northwestern continental Europe, and moved inland along the major rivers. From 860 to 880, notwithstanding the strength of the Wessex army of King Alfred, the Danes took eastern Mercia, East Anglia and most of Northumbria. This Danish-held and settled area became the Danelaw, at the centre of which were a group of five fortified towns in the East Midlands: Lincoln, Stamford, Nottingham, Leicester and Derby. A different wave of attacks and settlement occurred in the northwest of England, where from the early 10th century the Norwegians, mainly from the Dublin kingdom, occupied the region west of the Pennines up to the Solway Firth. Attempts were made to found a Norse kingdom east of the Pennines, at York, but a renewed campaign by the Mercian and Wessex kings reduced the area of the Danelaw. Danish raids on England were renewed early in the 10th century, resulting in the conquest and unification of the whole country except for the southwest, under Canute.

The largest area of Scandinavian settlement in England was the Danelaw, which was formally recognised in 886 by Alfred of Wessex and Guthrum. Its four principal regions were Northumbria, East Anglia, the southeast Midlands and the Five Boroughs. The laws and customs of the Danelaw differed from those of Anglo-Saxon England.

The Scandinavians also exercised powerful influence in Scotland, though Wales was less affected. In the 9th century Norwegians (Vikings) took the Orkneys and Shetlands and moved south from Caithness to the Moray Firth. They settled the Western Islands and founded kingdoms in Ireland and

the Isle of Man. There were frequent attacks by the Vikings from Dublin and the Isle of Man on the Welsh coast, and though no permanent settlements resulted the Scandinavian influence is seen in Norse topographical names of coastal features. The Scandinavian settlement affected both rural and urban life, producing an extension of arable cultivation and a stimulus to urban growth.

Against the background of conquest and war, the conversion of Britain to Christianity proceeded at varying pace and with development of different institutions. At the end of the 10th century a revival of monastic life in England occurred, mainly in the south and east, but the main extension of monasticism occurred after the Norman conquest. In Wales early monastic sites had been established by the 'Celtic' saints in the period from the 5th to the 7th century, and these monasteries were of great importance in Welsh religious life for a long period. There were bishops in Wales, but no division into sees, whereas in England the dioceses dated from the 7th-century Augustinian conversion, even though the territories of the sees changed rapidly during troubled times. In Scotland territorial bishoprics are evident by the 11th century, together with a crude parochial system (*see map page 150*). In England the development of a parochial system was well under way, though not complete by 1066.

Medieval Britain

On 14 October 1066, the Anglo-Saxon kingdom ended with the defeat in battle of Harold Godwinson by William, Duke of Normandy (a Norman duchy which had developed in the 10th century). The Conquest represents, however, less of a dramatic change in life in Britain than is sometimes thought, for many of the innovations with which the Normans are associated, including the feudal and manorial systems, were pre-Norman in origin. The administrative geography of Britain before and after the Norman Conquest was varied and complex. There existed in 1066 a number of earldoms— heritages from the Anglo-Saxon administrative system— including Northumbria, East Anglia and Wessex, which comprised groupings of shires. After the Conquest the existing administrative and judicial system of England was used, and co-operation envisaged with the existing officials such as sheriffs, bishops and abbots. The principal innovations of the new regime were a more rigid social structure and a greater emphasis on military skill and defensive systems. The latter was represented in the construction of a national system of royal and baronial castles, many in the larger towns and others constructed along the Welsh Marches and the Scots border.

From the end of the 10th century there began a period of economic expansion in Britain which had a profound effect on regional economies and on landscapes. This expansion began from a small population, a low-technology and predominantly rural economy, a limited urban and commercial base, and a pyramidal social structure. The population of England at the end of the 11th century was about two million, and by 1347 had reached between six and seven million. Little can be known of the equivalent figures for Wales, although one estimate for 1300 is of a population of less than 250,000. Estimates for Scotland suggest a population of c.250,000 for the late 11th century, reaching c.450,000 by the late 14th century. On the whole, what is postulated is a relatively general rapid increase in population in the 12th and 13th centuries, followed by a period of decline, though the rates of increase obviously varied locally and regionally. The population of 11th-century England had a highly uneven distribution, with the highest densities in the Lowlands, notably East Anglia, and the lowest in the Uplands, waste and forest areas. In the Lincolnshire fenland, for example, there were dramatic increases in the village populations in the 12th and 13th centuries. As there was still much under-used space, an inevitable consequence of the rising population was colonisation on a large scale. The major expansion of settlement in England took place in woodland areas, such as the Forest of Arden. Another indication of the advance of settlement and cultivation can be seen in the attempts at disafforestation of royal forest, that is to release some of the legal restraints on 'assarting' (or clearance) in them. Examples of this occurred in the 12th and 13th centuries in Surrey, Devon, Essex, Hampshire and the Southern Uplands of Scotland. Reclamation of marshland was another important feature of colonisation, with major drainage and settlement activity in the Somerset Levels, the Pevensey levels in Sussex, Holderness, the Romney and Walland marshes in Kent. Inroads were also made into the margins of the high moorland areas, including the Pennines, Dartmoor, Exmoor, and the uplands of Southern Scotland and central and north Wales. Much of the land reclamation of early medieval Britain was carried out by the initiative and under the control of the monastic orders, notably the Cistercians. The pace of colonisation was uneven, and in some areas there was already a shortage of land by the 14th century.

The nature of the rural economy in Britain in the 11th, 12th and 13th centuries is impossible to describe in detail, for local and regional variance was considerable. In those areas where arable cultivation was possible on a relatively large scale, much of the land was arranged and managed in 'open' or sub-divided fields (fields divided into tenurial strips), as in parts of the south and east Midlands, but in other areas, such as southwestern England and west Wales, much land was enclosed and held in severalty rather than in common. In many areas there was a mixture of 'open' and 'enclosed' land. The system of farming the open fields, particularly in heavy soil areas, involved the ploughing-up of substantial cultivation ridges, separated by drainage furrows, and these can still be seen, notably in Midland England, as 'ridge-and-furrow' topography. The most mature form of field-system was the two-and-three-field system, found in a broad belt of territory running from northeast England through the Midlands to south central England and with outliers in South Wales, and involving the

Britain to 1350 The Domesday survey of 1086 produced an unparalleled wealth of information about 11th-century England. Steady inroads were made by 1350 on the areas of unfarmed land covered by forest and marsh.

Late Medieval Britain The indication of farming regions at this date are only tentative, but the enclosures of the 15th and 16th centuries were primarily concentrated in regions of arable farming, converting them to sheep-rearing.

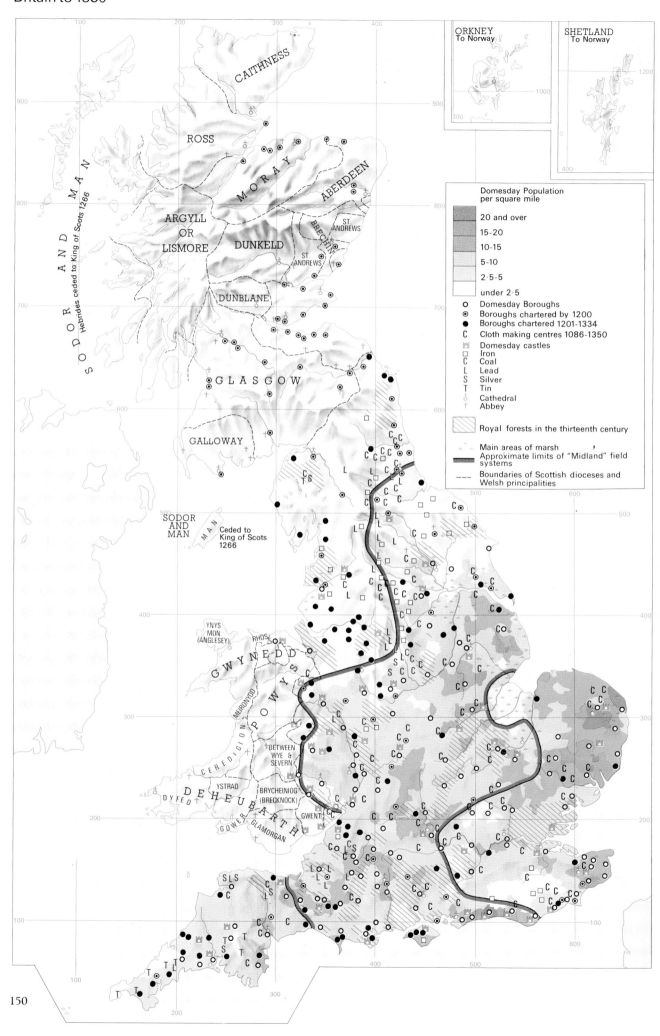

ORKNEY
To Norway

SHETLAND
To Norway

CAITHNESS

ROSS

M O R A Y

ABERDEEN

BRECHIN

ST. ANDREWS

ST. ANDREWS

DUNBLANE

S O D O R   A N D   M A N

Hebrides ceded to King of Scots 1266

ARGYLL
OR
LISMORE

DUNKELD

GLASGOW

GALLOWAY

SODOR
AND
MAN

Ceded to
King of Scots
1266

YNYS
MON
(ANGLESEY)

RHOS

G W Y N E D D

MEIRIONYDD

POWYS

CEREDIGION

YSTRAD

DYFED

D E H E U B A R T H

GOWER

GLAMORGAN

BETWEEN
WYE &
SEVERN

BRYCHEINIOG
(BRECKNOCK)

GWENT

Domesday Population
per square mile

20 and over
15–20
10–15
5–10
2·5–5
under 2·5

○ Domesday Boroughs
⊙ Boroughs chartered by 1200
● Boroughs chartered 1201-1334
C Cloth making centres 1086-1350
⌘ Domesday castles
□ Iron
C Coal
L Lead
S Silver
T Tin
⌖ Cathedral
† Abbey

Royal forests in the thirteenth century

Main areas of marsh

Approximate limits of "Midland" field
systems

Boundaries of Scottish dioceses and
Welsh principalities

150

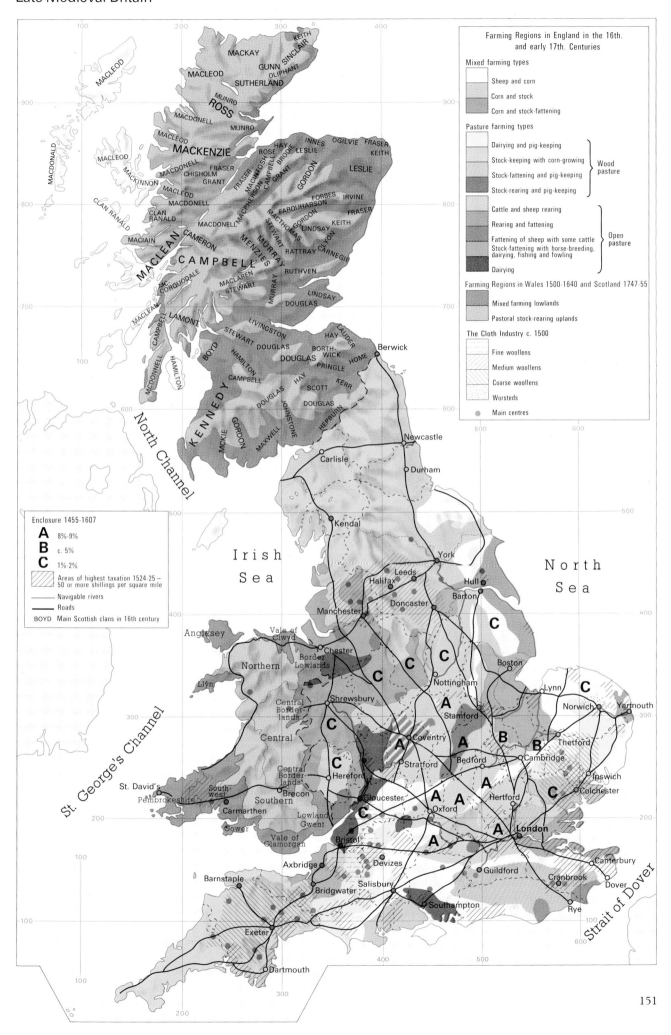

Farming Regions in England in the 16th.
and early 17th. Centuries

Mixed farming types

Sheep and corn

Corn and stock

Corn and stock-fattening

Pasture farming types

Dairying and pig-keeping

Stock-keeping with corn-growing

Stock-fattening and pig-keeping

Stock-rearing and pig-keeping

} Wood pasture

Cattle and sheep rearing

Rearing and fattening

Fattening of sheep with some cattle
Stock-fattening with horse-breeding,
dairying, fishing and fowling

Dairying

} Open pasture

Farming Regions in Wales 1500-1640 and Scotland 1747-55

Mixed farming lowlands

Pastoral stock-rearing uplands

The Cloth Industry c. 1500

Fine woollens

Medium woollens

Coarse woollens

Worsteds

Main centres

Enclosure 1455-1607

A 8%-9%
B c. 5%
C 1%-2%

Areas of highest taxation 1524-25 –
50 or more shillings per square mile

Navigable rivers

Roads

BOYD Main Scottish clans in 16th century

sub-division of the two or three major arable fields into furlongs, and the division of the arable area usually into three cropping zones, one of which was normally left fallow. Elsewhere, particularly in upland and heavy woodland areas, there were smaller fields and less regular cropping systems. In many of the upland and marshland areas there was no arable cultivation, except perhaps for very isolated pockets, and the rural economy was essentially pastoral, the main activity being the rearing of sheep and cattle. The large sheep flocks of the lowland coastal marshes, of Kent and Essex, for example, were paralleled by the 'vaccaries' of the Pennines and central Wales. Natural habitats, including woods and marshes, provided fodder and habitat for both domesticated animals and for wild game. An important feature of the medieval landscape was the royal forest and its diminutive form, the deer park. The rural settlements of medieval Britain varied widely in size and form from the undoubtedly large villages of parts of Midland England and East Anglia to the more isolated hamlets and farmsteads of many of the uplands and recently-colonised areas of the west and north of Britain.

The increase in monastic orders in Britain after the Conquest was a significant feature of medieval life. It is estimated that in 1066 there were about 280 religious houses in England and Wales, a figure that had increased to over 1,300 by the end of the 12th century (largely by the establishment of houses of monks, regular canons and nuns, military orders and hospitals). By the 14th century the number had increased to over 2,000, mainly with the addition of mendicant orders of friars after 1221, but the total had declined by 1500. The larger monastic houses were very substantial landowners, and are epitomised best by the relics of the spectacular Cistercian abbeys at Fountains, Rievaulx, Tintern and Melrose. In Scotland 'innovative' monasteries came later, beginning in the 12th century and including the founding of houses by the Augustinians and the Cistercians.

The towns of medieval Britain were small in comparison with their modern counterparts. According to the data of the Domesday Book of 1086, there were 111 boroughs in England, some of which were very small indeed. London was the largest, with a population of about 10,000. There was only one borough in Wales at this time – Rhuddlan. The period of economic expansion, however, witnessed a growth in the number of boroughs in England, which numbered 480 by the beginning of the 14th century. There was an increase in the towns in Wales consequent on the Norman Conquest, notably in south Wales and, in the late 13th century, in northwest Wales. In Scotland, urbanisation appears to have begun during the Norman period and notably after 1124 when David I became King of Scots. Prior to this date he had given burgh charters to Roxburgh and Berwick, and between 1124 and 1153 created eleven royal burghs, including Edinburgh, Stirling and Dunfermline. Burghs were also given charters by the Church, and the early ecclesiastical burghs include Glasgow and Aberdeen.

Industrial activity in medieval Britain was generally not highly location-specific, for the major industries were those that supplied the everyday needs of the populace – food, drink, clothing and materials for building – and were relatively ubiquitous. The towns were important centres of a wide variety of industries, though in the 13th century there are signs that some industries, notably textiles, moved away from the towns to the countryside. By the late Middle Ages the major textile regions of England included Wiltshire and Gloucestershire (producing broad cloth), the West Riding of Yorkshire (low-grade cloth), the Norwich worsted region and the cloth regions of Suffolk and Essex (which became progressively more specialised in production), and the cloth regions of Somerset and Devon. These developments reflected a general change from the export of wool to the export of cloth.

The principal areas of iron production were the Weald of Sussex and Kent, the Forest of Dean and the Cleveland Hills. The efficiency of production was increased by the introduction of a form of blast furnace. In the later Middle Ages there was also an increase in the production of coal, encouraged by a growing timber shortage. The main mining areas were the Tyne valley, south Nottinghamshire, west Yorkshire, south Wales and around the Forth and in Fife in Scotland. Lead, together with silver, was produced in Derbyshire, the Pennine valleys of Yorkshire and Durham, in Cumberland, and north and south Wales. Tin production took place in Cornwall, and copper ore was extracted in Devonshire, Cumberland and Wales. The products of the agriculture and industries of medieval Britain were mainly consumed and used within the mainland, but trade was nevertheless an important feature of economic activity. The largest ports were London, Southampton and Bristol. Much of the trade of the western ports, including Southampton, was with the Gascony wine area. Southampton and Bristol imported wine and exported wool and cloth. The east-coast ports mainly traded with the Baltic and the Low Countries, while London had trading connections with most parts of continental Europe.

The dynamic character and the vicissitudes of life in medieval Britain should be stressed, for the economic and human geographies of regions and settlements were continually changing. There was a decline in the population of England from six or seven million in 1348 to about 2·75 million in the early 16th century, with changes of a similar order in Wales and Scotland. This was mainly due to the effects of epidemic and infectious diseases. The best-known epidemic was the Black Death, which affected Britain from 1348 to 1350, though there were many other epidemics including tuberculosis, measles and smallpox. In some respects the decrease of population which began in the late 14th century was related to a weakening of a feudal mode of production, and paved the way for the early advent of rural and urban capitalism, culminating in the Agricultural and Industrial Revolutions. It has been suggested that in 1509, when Henry VIII succeeded to the throne of England, Britain was still medieval in many aspects: by the end of the Tudor dynasty this medievalism was rapidly disappearing, and nearly all traces of it had vanished by 1700.

The Agricultural Revolution Enclosures at this period affected both the commons and the open-fields that had been communally cultivated since medieval times. Agricultural societies formed an important channel for the spreading of new farming ideas and techniques.

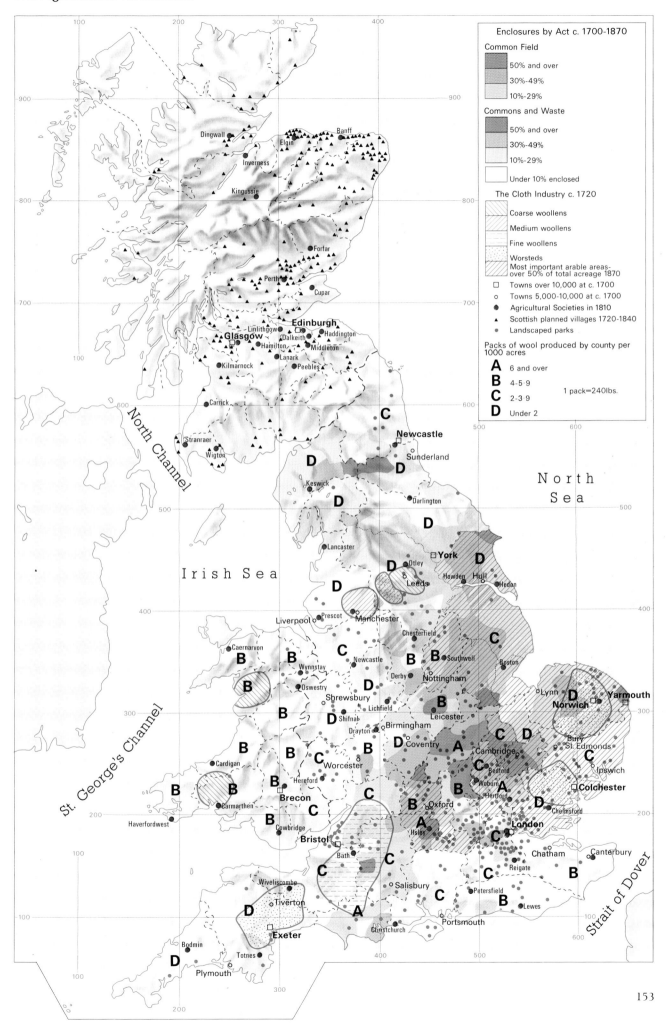

The Agricultural Revolution

Enclosures by Act c. 1700-1870

Common Field
- 50% and over
- 30%-49%
- 10%-29%

Commons and Waste
- 50% and over
- 30%-49%
- 10%-29%
- Under 10% enclosed

The Cloth Industry c. 1720
- Coarse woollens
- Medium woollens
- Fine woollens
- Worsteds
- Most important arable areas— over 50% of total acreage 1870
- □ Towns over 10,000 at c. 1700
- ○ Towns 5,000-10,000 at c. 1700
- ● Agricultural Societies in 1810
- ▲ Scottish planned villages 1720-1840
- • Landscaped parks

Packs of wool produced by county per 1000 acres

A 6 and over
B 4-5·9
C 2-3·9   1 pack=240lbs.
D Under 2

North Channel

North Sea

Irish Sea

St. George's Channel

Strait of Dover

Dingwall

Banff
Elgin
Inverness
Kingussie
Forfar
Perth
Cupar

Edinburgh
Linlithgow
Glasgow Dalkeith Haddington
Hamilton Middleton
Kilmarnock Lanark Peebles

Carrick

Stranraer
Wigton

Newcastle
Sunderland

Keswick

Darlington

Lancaster

York Howden Hull
Otley Hedon
Leeds

Liverpool Prescot Manchester

Chesterfield

Caernarvon
Wynnstay Newcastle Southwell Boston
Oswestry Derby Nottingham
Shrewsbury Lichfield Lynn **Norwich** **Yarmouth**
Shifnal Leicester
Drayton Birmingham Bury
Cardigan Coventry St. Edmonds
Worcester Cambridge Ipswich
Hereford Bedford **Colchester**
Carmarthen **Brecon** Woburn Chelmsford
Haverfordwest Cowbridge Hertford
Bristol Oxford **London**
Bath Ilsley Chatham
Canterbury
Wiveliscombe Salisbury Reigate
Tiverton Petersfield
Exeter Portsmouth Lewes
Bodmin Christchurch
Totnes
Plymouth

153

The Agricultural Revolution

The 16th and 17th centuries witnessed widespread change of an economic and political nature. In England population trends saw a continuing recovery, probably beginning after about 1470; in 1541 the total was about three million, increasing to four million by 1600, to 5·5 million by 1651, followed by a slight decline before further increase in the 18th century. Estimates for Scotland put the population at 550-800,000 for the late 16th century, and at between 800,000 and one million for 1700.

These population increases mirror the beginning of major changes in the sectoral and space-economies of the regions of Britain. Generally labelled the Agricultural and Industrial Revolutions, the phenomena thus classified were extremely complex and extending over quite a long period of time.

In the rural and agricultural sectors the main indices of change are well known, although their local and regional manifestations require further investigation. Enclosure and technical innovations are the best-known features. Enclosure had been a continuous process over a very long period of time, but accelerated in the 16th and 17th centuries prior to the major burst of 'Parliamentary' enclosure in the 18th and 19th centuries. In the late 15th and the 16th century the conversion of arable land to pasture, on account of the relative profitability of sheep farming, led to a 'de-populating' form of enclosure and the desertion of settlements, particularly in the Midlands. The amount of land enclosed in this fashion was quite small, although more 'silent' forms of enclosure also occurred. By 1600 there were regions which had few or no open fields (though these were mainly peripheral to the great central swathe of open fields), and during the 17th century various methods of enclosure, including enclosure 'by agreement', were used to continue the elimination of the open fields. Enclosure by private Act of Parliament was the major mechanism in the 18th and 19th centuries, and quantitatively was the most important method. In this period there were some 5286 Enclosure Acts, of which 3105 effected the enclosure of open-field arable. The total effect was the enclosure in England of nearly 2·8 million HA (seven million acres) or 21% of the total surface area. The counties most affected were Lincolnshire, West Yorkshire, Norfolk, Northamptonshire and East Yorkshire, and those least affected were Middlesex, Essex, Devon, Rutland, Sussex, Hereford, Cheshire, Monmouth, Cornwall and Kent. The degree of enclosure varied in time, but the periods of greatest intensity were 1760-80 and 1793-1815, the latter being the period of the Napoleonic wars. The acreage for Parliamentary enclosure in Wales is estimated to be 167,000 HA (414,000 acres), with the greatest intensity in the period 1793-1815.

The legal system of enclosure in Scotland differed from that of England and Wales, and landowners were not as constrained from enclosing. Acts of the late 16th century facilitated changes in land tenure, and the Act against Lands Lying in Run-rig of 1695 gave power for division of commons. In the Lowlands, arable enclosure was mainly completed by 1770 in Berwickshire and the Lothians, but had only just begun in Ayrshire and Perthshire. In addition, about 200,000 HA (500,000 acres) of common were enclosed in the Lowlands between 1720 and 1850. The pattern of enclosure in the Scottish Highlands was different, particularly after 1745 with the 'clearance' and amalgamation of Highland farms, which were subsequently let to Lowland sheep graziers. This process initially affected the Central Highlands, and later the northwest Highlands and Islands, leading to large-scale emigration.

The landscape effects of enclosure at this time are plain to see—in the form of regular, usually square or rectangular fields, mainly bounded by hedgerows or stone walls. The economic effects of enclosure in the shorter term are more difficult to measure, for in spite of its association with agricultural improvement it is difficult to prove direct causal relationships. The social consequences of enclosures have tended to be neglected, though opinions tend to polarise around the 'improvement' effects and the 'depopulation' effects.

Enclosure was but one of several manifestations of the advent of a capitalist system of production in the rural economy. We associate the Agricultural Revolution with technical improvements in farming, and usually with improvers, such as Thomas Coke of Norfolk, Robert Bakewell of Leicestershire, the Culleys of Northumberland, Jethro Tull and 'Turnip' Townshend. While it is more accurate to describe some of these as popularisers rather than direct innovators, it is certainly the case that many of the technical improvements of this period are associated with large estates, such as Coke's Norfolk estate, and the estates of innovating landlords in East Lothian. The technical innovations included the introduction of short leys with improved grasses (known as convertible husbandry), new crops (clover, turnips, the potato, ryegrass, sainfoin), new rotations (especially the Norfolk system), the application of fertilisers and the new implements such as Tull's seed drill. The area of improved land was increased by major reclamation schemes (notably the Fenland and of areas of moorland and heathland). The regional chronologies of adoption are very complex, and there is no overall pattern or 'national' picture. Incentives for improving and intensifying agricultural production included the rapidly growing population and the increase in the proportion of the population living in towns, particularly London and the towns of the industrial areas. Improvement is also seen in the newer residences, planned estate villages and the landscaped gardens and parks. What has been described as the flowering or re-building of rural England commenced in the late 16th century, but the architectural expression of the Agricultural Revolution is usually associated with the great buildings of the 18th century and the classical Palladian styles. Landscape gardening also reached its peak in the 18th century, the major practitioners being William Kent, Lancelot Brown and Humphrey Repton.

Agricultural change did not stop in the early 19th century, although progress and advancement were not always universal in rural areas. In the 19th century the legislative context of farming continued to change with

The Early Industrial Revolution The geography of early industrialisation depended on the availability of coal or water for power, and on canals for communications. The concentration of industry into relatively small areas was fed by a dramatic movement of people from rural areas to the towns.

154

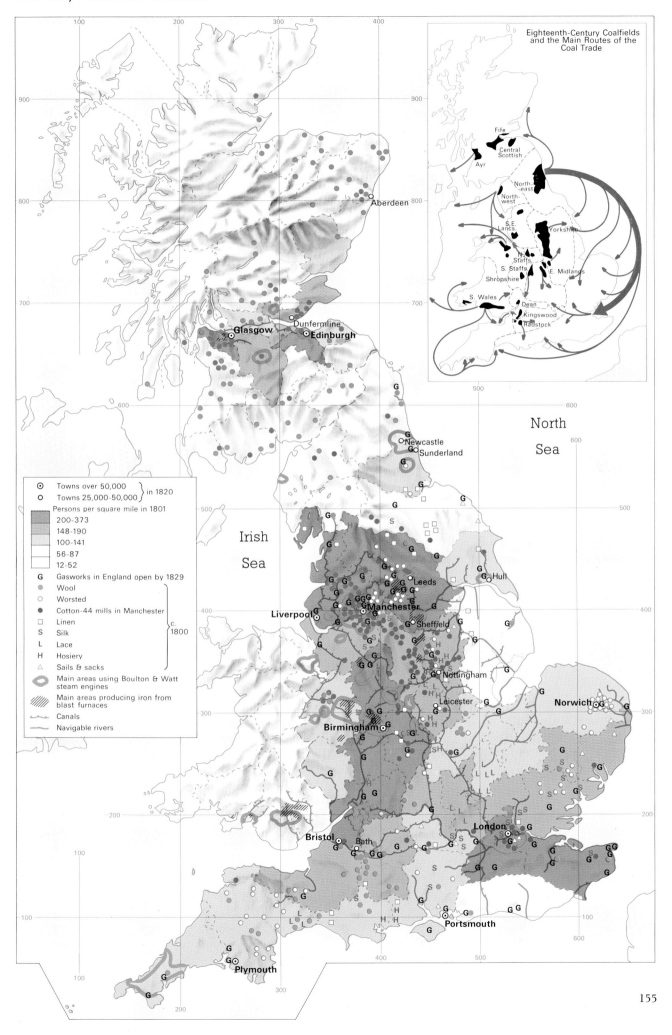

The Early Industrial Revolution

Eighteenth-Century Coalfields
and the Main Routes of the
Coal Trade

North
Sea

Irish
Sea

| Towns over 50,000 | ⊙ | in 1820 |
| Towns 25,000-50,000 | ○ | |

Persons per square mile in 1801
200-373
148-190
100-141
56-87
12-52

G Gasworks in England open by 1829
● Wool
○ Worsted
● Cotton-44 mills in Manchester
□ Linen
S Silk
L Lace
H Hosiery
△ Sails & sacks

Main areas using Boulton & Watt
steam engines
Main areas producing iron from
blast furnaces
Canals
Navigable rivers

c. 1800

Aberdeen

Glasgow   Dunfermline
Edinburgh

Newcastle
Sunderland

Hull

Liverpool   Leeds
Manchester
Sheffield

Nottingham

Leicester   Norwich

Birmingham

Bristol   Bath

London

Plymouth

Portsmouth

155

more Enclosure Acts and the repeal of the Corn Laws (ending the artificial maintenance of prices), the subsidy of land drainage by the Public Money Drainage Act of 1846, and the strengthening of the rights of tenants by the Agricultural Holdings Acts. Farming became a more and more capitally-intensive commercial enterprise, responding to the demands of a rapidly growing population for cheaper food. This process, assisted by new technology (including under-draining, chemical fertilisers and better transport to markets), resulted in improved productivity. It also produced a massive decline in the rural labour force in the course of the 19th century. High investment at the time of high farming could be very profitable, but at other times, particularly the 1880s and 1890s, low prices produced considerable depression and widespread bankruptcy, notably in eastern England.

The Industrial Revolution

The other 'revolution' of the 18th and 19th centuries was 'industrial', a term which has associations not merely with manufacturing and extractional industries but also with rapid urbanisation, rapid population increase and major changes in the transport system. In the mid-18th century the population of Britain was about eleven million, and this figure had risen spectacularly to 45 million by 1911 (of whom less than 10% were engaged in agriculture). The increase was most rapid in mid-century. In the late 18th century, a decline in the death-rate and rise in birth rate because of earlier age at marriage gave a national increase in population of about 40%. The overall figures do, however, mask regional and local variations: in the mid-19th century rural areas of Wales, Scotland and (to a lesser extent) England experienced population decline. Immigration from Ireland was important, though offset by overseas emigration from Britain, giving a net loss of over one million people in the period 1801 to 1911. For the 19th century population growth varied between 11% and 14% a decade, falling, however, to 10% in the first decade of the 20th century. Population growth was highest in the rapidly industrialising and urbanising regions of north and midland England, London, Clydeside and South Wales.

The Industrial Revolution did not start from a totally new base. The textile industries which had developed in the 16th and 17th centuries retained regional distinctiveness. Until the mid-18th century the woollen industry provided about 33% of Britain's industrial output. The wool textile regions changed balance, however, with the decline of the Somerset and Devon and Suffolk producers, and a greater concentration in Gloucestershire, Wiltshire, Norwich and the West Riding (*see map page 153*). The cotton industry experienced a rapid rise in the 18th century, particularly with the increased demand from the home market after 1750, and the technical advances after 1770. The major areas of production were Lancashire, the East Midlands and the Glasgow region. Coal output also increased rapidly in the 18th century: the total for 1700 was about 2·5 million tons, which increased to 10 million by 1800. The turning point for expansion in coal production was about 1770, with the beginning of the canal era providing a cheaper means of distribution. The largest coalfield was that of northeast England, much of whose

output was shipped down the east coast to London. Other smaller areas of production included the coalfields of the Midlands, Yorkshire, Lancashire, the Forest of Dean, the Rhondda and the Firth of Forth. Iron production was mainly concentrated in South Wales, Shropshire, Staffordshire, Yorkshire, and the Central valley of Scotland. Other major industries of the 18th century included silk textiles, glassmaking, and shipbuilding.

Changes in the form of power (especially steam) allied to technological changes—the smelting of iron using coal in the early 18th century, the advent of a wide range of machines and of the factory systems—accelerated industrial activity, particularly in the regions on the developing coalfields. By the mid-19th century the Industrial Revolution had reached its peak. Deeper mining and greater demand led to increased production—from 21 million tons in 1826 to 154 million tons in 1880, with the Northumberland and Durham field the major producer, followed by Lancashire, South Wales and Yorkshire. The iron industry was tied to coal production, and of the mid-century total of 2·7 million tons of pig-iron, the largest producers were Staffordshire, Scotland and South Wales. The working of the iron was not so tied, and metal industries were located in Sheffield and the Black Country, with different locations for shipbuilding and locomotive engineering. The textile industries experienced further concentration, with Lancashire dominating cotton production. There was less regional dominance by a single region in the woollen industry, although the major concentration was in West Yorkshire.

The railway age (from 1825 onwards) brought massive change in population distribution, with the increasing concentration in the towns of the coalfield and industrial regions. Over 50% of the English population were urban-dwellers in 1851, and 70% by 1881. Urban development was marked in Yorkshire, Lancashire, the Black Country and Birmingham, Tyneside, Central Scotland, London, South Wales and, later in the century, along the coast of southeast England.

As with agriculture, so there was also depression in industry in late-Victorian Britain, especially in the period 1873-1896, when industrial productivity fell, though new industries developed and partly offset decline elsewhere. These included the chemical and electrical engineering industries, food processing, and steel. On the eve of World War I the main trends of the Industrial Revolution had changed, as some of the older industrial areas began to lose population with a drift of population towards the south-east. These trends have continued to dominate throughout the 20th century.

Britain in the Late Nineteenth Century Between 1835 and 1900 the country was covered by a network of railways, often to the detriment of competing canals and roads. London's role as capital of the Empire helped to attract immigrants sufficient to make it one of the world's largest cities, despite a higher-than-normal mortality rate.

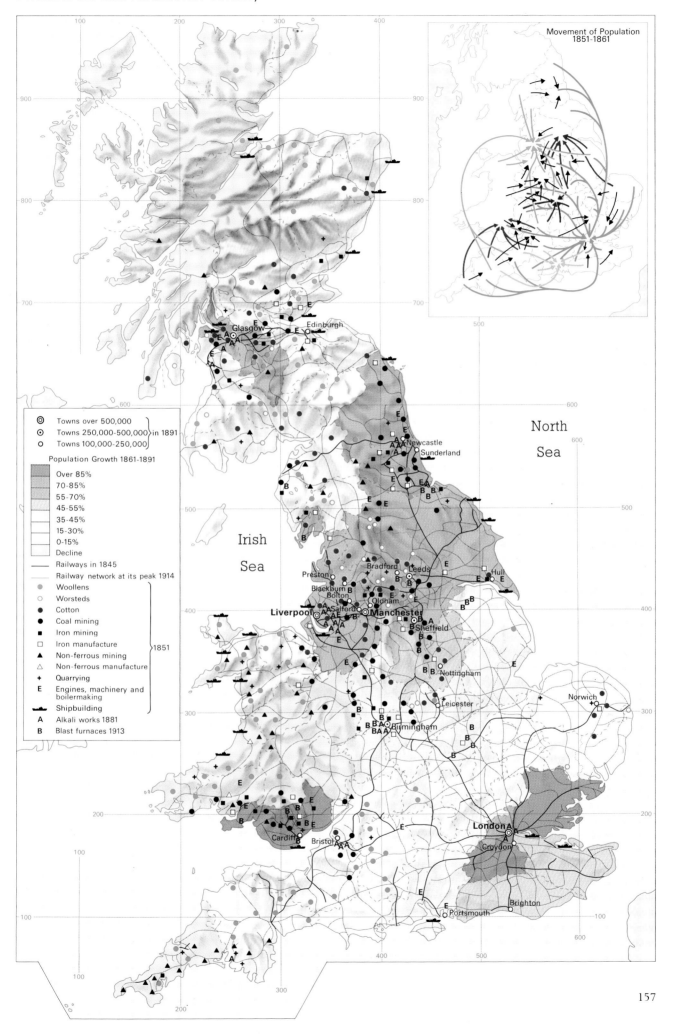

Movement of Population
1851-1861

North
Sea

Irish
Sea

Towns over 500,000
Towns 250,000-500,000 } in 1891
Towns 100,000-250,000

Population Growth 1861-1891

Over 85%
70-85%
55-70%
45-55%
35-45%
15-30%
0-15%
Decline

Railways in 1845
Railway network at its peak 1914
Woollens
Worsteds
Cotton
Coal mining
Iron mining
Iron manufacture
Non-ferrous mining
Non-ferrous manufacture
Quarrying
Engines, machinery and
boilermaking
Shipbuilding
Alkali works 1881
Blast furnaces 1913

} 1851

Glasgow
Edinburgh
Newcastle
Sunderland
Preston
Bradford
Leeds
Hull
Blackburn
Bolton
Oldham
Liverpool
Salford
Manchester
Sheffield
Nottingham
Leicester
Norwich
Birmingham
Cardiff
Bristol
London
Croydon
Brighton
Portsmouth

157

Modern Britain

The Legacy of the 1930s

Contrasts between the north and south of Britain are often made in the spirit of rivalry and jest. The Scottish people have their own history and pride. The people of the north of England, it has been remarked, offer 'the backbone of the country' and the superior robustness of the north is contrasted with the agility of intellect, but softer character, of the south. Behind the sometimes provocative jesting about the differences between Yorkshiremen and Londoners, Geordies and Brummies, there lay in the 1930s very great differences in the prosperity and ways of life of the 'two Britains'. Although there were exceptions to the rule, it was in the north that depression was concentrated, in the south that new industries were developing and the cities growing rapidly. Many northerners were moving away seeking the wider opportunities of London and the West Midlands. There was a 'drift' of population to the south of about 1,160,000 between 1923 and 1936. Wales, in this respect, was to be linked with the north rather than the south. Between 1923 and 1937 the insured population of the three southern divisions of the Ministry of Labour increased by 1,396,000 or 41% and the Midlands by 445,000 (27%). The insured population of the rest of Britain increased by only 576,000 or 10%. In terms of actual jobs, the three southern divisions increased by 47%, the Midlands by 32% and the North, Scotland and Wales by only 4%.

This situation was a product of the localisation of industries which had grown before 1914 but were now declining. There were falls in employment in cotton, coal, shipbuilding and some sectors of the iron and steel industries. The industrial districts of the north and Wales were heavily dependent on such industries. To pick out some extremes, unemployment rates in 1932 reached 60·9% in Merthyr Tydfil, 48·9% in Port Talbot, 46·7% in Sunderland, 44·6% in Barnsley, 44% in West Cumberland, 35% in Dundee. The Birmingham rate was 15·3%, Brighton's was 11·4%. Even East Ham in London was no more than 24·1%. And the unemployment rates fell more quickly in the south and the Midlands as economic recovery from the Great Depression began.

For it was in the southern part of Britain that the growing industries were concentrated. Here were the trades manufacturing for the home market and here could be found employment in the service and constructional industries. Motor-car manufacturing was well established in Dagenham, Luton, Oxford, Coventry and Birmingham. Industries linked to the assembly lines, like electrical engineering and the manufacture of components, tyres, car bodies and gear boxes, were in the south. The Birmingham metal trades prospered and the West Midlands, with its closely knit system of 'linkages' between trades, offered jobs to migrants from Wales and the North. Coventry was one of the fastest-growing cities, with an increase of population of 20% between 1931 and 1938 as against 3% for the country as a whole. Jobs were to be found in motor-car and cycle factories, electrical engineering, firms making components, machine-tool industries and in the rayon industry. With about one-fifth of the population of Great Britain, 'Greater London obtained five-sixths of the net increase in the number of factories between 1932 and 1937, two-fifths of all the employment in new factories and one-third of all the factory extensions'. New factories sprang up in the southeast, south, west and north of Greater London, many of them on speculatively built industrial estates along the main roads and railways out of London. Such estates can still be seen in Acton, Perivale, Park Royal and Wembley. Radio and electrical industries, automobile and aircraft engineering, pharmaceuticals, the food and drink trades, paper and printing, scientific instruments, and furniture, all nationally expanding industries, figured prominently.

While such development was in train the Clyde was in the grip of one of the worst concentrations of persistent unemployment lasting for almost all the inter-war period. Conditions on the Tyne were little, if any, better. The demand for action could not be resisted. The Special Areas Act of 1934 was the first of a series of Acts which gave limited powers to Commissioners for the Special Areas to take action to relieve unemployment in South Wales, northeast England, Cumberland and Clydeside. Industrial trading estates were set up, for example at Treforest (near Cardiff), Team Valley (Gateshead) and Hillington (Glasgow). Local authorities began to muster their resources. The Bank of England made available funds for the building of new blast furnaces, steel works and a continuous strip mill at Ebbw Vale: the original plan had been to build the plant on an iron-ore based location in Lincolnshire. Government plants making war materials were sited in the Special Areas. Government contracts, many for naval vessels, helped to bring life to the Clyde, the Tyne and to Barrow. Some of the depressed regions, eastern South Wales for example, profited more than others. Re-armament and the up-swing of trade achieved more than government policy. In 1938 the Royal Commission on the Distribution of the Industrial Population (the 'Barlow Commission') was established and its report was to influence post-war policy for regional development and industrial location.

The circumstances of regional contrast in employment had further consequences in terms of differences in personal incomes, quality of housing, access to medical and social services, opportunities for advancement. The Beveridge Report's recommendation of 1942 of a plan for 'Social Security as part of a general programme of social policy' must be viewed against this background.

The 1930s must not be seen wholly in terms of regional contrast. There was concern for example that the Axial Belt or 'Coffin' stretching from northwest to southeast from Lancashire to London was coming to house too great a share of the country's population (*see map page 173*). It was an age of technical change: the 'talkies' replaced the silent cinema, almost everybody could afford a radio, and the BBC under Sir John Reith's Directorship had a firm policy from which many young people benefited. New secondary schools were

The Crisis of the 1930s A study carried out in the late 1930s revealed the excessive dependence of many towns on a single industry as a structural problem exacerbating the impact of the depression. This map compares the distribution of these industries with the incidence of unemployment.

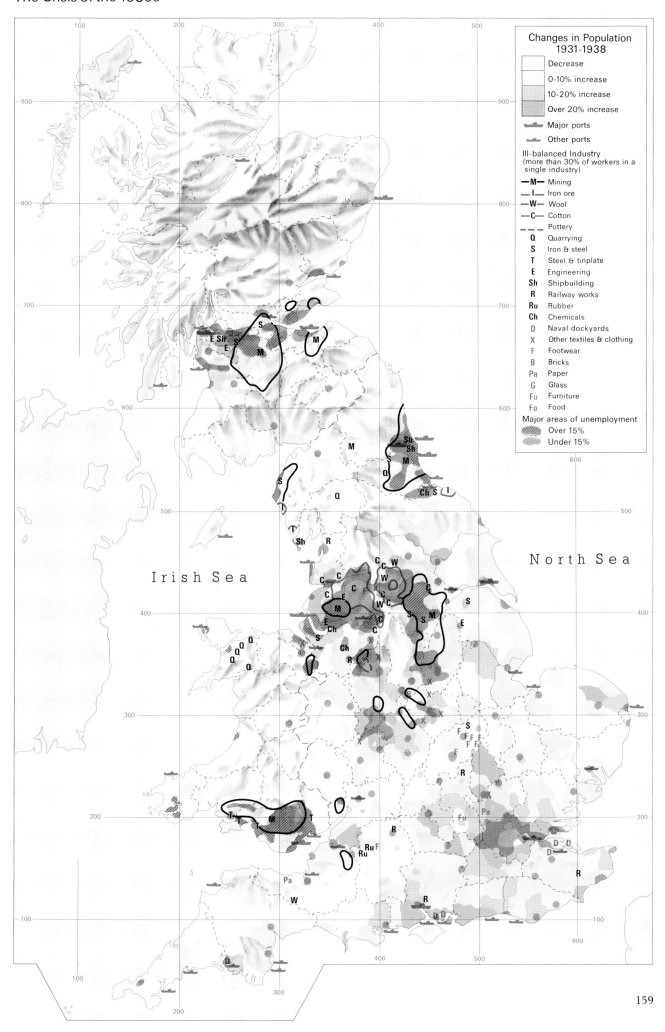

Changes in Population
1931-1938

Decrease

0-10% increase

10-20% increase

Over 20% increase

Major ports

Other ports

Ill-balanced Industry
(more than 30% of workers in a
single industry)

M — Mining

I — Iron ore

W — Wool

C — Cotton

Pottery

Q — Quarrying

S — Iron & steel

T — Steel & tinplate

E — Engineering

Sh — Shipbuilding

R — Railway works

Ru — Rubber

Ch — Chemicals

D — Naval dockyards

X — Other textiles & clothing

F — Footwear

B — Bricks

Pa — Paper

G — Glass

Fu — Furniture

Fo — Food

Major areas of unemployment

Over 15%

Under 15%

North Sea

Irish Sea

established. Motor-car ownership was extending as the Baby Austin and Morris Minor found ready markets. Some new roads were built, among them the Wolverhampton New Road across the derelict land of the Black Country and the North Circular Road linking the industrial areas of north London.

Competition between the railway companies, especially on the routes from London to Scotland, led to the introduction of new and more efficient steam locomotives and reductions in travel times. Air services to the Continent, notably from Croydon, grew in frequency and a network of internal air services was introduced. British passenger liners registered success in the competition for the Atlantic 'Blue Riband'. An Electricity Grid was built, helping, with the rise of road transport and the growth of light industries, to free industry from coal-based locations.

It was the age of suburbia. More than four million houses were built in Britain between the wars, most of them in the suburbs. The better council housing estates attempted to embody Garden City lines with curving, geometrically designed, tree-lined avenues and nearby playing fields and schools. It was a day for the speculative builder and the semi-detached home, increasingly with garage space or garage. There was some ribbon development but more building of estates with local shops and cinema.

Much of this often-criticised housing remains in the 1980s and commands high prices. As cities expanded outwards, trolley-buses and motor-buses began to supplement and then to supersede the electric tram. In Greater London underground lines were extended and Metroland grew in the northwest, backed by the Metropolitan Railway. Such urban sprawl aroused alarm on many counts. These included concern at the growing size and costs of urban growth, concern at the loss for ever of good agricultural land and, under the shadow of Guernica, forebodings about aerial bombardment. And, as the 1930s drew on, the news from the Continent, the increasing pressure of refugees from Nazi Germany and their stories of persecution led increasingly to the conviction that, at least for a time, domestic problems would have to take second place. But even at the worst times of the war preparation for the future of Britain was in progress and the Barlow Report and the Scott Report, together with the Beveridge Report, laid foundations for the planning of the post-war society.

Fuel and Energy Resources

King Coal provided the heat and energy for Britain's Industrial Revolution of the 18th and 19th centuries. Britain's coals are of Carboniferous age: the formerly-wide extent of the Carboniferous rocks has been broken into a number of separate coalfields by subsequent earth movements and by denudation. Except for the anthracite of the western part of the South Wales Coalfield, the coals in Britain are bituminous in type. Considerable variation in coal types exists, from the steam coals of South Wales (formerly so important in the export trade), to the coking coals such as those of Durham, to the general industrial coals which are widespread but best illustrated in the Yorkshire, Nottinghamshire and Derbyshire coalfields (*see maps pages 161 and 162*).

The Northumberland and Durham coalfields were the first to be developed on a large scale, having the advantages of river and sea transport. As demand increased, mining moved from the shallow pits sunk near the outcrops of the main coal seams to deeper pits working seams at depth and through the overlying later rocks on the 'concealed' coalfields. Coal production increased during the 19th century and reached 230 million tons by 1900 and its maximum of 287 million tons in 1913. Of that total about one-third was exported. South Wales produced 57 million tons, Northumberland and Durham 56 million, Yorkshire 44 million, Scotland 42 million, and Nottinghamshire, Derbyshire and Leicestershire 34 million tons.

Production never again rose to such levels. By 1938 total production had fallen to 227 million tons partly as a result of declining exports. Steamships were replaced by oil-fired vessels; production from South Wales was down to 35 million tons (partly due to the decline in steam-coal production), and from Northumberland and Durham to 33 million, though the East Midlands coalfields held stable.

The industry was nationalised in 1947 and the National Coal Board inherited many problems. Geological problems were increasingly encountered and too little investment in new methods and equipment had taken place. There were complex problems of labour relations, arising in part from the diverse local conditions of mining and the past history of management and of variable demand. Nine hundred and fifty collieries existed of which, according to the *Plan for Coal* of 1950, 250 were to be selected for modernisation and reconstruction to yield about 70% of a planned output of 240 million tons. There was now a high demand for coal, in the phase of economic reconstruction after 1945, and before oil began to invade the general market for industrial, railway and household coal. New mines were sunk, mechanical equipment installed and schemes for improved productivity developed. Open-cast working was introduced. The costs of coal production varied widely, being highest in Kent, South Wales, Lancashire, Durham and Scotland and lowest in the East Midlands and Yorkshire. Despite progress there remained until about 1957 a coal 'gap': the industry could not supply enough to meet the country's needs. Of the 221 million tons produced in that year the main users were power stations (46·5 million), industry (37·5 million), domestic users (35·1 million), coke ovens (30·7 million), gas works (26·4 million), and railways (11·4 million).

The change in the industry's position after this date was dramatic. Competition from other sources of energy and improvements in the efficiency of fuel-burning equipment led to declining demand for coal. By 1967 production had fallen to 174 million tons and by 1977 to 120 million. By 1977 the main users were power stations (77·7 million), coke ovens (19·3 million), domestic (10·4 million), industry (9·1 million); the railways had turned to oil and the gas industry had converted to natural gas. Great changes occurred in the geography of coal production as mines in the high-cost coalfields were closed. Now the coalfields of Yorkshire and

Mineral Resources The mining of metals is carried on commercially in a number of locations. The widespread availability of sand and gravel is vital to the construction industry, as is chalk and limestone.

Mineral Resources

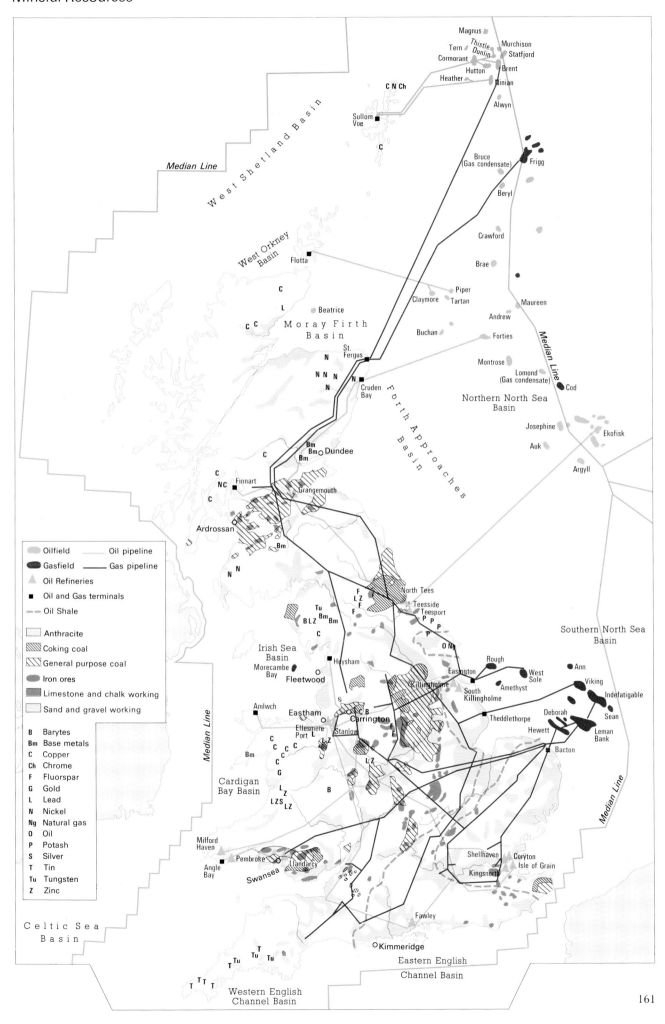

161

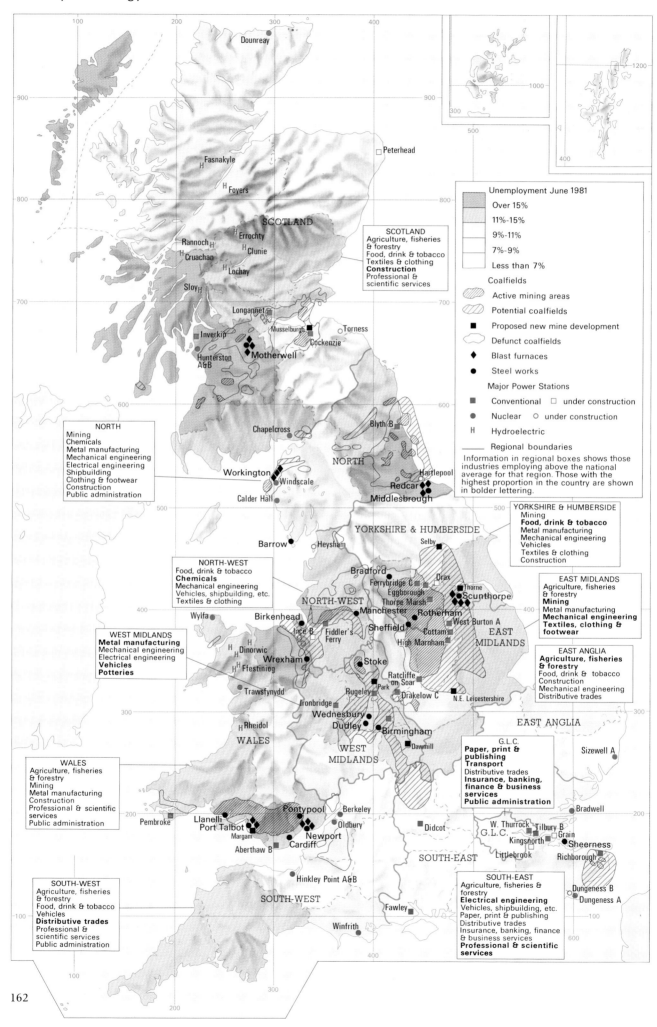

Unemployment June 1981
- Over 15%
- 11%-15%
- 9%-11%
- 7%-9%
- Less than 7%

Coalfields
- Active mining areas
- Potential coalfields
- ■ Proposed new mine development
- Defunct coalfields
- ◆ Blast furnaces
- ● Steel works

Major Power Stations
- ■ Conventional □ under construction
- ● Nuclear ○ under construction
- H Hydroelectric

—— Regional boundaries

Information in regional boxes shows those industries employing above the national average for that region. Those with the highest proportion in the country are shown in bolder lettering.

SCOTLAND
Agriculture, fisheries & forestry
Food, drink & tobacco
Textiles & clothing
Construction
Professional & scientific services

NORTH
Mining
Chemicals
Metal manufacturing
Mechanical engineering
Electrical engineering
Shipbuilding
Clothing & footwear
Construction
Public administration

YORKSHIRE & HUMBERSIDE
Mining
Food, drink & tobacco
Metal manufacturing
Mechanical engineering
Vehicles
Textiles & clothing
Construction

NORTH-WEST
Food, drink & tobacco
Chemicals
Mechanical engineering
Vehicles, shipbuilding, etc.
Textiles & clothing

EAST MIDLANDS
Agriculture, fisheries & forestry
Mining
Metal manufacturing
Mechanical engineering
Textiles, clothing & footwear

WEST MIDLANDS
Metal manufacturing
Mechanical engineering
Electrical engineering
Vehicles
Potteries

EAST ANGLIA
Agriculture, fisheries & forestry
Food, drink & tobacco
Construction
Mechanical engineering
Distributive trades

WALES
Agriculture, fisheries & forestry
Mining
Metal manufacturing
Construction
Professional & scientific services
Public administration

G.L.C.
Paper, print & publishing
Transport
Distributive trades
Insurance, banking, finance & business services
Public administration

SOUTH-WEST
Agriculture, fisheries & forestry
Food, drink & tobacco
Vehicles
Distributive trades
Professional & scientific services
Public administration

SOUTH-EAST
Agriculture, fisheries & forestry
Electrical engineering
Vehicles, shipbuilding, etc.
Paper, print & publishing
Distributive trades
Insurance, banking, finance & business services
Professional & scientific services

Dounreay

Fasnakyle H
Foyers H

SCOTLAND

Peterhead

Errochty H
Rannoch H
Cruachan H
Clunie H
Lochay H
Sloy H

Longannet
Inverkip
Hunterston A&B
Musselburgh
Cockenzie
Torness
Motherwell

Chapelcross
Blyth B

NORTH

Workington
Windscale
Calder Hall
Hartlepool
Redcar
Middlesbrough

Barrow
Heysham

YORKSHIRE & HUMBERSIDE

Selby

Bradford
Ferrybridge C
Drax
Eggborough
Thorpe Marsh
Thorne
Scunthorpe

NORTH-WEST

Wylfa
Birkenhead
Manchester
Rotherham
Sheffield
West Burton A
Cottam
High Marnham
Ince B
Fiddler's Ferry
Dinorwic
Wrexham
Ffestiniog
Stoke
Ratcliffe on Soar
Park
Drakelow C
N.E. Leicestershire

EAST
MIDLANDS

Trawsfynydd
Rheidol H
Ironbridge
Wednesbury
Dudley
Birmingham
Rugeley

WALES

WEST
MIDLANDS

EAST ANGLIA

Dawmill

Sizewell A

Pontypool
Berkeley
Pembroke
Llanelli
Port Talbot
Margam
Newport
Cardiff
Oldbury
Didcot
Bradwell

W. Thurrock
Tilbury B
Kingsnorth
Grain
Littlebrook
Sheerness
Richborough

Aberthaw B

G.L.C.

SOUTH-EAST

Dungeness B
Dungeness A

Hinkley Point A&B

SOUTH-WEST

Fawley

Winfrith

the East Midlands where costs were lowest and productivity highest produced over one-half of the total. A great local market existed in the thermal electricity generating stations which the Central Electricity Generating Board had erected along the River Trent and the rivers of Yorkshire (*see map page 162*). New reserves have been proved, for example at Selby in Yorkshire, where development is currently in progress, in North-East Leicestershire, where plans for development in the Vale of Belvoir have aroused controversy on environmental grounds, and elsewhere. However, the problem is not so much one of reserves (for there is enough coal for 400-500 years at present rates of production), but of price and convenience. Government strategies for fuel and energy propose an increase in production to about 165 million tons by the end of the century, but doubts have been expressed as to the existence of potential markets for that amount.

The ten years after 1965 saw a revolution in the geography of the UK fuel and power industries. The decline of coal was matched by the rise in importance of natural gas, first imported and then extracted from beneath the North Sea, the development of North Sea oil and the emergence of nuclear power.

The West Sole gas field was found in 1964 and offshore gas production began in 1967. By the early 1970s four major fields Leman, Indefatigable, Hewett and Viking were also in production. Since then, Frigg and Rough have been tapped and natural gas is also produced in association with oil in other fields in the northern North Sea. Four North Sea terminals, Bacton, Theddlethorpe, Easington and St Fergus are linked to the 5600-km (3500-mile) national high-pressure pipe-line system. North Sea gas meets some 81% of total natural gas supplies. Liquefied Natural Gas (LNG) is imported from Algeria to Canvey Island and has higher calorific value than North Sea gas. Further discoveries of natural gas, including the Morecambe field in the Irish Sea, ensure that indigenous production will continue to meet the major part of home needs for the next 30 years at least.

For many years small amounts of oil have been extracted from on-shore fields, notably from Eakring in Nottinghamshire. The discovery of oil in the North Sea in 1969 changed Britain's oil position dramatically, and the first oil flowed ashore in 1975. The scale of investment is indicated by the fact that by the end of 1979, 859 exploration or appraisal wells and 586 development wells had been drilled or begun. The North Sea provides a difficult environment for drilling, with high winds and steep waves, and costs are high. However, the oil is light and of low sulphur content and production is profitable. Among the largest fields in production and reserve are Forties, Brent, Piper and Ninian. Major investments have been made in 1200 km (750 miles) of pipeline and in terminal facilities, notably at Sullom Voe in Shetland. Although Britain still needs to import heavy grades of crude oil these have been

declining and exports have been increasing so that the country has become a net oil exporter.

Our picture of fuel and energy resources must be completed by references to nuclear energy and hydroelectricity (*see map page 162*). Electricity from a nuclear power station (Calder Hall) first entered the Grid in 1956. The commissioning of Berkeley and Bradwell in 1962 marked an important stage in the development of a civil nuclear power programme and 16 stations are now in operation (eleven of which are controlled by the electricity authorities). The government view nuclear energy as a major contributor to the future energy needs of the country and, in addition to the completion of the present construction programme, the search for sites for new stations has now begun. Controversy exists over the scale of the programme required and the best type of system. According to one projection nuclear power stations may provide nearly 20% of electricity generated in Britain by the end of the century.

The contribution of hydro-electricity is mainly in the more remote areas, especially in Scotland. Hydro-electric power supplies only 2% of electricity requirements overall. Most potential sites for other than very small stations have been employed already. Pumped storage schemes have been developed to increase the scale of power stations.

More will be heard of the search for alternative sources of energy. Studies of the possibilities of tidal energy from the Severn estuary have been made. Experiments with wave energy methods have been begun. Investigations into geothermal possibilities are in progress. There are advocates of the greater use of wind power. Unfortunately, Britain's climate does not encourage the large-scale development of solar energy even though solar water-heating systems do offer some promise. It will be many years yet before such alternative systems provide other than minor contributions to Britain's needs. Meanwhile there is much to be done in the field of energy conservation.

Industry

Since the end of World War II persistent efforts have been made to influence the location of Britain's industry. The Barlow Commission's Report of 1940 had drawn attention to the problems created by what was regarded as ill-balanced industrial growth in the southeast and the West Midlands, and the narrow industrial structures, declining industries and unemployment in South Wales, Tyneside, Clydeside and the northeast. Measures to remedy the lack of balance and to improve the diversity and the resilience of industries in the Development Areas, as they came to be called, were taken after the war. What has come to be called 'regional policy' developed. There have been, from time to time, changes in the boundaries of the areas delimited as requiring special help; the measures adopted have also varied in kind and in degree. Different governments have given more or less emphasis to regional policy, but the theme has remained a consistent one. Broadly, industrial firms seeking to expand their premises or to build new plant in the southeast and the West Midlands have been subject to control through the need to seek Industrial Development Certificates. Those expanding or establishing themselves in Development Areas have been eligible for various forms of financial assistance.

Industry and Energy The listing of major industries derives from regional employment statistics; as industries such as steel become confined to a very few locations, the provision of a wide range of employment regionally becomes important. The areas of potential coalfields shown on the map are exploratory; by no means all are likely to be exploited.

Industrial estates were built in Development Areas and some factories were constructed in advance of need as a further incentive. The original concept of Development Areas was amended over time, and new designations were introduced. These included Special Development Areas where acute problems, such as the rapid decline in coalmining employment, were judged to merit higher levels of assistance, and Intermediate Areas where lesser benefits were made available after 1969 for areas where employment levels or other signs of sluggish economic performance as well as environment problems such as derelict land, a legacy of previous industry, gave rise to concern.

The assisted areas, taken together, came in the 1970s to include about 40% of the country's employed population; too large a share, in the eyes of some, for regional policy to be really effective. Many attempts have been made to evaluate the economic results, especially in terms of employment creation, of a policy which, despite some variations in practice, carried for a long time a strong political consensus. But policy evaluations of this kind are difficult exercises, even employing sophisticated statistical techniques, for it is impossible to know exactly what would have happened in the absence of such policies. Many studies have made favourable assessments of the effects of the measures taken to encourage job creation. One such study estimates that about 241,000 jobs were created in four large development areas (Scotland, Wales, Northern Ireland, Northern England) in the years 1960-76. By contrast, another suggests that we cannot be absolutely certain that regional policy measures have had any serious effect on the national distribution of industrial activity. The balance of view appears to be that without a regional policy matters would have been considerably worse in the assisted areas.

During the later 1970s, years of increasing unemployment, critical voices have been raised. The high cost of the financial assistance (projected for 1982-83 in the 1978 White Paper as £609 million at 1979 price levels) was pointed out. It was argued that high levels of unemployment were appearing also in certain parts of the so-called growth regions, eg. in Birmingham and east London. The problem, therefore, was to encourage industrial growth and industrial location wherever it could be located. Industrial growth in the southeast should no longer be restricted for here, where scientific research was strongly located, were possibilities for developing science-based industries. And the southeast was well placed in relation to trade with the EEC.

At the time the Barlow Commission reported in 1940, manufacturing industry was, among the various sectors, the major employer of labour. The location of manufacturing industry was thus seen as the key to the location of employment and hence to the distribution of population. But times have changed and employment in manufacturing industry has declined both relatively and actually. By 1980 only 30·4% of Britain's employed workers were engaged in manufacturing, compared with 59·3% in the services group. And location policy had had only a limited effect on the distribution of the servicing industries. Between 1965 and 1980 manufacturing industries shed 1,730,000 workers or 21% of its workforce while jobs in the servicing group went up by 1,950,000.

Some writers refer to this change as a process of 'de-industrialisation', others refer to the 'de-skilling' that has arisen from the decline of jobs in the traditional industries located in the assisted areas. The location of manufacturing industry is no longer such an important factor in the general distribution of population as it once was. And, it is argued, the growth of multi-national corporations has placed decisions affecting important British industries in international, rather than national, hands.

A re-interpretation of regional policy in 1979 was intended to lead to substantial savings in expenditure in 1982-83. To achieve this, the plan was to reduce the areas eligible for assistance to include only about 25% of the employed population. Changes have been made in the status of some areas, for example, Wrexham, Kilmarnock and Ayr which assume Special Development Area status. Between 1980 and 1982 the map shows a significant reduction of the intermediate areas (see map page 173). Levels of financial assistance show a similar reduction. The new policy rests also on generating local enterprise, and the establishment of 'enterprise zones' in Tyneside, Clydeside, Merseyside, Manchester, Swansea, Dudley and London has been announced. Certain controls are relaxed and financial assistance given.

The emphasis so far has been on the effects of regional policy to influence industrial location. But there are many other ways in which governments influence industrial location. Some basic industries, like steel, are nationalised: the re-organisation of the steel industry in the late 1970s led to the closure of many plants (eg. Consett, Shelton, Bilston and Corby) and to substantial reductions in the labour force (see map page 162). Other industries such as cotton textiles and tinplate have been re-organised with help provided under Acts of Parliament. Since 1966 government bodies (currently the National Enterprise Board) have assisted rationalisation plans, have promoted new ventures and have held share-holdings in many companies. The list of industries in which the government has become involved is long. In addition to those already mentioned it includes shipbuilding, the motor-car industry, machine tools, the aerospace industries, not to mention oil, gas and electricity. Government decisions are also potent influences on the defence industries and on employment in the construction industry.

In recent years the trend towards an economy based on 'service industry' has continued. It has become clear that the 'regional problem', already discussed, is only one aspect of the changes in progress. There has also been a strong de-centralisation of employment from most of the major conurbations to the outer parts of the city regions and to medium and small towns and some rural areas. In the period 1971-77, for example, employment in the Greater London Conurbation declined by 6·6% or 282,000 persons, that in Merseyside by 8·7%, Clydeside by 3·1% and the West Midlands by 2·6%. By contrast, rates of growth in many medium-sized and small cities and towns were of the order of 10 to 13%.

Behind such changes lies the general problem of the decline in the total number of jobs, especially those for men. Male full-time employment declined by over 445,000 in the

years 1971-77, and although there has been a substantial growth in the number of part-time jobs for women, unemployment has become a major issue. In 1965 the general unemployment level was of the order of 1.5%: in 1982 it was over 11%. Some writers have given a picture, in this unhappy situation, of growing regional economic convergence with a more even distribution of employment than in 1965 (*see map page 162*). 'Big industrial areas such as the South-east, North West and West Midlands,' writes one, 'have declined rapidly relative to small rural or peripheral regions such as East Anglia, the South West, Wales and Northern England.' The appearance of unemployment rates in the West Midlands at levels almost as high as in some development areas has certainly come as an unwelcome shock to an area long renowned for its growth.

So the problems have become more complex than was formerly assumed. To the continuing problem of the development areas created by structural decline of employment in basic and long established industries must be added the changes created by declining employment in other manufacturing industries such as the motor-car and related industries. There have been, too, shifts from big cities to smaller ones, a large-scale decentralisation which has left behind problems of regenerating employment in inner cities. Particular local problems, such as that in East London arising from the closure of the docks, add to the complexity.

What will happen when the industrial recession, which has adversely affected industry and employment since 1974, fades and growth begins again? Probably large-scale unemployment will not disappear quickly. Those industries will benefit that have improved their productivity and international competitiveness. Science- and high-level engineering-based industries, many of which have survived and made progress, should grow further, but they are not mass employers of labour. Those service industries which are often termed 'quaternary industries', demanding high skills and providing international services, have also done well and should strengthen their position. There is great skill and much experience available and the development of imaginative education and re-training schemes could maximise the exploitation of future possibilities for the expansion of the economy.

Transport

'Good roads, canals and navigable rivers by diminishing the expenses of carriage put the remote parts of the country more nearly on a level with those in the neighbourhood of the town. They are upon that account the greatest of all improvements.' So wrote the great economist Adam Smith at the time of the Transport Revolution of the 18th century. However, it may be questioned whether the re-shaping of the British transport system in the past 30 years has had the same effect. It is arguable that recent improvements have emphasised the accessibility of places within the main inter-city network to the relative detriment of the more remote areas, and have worked to the advantage of some, and the disadvantage of other, groups of people.

The British economy depends upon an intensively developed efficient transport network for the rapid movement of people and goods between the principal industrial regions. About 60% of freight traffic is generated by or received in the 'axial belt' extending from Kent to Lancashire. The transport industries are themselves major employers with some 2.75 million people employed in transport and in industries like the manufacture and repair of motor-cars, railway vehicles and aircraft.

Changes in the use of the different modes of transport and technical changes have, at least over the most densely populated parts of the country, made for speed of transport and communication between cities. In terms of inland transport, road transport is now of the first importance. About 80% of all passenger travel is made by private car: there are some 14.3 million motor-cars in Britain. Over 80% of inland freight, by tonnage (two-thirds of tonne-kilometres), is carried by road. To meet the problems of congestion on roads that are among the most crowded in the world a major improvement programme was initiated in 1955 and the motorway and improved trunk road network is the product of this. About 2400 km (1500 miles) of motorway have been constructed. Many motorways, together with the improved A1(M), focus on London, around which the M25 is now under construction. From the M1/M6 junction in the east Midlands motorways extend northwards on both sides of the Pennines. The system extends into south Wales and southwest to Exeter. The midland valley of Scotland has its own network. Except for the M25 and the extension of the M40 towards Birmingham, few new major motorways are now planned; attention in road improvement will be given to congested roads to ports and to new roads, including by-passes, that will improve the environment of towns and villages. For much of the existing road network originated in the 18th and early 19th centuries. Towns grew around roads: now we are trying to take traffic around towns. But despite the introduction of traffic management schemes, problems of traffic congestion remain in the main cities, especially London. Birmingham's Inner Ring Road is one successful example of a major new road development within a major city.

About 11% of passenger transport is accounted for by buses and coaches. This is a significant decline since 1960. Much however has been done to improve the organisation of public transport services in the metropolitan counties and express bus services ply busily between the main cities.

The railway map exhibits a most dramatic re-shaping. A modernisation scheme of 1955 was overtaken by the Beeching Report of 1963 which brought subsequent closure of lines and stations and withdrawal of stopping train and local services on many other lines. The railway network has been reduced by about one-third to 17,973 km (11,168 miles) by the end of the 1970s. In 1962 there were 4347 stations open; ten years later this number had fallen to 2362. The emphasis has been on improving the inter-city services. The main-line permanent way has been re-laid and 3767 km (2341 miles) of line is electrified. The Inter-City 125 services, first introduced in 1976, are the world's fastest diesel rail services, amid other notable improvements (the Advanced Passenger Train came into service in late 1981). Less has been done to improve suburban services although, notably, the Tyne and Wear Metro was opened in 1980. Policy for freight has concentrated on long-distance and bulk traffic.

The Transport System

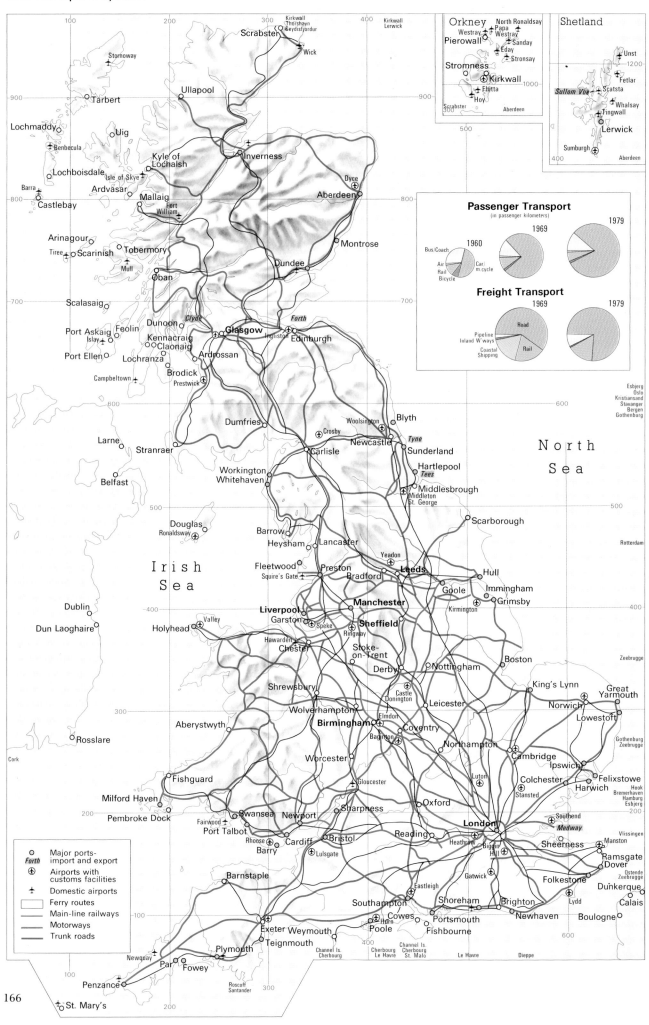

Coal and coke, iron and steel and petroleum products are the most important commodities carried.

Britain's seaports have always played a crucial role in its economic development handling imported materials for manufacture and the exported manufactures. The scale of British seaborne trade, as measured by tonne-kilometres, has declined since 1973, partly because of the economic recession, and partly through the decrease in crude oil imports and the increasing share of European (that is, short-distance) trade. London remains the leading sea-port though many of its older docks have now closed and much traffic is handled at Tilbury. Milford Haven has been the leading oil port but is being overtaken by Sullom Voe in Shetland. The handling of North Sea oil has increased the trade of Tees, Forth and Flotta, in Orkney. Tees, Immingham, Port Talbot and Clyde handle imported ores. Recent developments include the growth of container and roll-on traffic which has more than trebled since 1969, especially at Dover, Felixstowe, Tilbury, Southampton and Hull.

Inland waterways are much less important to the economy than in the days of the Industrial Revolution. Some of the old narrow canals have been closed; others are used by recreational craft. But the wider and deeper canals of Yorkshire and Humberside remain important and development of certain canals, such as that between Doncaster and Rotherham, and their re-equipment with push-tow barge trains are significant recent developments. The 58-km long (36-mile) Manchester Ship Canal remains important for ocean-going vessels.

Not the least important of recent changes in the transport network has been the construction of pipelines for the carriage of crude oil, petroleum products and natural gas (see map page 161). More than 570 km (350 miles) of submarine pipeline link the North Sea oilfields with the refineries and oil ports. Pipeline systems also carry refined products and natural gas to inland markets: one of the longest is the 500-km (300-mile) pipeline from Milford Haven to the Midlands and Manchester.

Of all the developments that illustrate the impact of technical change that of air transport stands out. The siting of Britain's airports reflects many circumstances, including the needs of the RAF in the face of threats from continental Europe, decisions by local authorities and the location of the markets for air traffic. Except for London, there has been little co-ordination in airport development. Plans for new airports such as the Third London Airport arouse high controversy especially on environmental grounds. A hierarchy of airports may be discerned ranging from major international (Heathrow) through those operating medium- and short-haul international and domestic services, those operating charter services, to the small airports with limited facilities mainly serving regional needs. Although much discussion of air transport is in terms of passenger movements, its contribution to freight transport should not be overlooked. Only about 1% of Britain's overseas trade measured by weight is carried by air but this amounts to more than 15% by value. This is heavily concentrated at London, which in terms of the value of freight handled is now Britain's leading port.

Many tasks remain, for example the Channel Tunnel, but the modernisation of the transport system has been a remarkable achievement. The Severn, Forth and Humber bridges, the High Speed Train, the Advanced Passenger Train, the Victoria and Jubilee Lines of London Transport, the North Sea pipelines are symbols of the change. But many argue that the changes which have been designed to link the major industrial areas and to promote resource development and trade have left many rural areas relatively worse off than before, bereft of railway services and with reduced bus services. Also relatively worse off are those like the poor and the elderly who do not own private transport and have been affected by reduced public transport services. But the problem in part reflects the shape of Britain and the concentration of its population. It is theoretically possible to devise a basic route network for a road or railway system of only 1550 km (970 miles) which would reach to within 9 km of half the population and a more extended network of 2800 km (1750 miles) to reach 70%. But to serve the most remote 30% an additional network of over 6000 km (3750 miles) would be required.

Planning for Land

One of the most fruitful aspects of planning since the 1939-45 war has been the care that has been taken over the use of the land of Britain. Although cities and urban life styles have spread outwards, our countryside, though not unchanged, retains its variety and its beauty, even though it provides more and more for the food, water and leisure of the urban population. The Committee on Land Utilisation in Rural Areas (the Scott Committee) in 1942 had expressed concern at the spread of cities over the countryside, and its recommendations provided pathways for fresh thinking and eventual legislation. Such a pathway led, after much discussion, to the National Parks and Access to the Countryside Act of 1949, applying to England and Wales (see map page 172). The National Parks protect some of the most exceptionally beautiful areas of the countryside: they also provide for access and enjoyment by the general public. In so highly developed a country as Britain, it was impossible to draw boundaries around such areas without also including large numbers of towns and villages—and so the National Parks also include the working environments of the communities within them. Out of this situation, many conflicts have developed on such questions as the emphasis that should be given to the preservation of scenery and wild life and how far development such as new limestone quarries in the Peak District, a new trunk road through the Lake District, minerals exploration in Snowdonia, should be permitted. In Scotland a different scheme was adopted, with the establishment of Forest Parks, and the Forestry Commission there as well as in some English forests has done much to improve the compatibility of tree production and the growing demand for recreation. The problems that exist over the objectives of National Parks should not be allowed to cloud the great benefits which the public have gained from the measures taken both to protect the parks and to display their individually distinctive characteristics.

It is not only in National Parks that special care is taken over new development. There are also 33 Areas of Outstanding Natural Beauty in England and Wales (9% of

Agriculture and Fisheries

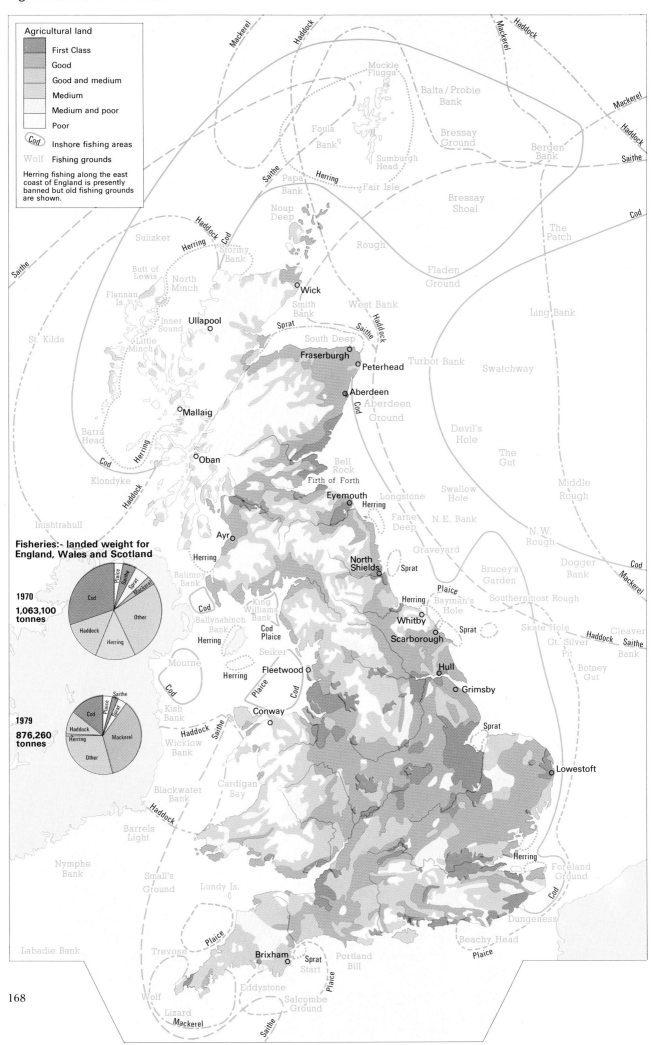

Agricultural land

- First Class
- Good
- Good and medium
- Medium
- Medium and poor
- Poor

Cod — Inshore fishing areas

Wolf — Fishing grounds

Herring fishing along the east coast of England is presently banned but old fishing grounds are shown.

Fisheries:- landed weight for England, Wales and Scotland

1970 1,063,100 tonnes

Pie chart: Cod, Plaice, Saithe, Sprat, Mackerel, Other, Herring, Haddock

1979 876,260 tonnes

Pie chart: Cod, Plaice, Saithe, Sprat, Mackerel, Other, Herring, Haddock

Place labels (map)

Mackerel, Haddock, Mackerel, Haddock, Muckle Flugga, Balta / Probie Bank, Bressay Ground, Bergen Bank, Mackerel, Haddock, Saithe, Foula Bank, Sumburgh Head, Bressay Shoal, Saithe, Papa Bank, Herring, Fair Isle, The Patch, Cod, Noup Deep, Rough, Fladen Ground, Sulizker, Haddock, Herring, Cod, Stormy Bank, Smith Bank, West Bank, Ling Bank, Wick, Butt of Lewis, North Minch, Flannan Is., Inner Sound, Ullapool, Sprat, South Deep, Saithe, Haddock, Turbot Bank, Swatchway, St. Kilda, Little Minch, Fraserburgh, Peterhead, Aberdeen, Aberdeen Ground, Devil's Hole, Mallaig, The Gut, Barra Head, Cod, Oban, Bell Rock, Firth of Forth, Middle Rough, Klondyke, Haddock, Eyemouth, Herring, Longstone, Swallow Hole, Inishtrahull, Herring, Ayr, Herring, Farne Deep, N.E. Bank, N.W. Rough, Graveyard, Balimoy Bank, North Shields, Sprat, Brucey's Garden, Dogger Bank, King Williams Bank, Plaice, Southernmost Rough, Cod, Mackerel, Ballynahinch Bank, Herring, Whitby, Bayman's Hole, Skate Hole, Haddock, Cleaver Bank, Herring, Cod Plaice, Scarborough, Sprat, Gt. Silver Pit, Saithe, Seiker, Hull, Botney Gut, Mourne, Herring, Fleetwood, Plaice, Cod, Grimsby, Cod, Kish Bank, Conway, Sprat, Haddock, Wicklow Bank, Lowestoft, Blackwater Bank, Cardigan Bay, Herring, Foreland Ground, Barrels Light, Haddock, Cod, Nymphe Bank, Small's Ground, Lundy Is., Dungeness, Beachy Head, Plaice, Labadie Bank, Trevose, Plaice, Brixham, Sprat, Portland Bill, Wolf, Start, Plaice, Eddystone, Salcombe Ground, Lizard, Mackerel, Saithe

Farming Types

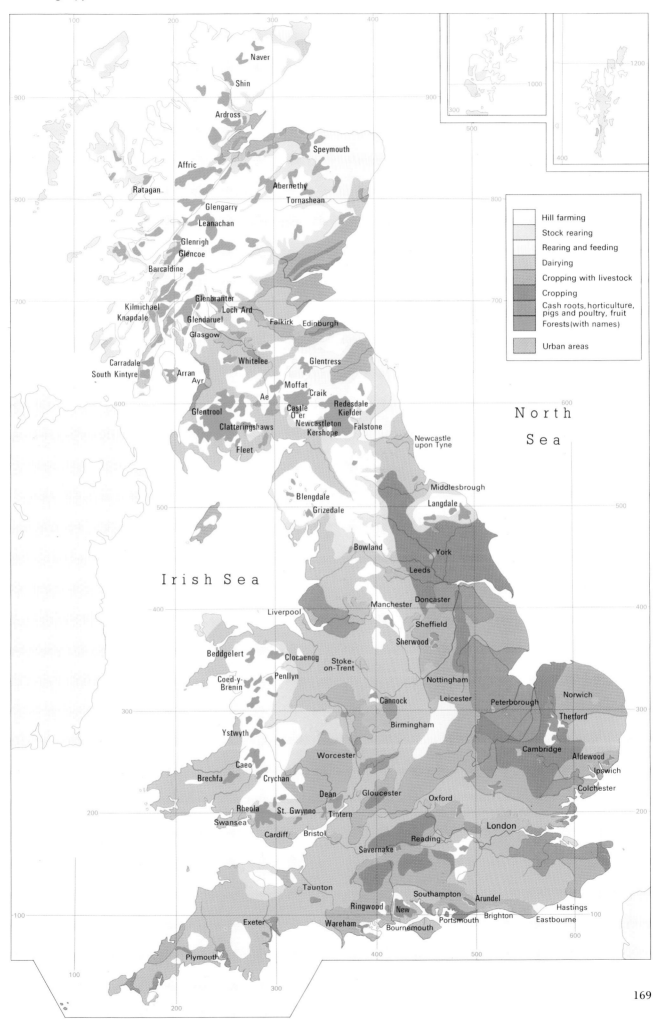

Naver
Shin
Ardross
Speymouth
Affric
Abernethy
Ratagan
Tornashean
Glengarry
Leanachan
Glenrigh
Glencoe
Barcaldine
Glenbranter
Loch Ard
Kilmichael
Glendaruel
Knapdale
Glasgow
Falkirk
Edinburgh
Whitelee
Glentress
Carradale
Arran
South Kintyre
Ayr
Moffat
Craik
Ae
Castle
Redesdale
Glentrool
O'er
Kielder
Newcastleton
Falstone
Clatteringshaws
Kershope
Fleet
Newcastle
upon Tyne

North
Sea

Blengdale
Langdale
Grizedale
Middlesbrough
Bowland
York
Leeds
Manchester
Doncaster

Irish Sea

Liverpool
Sheffield
Sherwood
Beddgelert
Clocaenog
Stoke-
on-Trent
Coed-y-
Penllyn
Brenin
Nottingham
Cannock
Leicester
Peterborough
Norwich
Birmingham
Thetford
Ystwyth
Cambridge
Aldewood
Caeo
Worcester
Ipswich
Brechfa
Crychan
Colchester
Dean
Gloucester
Oxford
Rheola
St. Gwynno
Tintern
Swansea
London
Cardiff
Bristol
Reading
Savernake
Taunton
Southampton
Arundel
Ringwood
Hastings
New
Wareham
Portsmouth
Brighton
Eastbourne
Exeter
Bournemouth
Plymouth

Legend

- Hill farming
- Stock rearing
- Rearing and feeding
- Dairying
- Cropping with livestock
- Cropping
- Cash roots, horticulture, pigs and poultry, fruit
- Forests (with names)
- Urban areas

the area) including areas such as the Shropshire hills, the Cotswolds, the Chilterns and the North and South Downs (*see map page 172*). Great progress has also been made in delimiting Heritage Coasts where development is carefully controlled by local authorities. Long-distance footpaths have been signposted and offer splendid opportunities alike for the serious walker and for the gentle stroller.

The need was later seen, and provided for in the Countryside Act of 1968, for recreational access to the smaller but often very lovely areas near to the main cities. By 1977 over 140 Country Parks and 180 Picnic Sites had been established, mainly by local authorities, with the aid of grants from the Countryside Commission for England and Wales. There is a similar, but separate, Commission for Scotland and its plans, based on the distinct landscape characteristics of Scotland and embodying a somewhat different approach from that adopted south of the border, also deserve careful study.

The Scott Committee also argued that good-quality agricultural land should not be used for urban development when land of lesser quality was available. In order to define the extent of the areas of good-, medium- and low-quality farmland a number of land classification schemes have been produced (*see map page 168*). Generally these gradings take account principally of physical conditions such as aspect, height, climate, soil type and drainage conditions but the quality of management is also an important consideration. At present the Ministry of Agriculture recognises five main grades of land and these gradings are used in planning decisions, such as those about urban growth or the lines selected for trunk roads. The amount of truly first-class land is small, about 3% of the total for England and Wales. Grade 2 land, which has minor limitations of soil texture, soil depth or drainage, accounts for about 15%. Including the better areas of Grade 3 (land with moderate limitations) it may be reckoned that about one-third of the agricultural area of England and Wales is of reasonably good quality. Grade 3 land is in fact of diverse qualities ranging from quite good to rather poor and the whole category includes 49% of the total land area. Grades 4 and 5 (poor land) account for a further one-third of England and Wales.

Taken with what has been written in the Introduction about climatic conditions, it will be seen that farming in Britain has to contend with a very diverse range of conditions. Generally speaking the farming patterns that result (*see map page 169*) represent a sophisticated adjustment to physical conditions, to market demands and to changing agricultural technology. Taken overall Britain is a country of mixed farming: the main arable areas are found mainly in the east and some parts of the Midlands and southern England. By contrast, in the west, where rainfall and relief make arable cropping difficult, grassland for livestock production predominates. The hill areas are very valuable for the production of young livestock.

There are about 270,000 farming units in the United Kingdom. However, many of these are part-time holdings and a recent estimate of the number of *bona fide* farm businesses puts the number at about 166,000, with an average overall size of 101 HA (250 acres). Less than a quarter employ more than four farm workers and the

number of regular farm workers has dropped from about 700,000 in 1946 to about 200,000 today. Of all the countries of Western Europe, Britain has the smallest percentage of its population engaged in agriculture. Output per man is high. Some 2·7% of the country's labour force produce two-thirds of the country's needs of temperate foodstuffs.

In part this happy situation is the product of greatly improved technology. The 350,000 horses who worked on farms in 1950 have almost all been replaced by machines. Farming has become capital- and energy-related. About one million tonnes of nitrogen fertilisers are applied to the land each year. Chemical pesticides have played their part. The farming industry has become much more closely related to manufacturing industry and rural-urban interdependence has, in this respect, been intensified.

A second factor behind this position is the support received from the State. After World War II the Government declared its intention to foster a healthy, prosperous and efficient agriculture and under the Agriculture Act of 1948 the Minister of Agriculture supported farmers by deficiency payments on certain commodities, as well as by grants and subsidies of various kinds. The system changed when Britain entered the EEC. Under the Common Agricultural Policy the farmers' prices are maintained by EEC intervention in the marketplace. Argument exists over the Common Agricultural Policy and its effects and it is probably in British interests to obtain changes in its operation. Nevertheless, the general climate of political support for farming in the post-war period has created a climate in agriculture in which 'the catalogue of achievement has grown by the day'.

While many rejoice in the achievements of the industry, others count the cost of change. Many small farms have been amalgamated into larger holdings. In many parts of the country woodlands and hedgerows have been removed, downland and moorland have been ploughed up, and the loss of wild landscape and wildlife is the result. Some complain that too much continuous cropping may eventually affect adversely the quality of the land, others attack factory farming and the over-use of fertilisers. The controversies were well brought out in Parliamentary debates on the Wildlife and Countryside Act (1981).

The argument may be extended to the fate of villages and rural communities. Some have lost population; churches and shops have closed and public transport services have been reduced or withdrawn. Others, nearer the great cities, have been overwhelmed by the influx of newcomers with urban ways of life, jobs in the city and homes in the countryside. The nature of change varies from area to area. But while the agricultural industry has its critics and while not all that has been done in its name may have been wise, it must be admitted that it has contributed greatly to the maintenance of the British countryside and to the improvement of the British economy.

Planning for the Environment and Regional Change

Several schemes for the future welfare and development of Britain were produced during and immediately after World War II. These included plans for the re-development of cities, many of which had been badly damaged by war-time

bombing and where inherited housing problems existed, plans for the more equitable distribution of industry and employment between the regions, and plans for the rural environment, including conservation of the scenic environment and the future prosperity of agriculture.

The Greater London Plan (1944) by Sir Patrick Abercrombie is a leading example of post-war planning. As was generally thought at the time, it assumed that population would not greatly increase: the problem was the re-distribution of people rather than of growth. It embodied the desire to prevent urban sprawl and to contain the growth of cities and employed the idea of a Green Belt on to which the London conurbation would not expand. The re-building of the bomb-damaged and the poor-quality housing of inner London was a priority. However, to accomplish lower densities and with more open space, it would be necessary to move large numbers of families and jobs out of London and New Towns were to be built for this purpose. The problems of the great city had to be solved on a regional scale. Abercrombie's ideas were applied for Greater London with modifications in detail and the eight New Towns which were begun, Crawley, Bracknell, Hemel Hempstead, Hatfield, Welwyn Garden City, Stevenage, Harlow and Basildon provided exciting opportunities for architects and town planners (see map page 173). Not all the New Towns built then and later have been equally successful and criticisms can be made with hindsight. Nevertheless the post-war New Towns are widely regarded as an achievement for British town planning.

Such ideas of regional-scale planning were not at first adopted so readily in other urban regions, such as in Manchester and Birmingham. However, much was done, especially in Birmingham, to demolish slums and to build a new inner-urban environment with an inner ring road, new housing areas and more green spaces. New Towns were begun also at Corby (Northamptonshire), Newton Aycliffe and Peterlee in the northeast, Cwmbran (south Wales) and East Kilbride, Glenrothes and Cumbernauld in Scotland.

The Town and Country Planning Act (1947) provided powers for local authorities on development control and land-use change. Green Belts were delimited around the conurbations and other cities of special quality.

The 1950s brought a changed situation. Population grew by 5% between 1951 and 1961 and the extra numbers had to be provided for. While, for the time being at least, employment remained concentrated in cities, people began to move their houses to towns and villages beyond the Green Belts. Widespread ownership of motor cars brought more flexibility in movements to work. Supplementary schemes were needed. Around London, 'expanded' towns like Ashford, Thetford and Bletchley were added to the New Towns programme. Cities like Birmingham, constrained by local authority boundaries, had to look outside their boundaries for housing land, and found themselves in conflict with the surrounding county councils. The decentralisation of population from major cities became a still more obvious phenomenon in the 1960s, accompanied now by a relative decentralisation of jobs. The older urban pattern of compact cities was changing into a pattern of 'city regions'. A second wave of New Town construction was

embarked upon involving the building, usually on a larger scale than in the first wave, of New Towns in the east Midlands (Peterborough, Northampton), the west Midlands (Redditch, Telford), the northwest (Skelmersdale, Runcorn, Warrington, Central Lancashire), the northeast (Washington), Wales (Newtown) and Scotland (Livingston, Irvine). Population grew by a further 5% between 1961 and 1971, and the expectations of a continued growth in numbers, coupled with the desire better to relate plans for town and country with those for transport, the provision of services, and employment, led to an important phase of re-thinking for planning on a regional scale in the mid- and later 1960s. Regional Economic Planning Councils (since discontinued) were established for this task and produced a series of interesting and useful reports. Broad 'structure' planning replaced detailed land-use based planning.

Meanwhile the larger cities continued to lose population and jobs, not only from the inner areas but also from suburban areas. The tendency for dispersion involving the growth of towns of medium and small sizes produced an extension of urban Britain, confirming the tendency towards 'megalopolis', the functionally-linked zone of city regions and high population densities extending from the Channel coast to Lancashire and Yorkshire. But the 1970s did not bring the expected continued growth in population (an increase of only 0·3% in Great Britain 1971-81), and, as one report put it, 'Britain's main cities are losing population in a big rush to the countryside'. The population of Greater London fell by 10·1% to 6·7 million, or below the 1901 population of the same area, with the inner London boroughs losing between 12% and 26% of their populations. In 1961 Southwark had 313,000 people; in 1981, 212,000. Manchester (−17%), Liverpool (−16%), Salford (−13%), Newcastle-upon-Tyne (−10%), Nottingham (−10%), Birmingham (−8%) also demonstrate the trend (see map page 174).

By contrast, population has been increasing in the outer rings around conurbations. There is a crescent of increase in the southeast from Norfolk to the Solent, and smaller but similar areas of increase around the west Midland conurbation, south of Manchester, in the east Midlands and beyond Glasgow and Edinburgh. Northeast Scotland has increased its population, mainly, no doubt, the result of oil and oil-related developments. So has the southwest peninsula to which many retired people have moved. The patterns of decentralisation and dispersion noted for the 1950s and 1960s have intensified and extended in the 1970s.

Thus, dynamic urban changes are in progress. Not all these changes are the direct results of town planning, though the policies of containing the outward spread of the

Planning for Leisure Preservation of the countryside for leisure purposes has involved planning both nationally—with the establishment of the National Parks, areas of outstanding natural beauty and long-distance footpaths—and regionally, by the tourist boards and county councils.

Planning for Industry Post-war planning has attempted to break out of the 'industrial coffin' by the encouragement of Development Areas and New Towns. Green belts and areas of outstanding natural beauty are subject to rigorous development constraints, whereas sites of scientific, landscape and historic interest are given varying degrees of protection.

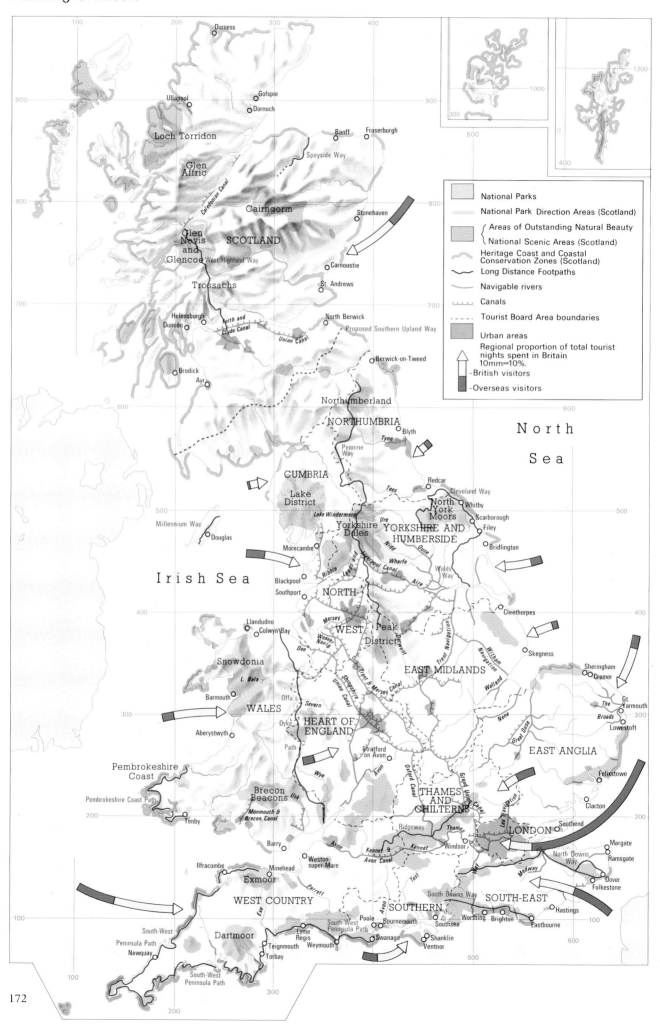

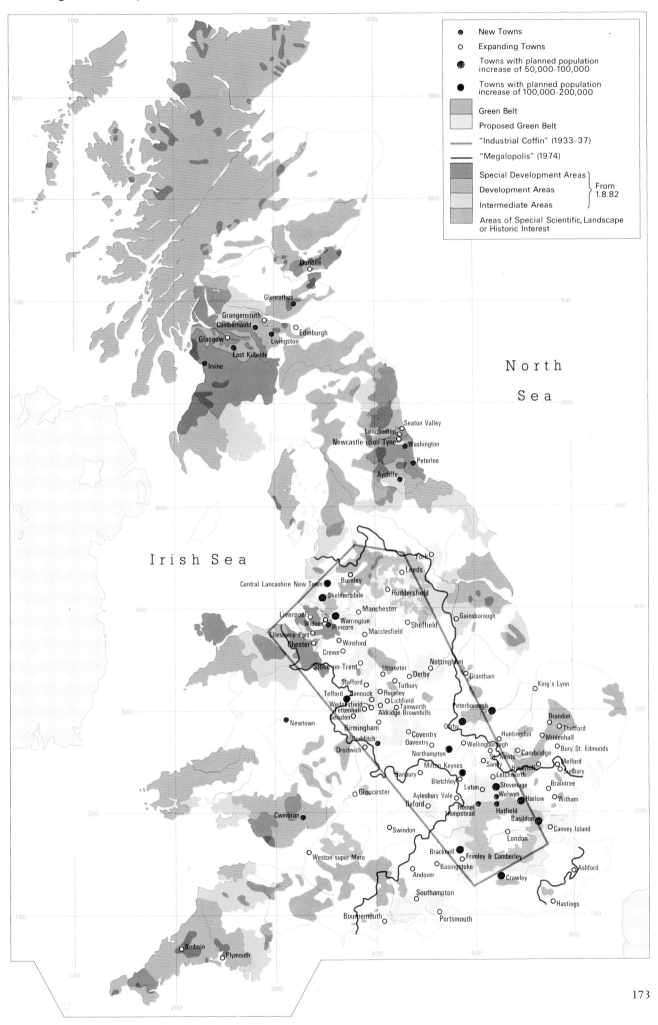

New Towns

Expanding Towns

Towns with planned population
increase of 50,000-100,000

Towns with planned population
increase of 100,000-200,000

Green Belt

Proposed Green Belt

"Industrial Coffin" (1933-37)

"Megalopolis" (1974)

Special Development Areas ⎫
Development Areas ⎬ From
Intermediate Areas ⎭ 1.8.82

Areas of Special Scientific, Landscape
or Historic Interest

North

Sea

Irish Sea

Dundee

Glenrothes

Grangemouth
Cumbernauld
Glasgow
East Kilbride
Irvine
Livingston
Edinburgh

Seaton Valley
Longbenton
Newcastle-upon-Tyne
Washington
Peterlee
Aycliffe

York
Leeds
Burnley
Central Lancashire New Town
Skelmersdale
Huddersfield
Manchester
Gainsborough
Liverpool
Warrington
Widnes
Runcorn
Sheffield
Ellesmere Port
Macclesfield
Chester
Winsford
Crewe
Stoke-on-Trent
Uttoxeter
Nottingham
Derby
Grantham
King's Lynn
Stafford
Tutbury
Telford
Cannock
Rugeley
Lichfield
Peterborough
Brandon
Wednesfield
Tamworth
Thetford
Tettenhall
Aldridge-Brownhills
Corby
Mildenhall
Seisdon
Newtown
Birmingham
Huntingdon
Bury St. Edmunds
Redditch
Coventry
Wellingborough
Cambridge
Droitwich
Daventry
Northampton
St. Neots
Melford
Sandy
Havehill
Sudbury
Banbury
Milton Keynes
Letchworth
Braintree
Bletchley
Luton
Stevenage
Witham
Gloucester
Aylesbury Vale
Welwyn
Oxford
Harlow
Hemel
Hempstead
Hatfield
Cwmbran
Basildon
Canvey Island
Swindon
London
Bracknell
Weston-super-Mare
Frimley & Camberley
Ashford
Basingstoke
Andover
Crawley
Southampton
Hastings
Bournemouth
Portsmouth
Bodmin
Plymouth

173

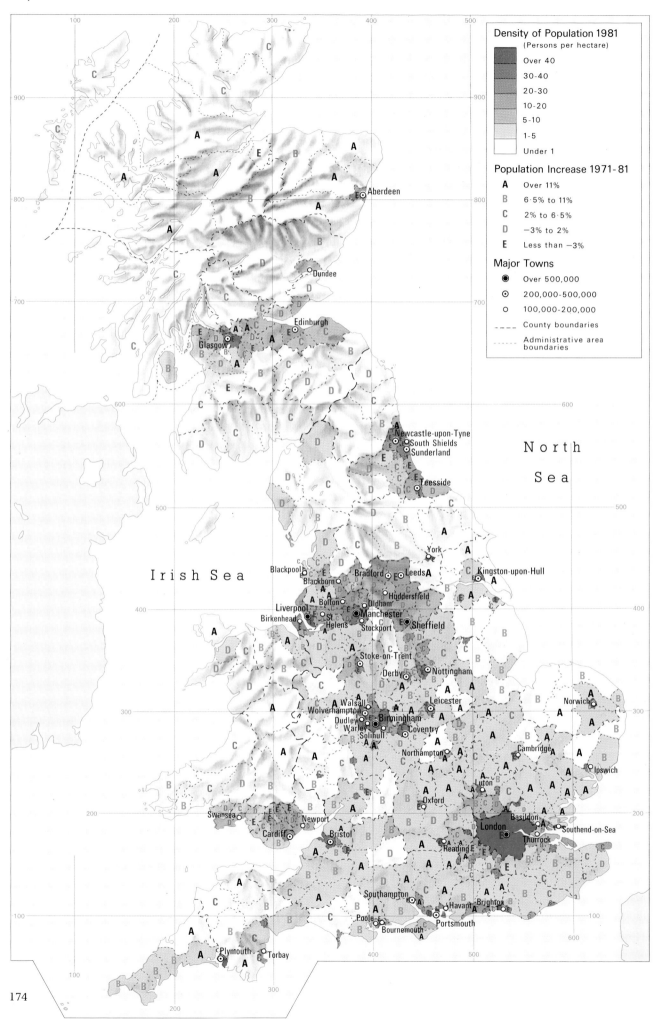

Density of Population 1981
(Persons per hectare)

- Over 40
- 30-40
- 20-30
- 10-20
- 5-10
- 1-5
- Under 1

Population Increase 1971-81

A   Over 11%
B   6·5% to 11%
C   2% to 6·5%
D   −3% to 2%
E   Less than −3%

Major Towns

◉   Over 500,000
⊙   200,000-500,000
○   100,000-200,000
– – –   County boundaries
·········   Administrative area boundaries

North Sea

Irish Sea

Aberdeen
Dundee
Edinburgh
Glasgow
Newcastle-upon-Tyne
South Shields
Sunderland
Teesside
York
Blackpool
Bradford
Leeds
Kingston-upon-Hull
Blackburn
Huddersfield
Bolton
Oldham
Liverpool
Manchester
Birkenhead
St. Helens
Stockport
Sheffield
Stoke-on-Trent
Derby
Nottingham
Walsall
Leicester
Norwich
Wolverhampton
Birmingham
Dudley
Warley
Coventry
Solihull
Northampton
Cambridge
Ipswich
Luton
Oxford
Swansea
Newport
Basildon
London
Southend-on-Sea
Cardiff
Bristol
Thurrock
Reading
Southampton
Brighton
Havant
Poole
Portsmouth
Bournemouth
Plymouth
Torbay

Cultural Diversity

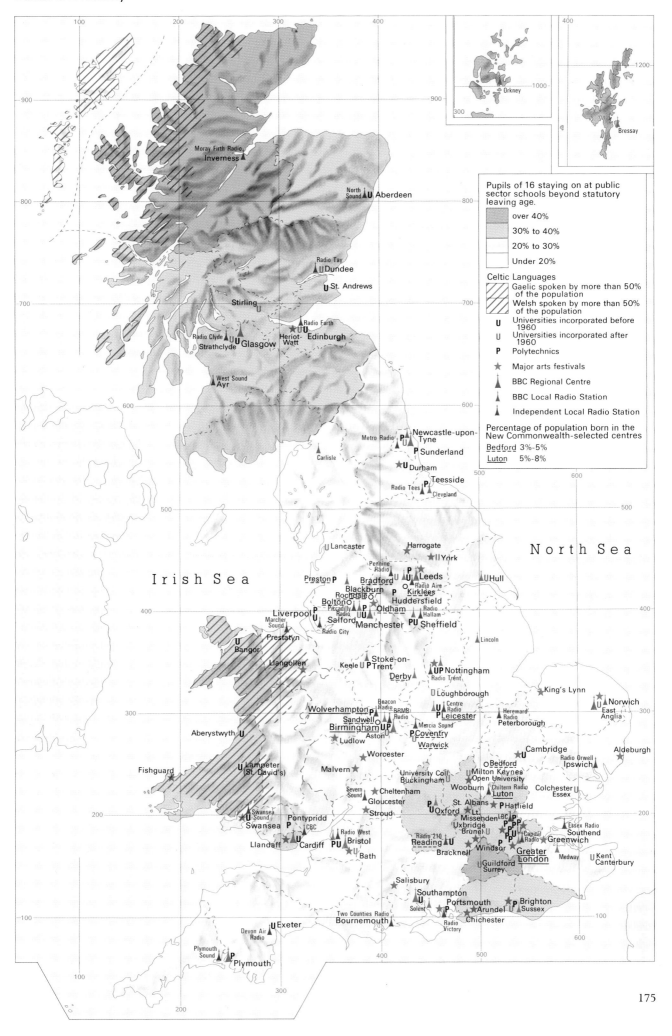

Legend:

Pupils of 16 staying on at public sector schools beyond statutory leaving age.

- over 40%
- 30% to 40%
- 20% to 30%
- Under 20%

Celtic Languages

- Gaelic spoken by more than 50% of the population
- Welsh spoken by more than 50% of the population
- U Universities incorporated before 1960
- U Universities incorporated after 1960
- P Polytechnics
- ★ Major arts festivals
- ▲ BBC Regional Centre
- ▲ BBC Local Radio Station
- ▲ Independent Local Radio Station

Percentage of population born in the New Commonwealth-selected centres

- Bedford 3%-5%
- Luton 5%-8%

Map labels (north to south):

Orkney
Bressay
Moray Firth Radio
Inverness
North Sound U Aberdeen
Radio Tay U Dundee
U St. Andrews
Stirling
Radio Forth
Radio Clyde U Heriot- Edinburgh
Strathclyde U Glasgow Watt
West Sound Ayr
Carlisle
Metro Radio Newcastle-upon-Tyne
P Sunderland
U Durham
Radio Tees P Teesside
Cleveland
U Lancaster
Harrogate
Pennine Radio U York
Preston P
Blackburn P Bradford U Leeds
Rochdale O Radio Aire
Bolton O P Kirklees
Piccadilly Huddersfield
Radio U P Oldham Radio
Liverpool P U Salford Hallam
Marcher Radio City Manchester P U Sheffield
Sound
Prestatyn
Bangor U
Llangollen
Keele U Stoke-on-Trent
Lincoln
P Derby U P Nottingham
Radio Trent
U Loughborough
King's Lynn
Beacon Centre Norwich
Radio Radio U P East
Wolverhampton P BRMB U Leicester Hereward Anglia
Sandwell Radio P Leicester Radio
Birmingham U P Mercia Sound Peterborough
Aston P Coventry
Aberystwyth U Ludlow Warwick
Cambridge
Worcester Aldeburgh
Fishguard Malvern Radio Orwell Ipswich
Lampeter University Coll Bedford
(St. David's) Buckingham Milton Keynes Colchester
Severn Cheltenham Woburn Open University Essex
Sound Gloucester Chiltern Radio Luton
Swansea Stroud St. Albans P Hatfield
Sound Missenden LBC
Swansea U Pontypridd Oxford U Lt. P P P Essex Radio
Llandaff CBC Radio West Uxbridge U P P Southend
P Brunel U P Capital Greenwich
Cardiff P U Bristol Radio 210 U Radio
Bath Reading U Windsor Greater
Bracknell London
Guildford Kent
Surrey Medway Canterbury
Salisbury
Southampton U
Two Counties Radio Portsmouth P Brighton
Bournemouth Solent P Arundel U Sussex
Radio Chichester
Victory
Devon Air U Exeter
Radio
Plymouth Sound P
P Plymouth

Irish Sea

North Sea

175

conurbations and decentralisation have set the general pattern. It is the consequences of these changes for the inner city that now cause concern. There is the contrast between the outer parts of the city regions peopled by young, middle-class families and many of the older parts of the inner city with older, poorer and less skilled workers living in pre-1914 houses or more recently-built high-rise blocks and council estates. Industries have moved out or have died. In some areas there are high proportions of immigrant families. The inner-city problem has been the most recent major town planning task. But while there is a general problem, each inner-city area presents its own distinctive problems. The London Docklands are very different from Lambeth and Brixton. The tasks of renewal in Inner Birmingham are not the same as in Liverpool or Glasgow. So planning for urban deprivation has taken precedence in the 1970s with many special studies and the emergence of special grants, programmes and partnership schemes between local and central government. The urban riots of 1981 drew further attention to the problem, especially in south London, Manchester and Liverpool. There are signs of progress but the re-creation of the environments of the inner cities continues to be a major task for the 1980s.

Local Government

The reforms of local government of 1888 and 1894, intended to produce a pattern adapted to the age of the industrial city, also confirmed the existence of units such as the county whose origins lay in early medieval times (*see map page 178*). By the late 1950s and 1960s it had become widely recognised that further major reforms were necessary in the wake of the changes in population distribution, changes in city size, shape and needs and the greater responsibilities, including housing and town planning, which local government had assumed. Royal Commissions on local government in London, England, Wales and Scotland were established. The first result was the establishment in 1963 of the Greater London Council responsible for certain functions for the whole of the London conurbation with a second tier of London Boroughs. The Report of the 'Maud' Royal Commission on Local Government in England in 1969, which included two possible sets of proposals, was hotly argued. The new pattern was set up in 1974 (*see map page 179*). It was based on a smaller number of counties (achieved, for instance, through the amalgamation of Herefordshire and Worcestershire) and county districts, but with metropolitan authorities for major conurbations (such as West Midlands, Merseyside, West Yorkshire, South Yorkshire, and Tyne and Wear). The boundaries of the metropolitan counties were tightly drawn and criticisms were made of the failure to establish regional authorities.

Population Patterns Although the 1981 census showed overall little growth since 1971, it gave evidence of considerable movement of people, especially from the old cities into the countryside around. Some inner city areas lost more than a quarter of their population.

Cultural Diversity The 1960s and 1970s saw a general growth in cultural activity outside the largest towns, sometimes spontaneous and sometimes deliberately fostered. The revival of Celtic traditions and new ethnic minorities in many towns have brought a new cultural mix to Britain.

Wales now has eight county councils (five with historic Welsh names) and 36 district councils; these replace 13 counties, four county boroughs and 164 district councils.

For Scotland, the 'Wheatley' Royal Commission reported in 1969. Its general principles were accepted with amendments and the pattern established by the Local Government (Scotland) Act 1973, by contrast with that in England, accepted the regional principle. It represents a more logical attempt to establish economic and social entities for cities and countryside. There are nine regions, 53 districts and three all-purpose island councils. Local government responsibilities in Scotland differ in certain respects from those in England.

Meanwhile the wider problems of the devolution of political and administrative responsibilities from Westminster were under study by the Kilbrandon Royal Commission on the Constitution, whose report appeared in 1973. Ever since the Union of Scotland and England in 1707 the arrangements for the government of Scotland have differed in some important respects from those in England. Scotland has its own systems of law and education. In 1885 the office of Secretary of State for Scotland was created, and he discharges functions that for England are exercised by the Home Office, the Departments of the Environment, Education and Science, some aspects of the Department of Health and Social Security, and the Ministry of Agriculture. A separate Welsh Ministry was established in 1951 and strengthened in 1964 but its responsibilities, while wide, are less than those of the Scottish Office.

The re-emergence of national feeling at the political level was channelled in the 1960s and early 1970s into campaigns for devolution. Proposals for devolution were brought forward by the government in 1974 and 1975 based on the preservation of the unity of the UK and rejecting federal solutions. Assemblies were proposed for Scotland and Wales, although that for Scotland was to have much the stronger set of powers. After extensive Parliamentary debates from 1976 the referenda required under the Acts failed to secure the necessary majorities and the issue died away, at least temporarily. But the issue of how to reconcile, in a parliamentary democracy, the need for centralised services with the aspiration of regional feeling, remains for further debate. This central question has a wider application than to Scotland and Wales. Cornishmen claim their own right to political expression, and if, say some, there is devolution to Wales and Cornwall, what of Yorkshire with its own rugged traditions? Too little is still known of the economic aspects of regionalism. And there is a long history of discussion, going back to the time of World War I, on how responsibilities for the government of the regions of England can best be arranged. Arguments on this question could gain strength from the recent trend towards the development of city regions.

Currently the relations between central and local government are under strain. Local governments see their powers diminishing and more power attaching to the centre: the centre is concerned at the levels of public expenditure incurred by local government. Local governments differ greatly in their ability to generate current income through the rating system (itself now requiring modification or

176

reform), and, even though a system of income equalisation exists through funds made available by central government under the Rate Support Grant (recently revised), considerable differences exist in the levels of expenditure and of services provided by local governments. What you may get from the social services depends to an extent on where you live. The suggestion is made, for example, that educational attainment is much influenced by the levels of expenditure of Local Education Authorities: some Welsh authorities where education has been highly valued come out well in this respect (*see map page 175*).

Maps which show variations in levels of service provision by local and national authorities tend to show the south and southeast as the best provided regions with a gradation downwards to Wales, to the industrial districts of Northern England and to Scotland. But at a more detailed level the pattern has to be modified to show the contrast between the poorly-provided inner cities and the better-off suburbs.

The issue of how exactly Britain should be governed at national, regional and local levels will not easily be resolved. Differences between central and local government must be seen in the context of a picture in which government has now become a main influence on the geography of life in Britain. Employment in the civil service, local government, nationalised industries and other government established bodies in itself a strong factor. Governments at different levels influence the geography of Britain through planning decisions, industrial location policies, decisions on the provision of basic services such as transport, energy, water and housing as well as the social services like health, welfare and education. There is still much room for argument on who should make which decisions and for what areas, how the money should be raised and how it should be disbursed.

Acknowledgements and Bibliography

The thematic maps in the Introduction and sections on historical geography and modern Britain were researched by Peter Furtado and made and drawn by Clyde Surveys Ltd., of Maidenhead.

The authors and publishers would like to acknowledge the following as some major sources for these maps:

Great Britain – Geology: Tectonic Map of Great Britain, the Institute of Geological Sciences 1966; and Oxford University Press.

Great Britain – Climate: *The Climate of the British Isles*, T J Chandler and S Gregory, Longman 1976.

The Dark Ages: *The Archaeology of Anglo-Saxon England* ed D M Wilson, Methuen 1976.

Britain to 1350: *A New Historical Geography of England* ed H C Darby, Cambridge University Press 1973. *Feudal Britain* G W S Barrow, Edward Arnold 1956.

Late Medieval Britain: *The Agrarian History of England and Wales IV* ed Joan Thirsk, Cambridge University Press 1967.

The Agricultural Revolution: *An Historical Geography of England and Wales* ed R A Dodgshon and R A Butlin, Academic Press 1978. *Man Made the Land* Alan R H Baker and J B Harley, David & Charles 1973

The Early Industrial Revolution: *The Early Industrial Revolution* E Pawson, Batsford 1979.

Britain in the Late Nineteenth Century: *The Movement of Population* C T Smith, Geographical Journal vol 117, 1951.

Mineral Resources: *The Mineral Resources of Britain* John Blunden, Hutchinson 1975. *A Geography of Energy in the UK* John Fernie, Longman 1981.

Industry and Energy: *Britain 1981* HMSO 1981.

Agriculture and Fisheries: *Fish from the Sea* The White Fish Authority. Fishing grounds – The Watt Committee on Energy, University of Glasgow 1979.

Farming Types: *Types of Farming in Britain* K Buchanan and D J Sinclair, Association of Agriculture 1966.

Planning for Industry: *The Containment of Urban England* Peter Hall, George Allen & Unwin 1974.

Countless books have been written about the history, geography and countryside of Britain. The following titles (as well as those mentioned above) might be of interest about the geography of Britain:

The Personality of Britain Sir Cyril Fox and L F Chitty, National Museum of Wales 1932.

The UK Space ed J W House, Weidenfeld and Nicolson 1977.

The British Isles: A Systematic Geography J W Watson and J B Sissons, Nelson 1964.

An Agricultural Atlas of Great Britain J T Coppock, Faber and Faber 1976.

Countryside Conservation Bryn Green, George Allen & Unwin 1981.

National Parks: Conservation or Cosmetics Ann and Malcolm McEwen, George Allen & Unwin 1982.

Britain's Structure and Scenery L D Stamp, Collins 1974.

Urban and Regional Planning Peter Hall, Penguin 1974.

Airport Strategy and Planning K R Sealy. Oxford University Press 1976.

Land Use and Living Space R H Best, Methuen 1981.

A Living History of the British Isles ed W G V Balchin, Country Life 1981.

A Natural History of the British Isles ed Pat Morris, Country Life 1979.

The Making of the English Landscape W G Hoskins, Penguin 1970.

Wales F V Emery, Longman 1969.

The Making of the Scottish Landscape R N Millman, Batsford 1975.

County Boundaries before 1974

1	KINCARDINESHIRE
2	DUNBARTONSHIRE
3	STIRLINGSHIRE
4	CLACKMANNANSHIRE
5	KINROSS-SHIRE
6	RENFREWSHIRE
7	WEST LOTHIAN
8	MIDLOTHIAN
9	PEEBLES-SHIRE
10	SELKIRKSHIRE

11	CAERNARVONSHIRE
12 13	FLINTSHIRE
14	MONTGOMERYSHIRE
15	RUTLAND
16	HUNTINGDON AND PETERBOROUGH
17	CAMBRIDGESHIRE AND ISLE OF ELY
18	BEDFORDSHIRE
19	MONMOUTHSHIRE
20	WORCESTERSHIRE

County Boundaries since 1974

ORKNEY

SHETLAND

WESTERN
ISLES

HIGHLAND
Inverness

GRAMPIAN
Aberdeen

S C O T L A N D

TAYSIDE
Dundee
Perth

FIFE

CENTRAL
Stirling
Dunfermline

Edinburgh
LOTHIAN

Glasgow
Motherwell

STRATHCLYDE

BORDERS

N O R T H

S E A

Ayr

DUMFRIES
AND
GALLOWAY

NORTHUMBERLAND

Newcastle-upon-Tyne
1
Sunderland

Carlisle

DURHAM
Darlington 2 Middlesbrough

C U M B R I A

NORTH YORKSHIRE

ISLE OF
MAN

Lancaster

York

I R I S H   S E A

Blackpool

LANCASHIRE Bradford Leeds

HUMBERSIDE
Kingston-upon-Hull

Burnley
3
Huddersfield

Grimsby

Wigan Bolton
5 Barnsley 4
Manchester Sheffield

Doncaster

Liverpool
6

E N G L A N D

CHESHIRE DERBY-

NOTTINGHAM-
SHIRE

LINCOLNSHIRE

G
W
Y
N
E
D
D

CLWYD

Stoke-on-Trent

SHIRE
Derby

Nottingham

STAFFORD-
SHIRE

Shrewsbury

LEICESTERSHIRE

N O R F O L K
Norwich

SHROPSHIRE

Leicester

Birmingham 7

NORTHAMPTON-
SHIRE

Peterborough

W A L E S

Coventry

CAMBRIDGE-
SHIRE

S U F F O L K
Ipswich

POWYS HEREFORD
AND
WORCESTER

Worcester

WARWICK-
SHIRE

Northampton

Cambridge

8

D Y F E D

Hereford

GLOUCESTER-
SHIRE

OXFORD-

B
U
C
K
I
N
G
H
A
M

Luton

HERTFORD-
SHIRE

E S S E X

10

GWENT

SHIRE
Oxford

GREATER

Swansea

11

Swindon

9 Reading

LONDON

Southend

12 Cardiff
Bristol
AVON

WILTSHIRE

SURREY

K E N T
Dover

SOMERSET

HAMPSHIRE

WEST
SUSSEX

EAST
SUSSEX

DEVON

D O R S E T
Bournemouth

Southampton

Brighton

CORNWALL
Plymouth

Exeter

ISLE OF
WIGHT

1 TYNE AND WEAR
2 CLEVELAND
3 WEST YORKSHIRE
4 SOUTH YORKSHIRE
5 GREATER MANCHESTER
6 MERSEYSIDE

7 WEST MIDLANDS
8 BEDFORDSHIRE
9 BERKSHIRE
10 WEST GLAMORGAN
11 MID GLAMORGAN
12 SOUTH GLAMORGAN

179

Index

Content
The Index lists all the definitive names shown in the map section of the Atlas. For each entry the Atlas page number is listed and the National Grid map reference is given to the nearest kilometre of the feature to which the name applies.

For long linear features, such as the River Thames, more than one reference is given. For these multiple entries and where a name applies to more than one feature the County, Region or Island Area name is also given.

Abbreviations used in the Index to identify the nature of certain named features and abbreviations for Counties used in the Index are also listed.

Method of Listing Names
Names are listed alphabetically in the Index as they appear on the map. For example, 'Ashdown Forest' appears under 'A', while 'Forest of Bere' is under 'F'. Similarly, 'Beaulieu River' appears under 'B' but 'River Thames' is under 'R'. When the definite article precedes a name, the name appears first. Thus, 'The Wash' becomes 'Wash, The' and is listed under 'W'. An exception to this rule is made in the case of Gaelic and Welsh place names. These are listed under the initial letter of the Gaelic or Welsh definite article. For example, 'An Ceannaich' is listed under 'A', and 'Y Llethr' is listed under 'Y'.

Example Use of Index
To find Dorking refer to the name in the index and read off the reference 28TQ 1649. The first number indicates that Dorking is shown on page 28. The remaining two letters and four figures signify that the town lies within the 100 kilometre square TQ (see diagram on front endpaper) and is 16 kilometres east and 49 kilometres north of the south west corner of the square. The 10 kilometre grid numbers '1' and '4' are shown on the edges of page 28 and the exact location of Dorking is found by estimating '6' tenths eastward from the grid line '1' and '9' tenths northwards from the grid line '4'. In the National Grid Reference system the Eastings (16 for Dorking) are always stated before the Northings (49 for Dorking).

Features can thus be located on the Atlas pages by referring to the page number and grid number only; the two letters are required for the full grid reference to locate a feature on any map which shows the National Grid.

List of County Names Showing Abbreviations Used in this Index

England
Avon	Avon
Bedfordshire	Beds.
Berkshire	Berks.
Buckinghamshire	Bucks.
Cambridgeshire	Cambs.
Cheshire	Ches.
Cleveland	Cleve.
Cornwall	Corn.
Cumbria	Cumbr.
Derbyshire	Derby.
Devon	Devon
Dorset	Dorset
Durham	Durham
East Sussex	E Susx
Essex	Essex
Gloucestershire	Glos.
Greater London	Gtr London
Greater Manchester	Gtr Mches.
Hampshire	Hants.
Hereford and Worcester	Here. and Worc.
Hertfordshire	Herts.
Humberside	Humbs.
Isle of Wight	I. of W.
Kent	Kent
Lancashire	Lancs.
Leicestershire	Leic.
Lincolnshire	Lincs.
Merseyside	Mers.
Norfolk	Norf.
North Yorkshire	N Yorks.
Northamptonshire	Northants.
Northumberland	Northum.
Nottinghamshire	Notts.
Oxfordshire	Oxon.
Shropshire	Shrops.
Somerset	Somer.
South Yorkshire	S Yorks.
Staffordshire	Staffs.
Suffolk	Suff.
Surrey	Surrey
Tyne and Wear	Tyne and Wear
Warwickshire	Warw.
West Midlands	W Mids
West Sussex	W Susx
West Yorkshire	W Yorks.
Wiltshire	Wilts.

Wales
Clwyd	Clwyd
Dyfed	Dyfed
Gwent	Gwent
Gwynedd	Gwyn.
Mid Glamorgan	Mid Glam.
Powys	Powys
South Glamorgan	S Glam.
West Glamorgan	W Glam.

Other Areas
Isle of Man	I. of M.
Isles of Scilly	Is. of Sc.

Region and Islands Area Names
Scotland
Regions
Borders	Borders
Central	Central
Dumfries and Galloway	Dumf. and Galwy.
Fife	Fife
Grampian	Grampn.
Highland	Highld.
Lothian	Lothian
Strathclyde	Strath.
Tayside	Tays.

Islands areas
Orkney	Orkney
Shetland	Shetld.
Western Isles	W Isles

Abbreviations which are used in this Index to identify the nature of certain named features
ant.	Antiquity
chan.	Channel or arm of the sea
dist.	District or name of an area
is.	Island
mt.	Mountain, mount or hill
pt.	Point or headland on coast
sbk.	Sandbank

Abbas Combe Alphington

A

Abbas Combe 25 ST 7022
Abberley 49 SO 7567
Abberley Hill 49 SO 7566
Abberton (Essex) 39 TM 0019
Abberton (Here. and Worc.) 50 SO 9953
Abberton Reservoir 39 TL 9818
Abberwick 91 NU 1213
Abbess Roding 37 TL 5711
Abbey 24 ST 1410
Abbey Brook 70 SK 1892
Abbey Burn 95 NS 9353
Abbeycwmhir 57 SO 0571
Abbey Dore 45 SO 3830
Abbey Head 87 NX 7343
Abbey Hulton 59 SJ 9148
Abbey St. Bathans 96 NT 7662
Abbeystead 77 SD 5654
Abbeytown 82 NY 1750
Abbey Wood 37 TQ 4779
Abbotrule 90 NT 6112
Abbots Bickington 22 SS 3813
Abbots Bromley 60 SK 0824
Abbotsbury 25 SY 5785
Abbotsford 96 NT 5034
Abbotsham 22 SS 4226
Abbotside Common 83 SD 8196
Abbotskerswell 21 SX 8569
Abbots Langley 36 TL 0902
Abbots Leigh 33 ST 5473
Abbotsley 53 TL 2256
Abbots Morton 50 SP 0255
Abbots Ripton 53 TL 2377
Abbot's Salford 50 SP 0650
Abbot's Way (ant.) 21 SX 6266
Abbotswood 26 SU 3722
Abbotts Ann 34 SU 3243
Abdon 48 SO 5786
Aber (Dyfed) 43 SN 4748
Aber (Gwyn.) 67 SH 6572
Aberaeron 56 SN 4562
Aberaman 41 SO 0101
Aberangell 57 SH 8409
Aberarder 116 NH 6225
Aberarder Forest 116 NN 4888
Aberargie 108 NO 1615
Aberarth 56 SN 4763
Aber-banc 43 SN 3541
Aberbargoed 41 SO 1500
Aberbeeg 41 SO 2102
Abercanaid 41 SO 0503
Abercarn 41 ST 2195
Abercegir 57 SH 8001
Aberchalder 115 NH 3403
Aberchalder Burn 116 NH 5618
Aberchalder Forest 115 NN 3499
Aberchirder 121 NJ 6252
Abercraf 41 SN 8212
Abercrombie 103 NO 5102
Abercych 43 SN 2441
Abercynon 41 ST 0894
Aberdalgie 108 NO 0720
Aberdare 41 SO 0002
Aberdaron 56 SH 1726
Aberdeen 119 NJ 9305
Aberdeen Airport 119 NJ 8712
Aberdour 102 NT 1885
Aberdovey Bar 56 SN 5994
Aberdulais 41 SS 7799
Aberdyfi 56 SN 6196
Aber Dysynni 56 SH 5603
Aberedw 44 SO 0747
Abereiddy 42 SM 7931
Abererch 66 SH 3936
Aber Falls 67 SH 6669
Aberfan 41 SO 0700
Aberfeldy 108 NN 8549
Aberffraw 66 SH 3568
Aberffrwd 57 SN 6878
Aberford 79 SE 4336
Aberfoyle 101 NN 5200
Abergavenny 45 SO 2914
Abergeldie Castle 117 NO 2895
Abergele 67 SH 9477
Abergele Roads 67 SH 9379
Abergorlech 43 SN 5833
Abergwesyn 44 SN 8552
Abergwili 43 SN 4421
Abergwynant 57 SH 6717
Abergwynfi 41 SS 8996
Abergynolwyn 57 SH 6706
Aberhosan 57 SN 8197
Aberkenfig 41 SS 8983
Aberlady 103 NT 4679
Aberlady Bay 103 NT 4581
Aberlemno 109 NO 5255
Aberllefenni 57 SH 7609
Abermenai Point 66 SH 4461
Abermeurig 43 SN 5655
Abermule 58 SO 1694
Abernaint 58 SJ 1221
Abernant (Dyfed) 43 SN 3423
Aber-nant (Mid Glam.) 41 SO 0103
Abernethy 108 NO 1816
Abernethy Forest 117 NH 9918
Abernyte 108 NO 2531
Aberporth 43 SN 2651
Aberporth Airfield 43 SN 2549
Aberscross 129 NC 7600
Abersoch 56 SH 3128
Abersychan 45 SO 2704
Abertillery 41 SO 2104
Abertridwr (Mid Glam.) 41 ST 1289
Abertridwr (Powys) 57 SJ 0319
Abertysswg 41 SO 1305
Aberuthven 108 NN 9715
Aberyscir 41 SN 9929
Aberystwyth 56 SN 5881
Abhainn a'Bhealaich 100 NM 9506
Abhainn a' Chadh' Bhuidhe 127 NH 1367
Abhainn a' Choilich 115 NH 0824
Abhainn a' Choire 132 NC 3526
Abhainn a' Gharbh Choire 123 NG 8769
Abhainn a' Ghiubhais Li 127 NH 2471
Abhainn a' Ghlinne Bhig 123 NG 8217
Abhainn a' Ghlinne Bhig 127 NH 3484
Abhainn an Fhasaigh 126 NH 0267
Abhainn an Loin 132 NC 3241
Abhainn an t-Sratha' Chàrnaig 129 NH 7198
Abhainn an t-Srathain 132 NC 2362
Abhainn an t-Srath Chuileannaich 128 NH 4393
Abhainn Bearraray 130 NB 0514
Abhainn Beinn nan Eun 128 NH 4673
Abhainn Bràigh-horrisdale 123 NG 8167
Abhainn Bruachaig 127 NH 0763
Abhainn Cam Linne 106 NM 9723
Abhainn Chòsaidh 114 NG 9201
Abhainn Chuaig 123 NG 7256
Abhainn Crò Chlach 116 NH 6205
Abhainn Cuileig 127 NH 1776
Abhainn Dalach 106 NN 0341
Abhainn Deabhag 115 NH 2724
Abhainn Dearg 126 NG 8847
Abhainn Droma 127 NH 2276
Abhainn Dubh (Highld.) 123 NG 7851
Abhainn Dubh (Highld.) 127 NH 0657
Abhainn Duibhe 107 NN 4253
Abhainn Fionain 106 NM 9518
Abhainn Geiraha 131 NB 5150
Abhainn Ghlas 98 NR 3166
Abhainn Ghleann Iubharnadeal 98 NR 4570
Abhainn Mhòr (Strath.) 99 NR 7377
Abhainn Mhòr (Strath.) 99 NR 7571
Abhainn na Clach Airigh 132 NC 1420
Abhainn na Cuile 99 NR 8269
Abhainn na Frithe 134 NC 8226
Abhainn na Glasa 128 NH 4579
Abhainn Rath 106 NN 2868
Abhainn Sgeamhaidh 133 NC 5616
Abhainn Sithidh 115 NH 0624
Abhainn Srath na Sealga 127 NH 0780
Abhainn Thràil 126 NG 9153
A'Bhrideanach (pt.) 110 NM 2999
A' Bhuidheanach Bheag 116 NN 6677
Abingdon 47 SU 4997
Abinger Common 28 TQ 1145
Abington 95 NS 9323
Abington Pigotts 53 TL 3044
Ab Kettleby 61 SK 7223
Ablington 46 SP 1007
Abney 70 SK 1979
Aboyne 119 NO 5298
Abram 69 SD 6001
Abriachan 116 NH 5535
Abridge 37 TQ 4696
Abthorpe 51 SP 6446
Abune-the-Hill 136 HY 2928
Aby 73 TF 4178
Acairseid Falaich 112 NF 8537
Acarsaid 111 NM 5871
Acaster Malbis 79 SE 5845
Acaster Selby 79 SE 5741
Accrington 78 SD 7528
Acha 110 NM 1854
Achachork 123 NG 4746
Achaglachgach Forest 99 NR 8064
Achahoish 99 NR 7877
A' Chailleach (Highld.) (mt.) 127 NH 1371
A' Chailleach (Highld.) (mt.) 116 NH 6804
A' Chailleach Am Bodach (pt.) 132 NC 2473
Achairn Burn 135 ND 2949
Achalader (Tays.) 108 NO 1245
Achallader (Strath.) 106 NN 3244
Achaluachrach 133 NC 6709
Achanalt 127 NH 2561
Achanamara 99 NR 7887
Achandunie 128 NH 6472
Ach' an Todhair 106 NN 0972
Achany 128 NC 5601
Achany Glen 128 NC 5704
Achaphubuil 115 NN 0875
Acharacle 111 NM 6767
Acharn (Highld.) 111 NM 7050
Acharn (Tays.) 107 NN 7543
Acharosson Burn 100 NR 9376
Achath 119 NJ 7311
Achavanich 135 ND 1742
Achduart 127 NC 0403
Achentoul 134 NC 8733
Achentoul Forest 134 NC 8638
Achfary 132 NC 2939
Achgarve 126 NG 8893
Achiemore (Highld.) 132 NC 3667
Achiemore (Highld.) 134 NC 8958
A' Chill 110 NG 2705
Achiltibuie 126 NC 0208
Achina 133 NC 7060
Achinduich 128 NC 5800
Achingills 135 ND 1663
Achinhoan Head 92 NR 7617
Achintee (Highld.) 126 NG 9441
Achintraid 123 NG 8438
Achintree House 115 NN 1273
Achleck 105 NM 4145
A'Chleit (Highld.) (is.) 132 NC 0320
A'Chlèit (Island of Mull) 105 NM 4118
A'Chlèit (Strath.) (pt.) 92 NR 6841
Achlyness 132 NC 2452
Achmelvich 132 NC 0524
Achmelvich Bay 132 NC 0525
Achmore (Central) 107 NN 5832
Achmore (Highld.) 123 NG 8533
Achmore (Isle of Lewis) 131 NB 3129
Achnaba 106 NM 9436
Achnacarnin 132 NC 0431
Achnacarry 115 NN 1787
Achnacloish 111 NG 5908
Achnacroish 105 NM 8541
Achnadrish 111 NM 4551
Achnagarron 128 NH 6870
Achnaha 111 NM 4668
Achnahanat 128 NH 5198
Achnahannet 117 NH 9727
Achnasaul 115 NN 1589
Achnasheen 127 NH 1658
Achnashellach Forest 126 NH 0247
Achnastank 117 NJ 2733
Achosnich 111 NM 4467
A' Chràlaig 115 NH 0914
Achranich 105 NM 7047
Achray Forest 101 NN 5103
Achreamie 135 ND 0166
Achriabhach 106 NN 1468
Achriesgill 132 NC 2554
A'Chruach (Isle of Arran) 92 NR 9633
A'Chruach (Strath.) 106 NM 9021
A'Chruach (Strath.) 92 NR 6110
A'Chruach (Strath.) 92 NR 7630
A Chruach (Tays.) 107 NN 3756
Achurch 52 TL 0283
Achuvoldrach 133 NC 5659
Achvaich 129 NH 7194
Achvarasdal 134 NC 9864
Achvarasdal Burn 134 NC 9862
Ackergill 135 ND 3553
Ackergill Tower 135 ND 3554
Acklam (Cleve.) 85 NZ 4817
Acklam (N Yorks.) 80 SE 7861
Ackleton 59 SO 7798
Acklington 91 NU 2201
Ackton 79 SE 4121
Ackworth Moor Top 71 SE 4316
Acle 65 TG 3910
Acock's Green 50 SP 1383
Acol 31 TR 3067
Acomb 90 NY 9366
Aconbury 45 SO 5133
Acre 78 SD 7824
Acrefair 58 SJ 2743
Acrise Place 31 TR 1942
Acton (Ches.) 59 SJ 6253
Acton (Gtr London) 37 TQ 2080
Acton (Shrops.) 48 SO 3184
Acton (Suff.) 54 TL 8945
Acton Beauchamp 49 SO 6750
Acton Bridge 69 SJ 5975
Acton Burnell 59 SJ 5301
Acton Green 49 SO 6950
Acton Pigott 59 SJ 5402
Acton Round 59 SO 6395
Acton Scott 48 SO 4589
Acton Trussell 59 SJ 9317
Acton Turville 33 ST 8080
Adbaston 59 SJ 7627
Adber 25 ST 5920
Adderbury 47 SP 4635
Adderley 59 SJ 6639
Adderstone 97 NU 1330
Addiewell 102 NS 9962
Addingham 78 SE 0749
Addington (Bucks.) 51 SP 7428
Addington (Kent) 30 TQ 6659
Addlestone 36 TQ 0464
Addlethorpe 73 TF 5469
Adeney 59 SJ 6918
Adfa 57 SJ 0501
Adforton 48 SO 4071
Adisham 31 TR 2253
Adlestrop 47 SP 2427
Adlingfleet 74 SE 8421
Adlington (Ches.) 69 SJ 9180
Adlington (Lancs) 69 SD 6013
Admaston (Shrops.) 59 SJ 6313
Admaston (Staffs.) 60 SK 0423
Admington 50 SP 1945
Adstock 51 SP 7329
Adstone 51 SP 5951
Adventurers' Fen 53 TL 5668
Advie 117 NJ 1234
Adwell 36 SU 6899
Adwick le Street 71 SE 5308
Adwick upon Dearne 71 SE 4601
Adziel 121 NJ 9453
Ae Village 88 NX 9889
Affleck 121 NJ 8623
Affleck Castle (ant.) 109 NO 4938
Affpuddle 25 SY 8093
Afon Aeron 43 SN 5757
Afon Afan 41 SS 8195
Afon Aled 67 SH 9570
Afon Alwen 67 SJ 0244
Afon Banwy neu Einion 58 SJ 1307
Afon Bidno 57 SN 8584
Afon Biga 57 SN 8589
Afon Cain 58 SJ 1618
Afon Cefni 66 SH 4370
Afon Ceirw 67 SH 9247
Afon Cennen 43 SN 6318
Afon Cerist 57 SH 8416
Afon Claerwen 57 SN 8664
Afon Cledwen 67 SH 8762
Afon Clywedog 57 SN 8890
Afon Cothi 43 SN 6033
Afon Cynin 43 SN 2621
Afon Cywyn 43 SN 3114
Afon Ddu 67 SH 7464
Afon Duad 43 SN 3729
Afon Dugoed 57 SH 9012
Afon Dulas (Gwyn.) 57 SH 7508
Afon Dulas (Powys) 57 SN 7699
Afon Dulyn 67 SH 7267
Afon Dwyfach 66 SH 4746
Afon Dwyfor 66 SH 4941
Afon Dyfi 57 SH 8715
Afon Dysynni 57 SH 6206
Afon Eden 67 SH 7029
Afon Gamlan 57 SH 6924
Afon Glaslyn 66 SH 5941
Afon Gronw 43 SN 2119
Afon Gwy 45 ST 5398
Afon Gwydderig 41 SN 8431
Afon Honddu 45 SO 2925
Afon Leri 57 SN 6588
Afon Llafar 67 SH 8535
Afon Lliw 40 SS 5999
Afon Llugwy 67 SH 6860
Afon Llwchwr 40 SS 4996
Afon Llynfi 41 SO 1331
Afon Lwyd 57 SN 8590
Afon Machno 67 SH 7748
Afon Marteg 57 SN 9974
Afon Mawddach 57 SH 7220
Afon Mellte 41 SN 9209
Afon Mynwy 45 SO 4717
Afon Nyfer 42 SN 1237
Afon Porth-llwyd 67 SH 7365
Afon Rheidol 57 SN 6778
Afon Rhiw 57 SJ 0200
Afon Senni 41 SN 9224
Afon Syfynwy 42 SN 0324
Afon Taf 43 SN 2116
Afon Tanat 58 SJ 1424
Afon Teifi 43 SN 5346
Afon Trannon 57 SN 9890
Afon Troddi (River Trothy) 45 SO 4314
Afon Tryweryn 67 SH 8839
Afon Twrch (Dyfed) 43 SN 6445
Afon Twrch (Dyfed) 41 SN 7715
Afon Twrch (Powys) 57 SH 9714
Afon Twymyn 57 SN 8797
Afon Tywi 43 SN 6624
Afon Vyrnwy 58 SJ 1614
Afon Wnion 57 SH 8021
Afon Yscir 41 SN 9934
Afon Ystrad 67 SJ 0162
Afon Ystwyth 57 SN 6276
Afton Bridgend 88 NS 6212
Afton Resr. 88 NS 6304
Afton Water 88 NS 6307
Agden Resr. 71 SK 2592
Agglethorpe 78 SE 0886
A' Ghairbhe 126 NH 0158
A' Ghlas-bheinn 114 NH 0023
A' Ghoil 132 NC 3571
Aigas Forest 128 NH 4341
Aignish 131 NB 4832
Aike 74 TA 0445
Aiker Ness (Orkney) 136 HY 3826
Aikerness (Westray) 138 HY 4552
Aikers 136 ND 4590
Aiketgate 83 NY 4846
Aikton 82 NY 2753
Ailey 45 SO 3348
Ailsa Craig 86 NX 0199
Ailsworth 62 TL 1199
Ainderby Quernhow 79 SE 3480
Ainderby Steeple 84 SE 3392
Aingers Green 39 TM 1120
Ainsdale 68 SD 3111
Ainshval (mt.) 110 NM 3794
Ainstable 83 NY 5346
Ainsworth 69 SD 7610
Aintree 68 SJ 3798
Aira Force 83 NY 3920
Aird (Dumf. and Galwy.) 86 NX 0960
Aird (Isle of Lewis) 131 NB 5635
Aird (Strath.) 99 NM 7600
Aird a' Mhòrain 124 NF 8379
Aird an Rùnair 124 NF 6970
Aird an Troim 131 NB 2316
Aird Barvas 131 NB 3553
Aird Brenish 130 NA 9727
Aird Dell 131 NB 4761
Aird-dhubh 123 NG 7040
Aird Dhubh 126 NG 9382
Airde, The 133 NC 5313
Aird Fada 105 NM 4424
Aird Fenish 130 NA 9929
Aird Luing 105 NM 7406
Aird Mhànais 125 NG 1188
Aird Mheadhonach 125 NG 1998
Aird Nisabost 124 NG 0497
Aird of Coigach 132 NC 0711
Aird of Kinloch 105 NM 5228
Aird of Sleat 111 NG 5900
Aird Riabhach 125 NG 2396
Airdrie 101 NS 7665
Airdriehill 101 NS 7867
Airds Bay 106 NN 0032
Airds Moss 94 NS 5724
Aird, The (Highld.) (dist) 128 NH 5241
Aird, The, (Island of Skye) 123 NG 4052
Aird, The, (Island of Skye) 123 NG 4375
Aird Thormaid 124 NF 9276
Aird Uig 130 NB 0437
Aird Vanish 124 NF 9999
Aire and Calder Navigation (N Yorks.) 71 SE 5820
Aire and Calder Navigation (N Yorks.) 71 SE 6119
Airedale 78 SE 0345
Airie Hill 88 NX 6268
Airies 86 NW 9767
Airlie Castle 108 NO 2952
Airmyn 74 SE 7224
Airntully 108 NO 0935
Airor 111 NG 7205
Airth 102 NS 8987
Airton 78 SD 9059
Aisby (Lincs.) 72 SK 8792
Aisby (Lincs.) 62 TF 0138
Aiskew 79 SE 2788
Aislaby (Cleve) 85 NZ 4012
Aislaby (N Yorks.) 80 NZ 8508
Aislaby (N Yorks.) 80 SE 7785
Aisthorpe 72 SK 9479
Aith (Fetlar) 143 HU 6390
Aith (Orkney) 136 HY 2417
Aith (Shetld.) 141 HU 3455
Aith (Stronsay) 137 HY 6525
Aith Hope 136 ND 2989
Aith Ness 141 HU 5144
Aithsting (dist.) 141 HU 3455
Aith Voe (Shetld.) 141 HU 3458
Aith Voe (Shetld.) 141 HU 4328
Aith Wick 141 HU 4429
Aitnoch 117 NH 9839
Akeld 97 NT 9529
Akeley 51 SP 7037
Akeman Street (Bucks.) (ant.) 36 SP 7316
Akeman Street (Oxon.) (ant.) 47 SP 3213
Akenham 55 TM 1448
Akermoor Loch 89 NT 4020
Alavna Roman Fort (ant.) 82 NY 0437
Albaston 20 SX 4270
Alberbury 58 SJ 3514
Albourne 28 TQ 2616
Albrighton (Shrops.) 59 SJ 4918
Albrighton (Shrops.) 59 SJ 8103
Alburgh 55 TM 2786
Albury (Herts.) 37 TL 4324
Albury (Surrey) 28 TQ 0547
Alby Hill 65 TG 1934
Alcaig 128 NH 5657
Alcaston 48 SO 4587
Alcester 50 SP 0857
Alciston 29 TQ 5005
Alconbury 52 TL 1875
Alconbury Weston 52 TL 1777
Aldbar Castle (ant.) 109 NO 5757
Aldborough (Norf.) 65 TG 1834
Aldborough (N Yorks.) 79 SE 4065
Aldbourne 34 SU 2675
Aldbrough (Humbs.) 75 TA 2338
Aldbrough St. John 84 NZ 2011
Aldbury 36 SP 9612
Aldclune 108 NN 9064
Aldeburgh 55 TM 4656
Aldeburgh Bay 55 TM 4755
Aldeby 65 TM 4593
Aldenham 37 TQ 1198
Alderbury 26 SU 1827
Alderford 65 TG 1218
Alderholt 26 SU 1212
Alderley 33 ST 7690
Alderley Edge 69 SJ 8478
Aldermaston 35 SU 5965
Aldermaston Soke 36 SU 6263
Aldermaston Wharf 35 SU 6067
Alderminster 50 SP 2248
Aldershot 35 SU 8650
Alderton (Glos.) 46 SP 0033
Alderton (Northants.) 51 SP 7346
Alderton (Shrops.) 59 SJ 4923
Alderton (Suff.) 55 TM 3441
Alderton (Wilts.) 33 ST 8382
Alderwasley 60 SK 3153
Aldfield 79 SE 2669
Aldford 68 SJ 4159
Aldham 54 TL 9125
Aldingbourne 28 SU 9205
Aldingham 77 SD 2871
Aldington (Here. and Worc.) 50 SP 0644
Aldington (Kent) 31 TR 0736
Aldochlay 100 NS 3591
Aldreth 53 TL 4473
Aldridge 60 SK 0500
Aldringham 55 TM 4460
Aldsworth 47 SP 1509
Aldunie 121 NJ 3626
Aldwark (Derby.) 71 SK 2257
Aldwark (N Yorks.) 79 SE 4663
Aldwick 28 SZ 9199
Aldwincle 52 TL 0081
Aldworth 35 SU 5579
Aled Isat Resr. 67 SH 9159
Alemoor Loch 89 NT 4015
Ale Water (Borders) 89 NT 4317
Ale Water (Borders) 97 NT 8764
Alexandria 101 NS 3979
Alfardisworthy 22 SS 2911
Alfington 24 SY 1197
Alfold 28 TQ 0333
Alford (Grampn.) 119 NJ 5715
Alford (Lincs.) 73 TF 4575
Alford (Somer.) 25 ST 6032
Alfred's Tower 25 ST 7435
Alfreton 60 SK 4155
Alfrick 49 SO 7453
Alfriston 29 TQ 5103
Alhampton 25 ST 6234
Alhang (mt.) 88 NS 6400
Aline Lodge 131 NB 1911
Alkborough 74 SE 8721
Alkerton 50 SP 3743
Alkham 31 TR 2441
Alkington 59 SJ 5239
Alkmonton 60 SK 1838
Alladale Lodge 128 NH 4389
Alladale River 128 NH 4188
Allaleigh 21 SX 8053
Allanaquoich 117 NO 1191
Allangrange House 128 NH 6251
Allanton (Borders) 97 NT 8654
Allanton (Strath.) 95 NS 8457
Allan Water (Borders) 89 NT 4606
Allan Water (Central) 101 NN 7802
Allardice 119 NO 8174
All Cannings 34 SU 0661
Allendale Common 84 NY 8651
Allendale Town 83 NY 8455
Allenheads 84 NY 8645
Allensmore 45 SO 4635
Aller 24 ST 4029
Allerby 82 NY 0839
Aller Dean 97 NT 9847
Allerford 23 SS 9047
Allermuir Hill 103 NT 2266
Allerston 81 SE 8782
Allerthorpe 74 SE 7847
Allerton 68 SJ 3986
Allerton Bywater 79 SE 4127
Allestree 60 SK 3439
Allexton 62 SK 8100
Allgreave 70 SJ 9767
Allhallows 30 TQ 8377
Alligin Shuas 123 NG 8358
Allimore Green 59 SJ 8519
Allington (Lincs.) 62 SK 8540
Allington (Wilts.) 34 SU 0663
Allington (Wilts.) 34 SU 2039
Allithwaite 77 SD 3876
Allnabad 133 NC 4641
Alloa 102 NS 8893
Allonby 82 NY 0842
Allonby Bay 82 NY 0541
Alloway 93 NS 3318
All Saints South Elmham 55 TM 3482
All Stretton 58 SO 4395
Allt a'Bhunn 133 NC 4812
Allt Ach' a' Bhàthàich 134 NC 8116
Allt a' Chaoil-réidhe 116 NN 5175
Allt a' Chaorainn 114 NM 9587
Allt a' Chaoruinn (Highld.) 127 NC 2703
Allt a' Chireachain 107 NN 7872
Allt a' Choire Mhóir 127 NH 1968
Allt a' Chonais 127 NH 0548
Allt a'Choromaig 106 NM 9120
Allt a' Chraois 133 NC 4438
Allt à Gheallaidh 117 NJ 1238
Allt a' Ghiubhais 123 NG 7968
Allt Airigh-dhamh 134 NC 8238
Allt a' Mhadaidh 127 NH 2274
Allt a' Mhuilinn (Highld.) 134 NC 8312
Allt a' Mhuilinn (Tays.) 116 NN 7675
Alltan Dearg 133 NC 6359
Allt an Dùin 134 NC 8125
Allt an Ealaidh 133 NC 7027
Allt an Stacain 106 NN 1220
Allt an Tairbh 98 NR 5488
Allt an Tiaghaich 132 NC 1623
Allt an t-Srathain 123 NG 7155
Allt Arnan 106 NN 2918
Allt Bail 'a' Mhuilinn 107 NN 5743
Allt Beinn Dònuill 127 NH 2399
Allt Beitheach 111 NM 7551
Allt Beochlich 106 NN 0115
Allt Bhlàraidh 115 NH 3518
Allt Bhran 116 NN 7889
Allt Braglenmore 106 NM 9119
Allt Breinag 116 NH 4707
Allt Càm (Highld.) 116 NN 4477
Allt Càm (Highld.) 116 NN 5178
Allt Càm Ban 116 NH 5606
Allt Camgharaidh 114 NM 9788
Allt Camghouran 107 NN 5253
Allt Car 133 NC 4317
Allt Chaiseagail 133 NC 5810
Alltchaorunn 106 NN 1950
Allt Choire a' Bhalachain 115 NN 0995
Allt Chomhraig 116 NN 8197
Allt Chonoghlais 106 NN 3336
Allt Cinn-locha 99 NR 7879
Allt Coire a'Chaolain 106 NN 2048
Allt Coire an Eoin 106 NN 2172
Allt Coire Lain Oig 116 NN 5198
Allt Coire na Saigh Duibhe 133 NC 4736
Allt Con 107 NN 6967
Allt Conait 107 NN 5245
Allt Connie 117 NO 0786
Allt Crunachdain 116 NN 5291
Allt Cuaich 116 NN 6686
Allt Darrarie 118 NO 3181
Allt Dearg 129 NH 8246
Allt Dochard 106 NN 2045
Allt Doe 116 NH 4107
Allt Easach 106 NN 0642
Allt Eigheach 107 NN 4360
Allt Eileag 127 NC 3107
Allt Fearna 106 NN 1222
Allt Féith Thuill 107 NN 3872
Allt Fionn Ghlinne 106 NN 3122
Alltforgan 57 SH 9624
Allt Forsiescye 135 ND 0158
Allt Garbh 115 NH 1619
Allt Garbh-airigh 128 NH 6399
Allt Garbh Buidhe 117 NN 9981
Allt Gharbh Ghaig 116 NN 7682
Allt Ghlas 107 NN 5364
Allt Glas Choire 116 NN 7378
Allt Glas Dhoire 115 NN 3084
Allt Gleann Da-Eig 107 NN 5944
Allt Gleann nam Meann 101 NN 5114
Allt Gleann Udalain 123 NG 8629
Allt Glen Loch 108 NO 0071
Allt Goibhre 128 NH 4148
Allt Hallater 106 NN 1338
Allt Làire 115 NN 3175
Allt Lon a' Chuil 134 NC 7240
Allt Loraich 115 NN 3878
Allt Lorgy 117 NH 8716
Allt Lundie 115 NH 2807
Allt Madagain 116 NN 6298
Alltmawr 44 SO 0647
Allt Mhoille 106 NN 1031
Allt Mhucarnaich 127 NH 2678
Allt Mór (Highld.) 116 NH 7404
Allt Mór (Highld.) 117 NN 8295
Allt Mór (Island of Skye) 123 NG 7221
Allt Mór (Tays.) 107 NN 7453
Allt na Bogair 107 NN 5954
Alltnacaillich 133 NC 4645
Allt na Caim 107 NN 3763
Allt na Doire Gairbhe 114 NH 0328
Allt na Gile 98 NR 4778
Allt na Glaise 107 NN 5769
Allt na h-Airbhe 127 NH 1193
Allt na h-Eirigh 123 NG 7054
Allt na Lairige (Highld.) 106 NN 2872
Allt na Lairige (Strath.) 106 NN 2316
Allt na Lairige Móire 106 NN 1163
Allt na Lùibe 133 NC 6410
Allt na Muic 115 NH 2515
Allt nan Achaidhean 134 NC 7729
Allt nan Airighèan 98 NR 3650
Allt nan Caorach 128 NH 5267
Allt nan Ramh 132 NC 2237
Allt Odhar 116 NH 5104
Allt Phocaichain 115 NH 3009
Allt Riabhach 115 NH 2219
Allt Riobain 107 NN 4530
Allt Ruighe nan Saorach 107 NN 6463
Allt Sleibh 107 NN 6566
Allt Smeòrail 134 NC 8511
Allt Srath a'Ghlinne 107 NN 6719
Allt Tolaghan 106 NN 2440
Allt Tuileach 117 NJ 2208
Allt Uisg an t-Sithein 116 NH 5921
Alltwalis 43 SN 4431
Alltwen 40 SN 7303
Allweston 25 ST 6614
Almeley 45 SO 3351
Almer 25 SY 9098
Almington 59 SJ 7034
Almondbank 108 NO 0626
Almondbury 70 SE 1614
Almondsbury 33 ST 6083
Alne 79 SE 4965
Alness 128 NH 6569
Alness Bay 128 NH 6367
Alnham 91 NT 9910
Alnmouth 91 NU 2410
Alnmouth Bay 91 NU 2510
Alnwick 91 NU 1912
Alphamstone 54 TL 8735
Alpheton 54 TL 8850
Alphington 21 SX 9190

Auchingilloch (mt.) Battleton

Auchingilloch (mt.)	94	NS 7035
Auchininna	121	NJ 6446
Auchinleck (Dumf. and Galwy.)	87	NX 4570
Auchinleck (Strath.)	93	NS 5422
Auchinloch	101	NS 6670
Auchintoul	119	NJ 5316
Auchleuchries	121	NK 0136
Auchleven	121	NJ 6224
Auchlochan	95	NS 8037
Auchlossan	119	NJ 5701
Auchlunies	119	NO 8999
Auchlyne	107	NN 5129
Auchlyne West Burn	107	NN 4830
Auchmacoy	121	NJ 9930
Auchmillan	93	NS 5129
Auchmithie	109	NO 6744
Auchmuirbridge	103	NO 2101
Auchmull	119	NO 5874
Auchnacloich	106	NM 9533
Auchnacree	109	NO 4663
Auchnafree	107	NN 8133
Auchnafree Hill	107	NN 8030
Auchnagallin	117	NJ 0533
Auchnagatt	121	NJ 9341
Aucholzie	118	NO 3490
Auchope Cairn	90	NT 8819
Auchronie	118	NO 4480
Auchterarder	102	NN 9312
Auchterderran	103	NT 2195
Auchterhouse	108	NO 3337
Auchtermuchty	103	NO 2311
Auchterneed	128	NH 4959
Auchtertool	103	NT 2190
Auchtertyre Hill	123	NG 8329
Auchter Water	95	NS 8754
Auchtitench Hill	88	NS 7118
Auchtoo	107	NN 5620
Auckengill	135	ND 3764
Auckley	71	SE 6501
Audenshaw	69	SJ 9196
Audlem	59	SJ 6543
Audley	59	SJ 7950
Audley End (ant.)	53	TL 5237
Audley End Station	53	TL 5136
Auds	121	NJ 6564
Aughton (Humbs.)	74	SE 7038
Aughton (Lancs.)	68	SD 3804
Aughton (Lancs.)	77	SD 5467
Aughton (S Yorks.)	71	SK 4586
Aughton Park	68	SD 4106
Auld Darkney (mt.)	109	NO 4266
Auldearn	129	NH 9155
Aulden	45	SO 4654
Auldhame	103	NT 5984
Auldhouse	94	NS 6250
Auldton Fell	89	NT 1108
Aulich Burn	107	NN 5961
Auliston Point	111	NM 5457
Ault a' chruinn	114	NG 9420
Aultanrynie	132	NC 3436
Aultbea	126	NG 8789
Aultdearg	127	NH 2865
Aultgrishan	126	NG 7485
Aultguish Inn	127	NH 3570
Aultibea	135	ND 0423
Aultiphurst	134	NC 8065
Aultmore (Grampn.)	121	NJ 4053
Aultmore (Grampn.) (dist.)	121	NJ 4557
Ault-na-goire	116	NH 5423
Aultnamain Inn	128	NH 6681
Aulton	121	NJ 6028
Aundorach	117	NH 9716
Aunsby	62	TF 0438
Auquhorthies	121	NJ 8329
Auskerry (is.)	137	HY 6716
Auskerry Sound	137	HY 6618
Aust	33	ST 5789
Austerfield	71	SK 6594
Austrey	60	SK 2906
Austwick	78	SD 7668
Authorpe	73	TF 3980
Authorpe Row	73	TF 5373
Avebury	34	SU 0969
Avebury (ant.)	34	SU 1070
Aveley	37	TQ 5680
Avening	46	ST 8797
Averham	61	SK 7654
Aveton Gifford	21	SX 6947
Avielochan	117	NH 9016
Aviemore	117	NH 8912
Avington	34	SU 3767
Avoch	128	NH 6955
Avoch Bay	129	NH 7054
Avon	26	SZ 1498
Avonbridge	102	NS 9072
Avon Castle	26	SU 1303
Avon Dam Resr.	21	SX 6765
Avon Dassett	50	SP 4150
Avonmouth	33	ST 5177
Avon Water	94	NS 7143
Avon Wick	21	SX 7158
Awbridge	26	SU 3323
Awkley	33	ST 5885
Awliscombe	24	ST 1301
Awre	46	SO 7008
Awsworth	61	SK 4843
Axbridge	33	ST 4254
Axe Edge	70	SK 0370
Axford (Hants.)	35	SU 6043
Axford (Wilts.)	34	SU 2369
Axminster	24	SY 2998
Axmouth	24	SY 2591
Aylburton	45	SO 6101
Ayle	83	NY 7149
Aylesbeare	24	SY 0391
Aylesbury	36	SP 8213
Aylesby	75	TA 2007
Aylesford	30	TQ 7359
Aylesham	31	TR 2352
Aylestone	61	SK 5701
Aylmerton	65	TG 1839
Aylsham	65	TG 1926
Aylton	49	SO 6537
Aymestrey	48	SO 4265
Aynho	47	SP 5133
Ayot St. Lawrence	37	TL 1916
Ayot St. Peter	37	TL 2115
Ayr	93	NS 3321
Ayres, The	76	NX 4303
Aysgarth	78	SE 0088
Ayside	77	SD 3983
Ayston	62	SK 8601
Aythorpe Roding	37	TL 5815
Ayton (Borders)	97	NT 9260
Ayton (N Yorks.)	81	SE 9884
Aywick (Yell)	143	HU 5386
Ay Wick (Yell)	143	HU 5486
Azerley	79	SE 2574

B

Baa Taing (Auskerry)	137	HY 6715
Baa Taing (Shetld.)	142	HU 2774
Babbacombe	21	SX 9365
Babbacombe Bay	21	SX 9568
Babbet Ness	103	NO 5914
Babbinswood	58	SJ 3329
Babcary	25	ST 5628
Babel	41	SN 8235
Babell	68	SJ 1574
Babeny	21	SX 6775
Babingley River	64	TF 6825
Babraham	53	TL 5150
Babworth	72	SK 6880
Bac an Eich	127	NH 2249
Bac Beag (is.)	104	NM 2337
Bach Camp (ant.)	45	SO 5460
Bache Hill	48	SO 2163
Bach Island	105	NM 7726
Bachlaig	98	NR 4175
Back	131	NB 4840
Backaland	138	HY 5630
Backaskail Bay	139	HY 6438
Backaskaill	138	HY 4850
Backbarrow	77	SD 3584
Backfolds	121	NK 0252
Backford	68	SJ 3971
Backhill (Grampn.)	121	NJ 7939
Backhill (Grampn.)	121	NK 0039
Backhill of Clackriach	121	NJ 9246
Backhill of Trustach	119	NO 6397
Backies	129	NC 8302
Backlass	135	ND 2053
Backmuir of New Gilston	103	NO 4308
Back of Keppoch	111	NM 6587
Backstane Hill	95	NS 9127
Backwater Reservoir	108	NO 2560
Backwell	33	ST 4868
Backworth	91	NZ 2972
Bac Mór or Dutchman's Cap	104	NM 2438
Bacon End	38	TL 6018
Baconsthorpe	65	TG 1237
Bacton (Here. and Worc.)	45	SO 3732
Bacton (Norf.)	65	TG 3434
Bacton (Suff.)	54	TM 0466
Bacup	78	SD 8622
Bad a'Chreamha	123	NG 8536
Badachro	123	NG 7873
Badandun HiLL	108	NO 2067
Badanloch Forest	134	NC 7935
Badanloch Lodge	134	NC 7933
Badavanich	127	NH 1058
Bad Bog	126	NG 9281
Badbury	34	SU 1980
Badbury Hill	47	SU 2694
Badbury Rings (ant.)	26	ST 9602
Badby	51	SP 5559
Badcall (Highld.)	132	NC 1541
Badcall (Highld.)	132	NC 2355
Badcall Bay	132	NC 1541
Badcaul	126	NH 0191
Baddeley Green	59	SJ 9250
Baddesley Ensor	60	SP 2798
Baddidarach	132	NC 0923
Baddinsgill Reservoir	95	NT 1255
Baddoch	117	NO 1382
Baddoch (mt.)	117	NJ 0719
Badenoch (dist.)	116	NN 7091
Badenscoth	121	NJ 7038
Badentarbat Bay	126	NC 0008
Badenyon	118	NJ 3419
Badger	59	SO 7699
Badgers Mount	37	TQ 5061
Badgeworth (Glos.)	46	SO 9019
Badgworth (Somer.)	32	ST 3952
Badingham	55	TM 3067
Badlesmere	31	TR 0154
Badlipster	135	ND 2049
Badluarach	126	NG 9994
Badminton	33	ST 8082
Badminton House	33	ST 8082
Badmondisfield Hall (ant.)	54	TL 7457
Badninish	129	NH 7694
Badrallach	127	NH 0691
Badsey	50	SP 0743
Badsworth	71	SE 4614
Badwell Ash	54	TL 9969
Bagby	79	SE 4680
Bagendon	46	SP 0006
Bage, The	45	SO 2943
Baggrave Hall	61	SK 6909
Baggy Point	22	SS 4140
Bagh an Tailleir (pt.)	99	NR 8481
Bagh Feisdlum	110	NM 2458
Bàgh Loch an Ròin	132	NC 1954
Bàgh na Doide	99	NR 6976
Bàgh nam Faoileann	124	NF 8444
Bàgh nan Gunnaichean	123	NG 4574
Bàgh Tigh-an-Droighinn	99	NR 8579
Bagillt	68	SJ 2175
Bagillt Bank (sbk.)	68	SJ 2376
Baginton	50	SP 3474
Baglan	41	SS 7493
Bagley	58	SJ 4027
Bagnall	59	SJ 9250
Bagshot (Surrey)	36	SU 9163
Bagshot (Wilts.)	34	SU 3165
Bagshot Heath	36	SU 9061
Bagthorpe (Norf.)	64	TF 7932
Bagthorpe (Notts.)	61	SK 4751
Bagworth	61	SK 4408
Bagwy Llydiart	45	SO 4427
Baidland Hill	93	NS 2552
Baildon	78	SE 1539
Baile	124	NF 9381
Bailebeag	116	NH 5018
Baile Boidheach	99	NR 7473
Baile Mór	104	NM 2824
Bailey Hill	48	SO 2472
Bailiesward	121	NJ 4737
Baillieston	101	NS 6764
Bail Uachdraich	124	NF 8160
Bainbridge	84	SD 9390
Bainton (Cambs.)	62	TF 0906
Bainton (Humbs.)	81	SE 9652
Bairnkine	90	NT 6515
Bait or St. Mary's Island	91	NZ 3575
Bakers End	37	TL 3917
Baker Street	38	TQ 6381
Bakewell	70	SK 2168
Bala	67	SH 9236
Balachuirn	123	NG 5540
Balaglas	124	NF 8457
Bala Lake or Llyn Tegid	67	SH 9033
Balallan	131	NB 2920
Balbeg	116	NH 4924
Balbeggie	108	NO 1629
Balbegno Castle	109	NO 6372
Balbithan	119	NJ 7917
Balbithan House	119	NJ 8018
Balblair	129	NH 7066
Balcary Point	87	NX 8249
Balcherry	129	NH 8182
Balchladich	132	NC 0330
Balchraggan	128	NH 5343
Balchrick	132	NC 1960
Balcombe	29	TQ 3130
Balcomie	103	NO 6209
Balcurvie	103	NO 3400
Balderhead Resr.	84	NY 9118
Baldersby	79	SE 3578
Balderstone	77	SD 6332
Balderton	62	SK 8151
Baldhu	18	SW 7743
Baldinnie	103	NO 4311
Baldock	53	TL 2434
Baldoon Sands	87	NX 4552
Baldrine	76	SC 4281
Balduff Hill	108	NO 2253
Baldwin	76	SC 3581
Baldwinholme	82	NY 3351
Baldwin's Gate	59	SJ 7939
Bale	64	TG 0136
Balemartine	104	NL 9841
Balephetrish Bay	104	NM 0047
Balephuil	104	NL 9640
Balephuil Bay	104	NL 9440
Balerno	102	NT 1666
Baleshare (is.)	124	NF 7861
Balevullin	104	NL 9546
Balfield	109	NO 5468
Balfour	136	HY 4716
Balfour Castle	136	HY 4716
Balfron	101	NS 5488
Balgaveny	121	NJ 6640
Balgavies	109	NO 5351
Balgedie	102	NO 1603
Balgonar	102	NT 0293
Balgove	121	NJ 8133
Balgowan	116	NN 6394
Balgowan Point	86	NX 1242
Balgown	122	NG 3868
Balgray	109	NO 4138
Balgray Reservoir	93	NS 5157
Balgrochan	101	NS 6278
Balgy	123	NG 8454
Balhalgardy	121	NJ 7623
Balhary	108	NO 2646
Baliasta	143	HP 6009
Baligill	134	NC 8566
Balintore (Highld.)	129	NH 8675
Balintore (Tays.)	108	NO 2859
Balintraid	129	NH 7370
Balivanich	124	NF 7755
Balkeerie	108	NO 3244
Balkholme	74	SE 7828
Balkissock	86	NX 1381
Ball	58	SJ 3026
Balla	112	NF 7811
Ballabeg	76	SC 2470
Ballacannell	76	SC 4382
Ballacarnane Beg	76	SC 3088
Ballachulish	106	NN 0857
Ballageich Hill	93	NS 5350
Ballagyr	76	SC 2685
Ballajora	76	SC 4790
Ballamodha	76	SC 2773
Ballantrae	86	NX 0882
Ballantrae Bay	86	NX 0783
Ballantrushal	131	NB 3753
Ballard Point	26	SZ 0481
Ballasalla (I. of M.)	76	SC 2870
Ballasalla (I. of M.)	76	SC 3497
Ballater	118	NO 3695
Ballaugh	76	SC 3493
Ballechin	108	NN 9353
Ballencleuch Law	88	NS 9304
Ballencrieff	103	NT 4878
Ball Hill	34	SU 4263
Balliekine	92	NR 8739
Balliemore (Strath.)	105	NM 8228
Balliemore (Strath.)	100	NS 0584
Ballig	76	SC 2882
Ballikinrain Castle	101	NS 5687
Ballimore (Central)	107	NN 5217
Ballimore (Strath.)	100	NR 9283
Ballinaby	98	NR 2267
Ballindean	108	NO 2529
Ballinger Common	36	SP 9103
Ballingham	45	SO 5731
Ballingry	102	NT 1797
Ballinlick	108	NN 9840
Ballinloan Burn	108	NN 9442
Ballinluig	108	NN 9852
Ballintuim	108	NO 1054
Balloch (Highld.)	129	NH 7346
Balloch (Strath.)	101	NS 3981
Balloch (Tays.)	107	NN 8419
Balloch (Tays.)	109	NO 3557
Ballochan	119	NO 5290
Ballochbuie Forest	117	NO 1989
Balloch Castle	101	NS 3983
Ballochroy	92	NR 7252
Balloch, The (mt.)	121	NJ 4648
Ballo Resr.	103	NO 2204
Balls Cross	28	SU 9826
Ballygown	105	NM 4343
Ballygrant	98	NR 3966
Ballyhaugh	110	NM 1758
Ballymichael	92	NR 9231
Balmacaan Forest	115	NH 3925
Balmacara	123	NG 8127
Balmaclellan	88	NX 6578
Balmacneil	108	NN 9850
Balmae	87	NX 6845
Balmaha	101	NS 4290
Balmalcolm	103	NO 3108
Balmanno Hill	102	NO 1414
Balmartin	124	NF 7273
Balmedie	119	NJ 9617
Balmerino	109	NO 3524
Balmerlawn	26	SU 3003
Balmoral Castle	117	NO 2595
Balmoral Forest	117	NO 2587
Balmore	101	NS 6073
Balmore Forest	115	NH 3333
Balmullo	109	NO 4220
Balmungie	129	NH 7459
Balmurrie	86	NX 2066
Balnabodach	112	NF 7101
Balnacoil	134	NC 8011
Balnacra	126	NG 9746
Balnafoich	116	NH 6835
Balnaglaic	116	NH 4430
Balnagown Castle	129	NH 7675
Balnaguard	108	NN 9451
Balnaguard Burn	108	NN 9249
Balnaguisich	128	NH 6771
Balnahara	105	NM 4534
Balnahard	98	NR 4199
Balnakeil	132	NC 3968
Balnakeil Bay	132	NC 3869
Balnaknock	123	NG 4162
Balnamoon	109	NO 5463
Balnapaling	129	NH 7969
Balquhidder	107	NN 5320
Balranald	124	NF 7169
Balsall Common	50	SP 2377
Balscote	50	SP 3841
Balsham	53	TL 5850
Balta (is.)	143	HP 6608
Baltasound (Unst)	143	HP 6208
Balta Sound (Unst)	143	HP 6508
Baltasound Aerodrome	143	HP 6207
Balterley	59	SJ 7550
Balthangie	121	NJ 8351
Baltonsborough	25	ST 5434
Balvaird	128	NH 5452
Balvarran	108	NO 0762
Balvenie Castle (ant.)	121	NJ 3240
Balvicar	105	NM 7616
Balvraid	117	NH 8231
Bamber Bridge	77	SD 5626
Bamburgh	97	NU 1834
Bamff	108	NO 2251
Bamford	70	SK 2083
Bampton (Cumbr.)	83	NY 5118
Bampton (Devon)	23	SS 9522
Bampton (Oxon.)	47	SP 3103
Bampton Common	83	NY 4716
Banavie	115	NN 1177
Banbury	51	SP 4540
Banc Cwmhelen	40	SN 6811
Banchory	119	NO 6995
Banchory-Devenick	119	NJ 9002
Banc Nant Rhys	57	SN 8279
Bancyfelin	43	SN 3218
Banc-y-ffordd	43	SN 4037
Bandirran House	108	NO 1930
Banff	121	NJ 6863
Bangor	66	SH 5872
Bangor-Is-coed	58	SJ 3945
Banham	54	TM 0688
Bank	26	SU 2807
Bankend (Dumf. and Galwy.)	88	NY 0268
Bankend (Strath.)	95	NS 8033
Bankfoot	108	NO 0635
Bankglen	88	NS 5912
Bankhead (Grampn.)	119	NJ 6608
Bankhead (Grampn.)	119	NJ 8910
Bank Newton	78	SD 9152
Banknock	101	NS 7779
Banks (Cumbr.)	90	NY 5664
Banks (Lancs)	68	SD 3820
Bankshill	89	NY 1981
Banks Sands	77	SD 3724
Bank Street	49	SO 6362
Banningham	65	TG 2129
Banniskirk House	135	ND 1657
Bannister Green	38	TL 6920
Bannockburn	101	NS 8190
Ban Rubha	105	NM 7106
Banstead	37	TQ 2559
Bantham	21	SX 6643
Banton	101	NS 7479
Banwell	32	ST 3959
Baosbheinn (mt.)	123	NG 8765
Bapchild	30	TQ 9363
Baramore	111	NM 6474
Barassie	93	NS 3232
Barbaraville	129	NH 7472
Barber Booth	70	SK 1184
Barbon	77	SD 6282
Barbreck House	105	NM 8306
Barbreck River	105	NM 8306
Barbrook	23	SS 7147
Barbrook Reservoir	71	SK 2777
Barbury Castle (ant.)	34	SU 1476
Barby	51	SP 5470
Barcaldine Castle (ant.)	106	NM 9140
Barcaldine Forest	106	NM 9741
Barcaldine House	106	NM 9641
Barcheston	50	SP 2639
Barcloy Hill	87	NX 7552
Barcombe	29	TQ 4214
Barcombe Cross	29	TQ 4216
Barcraigs Resr.	93	NS 3857
Barden	84	SE 1493
Barden Fell	78	SE 0858
Barden Resrs.	78	SE 0257
Bardfield Saling	54	TL 6826
Bard Head	141	HU 5135
Bardister	142	HU 3577
Bardney	73	TF 1169
Bardon Mill	90	NY 7764
Bardowie	101	NS 5873
Bardrainney	100	NS 3372
Bardsea	77	SD 3074
Bardsey	79	SE 3643
Bardsey Island (Ynys Enlli)	56	SH 1221
Bardsey Sound	56	SH 1323
Bardsley	69	SD 9201
Bardwell	54	TL 9473
Barewood	45	SO 3856
Barford (Norf.)	65	TG 1007
Barford (Warw.)	50	SP 2660
Barford St. Martin	26	SU 0531
Barford St. Michael	47	SP 4332
Barfrestone	31	TR 2650
Bargatton Loch	88	NX 6962
Bargoed	41	SO 1500
Bargrennan	86	NX 3476
Barham (Cambs.)	52	TL 1375
Barham (Kent)	31	TR 2050
Barham (Suff.)	55	TM 1451
Bar Hill	53	TL 3863
Barholm	62	TF 0811
Barkby	61	SK 6309
Barkestone-le-Vale	61	SK 7734
Barkham	36	SU 7866
Barking	37	TQ 4785
Barking (Suff.)	54	TM 0653
Barkingside	37	TQ 4489
Barkin Isles	131	NB 4023
Barkisland	70	SE 0419
Barkston (Lincs.)	62	SK 9241
Barkston (N Yorks.)	79	SE 4936
BarkwAY	53	TL 3835
Barkwith	73	TF 1681
Barlaston	59	SJ 8938
Barlavington	28	SU 9716
Barlborough	71	SK 4777
Barlby	79	SE 6334
Barlestone	60	SK 4205
Barley (Herts.)	53	TL 4038
Barley (Lancs.)	78	SD 8240
Barleythorpe	62	SK 8409
Barling	38	TQ 9289
Barlow (Derby.)	71	SK 3474
Barlow (N Yorks.)	79	SE 6428
Barlow (Tyne and Wear)	91	NZ 1560
Barmby Moor	80	SE 7748
Barmby on the Marsh	74	SE 6828
Barmekin Hill	119	NJ 7207
Barmer	64	TF 8133
Barmoor Castle	97	NT 9939
Barmore Island	99	NR 8771
Barmouth	56	SH 6115
Barmouth Bay	56	SH 5612
Barmpton	84	NZ 3118
Barmston	81	TA 1659
Barnack	62	TF 0705
Barnacle	50	SP 3884
Barnard Castle	84	NZ 0516
Barnard Gate	47	SP 4010
Barnardiston	54	TL 7148
Barnbougle Castle (ant.)	102	NT 1678
Barnburgh	71	SE 4803
Barnby	55	TM 4789
Barnby Dun	71	SE 6109
Barnby IN THE Willows	62	SK 8552
Barnby Moor	71	SK 6684
Barnes	37	TQ 2276
Barnet	37	TQ 3395
Barnetby le Wold	74	TA 0509
Barney	64	TF 9932
Barnham (Suff.)	54	TL 8779
Barnham (W Susx)	28	SU 9604
Barnham Broom	65	TG 0807
Barnhead	109	NO 6657
Barnhill	129	NJ 1457
Barnhills	86	NW 9871
Barnhourie (sbk.)	82	NX 9350
Barningham (Durham)	84	NZ 0810
Barningham (Suff.)	54	TL 9676
Barnoldby le Beck	75	TA 2303
Barnoldswick	78	SD 8746
Barns Green	28	TQ 1227
Barnsley (Glos.)	46	SP 0705
Barnsley (S Yorks.)	71	SE 3406
Barns Ness	96	NT 7277
Barnstaple	23	SS 5533
Barnstaple or Bideford Bay	22	SS 3432
Barnston (Essex)	38	TL 6519
Barnston (Mers.)	68	SJ 2783
Barnt Green	50	SP 0073
Barnton	69	SJ 6374
Barnwell	52	TL 0485
Barnwood	46	SO 8518
Barochan House (ant.)	101	NS 4168
Barons Point	100	NS 2280
Barony, The	136	HY 2527
Barr	86	NX 2794
Barra (is.)	112	NF 6801
Barra Castle	121	NJ 7925
Barrachan	86	NX 3649
Barrack	121	NJ 8942
Barraer Fell	86	NX 3761
Barraglom	131	NB 1634
Barra Head	112	NL 5579
Barrahormid	99	NR 7184
Barrapol	104	NL 9542
Barras	119	NO 8580
Barrasford	90	NY 9273
Barravullin	105	NM 7907
Barr Castle (ant.)	100	NS 3458
Barregarrow	76	SC 3288
Barrel of Butter (is.)	136	HY 3500
Bàrr Ganuisg	100	NR 9280
Barr Glen	92	NR 6936
Barrhead	101	NS 5058
Barr Hill (Dumf. and Galwy.)	88	NX 7781
Barrhill (Strath.)	86	NX 2382
Barrington (Cambs.)	53	TL 3949
Barrington (Somer.)	24	ST 3918
Barripper	18	SW 6338
Barrisdale Bay	111	NG 8605
Barr Liath	100	NR 9673
Barrmill	93	NS 3651
Barr Mór (Strath.)	105	NM 8138
Barr Mór (Strath.)	100	NN 1312
Barrock	135	ND 2571
Barrock House	135	ND 2862
Barrow (Lancs.)	77	SD 7338
Barrow (Leic.)	62	SK 8815
Barrow (Shrops.)	59	SJ 6500
Barrow (Somer.)	25	ST 7231
Barrow (Suff.)	54	TL 7663
Barroway Drove	63	TF 5703
Barrowby	62	SK 8736
Barrow Deep (lightship)	39	TM 3004
Barrowden	62	SK 9400
Barrowford	78	SD 8538
Barrow Gurney	33	ST 5267
Barrow-in-Furness	76	SD 1969
Barrow Street	25	ST 8330
Barrow upon Humber	74	TA 0721
Barrow upon Soar	61	SK 5717
Barrow upon Trent	60	SK 3528
Barr Water	92	NR 6836
Barry (S Glam.)	41	ST 1168
Barry (Tays.)	109	NO 5334
Barry Island	41	ST 1166
Barry Links	109	NO 5431
Barry Links Station	109	NO 5433
Barsalloch Point	86	NX 3441
Barsby	61	SK 6911
Barsham	55	TM 3989
Barston	50	SP 2078
Bartestree	45	SO 5641
Bar, The (Dyfed)	56	SN 5780
Bar, The (Gwyn.)	66	SH 4161
Bar, The (Gwyn.)	56	SH 6014
Barth Head	136	ND 4285
Barthol Chapel	121	NJ 8134
Barthomley	59	SJ 7652
Bartley	26	SU 3012
Bartlow	53	TL 5845
Barton (Cambs.)	53	TL 4055
Barton (Ches.)	58	SJ 4454
Barton (Devon)	21	SX 9067
Barton (Glos.)	46	SP 0925
Barton (Lancs.)	77	SD 5136
Barton (N Yorks.)	84	NZ 2208
Barton (Warw.)	50	SP 1051
Barton Aerodrome	69	SJ 7397
Barton Bendish	64	TF 7105
Barton Hartshorn	51	SP 6431
Barton in Fabis	61	SK 5232
Barton in the Beans	60	SK 3906
Barton-le-Clay	52	TL 0831
Barton-le-Street	80	SE 7274
Barton-le-Willows	80	SE 7163
Barton Mills	54	TL 7273
Barton Moss	69	SJ 7397
Barton on Sea	26	SZ 2493
Barton-on-the-Heath	47	SP 2532
Barton Seagrave	52	SP 8877
Barton Stacey	34	SU 4340
Barton Stacey Camp	34	SU 4342
Barton St. David	25	ST 5431
Barton Turf	65	TG 3522
Barton-under-Needwood	60	SK 1818
Barton-Upon-Humber	74	TA 0222
Barvas	131	NB 3649
Barway	53	TL 5475
Barwell	61	SP 4496
Barwick	25	ST 5513
Barwick in Elmet	79	SE 3937
Baschurch	58	SJ 4222
Bascote	50	SP 4063
Basford Green	60	SJ 9951
Bashall Eaves	77	SD 6943
Bashley	26	SZ 2496
Basildon	38	TQ 7189
Basing	35	SU 6652
Basingstoke	35	SU 6351
Basingstoke Canal	35	SU 8453
Baslow	71	SK 2572
Bason Bridge	32	ST 3445
Bassaleg	68	SJ 2787
Bassenthwaite	82	NY 2332
Bassenthwaite Lake	82	NY 2129
Bassett	26	SU 4116
Bassingbourn	53	TL 3344
Bassingfield	61	SK 6137
Bassingham	72	SK 9059
Bassingthorpe	62	SK 9628
Bass Rock	103	NT 6087
Basta	143	HU 5294
Basta Voe	143	HU 5296
Baston	62	TF 1114
Bastwick	65	TG 4217
Batcombe (Dorset.)	25	ST 6104
Batcombe (Somer.)	33	ST 6838
Bate Heath	69	SJ 6879
Bath	33	ST 7464
Bathampton	33	ST 7765
Bathealton	24	ST 0724
Batheaston	33	ST 7767
Bathford	33	ST 7866
Bathgate	102	NS 9768
Bathley	72	SK 7759
Bathpool	20	SX 2874
Batley	79	SE 2424
Batsford	47	SP 1834
Battersby	85	NZ 5908
Battersea	37	TQ 2876
Battery Point	33	ST 4677
Battisford	54	TM 0554
Battisford Tye	54	TM 0254
Battle (E Susx.)	29	TQ 7416
Battle (Powys)	41	SO 0031
Battlefield	59	SJ 5117
Battlesbridge	38	TQ 7794
Battlesbury (ant.)	33	ST 8945
Battlesden	52	SP 9628
Battleton	23	SS 9127

Battramsley

Bettws

Battramsley	26	SZ	3099
Bauds of Cullen	121	NJ	4766
Baugh Fell	83	SD	7493
Baughurst	35	SU	5859
Baulking	34	SU	3190
Baumber	73	TF	2174
Baunton	46	SP	0204
Bavelaw Castle (ant.)	102	NT	1662
Baverstock	26	SU	0231
Bawburgh	65	TG	1508
Bawden Rocks or Man and his man	18	SW	6953
Bawdeswell	64	TG	0420
Bawdrip	32	ST	3339
Bawdsey	55	TM	3440
Bawtry	71	SK	6592
Baxenden	78	SD	7726
Baxterley	60	SP	2796
Bayble	131	NB	5231
Bayble Bay	131	NB	5330
Bayble Hill	131	NB	5030
Baycliff	77	SD	2872
Baydon	34	SU	2877
Bayford	37	TL	3108
Bayham Abbey	29	TQ	6436
Bayhead	124	NF	7468
Bayles	83	NY	7044
Baylham	55	TM	1051
Bay of Backaland	138	HY	5730
Bay of Bomasty	137	HY	6123
Bay of Brough	139	HY	6541
Bay of Cleat	138	HY	4646
Bay of Cruden	121	NK	0934
Bay of Deepdale	140	HU	1754
Bay of Firth	136	HY	3814
Bay of Fladdabister	141	HU	4332
Bay of Furrowend	136	HY	4719
Bay of Holland	137	HY	6422
Bay of Houseby	137	HY	6821
Bay of Ireland	136	HY	2809
Bay of Isbister	136	HY	4018
Bay of Keisgaig	132	NC	2469
Bay of Kirkwall	136	HY	4413
Bay of Laig	111	NM	4688
Bay of Linton	137	HY	5318
Bay of London	138	HY	5634
Bay of Lopness	139	HY	7443
Bay of Meil	136	HY	4812
Bay of Newark	139	HY	7139
Bay of Noup	138	HY	4149
Bay of Quendale	141	HU	3712
Bay of Sandoyne	136	HY	4602
Bay of Sandquoy	139	HY	7345
Bay of Skaill (Orkney)	136	HY	2319
Bay of Skaill (Papa Westray)	138	HY	4651
Bay of Stoer	132	NC	0328
Bay of Stove	139	HY	6134
Bay of Swartmill	138	HY	4846
Bay of the Tongue	136	HY	2004
Bay of Tuquoy	138	HY	4644
Bay River	122	NG	2752
Baysdale Beck	85	NZ	6207
Bayston Hill	59	SJ	4809
Bayton	49	SO	6973
Beachampton	51	SP	7737
Beachamwell	64	TF	7505
Beachamwell Warren	64	TF	7607
Beachans	129	NJ	0246
Beacharr	92	NR	6943
Beachborough	31	TR	1638
Beachley	33	ST	5591
Beach River	105	NM	4623
Beachy Head	29	TV	5895
Beacon	24	ST	1705
Beacon End	38	TL	9524
Beacon Fell	77	SD	5642
Beacon Hill (Dorset)	26	SY	9794
Beacon Hill (Hants.) (ant.)	35	SU	4557
Beacon Hill (Powys)	48	SO	1677
Beacon Hill (Wilts.)	34	SU	2043
Beacon Point (Durham)	85	NZ	4445
Beacon Point (Northum.)	91	NZ	3189
Beacon's Bottom	36	SU	7895
Beaconsfield	36	SU	9490
Beacons Reservoir	41	SN	9818
Beacontree	37	TQ	4886
Beacravik	125	NG	1190
Beadlam	79	SE	6584
Beadnell	97	NU	2329
Beadnell Bay	97	NU	2327
Beaford	23	SS	5514
Beal (Northum.)	97	NU	0642
Beal (N Yorks.)	79	SE	5325
Bealings	55	TM	2348
Beaminster	25	ST	4801
Beamish	84	NZ	2253
Beamsley	78	SE	0752
Bean	30	TQ	5972
Beanacre	33	ST	9066
Bean Hill	86	NX	0554
Beanley	91	NU	0818
Beaquoy	136	HY	3022
Beare Green	28	TQ	1842
Bearley	50	SP	1760
Bearneas	126	NH	0242
Bearpark	84	NZ	2343
Bearreraig Bay	123	NG	5153
Bearsbridge	83	NY	7857
Bearsden	101	NS	5471
Bearsted	30	TQ	8055
Bearwood	26	SZ	0496
Beatshach	117	NJ	2737
Beattock	89	NT	0702
Beauchamp Roding	37	TL	5809
Beauchief	71	SK	3381
Beaufort	41	SO	1611
Beaufort Castle	128	NH	5042
Beaulieu	26	SU	3801
Beaulieu Heath (Hants.)	26	SU	3400
Beaulieu Heath (Hants.)	26	SU	4104
Beaulieu River	26	SU	3901
Beaulieu Road Station	26	SU	3405
Beauly	128	NH	5246
Beauly Firth	128	NH	6147
Beaumaris	66	SH	6076
Beaumont (Cumbr.)	89	NY	3459
Beaumont (Essex)	55	TM	1725
Beauport Park	30	TQ	7813
Beaupre Castle (ant)	41	ST	0071
Beausale	50	SP	2470
Beauty Hill	121	NJ	9020
Beaver Dyke Resrs.	79	SE	2254
Beaworthy	20	SX	4699
Beazley End	54	TL	7428
Bebington	68	SJ	3384
Bebside	91	NZ	2881
Beccles	55	TM	4290
Becconsall	77	SD	4422
Beckbury	59	SJ	7601
Beckbury Camp (ant.)	46	SP	0629
Beckenham	37	TQ	3769
Beckermet	82	NY	0206
Beckfoot (Cumbr.)	82	NY	0949
Beckfoot (Cumbr.)	82	NY	1600
Beck Foot (Cumbr.)	83	SD	6196
Beckford	46	SO	9735
Beckhampton	34	SU	0868
Beck Hole	80	NZ	8102
Beckingham (Lincs.)	62	SK	8753
Beckingham (Notts.)	72	SK	7790
Beckington	33	ST	7951
Beckley (E Susx.)	30	TQ	8423
Beckley (Oxon)	47	SP	5611
Beck Row	54	TL	6977
Beck Side	76	SD	2382
Beckton	37	TQ	4381
Beckwithshaw	79	SE	2653
Beda Fell	83	NY	4216
Bedale	79	SE	2688
Bedburn	84	NZ	1031
Beddau	41	ST	0585
Beddgelert	66	SH	5848
Beddingham	29	TQ	4408
Beddington	37	TQ	3165
Bedfield	55	TM	2266
Bedford	52	TL	0449
Bedford Level (Middle Level) (dist.)	63	TL	3393
Bedford Level (North Level) (dist.)	63	TF	2404
Bedford Level (South Level) (dist.)	54	TL	5985
Bedgebury Forest	29	TQ	7233
Bedhampton	27	SU	6906
Bedingfield	55	TM	1768
Bedlington	91	NZ	2581
Bedlinog	41	SO	0901
Bedmond	36	TL	0903
Bednall	60	SJ	9517
Bedrule	90	NT	6017
Bedruthan Steps	19	SW	8569
Bedstone	48	SO	3675
Bedwas	41	ST	1689
Bedworth	50	SP	3587
Beeby	61	SK	6608
Beech (Hants.)	35	SU	6938
Beech (Staffs.)	59	SJ	8538
Beech Hill	36	SU	6964
Beechingstoke	34	SU	0859
Beedon	35	SU	4877
Beeford	81	TA	1254
Beefstand Hill	90	NT	8214
Beeley	71	SK	2667
Beelsby	75	TA	2001
Beenham	35	SU	5868
Beer	24	SY	2289
Beercrocombe	24	ST	3220
Beer Hackett	25	ST	5911
Bee Head	24	SY	2287
Beesands	21	SX	8140
Beesby	73	TF	4680
Beeson	21	SX	8140
Beeston (Beds.)	52	TL	1648
Beeston (Ches.)	69	SJ	5358
Beeston (Norf.)	64	TF	9015
Beeston (Notts.)	61	SK	5336
Beeston (W Yorks.)	79	SE	2930
Beeston Regis	65	TG	1742
Beeswing	88	NX	8969
Beetham	77	SD	4979
Beetley	64	TF	9718
Begbroke	47	SP	4613
Begelly	42	SN	1107
Beguildy	48	SO	1979
Begwns, The	44	SO	1544
Beich Burn	107	NN	6228
Beighton (Norf.)	65	TG	3808
Beighton (S Yorks.)	71	SK	4483
Beinn a' Bha'ach Ard	127	NH	3643
Beinn a' Bheithir	106	NN	0455
Beinn a' Bhoth	131	NB	1316
Beinn a' Bhragaidh	129	NC	8100
Beinn a' Bhràghad	123	NG	4125
Beinn a' Bhuird	117	NO	0898
Beinn a'Bhùiridh	106	NN	0928
Beinn a' Bhùtha	132	NC	2934
Beinn a' Chàisgein Beag	126	NG	9682
Beinn a'Chàisgein Mór	126	NG	9878
Beinn a Chaisil	105	NM	7847
Beinn a' Chaisteil	127	NH	3781
Beinn Achaladair	106	NN	3443
Beinn a' Chaoinich	123	NG	8618
Beinn a'Chaol-airigh	104	NM	3517
Beinn a' Chaolais	125	NG	2199
Beinn a' Chaorainn (Grampn.)	117	NJ	0401
Beinn a' Chaorrainn (Highld.)	115	NN	3884
Beinn a' Chapuill	123	NG	8215
Beinn a' Charnain	124	NF	8988
Beinn a' Chearcaill	123	NG	4650
Beinn a' Chlachain	123	NG	7147
Beinn a' Chlachair	116	NN	4778
Beinn a' Chlaidheimh	127	NH	0677
Beinn a'Choin	100	NN	3512
Beinn a'Chreachain	107	NN	3743
Beinn a'Chroin	107	NN	3918
Beinn a'Chrùlaiste	106	NN	2456
Beinn a'Chuallaich	107	NN	6861
Beinn a' Chùirn	123	NG	8621
Beinn a'Ghlinne Bhig	123	NG	3945
Beinn a' Ghlinne Mhóir	104	NM	3421
Beinn a' Ghlo	117	NN	9673
Beinn a' Ghràig	105	NM	5437
Beinn Aird da Loch	132	NC	2831
Beinn Airein	111	NM	4079
Beinn Airigh Charr	126	NG	9376
Beinn Alligin	123	NG	8661
Beinn a'Mhanaich	100	NS	2694
Beinn a' Mhùinidh	126	NH	0366
Beinn an Amair	132	NC	3565
Beinn an Dòthaidh	106	NN	3240
Beinn an Eòin (Highld.)	127	NC	3808
Beinn an Eòin (Highld.)	126	NG	9064
Beinn an Lochain	100	NN	2107
Beinn an Oir	98	NR	4974
Beinn an t-Sneachda	114	NM	9880
Beinn an Tuirc	92	NR	7536
Beinn a'Sgà	123	NG	4356
Beinn Bhalgairean	106	NN	2023
Beinn Bhàn (Highld.)	123	NG	8044
Beinn Bhàn (Highld.)	115	NN	1285
Beinn Bhàn (Islay)	98	NR	4056
Beinn Bharrain	92	NR	8942
Beinn Bheag (Highld.)	115	NH	0800
Beinn Bheag (Strath.)	100	NS	1293
Beinn Bheigeir	98	NR	4356
Beinn Bheula	100	NS	1598
Beinn Bhreac (Central)	101	NN	4713
Beinn Bhreac (Central)	101	NS	4196
Beinn Bhreac (Colonsay)	98	NR	3796
Beinn Bhreac (Grampn.)	117	NO	0596
Beinn Bhreac (Highld.)	133	NC	6056
Beinn Bhreac (Highld.)	123	NG	8363
Beinn Bhreac (Highld.)	116	NH	7527
Beinn Bhreac (Highld.)	116	NH	7837
Beinn Bhreac (Highld.)	111	NM	5969
Beinn Bhreac (Island of Arran)	92	NR	9531
Beinn Bhreac (Island of Skye)	122	NG	2553
Beinn Bhreac (Island of Skye)	122	NG	3426
Beinn Bhreac (Island of Skye)	123	NG	4328
Beeinn Bhreac (Islay)	98	NR	3571
Beinn Bhreac (Jura)	98	NR	5377
Beinn Bhreac (Jura)	98	NR	5990
Beinn Bhreac (Soay, Island of Skye)	123	NG	4615
Beinn Bhreac (Strath.)	106	NM	9940
Beinn Bhreac (Strath.)	100	NN	0210
Beinn Bhreac (Strath.)	92	NR	7538
Beinn Bhreac (Strath.)	92	NR	7847
Beinn Bhreac (Strath.)	100	NR	9877
Beinn Bhreac (Strath.)	100	NS	0576
Beinn Bhreac (Strath.)	100	NS	3299
Beinn Bhreac (Tays.)	107	NN	7340
Beinn Bhreac (Tays.)	117	NN	8682
Beinn Bhreac-liath	106	NN	3033
Beinn Bhreac Mhór	116	NH	6719
Beinn Bhrotain	117	NN	9592
Beinn Bhuidhe (Highld.)	111	NM	6053
Beinn Bhuidhe (Highld.)	111	NM	8296
Beinn Bhuidhe (Strath.)	105	NM	5940
Beinn Bhuidhe (Strath.)	106	NN	2018
Beinn Bhuidhe Mhór	116	NH	7840
Beinn Bragar	131	NB	2643
Beinn Ceannabeinne	133	NC	4264
Beinn Chàiteag	135	ND	1347
Beinn Chaorach	100	NS	2892
Beinn Chapull	106	NM	9319
Beinn Charnach Bheag	122	NG	2757
Beinn Cheathaich	107	NN	4432
Beinn Chlaonleud	111	NM	7352
Beinn Chlianaig	115	NN	2978
Beinn Chreagach (Island of Mull)	105	NM	5121
Beinn Chreagach (Island of Skye)	122	NG	2853
Beinn Chreagach (Ulva)	105	NM	4040
Beinn Chreagach Mhór	105	NM	6339
Beinn Churalain	106	NM	9846
Beinn Damh	126	NG	8851
Beinn Dearg (Central)	101	NN	5803
Beinn Dearg (Highld.)	132	NC	2765
Beinn Dearg (Highld.)	127	NH	2581
Beinn Dearg (Highld.)	127	NH	2868
Beinn Dearg (Strath.)	100	NN	0204
Beinn Dearg (Tays.)	117	NN	8577
Beinn Dearg Bad Chailleach	126	NG	9187
Beinn Dearg Mhór	126	NG	8692
Beinn Dearg Mór	126	NH	0379
Beinn Dhorain	134	NC	9215
Beinn Dhubh	125	NB	0800
Beinn Domhnaill	128	NH	6796
Beinn Donachain	106	NN	1931
Beinn Donn	106	NM	9647
Beinn Dòrain	106	NN	3238
Beinn Dronaig	114	NH	0237
Beinn Dubh (Central)	101	NN	4004
Beinn Dubh (Islay)	98	NR	4263
Beinn Dubhain	134	NC	9320
Beinn Dubhchraig	106	NN	3025
Beinn Each	107	NN	6015
Beinn Edra	123	NG	4562
Beinn Eich	100	NS	3094
Beinn Eighe	126	NG	9659
Beinn Eighe National Nature Reserve	126	NG	9861
Beinn Eilde	116	NN	5684
Beinn Eilideach	127	NH	1692
Beinn Enaiglair	127	NH	2280
Beinn Eunaich	106	NN	1332
Beinneun Forest	115	NH	2207
Beinn Fhada or Ben Attow	114	NH	0118
Beinn Fhionnlaidh	106	NN	0949
Beinn Gàire	111	NM	7874
Beinn Gharbh	132	NC	2122
Beinn Ghlas (Strath.)	106	NM	9525
Beinn Ghlas (Strath.)	106	NN	1318
Beinn Ghlas (Strath.)	100	NR	9899
Beinn Ghobhlach	127	NH	0594
Beinn Ghuilbin	117	NH	8917
Beinn Ghuilean	92	NR	7217
Beinn Heasgarnich	107	NN	4138
Beinn Iadain	111	NM	6955
Beinn Iaruinn	115	NN	2989
Beinn Ime	100	NN	2508
Beinn Inverveigh	106	NN	2738
Beinn Iutharn Mhór	117	NO	0479
Beinn Làir	126	NG	9873
Beinn Leabhain	107	NN	5728
Beinn Leòid	132	NC	3229
Beinn Liath Bheag	127	NH	2473
Beinn Liath Mhór a'Ghiubhais Li	127	NH	2871
Beinn Lochain (Strath.)	100	NN	1500
Beinn Lochain (Strath.)	92	NR	9037
Beinn Loinne	115	NH	1507
Beinn Lunndaidh	129	NC	7802
Beinn Maol Chaluim	106	NN	1351
Beinn Mhanach	107	NN	3741
Beinn Mheadhoin (Highld.)	111	NM	7951
Beinn Mheadhoin (Highld.)	106	NM	8869
Beinn Mheadhonach (Isle of Lewis)	131	NB	0923
Beinn Mheadhonach (Strath.)	106	NN	0236
Beinn Mhic-Mhonaidh	106	NN	2034
Beinn Mholach (Isle of Lewis)	131	NB	3538
Beinn Mholach (Tays.)	107	NN	5865
Beinn Mhór (Grampn.)	117	NH	9928
Beinn Mhór (Islay)	98	NR	2940
Beinn Mhór (Isle of Lewis)	131	NB	2509
Beinn Mhór (North Uist)	124	NF	8976
Beinn Mhór (South Uist)	112	NF	8031
Beinn Mhór (Strath.)	105	NM	7921
Beinn Mhór (Strath.)	100	NS	1090
Beinn na Boineid	122	NG	2339
Beinn na Caillich (Highld.)	111	NG	7906
Beinn na Caillich (Island of Skye)	123	NG	6023
Beinn Na Cille	111	NM	8554
Beinn na Crò	123	NG	5623
Beinn na Croise	105	NM	5625
Beinn na Drise	105	NM	4742
Beinn na Greine	123	NG	4541
Beinn na Gucaig	106	NN	0665
Beinn na h-Uamha	111	NM	6853
Beinn na Lap	107	NN	3769
Beinn na Lice	92	NR	6008
Beinn nam Bad Mór	134	NC	9955
Beinn nam Beathrach	111	NM	7556
Beinn nam Bò	134	NC	7858
Beinn nan Aighenan	106	NN	1440
Beinn nan Cabar	111	NM	7686
Beinn nan Caorach	123	NG	8712
Beinn nan Càrn	123	NG	6318
Beinn nan Cuithean	122	NG	3129
Beinn nan Eun	128	NH	4475
Beinn nan Imirean	107	NN	4130
Beinn nan Losgann	111	NM	5365
Beinn nan Lus	106	NN	1337
Beinn nan Ramh	127	NH	1466
Beinn na Seamraig	123	NG	7318
Beinn na Seilg	111	NM	4564
Beinn na Srèine	105	NM	4530
Beinn na Sròine	106	NN	2328
Beinn Odhar	106	NN	3333
Beinn Odhar Bheag	111	NM	8477
Beinn Ràtha	134	NC	9561
Beinn Resipol	111	NM	7665
Beinn Rifa-gil	134	NC	7448
Beinn Ruadh (Highld.)	134	NC	8459
Beinn Ruadh (Strath.)	100	NS	1371
Beinn Ruadh (Strath.)	100	NS	1588
Beinn Ruisg	100	NS	3291
Beinn Sgaillinish	98	NR	6184
Beinn Sgeireach	133	NC	4511
Beinn Sgreamhaidh	133	NC	4415
Beinn Sgritheall	123	NG	8312
Beinn Sgulaird	106	NN	0545
Beinn Shléibhe	124	NF	9283
Beinn Sholum	98	NR	3949
Beinn Spionnaidh	132	NC	3657
Beinn Stumanadh	133	NC	6449
Beinn Suidhe	106	NN	2139
Beinn Talaidh	105	NM	6234
Beinn Tarsuinn	92	NR	9541
Beinn Tart a'Mhill	98	NR	2056
Beinn Teallach	115	NN	3686
Beinn Tharsuinn (Highld.)	127	NH	0543
Beinn Tharsuinn (Highld.)	128	NH	4182
Beinn Tharsuinn (Highld.)	128	NH	6079
Beinn Trilleachan	106	NN	0843
Beinn Tulaichean	107	NN	4119
Beinn Udlaidh	106	NN	2732
Beinn Udlamain	116	NN	5874
Beinn Uidhe	132	NC	2825
Beinn Uird	101	NS	3998
Beinn Ulbhaidh	128	NH	4396
Beinn Uraraidh	98	NR	4054
Beith	93	NS	3454
Bekesbourne	31	TR	1955
Belaugh	65	TG	2818
Belbroughton	49	SO	9177
Belchamp Otten	54	TL	8041
Belchamp St. Paul	54	TL	7942
Belchamp Walter	54	TL	8240
Belchford	73	TF	2975
Belford	97	NU	1033
Belhelvie	119	NJ	9417
Bellabeg	118	NJ	3513
Bellanoch	99	NR	7992
Bellaty	108	NO	2459
Bell Busk	78	SD	9056
Bell Craig	89	NT	1812
Belleau	73	TF	4078
Bellehiglash	117	NJ	1837
Belle Isle	83	SD	3996
Bellerby	84	SE	1192
Bell Hill	90	NT	8409
Belliehill	109	NO	5663
Bellingdon	36	SP	9405
Bellingham	90	NY	8383
Belloch	92	NR	6737
Bellochantuy	92	NR	6632
Bellochantuy Bay	92	NR	6432
Bell Rock or Inchcape	109	NO	7626
Bellsbank	93	NS	4804
Bellshill (Northum.)	97	NU	1230
Bellshill (Strath.)	101	NS	7360
Bellsmyre	101	NS	4076
Bellspool	95	NT	1635
Bellsquarry	102	NT	0465
Bells Yew Green	29	TQ	6136
Bellybought Hill	88	NX	9099
Bellymore	86	NX	2386
Belmaduthy	128	NH	6556
Belmesthorpe	62	TF	0410
Belmont (Lancs.)	69	SD	6715
Belmont (Unst)	143	HP	5600
Belmont Castle	108	NO	2843
Belmont Resr.	69	SD	6717
Belnacraig	118	NJ	3716
Belnahua Fladda	105	NM	7112
Belowda	19	SW	9661
Belper	60	SK	3447
Belsay	91	NZ	1078
Belses	96	NT	5725
Belsford	21	SX	7659
Belstead	55	TM	1341
Belston	93	NS	3820
Belstone	21	SX	6193
Belthorn	77	SD	7124
Beltoft	74	SE	8006
Belton (Humbs.)	74	SE	7806
Belton (Leic.)	61	SK	4420
Belton (Leic.)	62	SK	8101
Belton (Lincs.)	62	SK	9239
Belton (Norf.)	65	TG	4802
Belvedere	37	TQ	4978
Belvide Resr.	59	SJ	8610
Belvoir	62	SK	8133
Bembridge	27	SZ	6488
Bembridge Airport	27	SZ	6387
Bembridge Point	27	SZ	6488
Bemersyde	96	NT	5933
Bempton	81	TA	1972
Benachally	108	NO	0649
Benachie Forest	121	NJ	6820
Benacre	55	TM	5184
Ben Aigan	120	NJ	3048
Ben Alder	107	NN	4971
Ben Alder Forest	116	NN	5375
Ben Alder Lodge	116	NN	5778
Ben Alisky	135	ND	0438
Ben An	101	NN	5008
Benaquhallie	119	NJ	6008
Ben Armine	133	NC	6828
Ben Armine Forest	133	NC	6621
Ben Armine Lodge	133	NC	7019
Ben Arnaboll	133	NC	4559
Ben Arthur	100	NN	2505
Benarty Hill	102	NT	1597
Ben Aslak	123	NG	7519
Ben Attow or Beinn Fhada	114	NH	0118
Ben Auskaird	132	NC	2140
Ben Avon	117	NJ	1401
Benbecula (is.)	124	NF	8251
Benbecula Aerodrome	124	NF	7856
Benbeoch	93	NS	4908
Benbrack (Dumf. and Galwy.)	87	NS	5300
Benbrack (Dumf. and Galwy.)	88	NX	5975
Benbrack (Dumf. and Galwy.)	88	NX	6796
Benbrack (Strath.)	93	NS	5305
Ben Buie	105	NM	6027
Benbuie	88	NX	7196
Ben Casgro	131	NB	4126
Ben Challum	107	NN	3832
Ben Chonzie	107	NN	7730
Ben Clach	107	NN	7515
Ben Cleuch	102	NN	9000
Ben Cliad	112	NF	6704
Ben Connan	122	NG	1940
Ben Corkeval	122	NG	1844
Ben Cruachan	106	NN	0730
Ben-damph Forest	126	NG	8852
Bendcallt (mt.)	128	NH	5570
Bendeallt	128	NH	5570
Ben Dell	131	NB	5056
Benderloch	106	NM	9038
Benderloch (dist.)	106	NM	9139
Ben Donich	100	NN	2104
Bendronaig Lodge	114	NH	0138
Ben Duagrich	123	NG	3938
Ben Earb	108	NO	0769
Benenden	30	TQ	8033
Beneraird	86	NX	1378
Ben Ettow	122	NG	1752
Benfield	86	NX	3764
Bengairn	87	NX	7654
Ben Garrisdale	99	NR	6394
Bengate	65	TG	3027
Ben Geary	122	NG	2561
Ben Glas	106	NN	3419
Ben Glas Burn	106	NN	3218
Bengray	88	NX	6259
Ben Griam Beg	134	NC	8341
Ben Griam Mór	134	NC	8039
Ben Gulabin	108	NO	1072
Ben Halton	107	NN	7220
Ben Hee	133	NC	4234
Ben Hiant	111	NM	5363
Ben Hogh	110	NM	1858
Benholm	109	NO	8069
Ben Hope	133	NC	4749
Ben Horn	129	NC	8006
Ben Hutig	133	NC	5365
Ben Idrigill	122	NG	2338
Beningbrough	79	SE	5257
Benington (Herts.)	37	TL	3023
Benington (Lincs.)	63	TF	3946
Beninner	88	NX	6096
Ben Klibreck	133	NC	6131
Ben Laga	111	NM	6462
Ben Lawers	107	NN	6341
Ben Ledi	101	NN	5609
Ben Lee	123	NG	5033
Benllech	66	SH	5182
Ben Lomond	101	NN	3602
Ben Loyal	133	NC	5748
Ben Lui	106	NN	2626
Ben Luskentyre	125	NG	0999
Ben Macdui (Beinn MacDuibh)	117	NN	9898
Ben Meabost	123	NG	5316
Ben Mór Coigach	127	NC	0904
Benmore (Central)	107	NN	4125
Ben More (Central)	107	NN	4324
Ben More (Island of Mull)	105	NM	5233
Benmore (Strath.)	100	NS	1385
Ben More Assynt	132	NC	3120
Benmore Forest (Highld.)	132	NC	3216
Benmore Forest (Strath.)	100	NS	1682
Benmore Lodge	132	NC	3211
Bennachie	121	NJ	6522
Bennacott	20	SX	2991
Bennan (Dumf. and Galwy.)	88	NX	5679
Bennan (Dumf. and Galwy.)	88	NX	7995
Bennan (Island of Arran)	92	NR	9821
Bennane Head	86	NX	0986
Bennan Head	92	NR	9920
Bennecarrigan	92	NR	9423
Ben Nevis	106	NN	1671
Benniworth	73	TF	2081
Benover	29	TQ	7048
Ben Raah	124	NB	0301
Ben Rinnes	117	NJ	2435
Ben Scrien	112	NF	7911
Ben Shieldaig	123	NG	8451
Benson	36	SU	6191
Ben Stack	132	NC	2642
Ben Starav	106	NN	1242
Ben Strome	132	NC	2436
Ben Tangaval	112	NL	6399
Ben Tee	115	NN	2497
Benthall (Northum.)	97	NU	2328
Benthall (Shrops.)	59	SJ	6602
Bentham	46	SO	9116
Benthoul	119	NJ	8003
Ben Tianavaig	123	NG	5140
Ben Tirran	118	NO	3774
Bentley (Hants.)	35	SU	7844
Bentley (Here. and Worc.)	50	SO	9966
Bentley (Humbs.)	74	TA	0135
Bentley (S Yorks.)	71	SE	5605
Bentley (Warw.)	60	SP	2895
Bentley Heath	50	SP	1676
Benton	23	SS	6536
Bentpath	89	NY	3190
Bentworth	35	SU	6640
Benty Cowan Hill	88	NS	5808
Ben Uigshader	122	NG	3649
Benvane (Central)	101	NN	5313
Benvane (Strath.)	100	NN	2709
Ben Venue	101	NN	4706
Benvie	108	NO	3231
Ben Vorlich (Strath.)	100	NN	2912
Ben Vorlich (Tays.)	107	NN	6319
Ben Vrackie	108	NN	9563
Ben Vuirich	108	NN	9969
Benwick	53	TL	3490
Ben Wyvis	128	NH	4668
Benyellary	86	NX	4183
Beoley	50	SP	0669
Beoraidbeg	111	NM	6793
Beorgs of Skelberry	142	HU	3588
Bepton	27	SU	8518
Berden	53	TL	4629
Berea	42	SM	7929
Bere Alston	20	SX	4466
Bere Ferrers	20	SX	4563
Berepper	18	SW	6522
Bere Regis	25	SY	8494
Bergh Apton	65	TG	3000
Berinsfield	47	SU	5696
Berkeley	46	ST	6899
Berkhamsted	36	SP	9907
Berkley	33	ST	8049
Berkswell	50	SP	2479
Bermondsey	37	TQ	3579
Bernard Wharf (sbk.)	77	SD	3550
Bernera	123	NG	8020
Bernera Island	105	NM	7939
Berneray (North Uist)	124	NF	9182
Berneray (W Isles)	112	NL	5680
Berney Arms Station	65	TG	4505
Bernice	100	NS	1391
Bernisdale	123	NG	4050
Berrick Salome	36	SU	6293
Berriedale	135	ND	1223
Berriedale Water	135	ND	0630
Berrier	83	NY	3929
Berriew	58	SJ	1801
Berrington (Northum.)	97	NU	0043
Berrington (Shrops.)	59	SJ	5206
Berrow	32	ST	2952
Berrow Flats (sbk.)	32	ST	2854
Berrow Green	49	SO	7458
Berry Head	21	SX	9456
Berry Hill	45	SO	5712
Berryhillock	121	NJ	5060
Berryl's Point	19	SW	8467
Berrynarbor	23	SS	5546
Berry Pomeroy	21	SX	8261
Berry, The (mt.)	136	ND	2490
Berry Top (mt.)	119	NO	8695
Bersham	58	SJ	3048
Berstane	136	HY	4610
Bersted	28	SU	9300
Berst Ness	138	HY	4441
Berth, The (ant.)	58	SJ	4323
Bervie Bay	109	NO	8372
Bervie Water	119	NO	7774
Berwick	29	TQ	5105
Berwick Bassett	34	SU	0973
Berwick Hill	91	NZ	1775
Berwick St. James	34	SU	0739
Berwick St. John	26	ST	9421
Berwick St. Leonard	25	ST	9233
Berwick-upon-Tweed	97	NT	9953
Berwyn (mt.)	67	SJ	0632
Bescar Lane Station	68	SD	3914
Besford	49	SO	9144
Bessacarr	71	SE	6101
Bessels Leigh	47	SP	4501
Bessingham	65	TG	1636
Besthorpe (Norf.)	64	TM	0695
Besthorpe (Notts.)	72	SK	8264
Beswick	81	TA	0148
Betchworth	28	TQ	2149
Bethel	66	SH	5265
Bethersden	30	TQ	9240
Bethesda (Dyfed)	42	SN	0918
Bethesda (Gwyn.)	67	SH	6266
Bethlehem	40	SN	6825
Bethnal Green	37	TQ	3583
Betley	59	SJ	7548
Betsham	30	TQ	6071
Betteshanger	31	TR	3152
Bettiscombe	24	SY	3999
Bettisfield	58	SJ	4535
Betton (Shrops.)	58	SJ	3102
Betton (Shrops.)	59	SJ	6836
Bettws	45	SO	2919

Boot Brobury

Boot 82 NY 1700
Boothby Graffoe 72 SK 9859
Boothby Pagnell 62 SK 9730
Boothstown 69 SD 7200
Booth Wood Resr. 70 SE 0215
Bootle (Cumbr.) 76 SD 1088
Bootle (Mers.) 68 SJ 3394
Bootle Fell 76 SD 1488
Bootle Station 82 SD 0989
Boquhan 101 NS 5387
Boraston 50 SO 6170
Borden 30 TQ 8863
Bordley 78 SD 9465
Bordon Camp 27 SU 7935
Boreham (Essex) 38 TL 7509
Boreham (Wilts.) 33 ST 8944
Boreham Street 29 TQ 6611
Borehamwood 37 TQ 1996
Boreland (Central) 107 NN 5534
Boreland (Dumf. and Galwy.) 89 NY 1790
Boreland Hill 88 NX 9460
Boreray (North Uist) 124 NF 8581
Boreray (St. Kilda or Hirta) 124 NA 1505
Bore Stane 102 NT 1459
Bore, The 138 HY 4956
Borgie 133 NC 6759
Borgie Forest 133 NC 6655
Borgue (Dumf. and Galwy.) 87 NX 6248
Borgue (Highld.) 135 ND 1325
Borle Brook 49 SO 7087
Borley 54 TL 8442
Bornesketaig 122 NG 3771
Borness 87 NX 6145
Borness Point 87 NX 6144
Boroughbridge 79 SE 3966
Borough Green 29 TQ 6057
Borras Head 58 SJ 3653
Borreraig 122 NG 1853
Borrobol Forest 134 NC 7726
Borrobol Lodge 134 NC 8626
Borrodale Burn 111 NM 7086
Borrowash 60 SK 4134
Borrow Beck 83 NY 5205
Borrowby 85 SE 4289
Borrowdale (Cumbr.) 82 NY 2416
Borrowdale (Cumbr.) 82 NY 2514
Borrowdale (Cumbr.) 83 NY 5703
Borrowdale Fells 82 NY 2512
Borrowfield 119 NO 8293
Borth 56 SN 6089
Borthwickbrae 89 NT 4113
Borthwickshiels 89 NT 4315
Borthwick Water 89 NT 4112
Borve (Barra) 112 NF 6501
Borve (Berneray, North Uist) 124 NF 9181
Borve (Harris, W Isles) 124 NG 0294
Borve (Island of Skye) 123 NG 4448
Borve Point 112 NF 6402
Borve River 131 NB 4254
Borwick 77 SD 5273
Bosavern 18 SW 3730
Bosbury 49 SO 6943
Boscastle 20 SX 0990
Boscobel House (ant.) 59 SJ 8308
Boscombe (Dorset) 26 SZ 1191
Boscombe (Wilts.) 34 SU 2038
Boscoppa 19 SX 0353
Bosham 27 SU 8004
Bosherston 42 SR 9694
Boskednan 18 SW 4434
Bosley 69 SJ 9165
Bossall 80 SE 7160
Bossiney 20 SX 0688
Bossingham 31 TR 1549
Bostock Green 69 SJ 6769
Boston 63 TF 3244
Boston Aerodrome 63 TF 2943
Boston Deeps (chan.) 63 TF 4947
Boston Spa 79 SE 4245
Boswinger 19 SW 9941
Botallack 18 SW 3632
Botany Bay 37 TQ 2999
Botcheston 61 SK 4804
Botesdale 54 TM 0475
Bothal 91 NZ 2386
Bothamsall 71 SK 6773
Bothel 82 NY 1838
Bothenhampton 25 SY 4791
Bothwell 101 NS 7058
Bothwell Water 103 NT 6666
Botley (Bucks.) 36 SP 9802
Botley (Hants.) 27 SU 5112
Botley (Oxon.) 47 SP 4806
Botolphs 28 TQ 1909
Bottacks 128 NH 4860
Bottesford (Humbs.) 74 SE 9107
Bottesford (Leic.) 61 SK 8038
Bottisham 53 TL 5460
Bottle Island 126 NB 9502
Bottomcraig 109 NO 3724
Bottoms 78 SD 9321
Botton Head 77 SD 6661
Botusfleming 20 SX 4061
Botwnnog 66 SH 2631
Boughrood 44 SO 1239
Boughspring 45 ST 5597
Boughton (Norf.) 64 TF 7002
Boughton (Northants.) 51 SP 7565
Boughton (Notts.) 71 SK 6768
Boughton Aluph 31 TR 0348
Boughton Green 29 TQ 7651
Boughton House (ant.) 52 SP 9081
Boughton Lees 31 TR 0247
Boughton Malherbe 30 TQ 8849
Boughton Street 31 TR 0559
Boulby 85 NZ 7519
Bouldon 48 SO 5485
Boulmer 91 NU 2614
Boulmer Haven 91 NU 2613
Boulston 42 SM 9812
Boulsworth Hill 78 SD 9335
Boultenstone 118 NJ 4110
Boultham 72 SK 9568
Bourn 53 TL 3256
Bourne 62 TF 0920
Bourne End (Beds.) 52 SP 9644
Bourne End (Bucks.) 36 SU 8987
Bourne End (Herts.) 36 TL 0206
Bournemouth 26 SZ 0991
Bournemouth (Hurn) Airport 26 SZ 1198
Bournes Green 46 SO 9104
Bournheath 49 SO 9474
Bournmoor 84 NZ 3051
Bournville 50 SP 0480
Bourton (Avon) 32 ST 3864
Bourton (Dorset) 25 ST 7630
Bourton (Oxon.) 34 SU 2387
Bourton (Shrops.) 59 SO 5996
Bourton on Dunsmore 50 SP 4370
Bourton-on-the-Hill 47 SP 1732
Bourton-on-the-Water 47 SP 1620
Bousd 110 NM 2563
Boveney 36 SU 9377
Boverton 41 SS 9868
Bovey Tracey 21 SX 8178
Bovingdon 36 TL 0103
Bovington Camp 25 SY 8389
Bow 37 TQ 3783
Bow (Devon) 23 SS 7201
Bow (Flotta, Orkney) 136 ND 3693
Bowbank 84 NY 9423
Bow Brickhill 52 SP 9034
Bowburn 84 NZ 3038
Bowcombe 27 SZ 4786
Bowd 24 SY 1190
Bowden (Borders) 96 NT 5530
Bowden (Devon) 21 SX 8448
Bowden Hill 34 ST 9367
Bowdon 69 SJ 7586
Bower 90 NY 7583
Bowerchalke 26 SU 0122
Bowermadden 135 ND 2364
Bowers Gifford 38 TQ 7588
Bowershall 102 NT 0991
Bowertower 135 ND 2362
Bowes 84 NY 9913
Bowes Moor 84 NY 9311
Bow Fell 82 NY 2406
Bow Head 138 HY 4553
Bowhill 96 NT 4227
Bowland 96 NT 4540
Bowland Bridge 83 SD 4189
Bowley 45 SO 5352
Bowlhead Green 28 SU 9138
Bowling 101 NS 4473
Bowling Bank 58 SJ 3948
Bowling Green 49 SO 8151
Bowmanstead 82 SD 3096
Bowmont Forest 96 NT 7328
Bowmont Water 97 NT 8125
Bowmore 98 NR 3159
Bowness-on-Solway 89 NY 2262
Bowness-on-Windermere 83 SD 4097
Bow of Fife 103 NO 3112
Bowood House 34 ST 9769
Bowsden 97 NT 9941
Bowside Lodge 134 NC 8261
Bow Street 57 SN 6284
Bowthorpe 65 TG 1709
Box (Glos.) 46 SO 8600
Box (Wilts.) 33 ST 8268
Boxbush 46 SO 7412
Boxford (Berks.) 34 SU 4271
Boxford (Suff.) 54 TL 9640
Boxgrove 27 SU 9007
Boxley 30 TQ 7759
Boxted (Essex) 54 TM 0033
Boxted (Suff.) 54 TL 8250
Boxted Cross 54 TM 0032
Boxworth 53 TL 3464
Boylestone 60 SK 1835
Boyndie 121 NJ 6463
Boyndie Bay 121 NJ 6765
Boyndlie 121 NJ 9162
Boyne Bay 121 NJ 6166
Boynton 81 TA 1368
Boysack 109 NO 6249
Boyton (Corn.) 20 SX 3192
Boyton (Suff.) 55 TM 3747
Boyton (Wilts.) 34 ST 9539
Bozeat 52 SP 9059
Braaid 76 SC 3176
Braal Castle 135 ND 1360
Brabling Green 55 TM 2964
Brabourne 31 TR 1041
Brabourne Lees 31 TR 0840
Brabster 135 ND 3269
Bracadale 122 NG 3538
Braceborough 62 TF 0713
Bracebridge Heath 72 SK 9767
Braceby 62 TF 0135
Bracewell 78 SD 8648
Brackenfield 71 SK 3759
Brackenthwaite 82 NY 1522
Bracklesham Bay 27 SU 8095
Brackletter 115 NN 1882
Brackley (Northants.) 51 SP 5837
Brackley (Strath.) 92 NR 7941
Bracknell 36 SU 8769
Braco 108 NN 8309
Bracobrae 121 NJ 5053
Braco Castle (ant.) 101 NN 8211
Bracon Ash 65 TM 1899
Bracora 111 NM 7192
Bracorina 111 NM 7292
Bradbourne 60 SK 2052
Bradbury 84 NZ 3128
Bradda 76 SC 1970
Bradda Head 76 SC 1870
Bradden 51 SP 6448
Braddock 19 SX 1662
Bradenham 36 SU 8297
Bradenham 64 TF 9208
Bradenstoke 34 SU 0079
Bradfield (Berks.) 35 SU 6072
Bradfield (Essex) 55 TM 1430
Bradfield (Norf.) 65 TG 2633
Bradfield Combust 54 TL 8957
Bradfield Green 69 SJ 6859
Bradfield Moors 71 SK 2292
Bradfield St. Clare 54 TL 9057
Bradfield St. George 54 TL 9059
Bradford (Devon) 22 SS 4207
Bradford (Northum.) 97 NU 1532
Bradford (W Yorks.) 78 SE 1633
Bradford Abbas 25 ST 5814
Bradford Leigh 33 ST 8362
Bradford-on-Avon 33 ST 8260
Bradford-on-Tone 24 ST 1722
Bradford Peverell 25 SY 6592
Brading 27 SZ 6087
Bradley (Derby.) 60 SK 2145
Bradley (Hants.) 35 SU 6341
Bradley (Here. and Worc.) 50 SO 9860
Bradley (Humbs.) 75 TA 2406
Bradley (Staffs.) 59 SJ 8717
Bradley Green 50 SO 9861
Bradley in the Moors 60 SK 0541
Bradmore 61 SK 5831
Bradninch 23 SS 9903
Bradnop 60 SK 0155
Bradpole 25 SY 4794
Bradshaw 69 SD 7312
Bradstone 20 SX 3880
Bradwell (Bucks.) 52 SP 8339
Bradwell (Derby.) 70 SK 1781
Bradwell (Essex) 38 TL 8023
Bradwell (Norf.) 65 TG 5003
Bradwell Green 69 SJ 7563
Bradwell Grove 47 SP 2308
Bradwell-on-Sea 39 TM 0006
Bradwell Waterside 39 TL 9907
Bradworthy 22 SS 3213
Brae (Highld.) 128 NC 4300
Brae (Highld.) 126 NG 8185
Brae (Highld.) 128 NH 6663
Brae (Shetld.) 141 HU 3567
Braeantra 128 NH 5678
Braedownie 117 NO 2875
Braefield 116 NH 4130
Braegrum 108 NO 0024
Braehead (Orkney) 136 HY 5101
Braehead (Strath.) 95 NS 8134
Braehead (Strath.) 95 NS 9550
Braehead (Tays.) 109 NO 6852
Braehead (Westray) 138 HY 4447
Braehead (Wigtown.) 87 NX 4252
Braehoulland 142 HU 2479
Braelangwell Lodge 128 NH 5192
Braemar (Grampn.) 117 NO 1591
Braemar (Grampn.) (dist.) 117 NO 1493
Braemore 135 ND 0630
Braemore Forest 127 NH 2076
Brae of Achnahaird 132 NC 0013
Brae of Glenbervie 119 NO 7684
Brae of Moan 138 HY 3733
Braeriach (Braigh Riabhach) 117 NN 9599
Braeroy Forest 115 NN 3791
Brae Roy Lodge 115 NN 3391
Braeside 100 NS 2375
Braes of Abernethy 117 NJ 0715
Braes of Balquhidder 107 NN 4921
Braes of Doune 101 NN 7005
Braes of Glenlivet 117 NJ 2522
Braes of Lorn 105 NM 8717
Braes of Ogilvie 102 NN 8907
Braes of the Carse 108 NO 2530
Braes o' Lochaber 115 NN 3280
Braes, The 123 NG 5234
Braeswick 139 HY 6037
Brae Wick 142 HU 2477
Brafferton (Durham) 84 NZ 2921
Brafferton (N Yorks.) 79 SE 4370
Brafield-on-the-Green 52 SP 8158
Braga Ness 140 HU 1948
Bragar 131 NB 2947
Bragbury End 37 TL 2621
Bragleenmore 106 NM 9020
Braich Anelog 56 SH 1427
Braich y Pwll 56 SH 1325
Braides 77 SD 4350
Braid Fell 86 NX 1166
Braid Hills 103 NT 2569
Braidley 78 SE 0380
Braidon Bay 119 NO 8777
Braidwood 95 NS 8448
Bràigh Mòr 130 NA 9916
Bràigh-nam-bàgh 125 NG 0889
Braigh Riabhach 117 NN 9599
Braigh Sròn Ghorm 117 NN 9078
Braigo 98 NR 2369
Brailes 50 SP 3139
Brailsford 60 SK 2541
Braintree 38 TL 7622
Braiseworth 55 TM 1371
Braishfield 26 SU 3725
Braithwaite 82 NY 2323
Braithwell 71 SK 5394
Bramber 28 TQ 1810
Bramcote 61 SK 5037
Bramdean 27 SU 6128
Bramerton 65 TG 2904
Bramfield (Herts.) 37 TL 2915
Bramfield (Suff.) 55 TM 4073
Bramford 55 TM 1246
Bramhall 69 SJ 8984
Bramham 79 SE 4242
Bramhope 79 SE 2443
Bramley (Hants.) 36 SU 6358
Bramley (Surrey) 28 TQ 0044
Bramley (S Yorks.) 71 SK 4892
Brampford Speke 21 SX 9298
Brampton (Cambs.) 52 TL 2170
Brampton (Cumbr.) 90 NY 5361
Brampton (Cumbr.) 83 NY 6723
Brampton (Lincs.) 72 SK 8479
Brampton (Norf.) 65 TG 2224
Brampton (Suff.) 55 TM 4381
Brampton (S Yorks.) 71 SE 4101
Brampton Abbotts 45 SO 6026
Brampton Ash 51 SP 7887
Brampton Bryan 48 SO 3672
Brampton Station 55 TM 4183
Bramshall 60 SK 0633
Bramshaw 26 SU 2615
Bramshill 36 SU 7461
Bramshill Plantation 36 SU 7562
Bramshott 27 SU 8432
Brancaster 64 TF 7743
Brancaster Bay 64 TF 7546
Brancaster Roads 64 TF 8049
Brancepeth 84 NZ 2238
Branchill 129 NJ 0852
Branderburgh 120 NJ 2371
Brandesburton 75 TA 1147
Brandeston 55 TM 2460
Brandiston 65 TG 1321
Brandon (Durham) 84 NZ 2439
Brandon (Lincs.) 62 SK 9048
Brandon (Northum.) 91 NU 0417
Brandon (Suff.) 54 TL 7886
Brandon (Warw.) 50 SP 4076
Brandon Bank 54 TL 6289
Brandon Creek 54 TL 6091
Brandon Park 54 TL 7784
Brandon Parva 64 TG 0708
Brandsby 79 SE 5872
Brands Hatch 37 TQ 5764
Brand Side 70 SK 0468
Brane 18 SW 4028
Bran End 54 TL 6525
Branksome Park 26 SZ 0490
Brannie Burn 106 NN 1616
Branscombe 24 SY 1988
Bransdale 85 SE 6296
Bransford 49 SO 7952
Bransgore 26 SZ 1897
Bransly Hill 103 NT 6770
Branston (Leic.) 61 SK 8029
Branston (Lincs.) 72 TF 0167
Branston (Staffs.) 60 SK 2221
Branstone 27 SZ 5583
Brant Broughton 62 SK 9154
Brant Fell 83 SD 6595
Brantham 55 TM 1034
Branthwaite 82 NY 0525
Brantingham 74 SE 9429
Branton 91 NU 0416
Branton 71 SE 6501
Branxholme 89 NT 4611
Branxholm Park 89 NT 4612
Branxton 97 NT 8937
Brassington 60 SK 2354
Brasted 29 TQ 4755
Brasted Chart 29 TQ 4653
Brat Bheinn 98 NR 4966
Brathens 119 NO 6798
Bratoft 73 TF 4765
Brattleby 72 SK 9480
Bratton 33 ST 9152
Bratton Castle (ant.) 33 ST 9051
Bratton Clovelly 20 SX 4691
Bratton Fleming 23 SS 6437
Bratton Seymour 25 ST 6729
Braughing 53 TL 3925
Braunston (Leic.) 62 SK 8306
Braunston (Northants.) 51 SP 5366
Braunstone 61 SK 5502
Braunton 22 SS 4836
Braunton Burrows 22 SS 4535
Brawby 80 SE 7378
Brawl 134 NC 8066
Brawlbin 135 ND 0757
Bray 36 SU 9079
Braybrooke 51 SP 7684
Brayford 23 SS 6834
Bray Shop 20 SX 3374
Braystones 82 NY 0006
Brayton 79 SE 6030
Brazacott 20 SX 2691
Breabag (mt.) 132 NC 2917
Breachacha Castle 110 NM 1553
Breachwood Green 37 TL 1522
Breackerie Water 92 NR 6413
Breaclete 131 NB 1536
Breadalbane (dist.) 107 NN 4735
Breadsall 60 SK 3639
Breadstone 46 SO 7000
Breagach Hill 118 NJ 3313
Breage 18 SW 6128
Breakachy 128 NH 4644
Breakish 123 NG 6723
Breaksea Point 41 ST 0265
Bream 45 SO 6005
Breamore 26 SU 1517
Brean 32 ST 2955
Brean Down 32 ST 2858
Brearton 79 SE 3260
Breasclete 131 NB 2135
Breaston 61 SK 4533
Breast Sand 63 TF 5427
Brechfa 43 SN 5230
Brechin 109 NO 5960
Breckles 64 TL 9594
Breck Ness 136 HY 2209
Breckrey 123 NG 5162
Breck, The 142 HU 3292
Brecon 41 SO 0428
Brecon and Abergavenny Canal 41 SO 1122
Brecon Beacons (mt.) 41 SO 0121
Bredbury 69 SJ 9292
Brede 30 TQ 8218
Bredenbury 45 SO 6056
Bredfield 55 TM 2653
Bredgar 30 TQ 8860
Bredhurst 30 TQ 7962
Bredon 49 SO 9236
Bredon Hill 50 SO 9640
Bredon's Norton 49 SO 9339
Bredwardine 45 SO 3344
Breedon on the Hill 60 SK 4022
Breich 102 NS 9560
Breighton 74 SE 7033
Breinton 45 SO 4739
Breiti Stack 139 HZ 2072
Brei Wick 141 HU 4740
Bremenium (ant.) 90 NY 8398
Bremhill 34 ST 9873
Bremia (ant.) 43 SN 6456
Brenchley 29 TQ 6741
Brendon 23 SS 7648
Brendon Common 23 SS 7645
Brendon Hills 24 ST 0135
Brenfield Bay 99 NR 8582
Brenig Resr. 67 SH 9857
Brenish 130 NA 9926
Brenish Point 124 NF 9089
Brent Eleigh 54 TL 9447
Brentford 37 TQ 1778
Brent Knoll 32 ST 3350
Brent Pelham 53 TL 4330
Brentwood 38 TQ 5993
Brenzett 31 TR 0027
Brereton 60 SK 0516
Brereton Green 69 SJ 7764
Brereton Heath 69 SJ 8064
Bressay 141 HU 5040
Bressay Sound 141 HU 4841
Bressingham 54 TM 0780
Brest Rocks 93 NS 1904
Brest Twrch 41 SN 8120
Bretby 60 SK 2923
Bretford 50 SP 4277
Bretforton 50 SP 0943
Bretherdale Head 83 NY 5705
Bretherton 69 SD 4720
Brettabister 141 HU 4857
Brettenham (Norf.) 54 TL 9383
Brettenham (Suff.) 54 TL 9653
Bretton 68 SJ 3563
Brevig 112 NL 6998
Brewham 25 ST 7136
Brewlands Bridge 108 NO 1961
Brewood 59 SJ 8808
Breydon Water 65 TG 4907
Briantspuddle 25 SY 8193
Brickendon 37 TL 3208
Bricket Wood 37 TL 1301
Bricklehampton 50 SO 9842
Bride 76 NX 4501
Bridekirk 82 NY 1133
Bridell 42 SN 1742
Bride's Ness 139 HY 7752
Bridestowe 20 SX 5189
Bridestowe and Sourton Common 21 SX 5688
Brideswell 121 NJ 5739
Bridford 21 SX 8186
Bridge 31 TR 1854
Bridge End (Lincs.) 62 TF 1436
Bridgefoot 82 NY 0529
Bridge Green 53 TL 4636
Bridgemary 27 SU 5702
Bridgend (Cumbr.) 83 NY 3914
Bridgend (Dumf. and Galwy.) 89 NT 0708
Bridgend (Fife) 103 NO 3911
Bridgend (Grampn.) 121 NJ 3731
Bridgend (Grampn.) 121 NJ 5135
Bridgend (Islay) 98 NR 3362
Bridgend (Lothian) 102 NT 0475
Bridgend (Mid Glam.) 41 SS 9079
Bridgend (Strath.) 99 NR 8592
Bridgend (Strath.) 101 NS 6970
Bridgend (Tays.) 108 NO 1224
Bridgend (Tays.) 109 NO 5368
Bridgend of Lintrathen 108 NO 2854
Bridge of Alford 119 NJ 5617
Bridge of Allan 101 NS 7897
Bridge of Avon 117 NJ 1835
Bridge of Balgie 107 NN 5746
Bridge of Brown 117 NJ 1220
Bridge of Buchat 118 NJ 3915
Bridge of Cally 108 NO 1351
Bridge of Canny 119 NO 6597
Bridge of Craigisla 108 NO 2553
Bridge of Dee 88 NX 7360
Bridge of Don 119 NJ 9409
Bridge of Dun 109 NO 6658
Bridge of Dye 119 NO 6585
Bridge of Earn 108 NO 1318
Bridge of Ericht 107 NN 5258
Bridge of Feugh 119 NO 7094
Bridge of Forss 135 ND 0368
Bridge of Gairn 118 NO 3597
Bridge of Gaur 107 NN 5056
Bridge of Muchalls 119 NO 8991
Bridge of Orchy 106 NN 2939
Bridge of Tilt 108 NN 8765
Bridge of Waithe 136 HY 2811
Bridge of Walls 140 HU 2651
Bridge of Weir 101 NS 3865
Bridgerule 22 SS 2803
Bridges 58 SO 3996
Bridge Sollers 45 SO 4142
Bridge Street 54 TL 8749
Bridgetown 23 SS 9233
Bridge Trafford 68 SJ 4471
Bridgewater Canal 69 SJ 7186
Bridgeyate 33 ST 6873
Bridgham 54 TL 9686
Bridgnorth 59 SO 7193
Bridgtown 60 SJ 9808
Bridgwater 24 ST 3037
Bridgwater Bay 32 ST 1852
Bridlington 81 TA 1766
Bridlington Bay 81 TA 1964
Bridport 25 SY 4692
Bridstow 45 SO 5824
Brierfield 78 SD 8436
Brierley (Glos.) 45 SO 6215
Brierley (Here. and Worc.) 45 SO 4956
Brierley (S Yorks.) 71 SE 4011
Brierley Hill 49 SO 9187
Briga Head 135 ND 1875
Brigg 74 TA 0007
Brigham (Cumbr.) 82 NY 0830
Brigham (Humbs.) 81 TA 0753
Brighouse 78 SE 1423
Brighstone 26 SZ 4282
Brighstone Bay 26 SZ 4180
Brighstone Forest 26 SZ 4285
Brightgate 71 SK 2659
Brighthampton 47 SP 3803
Brightling 29 TQ 6821
Brightlingsea 39 TM 0816
Brighton (Corn.) 19 SW 9054
Brighton (E Susx) 29 TQ 3105
Brighton, Hove & Worthing Municipal Airport 28 TQ 2005
Brightons 102 NS 9277
Brightwalton 34 SU 4278
Brightwell 55 TM 2543
Brightwell Baldwin 36 SU 6594
Brightwell-cum-Sotwell 35 SU 5790
Brignall 84 NZ 0712
Brig o'Turk 101 NN 5306
Brigsley 75 TA 2501
Brigsteer 83 SD 4889
Brigstock 52 SP 9485
Brill 36 SP 6513
Brilley 45 SO 2549
Brimfield 48 SO 5267
Brimington 71 SK 4073
Brimmond Hill 119 NJ 8509
Brimpsfield 46 SO 9312
Brimpton 35 SU 5564
Brims 136 ND 2888
Brims Ness (Highld.) 135 ND 0471
Brims Ness (Hoy, Orkney) 136 ND 2988
Brind 74 SE 7430
Brindister (Shetld.) 140 HU 2757
Brindister (Shetld.) 141 HU 4337
Brindle 77 SD 5924
Brindley Ford 59 SJ 8754
Brindley Heath 60 SJ 9914
Brineton 59 SJ 8013
Bring Deeps (chan.) 136 HY 2902
Bringewood Chase 48 SO 4573
Bring Head (Hoy, Shetld.) 136 HY 2702
Bring Head (Rousay) 138 HY 3733
Bringhurst 52 SP 8492
Brington 52 TL 0875
Briningham 64 TG 0334
Brinkburn Priory (ant.) 91 NZ 1198
Brinkhill 73 TF 3773
Brinkley 54 TL 6254
Brinklow 50 SP 4379
Brinkworth 34 SU 0184
Brinscall 77 SD 6321
Brinsley 61 SK 4548
Brinsop 45 SO 4344
Brinsworth 71 SK 4190
Brinton 64 TG 0335
Brinyan 136 HY 4327
Brisley 64 TF 9421
Brislington 33 ST 6170
Brisons, The 18 SW 3331
Bristol 33 ST 5872
Bristol Airport 33 ST 5064
Bristol Channel 40 SS 4267
Briston 64 TG 0632
Britannia 78 SD 8821
Britford 26 SU 1528
Briton Ferry 40 SS 7394
Britwell Salome 36 SU 6792
Brixham 21 SX 9255
Brixton 21 SX 5452
Brixton 37 TQ 3175
Brixton Deverill 33 ST 8638
Brixworth 51 SP 7470
Brize Norton 47 SP 2907
Broad Bay or Loch a Tuath 131 NB 5037
Broad Bench (pt.) 25 SY 8978
Broad Blunsdon 34 SU 1490
Broadbottom 70 SJ 9993
Broadbridge 27 SU 8105
Broadbridge Heath 28 TQ 1431
Broadbury (dist.) 20 SX 4596
Broad Cairn 117 NO 2481
Broad Campden 50 SP 1537
Broad Chalke 26 SU 0325
Broadclyst 21 SX 9897
Broad Clyst Station 21 SX 9995
Broad Down 24 SY 1793
Broadford 123 NG 6423
Broadford Aerodrome 123 NG 6925
Broadford Bay 123 NG 6524
Broad Green 49 SO 7656
Broadhaugh 89 NT 4509
Broad Haven 42 SM 8613
Broad Head 89 NY 3394
Broadheath (Gtr Mches.) 69 SJ 7689
Broadheath (Here. and Worc.) 49 SO 6665
Broadheath (Here. and Worc.) 49 SO 8156
Broadhembury 24 ST 1004
Broadhempston 21 SX 8066
Broad Hill (Cambs.) 54 TL 5976
Broadhill (Strath.) 95 NT 0029
Broad Hinton 34 SU 1076
Broadlands House 26 SU 3520
Broad Law 95 NT 1423
Broad Laying 34 SU 4362
Broadley (Grampn.) 121 NJ 4161
Broadley (Gtr Mches.) 69 SD 8716
Broadley Common 37 TL 4207
Broad Marston 50 SP 1346
Broadmayne 25 SY 7286
Broadmeadows 96 NT 4130
Broadmere 35 SU 6247
Broad Oak (Cumbr.) 82 SD 1194
Broadoak (Dorset) 25 SY 4496
Broadoak (E Susx) 29 TQ 6022
Broad Oak (E Susx) 30 TQ 8320
Broad Oak (Here. and Worc.) 45 SO 4721
Broadoak (Kent) 31 TR 1661
Broadrashes 121 NJ 4354
Broadsea Bay 86 NW 9659
Broad Sound (Dyfed) 42 SM 7307
Broad Sound (Is. of Sc.) 18 SV 8309
Broadstairs 31 TR 3967
Broadstone (Dorset) 26 SZ 0095
Broadstone (Shrops.) 48 SO 5389
Broad Street 30 TQ 8356
Broad Taing 136 HY 4217
Broad Town 34 SU 0977
Broadwas 49 SO 7555
Broadwater 28 TQ 1504
Broadway (Here. and Worc.) 50 SP 0937
Broadway (Somer.) 24 ST 3215
Broadway Hill 50 SP 1136
Broadwell (Glos.) 47 SP 2027
Broadwell (Oxon.) 47 SP 2503
Broadwell (Warw.) 51 SP 4565
Broadwell House 84 NY 9153
Broadwell Lane End 45 SO 5811
Broadwey 25 SY 6683
Broadwindsor 25 ST 4302
Broadwood-Kelly 23 SS 6105
Broadwoodwidger 20 SX 4089
Brobury 45 SO 3444

Brochel Caergwrle

Brochel 123 NG 5846
Brockbridge 27 SU 6018
Brockdam 97 NU 1624
Brockdish 55 TM 2179
Brockenhurst 26 SU 2902
Brocketsbrae 95 NS 8239
Brockford Street 55 TM 1166
Brockhall 51 SP 6362
Brockham 28 TQ 2049
Brockhampton 45 SO 5932
Brockholes 70 SE 1411
Brocklesby 75 TA 1311
Brockley 33 ST 4666
Brockley Green 54 TL 8254
Brockloch Hill (Dumf. and Galwy.) 87 NX 5173
Brockloch Hill (Dumf. and Galwy.) 88 NX 8179
Brockloch Rig 88 NS 5801
Brockton (Shrops.) 58 SJ 3104
Brockton (Shrops.) 59 SJ 7103
Brockton (Shrops.) 48 SO 3285
Brockton (Shrops.) 59 SO 5793
Brockweir 45 SO 5301
Brockwood Park 27 SU 6226
Brockworth 46 SO 8916
Brocolitia (ant.) 90 NY 8570
Brocton 60 SJ 9619
Brodick 92 NS 0136
Brodick Bay 92 NS 0237
Brodie Castle 129 NH 9757
Brodsworth 71 SE 5007
Brogborough 52 SP 9638
Brokenborough 33 ST 9189
Broken Cross (Ches.) 69 SJ 6872
Broken Cross (Ches.) 69 SJ 8973
Broken Cross Muir (mt.) 95 NS 8436
Brolass (dist.) 105 NM 4923
Bromborough 68 SJ 3582
Brome 55 TM 1376
Brome Street 55 TM 1576
Bromeswell 55 TM 3050
Bromfield (Cumbr.) 82 NY 1746
Bromfield (Salop) 48 SO 4876
Bromham (Beds.) 52 TL 0051
Bromham (Wilts.) 34 ST 9665
Bromley (Gtr London) 37 TQ 4069
Bromley Common 37 TQ 4266
Brompton (Kent) 30 TQ 7668
Brompton (N Yorks.) 85 SE 3796
Brompton (N Yorks.) 81 SE 9482
Brompton-on-Swale 84 SE 2199
Brompton Ralph 24 ST 0832
Brompton Regis 23 SS 9531
Bromsash 46 SO 6424
Bromsgrove 50 SO 9570
Bromyard 49 SO 6554
Bromyard Downs 49 SO 6655
Bronaber 67 SH 7131
Bronant 57 SN 6467
Bronington 59 SJ 4839
Bronllys 41 SO 1435
Bronygarth 58 SJ 2636
Brook (Hants.) 26 SU 2713
Brook (Hants.) 26 SU 3428
Brook (I. of W.) 26 SZ 3983
Brook (Kent) 31 TR 0644
Brook (Surrey) 28 SU 9338
Brooke (Leic.) 62 SK 8405
Brooke (Norf.) 65 TM 2999
Brookfield 101 NS 4164
Brookhouse 77 SD 5464
Brookhouse Green 69 SJ 8061
Brookland 31 TQ 9825
Brookmans Park 37 TL 2404
Brooks 58 SO 1499
Brook Street 37 TQ 5792
Brookthorpe 46 SO 8312
Brookwood 28 SU 9557
Broom (Beds.) 52 TL 1743
Broom (Warw.) 50 SP 0953
Broome (Here. and Worc.) 49 SO 9078
Broome (Norf.) 55 TM 3591
Broome (Shrops.) 48 SO 3981
Broome Park 91 NU 1112
Broomer's Corners 28 TQ 1221
Broomfield (Essex) 38 TL 7009
Broomfield (Grampn.) 121 NJ 9532
Broomfield (Kent) 30 TQ 8452
Broomfield (Kent) 31 TR 2066
Broomfield (Somer.) 24 ST 2231
Broomfleet 74 SE 8727
Broom Hall Airfield 66 SH 4137
Broomhead Resr. 71 SK 2695
Broom Hill (Dorset) 26 SU 0302
Broomhill (Northum.) 91 NU 2400
Broomlee Lough 90 NY 7969
Broomy Law 96 NT 4131
Broomy Lodge 26 SU 2111
Brora 129 NC 9003
Brosdale Island 98 NR 4962
Broseley 59 SJ 6701
Brother Isle 143 HU 4281
Brothers Water 83 NY 4012
Brothertoft 63 TF 2746
Brotherton 79 SE 4825
Brotton 85 NZ 6819
Broubster 135 ND 0360
Brough (Bressay) 141 HU 5141
Brough (Cumbr.) 83 NY 7914
Brough (Derby.) 70 SK 1882
Brough (Highld.) 135 ND 2273
Brough (Humbs.) 74 SE 9326
Brough (Notts.) 72 SK 8358
Brough (Shetld.) 143 HU 4377
Brough (Whalsay) 141 HU 5564
Brough (Yell) 143 HU 5179
Broughall 59 SJ 5641
Brough Head (Highld.) 135 ND 3663
Brough Head (Orkney) 136 HY 2328
Brough Lodge 143 HU 5892
Brough Ness 136 ND 4482
Brough of Deerness (pt.) 137 HY 5908
Brough Sowerby 83 NY 7912
Brough Taing 143 HP 6304
Brough, The 142 HU 2982
Broughton (Borders) 95 NT 1136
Broughton (Bucks.) 52 SP 8940
Broughton (Cambs.) 53 TL 2878
Broughton (Clwyd) 68 SJ 3363
Broughton (Cumbr.) 82 NY 0731
Broughton (Gtr Mches.) 69 SD 8201
Broughton (Hants.) 26 SU 3132
Broughton (Humbs.) 74 SE 9508
Broughton (Lancs.) 77 SD 5234
Broughton (Mid Glam.) 41 SS 9271
Broughton (Northants.) 52 SP 8375
Broughton (N Yorks.) 78 SD 9451
Broughton (N Yorks.) 80 SE 7673
Broughton (Oxon.) 50 SP 4238
Broughton (Westray) 138 HY 4448
Broughton Astley 51 SP 5292
Broughton Beck 77 SD 2882
Broughton Gifford 33 ST 8763
Broughton Hackett 49 SO 9254
Broughton Heights 95 NT 1241
Broughton in Furness 76 SD 2087
Broughton Mills 82 SD 2290
Broughton Moor 82 NY 0533
Broughton Poggs 47 SP 2303
Broughtown 139 HY 6540
Broughty Ferry 109 NO 4630
Browland 140 HU 2750
Brown Bank Head (mt.) 78 SE 1057
Brown Candover 35 SU 5839
Brown Carrick Hill 93 NS 2815
Brown Caterthun (mt.) 109 NO 5566
Brown Clee Hill 49 SO 5985
Brown Cow Hill 117 NJ 2204
Brown Edge 59 SJ 9053
Brown Head 92 NR 8925
Brownhill (Grampn.) 121 NJ 8640
Brownhills (W Mids) 60 SK 0405
Brownlow Heath 69 SJ 8360
Brownmoor Hill 88 NX 9991
Brownmuir 119 NO 7477
Brown Ridge 78 SD 3873
Brownsea Island 26 SZ 0187
Brownston 21 SX 6952
Brown Willy (mt.) 19 SX 1579
Browsholme Hall (ant.) 77 SD 6845
Broxbourne 37 TL 3707
Broxburn (Lothian) 102 NT 0872
Broxburn (Lothian) 96 NT 6977
Broxted 53 TL 5727
Broxwood 45 SO 3654
Bruach, The (mt.) 117 NJ 1105
Bruan 135 ND 3039
Bruar Lodge 117 NN 8376
Bruar Water (Tays.) 107 NN 8269
Bruar Water (Tays.) 117 NN 8375
Bruchag Point 93 NS 1157
Bruddans, The 142 HU 2077
Brue 131 NB 3349
Bruera 68 SJ 4360
Bruern Abbey 47 SP 2620
Bruernish 112 NF 7102
Bruernish Point 112 NF 7300
Bruichladdich 98 NR 2661
Bruisyard 55 TM 3266
Bruisyard Street 55 TM 3365
Brumby 74 SE 8809
Brund 70 SK 1061
Brundall 65 TG 3208
Brundish 55 TM 2669
Brundish Street 55 TM 2671
Brunerican Bay 92 NR 7007
Brunt Hill 96 NT 6874
Bruntingthorpe 51 SP 6090
Brunton (Fife) 108 NO 3220
Brunton (Northum.) 97 NU 2024
Bruntshiel Hill 89 NY 4182
Bruray 143 HU 6972
Brushford 23 SS 9225
Brushford Barton 23 SS 6707
Bruton 25 ST 6834
Bruton Forest 33 ST 7438
Bruxie Hill 119 NO 8280
Bryanston 25 ST 8706
Brydekirk 89 NY 1870
Bryher (is.) 18 SV 8714
Brymbo 58 SJ 2953
Bryn (Gtr Mches.) 69 SD 5701
Bryn (Powys) 44 SN 9055
Bryn (Shrops.) 48 SO 2985
Bryn (W Glam.) 41 SS 8192
Brynamlwg 57 SN 9297
Brynamman 40 SN 7114
Brynberian 42 SN 1035
Bryn Brawd 44 SN 6951
Bryncae 41 SS 9983
Bryn-celli-ddu (ant.) 66 SH 5070
Bryncethin 41 SS 9184
Bryncir 66 SH 4641
Bryn-côch 41 SS 7499
Bryncroes 66 SH 2231
Bryncrug 56 SH 6003
Bryn Crwn 44 SN 8258
Bryn-du (Clwyd) 58 SJ 1435
Bryn-du (Powys) 44 SN 9342
Bryneglwys 58 SJ 1447
Brynford 68 SJ 1774
Bryn Garw (Dyfed) 57 SN 8077
Bryn Garw (Powys) 57 SN 8361
Bryn Gates 69 SD 5901
Brynglas Station 57 SH 6203
Bryngwran 66 SH 3477
Bryngwyn (Gwent) 45 SO 3909
Bryngwyn (Powys) 45 SO 1849
Bryn-henllan 42 SN 0139
Brynhoffnant 43 SN 3351
Brynmawr 41 SO 1911
Brynmenyn 41 SS 9084
Brynna 41 SS 9883
Bryn Nicol 44 SN 8243
Brynrefail 66 SH 4786
Brynsadler 41 ST 0380
Brynsiencyn 66 SH 4867
Brynteg 66 SH 4982
Bryn, The 45 SO 3309
Bryntitley 57 SN 9375
Bryn Trillyn 67 SH 9459
Bryn y Castell 57 SH 9704
Bryn-y-maen (Clwyd) 67 SH 8376
Bryn-y-maen (Powys) 45 SO 1657
Buachaille Etive Beag 106 NN 1854
Buachaille Etive Mòr 106 NN 2254
Buail' a' Ghoill 112 NF 8130
Bualintur 123 NG 4020
Bubbenhall 50 SP 3672
Bubwith 74 SE 7136
Buccleuch 89 NT 3214
Buchan (dist.) 121 NJ 9749
Buchanan Smithy 101 NS 4689
Buchan Burn 86 NX 4181
Buchan Hill 87 NX 4281
Buchan Ness 121 NK 1342
Buchanty 108 NN 9328
Buchlyvie 101 NS 5793
Buckabank 83 NY 3749
Buckden (Cambs.) 52 TL 1967
Buckden (N Yorks.) 78 SD 9477
Buckden Pike 78 SD 9678
Buckenham 65 TG 3505
Buckerell 24 ST 1200
Buckfast 21 SX 7367
Buckfastleigh 21 SX 7466
Buckhaven 103 NT 3598
Buckholm 96 NT 4838
Buckhorn Weston 25 ST 7524
Buckhurst Hill 37 TQ 4193
Buckie 121 NJ 4265
Buckies 135 ND 1063
Buckingham 51 SP 6933
Buckland (Bucks.) 36 SP 8812
Buckland (Devon) 21 SX 6743
Buckland (Glos.) 50 SP 0836
Buckland (Herts.) 53 TL 3533
Buckland (Kent) 31 TR 2942
Buckland (Oxon.) 47 SU 3497
Buckland (Surrey) 28 TQ 2250
Buckland Abbey (ant.) 20 SX 4866
Buckland Brewer 22 SS 4120
Buckland Common 36 SP 9306
Buckland Dinham 33 ST 7550
Buckland Filleigh 22 SS 4609
Buckland in the Moor 21 SX 7273
Buckland Monachorum 20 SX 4868
Buckland Newton 25 ST 6905
Buckland St. Mary 24 ST 2713
Buckland-Tout-Saints 21 SX 7546
Bucklebury 35 SU 5570
Bucklerheads 109 NO 4636
Bucklers Hard 26 SZ 4099
Bucklesham 55 TM 2442
Buckley 68 SJ 2764
Buckminster 62 SK 8722
Bucknall (Lincs.) 73 TF 1668
Bucknall (Staffs.) 59 SJ 9147
Bucknell (Oxon.) 47 SP 5525
Bucknell (Shrops.) 48 SO 3574
Bucksburn 119 NJ 8909
Buck's Cross 22 SS 3422
Bucks Green 28 TQ 0732
Bucks Hill 36 TL 0500
Bucks Horn Oak 35 SU 8142
Buck's Mills 22 SS 3523
Buck, The (mt.) 121 NJ 4123
Buckton (Here. and Worc.) 48 SO 3873
Buckton (Northum.) 97 NU 0838
Buckworth 52 TL 1476
Budbrooke 50 SP 2565
Budby 71 SK 6169
Buddo Ness 109 NO 5515
Buddon Ness 109 NO 5530
Bude 22 SS 2006
Bude Bay 22 SS 1706
Bude Haven 22 SS 2006
Budlake 21 SS 9700
Budle 97 NU 1534
Budle Bay 97 NU 1535
Budleigh Salterton 24 SY 0682
Budock Water 19 SW 7832
Buerton 59 SJ 6843
Bugbrooke 51 SP 6757
Bugeilyn 57 SN 8292
Bught Fell 86 NX 2062
Bugle 19 SX 0158
Bugthorpe 80 SE 7757
Buidhe Bheinn 114 NG 9508
Builg Burn 119 NO 6687
Builth Road 44 SO 0253
Builth Wells 44 SO 0351
Bulbarrow Hill 25 ST 7705
Bulby 62 TF 0526
Buldoo 134 NC 9967
Bulford 34 SU 1643
Bulg (mt.) 119 NO 5476
Bulgham Bay 76 SC 4685
Bulkeley 59 SJ 5254
Bulkington (Warw.) 50 SP 3986
Bulkington (Wilts.) 34 ST 9458
Bulkworthy 22 SS 3914
Bull (lightship) 75 TA 3809
Bull Bay (Gwyn.) 66 SH 4294
Bull Bay (Gwyn.) 66 SH 4394
Bulldog Sand 64 TF 6027
Bulley 46 SO 7519
Bullie Burn 101 NN 7809
Bull Point 22 SS 4646
Bullpot Farm 77 SD 6681
Bullwood 100 NS 1674
Bulmer (Essex) 54 TL 8440
Bulmer (N Yorks.) 80 SE 6967
Bulmer Tye 54 TL 8438
Bulphan 38 TQ 6385
Bulverhythe 30 TQ 7809
Bulwark 121 NJ 9345
Bulwell 61 SK 5345
Bulwick 62 SP 9694
Bumble's Green 37 TL 4005
Bunacaimb 111 NM 6588
Bun Allt na Criche 106 NM 9256
Bun an Leoib (chan.) 105 NM 4023
Bunarkaig 115 NN 1887
Bunavoneadar 125 NB 1304
Bunbury 69 SJ 5658
Bunchrew 128 NH 6145
Buncton 28 TQ 1413
Bundalloch 114 NG 8927
Bu Ness (Fair Isle) 139 HZ 2272
Buness (Unst) 143 HP 6209
Bunessan 104 NM 3821
Bungay 55 TM 3389
Bunloinn Forest 115 NH 1608
Bunnahabhainn 98 NR 4173
Bunny 61 SK 5829
Buntait 115 NH 3930
Buntingford 53 TL 3629
Bunwell 65 TM 1293
Burach 115 NH 3814
Burbage (Derby.) 70 SK 0472
Burbage (Leic.) 51 SP 4492
Burbage (Wilts.) 34 SU 2261
Burcombe (Somer.) (dist.) 23 SS 7538
Burcombe (Wilts.) 26 SU 0630
Burcot 47 SU 5595
Burdale 81 SE 8762
Bures 54 TL 9034
Burfa Camp (ant.) 48 SO 2861
Burford 47 SP 2512
Burg 104 NM 3745
Burgar 136 HY 3427
Burga Water 140 HU 2354
Burgess Hill 29 TQ 3118
Burgh (Island of Mull) 105 NM 4226
Burgh (Suff.) 55 TM 2251
Burgh by Sands 89 NY 3259
Burgh Castle 65 TG 4805
Burghclere 35 SU 4660
Burghead 129 NJ 1168
Burghead Bay 129 NJ 0767
Burghfield 36 SU 6668
Burghfield Common 36 SU 6466
Burghfield Hill 36 SU 6567
Burgh Head 137 HY 6923
Burgh Heath 37 TQ 2458
Burghill 45 SO 4744
Burgh Island 21 SX 6443
Burgh Le Marsh 73 TF 5065
Burghley House (ant.) 62 TF 0406
Burgh Muir 121 NJ 7622
Burgh next Aylsham 65 TG 2125
Burgh on Bain 73 TF 2186
Burgh St. Margaret 65 TG 4413
Burgh St. Peter 65 TM 4693
Burghwallis 71 SE 5312
Burgi Geos 143 HP 4703
Burham 30 TQ 7262
Burifa Hill 135 ND 2075
Buriton 27 SU 7319
Burland 59 SJ 6153
Burlawn 19 SW 9970
Burlescombe 24 ST 0716
Burleston 25 SY 7794
Burley (Hants.) 26 SU 2103
Burley (Leic.) 62 SK 8810
Burleydam 59 SJ 6042
Burley Gate 45 SO 5947
Burley in Wharfedale 78 SE 1646
Burley Lodge 26 SU 2305
Burley Street 26 SU 2004
Burlingjobb 45 SO 2558
Burlton 58 SJ 4526
Burmarsh 31 TR 1032
Burmington 50 SP 2637
Burn 79 SE 5928
Burnage 69 SJ 8692
Burnaston 60 SK 2832
Burnby 74 SE 8346
Burncrooks Resr. 101 NS 4879
Burneside 83 SD 5095
Burness 139 HY 6644
Burneston 79 SE 3084
Burnett 33 ST 6665
Burn Farm, The 109 NO 6072
Burnfoot (Borders) 89 NT 4113
Burnfoot (Borders) 90 NT 5116
Burnfoot (Tays.) 102 NN 9804
Burnfoot Resr. 93 NS 4544
Burnham (Berks. - Bucks.) 36 SU 9382
Burnham (Humbs.) 74 TA 0517
Burnham Beeches 36 SU 9585
Burnham Deepdale 64 TF 8044
Burnham Green 37 TL 2616
Burnham Market 64 TF 8342
Burnham Norton 64 TF 8243
Burnham-on-Crouch 38 TQ 9496
Burnham-on-Sea 32 ST 3049
Burnham Overy Staithe 64 TF 8444
Burnham Overy Town 64 TF 8442
Burnham Thorpe 64 TF 8541
Burnhaven 121 NK 1244
Burnhead 88 NX 8595
Burnhervie 119 NJ 7319
Burnhill Green 59 SJ 7800
Burnhope 84 NZ 1948
Burnhope Reservoir 83 NY 8328
Burnhope Seat (mt.) 83 NY 7837
Burnhouse 93 NS 3850
Burn Howe Rigg (mt.) 81 SE 9099
Burniston 81 TA 0193
Burnley 78 SD 8332
Burn Moor 77 SD 7064
Burn Moor Fell 77 SD 7064
Burnmoor Tarn 82 NY 1804
Burnmouth 97 NT 9560
Burnock Water 93 NS 5017
Burn of Acharole 135 ND 2351
Burn of Agie 115 NN 3691
Burn of Arisdale 143 HU 4783
Burn of Aultmore 121 NJ 4556
Burn of Boyne 121 NJ 5858
Burn of Branny 118 NO 4484
Burn of Calletar 109 NO 4769
Burn of Cambus 101 NN 7003
Burn of Cattie 119 NO 5795
Burn of Corrichie 119 NJ 7002
Burn of Dale 140 HU 2053
Burn of Hillside 136 HY 3023
Burn of Houstry 135 ND 1436
Burn of Laxdale 141 HU 4131
Burn of Lochy 117 NJ 1221
Burn of Loin 117 NJ 1409
Burn of Lyth 135 ND 2961
Burn of Ore 136 ND 2893
Burn of Rothes 120 NJ 2248
Burn of Sandvoe 142 HU 3590
Burn of Sandwater 141 HU 4153
Burn of Sheeoch 119 NO 7589
Burn of Tennet 118 NO 5082
Burn of Tulchan 117 NJ 0838
Burn of Turret 119 NO 5480
Burnopfield 84 NZ 1756
Burnsall 78 SE 0361
Burns Cottage 93 NS 3318
Burnside (Fife) 102 NO 1607
Burnside (Lothian) 102 NT 0971
Burnside (Shetld.) 142 HU 2778
Burnside (Strath.) 88 NS 5811
Burnside (Tays.) 109 NO 4259
Burnside (Tays.) 109 NO 5050
Burnside of Duntrune 109 NO 4434
Burnswark 89 NY 1878
Burnt Fen 54 TL 6085
Burn, The 109 NO 5971
Burnt Hill 100 NS 3058
Burntisland 103 NT 2385
Burntwood 60 SK 0609
Burnt Yates 79 SE 2461
Burpham (Surrey) 28 TQ 0151
Burpham (W Susx) 28 TQ 0408
Burrach Mòr 116 NH 5808
Burradon (Northum.) 91 NT 9806
Burradon (Tyne and Wear) 91 NZ 2772
Burrafirth (Unst.) 143 HP 6113
Burra Firth (Unst) 143 HP 6116
Burraland (Shetld.) 140 HU 2249
Burraland (Shetld.) 142 HU 3475
Burra Ness 143 HU 5595
Burras 18 SW 6835
Burra Sound 136 HY 2404
Burrator Resr. 21 SX 5568
Burravoe (Shetld.) 141 HU 3667
Burra Voe (Shetld.) 142 HU 3689
Burra Voe (Yell) 143 HU 5279
Burravoe (Yell) 143 HU 5280
Burray 136 ND 4796
Burray Haas 136 ND 4998
Burray Ness 136 ND 5096
Burrelton 108 NO 1936
Burridge 27 SU 5110
Burrier Wick 142 HU 3192
Burries Ness 142 HU 2783
Burrill 79 SE 2387
Burringham 74 SE 8309
Burrington (Avon) 33 ST 4759
Burrington (Devon) 23 SS 6316
Burrington (Here. and Worc.) 48 SO 4472
Burrough Green 54 TL 6355
Burrough on the Hill 61 SK 7510
Burrow Bridge 24 ST 3530
Burrow Head 87 NX 4534
Burrowhill 36 SU 9763
Burrows Hole 97 NU 1340
Burry Holms 40 SS 3992
Burry Port 40 SN 4400
Burscough 68 SD 4310
Burscough Bridge 68 SD 4411
Bursea 74 SE 8033
Burshill 81 TA 0948
Bursledon 27 SU 4809
Burslem 59 SJ 8749
Burstall 54 TM 0944
Burstock 25 ST 4202
Burston (Norf.) 55 TM 1383
Burston (Staffs.) 59 SJ 9330
Burstow 29 TQ 3141
Burstwick 75 TA 2228
Burtersett 84 SD 8989
Burtle 32 ST 3943
Burton (Ches.) 68 SJ 3174
Burton (Ches.) 69 SJ 5063
Burton (Dorset) 26 SZ 1794
Burton (Dyfed) 42 SM 9805
Burton (Lincs.) 72 SK 9574
Burton (Northum.) 97 NU 1732
Burton (Somer.) 32 ST 1944
Burton (Wilts.) 33 ST 8179
Burton Agnes 81 TA 1063
Burton Bradstock 25 SY 4889
Burton Constable 75 TA 1836
Burton Fleming 81 TA 0872
Burton Green (Clwyd) 68 SJ 3458
Burton Green (Warw.) 50 SP 2675
Burton Hastings 50 SP 4189
Burton-in-Kendal 77 SD 5376
Burton in Lonsdale 77 SD 6572
Burton Joyce 61 SK 6443
Burton Latimer 52 SP 9074
Burton Lazars 61 SK 7716
Burton-Le-Coggles 62 SK 9725
Burton Leonard 79 SE 3263
Burton on the Wolds 61 SK 5821
Burton Overy 61 SP 6798
Burton Pedwardine 62 TF 1142
Burton Pidsea 75 TA 2431
Burton Salmon 79 SE 4827
Burton upon Stather 74 SE 8617
Burton upon Trent 60 SK 2423
Burtonwood 69 SJ 5692
Burwardsley 59 SJ 5156
Burwarton 49 SO 6185
Burwash 29 TQ 6724
Burwash Common 29 TQ 6423
Burwell (Cambs.) 53 TL 5866
Burwell (Lincs.) 73 TF 3579
Bur Wick (Shetld.) 141 HU 3840
Burwick (Shetld.) 141 HU 3940
Burwick (S. Ronaldsay) 136 ND 4384
Bury (Cambs.) 53 TL 2883
Bury (Gtr Mches.) 69 SD 8010
Bury (Somer.) 23 SS 9427
Bury (W Susx) 28 TQ 0113
Bury Ditches (ant.) 48 SO 3283
Bury Green 37 TL 4521
Bury Hill 34 SU 3443
Bury St. Edmunds 54 TL 8564
Burythorpe 80 SE 7964
Bury Walls (ant.) 59 SJ 5727
Busbie Muir Resr. 93 NS 2446
Busbridge 28 SU 9842
Busby (Strath.) 94 NS 5856
Busby (Tays.) 108 NO 0327
Buscot 47 SU 2297
Bushbury 59 SJ 9202
Bush Crathie 117 NO 2596
Bushey 37 TQ 1395
Bushey Heath 37 TQ 1594
Bush Green 55 TM 2187
Bushley 46 SO 8734
Bushton 34 SU 0677
Bushy Park 37 TQ 1569
Buss Craig 97 NT 9464
Busta 141 HU 3466
Busta Voe 141 HU 3566
Butcher's Pasture 38 TL 6024
Butcombe 33 ST 5161
Butleigh 25 ST 5233
Butleigh Wootton 25 ST 5034
Butlers Marston 50 SP 3150
Butley 55 TM 3651
Butser Hill 27 SU 7120
Butsfield 84 NZ 1044
Butterburn 90 NY 6774
Buttercrambe 80 SE 7358
Butterknowle 84 NZ 1025
Butterleigh 23 SS 9708
Butterley Reservoir 70 SE 0514
Buttermere (Cumbr.) 82 NY 1717
Buttermere (Cumbr.) 82 NY 1815
Buttermere (Wilts.) 34 SU 3361
Buttershaw 78 SE 1329
Butterstone 108 NO 0646
Butterton 60 SK 0756
Butterwick (Humbs.) 74 SE 8305
Butterwick (Lincs.) 63 TF 3845
Butterwick (N Yorks.) 80 SE 7377
Butterwick (N Yorks.) 81 SE 9971
Butterwick Low (sbk.) 63 TF 4243
Butt Green 59 SJ 6651
Buttington 58 SJ 2408
Buttock Point 100 NS 0074
Butt of Lewis 131 NB 5166
Button Hills 143 HU 3968
Buttonoak 49 SO 7578
Buxey Sand 39 TM 1103
Buxhall 54 TM 0057
Buxted 29 TQ 4923
Buxton (Derby.) 70 SK 0673
Buxton (Norf.) 65 TG 2222
Buxton Heath 65 TG 1821
Bwlch 41 SO 1422
Bwlchgwyn 58 SJ 2653
Bwlchllan 43 SN 5758
Bwlch Mawr (mt.) 66 SH 4247
Bwlchtocyn 56 SH 3126
Bwlch-y-cibau 58 SJ 1717
Bwlch-y-ffridd 57 SO 0695
Bwlch-y-groes (Dyfed) 43 SN 2436
Bwlch-y-groes (Gwyn.) 57 SH 9023
Bwlch-y-sarnau 57 SO 0274
Byerhope Resr 83 NY 8546
Byers Green 84 NZ 2234
Byfield 51 SP 5153
Byfleet 36 TQ 0461
Byford 45 SO 3943
Bygrave 53 TL 2636
Byker 91 NZ 2763
Byland Abbey (ant.) 79 SE 5478
Bylchau 67 SH 9762
Bylchau Rhos-faen 41 SN 7416
Byley 69 SJ 7269
Bynack Burn 117 NN 9784
Bynack More 117 NJ 0406
Byne Hill 86 NX 1794
Byrehope Mount 95 NT 1054
Bythorn 52 TL 0575
Byton 48 SO 3664
Byworth 28 SU 9921

C

Caaf Resr. 93 NS 2450
Caar Bheinn 114 NM 9986
Cabaan Forest 127 NH 3650
Caban Coch Resr. 57 SN 9163
Cabourne 75 TA 1301
Cabrach (Grampn.) 121 NJ 3826
Cabrach (Jura) 98 NR 4964
Cadbury 23 SS 9105
Cadbury Barton 23 SS 6917
Cadbury Camp 33 ST 4572
Cadbury Castle 25 ST 6225
Cadder 101 NS 6172
Caddington 36 TL 0619
Caddonfoot 96 NT 4534
Caddon Water 96 NT 4041
Cadeby (Leic.) 60 SK 4202
Cadeby (S Yorks.) 71 SE 5100
Cadeleigh 23 SS 9107
Cademuir Hill 95 NT 2437
Cader Fawr 41 SN 9712
Cader Idris 57 SH 7013
Cade Street 29 TQ 6021
Cadgwith 18 SW 7214
Cadham 103 NO 2701
Cadha na Gaoidhsich (pt.) 125 NG 4399
Cadishead 69 SJ 7091
Cadle 40 SS 6297
Cadley 34 SU 2066
Cadmore End 36 SU 7892
Cadnam 26 SU 2913
Cadney 74 TA 0103
Cadole 68 SJ 2062
Cadzow Resr. 94 NS 6951
Cae Afon 57 SH 8174
Caeathro 66 SH 5061
Caehopkin 41 SN 8212
Caenlochan Forest 117 NO 1875
Caeo 44 SN 6739
Caerau (Mid Glam.) 41 SS 8594
Caerau (S Glam.) 41 ST 1375
Caer Caradoc (ant.) 48 SO 3075
Caer Caradoc (ant.) 59 SO 4795
Caerdeon 57 SH 6418
Caergeiliog 66 SH 3178
Caergwrle 68 SJ 3057

Caergybi (ant.) Castle Heaton

Caergybi (ant.) 66 SH 2682
Caerlaverock Castle (ant.) 88 NY 0265
Caerleon 32 ST 3390
Caer Llan 45 SO 4908
Caernarfon 66 SH 4862
Caernarfon Bay 66 SH 3055
Caerphilly 41 ST 1587
Caersws 57 SO 0392
Caerwent 33 ST 4790
Caerwys 68 SJ 1272
Caesar's Camp (Berks.) (ant.) 36 SU 8665
Caesar's Camp (Hants.) (ant.) 35 SU 8350
Caethle 56 SN 6099
Cagar Feosaig 129 NC 8404
Cailiness Point 86 NX 1535
Cailleach Head 126 NG 9898
Cailleach Uragaig 98 NR 3898
Cairidh nan Ob 122 NG 3570
Cairnacay 117 NJ 2032
Cairn Avel (ant.) 88 NX 5692
Cairnbaan 99 NR 8390
Cairn Baddoch 108 NO 2770
Cairn Bannoch 117 NO 2282
Cairnbanno House 121 NJ 8444
Cairnborrow 121 NJ 4640
Cairnbrallan 121 NJ 3324
Cairnbrogie 121 NJ 8527
Cairnbulg Castle 121 NK 0164
Cairnbulg Point 121 NK 0365
Cairn Cattoch 120 NJ 2247
Cairncross 118 NO 4979
Cairncross 97 NT 8963
Cairndow 100 NN 1810
Cairn Edward Forest 88 NX 6171
Cairness 121 NK 0360
Cairneyhill 102 NT 0486
Cairnfield House 121 NJ 4162
Cairngaan 86 NX 1232
Cairn Galtar 112 NL 6491
Cairngarroch (Dumf. and Galwy.) 86 NX 0649
Cairngarroch (Dumf. and Galwy.) 87 NX 4977
Cairngarroch Bay 86 NX 0449
Cairn Geldie 117 NN 9988
Cairn Gibbs 108 NO 1859
Cairn Gorm 117 NJ 0004
Cairngorm Mountains 117 NJ 0103
Cairngorms Nature Reserve 117 NN 9598
Cairnharrow 87 NX 5356
Cairn Head 87 NX 4838
Cairnhill (Dumf. and Galwy.) 88 NS 8506
Cairnhill (Grampn.) 121 NJ 6732
Cairn Hill (Strath.) 86 NX 3090
Cairn Holy (ant.) 87 NX 5154
Cairnie 121 NJ 4945
Cairn Inks 108 NO 3072
Cairnkinna Hill 88 NS 7901
Cairn Kinny 88 NS 7821
Cairn Leuchan 118 NO 3791
Cairn Mona Gowan 117 NJ 3305
Cairn-mon-earn 119 NO 7891
Cairn Muldonich 117 NJ 2326
Cairn na Burgh Beg 104 NM 3044
Cairnoch Hill 101 NS 6985
Cairn of Barns 108 NO 3171
Cairn o'Mount 119 NO 6480
Cairnorrie 121 NJ 8640
Cairnpapple (ant.) 102 NS 9871
Cairn Pat 86 NX 0456
Cairn Point 86 NX 0668
Cairnryan 86 NX 0668
Cairnscarrow 86 NX 1364
Cairnsmore of Corsphairn 88 NX 5997
Cairnsmore of Fleet 87 NX 5066
Cairns of Coll (is.) 110 NM 2866
Cairntable (Strath.) 93 NS 4313
Cairn Table (Strath.) 94 NS 7224
Cairn Toul (Carn ant-Sabhail) 117 NN 9697
Cairn Uish 129 NJ 1750
Cairn Water 88 NX 8681
Cairnwell, The (mt.) 117 NO 1377
Cairn William 119 NJ 6516
Cairnywellan Head 86 NX 0940
Caisteal Abhail 92 NR 9644
Caister-on-Sea 65 TG 5212
Caistor 75 TA 1101
Caistor St.Edmund 65 TG 2303
Caistron 91 NT 9901
Caiteshal (mt.) 125 NB 2404
Calair Burn 107 NN 5317
Calback Ness 143 HU 3977
Calbha Beag (is.) 132 NC 1536
Calbha Mòr (is.) 132 NC 1636
Calbost 131 NB 4117
Calbourne 26 SZ 4286
Calcot 36 SU 6672
Caldback 143 HP 6006
Caldbeck 82 NY 3239
Caldbergh 78 SE 0984
Caldecote (Cambs.) 52 TL 1488
Caldecote (Cambs.) 53 TL 3456
Caldecote (Herts.) 53 TL 2338
Caldecott (Leic.) 62 SP 8693
Caldecott (Northants.) 52 SP 9968
Calderbank 101 NS 7662
Calder Bridge 82 NY 0405
Calderbrook 69 SD 9418
Calder Burn 115 NN 3399
Caldercruix 101 NS 8167
Calder Dam 100 NS 2965
Calder Fell 77 SD 5648
Calder Mains 135 ND 0959
Caldermill 94 NS 6641
Calder Vale 77 SD 5345
Calder Water 94 NS 6041
Caldey Island 42 SS 1496
Caldey Sound 42 SS 1297
Caldhame 109 NO 4748
Caldicot 33 ST 4888
Caldicot Level 33 ST 4285
Caldon Canal (Staffs.) 59 SJ 9453
Caldon Canal (Staffs.) 60 SJ 9949
Caldwell 84 NZ 1613
Caldwell (Derby.) 60 SK 2517
Caldy 68 SJ 2285
Caledonian Canal (Highld.) 127 NH 1380
Caledonian Canal (Highld.) 115 NH 3405
Caledonian Canal (Highld.) 116 NH 6240
Caledrhydiau 43 SN 4753
Calf of Eday 138 HY 5839
Calf of Flotta 136 ND 3896
Calf of Man 76 SC 1565
Calfsound (Eday) 138 HY 5738
Calf Sound (Eday) 138 HY 5739
Calf, The (mt.) 83 SD 6696
Calf Top 77 SD 6585
Calgary 110 NM 3751
Calgary Bay 110 NM 3550
Calgary Point 110 NM 1052
Caliach Point 110 NM 3454
Califer 129 NJ 0857
California (Central) 102 NS 9076
California (Norf.) 65 TG 5114
Calke 60 SK 3722
Calkin Rig 89 NY 2987
Callaly 91 NU 0509
Callander 101 NN 6208
Callanish 131 NB 2133
Callater Burn 117 NO 1687
Callestick 18 SW 7750
Calligarry 111 NG 6202
Callington 20 SX 3669
Callop River 114 NM 9180
Callow 45 SO 4934
Callow End 49 SO 8349
Callow Hill (Here. and Worc.) 49 SO 7473
Callow Hill (Wilts.) 34 SU 0385
Callows Grave 49 SO 5966
Calmore 26 SU 3314
Calmsden 46 SP 0408
Calne 34 ST 9971
Calow 71 SK 4071
Calpa Mòr 116 NH 6710
Calshot 27 SU 4701
Calshot Castle (ant.) 27 SU 4802
Calshot Spit (lightship) 27 SU 4901
Calstock 20 SX 4368
Calstone Wellington 34 SU 0268
Calthorpe 65 TG 1831
Calthwaite 83 NY 4640
Caltinish 124 NF 8341
Calton (N Yorks.) 78 SD 9059
Calton (Staffs.) 60 SK 1050
Calvay (South Uist) 112 NF 7728
Calvay (South Uist) 112 NF 8218
Calve Island 111 NM 5254
Calveley 69 SJ 5958
Calver 71 SK 2374
Calverhall 59 SJ 6037
Calver Hill 45 SO 3748
Calverleigh 23 SS 9214
Calverley 78 SE 2036
Calvert 36 SP 6824
Calverton (Bucks.) 51 SP 7938
Calverton (Notts.) 61 SK 6149
Calvine 107 NN 8066
Cam 46 ST 7599
Cama Choire 116 NN 6879
Camas Airigh Shamhraidh 105 NM 8448
Camas Allt nam Bearnach 125 NB 3608
Camas a' Mhoil 130 NA 9825
Camas Baravaig 123 NG 6909
Camas chil Mhalieu 106 NM 9055
Camas Coille 132 NC 0016
Camas Eilean Ghlais 132 NB 9615
Camas Geodhachan an Duilisg 130 NB 0438
Camas Ghaoideil 111 NM 6683
Camas Gorm 105 NM 7742
Camas-luinie 114 NG 9128
Camas Mòr (Highld.) 127 NC 1000
Camas Mòr (Highld.) 126 NG 7592
Camas Mòr (Island of Skye) 122 NG 3770
Camas na Ceardaich 100 NR 9162
Camas Nathais 105 NM 8737
Camas Pliasgaig 111 NG 4002
Camastianavaig 123 NG 5039
Camas Uig 130 NB 0233
Camasunary 123 NG 5118
Camault Muir 116 NH 5040
Camb 143 HU 5192
Cambeak (pt.) 20 SX 1296
Cam Beck 78 SD 7978
Camber 31 TQ 9619
Camber Castle (ant.) 30 TQ 9218
Camberley 36 SU 8760
Camberwell 37 TQ 3376
Camblesforth 79 SE 6425
Cambo 91 NZ 0285
Camboglanna (ant.) 90 NY 6166
Cambois 91 NZ 3083
Cambo Ness 103 NO 6011
Camborne 18 SW 6440
Cambrian Mountains 57 SH 8809
Cambridge 53 TL 4658
Cambridge Airport 53 TL 4858
Cambus 102 NS 8593
Cambusavie 129 NH 7796
Cambusbarron 101 NS 7792
Cambuscurrie Bay 129 NH 7285
Cambuskenneth 101 NS 8094
Cambuslang 101 NS 6459
Cambusmore Lodge 129 NH 7697
Cam Chreag 107 NN 5349
Camddwr 44 SN 7755
Camden Town 37 TQ 2784
Camelford 20 SX 1083
Camelon 102 NS 8680
Cameron Burn 103 NO 4912
Cameron Resr. 103 NO 4711
Camerory 117 NJ 0231
Camerton (Avon) 33 ST 6857
Camerton (Cumbr.) 82 NY 0330
Camesdale 101 SU 8932
Cam Fell 78 SD 8080
Camghouran 107 NN 5556
Cam Loch (Highld.) 132 NC 2113
Càm Loch (Strath.) 99 NR 8187
Camlo Hill 57 SO 0370
Cammachmore 119 NO 9295
Cammachmore Bay 119 NO 9295
Cammeringham 72 SK 9482
Cammoch Hill 108 NN 8959
Campay 131 NB 1442
Campbells Hill 93 NS 5201
Campbelton 93 NS 1950
Campbeltown 92 NR 7120
Campbeltown Loch 92 NR 7420
Camperdown House 109 NO 3532
Camphill Resr. 93 NS 2655
Campmuir 108 NO 2137
Campsall 71 SE 5313
Campsey Ash 55 TM 3356
Campsie Fells 101 NS 6082
Camps Resr. 95 NT 0022
Camps Water 95 NS 9622
Camps, The 46 SO 9109
Campton 52 TL 1238
Camrose 42 SM 9220
Camserney 107 NN 8149
Camster 135 ND 2641
Camster Burn 135 ND 2348
Camulodunum (ant.) 54 TM 0025
Camus Geodhachan an Duilisg 130 NB 0438
Camus-luinie 114 NG 9428
Camusnagaul (Highld.) 127 NH 0689
Camusnagaul (Highld.) 115 NN 0975
Camusrory 111 NM 8595
Camusteel 123 NG 7042
Camusterrach 123 NG 7141
Camusvrachan 107 NN 6248
Camy (pt.) 137 HY 5401
Canada 26 SU 2817
Canal Foot 77 SD 3177
Canaston Bridge 42 SN 0515
Candacraig House 118 NJ 3411
Candlesby 73 TF 4567
Candy Mill 95 NT 0741
Cane End 36 SU 6779
Canewdon 38 TQ 8994
Canford Bottom 26 SU 0300
Canford Cliffs 26 SZ 0689
Canford Heath 26 SZ 0294
Canisbay 135 ND 3472
Canis Dale 143 HU 5082
Canisp (mt.) 132 NC 2018
Cann 25 ST 8620
Canna (is.) 110 NG 2405
Canna Harbour 110 NG 2804
Cann Common 25 ST 8920
Cannich 115 NH 3331
Cannington 32 ST 2539
Cannock 60 SJ 9710
Cannock Chase 60 SJ 9816
Cannock Wood 60 SK 0412
Cannon Street Station 37 TQ 3280
Canonbie 89 NY 3976
Canon Bridge 45 SO 4341
Canon Frome 49 SO 6543
Canon Pyon 45 SO 4549
Canons Ashby 51 SP 5750
Canonstown 18 SW 5335
Canterbury 31 TR 1557
Cantick Head 136 ND 3489
Cantley (Norf.) 65 TG 3704
Cantley (S Yorks.) 71 SE 6202
Cantlop 59 SJ 5205
Canton 41 ST 1577
Cantraydoune 129 NH 7946
Cantraywood 129 NH 7847
Cantref Resr. 41 SN 9915
Cantsfield 77 SD 6172
Canvey Island 38 TQ 7783
Canwell Hall 60 SK 1400
Canwick 72 SK 9869
Canworthy Water 20 SX 2291
Caol 115 NN 1175
Caolard Rubha 99 NR 8783
Caolas a' Mhòrain 124 NF 8480
Caolas an Eilein 130 NA 9821
Caolas an Scarp 130 NA 9913
Caolas Bàn 110 NM 1151
Caolas Beag 126 NG 7478
Caolas Mòr (Highld.) 123 NG 7135
Caolas Mòr (Strath.) 98 NR 3586
Caolas Scalpay 123 NG 6127
Caoles 104 NM 0848
Caol Ghleann 100 NS 0693
Caolis 112 NL 6397
Caol Lairig 115 NN 2783
Caol Mòr 123 NG 5733
Caol Raineach (chan.) 133 NC 6364
Caol Rona 123 NG 6153
Cape Cornwall 18 SW 3431
Capel 28 TQ 1740
Cape Law 89 NT 1314
Capel Bangor 57 SN 6580
Capel Betws Lleucu 43 SN 6058
Capel Carmel 56 SH 1628
Capel Coch 66 SH 4582
Capel Curig 67 SH 7258
Capel Cynon 43 SN 3849
Capel Dewi 43 SN 4542
Capel Fell 89 NT 1607
Capel Garmon 67 SH 8155
Capel Gwyn (Dyfed) 433 SN 4622
Capel Gwyn (Gwyn.) 66 SH 3575
Capel Gwynfe 40 SN 7222
Capel Hendre 43 SN 5911
Capel Isaac 43 SN 5927
Capel Iwan 43 SN 2836
Capel-le-Ferne 31 TR 2439
Capel Llaniltern 41 ST 0979
Capel Parc 66 SH 4486
Capel St. Mary 55 TM 0838
Capel-y-ffin 45 SO 2531
Capenhurst 68 SJ 3673
Capernwray 77 SD 5372
Cape Wrath 132 NC 2574
Capheaton 91 NZ 0380
Capler Camp (ant.) 45 SO 5932
Caplestone Fell 90 NY 5888
Cappercleuch 95 NT 2423
Capstone 30 TQ 7865
Capton 21 SX 8353
Caputh 108 NO 0940
Caradon Hill 20 SX 2770
Cara Island 92 NR 6444
Carbh-Bheinn 123 NG 5323
Carbis Bay 18 SW 5339
Carbost (Island of Skye) 122 NG 3731
Carbost (Island of Skye) 123 NG 4248
Carbrooke 64 TF 9402
Carburton 71 SK 6173
Carcary 109 NO 6455
Carclew 19 SW 7838
Car Colston 61 SK 7142
Carcroft 71 SE 5409
Cardenden 103 NT 2195
Carden Hall (ant.) 58 SJ 4553
Cardeston 58 SJ 3912
Cardiff 41 ST 1877
Cardiff-Wales Airport 41 ST 0667
Cardigan 43 SN 1846
Cardigan Bay 44 SN 4080
Cardigan Island 42 SN 1651
Cardington (Beds.) 52 TL 0847
Cardington (Shrops.) 59 SO 5095
Cardinham 19 SX 1268
Cardney House 108 NO 0545
Cardno 121 NJ 9663
Cardoness Castle (ant.) 87 NX 5955
Cardow 120 NJ 1942
Cardrona 96 NT 3038
Cardrona Forest 96 NT 3036
Cardross (Central) (ant.) 101 NS 6097
Cardross (Strath.) 100 NS 3477
Cardurnock 89 NY 1758
Car Dyke (Cambs.) (ant.) 53 TL 4769
Car Dyke (Lincs.) (ant.) 62 TF 1437
Car Dyke (Northants.) (ant.) 62 TF 1508
Careby 62 TF 0216
Careston 109 NO 5260
Carew 42 SN 0403
Carew Cheriton 42 SN 0402
Carew Newton 42 SN 0404
Carey 45 SO 5631
Carfrae 103 NT 5769
Cargen 88 NX 9672
Cargenbridge 88 NX 9474
Cargill 108 NO 1536
Cargo 89 NY 3659
Cargreen 20 SX 4262
Carham 97 NT 7938
Carhampton 23 ST 0042
Carharrack 18 SW 7241
Carie (Tays.) 107 NN 6157
Carie (Tays.) 107 NN 6437
Carines 19 SW 7959
Carinish 124 NF 8159
Carisbrooke 27 SZ 4888
Cark 77 SD 3676
Carland Cross 19 SW 8554
Carlby 62 TF 0414
Carleatheran 101 NS 6892
Carlecotes 70 SE 1703
Carleton (Cumbr.) 83 NY 4253
Carleton (Lancs.) 77 SD 3339
Carleton (N Yorks.) 78 SD 9749
Carleton Forehoe 65 TG 0805
Carleton Rode 55 TM 1192
Carlingcott 33 ST 6958
Carlingwark Loch 88 NX 7661
Carlin Tooth 90 NT 6302
Carlisle 83 NY 3955
Carlisle Airport 89 NY 4860
Carlock Hill 86 NX 0877
Carlops 95 NT 1656
Carloway 131 NB 2042
Carlton (Beds.) 52 SP 9555
Carlton (Cambs.) 54 TL 6453
Carlton (Cleve.) 85 NZ 3921
Carlton (Leic.) 60 SK 3905
Carlton (Notts.) 61 SK 6141
Carlton (N Yorks.) 78 SE 0684
Carlton (N Yorks.) 79 SE 6086
Carlton (N Yorks.) 79 SE 6423
Carlton (Suff.) 55 TM 3864
Carlton (S Yorks.) 71 SE 3610
Carlton (W Yorks.) 79 SE 3327
Carlton Colville 55 TM 5190
Carlton Curlieu 61 SP 6997
Carlton Husthwaite 79 SE 4976
Carlton in Cleveland 85 NZ 5004
Carlton in Lindrick 71 SK 5984
Carlton-le-Moorland 72 SK 9058
Carlton Miniott 79 SE 3980
Carlton Moor 78 SE 0383
Carlton-on-Trent 72 SK 7963
Carlton Scroop 62 SK 9445
Carluke 95 NS 8450
Carl Wark (ant.) 71 SK 2681
Carmacoup 94 NS 7927
Carmarthen 43 SN 4120
Carmarthen Bay 40 SN 2400
Carmel (Clwyd) 68 SJ 1676
Carmel (Dyfed) 43 SN 5816
Carmel (Gwyn.) 66 SH 3882
Carmel (Gwyn.) 66 SH 4954
Carmel Head 66 SH 2992
Carminish 124 NG 0284
Carminish Islands 124 NG 0185
Carmont 119 NO 8084
Carmunnock 94 NS 5957
Carmyle 101 NS 6461
Carmyllie 109 NO 5542
Carna 111 NM 6259
Carn a' Bhiorain 127 NH 1483
Carn a Bhodaich 116 NH 5637
Carnaby 81 TA 1465
Carnach (Harris) 125 NG 2297
Carnach (Highld.) 114 NH 0228
Carn a' Chaochain 115 NH 2317
Carn a' Choin Deirg 127 NH 3992
Carn a' Choire Mhòir 117 NH 8428
Carn a' Chrasgie 129 NH 8642
Carn a' Chuilinn 116 NH 4103
Carn a' Ghaill 110 NG 2606
Carn a' Gheòidh 117 NO 1076
Carn a' Ghlinne 127 NH 0660
Carn a' Mhaim 117 NN 9995
Carnan (mt.) 112 NL 5582
Carn an Daimh 106 NN 1371
Carnan Eoin 98 NR 4098
Carn an Fhidhleir or Carn Ealar 117 NN 9084
Carn an Fhreiceadain 116 NH 7207
Carnan Mòr 104 NL 9640
Carn an Rìgh 117 NO 0277
Carn an t-Sabhail 117 NN 9697
Carn an t-Sean liathanaich 117 NH 8632
Carn an t-Suidhe 117 NJ 2726
Carn an Tuire 117 NO 1780
Carn Bàn (Highld.) 127 NH 3341
Carn Bàn (Highld.) 127 NH 3387
Carn Bàn (Highld.) 116 NH 6303
Carn Ban (Island of Mull) 105 NM 7229
Carn Bàn Mòr 117 NN 8896
Carn Beag 127 NH 1055
Carnbee 103 NO 5306
Carn Bhac 117 NO 0482
Carn Bheadhair 117 NJ 0511
Carn Bhrain 128 NH 5287
Carnbo 102 NO 0503
Carn Brea 18 SW 6741
Carn Breac 127 NH 0452
Carn Breac Beag 127 NH 1879
Carn Breugach 105 NM 8127
Carn Cas nan Gabhar 128 NH 5280
Carn Chòis 107 NN 7927
Carn Chuinneag 128 NH 4883
Carn Coire na Creiche 116 NH 6208
Carn Coire na h-Easgainn 116 NH 7313
Carn Daimh 117 NJ 1824
Càrn Dearg 116 NN 5076
Carn Dearg (Highld.) 116 NH 6202
Carn Dearg (Highld.) 115 NN 3488
Carn Dearg (Highld.) 115 NN 3596
Carn Dearg (Highld.-Tays.) 107 NN 4166
Carn Dearg (Strath.) 106 NM 8918
Carn Dearg Mòr 117 NN 8291
Carn Dubh 'Ic an Deòir 116 NH 7719
Carn Duchara 100 NM 8910
Carnduncan 98 NR 2467
Carne 19 SW 9138
Carn Ealar or Carn an Fhidhleir 117 NN 9084
Carn Ealasaid 117 NJ 2211
Carn Eàs 117 NO 1298
Carn Easgann Bàna 116 NH 4806
Carneddau (mt.) 44 SO 0654
Carnedd Dafydd 67 SH 6663
Carnedd Iago 67 SH 7840
Carnedd Llewelyn 67 SH 6864
Carnedd Moel-siabod 67 SH 7054
Carn Eige 115 NH 1226
Carn Eilrig 117 NH 9305
Carnell 93 NS 4632
Car Ness 136 HY 4614
Carn fadrun (ant.) 66 SH 2835
Carnferg 119 NO 5293
Carnforth 77 SD 4970
Carn Garbh 127 NH 2858
Carn Geuradainn 114 NG 9839
Carn Ghriogair 116 NH 6520
Carn Glas-choire 117 NH 8929
Carn Gorm (Highld.) 127 NH 1349
Carn Gorm (Highld.) 115 NH 3235
Carn Gorm (Highld.) 128 NH 4362
Carn Gorm (Highld.) 128 NH 4570
Carn Gorm (Tays.) 107 NN 6350
Carnhell Green 18 SW 6137
Carnie 119 NJ 8105
Carn Kitty 129 NJ 0942
Carn Leac 115 NN 4097
Carn Leac Saighdeir 117 NJ 2706
Carn Liath (Grampn.) 117 NJ 1827
Carn Liath (Grampn.) 117 NJ 2515
Carn Liath (Grampn.) 117 NO 0386
Carn Liath (Highld.) 116 NH 4790
Carn Liath (Tays.) 108 NN 9369
Carn Mairg 107 NN 6851
Carn Meadhonach 117 NJ 1317
Carn Mhartuin 127 NH 1754
Carn Mòr (Grampn.) 117 NJ 2618
Carn Mòr (Highld.) 127 NH 2487
Carn Mòr (Highld.) 128 NH 4271
Carn Mòr (Highld.) 116 NH 4334
Carn Mòr (Highld.) 114 NM 9090
Carn Mòr (Island of Mull) 105 NM 3948
Carn na Cailliche 129 NJ 1847
Carn na Caim 116 NN 6782
Carn na Cloiche Mòire 127 NH 3753
Carn na Còinnich 127 NH 3251
Carn na Drochaide 117 NO 1293
Carn na Dubh Choille 127 NH 3867
Carn na Farraidh 117 NJ 1114
Carn na Feannaige 117 NJ 0908
Carn na h-Easgainn 116 NH 7432
Carn na Làraiche Maoile 116 NH 5811
Carn na Lòine 117 NJ 0636
Carn nam Bad 115 NH 4033
Carn nam Bain-tighearna 117 NH 8425
Carn nam Buailtean 126 NH 0087
Carn nan Con Ruadha 128 NH 4174
Carn nan Iomairean 114 NG 9135
Carn nan Sgeir (is.) 126 NC 0101
Carn nan Tri-tighearnan 117 NH 8239
Carn na Saobhaidh 116 NH 6724
Carn na Saobhaidhe 116 NH 5914
Carn na Sean-lùibe 114 NH 0235
Carno 57 SN 9696
Carnock 102 NT 0489
Carn Odhar 116 NH 6317
Carnon Downs 19 SW 7940
Carnousie 121 NJ 6650
Carnoustie 109 NO 5634
Carn Phris Mhòir 116 NH 8021
Carn Ruigh Chorrach 117 NH 9834
Carn Sgùlain 116 NH 6909
Carn Sgùmain 117 NH 8740
Carn Sleamhuinn 117 NH 8516
Carn Towan 18 SW 3626
Carnwath 95 NS 9746
Carnyorth 18 SW 3733
Carperby 84 SE 0089
Carracks, The 18 SW 4640
Carradale 92 NR 8138
Carradale Bay 92 NR 8137
Carradale Point 92 NR 8136
Carradale Water 92 NR 7843
Carragreich 125 NG 1998
Carraig Bhàn 98 NR 2572
Carraig Dhubh 98 NR 3062
Carraig Fhada 98 NR 3444
Carraig Mhòr 98 NR 4656
Carrbridge 117 NH 9022
Carr Brigs (pt.) 103 NO 6411
Carreg Ddu 66 SH 2742
Carreg-gwylan-fach 42 SM 7730
Carreglefn 66 SH 3889
Carreg-lem 41 SN 8017
Carreg-lwyd 41 SN 8615
Carreg Ti-pw 56 SN 5370
Carregwastad Point 42 SM 9340
Carreg yr Imbill 56 SH 3834
Carr End (pt.) 97 NU 2232
Carrick (Fife) 109 NO 4422
Carrick (Strath.) 100 NR 9087
Carrick (Strath.) 86 NS 1994
Carrick (Strath.) (dist.) 86 NX 3394
Carrick Forest 86 NX 4093
Carrick House 138 HY 5638
Carrick Roads 19 SW 8335
Carriden 102 NT 0181
Carrine 92 NR 6709
Carrington (Gtr Mches.) 69 SJ 7492
Carrington (Lincs.) 63 TF 3155
Carrington (Lothian) 103 NT 3160
Carrington Moss 69 SJ 7491
Carrog 67 SJ 1043
Carron (Central) 102 NS 8882
Carron (Grampn.) 120 NJ 2241
Carron Bridge (Central) 101 NS 7483
Carronbridge (Dumf. and Galwy.) 88 NX 8697
Carronshore 102 NS 8983
Carron Valley Forest 101 NS 6982
Carron Valley Resr. 101 NS 6983
Carrot Hill 109 NO 4540
Carr Shield 83 NY 8047
Carrs, The 81 SE 9678
Carrutherstown 89 NY 1071
Carruth House 100 NS 3566
Carr Vale 71 SK 4669
Carrville 84 NZ 3043
Carrycoats Hall 90 NY 9279
Carsaig 105 NM 5421
Carsaig Bay 105 NM 5320
Carscreugh 86 NX 2260
Carsegowan 87 NX 4258
Carse Gray 109 NO 4653
Carse House 99 NR 7461
Carse of Gowrie (dist.) 108 NO 2726
Carseriggan 86 NX 3167
Carsethorn 88 NX 9959
Carsgailoch Hill 93 NS 5414
Carshalton 37 TQ 2764
Carsington 60 SK 2553
Carsington Reservoir 60 SK 2652
Carskiey 92 NR 6508
Carsluith 87 NX 4854
Carsphairn 88 NX 5693
Carsphairn Forest 88 NS 5701
Carstairs 95 NS 9345
Carstairs Junction 95 NS 9545
Carswell Marsh 47 SU 3198
Carter Bar 90 NT 6906
Carter's Clay 26 SU 3024
Carterton 47 SP 2706
Carterway Heads 84 NZ 0451
Carthagena Bank (sbk.) 108 NO 2722
Carthew 19 SX 0055
Carthorpe 79 SE 3083
Cartington 91 NU 0304
Cartland 95 NS 8646
Cartmel 77 SD 3778
Cartmel Fell 77 SD 4188
Cartmel Sands 77 SD 3375
Cartmel Wharf (sbk.) 77 SD 3668
Carway 43 SN 4606
Cas 99 NR 7064
Cashel Loch 88 NX 6086
Cashel Dhu 133 NC 4450
Cashlie 107 NN 4942
Cashmoor 26 ST 9813
Cashtel yn Ard (ant.) 76 SC 4689
Cassington 47 SP 4510
Cassiobury Park 36 TQ 0897
Casswell's Bridge 62 TF 1627
Castallack 18 SW 4525
Castellau 41 ST 0586
Castell Dinas (ant.) 45 SO 1730
Castell Howell 43 SN 4448
Castell Odo (ant.) 56 SH 1828
Castell y Bere (ant.) 57 SH 6708
Castell-y-bwch 32 ST 2792
Castell-y-geifr 41 SN 8216
Casterley Camp (ant.) 34 SU 1153
Casterton 77 SD 6279
Castle 136 HY 2113
Castle Acre 64 TF 8115
Castle-an-Dinas (ant.) 19 SW 9462
Castle Ashby 52 SP 8659
Castlebay 112 NL 6698
Castle Bolton 84 SE 0391
Castle Bromwich 50 SP 1489
Castle Bytham 62 SK 9818
Castlebythe 42 SN 0229
Castle Caereinion 58 SJ 1605
Castle Campbell (ant.) 102 NS 9699
Castle Camps 54 TL 6343
Castle Carrock 83 NY 5455
Castle Cary (Somer.) 25 ST 6332
Castlecary (Strath.) 101 NS 7878
Castle Combe 33 ST 8477
Castlecraig (Borders) 95 NT 1344
Castlecraig (Highld.) 129 NH 8169
Castle Ditches (Hants.) (ant.) 26 SU 1219
Castle Ditches (S Glam.) (ant.) 41 ST 0570
Castle Ditches (W Glam.) (ant.) 41 SS 9667
Castle Donington 61 SK 4427
Castle Douglas 88 NX 7662
Castle Eaton 47 SU 1495
Castle Eden 85 NZ 4338
Castle Forbes 119 NJ 6219
Castleford 79 SE 4225
Castle Fraser 119 NJ 7212
Castle Frome 49 SO 6645
Castle Gresley 60 SK 2718
Castle Haven 119 NO 8884
Castle Heaton 97 NT 9041

Cruachan Min Dogmersfield

Cruachan Min	105	NM	4421
Cruachan Odhar	104	NM	3846
Cruachan Reservoir	106	NN	0828
Cruach an Tailleir	99	NR	7469
Cruach an Uillt Fheàrna	99	NR	6290
Cruach a'Phubuill	99	NR	8276
Cruach Brenfield	99	NR	8283
Cruach Chuilceachan	100	NR	9887
Cruach Ionnastail	99	NR	6491
Cruach Lagain	99	NR	7466
Cruach Lusach	99	NR	7883
Cruach Maolachy	100	NM	8914
Cruach Mhic Fhionnlaidh	100	NM	9402
Cruach Mhic-Gougain	92	NR	7550
Cruach Mhór	100	NN	0514
Cruach nam Fiadh (Strath.)	99	NR	8085
Cruach nam Fiadh (Strath.)	92	NR	8256
Cruach nan Caorach	100	NR	9980
Cruach nan Capull (Strath.)	100	NN	1405
Cruach nan Capull (Strath.)	100	NS	0797
Cruach nan Capull (Strath.)	100	NS	0979
Cruach nan Cuilean	100	NS	0484
Cruach nan Gabhar	92	NR	7542
Cruach nan Tarbh	100	NR	9782
Cruach na Seilcheig	99	NR	6898
Cruach Rarey	105	NM	8116
Cruach Scarba	105	NM	6904
Cruach Tairbeirt	100	NN	3105
Crùban Beag	116	NN	6692
Crubenmore Lodge	116	NN	6791
Cruckmeole	58	SJ	4309
Cruckton	58	SJ	4210
Crucymel (ant.)	41	SO	2220
Cruden Bay	121	NK	0936
Crudgington	59	SJ	6317
Crudwell	34	ST	9592
Crûg	48	SO	1872
Crugmeer	19	SW	9076
Cruib (mt.)	98	NR	5684
Cruick Water	109	NO	5462
Cruinn a'Bheinn	101	NN	3605
Cruinn Bheinn	101	NN	4312
Cruivie Castle (ant.)	109	NO	4122
Crulivig	131	NB	1733
Crumlin	41	ST	2198
Crummock Water	82	NY	1519
Crumpton Hill	89	NY	3491
Crundale (Dyfed.)	42	SM	9718
Crundale (Kent)	31	TR	0749
Crunwear	43	SN	1810
Cruwys Morchard	23	SS	8712
Crux Easton	34	SU	4256
Cruys (mt.)	118	NO	4275
Crwbin	43	SN	4713
Crychan Forest	44	SN	8540
Crymmych	43	SN	1833
Crynant	41	SN	7905
Crystal Palace	37	TQ	3470
Cuaig	123	NG	7057
Cubbington	50	SP	3368
Cubert	19	SW	7857
Cublington	36	SP	8422
Cuckfield	29	TQ	3024
Cucklington	25	ST	7527
Cuckmere River	29	TQ	5408
Cuckney	71	SK	5671
Cudden Point	18	SW	5427
Cuddesdon	47	SP	5902
Cuddington (Bucks.)	36	SP	7311
Cuddington (Ches.)	69	SJ	5971
Cuddington Heath	58	SJ	4646
Cuddy Hill	77	SD	4937
Cudham	37	TQ	4459
Cudliptown	21	SX	5278
Cudworth (Somer.)	24	ST	3810
Cudworth (S Yorks.)	71	SE	3808
Cuffley	37	TL	3002
Cuiashader	131	NB	5458
Cuilags (mt.)	136	HY	2003
Cuil Bay	106	NM	9755
Cuillin Hills	123	NG	4422
Culachy Forest	115	NN	3999
Culardoch (mt.)	117	NO	1998
Cùl Beag (mt.)	127	NC	1408
Culbin Forest	129	NH	9862
Culblean Hill	118	NJ	3901
Culbo	128	NH	6360
Culbokie	128	NH	6059
Culbone Hill	23	SS	8247
Culburnie	128	NH	4941
Culcabock	128	NH	6844
Culcharry	129	NH	8650
Cùl Doirlinn	111	NM	6672
Culdrain	121	NJ	5133
Culduie	123	NG	7140
Culford	54	TL	8370
Culgaith	83	NY	6129
Culham	47	SU	5095
Culkein	132	NC	0333
Culkerton	46	ST	9296
Cullachie	117	NH	9720
Cullaloe Resr.	102	NT	1887
Cullen	121	NJ	5166
Cullen Bay	121	NJ	5068
Cullercoats	91	NZ	3571
Cullerlie	119	NJ	7603
Cullicudden	128	NH	6564
Culligran Falls	115	NH	3640
Cullingworth	78	SE	0636
Cullipool	105	NM	7313
Cullisse	129	NH	8275
Cullivoe	143	HP	5402
Culloch	107	NN	7818
Culloden Forest	129	NH	7647
Culloden Muir	129	NH	7345
Cullompton	24	ST	0207
Culmaily	129	NH	8099
Culmark Hill	88	NX	6489
Culmington	48	SO	4982
Cul Mór (mt.)	132	NC	1611
Culmstock	24	ST	1013
Culm Valley	24	ST	1013
Culnacraig	127	NC	0603
Culrain	128	NH	5794
Culross	102	NS	9885
Culroy	93	NS	3114
Culsh (Grampn.)	121	NJ	8848
Culsh (Grampn.)	118	NO	3497
Culswick	140	HU	2745
Culter Cleuch Shank (mt.)	95	NT	0422
Cultercullen	121	NJ	9124
Culter Fell	95	NT	0529
Culter Water	95	NT	0329
Culter Waterhead Resr.	95	NT	0427
Cult Hill	102	NT	0296
Cults (Grampn.)	121	NJ	5331
Cults (Grampn.)	119	NJ	8903
Culver Cliff	27	SZ	6385
Culverstone Green	30	TQ	6363
Culverthorpe	62	TF	0240
Culworth	51	SP	5447
Culzean Bay	93	NS	2311
Culzean Castle	93	NS	2310
Culzie Lodge	128	NH	5171
Cumb	143	HU	5292
Cumbernauld	101	NS	7676
Cumberworth	73	TF	5073
Cumbrian Mountains	82	NY	2716
Cuminestown	121	NJ	8050
Cummersdale	83	NY	3952
Cummertrees	89	NY	1366
Cummingstown	129	NJ	1368
Cumnock	88	NS	5619
Cumnor	47	SP	4604
Cumrew	83	NY	5450
Cumrew	83	NY	5550
Cumwhinton	83	NY	4552
Cumwhitton	83	NY	5052
Cundall (N Yorks.)	79	SE	4272
Cunndal (Isle of Lewis)	131	NB	5065
Cunnigill Hill	141	HU	4367
Cunninghame (dist.)	93	NS	4047
Cunninghamhead	93	NS	3741
Cunningsburgh (dist.)	141	HU	4130
Cunnister	143	HU	5296
Cupar	103	NO	3714
Cupar Muir	103	NO	3613
Curbar	71	SK	2574
Curbridge (Hants.)	27	SU	5211
Curbridge (Oxon.)	47	SP	3208
Curdridge	27	SU	5313
Curdworth	50	SP	1892
Curland	24	ST	2716
Curragh's, The	76	SC	3694
Currarie	86	NX	1690
Currarie Port	86	NX	0577
Currie	102	NT	1867
Curr, The (mt.)	97	NT	8523
Curry Mallet	24	ST	3221
Curry Rivel	24	ST	3824
Curtisden Green	29	TQ	7440
Curtisknowle	21	SX	7353
Cury	18	SW	6721
Cushat Law	90	NT	9213
Cushnie	121	NJ	7962
Cushuish	24	ST	1930
Cusop	45	SO	2341
Cut Hill	21	SX	5982
Cutiau	57	SH	6317
Cutnall Green	49	SO	8768
Cutsdean	46	SP	0830
Cutthorpe	71	SK	3473
Cutts	141	HU	4038
Cuxham	36	SU	6695
Cuxton	30	TQ	7166
Cuxwold	75	TA	1701
Cwm (Clwyd)	67	SJ	0677
Cwm (Gwent)	41	SO	1805
Cwm (W Glam.)	40	SS	6895
Cwmafan	41	SS	7892
Cwmaman	41	SS	9999
Cwmbach (Dyfed)	43	SN	2525
Cwmbach (Mid Glam.)	41	SO	0201
Cwmbelan	57	SN	9481
Cwmbran	45	ST	2894
Cwmcarn	41	ST	2293
Cwmcarvan	45	SO	4707
Cwm Ceulan	57	SN	6890
Cwm-Cewydd	57	SH	8713
Cwmcoy	43	SN	2941
Cwm Croes	57	SH	8825
Cwm Cynllwyd	57	SH	8827
Cwmdare	41	SN	9803
Cwmdu (Dyfed)	43	SN	6330
Cwmdu (Powys)	41	SO	1823
Cwmduad	43	SN	3731
Cwm Einion	57	SN	6994
Cwmfelin Boeth	43	SN	1919
Cwmfelinfach	41	ST	1891
Cwmfelin Mynach	43	SN	2324
Cwmffrwd	43	SN	4217
Cwmgwrach	41	SN	8605
Cwm Irfon	44	SN	8549
Cwmisfael	43	SN	4915
Cwm-Llinau	57	SH	8407
Cwmllynfell	41	SN	7413
Cwm Owen	44	SO	0144
Cwmparc	41	SS	9496
Cwmpengraig	43	SN	3436
Cwm Prysor	67	SH	7536
Cwmsychpant	43	SN	4746
Cwmtillery	41	SO	2106
Cwmtudu	43	SN	3557
Cwm-y-glo	66	SH	5562
Cwmyoy	45	SO	2923
Cwmystwyth	57	SN	7873
Cwrt-newydd	43	SN	4847
Cwrt-y-gollen	45	SO	2317
Cyffylliog	67	SJ	0557
Cymer Abbey (ant.)	57	SH	7219
Cymmer (Mid Glam.)	41	ST	0290
Cymmer (W Glam.)	41	SS	8696
Cymyran Bay	66	SH	2974
Cynfall Falls	67	SH	7041
Cynghordy	44	SN	8139
Cynwyd	67	SJ	0541
Cynwyl Elfed	43	SN	3727
Cyrn-y-Brain (mt.)	58	SJ	2149

D

Daaey	143	HU	6094
Dacre (Cumbr.)	83	NY	4526
Dacre (N Yorks.)	78	SE	1960
Dacre Banks	78	SE	1961
Daddry Shield	84	NY	8937
Dadford	51	SP	6638
Dadlington	60	SP	4098
Daer Resr.	88	NS	9707
Dafen	40	SN	5201
Daffy Green	64	TF	9609
Dagenham	37	TQ	5084
Daglingworth	46	SO	9905
Dagnall	36	SP	9916
Daill	98	NR	3662
Dailly	93	NS	2701
Dairsie or Osnaburgh	109	NO	4117
Dalavich	100	NM	9612
Dalbeattie	88	NX	8361
Dalbeattie Forest	87	NX	8557
Dalbeg	131	NB	2345
Dalbeg Bay	131	NB	2246
Dalblair	88	NS	6419
Dalbog	109	NO	5871
Dalby	76	SC	2178
Dalby Point	76	SC	2178
Dalcapon	108	NN	9755
Dalchalloch	107	NN	7264
Dalchenna	100	NN	0706
Dalchork	133	NC	5710
Dalchreichart	115	NH	2912
Dalchruin	107	NN	7116
Dalcross	129	NH	7748
Dalderby	73	TF	2465
Dale (Derby.)	60	SK	4338
Dale (Dyfed)	42	SM	8005
Dale (Shetld.)	140	HU	1852
Dale Dike Resr.	71	SK	2391
Dale Head	83	NY	4316
Dalelia	111	NM	7369
Dale Point	42	SM	8205
Dales Head Dike	73	TF	1463
Dales Voe (Shetld.)	143	HU	4270
Dales Voe (Shetld.)	141	HU	4545
Dalgarven	93	NS	2945
Dalgety Bay	102	NT	1783
Dalgig	93	NS	5512
Dalginross	107	NN	7721
Dalguise	108	NN	9947
Dalhalvaig	134	NC	8954
Dalham	54	TL	7261
Daliburgh	112	NF	7421
Dalinlongart Hill	100	NS	1481
Dalkeith	103	NT	3367
Dall	107	NN	5956
Dallas	129	NJ	1252
Dallas Forest	129	NJ	1253
Dall Burn	107	NN	5654
Dalleagles	88	NS	5710
Dalle Crucis Abbey (ant.)	58	SJ	2044
Dallinghoo	55	TM	2654
Dallington	29	TQ	6519
Dallowgill Moor	78	SE	1770
Dalmacallan Forest	88	NX	8087
Dalmally	106	NN	1527
Dalmary	101	NS	5195
Dalmellington	93	NS	4705
Dalmeny	102	NT	1477
Dalmeny House	102	NT	1678
Dalmigavie	116	NH	7419
Dalmigavie Lodge	116	NH	7523
Dalmore (Highld.)	128	NH	6668
Dalmore (Isle of Lewis)	131	NB	2244
Dalmunzie Hotel	108	NO	0971
Dalnabreck	111	NM	7069
Dalnacardoch Forest	116	NN	6775
Dalnacardoch Lodge	107	NN	7270
Dalnaglar Castle	108	NO	1464
Dalnamein Forest	116	NN	7777
Dalnaspidal Lodge	107	NN	6472
Dalnavie	128	NH	6473
Dalnawillan Lodge	135	ND	0240
Dalness	106	NN	1751
Dalnessie	133	NC	6315
Da Logat	140	HT	9541
Dalqueich	102	NO	0704
Dalquhairn	86	NX	3296
Dalquharran Castle	93	NS	2702
Dalreavoch	129	NC	7508
Dalry	93	NS	2949
Dalrymple	93	NS	3514
Dalserf	94	NS	7950
Dalston	83	NY	3750
Dalswinton	88	NX	9385
Dalton (Dumf. and Galwy.)	89	NY	1173
Dalton (Lancs.)	69	SD	4907
Dalton (Northum.)	90	NY	9158
Dalton (Northum.)	91	NZ	1172
Dalton (N Yorks.)	84	NZ	1108
Dalton (N Yorks.)	79	SE	4376
Dalton (N Yorks.)	71	SK	4593
Dalton-in-Furness	76	SD	2374
Dalton-le-Dale	85	NZ	4047
Dalton-on-Tees	84	NZ	2908
Dalton Piercy	85	NZ	4631
Dalveich	107	NN	6124
Dalvina Lodge	133	NC	6944
Dalwhat Water	88	NX	7194
Dalwhinnie	116	NN	6384
Dalwood	24	ST	2400
Damerham	26	SU	1015
Damflask Resr.	71	SK	2791
Damgate	65	TG	3909
Damnaglaur	86	NX	1235
Dam of Hoxa	136	ND	4294
Damsay	136	HY	3913
Danbury	38	TL	7805
Danby	80	NZ	7009
Danby Low Moor	85	NZ	7110
Danby Wiske	84	SE	3398
Dandaleith	120	NJ	2845
Danderhall	103	NT	3069
Danebridge	70	SJ	9665
Danebury (ant.)	26	SU	3237
Dane End	37	TL	3321
Danehill	29	TQ	4027
Dane Hills	61	SK	5605
Danesborough (ant.)	52	SP	9234
Dane's Brook	23	SS	8331
Danes' Dyke (ant.)	81	TA	2172
Danskine	103	NT	5667
Darden Lough	91	NY	9795
Daren-felen	41	SO	2212
Darenth	37	TQ	5671
Daresbury	69	SJ	5782
Darfield	71	SE	4104
Dargate	31	TR	0861
Darite	19	SX	2569
Darlaston	60	SO	9796
Darleith House	100	NS	3480
Darlingscote	50	SP	2342
Darlington	84	NZ	2914
Darliston	59	SJ	5833
Darlochan	92	NR	6723
Darlton	72	SK	7773
Darnaw (mt.)	87	NX	5176
Darnaway Forest	129	NH	9751
Darnbrook Fell	78	SD	8872
Darowen	57	SH	8302
Darra	121	NJ	7447
Darras Hall	91	NZ	1571
Darrington	71	SE	4919
Darsham	55	TM	4170
Dartford	37	TQ	5474
Dartington	21	SX	7862
Dartmeet	21	SX	6773
Dartmoor Forest	21	SX	6180
Dartmouth	21	SX	8751
Darton	71	SE	3110
Darvel	94	NS	5637
Darwell Resr.	29	TQ	7121
Darwen	77	SD	6922
Da Scrodhurdins	140	HT	9339
Datchet	36	SU	9876
Datchworth	37	TL	2619
Daugh of Cairnborrow	121	NJ	4542
Daugh of Carron	117	NJ	2339
Daugh of Invermarkie	121	NJ	4141
Daugh of Kinermony	120	NJ	2441
Dauntsey	34	ST	9882
Davenham	69	SJ	6570
Daventry	51	SP	5762
Daventry Resr.	51	SP	5763
Davidstow	20	SX	1587
Davington	89	NT	2302
Daviot (Grampn.)	121	NJ	7528
Daviot (Highld.)	116	NH	7239
Davoch of Grange	121	NJ	4951
Dawes Heath	38	TQ	8188
Dawley	59	SJ	6807
Dawlish	21	SX	9676
Dawlish Warren	21	SX	9778
Dawn	67	SH	8672
Dawpool Bank (sbk.)	68	SJ	2281
Dawsmere	63	TF	4430
Daylesford	47	SP	2425
Ddyle	57	SO	0575
Deadh Choimhead	106	NM	9428
Deadwater	90	NY	6096
Deal	31	TR	3752
Deal Hall	39	TR	0097
Dean (Cumbr.)	82	NY	0725
Dean (Devon)	21	SX	7364
Dean (Hants.)	27	SU	5619
Dean (Somer.)	33	ST	6743
Deanburnhaugh	89	NT	3911
Deane	35	SU	5450
Dean Hill	26	SU	2526
Deanich Lodge	127	NH	3683
Deanland	26	ST	9918
Dean Prior	21	SX	7363
Dean Row	69	SJ	8781
Deans	102	NT	0268
Deanscale	82	NY	0926
Deanshanger	51	SP	7639
Deanston	101	NN	7101
Dean Water	109	NO	3548
Dearg Abhainn	106	NM	9739
Dearham	82	NY	0736
Dearne	71	SE	4505
Deasker (is.)	124	NF	6466
Debach	55	TM	2454
Debden	53	TL	5533
Debden Green	53	TL	5832
Debenham	55	TM	1763
Dechmont	102	NT	0370
Deddington	47	SP	4631
Dedham	54	TM	0533
Dedridge	102	NT	0566
Deene	52	SP	9492
Deenethorpe	52	SP	9592
Deepcar	71	SK	2897
Deepcut	35	SU	9057
Deepdale (Cumbr.)	77	SD	7284
Deep Dale (Durham)	84	NY	9615
Deeping Fen	62	TF	1916
Deeping Gate	62	TF	1509
Deeping St. James	62	TF	1609
Deeping St. Nicholas	62	TF	2115
Deeps, The (chan.)	141	HU	3241
Deerhill	121	NJ	4556
Deerhurst	46	SO	8729
Deer Law	95	NT	2225
Deerlee Knowe	90	NT	7208
Deerness	137	HY	5606
Deer's Hill	121	NJ	8045
Deer Sound	137	HY	5307
Defford	49	SO	9143
Defynnog	41	SN	9227
Deganwy	67	SH	7779
Deighton (N Yorks.)	85	NZ	3801
Deighton (N Yorks.)	79	SE	6244
Deil's Caldron	107	NN	7623
Deil's Heid, The (pt.)	109	NO	6741
Deil's or Celtic Dike (ant.)	88	NS	7011
Deiniolen	66	SH	5863
Delabole	20	SX	0683
Delamere	69	SJ	5668
Delamere Forest	69	SJ	5570
Delamere Station	69	SJ	5570
De Lank River	19	SX	1175
Delfrigs	121	NJ	9721
Delgatie Castle	121	NJ	7550
Delgaty Forest	121	NJ	7748
Dell	131	NB	4861
Delliefure	117	NJ	0731
Dell Lodge	117	NJ	0119
Dell River	131	NB	5058
Delnadamph Lodge	117	NJ	2208
Delny Dock	129	NH	7569
Delph	70	SD	9807
Delph Bank	63	TF	3721
Delph Resr.	69	SD	6916
Delph, The	54	TL	7080
Delvine	108	NO	1240
Dembleby	62	TF	0437
Denbigh	67	SJ	0566
Denbury	21	SX	8268
Denby	60	SK	3946
Denby Dale	71	SE	2208
Denchworth	34	SU	3891
Dene Mouth	85	NZ	4640
Denend	121	NJ	6038
Denford	52	SP	9976
Denge Beach	31	TR	0717
Denge Marsh	31	TR	0419
Dengie	39	TL	9801
Dengie Flat (sbk.)	39	TM	0404
Denham (Bucks.)	36	TQ	0386
Denham (Suff.)	54	TL	7561
Denham (Suff.)	55	TM	1974
Denham Aerodrome	36	TQ	0288
Denham Castle	54	TL	7462
Denham Green	36	TQ	0388
Denhead (Fife)	103	NO	4613
Denhead (Grampn.)	121	NJ	9952
Denhead of Arbirlot	109	NO	5742
Denhead of Gray	109	NO	3431
Denholm	90	NT	5718
Denholme	78	SE	0633
Denmead	27	SU	6511
Denmore	119	NJ	9411
Denne Park	28	TQ	1729
Dennington	55	TM	2866
Dennis Head	139	HY	7855
Denny	101	NS	8182
Dennyloanhead	101	NS	8180
Denny Lodge	26	SU	3305
Denside	119	NO	8095
Densole	31	TR	2141
Denston	54	TL	7652
Denstone	60	SK	0940
Dent	77	SD	7087
Dentdale	77	SD	7286
Den, The	93	NS	3251
Denton (Cambs.)	52	TL	1487
Denton (Durham)	84	NZ	2118
Denton (E Susx)	29	TQ	4502
Denton (Gtr Mches.)	69	SJ	9295
Denton (Kent)	31	TR	2146
Denton (Lincs.)	62	SK	8632
Denton (Norf.)	55	TM	2888
Denton (Northants.)	52	SP	8357
Denton (N Yorks.)	78	SE	1448
Denton (Oxon.)	47	SP	5902
Denton Fell	90	NY	6162
Denton Resr.	62	SK	8633
Denver	64	TF	6101
Denwick (Northum.)	91	NU	2014
Den Wick (Orkney)	137	HY	5709
Deopham	64	TG	0400
Deopham Green	64	TM	0499
Depden Green	54	TL	7756
Deptford (Gtr London)	37	TQ	3676
Deptford (Wilts.)	34	SU	0038
Derby	60	SK	3435
Derbyhaven	76	SC	2867
Dere Street (Durham) (ant.)	84	NZ	2120
Dere Street (Northum.) (ant.)	90	NY	9179
Dere Street (Northum.) (ant.)	84	NZ	0757
Dere Street (N Yorks.) (ant.)	79	SE	4363
Dergoals	86	NX	2459
Deri	41	SO	1202
Dernaglar Loch	86	NX	2658
Derringstone	31	TR	2049
Derrington	59	SJ	8822
Derry Burn	117	NO	0396
Derry Cairngorm	117	NO	0198
Derryguaig	105	NM	4835
Derry Hill	34	ST	9670
Derrythorpe	74	SE	8208
Dersalloch Hill	93	NS	4204
Dersingham	64	TF	6830
Dervaig	111	NM	4351
Derventio Roman Fort (ant.)	82	NY	1031
Derwen	67	SJ	0650
Derwent Fells	82	NY	2218
Derwent Reservoir (Derby. - S Yorks.)	70	SK	1790
Derwent Reservoir (Durham - Northum.)	84	NZ	0152
Derwent Water	82	NY	2621
Desborough	51	SP	8083
Desford	61	SK	4703
Deskry Water	118	NJ	3807
Detchant	97	NU	0836
Dethenydd (dist.)	57	SO	0082
Detling	30	TQ	7958
Deuchar Hill	109	NO	4662
Deuchar Law	95	NT	2829
Deuchary Hill	108	NO	0348
Deuddwr	58	SJ	2317
Deva (ant.)	68	SJ	4066
Devauden	45	ST	4899
Devilla Forest	102	NS	9588
Devil's Beef Tub	89	NT	0713
Devil's Bridge	57	SN	7477
Devil's Causeway (Northum.) (ant.)	97	NU	0046
Devil's Causeway (Northum.) (ant.)	97	NU	0426
Devil's Causeway (Northum.) (ant.)	91	NU	1203
Devil's Causeway (Northum.) (ant.)	91	NZ	0478
Devil's Ditch (ant.)	54	TL	6062
Devil's Dyke (Norf.) (ant.)	64	TF	7408
Devil's Dyke (W Susx) (ant.)	28	TQ	2611
Devil's Elbow	117	NO	1476
Devil's Point, The (mt.)	117	NN	9795
Devil's Water	84	NY	9356
Devizes	34	SU	0061
Devoke Water	82	SD	1596
Devonport	20	SX	4554
Devonside	102	NS	9296
Devoran	19	SW	7939
Dewi Fawr	43	SN	3023
Dewlish	25	SY	7798
Dewsall Court	45	SO	4833
Dewsbury	79	SE	2422
Dhoon	76	SC	4586
Dhoor	76	SC	4396
Dhowin	76	NX	4101
Dial Post	28	TQ	1519
Diaval (mt.)	131	NB	4552
Dibden	26	SU	3908
Dibden Purlieu	26	SU	4106
Dibyn Du (mt.)	57	SN	7865
Dickleburgh	55	TM	1682
Didbrook	46	SP	0531
Didcot	35	SU	5290
Diddington	52	TL	1965
Diddlebury	48	SO	5085
Didley	45	SO	4432
Didmarton	33	ST	8287
Didsbury	69	SJ	8490
Didworthy	21	SX	6862
Diebidale Forest	128	NH	4584
Diebidale River	128	NH	4383
Diffwys	57	SH	6523
Digby	62	TF	0754
Diggle	70	SE	0008
Dighty Water	109	NO	4232
Dihewyd	43	SN	4855
Dilham	65	TG	3325
Dilhorne	60	SJ	9743
Dilston	91	NY	9763
Dilton Marsh	33	ST	8449
Dilwyn	45	SO	4154
Dinam	67	SJ	0033
Dinas (Dyfed)	42	SN	0139
Dinas (Dyfed)	43	SN	2730
Dinas (Gwyn.)	66	SH	2736
Dinas Head	42	SN	0041
Dinas-Mawddwy	57	SH	8514
Dinas Powys	41	ST	1571
Dinchope	48	SO	4583
Dinder	33	ST	5744
Dinedor	45	SO	5336
Din Fell	89	NY	4696
Dingeston	45	SO	4115
Dingley	51	SP	7687
Dingwall	128	NH	5458
Din Lligwy (ant.)	66	SH	5085
Dinnet	118	NO	4698
Dinnings Hill	89	NY	2297
Dinnington (Somer.)	24	ST	4012
Dinnington (S Yorks.)	71	SK	5386
Dinnington (Tyne and Wear)	91	NZ	2073
Dinorben (ant.)	67	SH	9575
Dinorwic	66	SH	5961
Dinorwig (ant.)	66	SH	5565
Dinsdale Station	85	NZ	3413
Dinton	26	SU	0131
Dinwoodie Mains	89	NY	1090
Dinworthy	22	SS	3015
Diollaid Mhór	92	NR	7739
Dippen	92	NR	7937
Dippen Hall	35	SU	8146
Dippin	92	NS	0422
Dippin Head	92	NS	0522
Dipple (Grampn)	121	NJ	3258
Dipple (Strath.)	93	NS	2002
Diptford	21	SX	7256
Dipton	84	NZ	1554
Dirleton	103	NT	5183
Dirrie More	127	NH	2475
Dirrington Great Law	96	NT	6954
Dirrington Little Law	96	NT	6853
Discoed	48	SO	2764
Diseworth	61	SK	4524
Dishes	137	HY	6523
Dishforth	79	SE	3873
Disley	70	SJ	9784
Diss	55	TM	1179
Disserth	44	SO	0458
Distington	82	NY	0023
Ditcheat	25	ST	6236
Ditchingham	55	TM	3391
Ditchling	29	TQ	3215
Ditchling Beacon	29	TQ	3313
Dittisham	21	SX	8655
Ditton (Ches.)	69	SJ	4986
Ditton (Kent)	30	TQ	7158
Ditton Green	54	TL	6658
Ditton Priors	49	SO	6089
Dixton (Glos.)	46	SO	9830
Dixton (Gwent)	45	SO	5114
Dizzard Point	20	SX	1699
Dobwalls	19	SX	2165
Doccombe	21	SX	7786
Dochfour House	116	NH	6039
Dochgarroch	116	NH	6140
Dochrie Hill	102	NO	0808
Docking	64	TF	7637
Docklow	45	SO	5657
Dockray	83	NY	3921
Doctor's Gate (ant.)	70	SK	0794
Dodburn	89	NT	4707
Dodd Fell	78	SD	8484
Dodd Hill	88	NX	5697
Doddinghurst	38	TQ	5998
Doddington (Cambs.)	53	TL	4090
Doddington (Kent)	30	TQ	9357
Doddington (Lincs.)	72	SK	8970
Doddington (Northum.)	97	NU	0032
Doddington (Salop)	49	SO	6176
Doddiscombsleigh	21	SX	8586
Dodford (Here. and Worc.)	49	SO	9273
Dodford (Northants.)	51	SP	6160
Dodington (Avon)	33	ST	7579
Dodleston	68	SJ	3661
Dodman Point	19	SX	0039
Dodworth	71	SE	3105
Doe Lea	71	SK	4566
Dog Bank (sbk.)	108	NO	3025
Dogdyke	62	TF	2055
Dogmersfield	35	SU	7852

Esgair y Maesnant Ford (Mers.)

Esgair y Maesnant 57 SN 8386
Esh 84 NZ 1944
Esha Ness 142 HU 2279
Esher 37 TQ 1464
Eshott 91 NZ 2097
Eshton 78 SD 9356
Esh Winning 84 NZ 1942
Eskadale 116 NH 4539
Eskbank 103 NT 3266
Eskdale (Cumbr.) 82 NY 1800
Eskdale (Dumf. and Galwy.) 89 NY 3489
Esk Dale (N Yorks.) 80 NZ 7407
Eskdale Green 82 NY 1400
Eskdalemuir 89 NY 2597
Eskdalemuir Forest 89 NT 2503
Eskielawn (mt.) 108 NO 2766
Esknish 98 NR 3664
Espley Hall 91 NZ 1790
Esprick 77 SD 4035
Essendine 62 TF 0412
Essendon 37 TL 2708
Essich 116 NH 6539
Essington 60 SJ 9603
Esslemont 121 NJ 9329
Esthwaite Water 82 SD 3596
Eston 85 NZ 5518
Etal 97 NT 9339
Etchilhampton 34 SU 0460
Etchingham 29 TQ 7126
Etchinghill (Kent) 31 TR 1639
Etchinghill (Staffs.) 60 SK 0218
Ethie Castle 109 NO 6846
Eton 36 SU 9678
Etteridge 116 NN 6892
Ettington 50 SP 2649
Etton (Humbs.) 74 SE 9743
Etton (Northants.) 62 TF 1306
Ettrick 89 NT 2714
Ettrick Bay 100 NS 0365
Ettrickbridge 96 NT 3824
Ettrick Forest 96 NT 3724
Ettrick Pen 89 NT 1907
Ettrick Water 89 NT 3118
Etwall 60 SK 2732
Euchan Water 88 NS 7206
Euston 54 TL 8978
Euston Station 37 TQ 2982
Euximoor Fen 63 TL 4799
Euxton 69 SD 5518
Evanton 128 NH 6066
Evedon 62 TF 0947
Evelix 129 NH 7691
Evenjobb 48 SO 2662
Evenley 47 SP 5834
Evenlode 47 SP 2229
Eventide Home 119 NJ 9618
Evenwood 84 NZ 1524
Everbay 137 HY 6724
Evercreech 33 ST 6438
Everdon 51 SP 5957
Everingham 74 SE 8042
Everleigh 34 SU 1953
Everley 81 SE 9789
Eversholt 52 SP 9933
Evershot 25 ST 5704
Eversley 36 SU 7762
Eversley Cross 36 SU 7961
Everton (Beds.) 52 TL 2051
Everton (Hants.) 26 SZ 2993
Everton (Notts.) 72 SK 6891
Evertown 89 NY 3576
Evesbatch 49 SO 6848
Evesham 50 SP 0344
Evington 61 SK 6203
Ewden Village 71 SK 2796
Ewe Hill 95 NT 0540
Ewelairs Hill 89 NT 1602
Ewell 37 TQ 2262
Ewell Minnis 31 TR 2643
Ewelme 36 SU 6491
Ewen 46 SU 0097
Ewenny 41 SS 9077
Ewerby 62 TF 1247
Ewes 89 NY 3690
Eweslees Knowe 89 NT 3201
Ewesley 91 NZ 0592
Ewes Water 89 NY 3791
Ewhurst (Surrey) 28 TQ 0940
Ewhurst Green 30 TQ 7924
Ewloe 68 SJ 3066
Eworthy 20 SX 4494
Ewshot 35 SU 8149
Ewyas Harold 45 SO 3828
Exbourne 23 SS 6002
Exbury 26 SU 4200
Exebridge 23 SS 9324
Exelby 79 SE 2986
Exeter 21 SX 9292
Exeter Airport 21 SX 9993
Exe Valley 23 SS 9415
Exford 23 SS 8538
Exhall 50 SP 1055
Exminster 21 SX 9487
Exmoor Forest 23 SS 7642
Exmouth 21 SY 0080
Exnaboe 141 HU 3912
Exning 54 TL 6265
Exton (Devon) 21 SX 9886
Exton (Hants.) 27 SU 6121
Exton (Leic.) 62 SK 9211
Exton (Somer.) 23 SS 9233
Eyam 70 SK 2176
Ey Burn 117 NO 0886
Eydon 51 SP 5450
Eye (Here. and Worc.) 48 SO 4963
Eye (Northants.) 63 TF 2202
Eye (Suffolk) 55 TM 1473
Eye Brook 61 SK 7602
Eyebrook Resr. 62 SP 8595
Eyebroughy (pt.) 103 NT 4986
Eyemouth 97 NT 9464
Eye Peninsula 131 NB 5332
Eye Water 97 NT 8263
Eyeworth 53 TL 2545
Eyhorne Street 30 TQ 8354
Eyke 55 TM 3151
Eynesbury 52 TL 1859
Eynhallow (is.) 136 HY 3529
Eynhallow Sound 136 HY 3827
Eynort 122 NG 3826
Eynort River 122 NG 3727
Eynsford 37 TQ 5365
Eynsham 47 SP 4309
Eype 25 SY 4491
Eyre 123 NG 4152
Eyre Point 123 NG 5834
Eythorne 31 TR 2849
Eyton (Here. and Worc.) 48 SO 4761
Eyton (Salop) 48 SO 3687
Eyton upon the Weald Moors 59 SJ 6414

F

Faan Hill 142 HU 3480
Faccombe 34 SU 3857
Faceby 85 NZ 4903
Faddiley 59 SJ 5752
Fadmoor 85 SE 6789
Faifley 101 NS 5073
Failand 33 ST 5272
Failford 93 NS 4526
Failsworth 69 SD 9002
Fairbourne 56 SH 6113
Fairburn 79 SE 4727
Fairfield 49 SO 9475
Fairford 47 SP 1501
Fairham Brook 61 SK 5531
Fair Isle 139 HZ 2172
Fairlie 93 NS 2155
Fairlie Roads 93 NS 1753
Fairlight 30 TQ 8612
Fairmile 24 SY 0997
Fairmilehead 103 NT 2567
Fairnington House 96 NT 6427
Fair Oak (Hants.) 27 SU 4918
Fairoak (Staffs.) 59 SJ 7632
Fairoaks Airport 36 TQ 0062
Fairseat 30 TQ 6261
Fair Snape Fell 77 SD 5947
Fairstead (Essex) 38 TL 7616
Fairwarp 29 TQ 4626
Fairy Cross 22 SS 4024
Fairy Glen 67 SH 8054
Faither, The (pt.) 142 HU 2585
Fakenham 64 TF 9229
Fala 103 NT 4361
Fala Dam 103 NT 4261
Falahill 96 NT 3956
Fala Moor 103 NT 4258
Faldingworth 72 TF 0684
Falfield 46 ST 6893
Falkenham 55 TM 2939
Falkirk 102 NS 8880
Falkland 103 NO 2507
Falla 90 NT 7013
Fallin 101 NS 8391
Fall of Glomach 114 NH 0325
Fall of Warness (chan.) 137 HY 5427
Fallowlees Burn 91 NY 9992
Falls of Acharn 107 NN 7543
Falls of Bruar The 107 NN 8267
Falls of Cruachan 106 NN 0727
Falls of Falloch 106 NN 3420
Falls of Garbh Allt 117 NO 2089
Falls of Keltie 108 NN 8625
Falls of Lochay 107 NN 5434
Falls of Lora 106 NM 9134
Falls of Moness 108 NN 8547
Falls of Rogie 128 NH 4458
Falls of Tummel 108 NN 9159
Falmer 29 TQ 3508
Falmouth 19 SW 8032
Falmouth Bay 19 SW 8130
Falstone 90 NY 7287
Fambridge Station 38 TQ 8597
Fanagmore 132 NC 1750
Fan Fawr 41 SN 9619
Fangdale Beck 85 SE 5694
Fangfoss 80 SE 7653
Fan-Gihirych 41 SN 8819
Fan Hill 57 SN 9388
Fan Hir (mt.) 41 SN 8220
Fan Llia 41 SN 9318
Fanmore 105 NM 4244
Fanna Hill 90 NT 5603
Fannich Forest 127 NH 1968
Fannich Lodge 127 NH 2166
Fannyside Lochs 101 NS 8073
Fans 96 NT 6140
Fara (is.) 136 ND 3295
Faraclett Head 138 HY 4433
Faraid Head 132 NC 3971
Faray 138 HY 5336
Farcet 62 TL 2094
Farcet Fen 53 TL 2392
Far Cotton 51 SP 7458
Farden 48 SO 5776
Fareham 27 SU 5806
Farewell 60 SK 0811
Farigaig Forest 116 NH 5221
Faringdon 47 SU 2895
Farington 77 SD 5425
Farlam 90 NY 5558
Farland Head 93 NS 1748
Farlary 129 NC 7606
Farleigh 37 TQ 3660
Farleigh Hungerford 33 ST 7957
Farleigh Wallop 35 SU 6246
Farlesthorpe 73 TF 4774
Farleton 77 SD 5380
Farley (Shrops.) 58 SJ 3808
Farley (Staffs.) 60 SK 0644
Farley (Wilts.) 26 SU 2229
Farley Green 28 TQ 0645
Farley Hill 36 SU 7564
Farley Mount 26 SU 4029
Farleys End 46 SO 7615
Farlington 79 SE 6167
Farlow 49 SO 6380
Farmborough 33 ST 6560
Farmcote 46 SP 0629
Farmers 43 SN 6444
Farmington 47 SP 1315
Farmoor 47 SP 4407
Farmoor Resr. 47 SP 4406
Farmtown 121 NJ 5051
Farnborough (Berks.) 34 SU 4381
Farnborough (Gtr London) 37 TQ 4464
Farnborough (Hants.) 35 SU 8753
Farnborough (Warw.) 50 SP 4349
Farncombe 28 SU 9755
Farndale 80 SE 6895
Farndale Moor 85 NZ 6500
Farndish 52 SP 9263
Farndon (Ches.) 58 SJ 4154
Farndon (Notts.) 61 SK 7651
Farne Islands 97 NU 2337
Farnell 109 NO 6255
Farnham (Dorset) 26 ST 9514
Farnham (Essex) 37 TL 4724
Farnham (N Yorks.) 79 SE 3460
Farnham (Suff.) 55 TM 3660
Farnham (Surrey) 35 SU 8446
Farnham Common 36 SU 9584
Farnham Green 53 TL 4625
Farnham Royal 36 SU 9682
Farningham 37 TQ 5566
Farnley 78 SE 2147
Farnley Tyas 70 SE 1612
Farnsfield 61 SK 6456
Farnworth (Ches.) 69 SJ 5187
Farnworth (Gtr Mches.) 69 SD 7305
Farquhar's Point 111 NM 6272
Farr (Highld.) 116 NC 7163
Farr (Highld.) 116 NH 6833
Farr (Highld.) 117 NH 8203
Farragon Hill 107 NN 8455
Farr Bay 133 NC 7063
Farr House 116 NH 6831
Farringdon 24 SY 0191
Farrington Gurney 33 ST 6255
Farrmheall (mt.) 132 NC 3058
Farr Point 134 NC 7164
Farsley 78 SE 2135
Farthinghoe 51 SP 5339
Farthingstone 51 SP 6155
Farway 24 SY 1895
Fascadale 111 NM 5070
Faseny Water 103 NT 6162
Fasheilach 118 NO 3485
Fashven (mt.) 132 NC 3167
Faslane Bay 100 NS 2489
Fasnacloich 106 NN 0247
Fasnakyle 115 NH 3128
Fasnakyle Forest 115 NH 2630
Fasque 119 NO 6475
Fassfern 114 NN 0278
Fast Castle (ant.) 97 NT 8671
Fastheugh Hill 96 NT 3927
Fatfield 84 NZ 3053
Fathan Glinne 107 NN 4917
Fattahead 121 NJ 6657
Faugh 83 NY 5155
Fauldhouse 102 NS 9260
Faulkbourne 38 TL 7917
Faulkland 33 ST 7354
Fauls 59 SJ 5933
Faversham 31 TR 0161
Favillar 117 NJ 2734
Fawfieldhead 70 SK 0763
Fawkham Green 37 TQ 5865
Fawler 47 SP 3717
Fawley (Berks.) 34 SU 3981
Fawley (Bucks.) 36 SU 7586
Fawley (Hants.) 27 SU 4503
Fawley Chapel 45 SO 5829
Faw Side (mt.) 89 NY 3596
Faxfleet 74 SE 8624
Faygate 28 TQ 2134
Fazeley 60 SK 2001
Feadda Ness 141 HU 5438
Feall Bay 110 NM 1354
Fearby 78 SE 1981
Feardar Burn 117 NO 1995
Fearnan 107 NN 7244
Fearnbeg 123 NG 7359
Fearnhead 69 SJ 6290
Fearn Lodge 128 NH 6387
Fearnmore 123 NG 7260
Fearnoch Forest 106 NM 9631
Fearn Station 129 NH 8178
Featherbed Top 70 SK 0892
Featherstone (Staffs.) 59 SJ 9305
Featherstone (W Yorks.) 79 SE 4222
Featherstone Castle 90 NY 6761
Feckenham 50 SP 0061
Fedderate 121 NJ 8949
Feering 38 TL 8720
Feetham 84 SD 9898
Feinne-bheinn Mhór 133 NC 4346
Fèith a'Chaoruinn 133 NC 5522
Fèith Gaineimh Mhór 134 NC 9332
Fèith Talagain 116 NN 5497
Feizor 78 SD 7968
Felbridge 29 TQ 3739
Felbrigg 65 TG 2039
Felcourt 29 TQ 3841
Felden 36 TL 0404
Felindre (Dyfed) 40 SN 7027
Felindre (Powys) 48 SO 1681
Felindre (W Glam.) 40 SN 6302
Felinfach 41 SO 0933
Felinfoel 40 SN 5202
Felingwm Uchaf 43 SN 5024
Felixkirk 79 SE 4684
Felixstowe 55 TM 3034
Felkington 97 NT 9444
Felling 91 NZ 2762
Fell of Barhullion 86 NX 3742
Fell of Carleton 86 NX 4037
Fell of Fleet 88 NX 5670
Fell Side 82 NY 3037
Fell Top 77 SD 5751
Felmersham 52 SP 9957
Felmingham 65 TG 2529
Felpham 28 SZ 9599
Felsham 54 TL 9457
Felsted 38 TL 6720
Feltham 37 TQ 1072
Felthorpe 65 TG 1618
Felton (Avon) 33 ST 5165
Felton (Here. and Worc.) 45 SO 5748
Felton (Northum.) 91 NU 1800
Felton Butler 58 SJ 3917
Feltwell 54 TL 7190
Feltwell Anchor 54 TL 6789
Fence 78 SD 8237
Fencote 84 SE 2893
Fender Burn 108 NN 9169
Fendike Corner 73 TF 4560
Fen Ditton 53 TL 4860
Fen Drayton 53 TL 3468
Fen End 50 SP 2274
Feniscowles 77 SD 6425
Feniton 24 SY 1199
Fenn's Moss 59 SJ 4937
Fenny Bentley 60 SK 1750
Fenny Bridges 24 SY 1198
Fenny Compton 50 SP 4152
Fenny Drayton 60 SP 3597
Fenny Stratford 52 SP 8834
Fen Road (ant.) 63 TL 4698
Fenrother 91 NZ 1792
Fenstanton 53 TL 3168
Fenton (Cambs.) 53 TL 3279
Fenton (Lincs.) 72 SK 8476
Fenton (Lincs.) 62 SK 8750
Fenton (Staffs.) 59 SJ 8944
Fenwick (Northum.) 97 NU 0639
Fenwick (Northum.) 91 NZ 0572
Fenwick (Strath.) 93 NS 4643
Fenwick (S Yorks.) 71 SE 5916
Fenwick Water 93 NS 4541
Feochaig 92 NR 7613
Feochan Bheag 106 NM 8824
Feock 19 SW 8238
Feolin Ferry 98 NR 4469
Feriniquarrie 122 NG 1750
Fern 109 NO 4861
Ferndale 41 SS 9997
Ferndown 26 SU 0700
Ferness 129 NH 9645
Fernham 34 SU 2991
Fernhill Heath 49 SO 8659
Fernhurst 27 SU 9028
Fernie 108 NO 3115
Ferniehirst Castle (ant.) 90 NT 6517
Fernilea 122 NG 3634
Fernilee 70 SK 0178
Fernilee Resr. 70 SK 0176
Fernworthy Reservoir 21 SX 6684
Ferrensby 79 SE 3660
Ferring 28 TQ 0902
Ferrybridge 79 SE 4824
Ferryden 109 NO 7156
Ferryhill 84 NZ 2832
Ferryside 43 SN 3610
Fersfield 54 TM 0682
Fersit 115 NN 3577
Fers Ness 138 HY 5334
Fersness Bay 138 HY 5434
Fersness Hill 138 HY 5332
Feshiebridge 117 NH 8504
Fetcham 28 TQ 1555
Fethaland 143 HU 3793
Fetlar (is.) 143 HU 6291
Fetterangus 121 NJ 9850
Fettercairn 119 NO 6573
Fetteresso Forest 119 NO 7786
Fewston 78 SE 1954
Fewston Resr. 78 SE 1754
Ffairfach 43 SN 6220
Ffestiniog 67 SH 7042
Fforest 43 SN 5804
Fforest Fach (Powys) 41 SN 9027
Fforest-fach (Powys) 48 SO 1867
Fforest-fach (W Glam.) 40 SS 6396
Fforest Fawr 41 SN 9018
Ffostrasol 43 SN 3747
Ffridd 57 SH 9603
Ffridd Faldwyn (ant.) 58 SO 2196
Ffridd Fawr 67 SJ 0560
Ffridd-uchaf 66 SH 5751
Ffrith 58 SJ 2855
Ffrwdgrech 41 SO 0227
Ffynnonddrain 43 SN 4021
Ffynnongroew 68 SJ 1382
Ffynnon Llugwy Reservoir 67 SH 6962
Fiag Lodge (ruin) 133 NC 4528
Fiarach (mt.) 106 NN 3425
Fiaray 112 NF 7010
Fiavig Bàgh 130 NB 0335
Fidden 104 NM 3021
Fiddes 119 NO 8181
Fiddington (Glos.) 46 SO 9231
Fiddington (Somer.) 32 ST 2140
Fiddlers Hamlet 37 TL 4701
Fidra (is.) 103 NT 5186
Field 60 SK 0233
Field Broughton 77 SD 3881
Field Dalling 64 TG 0039
Field Head 61 SK 4909
Fifehead Magdalen 25 ST 7721
Fifehead Neville 25 ST 7610
Fife Ness 103 NO 6309
Fifield (Berks.) 36 SU 9076
Fifield (Oxon.) 47 SP 2318
Figheldean 34 SU 1547
Figsbury Ring (ant.) 26 SU 1833
Filby 65 TG 4613
Filey 81 TA 1180
Filey Bay 81 TA 1378
Filgrave 52 SP 8748
Filkins 47 SP 2304
Filla (is.) 143 HU 6668
Filleigh (Devon) 23 SS 6628
Filleigh (Devon) 23 SS 7410
Fill Geo 143 HP 5708
Fillingham 72 SK 9485
Fillongley 50 SP 2787
Filton 33 ST 6079
Filton Airfield 33 ST 5880
Fimber 81 SE 8960
Finalty Hill 117 NO 2074
Finavon 109 NO 4957
Finavon Castle 109 NO 4956
Finbracks (mt.) 109 NO 4070
Finchale Priory (ant.) 84 NZ 2947
Fincham 64 TF 6806
Finchampstead 36 SU 7963
Fincharn 106 NM 9003
Finchdean 27 SU 7312
Finchingfield 54 TL 6832
Finchley 37 TQ 2890
Findern 60 SK 3030
Findhorn 129 NJ 0464
Findhorn Bay 129 NJ 0462
Findhorn Bridge 116 NH 8027
Findhu Glen 107 NN 7115
Findochty 121 NJ 4667
Findo Gask 108 NO 0020
Findon (Grampn.) 119 NO 9397
Findon (W Susx) 28 TQ 1208
Findon Forest 128 NH 6458
Findon Mains 128 NH 6060
Findon Ness 119 NO 9497
Findrack House 119 NJ 6004
Finedon 52 SP 9272
Fingal's Cave 104 NM 3234
Fingal Street 55 TM 2169
Fingask 121 NJ 7827
Fingask Castle 108 NO 2227
Fingest 36 SU 7791
Finghall 84 SE 1889
Fingland 88 NS 7517
Fingland Fell 89 NY 1495
Finglen Burn 107 NN 6734
Finglen Rig 95 NT 1332
Fingringhoe 39 TM 0220
Finiskaig 111 NM 8694
Finlarig 107 NN 5733
Finlas Water 100 NS 3389
Finlaystone House 101 NS 3673
Finmere 51 SP 6333
Finnart 107 NN 5157
Finnarts Bay 86 NX 0472
Finningham 54 TM 0669
Finningly 71 SK 6699
Finnygaud 121 NJ 6054
Finsbay 125 NG 0786
Finsbury 37 TQ 3282
Finsthwaite 77 SD 3687
Finstock 47 SP 3516
Finstown 136 HY 3513
Fintry (Central) 101 NS 6186
Fintry (Grampn.) 121 NJ 7554
Fionn Bheinn 127 NH 1462
Fionn Bheinn Mhòr 127 NC 3704
Fionn Lighe 114 NM 9682
Fionn Loch (Highld.) 132 NC 1317
Fionn Loch (Highld.) 126 NG 9578
Fionn Loch Mòr 132 NC 3323
Fionnphort (Island of Mull) 104 NM 2923
Fionn Phort (Strath.) 98 NR 9065
Firbank 83 SD 6294
Firbeck 71 SK 5688
Fire Beacon Point 20 SX 1092
Firgrove 69 SD 9113
Firle Beacon 29 TQ 4806
Firsby 73 TF 4563
Firth 143 HU 4473
Firth of Clyde 93 NS 1354
Firth of Forth 103 NT 3786
Firth of Lorn 105 NM 7221
Firth of Tay 109 NO 3727
Firths Voe 143 HU 4474
Firth, The 141 HU 3450
Fir Tree 84 NZ 1334
Fishbourne (I. of W.) 27 SZ 5592
Fishbourne (W Susx) 27 SU 8304
Fishburn 85 NZ 3632
Fishcross 102 NS 8995
Fisherfield Forest 126 NH 0080
Fisherford 121 NJ 6635
Fisher's Pond 27 SU 4820
Fisherstreet 28 SU 9531
Fisher Tarn Reservoir 83 SD 5592
Fisherton (Highld.) 129 NH 7451
Fisherton (Strath.) 93 NS 2717
Fishguard 42 SM 9637
Fishguard Bay 42 SM 9839
Fish Holm 143 HU 4774
Fishlake 71 SE 6513
Fishnish Bay 105 NM 6442
Fishpool 69 SD 8009
Fishtoft 63 TF 3642
Fishtoft Drove 63 TF 3148
Fishtown of Usan 109 NO 7254
Fishwick 97 NT 9151
Fiskavaig 122 NG 3234
Fiskerton (Lincs.) 72 TF 0472
Fiskerton (Notts.) 61 SK 7351
Fistral Bay 19 SW 7862
Fitful Head 141 HU 3413
Fittleton 34 SU 1449
Fittleworth 28 TQ 0119
Fitton End 63 TF 4312
Fitty Hill 138 HY 4244
Fitz 58 SJ 4417
Fitzhead 24 ST 1228
Fitzwilliam 71 SE 4115
Fiunary 105 NM 6246
Fiunary Forest 105 NM 6447
Five Ashes 29 TQ 5525
Fivehead 24 ST 3522
Five Oak Green 29 TQ 6445
Five Oaks 28 TQ 0928
Five Penny Borve 131 NB 4056
Five Penny Ness 131 NB 5364
Five Roads 43 SN 4905
Five Sisters 114 NG 9617
Flackwell Heath 36 SU 8890
Fladbury 50 SO 9946
Fladda (is.) 104 NM 2943
Fladdabister 141 HU 4332
Fladda-chùain (is.) 125 NG 3681
Flag Fen 63 TL 2894
Flagg 70 SK 1368
Flamborough 81 TA 2270
Flamborough Head 81 TA 2570
Flamstead 36 TL 0814
Flanders Moss (Central) 101 NS 5595
Flanders Moss (Central) 101 NS 6398
Flannan Isles 130 NA 7146
Flansham 28 SU 9601
Flasby 78 SD 9456
Flash 70 SK 0267
Flashader 122 NG 3553
Flashes, The (pt.) 85 NZ 6125
Flat Holm (is.) 41 ST 2265
Flatt, The 90 NY 5678
Flaunden 36 TL 0100
Flawborough 61 SK 7842
Flawith 79 SE 4865
Flax Bourton 33 ST 5069
Flaxby 79 SE 3957
Flaxley 46 SO 6915
Flaxpool 24 ST 1435
Flaxton 79 SE 6762
Fleam Dyke (ant.) 53 TL 5553
Fleckney 61 SP 6493
Flecknoe 51 SP 5163
Fleet (Hants.) 35 SU 8054
Fleet (Lincs.) 63 TF 3823
Fleet Bay 87 NX 5651
Fleet Hargate 63 TF 3925
Fleetwood 77 SD 3247
Flemingston 41 ST 0170
Flemington 101 NS 6559
Flempton 54 TL 8169
Fleshwick Bay 76 SC 2071
Fletching 29 TQ 4323
Flexford 28 SU 9350
Flimby 82 NY 0233
Flimwell 29 TQ 7131
Flint 68 SJ 2472
Flintham 61 SK 7446
Flint Mountain 68 SJ 2369
Flinton 75 TA 2136
Flitcham 64 TF 7226
Flitton 52 TL 0536
Flitwick 52 TL 0335
Flixborough 74 SE 8715
Flixton (Gtr Mches.) 69 SJ 7494
Flixton (N Yorks.) 81 TA 0479
Flixton (Suff.) 55 TM 3186
Float Bay 86 NX 0647
Flockton 71 SE 2314
Flodabay 125 NG 0988
Floday (Isle of Lewis) 131 NB 1033
Floday (Isle of Lewis) 131 NB 1241
Flodda (is.) 124 NF 8455
Flodday (Barra) 112 NF 7502
Flodday (W Isles) 112 NL 6192
Floddaybeg 124 NF 9158
Floddaymore 124 NF 9157
Flodden 97 NT 9235
Flodigarry 123 NG 4671
Flookburgh 77 SD 3675
Floors Castle 96 NT 7134
Flordon 65 TM 1897
Flore 51 SP 6460
Flossnan 122 NG 2337
Flotta (Orkney) (is.) 136 ND 3593
Flotta (Shetld.) (is.) 141 HU 3746
Flotterton 91 NT 9902
Flowerdale Forest 126 NG 8867
Flowton 55 TM 0847
Flushing (Corn.) 19 SW 8034
Flushing (Grampn.) 121 NK 0546
Flyford Flavell 50 SO 9754
Fobbing 38 TQ 7183
Fochabers 121 NJ 3458
Fochno 57 SN 6493
Fochriw 41 SO 1005
Fockerby 74 SE 8419
Fodder Fen 53 TL 5287
Fodderletter 117 NJ 1421
Fodderty 128 NH 5159
Foel 57 SH 9911
Foel-cwmcerwyn 42 SN 0931
Foel-drych 42 SN 1630
Foeleryr 42 SN 0632
Foel Fenlli (ant.) 68 SJ 1660
Foel Figenau 57 SH 9128
Foel Fraith 41 SN 7517
Foel-Fras 67 SH 6968
Foel Fynyddau 41 SS 7893
Foel Goch 67 SH 9542
Foel Gurig 57 SN 9279
Foel Rhiwlas 58 SJ 2032
Foel Rhudd 57 SH 8924
Foel Wen 57 SJ 0933
Foel-y-ffridd 57 SH 8312
Foel y Geifr 57 SH 9327
Foffarty 109 NO 4145
Foggathorpe 74 SE 7537
Fogla Skerry 140 HU 1461
Fogo 96 NT 7749
Foinaven (mt.) 132 NC 3149
Foindle 132 NC 1948
Folda 108 NO 1964
Fole 60 SK 0437
Foleshill 50 SP 3582
Folke 25 ST 6513
Folkestone 31 TR 2336
Folkingham 62 TF 0733
Folkington 29 TQ 5604
Folksworth 52 TL 1490
Folkton 81 TA 0579
Folla Rule 121 NJ 7333
Follifoot 79 SE 3452
Folly Gate 21 SX 5797
Fontburn Resr. 91 NZ 0493
Fonthill Bishop 26 ST 9332
Fonthill Gifford 25 ST 9231
Fonthill Magna 25 ST 8616
Fontwell 28 SU 9407
Foolow 70 SK 1976
Foots Cray 37 TQ 4770
Foot, The 137 HY 5316
Fora Ness (Shetld.) 141 HU 3517
Fora Ness (Shetld.) 143 HU 4571
Forcett 84 NZ 1712
Ford (Bucks.) 36 SP 7709
Ford (Devon) 21 SX 7840
Ford (Glos.) 46 SP 0829
Ford (Mers.) 68 SJ 3598

Grappenhall Hamble

Grappenhall 69 SJ 6385
Grasby 74 TA 0804
Grasmere (Cumbr.) 82 NY 3307
Grasmere (Cumbr.) 82 NY 3406
Grasscroft 70 SD 9804
Grassendale 68 SJ 3985
Grassholme 84 NY 9221
Grassholme Resr. 84 NY 9422
Grassington 78 SE 0064
Grassmoor 71 SK 4067
Grass Point 105 NM 7430
Grassthorpe 72 SK 7967
Grassy Cletts 136 ND 2887
Grateley 34 SU 2741
Gratwich 60 SK 0231
Graveley (Cambs.) 53 TL 2564
Graveley (Herts.) 53 TL 2328
Gravelly Hill 50 SP 1090
Gravels 58 SJ 3300
Graveney 31 TR 0562
Gravesend 30 TQ 6473
Gravir 131 NB 3815
Grayingham 72 SK 9395
Grayrigg 83 SD 5797
Grays 30 TQ 6177
Grayshott 27 SU 8735
Grayswood 28 SU 9234
Graythorp 85 NZ 5227
Grazeley 36 SU 6966
Grèabhal (mt.) 124 NG 0089
Grean 112 NF 6703
Greanamul (Barra) 112 NF 7305
Greanamul (W Isles) 112 NL 6289
Greanamul Deas 124 NF 8848
Greasbrough 71 SK 4195
Greasby 68 SJ 2587
Great Abington 53 TL 5348
Great Addington 52 SP 9575
Great Alne 50 SP 1159
Great Altcar 68 SD 3206
Great Amwell 37 TL 3712
Great Asby 83 NY 6813
Great Ashfield 54 TM 0068
Great Ayton 85 NZ 5510
Great Baddow 38 TL 7204
Great Bardfield 54 TL 6730
Great Barford 52 TL 1352
Great Barr 60 SP 0495
Great Barrington 47 SP 2013
Great Barrow 68 SJ 4668
Great Barton 54 TL 8967
Great Barugh 80 SE 7478
Great Bavington 91 NY 9880
Great Bedwyn 34 SU 2764
Great Bentley 39 TM 1121
Great Bernera (is.) 131 NB 1635
Great Billing 52 SP 8162
Great Bircham 64 TF 7632
Great Blakenham 55 TM 1150
Great Bolas 59 SJ 6421
Great Bookham 28 TQ 1454
Great Borne (mt.) 82 NY 1216
Great Bosullow 18 SW 4133
Great Bourton 51 SP 4545
Great Bowden 51 SP 7488
Great Bradley 54 TL 6753
Great Braxted 38 TL 8614
Great Bricett 54 TM 0350
Great Brickhill 52 SP 9030
Great Bridgeford 59 SJ 8827
Great Brington 51 SP 6665
Great Bromley 55 TM 0826
Great Broughton 85 NZ 5406
Great Budworth 69 SJ 6677
Great Burbo Bank (sbk.) 68 SJ 2597
Great Burdon 84 NZ 3116
Great Burstead 38 TQ 6892
Great Busby 85 NZ 5105
Great Calva 82 NY 2831
Great Canfield 38 TL 5917
Great Carlton 73 TF 4185
Great Casterton 62 TF 0009
Great Chart 31 TQ 9842
Great Chatwell 59 SJ 7914
Great Chesterford 53 TL 5042
Great Cheverell 34 ST 9858
Great Chishill 53 TL 4238
Great Clacton 39 TM 1716
Great Coates 75 TA 2310
Great Comberton 50 SO 9542
Great Corby 83 NY 4754
Great Cornard 54 TL 8840
Great Coxwell 47 SU 2693
Great Cransley 52 SP 8376
Great Cressingham 64 TF 8501
Great Crosby 68 SJ 3199
Great Cubley 60 SK 1637
Great Cumbrae Island 93 NS 1656
Great Dalby 61 SK 7414
Great Dodd (mt.) 82 NY 3420
Great Doddington 52 SP 8864
Great Driffield 81 TA 0257
Great Dunham 64 TF 8714
Great Dunmow 38 TL 6221
Great Durnford 34 SU 1338
Great Easton (Essex) 54 TL 6125
Great Easton (Leic.) 62 SP 8493
Great Eau 73 TF 4485
Great Eccleston 77 SD 4240
Great Edstone 80 SE 7084
Great Ellingham 64 TM 0196
Great Elm 33 ST 7449
Great End (mt.) 82 NY 2208
Great Eversden 53 TL 3653
Great Fen 54 TL 5978
Great Finborough 54 TM 0157
Greatford 62 TF 0811
Great Fransham 64 TF 8913
Great Gable 82 NY 2110
Great Gaddesden 36 TL 0211
Great Gidding 52 TL 1183
Great Givendale 80 SE 8153
Great Glemham 55 TM 3361
Great Glen 61 SP 6597
Great Gonerby 62 SK 8938
Great Gransden 53 TL 2756
Great Green (Norf.) 55 TM 2789
Great Green (Suff.) 54 TL 9155
Great Habton 80 SE 7576
Great Hallingbury 37 TL 5119
Greatham (Cleve.) 85 NZ 4927
Greatham (Hants.) 27 SU 7730
Greatham (W Susx) 28 TQ 0415
Great Hampden 36 SP 8402
Great Harrowden 52 SP 8871
Great Harwood 77 SD 7332
Great Haseley 36 SP 6401
Great Hatfield 75 TA 1842
Great Haw (mt.) 78 SE 0779
Great Haywood 60 SJ 9922
Great Heck 71 SE 5920
Great Henny 54 TL 8738
Great Hill 88 NX 9492
Great Hinton 33 ST 9058
Great Hockham 54 TL 9592
Great Holland 39 TM 2119
Great Horkesley 54 TL 9731
Great Hormead 53 TL 4030
Great Horwood 51 SP 7731
Great Houghton (Northants.) 51 SP 7958
Great Houghton (S Yorks.) 71 SE 4206
Great Hucklow 70 SK 1777
Great Kelk 81 TA 1058
Great Kingshill 36 SU 8798
Great Lake (Notts.) 71 SK 5773
Great Lake (N Yorks.) 80 SE 7170
Great Langton 84 SE 2996
Great Law 96 NT 4047
Great Leighs 38 TL 7317
Great Limber 75 TA 1308
Great Linford 52 SP 8542
Great Livermere 54 TL 8871
Great Longstone 70 SK 1971
Great Lumley 84 NZ 2949
Great Lyth 58 SJ 4507
Great Malvern 49 SO 7845
Great Maplestead 54 TL 8034
Great Marton 77 SD 3335
Great Massingham 64 TF 7922
Great Mew Stone (is.) 20 SX 5047
Great Milton 36 SP 6302
Great Missenden 36 SP 8901
Great Mis Tor 21 SX 5676
Great Mitton 77 SD 7138
Great Mongeham 31 TR 3451
Greatmoor Hill 89 NT 4800
Great Moulton 55 TM 1690
Great Musgrave 83 NY 7613
Great Ness 58 SJ 3918
Great Oakley (Essex) 55 TM 1927
Great Oakley (Northants.) 52 SP 8686
Great Offley 52 TL 1427
Great Ormes Head 67 SH 7584
Great Ormside 83 NY 7017
Great Orton 82 NY 3254
Great Oxendon 51 SP 7383
Great Palgrave 64 TF 8312
Great Parndon 37 TL 4308
Great Paxton 52 TL 2164
Great Pinseat (mt.) 84 NY 9702
Great Plumstead 65 TG 2910
Great Ponton 62 SK 9230
Great Postland 63 TF 2612
Great Preston 79 SE 4029
Great Raveley 53 TL 2581
Great Ridge 25 ST 9236
Great Rissington 47 SP 1917
Great Rollright 47 SP 3231
Great Ryburgh 64 TF 9527
Great Ryle 91 NU 0212
Great Saling 54 TL 7025
Great Salkeld 83 NY 5536
Great Sampford 54 TL 6435
Great Sankey 69 SJ 5688
Great Saxham 54 TL 7862
Great Shefford 34 SU 3875
Great Shelford 53 TL 4652
Great Shunner Fell 83 SD 8497
Great Shutter Rock 22 SS 1343
Great Smeaton 85 NZ 3404
Great Snoring 64 TF 9434
Great Somerford 34 ST 9682
Great Stainton 84 NZ 3322
Great Stambridge 38 TQ 8991
Great Staughton 52 TL 1264
Great Steeping 73 TF 4364
Great Stonar 31 TR 3359
Greatstone-on-Sea 31 TR 0822
Great Stour 31 TR 0651
Great Strickland 83 NY 5522
Great Stukeley 53 TL 2275
Great Sturton 73 TF 2176
Great Swinburne 90 NY 9375
Great Tew 47 SP 3929
Great Tey 54 TL 8925
Great Torrington 22 SS 4919
Great Tosson 91 NU 0300
Great Totham (Essex) 38 TL 8511
Great Totham (Essex) 38 TL 8613
Great Wakering 38 TQ 9487
Great Waldingfield 54 TL 9143
Great Walsingham 64 TF 9437
Great Waltham 38 TL 6913
Great Warley 37 TQ 5890
Great Washbourne 46 SO 9834
Great Welnetham 54 TL 8759
Great Wenham 54 TM 0738
Great Whernside (mt.) 78 SE 0074
Great Whittington 91 NZ 0070
Great Wigborough 39 TL 9615
Great Wilbraham 53 TL 5557
Great Wishford 26 SU 0835
Great Witcombe 46 SO 9014
Great Witley 49 SO 7566
Great Wolford 47 SP 2434
Greatworth 51 SP 5542
Great Wratting 54 TL 6848
Great Wyrley 60 SJ 9907
Great Wytheford 59 SJ 5719
Great Yarmouth 65 TG 5207
Great Yeldham 54 TL 7638
Greave 104 NM 2420
Greeb Point 19 SW 8733
Greenbooth Resr. 69 SD 8515
Greenburn 102 NS 9360
Greendikes 97 NU 0628
Greenfield (Beds.) 52 TL 0534
Greenfield (Clwyd) 68 SJ 1977
Greenfield (Gtr Mches.) 70 SD 9904
Greenfield (Highld.) 115 NH 2000
Greenfield (Oxon.) 36 SU 7191
Greenford 37 TQ 1382
Greengairs 101 NS 7870
Greenham 35 SU 4865
Green Hammerton 79 SE 4656
Greenhaugh 90 NY 7987
Green Head (Hoy, Orkney) 136 ND 3099
Greenhead (Northum.) 90 NY 6665
Greenhill (Central) 101 NS 8278
Greenhill (Gtr London) 37 TQ 1688
Green Hill (Northum.) 84 NY 8647
Greenhill (S Yorks.) 71 SK 3481
Green Hill (Wilts.) 34 SU 0686
Greenhithe 30 TQ 5974
Greenholm 94 NS 5637
Greenholme 83 NY 5905
Greenhouse 96 NT 5523
Greenhow Hill 78 SE 1164
Greenigo 136 HY 4107
Greenland 135 ND 2367
Green Law (Borders) 90 NT 6304
Greenlaw (Borders) 96 NT 7145
Greenlee Lough 90 NY 7669
Greenli Ness 137 HY 6221
Greenloaning 101 NN 8307
Green Lowther 88 NS 8911
Green Mount 69 SD 7714
Greenock 100 NS 2776
Greenodd 77 SD 3182
Green Ore 33 ST 5749
Green Road Station 76 SD 1984
Green Scar 42 SM 7922
Greenside 91 NZ 1362
Greensidehill 91 NT 9716
Greenside Reservoir 101 NS 4775
Greensides (mt.) 86 NX 2889
Greenskairs 121 NJ 7863
Greens Norton 51 SP 6649
Greenstead Green 54 TL 8227
Greensted 37 TL 5302
Greenstone Point 126 NG 8598
Green Street 37 TQ 1998
Green Street Green 37 TQ 4563
Green, The (Cumbr.) 76 SD 1784
Green, The (Wilts.) 25 ST 8731
Greenwich 37 TQ 4077
Greet 46 SP 0230
Greeta River or River Creed 131 NB 3632
Greete 49 SO 5770
Greetham (Leic.) 62 SK 9214
Greetham (Lincs.) 73 TF 3070
Greetland 78 SE 0821
Greg Ness 119 NJ 9704
Gregson Lane 77 SD 5926
Greian Head 112 NF 6404
Greinton 24 ST 4136
Gremista 141 HU 4643
Grendon (Northants.) 52 SP 8760
Grendon (Warw.) 60 SP 2799
Grendon Common 60 SP 2799
Grendon Green 45 SO 5957
Grendon Underwood 36 SP 6720
Grenitote 124 NF 8275
Grenoside 71 SK 3394
Gresford 58 SJ 3454
Gresham 65 TG 1738
Greshornish 122 NG 3454
Greshornish Point 122 NG 3456
Gress 131 NB 4942
Gressenhall 64 TF 9615
Gressenhall Green 64 TF 9616
Gressingham 77 SD 5769
Gress River 131 NB 4545
Greta Bridge 84 NZ 0813
Gretna 89 NY 3167
Gretna Green 89 NY 3268
Gretton (Glos.) 46 SP 0030
Gretton (Northants.) 62 SP 8994
Gretton (Shrops.) 59 SO 5195
Grewelthorpe 79 SE 2276
Grey Cairns (ant.) 135 ND 2544
Greygarth 78 SE 1872
Grey Head 138 HY 5740
Grey Hill 86 NX 1692
Grey Mare's Tail (mt.) 89 NT 1814
Greysouthen 82 NY 0729
Greystoke 83 NY 4330
Greystone 109 NO 5343
Greywell 35 SU 7151
Gribbin Head 19 SX 0949
Gribun 105 NM 4533
Grice Ness 137 HY 6728
Griff 50 SP 3588
Griffithstown 45 ST 2999
Grif Skerry 141 HU 6362
Grigghall 83 SD 4691
Grike (mt.) 82 NY 0814
Grimeford Village 69 SD 6112
Grime's Graves (ant.) 54 TL 8189
Grimes Hill 77 SD 6286
Grimethorpe 71 SE 4109
Griminish 124 NF 7851
Griminish Point 124 NF 7276
Grimister 143 HU 4693
Grimley 49 SO 8360
Grimness (S. Ronaldsay) 136 ND 4793
Grim Ness (S.Ronaldsay) 136 ND 4992
Grimoldby 73 TF 3988
Grimsargh 77 SD 5834
Grimsay 124 NF 8656
Grimsby 75 TA 2810
Grimscote 51 SP 6553
Grimscott 22 SS 2606
Grimshader 131 NB 4025
Grimspound (ant.) 21 SX 7080
Grimsthorpe 62 TF 0423
Grimston (Leic.) 61 SK 6821
Grimston (Norf.) 64 TF 7221
Grimstone 25 SY 6393
Grimwith Resr. 78 SE 0664
Grindale 81 TA 1371
Grindle 59 SJ 7403
Grindleford 71 SK 2477
Grindleton 78 SD 7545
Grindlow 70 SK 1877
Grind of the Navir (pt.) 142 HU 2180
Grindon (Northum.) 97 NT 9144
Grindon (Staffs.) 60 SK 0854
Grindstone Law 90 NT 7607
Gringley on the Hill 72 SK 7390
Grinsdale 89 NY 3758
Grinshill 59 SJ 5223
Grinton 84 SE 0498
Griomaval (mt.) 130 NB 0122
Grisedale 83 NY 3715
Grisedale Pike 82 NY 1922
Grisedale Tarn 82 NY 3512
Grishipoll 110 NM 1959
Griskerry 141 HU 3622
Gristhorpe 81 TA 0882
Griston 64 TL 9499
Gritley 137 HY 5605
Grittenham 34 SU 0382
Grittleton 33 ST 8579
Grizebeck 76 SD 2384
Grizedale 82 SD 3394
Grizedale Forest 82 SD 3394
Groatay 124 NF 9773
Groay 124 NG 0079
Groban (mt.) 127 NH 0970
Grob Bàgh 92 NR 6346
Grobister 137 HY 6524
Groby 61 SK 5207
Groemeshall Burn 136 HY 4704
Groes (Clwyd) 67 SJ 0064
Groes (W Glam.) 41 SS 7986
Groes-faen 41 ST 0780
Groesffordd Marli 67 SJ 0073
Groeslon 66 SH 4755
Grogport 92 NR 8044
Gronant 67 SJ 0883
Groombridge 29 TQ 5337
Grosebay 125 NG 1592
Grosmont (Gwent) 45 SO 4024
Grosmont (N Yorks.) 80 NZ 8205
Groton 54 TL 9641
Grove (Dorset) 25 SY 6972
Grove (Kent) 31 TR 2362
Grove (Notts.) 72 SK 7379
Grove (Oxon.) 34 SU 4090
Grovely Wood 26 SU 0534
Grove Park 37 TQ 4172
Grovesend 40 SN 5900
Grudie Burn 128 NC 5305
Grudie River 132 NC 3161
Gruids 128 NC 5604
Gruinard Bay 126 NG 9293
Gruinard House 126 NG 9492
Gruinard Island 126 NG 9494
Gruinard River 126 NG 9789
Gruinart 98 NR 2866
Grula 122 NG 3826
Gruline 105 NM 5440
Gruline House 105 NM 5539
Grumbla 18 SW 4029
Grumby Rock 133 NC 7010
Gruna (is.) 140 HU 2859
Grunasound 141 HU 3733
Gruna Stack 142 HU 2886
Grunay 143 HU 6971
Grundisburgh 55 TM 2251
Gruney (is.) 143 HU 3896
Grunka Hellier 143 HP 5815
Gruting 140 HU 2849
Gruting Voe 140 HU 2647
Grutness 141 HU 4009
Grut Wick 141 HU 5138
Grwyne Fechan 45 SO 2324
Gryfe Reservoirs 100 NS 2871
Gualachulain 106 NN 1145
Gualann (mt.) 101 NS 4594
Gualin House 132 NC 3056
Gualann Mhòr 100 NR 9062
Guardbridge 109 NO 4519
Guarlford 49 SO 8145
Guay 108 NO 0049
Guens, The (is.) 143 HU 6568
Guestling Green 30 TQ 8513
Guestwick 64 TG 0627
Gugh 18 SV 8908
Guide Post 91 NZ 2585
Guilden Morden 53 TL 2744
Guilden Sutton 68 SJ 4468
Guildford 28 TQ 0049
Guildtown 108 NO 1331
Guillamon Island 123 NG 6327
Guilsborough 51 SP 6773
Guilsfield 58 SJ 2111
Guirasdeal 105 NM 6907
Guirdil Bay 110 NG 3101
Guisachan Forest 115 NH 2520
Guisborough 85 NZ 6115
Guiseley 78 SE 1941
Guist 64 TF 9925
Guith 138 HY 5536
Guiting Power 46 SP 0924
Gulber Wick 141 HU 4438
Gulf of Corryvreckan 99 NM 6901
Gulland Rock 19 SW 8778
Gullane 103 NT 4882
Gullane Bay 103 NT 4783
Gull Point 93 NS 1450
Gulvain or Gaor Bheinn 114 NM 9987
Gulval 18 SW 4831
Gumfreston 42 SN 1101
Gumley 51 SP 6890
Gunby (Humbs.) 74 SE 7135
Gunby (Lincs.) 62 SK 9021
Gundleton 27 SU 6133
Gunfleet Sand 39 TM 2611
Gunn 23 SS 6333
Gunna (is.) 110 NM 0951
Gunnerside 84 SD 9598
Gunnerton 90 NY 9074
Gunness 74 SE 8411
Gunnislake 20 SX 4371
Gunnista 141 HU 5043
Gunthorpe (Norf.) 64 TG 0135
Gunthorpe (Notts.) 61 SK 6744
Gunton Hall 65 TG 2234
Gunton Sta 65 TG 2535
Gunver Head 19 SW 8977
Gunwalloe Fishing Cove 18 SW 6522
Gurnard 27 SZ 4795
Gurnard Bay 27 SZ 4795
Gurnard's Head 18 SW 4338
Gurn Ddu 66 SH 4046
Gurney Slade 33 ST 6249
Gurnos 41 SN 7709
Gussage All Saints 26 SU 0010
Gussage St. Michael 26 ST 9811
Guston 31 TR 3244
Gutcher 143 HU 5498
Guthrie 109 NO 5650
Gutter Sound 136 ND 3197
Guyhirn 63 TF 3903
Guy's Head 63 TF 4825
Guy's Marsh 25 ST 8420
Guyzance 91 NU 2103
Gwaelod-y-garth 41 ST 1183
Gwaenysgor 67 SJ 0780
Gwalchmai 66 SH 3975
Gwastad 45 SO 2305
Gwastedyn Hill 57 SN 9866
Gwaun-Cae-Gurwen 40 SN 7011
Gwaunceste Hill 44 SO 1555
Gwaun Nant-ddu 41 SO 0017
Gwaynynog 67 SJ 0365
Gwbert-on-Sea 42 SN 1650
Gweek 18 SW 7026
Gwehelog 45 SO 3804
Gwenddwr 44 SO 0643
Gwendraeth (sbk.) 43 SN 3606
Gwendraeth Fâch 43 SN 4714
Gwendraeth Fawr 43 SN 5011
Gwennap 18 SW 7340
Gwennap Head 18 SW 3621
Gwenter 18 SW 7418
Gwernaffield 68 SJ 2064
Gwernesney 45 SO 4101
Gwernogle 43 SN 5234
Gwernymynydd 68 SJ 2162
Gwespyr 68 SJ 1183
Gwinear 18 SW 5937
Gwithian 18 SW 5841
Gwrhyd 44 SN 9339
Gwrych Castle 67 SH 9277
Gwyddelwern 67 SJ 0746
Gwyddgrug 43 SN 4635
Gwytherin 67 SH 8761
Gylchedd 67 SH 8644
Gypsey Race 81 TA 0970

H

Haaf Gruney (is.) 143 HU 6398
Haa, The (pt.) 141 HU 5560
Habberley (Here. and Worc.) 49 SO 8077
Habberley (Shrops.) 58 SJ 3903
Habitancum (ant.) 90 NY 8986
Habost (Isle of Lewis) 131 NB 3219
Habost (Isle of Lewis) 131 NB 5262
Habrough 75 TA 1514
Haccombe 21 SX 8970
Haceby 62 TF 0236
Hacheston 55 TM 3059
Hackenthorpe 71 SK 4183
Hackford 64 TG 0502
Hackforth 84 SE 2493
Hackland 136 HY 3920
Hacklete 131 NB 1534
Hackleton 51 SP 8055
Hackley Head or Forvie Ness 121 NK 0226
Hackness (N Yorks.) 81 SE 9690
Hackness (South Walls) 136 ND 3391
Hackney 37 TQ 3585
Hacko's Ness 137 HY 5215
Hackpen Hill (Devon) 24 ST 1112
Hackpen Hill (Wilts.) 34 SU 1274
Hacks Ness 139 HY 6134
Hackthorn 72 SK 9882
Hackthorpe 83 NY 5423
Haconby 62 TF 1025
Hadden 97 NT 7836
Haddenham (Bucks.) 36 SP 7408
Haddenham (Cambs.) 53 TL 4675
Haddington 103 NT 5174
Haddiscoe 65 TM 4497
Haddock Sands (chan.) 141 HU 3443
Haddo House 121 NJ 8634
Haddon 52 TL 1392
Haddon Hall (ant.) 71 SK 2366
Haddon Hill 23 SS 9628
Hademore 60 SK 1708
Hadfield 70 SK 0296
Hadham Cross 37 TL 4218
Hadham Ford 37 TL 4321
Hadleigh (Essex) 38 TQ 8087
Hadleigh (Suff.) 54 TM 0242
Hadley 59 SJ 6712
Hadley End 60 SK 1320
Hadlow 29 TQ 6349
Hadlow Down 29 TQ 5324
Hadnall 59 SJ 5120
Hadrian's Wall (Cumbr.) (ant.) 89 NY 2661
Hadrian's Wall (Cumbr.) (ant.) 83 NY 3757
Hadrian's Wall (Cumbr.) (ant.) 89 NY 4561
Hadrian's Wall (Northum.) (ant.) 90 NY 7167
Hadrian's Wall (Northum.) (ant.) 90 NY 8069
Hadrian's Wall (Northum.) (ant.) 91 NZ 0568
Hadstock 53 TL 5645
Hadston Carrs (pt.) 91 NU 2800
Hadyard Hill 86 NX 2799
Hadzor 49 SO 9162
Haffenden Quarter 30 TQ 8841
Hafod-Dinbych 67 SH 8953
Haggbeck 89 NY 4774
Haggerston Castle 97 NU 0443
Hagley (Here. and Worc.) 45 SO 5641
Hagley (Here. and Worc.) 49 SO 9181
Hagshaw Hill 94 NS 7831
Hagworthingham 73 TF 3469
Haigh 69 SD 6108
Haighton Green 77 SD 5634
Haile 82 NY 0308
Hailes 46 SP 0530
Hailes Castle (ant.) 103 NT 5775
Hailey (Herts.) 37 TL 3710
Hailey (Oxon.) 47 SP 3512
Hailsham 29 TQ 5909
Hail Weston 52 TL 1662
Hainault 37 TQ 4691
Hainford 65 TG 2218
Hainton 73 TF 1784
Haisborough (lightship) 65 TG 4049
Haisthorpe 81 TA 1264
Halam 61 SK 6754
Halberry Head 135 ND 3037
Halberton 23 ST 0012
Halcro 135 ND 2260
Halcro Head 136 ND 4785
Hale (Ches.) 68 SJ 4682
Hale (Gtr Mches.) 69 SJ 7786
Hale (Hants.) 26 SU 1919
Hale (Lincs.) 62 TF 1443
Hale Bank 69 SJ 4784
Halebarns 69 SJ 7985
Hales (Norf.) 65 TM 3897
Hales (Staffs.) 59 SJ 7134
Halesowen 50 SO 9683
Hales Place 31 TR 1459
Hale Street 29 TQ 6749
Halesworth 55 TM 3877
Halewood 68 SJ 4585
Halford (Shrops.) 48 SO 4383
Halford (Warw.) 50 SP 2545
Halfpenny Green 49 SO 8292
Halfpenny Green Airport 49 SO 8291
Halfway (Berks.) 34 SU 4068
Halfway (Dyfed) 43 SN 6430
Halfway (Dyfed) 41 SN 8232
Halfway House 58 SJ 3411
Halfway Houses 30 TQ 9373
Halidon Hill 97 NT 9655
Halifax 78 SE 0825
Halistra 122 NG 2459
Halket 93 NS 4252
Halkirk 135 ND 1359
Halkyn 68 SJ 2071
Halkyn Mountain 68 SJ 1971
Halladale River 134 NC 8855
Halland 29 TQ 5016
Hallaton 61 SP 7896
Hallatrow 33 ST 6356
Hallbankgate 90 NY 5859
Hall Dunnerdale 82 SD 2195
Hallen 33 ST 5479
Hall Green 50 SP 1181
Hallhills Loch 89 NY 1688
Halliburton 96 NT 6748
Halliman Skerries 120 NJ 2172
Hallin 122 NG 2558
Halling 30 TQ 7063
Hallington 91 NY 9875
Hallington Resr. 91 NY 9776
Hallival (mt.) 111 NM 3996
Hall of Clestrain 136 HY 2907
Hall of Tankerness 137 HY 5208
Hall of the Forest 48 SO 2083
Halloughton 61 SK 6851
Hallow 49 SO 8258
Hall Road Station 68 SD 3000
Hallrule 90 NT 5914
Halls 103 NT 6572
Hallsands 21 SX 8138
Hall's Green 53 TL 2728
Hall, The 143 HU 6098
Hallthwaites 76 SD 1885
Hallworthy 20 SX 1787
Hallyburton Forest 108 NO 2333
Hallyburton House 108 NO 2438
Hallyne 95 NT 1940
Halmer End 59 SJ 7949
Halmore 46 SO 6902
Halmyre Mains 95 NT 1749
Halnaker 28 SU 9108
Halsall 68 SD 3710
Halse (Northants.) 51 SP 5640
Halse (Somer.) 24 ST 1327
Halsetown 18 SW 5038
Halsham 75 TA 2627
Halsinger 22 SS 5138
Halstead (Essex) 54 TL 8130
Halstead (Kent) 37 TQ 4961
Halstead (Leic.) 61 SK 7505
Halstock 25 ST 5308
Halstow Marshes 30 TQ 7877
Haltham 73 TF 2463
Haltoft End 63 TF 3645
Halton (Bucks.) 36 SP 8710
Halton (Ches.) 69 SJ 5381
Halton (Clwyd) 58 SJ 3039
Halton (Lancs.) 77 SD 5065
Halton East 78 SE 0454
Halton Gill 78 SD 8876
Halton Holegate 73 TF 4165
Halton Lea Gate 90 NY 6558
Halton West 78 SD 8454
Haltwhistle 90 NY 7064
Halvergate 65 TG 4206
Halvergate Marshes 65 TG 4506
Halwell 21 SX 7753
Halwill 20 SX 4299
Halwill Junction 20 SS 4400
Ham (Bressay) 141 HU 4939
Ham (Foula) 140 HT 9739
Ham (Glos.) 46 ST 6898
Ham (Gtr London) 37 TQ 1672
Ham (Highld.) 135 ND 2373
Ham (Kent) 31 TR 3354
Ham (Wilts.) 34 SU 3262
Hamar (pt.) 141 HU 5136
Hamara River 122 NG 1947
Hamars Ness 143 HU 5894
Hamble 27 SU 4806

Hamble Airfield Heskin Green

Hamble Airfield	27	SU 4707
Hambleden (Bucks.)	36	SU 7886
Hambledon (Hants.)	27	SU 6414
Hambledon (Surrey)	28	SU 9638
Hambledon Hill (ant.)	25	ST 8412
Hambleton (Lancs.)	77	SD 3742
Hambleton (N Yorks.)	79	SE 5430
Hambleton Hill	78	SE 1573
Hambleton Hills, The	79	SE 5286
Hambridge	24	ST 3921
Hambrook (Avon)	33	ST 6378
Hambrook (W Susx)	27	SU 7806
Hameldon Hill	78	SD 7928
Hameldown Tor	21	SX 7080
Hamera Head	141	HU 4862
Hameringham	73	TF 3167
Hamerton	52	TL 1379
Hametoun	140	HT 9637
Hamford Water	55	TM 2325
Ham Green (Avon)	33	ST 5575
Ham Green (Here. and Worc.)	50	SP 0063
Ham Hill (ant.)	25	ST 4816
Hamilton	94	NS 7255
Hamly Hill	136	HY 4904
Hammersmith	37	TQ 2279
Hammerwich	60	SK 0707
Hammond Beck	62	TF 2038
Hammond Street	37	TL 3304
Hammoon	25	ST 8114
Hamna Voe (Papa Stour)	140	HU 1659
Hamna Voe (Shetld.)	142	HU 2380
Hamnavoe (Shetld.)	142	HU 2381
Hamnavoe (Shetld.)	143	HU 4971
Hamnavoe (West Burra)	141	HU 3735
Hamna Voe (Yell)	143	HU 4879
Hamnavoe (Yell)	143	HU 4980
Ham of Muness	143	HP 6301
Hampden Park	29	TQ 6002
Hampnett	46	SP 0915
Hampole	71	SE 5010
Hampreston	26	SZ 0598
Hampstead	37	TQ 2485
Hampstead Norreys	35	SU 5276
Hampsthwaite	79	SE 2558
Hampton	50	SP 0243
Hampton (Gtr London)	37	TQ 1369
Hampton (Shrops.)	49	SO 7486
Hampton Bishop	45	SO 5538
Hampton Court (ant.)	37	TQ 1568
Hampton Heath	59	SJ 4949
Hampton in Arden	50	SP 2081
Hampton Lovett	49	SO 8865
Hampton Lucy	50	SP 2557
Hampton on the Hill	50	SP 2564
Hampton Poyle	47	SP 5015
Hamsey	29	TQ 4112
Hamstall Ridware	60	SK 1019
Hamstead (I. of W.)	26	SZ 3991
Hamstead (W Mids)	60	SP 0593
Hamstead Marshall	34	SU 4165
Hamsterley (Durham)	84	NZ 1131
Hamsterley (Durham)	84	NZ 1156
Hamsterley Forest	84	NZ 0328
Hamstreet (Kent)	31	TR 0034
Ham Street (Somer.)	25	ST 5534
Hamworthy	26	SY 9990
Hanbury (Here and Worc.)	50	SO 9663
Hanbury (Staffs.)	60	SK 1727
Hanchurch	59	SJ 8441
Handa Island	132	NC 1348
Handbridge	68	SJ 4164
Handcross	28	TQ 2630
Handfast Point or The Foreland	26	SZ 0582
Handforth	69	SJ 8883
Handley	68	SJ 4657
Handsacre	60	SK 0916
Handsworth (S Yorks.)	71	SK 4086
Handsworth (W Mids)	50	SP 0490
Hanford	59	SJ 8642
Hanging Langford	26	SU 0237
Hanham	33	ST 6372
Hankelow	59	SJ 6645
Hankerton	34	ST 9690
Hankham	29	TQ 6105
Hanley	59	SJ 8847
Hanley Castle	49	SO 8342
Hanley Childe	49	SO 6565
Hanley Swan	49	SO 8143
Hanley William	49	SO 6765
Hanlith	78	SD 9061
Hanmer	58	SJ 4540
Hanningfield Resr.	38	TQ 7398
Hannington (Hants.)	35	SU 5355
Hannington (Northants.)	52	SP 8171
Hannington (Wilts.)	47	SU 1793
Hannington Wick	47	SU 1795
Hanslope	51	SP 8046
Hanthorpe	62	TF 0824
Hanwell	50	SP 4343
Hanwood	58	SJ 4309
Hanworth (Gtr London)	37	TQ 1271
Hanworth (Norf.)	65	TG 1935
Happendon	95	NS 8533
Happisburgh	65	TG 3731
Happisburgh Common	65	TG 3729
Happyland Hall	84	NZ 0932
Hapsford	69	SJ 4774
Hapton (Lancs.)	78	SD 7931
Hapton (Norf.)	65	TM 1796
Harberton	21	SX 7758
Harbertonford	21	SX 7856
Harbledown	31	TR 1358
Harborne	50	SP 0384
Harborough Magna	51	SP 4779
Harbottle	90	NT 9304
Harbury	50	SP 3759
Harby (Leic.)	61	SK 7431
Harby (Notts.)	72	SK 8770
Harcombe	24	SY 1590
Harden	78	SE 0838
Hardgate	119	NJ 7801
Hardham	28	TQ 0317
Hardhorn	77	SD 3538
Hardingham	64	TG 0403
Hardingstone	51	SP 7657
Hardings Wood	59	SJ 8054
Hardington	33	ST 7452
Hardington Mandeville	25	ST 5111
Hardington Marsh	25	ST 5009
Hard Knott Pass	82	NY 2301
Hardley	26	SU 4205
Hardley Street	65	TG 3801
Hardmead	52	SP 9347
Hardrow	84	SD 8691
Hardstoft	71	SK 4463
Hardway (Hants.)	27	SU 6101
Hardway (Somer.)	25	ST 7134
Hardwick (Bucks.)	36	SP 8019
Hardwick (Cambs.)	53	TL 3758
Hardwick (Norf.)	55	TM 2290
Hardwick (Northants.)	52	SP 8569
Hardwick (Oxon.)	47	SP 3706
Hardwick (Oxon.)	47	SP 5729
Hardwicke (Glos.)	46	SO 7912
Hardwicke (Glos.)	46	SO 9127
Hardwick Hall (ant.)	71	SK 4663
Hareby	73	TF 3365
Hareden	77	SD 6350
Hare Faulds (ant.)	96	NT 5750
Harefield	36	TQ 0590
Hare Hatch	36	SU 8077
Hare Hill (Strath.)	88	NS 6509
Hare Hill (Strath.)	95	NS 9153
Harehope	91	NU 0920
Harelaw Dam	93	NS 4753
Hare Ness	119	NO 9599
Harescombe	46	SO 8410
Haresfield	46	SO 8110
Hareshaw Hill	94	NS 7629
Hare Street	53	TL 3929
Harewood	79	SE 3245
Harewood Forest	34	SU 3943
Harford	21	SX 6359
Hargrave (Ches.)	69	SJ 4862
Hargrave (Northants.)	52	TL 0370
Hargrave (Suff.)	54	TL 7759
Harker	89	NY 3960
Harkstead	55	TM 1935
Harland Hill	78	SE 0284
Harlaston	60	SK 2111
Harlaw House	121	NJ 7424
Harlaw Resr.	102	NT 1865
Harlaxton	62	SK 8832
Harlech	66	SH 5831
Harlesden	37	TQ 2383
Harleston (Devon)	21	SX 7945
Harleston (Norf.)	55	TM 2483
Harleston (Suff.)	54	TM 0160
Harlestone	51	SP 7064
Harle Syke	78	SD 8634
Harley	59	SJ 5901
Harling Road Station	54	TL 9788
Harlington	52	TL 0330
Harlosh	122	NG 2841
Harlosh Island	122	NG 2739
Harlosh Point	122	NG 2840
Harlow	37	TL 4711
Harlow Hill	91	NZ 0768
Harlthorpe	74	SE 7337
Harlton	53	TL 3852
Harman's Cross	26	SY 9880
Harmby	84	SE 1289
Harmer Green	37	TL 2516
Harmer Hill	59	SJ 4822
Harmston	72	SK 9762
Harnham	26	SU 1229
Harnhill	46	SP 0600
Harold Hill	37	TQ 5391
Haroldston West	42	SM 8615
Haroldswick (Unst)	143	HP 6312
Harold's Wick (Unst)	143	HP 6411
Harold Wood	37	TQ 5590
Harome	79	SE 6482
Harpenden	37	TL 1314
Harperleas Resr.	103	NO 2105
Harperrig Reservoir	102	NT 0961
Harper's Brook	52	SP 9286
Harpford	24	SY 0890
Harpham	81	TA 0961
Harpley (Here. and Worc.)	49	SO 6861
Harpley (Norf.)	64	TF 7826
Harpole	51	SP 6961
Harpsdale	135	ND 1256
Harpsden	36	SU 7680
Harpswell	72	SK 9389
Harpurhey	69	SD 8701
Harpur Hill	70	SK 0671
Harrabrough Head	136	ND 4190
Harrapool	123	NG 6522
Harrier	140	HT 9540
Harrietfield	108	NN 9829
Harrietsham	30	TQ 8753
Harrington (Cumbr.)	82	NX 9926
Harrington (Lincs.)	73	TF 3671
Harrington (Northants.)	51	SP 7780
Harringworth	62	SP 9197
Harris (Rhum)	110	NM 3395
Harris (W Isles) (dist.)	125	NG 1198
Harriseahead	59	SJ 8656
Harrogate	79	SE 3055
Harrold	52	SP 9456
Harrow	37	TQ 1388
Harrowbarrow	20	SX 3969
Harrowden	52	TL 0646
Harrow Hill	28	TQ 0810
Harrow on the Hill	37	TQ 1586
Harsgeir	131	NB 1040
Harston (Cambs.)	53	TL 4251
Harston (Leic.)	62	SK 8331
Hart	85	NZ 4735
Harta Corrie	123	NG 4723
Hartamul	112	NF 8311
Hartburn	91	NZ 0886
Harter Fell (Cumbr.)	83	NY 4609
Harter Fell (Cumbr.)	82	SD 2199
Hartest	54	TL 8352
Hart Fell (Dumf. and Galwy.)	89	NT 1113
Hart Fell (Dumf. and Galwy.)	89	NY 2289
Hartfield	29	TQ 4735
Hartford (Cambs.)	53	TL 2572
Hartford (Ches.)	69	SJ 6372
Hartfordbridge	35	SU 7757
Hartford End	38	TL 6817
Harthill (Ches.)	59	SJ 4955
Harthill (Lothian)	102	NS 9064
Harthill (S Yorks.)	71	SK 4980
Harthope Burn	97	NT 9623
Hartington	70	SK 1360
Hartland	22	SS 2624
Hartland Point	22	SS 2227
Hartland Quay	22	SS 2224
Hartlebury	49	SO 8470
Hartlepool	85	NZ 5032
Hartlepool Bay	85	NZ 5232
Hartley (Cumbr.)	83	NY 7808
Hartley (Kent)	30	TQ 6166
Hartley (Kent)	29	TQ 7634
Hartley (Northum.)	91	NZ 3475
Hartley Wespall	36	SU 6958
Hartley Wintney	35	SU 7756
Hartlip	30	TQ 8364
Harton (N Yorks.)	80	SE 7061
Harton (Shrops.)	48	SO 4888
Harton (Tyne and Wear)	91	NZ 3864
Hartpury	46	SO 7924
Hartshill	60	SP 3293
Hartshorne	60	SK 3221
Hartshorn Pike	90	NT 6201
Hartsop	83	NY 4013
Hartwell	51	SP 7850
Hartwood	101	NS 8459
Harvel	30	TQ 6563
Harvington	50	SP 0548
Harvington Cross	50	SP 0549
Harwell	35	SU 4989
Harwich	55	TM 2431
Harwich Harbour	55	TM 2632
Harwood (Durham)	83	NY 8133
Harwood (Gtr Mches.)	69	SD 7411
Harwood Beck	83	NY 8321
Harwood Dale	81	SE 9595
Harwood Forest	91	NY 9994
Harworth	71	SK 6291
Hascombe	28	TQ 0039
Hascosay	143	HU 5592
Hascosay Sound	143	HU 5492
Haselbech	51	SP 7177
Haselbury Plucknett	25	ST 4711
Haseley	50	SP 2368
Haselor	50	SP 1257
Hasfield	46	SO 8227
Hasguard	42	SM 8509
Haskayne	68	SD 3507
Haskeir Eagach (is.)	124	NF 5980
Haskeir Island	124	NF 6182
Hasketon	55	TM 2550
Hasland	71	SK 3969
Haslemere	27	SU 9032
Haslingden	78	SD 7823
Haslingden Grane	78	SD 7523
Haslingfield	53	TL 4052
Haslington	59	SJ 7355
Hassall	69	SJ 7657
Hassall Green	69	SJ 7758
Hassell Street	31	TR 0946
Hassendean	90	NT 5420
Hassingham	65	TG 3605
Hassocks	29	TQ 3015
Hassop	71	SK 2272
Hastigrow	135	ND 2661
Hastingleigh	31	TR 0945
Hastings	30	TQ 8009
Hastingwood	37	TL 4807
Hastoe	36	SP 9209
Haswell	85	NZ 3743
Hatch (Beds.)	52	TL 1547
Hatch (Hants.)	35	SU 6752
Hatch (Wilts.)	25	ST 9228
Hatch Beauchamp	24	ST 3020
Hatch End	37	TQ 1391
Hatching Green	37	TL 1313
Hatchmere	69	SJ 5571
Hatcliffe	75	TA 2100
Hatfield (Here. and Worc.)	45	SO 5859
Hatfield (Herts.)	37	TL 2309
Hatfield (S Yorks.)	71	SE 6609
Hatfield Aerodrome	37	TL 2009
Hatfield Broad Oak	37	TL 5516
Hatfield Chase	74	SE 7109
Hatfield Heath	37	TL 5215
Hatfield House (ant.)	37	TL 2308
Hatfield Moors	74	SE 7006
Hatfield Peverel	38	TL 7911
Hatfield Woodhouse	71	SE 6708
Hatford	47	SU 3394
Hatherden	34	SU 3450
Hatherleigh	23	SS 5404
Hathern	61	SK 5022
Hatherop	47	SP 1505
Hathersage	71	SK 2381
Hatherton (Ches.)	59	SJ 6847
Hatherton (Staffs.)	60	SJ 9610
Hatley St. George	53	TL 2851
Hatt	20	SX 3962
Hatterrall Hill	45	SO 3025
Hattingley	27	SU 6437
Hatton (Ches.)	69	SJ 5982
Hatton (Derby.)	60	SK 2130
Hatton (Grampn.)	121	NK 0537
Hatton (Gtr London)	37	TQ 1075
Hatton (Lincs.)	73	TF 1776
Hatton (Shrops.)	48	SO 4690
Hatton (Warw.)	50	SP 2367
Hatton Castle (ant.)	121	NJ 7546
Hattoncrook	121	NJ 8424
Hatton Heath	68	SJ 4561
Hatton of Fintray	119	NJ 8316
Hattons Lodge	34	SU 0688
Haugham	73	TF 3381
Haugh Head	97	NU 0026
Haughley	54	TM 0262
Haughley Green	54	TM 0364
Haugh of Glass	121	NJ 3239
Haugh of Urr	88	NX 8066
Haughs of Cromdale	117	NJ 0927
Haughton (Notts.)	71	SK 6772
Haughton (Shrops.)	58	SJ 3727
Haughton (Shrops.)	59	SJ 5516
Haughton (Shrops.)	59	SO 6795
Haughton (Staffs.)	59	SJ 8620
Haughton Common	90	NY 8172
Haughton Green	69	SJ 9393
Haughton Moss	59	SJ 5756
Haunn	104	NM 3347
Haunton	60	SK 2411
Hauxley	91	NU 2703
Hauxley Haven	91	NU 2902
Hauxton	53	TL 4351
Havant	27	SU 7106
Haven	45	SO 4054
Havengore Island	39	TQ 9788
Havenhouse Station	73	TF 5259
Havenstreet	27	SZ 5690
Haven, The	63	TF 3540
Haverfordwest	42	SM 9515
Haverhill	54	TL 6745
Haverigg	76	SD 1578
Havering-atte-Bower	37	TQ 5193
Haversham	52	SP 8343
Haverthwaite	77	SD 3483
Hawarden	68	SJ 3165
Hawarden Airport	68	SJ 3565
Hawes	84	SD 8789
Haweswater Resr.	83	NY 4814
Hawford	49	SO 8460
Hawick (Borders)	89	NT 5014
Ha Wick (Hoy, Orkney)	136	ND 2589
Hawkchurch	24	ST 3400
Hawkedon	54	TL 7952
Hawkeridge	33	ST 8653
Hawkerland	24	SY 0588
Hawkesbury	33	ST 7687
Hawkesbury Upton	33	ST 7786
Hawkes End	50	SP 2983
Hawkhill	91	NU 2212
Hawkhope	90	NY 7188
Hawkhurst	29	TQ 7630
Hawkinge	31	TR 2139
Hawkley	27	SU 7429
Hawkridge	23	SS 8630
Hawkridge Reservoir	24	ST 2036
Hawkshead	82	SD 3598
Hawksland	95	NS 8439
Hawks Ness	141	HU 4648
Hawkswick	78	SD 9570
Hawksworth (Notts.)	61	SK 7543
Hawksworth (W Yorks.)	78	SE 1641
Hawkwell	38	TQ 8691
Hawkwood Hill	94	NS 6838
Hawley (Hants.)	36	SU 8558
Hawley (Kent)	37	TQ 5571
Hawling	46	SP 0623
Hawnby	85	SE 5389
Haworth	78	SE 0337
Haworth Moor	78	SD 9935
Hawsker	81	NZ 9207
Hawstead	54	TL 8559
Hawthorn	85	NZ 4145
Hawthorn Hill	36	SU 8873
Hawthornthwaite Fell	77	SD 5752
Hawton	61	SK 7851
Haxby	79	SE 6057
Haxey	74	SK 7699
Haxton Down	34	SU 2049
Hay Bluff	45	SO 2436
Haycock	82	NY 1410
Haydock	69	SJ 5696
Haydon	25	ST 6615
Haydon Bridge	90	NY 8464
Haydon Dean	97	NT 9743
Haydon Wick	34	SU 1388
Haydown Hill	34	SU 3155
Haye	20	SX 3570
Hayes (Gtr London)	36	TQ 0980
Hayes (Gtr London)	37	TQ 4165
Hayfield	70	SK 0386
Hayhillock	109	NO 5242
Hayle	18	SW 5537
Hayling Bay	27	SZ 7198
Hayling Island	27	SU 7201
Haylot Fell	77	SD 5861
Haynes	52	TL 1042
Haynes Church End	52	TL 0841
Hay-on-Wye	45	SO 2342
Hayscastle	42	SM 8925
Hayscastle Cross	42	SM 9125
Hay Stacks	82	NY 2013
Hayton (Cumbr.)	82	NY 1041
Hayton (Cumbr.)	83	NY 5057
Hayton (Humbs.)	74	SE 8145
Hayton (Notts.)	72	SK 7284
Hayton's Bent	48	SO 5280
Haytor Vale	21	SX 7677
Haywards Heath	29	TQ 3324
Haywood Oaks	61	SK 6055
Hazelbank	95	NS 8344
Hazelbury Bryan	25	ST 7408
Hazeley	36	SU 7459
Hazel Grove	69	SJ 9287
Hazelrigg	97	NU 0533
Hazelslade	60	SK 0212
Hazelton Walls	108	NO 3321
Hazelwood	60	SK 3245
Hazlemere	36	SU 8895
Hazlerigg	91	NZ 2472
Hazleton	46	SP 0718
Heacham	64	TF 6737
Headbourne Worthy	27	SU 4831
Headcorn	30	TQ 8344
Headington	47	SP 5407
Headlam	84	NZ 1818
Headless Cross	50	SP 0365
Headley (Hants.)	35	SU 5162
Headley (Hants.)	27	SU 8236
Headley (Surrey)	28	TQ 2054
Head o' da Taing	140	HT 9739
Head of Bratta	143	HU 4799
Head of Brough	143	HU 4484
Head of Garness	121	NJ 7464
Head of Holland	136	HY 4812
Head of Hosta	143	HU 6791
Head of Lambhoga	143	HU 6287
Head of Moclett	138	HY 4949
Head of Muir	101	NS 8080
Head of Stanshi	142	HU 2180
Headon	72	SK 7476
Heads Nook	83	NY 4955
Heads of Ayr	93	NS 2818
Heage	60	SK 3650
Healabhal Bheag (mt.)	122	NG 2242
Healabhal Mhór (mt.)	122	NG 2244
Healaugh (N Yorks.)	84	SE 0198
Healaugh (N Yorks.)	79	SE 4947
Healaval (mt.)	122	NG 2464
Heald Green	69	SJ 8385
Heald Moor	78	SD 8726
Heale	23	SS 6446
Healey (Lancs.)	69	SD 8817
Healey (Northum.)	91	NZ 0158
Healey (N Yorks.)	78	SE 1780
Healeyfield	84	NZ 0648
Healing	75	TA 2110
Heamoor	18	SW 4631
Heanish	104	NM 0343
Heanor	60	SK 4346
Heanton Punchardon	22	SS 5035
Heapham	72	SK 8788
Hearnish (pt.)	124	NF 6263
Hearthstane	95	NT 1125
Heart Law	96	NT 7166
Heast	123	NG 6417
Heath (Derby.)	71	SK 4466
Heath (S Glam.)	41	ST 1779
Heath and Reach	52	SP 9228
Heathcote	70	SK 1460
Heath End (Hants.)	35	SU 5762
Heath End (Hants.)	35	SU 8550
Heather	60	SK 3910
Heathfield (Devon)	21	SX 8376
Heathfield (E Susx)	29	TQ 5821
Heathfield (Somer.)	24	ST 1526
Heathfield (Strath.)	100	NS 3262
Heathfield Moor	78	SE 1067
Heath Hayes	60	SK 0110
Heath Hill	59	SJ 7614
Heath House	32	ST 4146
Heathrow Airport - London	36	TQ 0875
Heath, The	54	TL 9043
Heathton	49	SO 8192
Heatley	69	SJ 6988
Heaton (Lancs.)	77	SD 4460
Heaton (Staffs.)	69	SJ 9462
Heaton (Tyne and Wear)	91	NZ 2665
Heaton Moor	69	SJ 8691
Heaval (mt.)	112	NL 6799
Heaverham	37	TQ 5758
Heaviley	69	SJ 9088
Hebburn	91	NZ 3265
Hebden	78	SE 0263
Hebden Bridge	78	SD 9927
Hebden Green	69	SJ 6365
Hebden Moor	78	SE 0465
Hebden Water	78	SD 9631
Hebrides or Western Isles	112	NG 0239
Hebron	91	NZ 1989
Heckfield	36	SU 7260
Heckington	62	TF 1444
Heckmondwike	78	SE 2123
Hecla (mt.)	112	NF 8234
Heddington	34	ST 9966
Heddle	136	HY 3512
Heddon-on-the-Wall	91	NZ 1366
Heddon's Mouth	23	SS 6549
Hedenham	65	TM 3193
Hedge End	27	SU 4812
Hedgehope Hill	90	NT 9419
Hedgerley	36	SU 9787
Hedging	24	ST 3029
Hedley on the Hill	91	NZ 0759
Hednesford	60	SK 0012
Hedon	75	TA 1828
Hedsor	36	SU 9086
Hegdon Hill	45	SO 5854
Heglibister	141	HU 3851
Heighington (Durham)	84	NZ 2522
Heighington (Lincs.)	72	TF 0269
Heights of Brae	128	NH 5161
Heights of Kinlochewe	127	NH 0764
Heilam	133	NC 4659
Heillia	142	HU 2684
Heishival Mór (mt.)	112	NL 6296
Heisker or Monach Islands	124	NF 6262
Heiskers (is.)	112	NL 5786
Heiton	96	NT 7130
Heldale Water	136	ND 2592
Heldon Hill	129	NJ 1257
Hele (Devon)	23	SS 5347
Hele (Devon)	23	SS 9902
Helensburgh	100	NS 2982
Helford	18	SW 7526
Helford River	18	SW 7626
Helhoughton	64	TF 8626
Helions Bumpstead	54	TL 6541
Hellabrick's Wick	140	HT 9536
Helland	19	SX 0770
Hellesdon	65	TG 1810
Helliar Holm	136	HY 4815
Hellidon	51	SP 5158
Hellifield	78	SD 8556
Helli Ness	141	HU 4628
Hellingly	29	TQ 5812
Hellington	65	TG 3103
Hellir (pt.)	143	HU 3892
Hellisay	112	NF 7504
Hellister	141	HU 3949
Hellmoor Loch	89	NT 3816
Hell's Glen	100	NN 1806
Hell's Mouth or Porth Neigwl	56	SH 2626
Helman Head	135	ND 3646
Helmdon	51	SP 5843
Helmingham	55	TM 1857
Helmsdale	135	ND 0215
Helmshore	78	SD 7821
Helmsley	79	SE 6183
Helmsley Moor	85	SE 5991
Helperby	79	SE 4369
Helperthorpe	81	SE 9570
Helpringham	62	TF 1340
Helpston	62	TF 1205
Helsby	69	SJ 4875
Helston	18	SW 6527
Helstone	20	SX 0881
Helton	83	NY 5122
Helvellyn (mt.)	82	NY 3315
Helwick (lightship)	40	SS 3281
Helwith Bridge	78	SD 8169
Hemblington	65	TG 3411
Hembury (ant.)	24	ST 1103
Hemel Hempstead	36	TL 0506
Hemingbrough	79	SE 6730
Hemingby	73	TF 2374
Hemingford Abbots	53	TL 2870
Hemingford Grey	53	TL 2970
Hemingstone	55	TM 1453
Hemington (Northants.)	52	TL 0985
Hemington (Somer.)	33	ST 7253
Hemley	55	TM 2842
Hempholme	81	TA 0850
Hempnall	65	TM 2494
Hempnall Green	65	TM 2593
Hempriggs	129	NJ 1064
Hempriggs House	135	ND 3547
Hempstead (Essex)	54	TL 6338
Hempstead (Norf.)	65	TG 4028
Hempsted (Glos.)	46	SO 8117
Hempsted (Norf.)	65	TG 1037
Hempton (Norf.)	64	TF 9129
Hempton (Oxon.)	47	SP 4431
Hemsby	65	TG 4917
Hemsby Hole	65	TG 5118
Hemswell	72	SK 9290
Hemsworth	71	SE 4213
Hemyock	24	ST 1313
Henbury (Avon)	33	ST 5478
Henbury (Ches.)	69	SJ 8873
Hendersyde Park	96	NT 7435
Hendon (Gtr London)	37	TQ 2389
Hendon (Tyne and Wear)	85	NZ 4055
Hendreys Course	102	NS 9758
Hendy	43	SN 5804
Heneglwys	66	SH 4276
Henfield	28	TQ 2116
Hen Gerrig	57	SH 9518
Hengistbury Head	26	SZ 1790
Hengoed (Mid Glam.)	41	ST 1495
Hengoed (Powys)	45	SO 2253
Hengoed (Shrops.)	58	SJ 2833
Hengrave	54	TL 8268
Hengynwydd-fawr	57	SN 9882
Henham	53	TL 5428
Heniarth	58	SJ 1108
Henley (Shrops.)	48	SO 5476
Henley (Somer.)	25	ST 4232
Henley (Suff.)	55	TM 1551
Henley (W Susx)	27	SU 8926
Henley-in-Arden	50	SP 1465
Henley-on-Thames	36	SU 7682
Henley Park	28	SU 9352
Henllan (Clwyd)	67	SJ 0268
Henllan (Dyfed)	43	SN 3540
Henllan Amgoed	43	SN 1820
Henllys	45	ST 2693
Henlow	52	TL 1738
Hennock	21	SX 8380
Henryd	67	SH 7674
Henry's Moat (Castell Hendre)	42	SN 0428
Hensall	79	SE 5923
Hensbarrow Downs	19	SW 9957
Henshaw	90	NY 7664
Henstead	55	TM 4986
Henstridge	25	ST 7219
Henstridge Marsh	25	ST 7420
Henton (Oxon.)	36	SP 7602
Henton (Somer.)	33	ST 4845
Henwick	49	SO 8354
Henwood	20	SX 2673
Heogan	141	HU 4743
Heoga Ness	143	HU 5379
Heol Senni	41	SN 9223
Heol-y-Cyw	41	SS 9484
Hepburn	97	NU 0724
Hepple	91	NT 9800
Hepscott	91	NZ 2284
Heptonstall	78	SD 9827
Heptonstall Moor	78	SD 9330
Hepworth (Suff.)	54	TL 9874
Hepworth (W Yorks.)	70	SE 1606
Herbrandston	42	SM 8707
Hereford	45	SO 5040
Hergest	45	SO 2655
Hergest Ridge	45	SO 2556
Heriot	96	NT 3952
Herma Ness	143	HP 6018
Hermaness Hill	143	HP 6017
Herman Law	89	NT 2115
Hermetray	124	NF 9874
Hermitage (Berks.)	35	SU 5072
Hermitage (Borders)	89	NY 5095
Hermitage (Dorset.)	25	ST 6306
Hermitage (Hants.)	27	SU 7505
Hermitage, The	28	TQ 2253
Hermon (Dyfed)	43	SN 2032
Hermon (Dyfed)	43	SN 3630
Hermon (Gwyn.)	66	SH 3868
Herne	31	TR 1866
Herne Bay	31	TR 1768
Herner	23	SS 5926
Herne, The	53	TL 2590
Hernhill	31	TR 0660
Herodsfoot	19	SX 2160
Herongate	38	TQ 6391
Heronsgate	36	TQ 0294
Herra, The	143	HU 4693
Herriard	35	SU 6645
Herringfleet	65	TM 4797
Herringswell	54	TL 7170
Herrington	85	NZ 3553
Herscha Hill	119	NO 7380
Hersden	31	TR 1961
Hersham	37	TQ 1164
Herstmonceux	29	TQ 6312
Herston	136	ND 4291
Herston Head	136	ND 4191
Hertford	37	TL 3212
Hertford Heath	37	TL 3511
Hertingfordbury	37	TL 3112
Hesketh Bank	77	SD 4323
Hesketh Lane	77	SD 6141
Hesket Newmarket	82	NY 3438
Heskin Green	69	SD 5315

Hesleden Howat's Hill

Hesleden 85 NZ 4438
Hesleyside 90 NY 8183
Heslington 79 SE 6250
Hessay 79 SE 5253
Hessenford 20 SX 3057
Hessett 54 TL 9361
Hessle 74 TA 0326
Hestan Island 87 NX 8350
Hest Bank 77 SD 4566
Hesti Geo 140 HT 9736
Heston 37 TQ 1277
Heswall 68 SJ 2682
Hethe 47 SP 5929
Hethersett 65 TG 1505
Hethersgill 89 NY 4767
Hethpool 97 NT 8928
Hett 84 NZ 2836
Hetton 78 SD 9658
Hetton-le-Hole 85 NZ 3548
Hetty Peglers Tump 46 SO 7900
Heugh 91 NZ 0873
Heugh-Head 118 NJ 3711
Hevdadale Head 142 HU 3089
Heveningham 55 TM 3372
Hever 29 TQ 4744
Heversham 77 SD 4983
Hevingham 65 TG 2022
Hewelsfield 45 SO 5602
Hewish (Avon) 32 ST 4064
Hewish (Somer.) 24 ST 4108
Hexham 90 NY 9364
Hexhamshire Common 84 NY 8853
Hextable 37 TQ 5170
Hexton 52 TL 1030
Hexworthy 21 SX 6572
Heybridge (Essex) 38 TL 8508
Heybridge (Essex) 38 TQ 6498
Heybridge Basin 38 TL 8707
Heybrook Bay 20 SX 4948
Heydon (Cambs.) 53 TL 4340
Heydon (Norf.) 65 TG 1127
Heydon Hill 24 ST 0327
Heydour 62 TF 0039
Heyford 51 SP 6558
Heylipol 104 NL 9643
Heylor 142 HU 2881
Heysham 77 SD 4161
Heysham Lake (chan.) 77 SD 3758
Heyshott 27 SU 8918
Heytesbury 33 ST 9242
Heythrop 47 SP 3527
Heywood (Gtr Mches.) 69 SD 8510
Heywood (Wilts.) 33 ST 8753
Hibaldstow 74 SE 9702
Hickleton 71 SE 4805
Hickling (Norf.) 65 TG 4124
Hickling (Notts.) 61 SK 6929
Hickling Green 65 TG 4023
Hickling Heath 65 TG 4022
Hidcote Boyce 50 SP 1742
High Ackworth 71 SE 4317
Higham (Derby.) 71 SK 3959
Higham (Kent) 30 TQ 7171
Higham (Lancs.) 78 SD 8036
Higham (Suff.) 54 TL 7465
Higham (Suff.) 54 TM 0335
Higham Dykes 91 NZ 1375
Higham Ferrers 52 SP 9669
Higham Gobion 52 TL 1033
Higham on the Hill 60 SP 3895
Highampton 22 SS 4804
Higham Wood 29 TQ 6048
High Banton 101 NS 7480
High Beach 37 TQ 4097
High Bentham 77 SD 6669
High Bickington 23 SS 5920
High Birkwith 78 SD 8076
High Blantyre 94 NS 6756
High Bonnybridge 101 NS 8378
High Bradfield 71 SK 2692
Highbridge 32 ST 3147
Highbrook 29 TQ 3630
Highburton 70 SE 1813
Highbury 33 ST 6849
High Buston 91 NU 2308
High Callerton 91 NZ 1670
High Catton 80 SE 7153
Highclere 34 SU 4360
Highclere Castle 34 SU 4358
Highcliffe 26 SZ 2193
High Cogges 47 SP 3709
High Coniscliffe 84 NZ 2215
High Cross (Hants.) 27 SU 7126
High Cross (Herts.) 37 TL 3618
High Cross Bank 60 SK 3018
High Easter 38 TL 6214
High Ellington 78 SE 1983
Higher Ansty 25 ST 7603
Higher Ballam 77 SD 3630
Higher Ercall 59 SJ 5917
Higher Penwortham 77 SD 5128
Higher Sharpnose Point 22 SS 1914
Higher Tale 24 ST 0601
Higher Town 18 SV 9315
Higher Walreddon 20 SX 4771
Higher Walton (Ches.) 69 SJ 5985
Higher Walton (Lancs.) 77 SD 5727
Higher Wych 59 SJ 4943
High Etherley 84 NZ 1628
Highfield (Northum.) 90 NY 7291
Highfield (Strath.) 93 NS 3050
Highfield (Tyne and Wear) 91 NZ 1459
Highfields 53 TL 3559
High Force 84 NY 8727
High Garrett 54 TL 7726
High Grange 84 NZ 1731
High Green (Here. and Worc.) 49 SO 8745
High Green (Norf.) 65 TG 1305
High Green (S Yorks.) 71 SK 3397
Highgreen Manor 90 NY 8191
High Halden 30 TQ 9037
High Halstow 30 TQ 7875
High Ham 25 ST 4231
High Hatton 59 SJ 6024
High Hesket 83 NY 4744
High Hoyland 71 SE 2710
High Hunsley 74 SE 9535
High Hurstwood 29 TQ 4926
High Knowes 90 NT 9612
Highland Hotel, The 100 NR 9986
High Lane 49 SO 6760
High Laver 37 TL 5208
Highleadon 46 SO 7623
High Legh 69 SJ 6984
Highleigh 27 SZ 8498
Highley 49 SO 7483
High Littleton 33 ST 6458
High Lorton 82 NY 1625
High Melton 71 SE 5001
Highmoor Cross 36 SU 7084
Highmoor Hill 33 ST 4689
High Moor of Killiemore 86 NX 3660
High Murdonochee 86 NX 1674
Highnam 46 SO 7919
High Neb (mt.) 71 SK 2385
High Newton 77 SD 4082
High Newton-by-the-Sea 97 NU 2325
High Offley 59 SJ 7826
High Ongar 37 TL 5603
High Onn 59 SJ 8216
High Peak (dist.) 70 SK 1187
High Pike 82 NY 3135
High Roding 38 TL 6017
High Salvington 28 TQ 1206
High Seat (mt.) 82 NY 2818
High Shaw 84 SD 8791
High Spen 91 NZ 1359
Highsted 30 TQ 9161
High Stile 82 NY 1714
High Street (Corn.) 19 SW 9753
High Street (Cumbr.) (ant.) 83 NY 4515
High Street (Cumbr.) (mt.) 83 NY 4411
High Street (Suff.) 55 TM 4355
High Street Green 54 TM 0055
Hightae 89 NY 0979
Hightown (Ches.) 69 SJ 8762
Hightown (Mers.) 68 SD 2903
High Toynton 73 TF 2869
High Trewhitt 91 NU 0105
Highway (Corn.) 19 SX 1453
Highway (Wilts.) 34 SU 0474
High White Stones (mt.) 82 NY 2809
High Willhays (mt.) 21 SX 5789
Highworth 34 SU 2092
High Wray 83 SD 3799
High Wych 37 TL 4614
High Wycombe 36 SU 8593
Hildasay 141 HU 3540
Hildenborough 29 TQ 5648
Hildersham 53 TL 5448
Hilderstone 59 SJ 9434
Hilderthorpe 81 TA 1765
Hilgay 64 TL 6298
Hilgay Fen 63 TL 5795
Hill 46 ST 6495
Hillam 79 SE 5028
Hillbeck 83 NY 7915
Hillberry 76 SC 3879
Hillborough (Kent) 31 TR 2168
Hillborough (Norf.) 64 TF 8200
Hillbrae (Grampn.) 121 NJ 6047
Hillbrae (Grampn.) 121 NJ 7923
Hill Brow 27 SU 7926
Hilldyke 63 TF 3447
Hill End (Durham) 84 NZ 0135
Hill End (Fife) 102 NT 0495
Hillend (Fife) 102 NT 1483
Hillend Reservoir 101 NS 8367
Hillesden 51 SP 6828
Hillesley 33 ST 7689
Hillfarrance 24 ST 1624
Hill Head (Devon) 21 SX 9053
Hill Head (Hants.) 27 SU 5402
Hillhead (Strath.) 93 NS 4219
Hillhead of Auchentumb 121 NJ 9258
Hillhead of Cocklaw 121 NK 0844
Hilliard's Cross 60 SK 1412
Hilliclay 135 ND 1764
Hillingdon 36 TQ 0882
Hillington 64 TF 7225
Hillmorton 51 SP 5374
Hill Ness 143 HP 6517
Hillockhead 118 NJ 3809
Hill of Aitnoch 117 NH 9739
Hill of Alyth 108 NO 2450
Hill of Arisdale 143 HU 4984
Hill of Bakkanalee 143 HP 4903
Hill of Barra 121 NJ 8025
Hill of Beath 102 NT 1690
Hill of Berran 109 NO 4471
Hill of Camb 143 HU 5092
Hill of Cammie 119 NO 5285
Hill of Cat 118 NO 4887
Hill of Colvadale 143 HP 6105
Hill of Corsegight 121 NJ 8550
Hill of Couternach 109 NO 3566
Hill of Crooksetter 143 HU 4178
Hill of Dalsetter 143 HU 5098
Hill of Dudwick 121 NJ 9737
Hill of Edendocher 119 NO 5985
Hill of Fare 119 NJ 6803
Hill of Fearn 129 NH 8377
Hill of Finavon 109 NO 4955
Hill of Fingray 119 NO 5681
Hill of Fishrie 121 NJ 8257
Hill of Foudland 121 NJ 6033
Hill of Garbet 109 NO 4668
Hill of Glansie 109 NO 4269
Hill of Maud Crofts 121 NJ 4661
Hill of Menmuir 109 NO 5266
Hill of Miffia 136 HY 2313
Hill of Mulderie 121 NJ 3851
Hill of Nigg 129 NH 8372
Hill of Oliclett 135 ND 2946
Hill of Rangag 135 ND 1843
Hill of Reafirth 143 HU 5087
Hill of Saughs 118 NO 4485
Hill of Shurton 141 HU 4440
Hill of Skilmafilly 121 NJ 8940
Hill of Stake 100 NS 2763
Hill of the Wangie 129 NJ 1353
Hill of Three Stones 121 NJ 3422
Hill of Tillymorgan 121 NJ 6534
Hill of Tomechole 129 NJ 0649
Hill of Towie 121 NJ 3847
Hill of Trusta 119 NO 7886
Hill of Wirren 119 NO 5273
Hill Ridware 60 SK 0718
Hill Row 53 TL 4475
Hill Row Doles 53 TL 4276
Hillside (Grampn.) 119 NO 9298
Hillside (Shetld.) 141 HU 4063
Hillside (Tays.) 109 NO 7061
Hills of Cromdale 117 NJ 1126
Hillswick 142 HU 2877
Hill, The 76 SD 1783
Hill Top (Hants.) 26 SU 4002
Hill Top (W Yorks.) 71 SE 3315
Hillwell 141 HU 3714
Hilmarton 34 SU 0175
Hilperton 33 ST 8759
Hilpsford Point 76 SD 2061
Hilsea 27 SU 6503
Hilton (Cambs.) 53 TL 2966
Hilton (Cleve.) 85 NZ 4611
Hilton (Cumbr.) 83 NY 7320
Hilton (Derby.) 60 SK 2430
Hilton (Dorset) 25 ST 7802
Hilton (Durham) 84 NZ 1621
Hilton (Grampn.) 121 NJ 9434
Hilton (Shrops.) 59 SO 7795
Hilton of Cadboll 129 NH 8776
Himbleton 49 SO 9458
Himley 49 SO 8891
Hincaster 77 SD 5184
Hinchingbrooke House (ant.) 53 TL 2271
Hinckley 60 SP 4294
Hinderclay 54 TM 0276
Hinderwell 85 NZ 7916
Hindford 58 SJ 3333
Hindhead 27 SU 8736
Hindhope Law 90 NY 7797
Hindlethwaite Moor 78 SE 0680
Hindley 69 SD 6104
Hindley Green 69 SD 6403
Hindlip 49 SO 8758
Hindolveston 64 TG 0329
Hindon 25 ST 9032
Hindringham 64 TF 9836
Hingham 64 TG 0202
Hinstock 59 SJ 6926
Hintlesham 55 TM 0843
Hinton (Avon) 33 ST 7376
Hinton (Hants.) 26 SZ 2095
Hinton (Northants.) 51 SP 5352
Hinton (Shrops.) 58 SJ 4008
Hinton Ampner 27 SU 5927
Hinton Blewett 33 ST 5956
Hinton Charterhouse 33 ST 7758
Hinton-in-the-Hedges 51 SP 5537
Hinton Marsh 27 SU 5827
Hinton Martell 26 SU 0106
Hinton on the Green 50 SP 0240
Hinton Parva 34 SU 2283
Hinton St. George 25 ST 4212
Hinton St. Mary 25 ST 7816
Hinton Waldrist 47 SU 3799
Hints (Shrops.) 49 SO 6175
Hints (Staffs.) 60 SK 1503
Hinwick 52 SP 9361
Hinxhill 31 TR 0442
Hinxton 53 TL 4945
Hinxworth 53 TL 2340
Hipperholme 78 SE 1225
Hipswell Moor 84 SE 1496
Hirfynydd 41 SN 8205
Hirn 119 NJ 7300
Hirnant 57 SJ 0423
Hirst 91 NZ 2787
Hirst Courtney 79 SE 6124
Hirta or St. Kilda (is.) 124 NF 0999
Hirwaun 41 SN 9505
Hirwaun Common 41 SN 9304
Hiscott 23 SS 5426
Hisehope Resr. 84 NZ 0246
Histon 53 TL 4363
Hitcham 54 TL 9851
Hitchin 52 TL 1829
Hither Green 37 TQ 3874
Hittisleigh 21 SX 7395
Hixon 60 SK 0026
Hoaden 31 TR 2759
Hoaldalbert 45 SO 3923
Hoar Cross 60 SK 1223
Hoarwithy 45 SO 5429
Hoath 31 TR 2064
Hobarris 48 SO 3078
Hobbister 136 HY 3807
Hobhole Drain 63 TF 3647
Hobkirk 90 NT 5810
Hobland Hall 65 TG 5101
Hobson 84 NZ 1755
Hoby 61 SK 6617
Hockering 64 TG 0713
Hockerton 61 SK 7156
Hockley 38 TQ 8293
Hockley Heath 50 SP 1572
Hockliffe 52 SP 9726
Hockwold cum Wilton 54 TL 7288
Hockwold Fens 54 TL 6887
Hockworthy 24 ST 0319
Hoddesdon 37 TL 3709
Hoddlesden 77 SD 7122
Hoddom Castle (ant.) 89 NY 1573
Hodge Beck 85 SE 6294
Hodgeston 42 SS 0399
Hod Hill 25 ST 8510
Hodnet 59 SJ 6128
Hodthorpe 71 SK 5476
Hoe 64 TF 9916
Hoe Gate 27 SU 6213
Hoe Point 122 NG 1641
Hoe Rape (pt.) 122 NG 1543
Hoe, The 122 NG 1641
Hoff 83 NY 6717
Hog Fell 89 NY 3989
Hoggeston 51 SP 8025
Hogh Bay 110 NM 1657
Hog Hill 89 NY 2895
Hoghton 77 SD 6125
Hognaston 60 SK 2350
Hog's Back 28 SU 9348
Hogs Law 96 NT 5555
Hogsthorpe 73 TF 5372
Holbeach 63 TF 3625
Holbeach Bank 63 TF 3627
Holbeach Drove 63 TF 3212
Holbeach Hurn 63 TF 3927
Holbeach Marsh 63 TF 3729
Holbeach St. Johns 63 TF 3418
Holbeach St. Marks 63 TF 3731
Holbeach St. Matthew 63 TF 4132
Holbeck 71 SK 5473
Holberrow Green 50 SP 0259
Holbeton 21 SX 6150
Holborn 37 TQ 3181
Holborn Head 135 ND 1071
Holbrook (Derby.) 60 SK 3645
Holbrook (Suff.) 55 TM 1636
Holbrook Bay 55 TM 1633
Holburn 97 NU 0436
Holbury 26 SU 4303
Holcombe (Devon) 21 SX 9574
Holcombe (Somer.) 33 ST 6649
Holcombe Rogus 24 ST 0519
Holcot 51 SP 7969
Holden 78 SD 7749
Holdenby 51 SP 6967
Holderness Drain 75 TA 1135
Holdgate 48 SO 5589
Holdingham 62 TF 0547
Holehouse Hill 88 NY 0195
Hole-in-the-Wall 45 SO 6128
Hole o' Row 136 HY 2218
Hole Park 30 TQ 8332
Holes of Scraada 142 HU 2179
Holestane 88 NX 8799
Hole Stone Bay 86 NX 0646
Holford 32 ST 1541
Holker 77 SD 3577
Holkham 64 TF 8944
Holkham Bay 64 TF 8746
Hollacombe 22 SS 3702
Holland (Papa Westray) 138 HY 4851
Holland (Stronsay) 137 HY 6622
Holland Fen 63 TF 2445
Holland-on-Sea 39 TM 2016
Hollandstoun 139 HY 7553
Hollesley 55 TM 3544
Hollesley Bay 55 TM 3844
Hollinfare 69 SJ 6990
Hollingbourne 30 TQ 8455
Hollington (Derby.) 60 SK 2239
Hollington (E Susx) 30 TQ 7911
Hollington (Staffs.) 60 SK 0538
Hollingworth 70 SK 0096
Hollingworth Lake 69 SD 9314
Hollins 69 SD 8108
Hollinsclough 70 SK 0666
Hollinswood 59 SJ 6909
Hollinwood 59 SJ 5236
Hollowell Point 23 TR 0396
Hollocombe 23 SS 6311
Holloway 60 SK 3256
Hollowell 51 SP 6972
Hollowell Resr. 51 SP 6873
Holl Resr. 103 NO 2203
Hollybush (Gwent) 41 SO 1603
Hollybush (Here. and Worc.) 49 SO 7636
Hollybush (Strath.) 93 NS 3914
Holly End 63 TF 4906
Hollym 75 TA 3425
Holm (Dumf. and Galwy.) 89 NY 2498
Holm (Isle of Lewis) 131 NB 4531
Holmbury St. Mary 28 TQ 1144
Holme (Cambs.) 52 TL 1987
Holme (Cumbr.) 77 SD 5278
Holme (Notts.) 72 SK 8059
Holme (W Yorks.) 70 SE 1005
Holme Chapel 78 SD 8728
Holme Hale 64 TF 8807
Holme Island 77 SD 4278
Holme Lacy 45 SO 5535
Holme Marsh 45 SO 3354
Holme next the Sea 64 TF 7043
Holme-on-Spalding-Moor 74 SE 8138
Holme on the Wolds 74 SE 9646
Holmer 45 SO 5042
Holmer Green 36 SU 9097
Holmes Chapel 69 SJ 7667
Holmesfield 71 SK 3277
Holmeswood 68 SD 4316
Holmewood 71 SK 4365
Holmfirth 70 SE 1408
Holmhead 88 NS 5620
Holm Island 123 NG 5251
Holm of Helliness 141 HU 4628
Holm of Huip 139 HY 6231
Holm of Melby 140 HU 1958
Holm of Noss 141 HU 5539
Holm of Papa 138 HY 5052
Holm of Skaw 143 HP 6617
Holm of West Sandwick 143 HU 4389
Holmpton 75 TA 3623
Holmrook 82 SD 0799
Holmsgarth 141 HU 4642
Holms of Ire 139 HY 6446
Holm Sound 136 ND 5099
Holms Water 95 NT 0831
Holmwood Station 28 TQ 1743
Holne 21 SX 7069
Holnest 25 ST 6509
Holnicote Estate 23 SS 8944
Holoman Bay 123 NG 5439
Holsworthy 22 SS 3403
Holsworthy Beacon 22 SS 3508
Holt (Clwyd) 58 SJ 4053
Holt (Dorset) 26 SU 0203
Holt (Here. and Worc.) 49 SO 8262
Holt (Norf.) 64 TG 0738
Holt (Wilts.) 33 ST 8661
Holtby 79 SE 6754
Holt End 50 SP 0769
Holt Heath 49 SO 8163
Holton (Oxon.) 47 SP 6006
Holton (Somerset) 25 ST 6826
Holton (Suff.) 55 TM 4077
Holton cum Beckering 73 TF 1181
Holton Heath 26 SY 9491
Holton le Clay 75 TA 2802
Holton le Moor 72 TF 0797
Holton St. Mary 54 TM 0537
Holwell 25 ST 7011
Holwell (Herts.) 52 TL 1633
Holwell (Leic.) 61 SK 7323
Holwell (Oxon.) 47 SP 2309
Holwick 84 NY 9026
Holworth 25 SY 7683
Holybourne 35 SU 7341
Holy Cross 49 SO 9279
Holyhead 66 SH 2482
Holyhead Bay 66 SH 2587
Holyhead Mountain 66 SH 2182
Holy Island (Gwyn.) 66 SH 2579
Holy Island (Island of Arran) 92 NS 0630
Holy Island (Northum.) 97 NU 1342
Holy Island Sands 97 NU 1041
Holy Loch 100 NS 1780
Holymoorside 71 SK 3369
Holyport 36 SU 8977
Holystone 90 NT 9502
Holytown 101 NS 7760
Holywell (Cambs.) 53 TL 3370
Holywell (Clwyd) 68 SJ 1875
Holywell (Corn.) 18 SW 7658
Holywell (Dorset) 25 ST 5904
Holywell Bank 68 SJ 2178
Holywell Bay 18 SW 7559
Holywell Green 70 SE 0918
Holywell Lake 24 ST 1020
Holywell Row 54 TL 7077
Holywood 88 NX 9480
Homer 59 SJ 6101
Homersfield 55 TM 2885
Hom Green 45 SO 5822
Homington 26 SU 1226
Honddu 44 SO 0137
Honeyborough 42 SM 9506
Honeybourne 50 SP 1144
Honeychurch 23 SS 6202
Honey Hill 31 TR 1161
Honiley 50 SP 2472
Honing 65 TG 3227
Honingham 65 TG 1011
Honington (Lincs.) 62 SK 9443
Honington (Suff.) 54 TL 9174
Honington (Warw.) 50 SP 2642
Honister Pass 82 NY 2214
Honiton 24 ST 1600
Honley 70 SE 1311
Hooe (Devon) 20 SX 5052
Hooe (E Susx) 29 TQ 6809
Hoo Green 55 TM 2559
Hook (Dyfed) 42 SM 9811
Hook (Hants.) 35 SU 7254
Hook (Humbs.) 74 SE 7525
Hook (Surrey) 37 TQ 1764
Hook (Wilts.) 34 SU 0784
Hooke (Dorset) 25 ST 5300
Hookgate 59 SJ 7435
Hook Norton 47 SP 3533
Hookway 21 SX 8598
Hookwood 29 TQ 2643
Hoole 68 SJ 4367
Hoo Stack 141 HU 5052
Hoo St. Werburgh 30 TQ 7872
Hooton 68 SJ 3679
Hooton Levitt 71 SK 5291
Hooton Pagnell 71 SE 4808
Hooton Roberts 71 SK 4897
Hope 133 NC 4760
Hope (Clwyd) 68 SJ 3058
Hope (Derby.) 70 SK 1783
Hope (Devon) 21 SX 6740
Hope (Powys) 58 SJ 2507
Hope (Shrops.) 58 SJ 3401
Hope Bagot 48 SO 5874
Hope Bowdler 48 SO 4792
Hope House 90 NY 6880
Hopeman 129 NJ 1469
Hope Mansell 45 SO 6219
Hopesay 48 SO 3883
Hope's Nose (pt.) 21 SX 9463
Hopes Resr. 103 NT 5462
Hopes Water 103 NT 5562
Hopetoun House 102 NT 0878
Hope under Dinmore 45 SO 5052
Hopton (Norf.) 65 TG 5200
Hopton (Shrops.) 59 SJ 5926
Hopton (Staffs.) 59 SJ 9426
Hopton (Suff.) 54 TL 9979
Hopton Cangeford 48 SO 5480
Hopton Castle 48 SO 3678
Hopton Titterhill 48 SO 3577
Hopton Wafers 49 SO 6476
Hopwas 60 SK 1705
Hopwood 50 SP 0375
Horam 29 TQ 5717
Horbling 62 TF 1135
Horbury 71 SE 2918
Horden 85 NZ 4441
Horden Point 85 NZ 4443
Horderley 48 SO 4086
Hordle 26 SZ 2795
Hordley 58 SJ 3730
Horeb 43 SN 3942
Horham 55 TM 2172
Horkstow 74 SE 9818
Horley (Oxon.) 50 SP 4143
Horley (W Susx) 29 TQ 2843
Hornblotton Green 25 ST 5833
Hornby (Lancs.) 77 SD 5868
Hornby (N Yorks.) 85 NZ 3605
Horncastle 73 TF 2669
Hornchurch 37 TQ 5487
Horncliffe 97 NT 9249
Horndean 27 SU 7013
Horndon on the Hill 38 TQ 6683
Horne 29 TQ 3344
Horn Hill 36 TQ 0292
Horniehaugh 109 NO 4161
Horning 65 TG 3417
Horninghold 61 SP 8097
Horninglow 60 SK 2324
Horningsea 53 TL 4962
Horningsham 33 ST 8241
Horningtoft 64 TF 9323
Hornish (pt.) 112 NF 7309
Hornish Point 124 NF 7547
Hornsby 83 NY 5150
Hornsea 75 TA 2047
Hornsea Mere 75 TA 1946
Hornsey 37 TQ 3089
Hornton 50 SP 3945
Horrabridge 20 SX 5169
Horringer 54 TL 8261
Horsanish 124 NA 9908
Horsea Island 27 SU 6304
Horse Bank (sbk.) 68 SD 3220
Horsebridge (E Susx) 29 TQ 5911
Horsebridge (Hants.) 26 SU 3430
Horse Bridge (Staffs.) 60 SJ 9553
Horsebrook 59 SJ 8810
Horsehay 59 SJ 6707
Horseheath 54 TL 6147
Horse Hope Hill 95 NT 2130
Horsehouse 78 SE 0481
Horse Island (Highld.) 126 NC 0204
Horse Island (Shetld.) 141 HU 3807
Horse Isle (Strath.) 93 NS 2142
Horseley Fen 53 TL 4083
Horseley Hill 97 NT 8362
Horsell 36 SU 9959
Horseman's Green 58 SJ 4441
Horse of Burravoe 143 HU 5381
Horse of Copinsay (is.) 137 HY 6202
Horse Sound 126 NC 0304
Horseway 53 TL 4287
Horsey 65 TG 4523
Horsey Island 39 TM 2324
Horsford 65 TG 1915
Horsforth 79 SE 2337
Horsham (Here. and Worc.) 49 SO 7357
Horsham (W Susx) 28 TQ 1730
Horsham St. Faith 65 TG 2114
Horsington (Lincs.) 73 TF 1868
Horsington (Somer.) 25 ST 7023
Horsley (Derby.) 60 SK 3744
Horsley (Glos.) 46 ST 8398
Horsley (Northum.) 90 NY 8496
Horsley (Northum.) 91 NZ 0966
Horsley Cross 55 TM 1227
Horsleycross Street 55 TM 1228
Horsleyhill 90 NT 5319
Horsley Woodhouse 60 SK 3945
Horsmonden 29 TQ 7040
Horspath 47 SP 5704
Horstead 65 TG 2619
Horsted Keynes 29 TQ 3828
Horton (Avon) 33 ST 7684
Horton (Berks.) 36 TQ 0175
Horton (Bucks.) 36 SP 9219
Horton (Dorset) 26 SU 0307
Horton (Lancs.) 78 SD 8550
Horton (Northants.) 52 SP 8254
Horton (Northum.) 97 NU 0230
Horton (Staffs.) 69 SJ 9457
Horton (W Glam.) 40 SS 4785
Horton (Wilts.) 34 SU 0463
Horton Court (ant.) 33 ST 7685
Horton-cum-Studley 47 SP 5912
Horton Green 58 SJ 4549
Horton Heath 27 SU 4916
Horton in Ribblesdale 78 SD 8172
Horton Kirby 37 TQ 5668
Horton Moor 78 SD 8274
Horwich 69 SD 6311
Horwood 22 SS 5027
Hose 61 SK 7329
Hoselaw Loch 97 NT 8031
Hoses 82 SD 2192
Hosh 108 NN 8523
Hoswick 141 HU 4123
Hotham 74 SE 8934
Hothfield 31 TQ 9644
Hoton 61 SK 5722
Hot Point 18 SW 7112
Hott Hill 89 NT 4210
Houbie 143 HU 6290
Hough 59 SJ 7151
Hougham 62 SK 8844
Hougharry 124 NF 7071
Hough Bay 104 NL 9346
Hough Green 69 SJ 4885
Hough-on-the-Hill 62 SK 9246
Hough Skerries 104 NL 9247
Houghton (Cambs.) 53 TL 2871
Houghton (Cumbr.) 89 NY 4159
Houghton (Dyfed) 42 SM 9807
Houghton (Hants.) 26 SU 3331
Houghton (W Susx) 28 TQ 0111
Houghton Conquest 52 TL 0441
Houghton House (ant.) 52 TL 0339
Houghton-le-Spring 85 NZ 3450
Houghton on the Hill 61 SK 6703
Houghton Regis 36 TL 0224
Houghton St. Giles 64 TF 9235
Houlsyke 80 NZ 7308
Hound Green 36 SU 7259
Houndslow 96 NT 6347
Houndwood 97 NT 8464
Hounslow 37 TQ 1276
Housa Water 140 HU 2844
Housay 143 HU 6771
Housedon Hill 97 NT 9032
House of Aquahorthies 121 NJ 7220
House of Daviot 116 NH 7240
House of Glenmuick 118 NO 3794
Housetter 142 HU 3684
Houss Ness 141 HU 3729
Houston 101 NS 4067
Houstry 135 ND 1534
Houton Head 136 HY 3003
Hove 29 TQ 2805
Hoveringham 61 SK 6946
Hoveton 65 TG 3018
Hovingham 79 SE 6675
How 83 NY 5056
Howardian Hills 79 SE 6472
Howat's Hill 89 NY 2279

Loch Urigill

Mansfield Woodhouse

Loch Urigill	*132*	NC 2409
Loch Urr	*88*	NX 7584
Loch Urrahag	*131*	NB 3247
Loch Ussie	*128*	NH 5057
Loch Vaich	*127*	NH 3477
Loch Valigan	*108*	NN 9769
Loch Valley	*87*	NX 4481
Loch Venachar	*101*	NN 5705
Loch Veyatie	*132*	NC 1813
Loch Voil	*107*	NN 5019
Loch Vrotachan	*117*	NO 1278
Loch Walton	*101*	NS 6686
Loch Watten	*135*	ND 2256
Loch Whinyeon	*88*	NX 6260
Lochwinnoch	*100*	NS 3558
Lochwood (Dumf. and Galwy.)	*89*	NY 0896
Lochwood (Strath.)	*101*	NS 6966
Lock Awe (Argyll.)	*100*	NM 9610
Lockengate	*19*	SX 0361
Lockerbie	*89*	NY 1381
Lockeridge	*34*	SU 1467
Lockerley	*26*	SU 2925
Lockerley Hall	*26*	SU 2928
Locking	*32*	ST 3659
Lockington (Humbs.)	*74*	SE 9947
Lockington (Leic.)	*61*	SK 4628
Lockleywood	*59*	SJ 6828
Lockmaddy	*124*	NF 9168
Locks Heath	*27*	SU 5207
Lockton	*80*	SE 8489
Lockwood Beck Resr.	*85*	NZ 6713
Loddington (Leic.)	*61*	SK 7802
Loddington (Northants.)	*52*	SP 8178
Loddiswell	*21*	SX 7148
Loddon	*65*	TM 3698
Lode	*53*	TL 5362
Loder Head	*141*	HU 5243
Loders	*25*	SY 4994
Lodsworth	*28*	SU 9223
Loe, The	*18*	SW 6425
Loft Hill	*90*	NT 8513
Lofthouse (N Yorks.)	*78*	SE 1073
Lofthouse (W Yorks.)	*79*	SE 3325
Loftus	*85*	NZ 7118
Logan	*88*	NS 5820
Loganlea Resr.	*103*	NT 1962
Logan Mains	*86*	NX 0942
Logan Rock	*18*	SW 3523
Logan Water	*94*	NS 7537
Loggerheads	*59*	SJ 7336
Loggie	*127*	NH 1490
Logie (Fife)	*109*	NO 4020
Logie (Grampn.)	*121*	NK 0356
Logie (Tays.)	*109*	NO 6963
Logiealmond (dist.)	*108*	NN 9731
Logiealmond Lodge	*108*	NN 9531
Logie Coldstone	*118*	NJ 4304
Logie Head	*121*	NJ 5267
Logie Hill	*129*	NH 7776
Logie Newton	*121*	NJ 6638
Logie Pert	*109*	NO 6664
Logierait	*108*	NN 9752
Login	*42*	SN 1623
Lolworth	*53*	TL 3664
Lomond Hills	*103*	NO 2106
Lonbain	*123*	NG 6852
Londesborough	*74*	SE 8645
Londinium (ant.)	*37*	TQ 3079
London	*37*	TQ 3079
London Airport (Eday)	*138*	HY 5634
London Airport (Gatwick)	*28*	TQ 2740
London Airport (Heathrow)	*36*	TQ 0875
London Bridge Station	*37*	TQ 3280
London Colney	*37*	TL 1603
Londonderry	*79*	SE 3087
Londonthorpe	*62*	SK 9537
Londubh	*126*	NG 8680
Lonemore	*129*	NH 7688
Longa Island	*126*	NG 7377
Longannet Point	*102*	NS 9485
Long Ashton	*33*	ST 5470
Longay	*123*	NG 6531
Long Bennington	*62*	SK 8344
Longbenton	*91*	NZ 2668
Longborough	*47*	SP 1729
Long Bredy	*25*	SY 5690
Longbridge (Warw.)	*50*	SP 2662
Longbridge (W Mids.)	*50*	SP 0178
Longbridge Deverill	*33*	ST 8640
Long Buckby	*51*	SP 6267
Longburton	*25*	ST 6412
Long Clawson	*61*	SK 7227
Longcliffe	*60*	SK 2255
Long Common	*27*	SU 5014
Long Compton (Staffs.)	*59*	SJ 8522
Long Compton (Warw.)	*47*	SP 2832
Longcot	*34*	SU 2790
Long Crag	*91*	NU 0606
Long Craig	*109*	NO 7254
Long Crendon	*36*	SP 6908
Long Crichel	*26*	ST 9710
Longcroft	*101*	NS 7979
Longden	*58*	SJ 4306
Longdendale	*70*	SK 0397
Long Ditton	*37*	TQ 1666
Longdon (Here. and Worc.)	*49*	SO 8336
Longdon (Staffs.)	*60*	SK 0714
Longdon on Tern	*59*	SJ 6215
Longdown	*21*	SX 8691
Longdowns	*18*	SW 7434
Long Drax	*79*	SE 6528
Long Duckmanton	*71*	SK 4371
Long Eaton	*61*	SK 4933
Long Fell	*88*	NX 9064
Longfield	*30*	TQ 6068
Longford (Derby.)	*60*	SK 2137
Longford (Glos.)	*46*	SO 8320
Longford (Gtr London)	*36*	TQ 0576
Longford (Shrops.)	*59*	SJ 6433
Longford (Shrops.)	*59*	SJ 7218
Longford (W Mids.)	*50*	SP 3583
Longford Castle (ant.)	*26*	SU 1626
Longforgan	*108*	NO 3129
Longformacus	*96*	NT 6957
Longframlington	*91*	NU 1201
Long Geo	*136*	HY 4404
Long Gill	*78*	SD 7858
Longham (Dorset)	*26*	SZ 0697
Longham (Norf.)	*64*	TF 9415
Long Hanborough	*47*	SP 4114
Long Haven	*121*	NK 1240
Long Hermiston	*102*	NT 1770
Longhirst	*91*	NZ 2289
Long Holcombe	*23*	SS 7636
Longhope (Glos.)	*46*	SO 6819
Longhope (Hoy, Orkney) (chan.)	*136*	ND 3191
Longhorsley	*91*	NZ 1494
Longhoughton	*91*	NU 2414
Long Itchington	*50*	SP 4165
Long Lawford	*51*	SP 4775
Longleat House (ant.)	*33*	ST 8042
Longley Green	*49*	SO 7350
Long Load	*25*	ST 4623
Long Loch (Strath.)	*93*	NS 4752
Long Loch (Tays.)	*108*	NO 2938
Longmanhill	*121*	NJ 7462
Longman Point	*128*	NH 6747
Long Man, The (ant.)	*29*	TQ 5403
Long Marston (Herts.)	*36*	SP 8915
Long Marston (N Yorks.)	*79*	SE 4951
Long Marston (Warw.)	*50*	SP 1548
Long Marton	*83*	NY 6624
Long Melford	*54*	TL 8646
Longmoor Camp	*27*	SU 7930
Longmorn	*120*	NJ 2358
Long Mountain	*58*	SJ 2808
Long Mynd, The (mt.)	*58*	SO 4093
Long Newnton (Glos.)	*33*	ST 9092
Longnewton (Borders)	*96*	NT 5827
Longnewton (Cleve.)	*85*	NZ 3816
Longnewton Forest	*96*	NT 6227
Longney	*46*	SO 7612
Longniddry	*103*	NT 4476
Longnor (Shrops.)	*59*	SJ 4800
Longnor (Staffs.)	*70*	SK 0864
Long Nose Spit	*31*	TR 3771
Longparish	*34*	SU 4344
Long Preston	*78*	SD 8357
Longridge (Lancs.)	*77*	SD 6037
Longridge (Lothian)	*102*	NS 9462
Longridge Fell	*77*	SD 6540
Longridge Towers	*97*	NT 9549
Longriggend	*101*	NS 8270
Long Riston	*75*	TA 1242
Long Sand	*63*	TF 5548
Longsdon	*60*	SJ 9554
Longships	*18*	SW 3225
Longside	*121*	NK 0347
Longsleddale	*83*	NY 4902
Longslow	*59*	SJ 6535
Longstanton	*53*	TL 3966
Longstock	*26*	SU 3536
Longstone Wells	*23*	SS 7633
Long Stowe	*53*	TL 3054
Long Stratton	*55*	TM 1992
Long Street	*51*	SP 7947
Long Sutton (Hants.)	*35*	SU 7347
Long Sutton (Lincs.)	*63*	TF 4322
Long Sutton (Somer.)	*25*	ST 4625
Long Taing	*143*	HU 3785
Longthorpe	*62*	TL 1698
Longton (Lancs.)	*77*	SD 4725
Longton (Staffs.)	*59*	SJ 9043
Longtown (Cumbr.)	*89*	NY 3768
Longtown (Here. and Worc.)	*45*	SO 3228
Long Valley	*35*	SU 8351
Longville in the Dale	*59*	SO 5393
Long Whatton	*61*	SK 4723
Longwick	*36*	SP 7805
Long Wittenham	*47*	SU 5493
Longwitton	*91*	NZ 0788
Longwood House	*27*	SU 5324
Longwood Warren	*27*	SU 5226
Longworth	*47*	SU 3899
Longyester	*103*	NT 5465
Lòn Liath	*111*	NM 6590
Lonmore	*122*	NG 2646
Looe	*19*	SX 2553
Looe Bay	*20*	SX 2753
Looe or St. George's Island	*19*	SX 2551
Loose	*29*	TQ 7552
Loosley Row	*36*	SP 8100
Lootcherbrae	*121*	NJ 6054
Lopcombe Corner	*26*	SU 2435
Lopen	*25*	ST 4214
Lop Ness	*139*	HY 7643
Loppington	*58*	SJ 4629
Lorbottle	*91*	NU 0306
Lorbottle Hall	*91*	NU 0407
Lord Arthur's Cairn	*118*	NJ 5019
Lord's Seat (mt.)	*82*	NY 2026
Lorn (dist.)	*106*	NN 0735
Lornty	*108*	NO 1746
Lornty Burn	*108*	NO 1048
Lorton	*82*	NY 1625
Lorton Vale	*82*	NY 1526
Loscoe	*60*	SK 4247
Lossie Forest	*120*	NJ 2767
Lossiemouth	*120*	NJ 2370
Lossit	*98*	NR 1856
Lossit Bay	*98*	NR 1755
Lossit Point	*98*	NR 1756
Lostock Gralam	*69*	SJ 6874
Lostock Junction	*69*	SD 6708
Lostwithiel	*19*	SX 1059
Lothbeg	*134*	NC 9410
Lothbeg Point	*134*	NC 9609
Lothersdale	*78*	SD 9545
Lothmore	*134*	NC 9611
Lotus Hill	*88*	NX 9067
Loudoun Hill	*94*	NS 6037
Loudwater	*36*	SU 8990
Loughborough	*61*	SK 5319
Loughor	*40*	SS 5898
Loughton (Bucks.)	*52*	SP 8337
Loughton (Essex)	*37*	TQ 4296
Loughton (Shrops.)	*49*	SO 6183
Lound (Lincs.)	*62*	TF 0618
Lound (Notts.)	*72*	SK 6986
Lound (Suff.)	*65*	TM 5099
Lount	*60*	SK 3819
Louth	*73*	TF 3287
Love Clough	*78*	SD 8126
Lover	*26*	SU 2120
Loversall	*71*	SK 5798
Loves Green	*38*	TL 6404
Loveston	*42*	SN 0808
Lovington	*25*	ST 5931
Low Bentham	*77*	SD 6469
Low Bradfield	*71*	SK 2691
Low Bradley	*78*	SE 0048
Low Braithwaite	*83*	NY 4242
Lowbridge House	*83*	NY 5301
Low Brunton	*90*	NY 9269
Low Burnham	*74*	SE 7702
Lowca	*82*	NX 9821
Low Catton	*80*	SE 7053
Low Coniscliffe	*84*	NZ 2514
Low Crosby	*89*	NY 4459
Lowdham	*61*	SK 6646
Low Dinsdale	*85*	NZ 3411
Low Eggborough	*79*	SE 5522
Lower Aisholt	*24*	ST 2035
Lower Assendon	*36*	SU 7484
Lower Basildon	*35*	SU 6078
Lower Beeding	*28*	TQ 2227
Lower Benefield	*52*	SP 9888
Lower Boddington	*51*	SP 4752
Lower Bullingham	*45*	SO 5038
Lower Cam	*46*	SO 7401
Lower Chapel	*41*	SO 0235
Lower Chute	*34*	SU 3153
Lower Cwmtwrch	*41*	SN 7710
Lower Darwen	*77*	SD 6824
Lower Diabaig	*123*	NG 7960
Lower Down	*48*	SO 3384
Lower Dunsforth	*79*	SE 4464
Lower Farringdon	*27*	SU 7035
Lower Frankton	*58*	SJ 3732
Lower Froyle	*35*	SU 7544
Lower Gledfield	*128*	NH 5990
Lower Green	*64*	TF 9837
Lower Halstow	*30*	TQ 8567
Lower Hardres	*31*	TR 1453
Lower Heyford	*47*	SP 4824
Lower Higham	*30*	TQ 7172
Lower Hope, The (chan.)	*30*	TQ 7077
Lower Hordley	*58*	SJ 3929
Lower Icknield Way (ant.)	*36*	SP 8912
Lower Killeyan	*98*	NR 2743
Lower Langford	*33*	ST 4660
Lower Largo	*103*	NO 4102
Lower Lemington	*47*	SP 2134
Lower Lye	*48*	SO 4067
Lower Machen	*41*	ST 2288
Lower Maes-coed	*45*	SO 3431
Lower Moor	*50*	SO 9847
Lower Nazeing	*37*	TL 3906
Lower Penarth	*41*	ST 1869
Lower Penn	*59*	SO 8696
Lower Pennington	*26*	SZ 3193
Lower Peover	*69*	SJ 7474
Lower Quinton	*50*	SP 1847
Lower Sharpnose Point	*22*	SS 1912
Lower Shelton	*52*	SP 9942
Lower Shiplake	*36*	SU 7779
Lower Shuckburgh	*51*	SP 4862
Lower Slaughter	*47*	SP 1622
Lower Stanton St. Quintin	*33*	ST 9180
Lower Sundon	*52*	TL 0526
Lower Swanwick	*27*	SU 4909
Lower Swell	*47*	SP 1725
Lower Tamar Lake	*22*	SS 2910
Lower Thurlton	*65*	TM 4299
Lower Tysoe	*50*	SP 3445
Lower Upham	*27*	SU 5219
Lower Vexford	*24*	ST 1135
Lower Weare	*32*	ST 4053
Lower Wield	*35*	SU 6340
Lower Winchendon or Nether Winchendon	*36*	SP 7312
Lower Woodend	*36*	SU 8088
Lower Woodford	*26*	SU 1235
Lowesby	*61*	SK 7207
Lowestoft	*65*	TM 5493
Lowestoft End	*65*	TM 5394
Loweswater	*82*	NY 1421
Loweswater Fell	*82*	NY 1319
Low Gate	*90*	NY 9064
Lowgill (Cumbr.)	*83*	SD 6297
Lowgill (Lancs.)	*77*	SD 6564
Low Ham	*25*	ST 4329
Low Hartsop	*83*	NY 4013
Low Hesket	*83*	NY 4646
Low Hesleyhurst	*91*	NZ 0997
Lowick (Cumbr.)	*77*	SD 2985
Lowick (Northants.)	*52*	SP 9781
Lowick (Northum.)	*97*	NU 0139
Lowlandman's Bay	*98*	NR 5672
Low Mill	*85*	SE 6795
Low Moor	*77*	SD 7241
Lownie Moor	*109*	NO 4848
Lowood	*96*	NT 5235
Low Redford	*84*	NZ 0731
Low Row (Cumbr.)	*90*	NY 5863
Low Row (N Yorks.)	*84*	SD 9897
Lowsonford	*50*	SP 1867
Lowther Castle	*83*	NY 5223
Lowther College	*67*	SH 9975
Lowther Hill	*88*	NS 8810
Lowther Hills	*88*	NS 8910
Lowthorpe	*81*	TA 0860
Lowton	*69*	SJ 6197
Lowton Common	*69*	SJ 6397
Low Torry	*102*	NT 0086
Low Waters	*94*	NS 7353
Low Worsall	*85*	NZ 3909
Loxbeare	*23*	SS 9116
Loxhill	*28*	TQ 0037
Loxhore	*23*	SS 6138
Loxley	*50*	SP 2553
Loxton	*32*	ST 3755
Loxwood	*28*	TQ 0431
Lubcroy	*127*	NC 3501
Lubenham	*51*	SP 7087
Lùb Score	*123*	NG 3973
Luccombe	*23*	SS 9144
Luccombe Chine	*27*	SZ 5879
Luccombe Village	*27*	SZ 5880
Luce Bay	*86*	NX 2244
Luce Sands	*86*	NX 1453
Lucker	*97*	NU 1530
Luckett	*20*	SX 3873
Luckington	*33*	ST 8383
Lucklawhill	*109*	NO 4222
Luckwell Bridge	*23*	SS 9038
Lucton	*48*	SO 4364
Ludag	*112*	NF 7714
Ludborough	*73*	TF 2995
Ludchurch	*42*	SN 1411
Luddenden	*78*	SE 0425
Luddenham Court	*31*	TQ 9963
Luddesdown	*30*	TQ 6766
Luddington	*74*	SE 8216
Lude House	*108*	NN 8865
Ludford (Lincs.)	*73*	TF 1989
Ludford (Shrops.)	*48*	SO 5173
Ludgershall (Bucks.)	*36*	SP 6617
Ludgershall (Wilts.)	*34*	SU 2650
Ludgvan	*18*	SW 5033
Ludham	*65*	TG 3818
Ludlow	*48*	SO 5175
Ludwell	*25*	ST 9122
Ludworth	*85*	NZ 3641
Luffincott	*20*	SX 3394
Lugar	*94*	NS 5821
Lugar Water	*93*	NS 5022
Lugate Water	*96*	NT 4145
Luggate Burn	*103*	NT 6074
Luggiebank	*101*	NS 7672
Lugton	*93*	NS 4152
Lugton Water	*93*	NS 3848
Luguvalium (ant.)	*83*	NY 3955
Lugwardine	*45*	SO 5441
Luib	*123*	NG 5627
Luing (is.)	*105*	NM 7410
Luinga Bheag (is.)	*111*	NM 6187
Luinga Mhór (is)	*111*	NM 6086
Luinne Bheinn	*111*	NG 8600
Luirsay Dubh	*112*	NF 8640
Luithaid	*131*	NB 1713
Lui Water	*117*	NO 0592
Lulham	*45*	SO 4041
Lullingstone Castle	*37*	TQ 5364
Lullington (Derby.)	*60*	SK 2513
Lullington (Somer.)	*33*	ST 7851
Lulsgate Bottom	*33*	ST 5065
Lulsley	*49*	SO 7455
Lulworth Cove	*25*	SY 8279
Lumb	*78*	SE 0221
Lumby	*79*	SE 4830
Lumley Moor Resr.	*79*	SE 2270
Lumloch	*101*	NS 6369
Lumphanan	*119*	NJ 5804
Lumphinnans	*102*	NT 1692
Lumsdaine	*97*	NT 8769
Lumsden	*121*	NJ 4722
Lunan	*109*	NO 6851
Lunan Bay	*109*	NO 7051
Lunan Burn	*108*	NO 1542
Lunanhead	*109*	NO 4752
Lunan Water	*109*	NO 6149
Luncarty	*108*	NO 0929
Lund (Humbs.)	*81*	SE 9648
Lund (N Yorks.)	*79*	SE 6532
Lund (Unst)	*143*	HP 5703
Lunda Wick	*143*	HP 5604
Lunderston Bay	*100*	NS 1873
Lundie (Highld.)	*115*	NH 1410
Lundie (Tays.)	*108*	NO 2836
Lundin Links	*103*	NO 4002
Lundy	*22*	SS 1443
Lune Forest	*83*	NY 8323
Lune Moor	*84*	NY 9023
Lunga (Island of Mull) (is.)	*104*	NM 2741
Lunga (Strath.) (is.)	*105*	NM 7008
Lunga Hotel	*105*	NM 7906
Lunna	*143*	HU 4869
Lunna Holm	*143*	HU 5274
Lunnasting (dist.)	*141*	HU 4865
Lunning	*141*	HU 5066
Lunning Sound	*141*	HU 5165
Lunsford's Cross	*29*	TQ 7210
Lunt	*68*	SD 3401
Luntley	*45*	SO 3955
Luppitt	*24*	ST 1606
Lupton	*77*	SD 5581
Lupton Beck	*77*	SD 5580
Lurgashall	*28*	SU 9326
Lurg Hill	*121*	NJ 5057
Lurg Mhór (mt.)	*115*	NH 0640
Lurgmore	*116*	NH 5937
Lusby	*73*	TF 3367
Luskentyre	*125*	NG 0699
Lusragan Burn	*106*	NM 9031
Luss	*100*	NS 3592
Lussa Loch	*92*	NR 7130
Lussa Point	*99*	NR 6486
Lussa River (Island of Mull)	*105*	NM 6531
Lussa River (Jura)	*99*	NR 6292
Lusta	*122*	NG 2756
Lustleigh	*21*	SX 7881
Luston	*48*	SO 4863
Luthermuir	*109*	NO 6568
Luther Water	*109*	NO 6870
Luthrie	*108*	NO 3219
Luton (Beds.)	*36*	TL 0821
Luton (Devon)	*21*	SX 9076
Luton (Kent)	*30*	TQ 7766
Luton Airport	*37*	TL 1221
Lutterworth	*51*	SP 5484
Lutton (Devon)	*21*	SX 5959
Lutton (Lincs.)	*63*	TF 4325
Lutton (Northants.)	*52*	TL 1187
Luxborough	*23*	SS 9738
Luxhay Reservoir	*24*	ST 2017
Luxulyan	*19*	SX 0458
Lybster	*135*	ND 2435
Lydbury North	*48*	SO 3486
Lydcott	*23*	SS 6936
Lydd	*31*	TR 0421
Lydd Airport	*31*	TR 0621
Lydden	*31*	TR 2645
Lyddington	*62*	SP 8797
Lydd-on-Sea	*31*	TR 0819
Lydeard St. Lawrence	*24*	ST 1232
Lydford (Devon)	*20*	SX 5084
Lydford (Somer.)	*25*	ST 5731
Lydgate	*78*	SD 9225
Lydham	*48*	SO 3391
Lydiard Millicent	*34*	SU 0986
Lydiate	*68*	SD 3604
Lydlinch	*25*	ST 7413
Lydney	*45*	SO 6203
Lydney Sand	*45*	ST 6399
Lydstep	*42*	SS 0898
Lye	*49*	SO 9284
Lye Green	*36*	SP 9703
Lyford	*47*	SU 3994
Lymbridge Green	*31*	TR 1243
Lyme Park (ant.)	*70*	SJ 9682
Lyme Regis	*24*	SY 3492
Lyminge	*31*	TR 1641
Lyminge Forest	*31*	TR 1545
Lymington	*26*	SZ 3295
Lymington River	*26*	SU 3102
Lyminster	*28*	TQ 0204
Lymm	*69*	SJ 6786
Lymore	*26*	SZ 2992
Lympne	*31*	TR 1235
Lympsham	*32*	ST 3454
Lympstone	*21*	SX 9984
Lynaberack	*116*	NN 7694
Lynchat	*116*	NH 7801
Lyn Cwmdulyn Reservoir	*66*	SH 4949
Lyndale House	*122*	NG 3654
Lyndale Point	*122*	NG 3657
Lyndhurst	*26*	SU 2907
Lyndhurst Road Station	*26*	SU 3309
Lyndon	*62*	SK 9004
Lyne	*36*	TQ 0166
Lyneal	*58*	SJ 4433
Lyneham (Oxon.)	*47*	SP 2720
Lyneham (Wilts.)	*34*	SU 0179
Lyne House	*28*	TQ 1938
Lynemouth	*91*	NZ 2991
Lyne of Gorthleck	*116*	NH 5420
Lyne of Skene	*119*	NJ 7610
Lyness	*136*	ND 3094
Lyne Water	*95*	NT 1645
Lyng (Norf.)	*64*	TG 0617
Lyng (Somer.)	*24*	ST 3328
Lynmouth	*23*	SS 7249
Lynn Deeps (chan.)	*63*	TF 5846
Lynn of Lorn	*105*	NM 8639
Lynsted	*30*	TQ 9461
Lynton	*23*	SS 7149
Lyon's Gate	*25*	ST 6605
Lyonshall	*45*	SO 3356
Lype Hill	*23*	SS 9537
Lyrawa Burn	*136*	ND 2699
Lyrie Geo	*136*	ND 2096
Lytchett Matravers	*26*	SY 9495
Lytchett Minster	*26*	SY 9593
Lyth	*135*	ND 2763
Lytham	*77*	SD 3727
Lytham St. Anne's	*77*	SD 3427
Lythe	*85*	NZ 8413
Lythes	*136*	ND 4589

M

Maaey Riabhach	*124*	NF 8850
Maaruig	*125*	NB 1906
Maa Water	*141*	HU 3755
Mabe Burnthouse	*18*	SW 7634
Mabie	*88*	NX 9570
Mablethorpe	*73*	TF 5085
Macaterick	*87*	NX 4390
Macclesfield	*69*	SJ 9173
Macclesfield Canal (Ches.)	*69*	SJ 9166
Macclesfield Canal (Ches.)	*69*	SJ 9482
Macclesfield Forest	*70*	SJ 9772
Macduff	*121*	NJ 7064
Macduff's Castle (ant.)	*103*	NT 3497
Machany Water	*107*	NN 8415
Macharioch	*92*	NR 7309
Machars, The (dist.)	*86*	NX 3753
Machen	*41*	ST 2189
Machir Bay	*98*	NR 1962
Machrie Bay	*92*	NR 8834
Machrie Water	*92*	NR 9334
Machrihanish	*92*	NR 6220
Machrihanish Airfield	*92*	NR 6622
Machrihanish Bay	*92*	NR 6423
Machrihanish Water	*92*	NR 6520
Machynlleth	*57*	SH 7401
Mackworth	*60*	SK 3137
Maclean's Nose	*111*	NM 5361
Macleod's Maidens (is.)	*122*	NG 2436
Macleod's Tables (mt.)	*122*	NG 2243
Macmerry	*103*	NT 4372
Madadh Gruamach (is.)	*124*	NF 9566
Madderty	*108*	NN 9522
Maddiston	*102*	NS 9476
Madehurst	*28*	SU 9810
Madeley (Shrops.)	*59*	SJ 6904
Madeley (Staffs.)	*59*	SJ 7744
Madingley	*53*	TL 3960
Madley	*45*	SO 4138
Madresfield	*49*	SO 8047
Madron	*18*	SW 4532
Mad Wharf (sbk.)	*68*	SD 2607
Maelienydd	*48*	SO 1271
Maenclochog	*42*	SN 0827
Maendy	*41*	ST 0176
Mae Ness	*138*	HY 4831
Maentwrog	*67*	SH 6640
Maer	*59*	SJ 7938
Maerdy (Clwyd)	*67*	SJ 0144
Maerdy (Mid Glam.)	*41*	SS 9798
Maesbrook	*58*	SJ 3121
Maesbury Marsh	*58*	SJ 3125
Maes-glas	*32*	ST 2985
Maesgwynne	*43*	SN 2024
Maeshafn	*68*	SJ 2061
Maes Howe (ant.)	*136*	HY 3112
Maesllyn	*43*	SN 3644
Maesmynis	*44*	SO 0148
Maesteg	*41*	SS 8591
Maesybont	*43*	SN 5616
Maesycwmmer	*41*	ST 1594
Maesyrchen Mountain	*58*	SJ 1846
Magdalen Laver	*37*	TL 5108
Maggieknockater	*121*	NJ 3145
Magham Down	*29*	TQ 6111
Maghannan	*131*	NB 0821
Maghull	*68*	SD 3702
Magor	*33*	ST 4287
Maiden Bradley	*33*	ST 8038
Maiden Castle (ant.)	*25*	SY 6688
Maidencombe	*21*	SX 9268
Maidenhead	*36*	SU 8881
Maidenhead Bay	*93*	NS 2008
Maiden Island	*105*	NM 8432
Maiden Law	*84*	NZ 1749
Maiden Newton	*25*	SY 5997
Maidenpap (Dumf. and Galwy.) (mt.)	*88*	NX 8961
Maiden Pap (Highld.) (mt.)	*135*	ND 0429
Maiden Paps (Borders) (mt.)	*89*	NT 5002
Maidens	*93*	NS 2107
Maiden Stone (ant.)	*121*	NJ 7024
Maiden Way (Cumbr.) (ant.)	*83*	NY 6535
Maiden Way (Northum.) (ant.)	*83*	NY 6756
Maidenwell	*19*	SX 1470
Maidford	*51*	SP 6052
Maids Moreton	*51*	SP 7035
Maidstone	*29*	TQ 7656
Maidwell	*51*	SP 7477
Mail	*141*	HU 4228
Mainland (Orkney)	*136*	HY 3711
Mainland (Shetld.)	*141*	HU 4051
Mains	*116*	NH 4239
Mains of Ardestie	*109*	NO 5034
Mains of Balhall	*109*	NO 5163
Mains of Ballindarg	*109*	NO 4051
Mains of Dalvey	*117*	NJ 1132
Mains of Dillavaird	*119*	NO 7481
Mains of Drum	*119*	NO 8099
Mains of Melgund	*109*	NO 5456
Mains of Thornton	*109*	NO 6871
Mainstone	*48*	SO 2687
Main Water of Luce	*86*	NX 1468
Maisemore	*46*	SO 8121
Maisgeir (is.)	*104*	NM 3539
Malasgair (mt.)	*131*	NB 3017
Malborough	*21*	SX 7039
Malcolm's Head	*139*	HZ 1970
Malcolm's Point	*105*	NM 4918
Maldon	*38*	TL 8506
Malham	*78*	SD 9062
Malham Tarn	*78*	SD 8966
Mallaig	*111*	NM 6796
Mallart River	*133*	NC 6737
Mallerstang Common	*83*	SD 7798
Mallowdale Fell	*77*	SD 6159
Malltraeth Bay	*66*	SH 3764
Malltraeth Marsh	*66*	SH 4471
Malltraeth Sands	*66*	SH 4066
Mallwyd	*57*	SH 8612
Malmesbury	*34*	ST 9387
Malpas (Ches.)	*59*	SJ 4847
Malpas (Cornwall)	*19*	SW 8442
Malpas (S Glam.)	*32*	ST 3091
Maltby (Cleve.)	*85*	NZ 4613
Maltby (S Yorks.)	*71*	SK 5392
Maltby le Marsh	*73*	TF 4681
Maltman's Hill	*30*	TQ 9043
Malton	*80*	SE 7871
Malvern Hills	*49*	SO 7641
Malvern Link	*49*	SO 7848
Malvern Wells	*49*	SO 7742
Màm an Staing	*123*	NG 7813
Mamble	*49*	SO 6871
Mam na Gualainn	*106*	NN 1162
Mamore Forest	*106*	NN 1765
Màm Sodhail	*115*	NH 1225
Màm Suim	*117*	NJ 0109
Mam Tor (ant.)	*70*	SK 1283
Manaccan	*18*	SW 7625
Manacle Point	*19*	SW 8121
Manacles, The (pt.)	*19*	SW 8120
Manafon	*58*	SJ 1102
Man and his man or Bawden Rocks	*18*	SW 6953
Manar House	*119*	NJ 7319
Manaton	*21*	SX 7481
Manby	*73*	TF 3986
Mancetter	*60*	SP 3196
Manchester	*69*	SJ 8397
Manchester Airport	*69*	SJ 8184
Manchester Ship Canal	*69*	SJ 6989
Mancot	*68*	SJ 3267
Mandally	*115*	NH 2900
Manea	*53*	TL 4789
Manfield	*84*	NZ 2213
Mangaster	*142*	HU 3270
Mangersta	*130*	NB 0131
Mangotsfield	*33*	ST 6676
Manish (Harris, W Isles)	*125*	NG 1089
Manish (Scarp)	*130*	NA 9513
Manish Point (Island of Raasay)	*123*	NG 5648
Manish Point (North Uist)	*124*	NF 7173
Mankinholes	*78*	SD 9523
Manley	*69*	SJ 5071
Manmoel	*41*	SO 1703
Mannal	*104*	NL 9840
Manningford Bohune	*34*	SU 1357
Manningford Bruce	*34*	SU 1359
Manning's Heath	*28*	TQ 2028
Mannington	*26*	SU 0605
Manningtree	*55*	TM 1031
Mannofield	*119*	NJ 9104
Manorbier	*42*	SS 0698
Manorhill	*96*	NT 6632
Manorowen	*42*	SM 9336
Manor Water	*95*	NT 2031
Man o' Scord (mt.)	*142*	HU 3283
Manquhill Hill	*88*	NX 6694
Mansell Gamage	*45*	SO 3944
Mansell Lacy	*45*	SO 4245
Mansergh	*77*	SD 6082
Mansfield (Notts.)	*71*	SK 5361
Mansfield (Strath.)	*88*	NS 6214
Mansfield Woodhouse	*71*	SK 5363

Mynydd Margam North Charford

Mynydd Margam 41 SS 8188
Mynyddmelyn 42 SN 0236
Mynydd Merddin 45 SO 3428
Mynydd Merthyr 41 ST 0599
Mynydd Myddfai 41 SN 8029
Mynydd Pen-bre 43 SN 4503
Mynydd Pencarreg 43 SN 5743
Mynydd Pennant 57 SH 6610
Mynydd Pen-y-fal 45 SO 2619
Mynydd Perfedd 67 SH 6262
Mynydd Preseli 42 SN 1032
Mynydd Resolfen 41 SN 8603
Mynydd Rhiw-Saeson 57 SH 9006
Mynydd Sylen 43 SN 5108
Mynydd Tan-y-coed 57 SH 6604
Mynydd Tarw 58 SJ 1132
Mynydd Trawsnant 44 SN 8249
Mynydd Troed 41 SO 1728
Mynydd Waun Fawr 57 SJ 0105
Mynydd y Betws 40 SN 6710
Mynydd y Cemais 57 SH 8707
Mynydd y Drum 41 SN 8109
Mynydd y Gadfa 57 SH 9914
Mynydd y Gaer 41 SS 9585
Mynydd-y-Garreg 43 SN 4409
Mynydd-y-glog 41 SN 9808
Mynydd y Gwair 43 SN 6607
Mynytho 66 SH 3031
Myrebird 119 NO 7498
Mytchett 35 SU 8855
Mytholm 78 SD 9827
Mytholmroyd 78 SE 0125
Myton-on-Swale 79 SE 4366

N

Naast 126 NG 8283
Naburn 79 SE 5945
Nackington 31 TR 1554
Nacton 55 TM 2240
Na Cuiltean (is.) 98 NR 5464
Naden Resrs. 69 SD 8516
Na Dromannan 127 NC 2101
Nafferton 81 TA 0559
Na Gamhnaichean (is.) 123 NG 4312
Nailsea 33 ST 4670
Nailstone 60 SK 4107
Nailsworth 46 ST 8499
Nairn 129 NH 8856
Nancegollan 18 SW 6632
Nancledra 18 SW 4936
Nanhoron 66 SH 2831
Nannau 57 SH 7420
Nannerch 68 SJ 1669
Nanpantan 61 SK 5017
Nanpean 19 SW 9556
Nant Bran 41 SN 9533
Nantclwyd Hall 58 SJ 1151
Nant Cynnen 43 SN 3522
Nant-ddu 41 SO 0015
Nanternis 43 SN 3756
Nant Ffrancon 67 SH 6363
Nantgaredig 43 SN 4921
Nantgarw 41 ST 1285
Nant-glâs 57 SN 9965
Nantglyn 67 SJ 0061
Nantgwynant 66 SH 6049
Nantlle 66 SH 5053
Nantmawr 58 SJ 2424
Nantmel 57 SO 0366
Nantmor 66 SH 6046
Nant Peris 66 SH 6058
Nantstallon 19 SX 0367
Nantwich 59 SJ 6552
Nant-y-derry 45 SO 3306
Nantyffyllon 41 SS 8492
Nantyglo 41 SO 1911
Nant-y-moch Resr. 57 SN 7587
Nant-y-moel 41 SS 9393
Nant yr Eira 57 SH 9505
Naphill 36 SU 9496
Nappa 78 SD 8553
Napton on the Hill 51 SP 4661
Narachan Burn 92 NR 7548
Narberth 42 SN 1114
Narborough (Leic.) 61 SP 5497
Narborough (Norf.) 64 TF 7413
Nare Head 19 SW 9136
Nare Point 19 SW 7925
Narrows of Raasay 123 NG 5435
Nasareth 66 SH 4749
Naseby 51 SP 6878
Naseby Field 51 SP 6879
Naseby Resr. 51 SP 6677
Nash (Bucks.) 51 SP 7734
Nash (Gwent) 32 ST 3483
Nash (Here. and Worc.) 48 SO 3062
Nash (Shrops.) 49 SO 6071
Nash Lee 36 SP 8408
Nash Point 41 SS 9168
Nassington 62 TL 0696
Nass, The (sbk.) 39 TM 0011
Nasty 37 TL 3624
Nateby (Cumbr.) 83 NY 7706
Nateby (Lancs.) 77 SD 4644
National Exhibition Centre 50 SP 1883
Natland 83 SD 5289
Naughton 54 TM 0249
Naunton (Glos.) 46 SP 1123
Naunton (Here. and Worc.) 49 SO 8739
Naunton Beauchamp 50 SO 9652
Navax Point 18 SW 5943
Nave Island 98 NR 2875
Navenby 72 SK 9857
Naver Forest 133 NC 6938
Navestock Heath 37 TQ 5397
Navestock Side 37 TQ 5697
Navio (ant.) 70 SK 1882
Naworth Castle (ant.) 90 NY 5662
Nawton 79 SE 6584
Nayland 54 TL 9734
Nazeing 37 TL 4106
Naze, The (pt.) 39 TM 2624
Neacroft 26 SZ 1897
Neal's Green 50 SP 3384
Neap 141 HU 5058
Neap of Skea 143 HU 3783
Near Cotton 60 SK 0646
Neasham 84 NZ 3210
Neath 41 SS 7597
Neatishead 65 TG 3421
Neaty Burn 127 NH 3542
Neave or Coomb Island 133 NC 6664
Neban Point 136 HY 2113
Neblonga (pt.) 136 HY 2111
Nebo (Dyfed) 56 SN 5465
Nebo (Gwyn.) 66 SH 4750
Nebo (Gwyn.) 67 SH 8356
Necton 64 TF 8709
Nedd 132 NC 1332
Nedging Tye 54 TM 0149
Needham 55 TM 2281
Needham Market 55 TM 0855
Needingworth 53 TL 3472
Needles, The (pt.) 26 SZ 2984
Needs Law 90 NT 6002
Needs Oar Point 27 SZ 4498
Needwood Forest 60 SK 1524
Neegirth (pt.) 143 HU 5171
Neen Savage 49 SO 6777
Neen Sollars 49 SO 6572
Neenton 49 SO 6487
Nefyn 66 SH 3040
Neidpath Castle (ant.) 95 NT 2340
Neil's Helly (pt.) 138 HY 5054
Neilston 93 NS 4657
Neilston Pad (mt.) 93 NS 4755
Neist 122 NG 1247
Nelson (Lancs.) 78 SD 8737
Nelson (Mid Glam.) 41 ST 1195
Nelson Village 91 NZ 2577
Nemphlar 95 NS 8544
Nempnett Thrubwell 33 ST 5360
Nenthead 83 NY 7743
Nenthorn 96 NT 6837
Nercwys 68 SJ 2260
Nereabolls 98 NR 2255
Nerston 94 NS 6457
Nesbit 97 NT 9833
Ness (Ches.) 68 SJ 3075
Ness (Isle of Lewis) (dist.) 131 NB 5261
Ness (N Yorks.) 80 SE 6878
Nesscliffe 58 SJ 3819
Ness Glen 93 NS 4701
Ness Head 135 ND 3866
Ness of Boray 136 HY 4321
Ness of Brough 139 HY 6542
Ness of Burravoe 143 HU 3890
Ness of Gossabrough 143 HU 5383
Ness of Hillswick 142 HU 2775
Ness of Houlland (Shetld.) 143 HU 3788
Ness of Houlland (Yell) 143 HP 5205
Ness of Ireland 141 HU 3723
Ness of Olnesfirth 142 HU 3076
Ness of Ork 137 HY 5422
Ness of Ramnageo 143 HU 6299
Ness of Sound (Shetld.) 141 HU 4638
Ness of Sound (Yell) 143 HU 4482
Ness of Trebister 141 HU 4538
Ness Point or North Cheek 81 NZ 9506
Ness, The (Orkney) 137 HY 5408
Ness, The (South Havra) 141 HU 3626
Ness, The (Stronsay) 139 HY 6630
Neston (Ches.) 68 SJ 2877
Neston (Wilts.) 33 ST 8667
Nether Alderley 69 SJ 8476
Netheravon 34 SU 1448
Nether Blainslie 96 NT 5443
Netherbrae 121 NJ 7959
Nether Broughton 61 SK 6925
Netherburn 94 NS 7947
Nether Burrow 77 SD 6174
Netherbury 25 SY 4799
Netherby 89 NY 3971
Nether Cerne 25 SY 6698
Nether Compton 25 ST 5907
Nether Crimond 121 NJ 8222
Nether Dallachy 121 NJ 3663
Netherend 45 SO 5900
Nether Exe 21 SS 9300
Netherfield 29 TQ 7018
Netherhampton 26 SU 1029
Nether Handwick 109 NO 3641
Nether Haugh 71 SK 4196
Nether Howecleuch 89 NT 0312
Nether Kellet 77 SD 5067
Nether Kinmundy 121 NK 0444
Nether Kirkton 93 NS 4757
Nether Langwith 71 SK 5371
Netherlaw 87 NX 7445
Netherley 119 NO 8593
Nethermill 89 NY 0487
Nethermuir 121 NJ 9143
Nether Padley 71 SK 2478
Netherplace 93 NS 5155
Nether Poppleton 79 SE 5654
Nether Row 82 NY 3237
Netherseal 60 SK 2813
Nether Silton 85 SE 4592
Nether Stowey 32 ST 1939
Netherthird 88 NS 5818
Netherthong 70 SE 1309
Netherthorpe Airfield 71 SK 5480
Netherton (Central) 101 NS 5579
Netherton (Devon) 21 SX 8971
Netherton (Here. and Worc.) 50 SO 9941
Netherton (Mers.) 68 SD 3500
Netherton (Northum.) 91 NT 9907
Netherton (Tays.) 108 NO 1452
Netherton (Tays.) 109 NO 5457
Netherton (W Yorks.) 71 SE 2716
Nethertown (Cumbr.) 82 NX 9807
Nethertown (Island of Stroma) 135 ND 3578
Nether Urquhart 102 NO 1808
Nether Wallop 26 SU 3036
Nether Wasdale 82 NY 1204
Nether Whitacre 60 SP 2393
Nether Winchendon or Lower Winchendon 36 SP 7312
Netherwitton 91 NZ 1090
Netherwood 94 NS 6528
Nether Worton 47 SP 4230
Nethy Bridge 117 NJ 0020
Netley 27 SU 4508
Netley Marsh 26 SU 3312
Nettlebed 36 SU 7086
Nettlebridge 33 ST 6448
Nettlecombe 25 SY 5195
Nettleden 36 TL 0210
Nettle Geo 137 HY 5319
Nettleham 72 TF 0075
Nettle Hill 83 NY 7107
Nettlestead 29 TQ 6852
Nettlestead Green 29 TQ 6850
Nettlestone 27 SZ 6290
Nettlestone Point 27 SZ 6391
Nettleton (Lincs.) 75 TA 1000
Nettleton (Wilts.) 33 ST 8178
Neuadd Reservoirs 41 SO 0218
Neuk, The 119 NO 7397
Nevendon 38 TQ 7390
Nevern 42 SN 0840
Nevis Forest 106 NN 1271
Nev of Stuis (pt.) 143 HU 4697
Nev, The (Shetld.) (pt.) 140 HU 2643
Nev, The (Shetld.) (pt.) 141 HU 3414
Nev, The (Unst) (pt.) 143 HP 6611
Nev, The (Westray) (pt.) 138 HY 4452
New Abbey 88 NX 9665
New Aberdour 121 NJ 8863
New Addington 37 TQ 3863
New Alresford 27 SU 5832
New Alyth 108 NO 2447
Newark (Northants.) 62 TF 2100
Newark (Sanday, Orkney) 139 HY 7242
Newark Bay (Orkney) 137 HY 5703
Newark Bay (S. Ronaldsay) 136 ND 4689
Newark Castle (Borders) (ant.) 96 NT 4229
Newark Castle (Strath.) (ant.) 93 NS 3217
Newark Castle (Strath.) (ant.) 100 NS 3274
Newark-on-Trent 61 SK 7953
New Arley 50 SP 2989
Newarthill 101 NS 7859
New Ash Green 30 TQ 6065
Newbald 74 SE 9136
New Bedford River or Hundred Foot Drain 53 TL 4987
New Bewick 91 NU 0620
Newbiggin (Cumbr.) 83 NY 4729
Newbiggin (Cumbr.) 83 NY 5649
Newbiggin (Cumbr.) 83 NY 6228
Newbiggin (Cumbr.) 76 SD 2669
Newbiggin (Durham) 84 NY 9127
Newbiggin (N Yorks.) 84 SD 9591
Newbiggin (N Yorks.) 78 SD 9985
Newbiggin-by-the-Sea 91 NZ 3187
Newbiggin Common 84 NY 9131
Newbigging (Strath.) 95 NT 0145
Newbigging (Tays.) 108 NO 2841
Newbigging (Tays.) 109 NO 4237
Newbigging (Tays.) 109 NO 4936
Newbiggin on Lune 83 NY 7005
Newbold (Derby.) 71 SK 3773
Newbold (Leic.) 60 SK 4018
Newbold on Avon 51 SP 4877
Newbold-on-Stour 50 SP 2446
Newbold Pacey 50 SP 2957
Newbold Verdon 61 SK 4403
New Bolingbroke 73 TF 3058
Newborough (Gwyn.) 66 SH 4265
Newborough (Northants.) 62 TF 2006
Newborough (Staffs.) 60 SK 1325
Newborough Warren 66 SH 4063
Newbottle 51 SP 5236
Newbourn 55 TM 2743
New Brancepeth 84 NZ 2241
Newbridge (Clwyd) 58 SJ 2841
Newbridge (Corn.) 18 SW 4231
Newbridge (Gwent) 41 ST 2197
Newbridge (Hants.) 26 SU 2915
Newbridge (I. of W.) 26 SZ 4187
Newbridge (Lothian) 102 NT 1272
Newbridge-on-Usk 45 ST 3894
Newbridge on Wye 44 SO 0158
New Brighton 68 SJ 3093
New Brinsley 61 SK 4550
Newbrough 90 NY 8767
New Buckenham 55 TM 0890
Newburgh (Fife) 108 NO 2318
Newburgh (Grampn.) 121 NJ 9925
Newburgh (Lancs.) 69 SD 4810
Newburgh Bar 121 NK 0023
Newburgh Priory 79 SE 5476
Newburn 91 NZ 1765
Newbury 35 SU 4666
Newby (Cumbr.) 83 NY 5921
Newby (N Yorks.) 85 NZ 5012
Newby (N Yorks.) 77 SD 7269
Newby Bridge 77 SD 3686
Newby East 89 NY 4758
Newby Hall (ant.) 79 SE 3467
Newby Moss 77 SD 7472
New Byth 121 NJ 8254
Newby West 82 NY 3653
Newby Wiske 79 SE 3687
Newcastle (Gwent) 45 SO 4417
Newcastle (Shrops.) 48 SO 2482
Newcastle Airport 91 NZ 1971
Newcastle Emlyn 43 SN 3040
Newcastleton 89 NY 4887
Newcastleton Forest 90 NY 5287
Newcastle-under-Lyme 59 SJ 8445
Newcastle upon Tyne 91 NZ 2464
Newchapel (Dyfed) 43 SN 2239
Newchapel (Staffs.) 59 SJ 8654
Newchapel (Surrey) 29 TQ 3642
Newchurch (Dyfed) 43 SN 3724
Newchurch (Gwent) 45 ST 4597
Newchurch (I. of W.) 27 SZ 5585
Newchurch (Kent) 31 TR 0531
Newchurch (Powys) 45 SO 2150
Newchurch in Pendle 78 SD 8239
New Clipstone 71 SK 5863
New Costessey 65 TG 1710
Newcott 24 ST 2309
New Cross 57 SN 6376
New Cumnock 88 NS 6113
New Deer 121 NJ 8846
Newdigate 28 TQ 2042
New Duston 51 SP 7162
New Earswick 79 SE 6155
New Edlington 71 SK 5399
New Ellerby 75 TA 1639
Newell Green 36 SU 8771
New Eltham 37 TQ 4573
New End 50 SP 0560
Newenden 30 TQ 8327
Newent 46 SO 7226
New Farnley 79 SE 2431
New Ferry 68 SJ 3385
Newfield (Durham) 84 NZ 2033
Newfield (Highld.) 129 NH 7877
New Forest 26 SU 2806
New Fryston 79 SE 4526
Newgale 42 SM 8422
New Galloway 88 NX 6377
Newgate 64 TG 0443
Newgate Street 37 TL 3005
New Gilston 103 NO 4207
Newgord 143 HP 5706
New Grimsby 18 SV 8815
New Grounds 46 SO 7204
Newhall 95 NT 1756
Newhall (Ches.) 59 SJ 6045
Newhall (Derby.) 60 SK 2821
Newhall House (Highld.) 128 NH 6965
Newham (Northum.) 97 NU 1728
Newham Hall 97 NU 1729
New Hartley 91 NZ 3076
Newhaven 29 TQ 4401
New Hedges 42 SN 1302
Newhey 69 SD 9311
New Holland 74 TA 0724
Newholm 85 NZ 8610
New Horton Grange 91 NZ 1975
New Houghton (Derby.) 71 SK 4965
New Houghton (Norf.) 64 TF 7827
Newhouse 101 NS 7961
New Houses 78 SD 8073
New Hutton 83 SD 5691
New Hythe 30 TQ 7159
Newick 29 TQ 4121
Newington (Kent) 30 TQ 8665
Newington (Kent) 31 TR 1737
Newington (Oxon.) 36 SU 6196
New Inn (Gwent) 45 SO 4800
New Inn (Gwent) 45 ST 3099
New Inn (N Yorks.) 78 SD 8072
New Invention 48 SO 2976
New Kelso 126 NG 9442
New Lanark 95 NS 8742
Newland (Glos.) 45 SO 5509
Newland (Here. and Worc.) 49 SO 7948
Newland (N Yorks.) 74 SE 6824
Newlandrig 103 NT 3662
Newlands (Borders) 90 NY 5194
Newlands (Grampn.) 120 NJ 3051
Newlands (Northum.) 84 NZ 0955
Newlands of Fleenas Wood 129 NH 9146
Newlands of Geise 135 ND 0865
Newlands Pass 82 NY 1917
New Lane 68 SD 4212
New Leake 73 TF 4057
New Leeds 121 NJ 9954
New Longton 77 SD 5125
New Luce 86 NX 1764
Newlyn 18 SW 4628
Newlyn Downs 19 SW 8354
Newmachar 119 NJ 8819
Newmains 95 NS 8256
New Mains of Ury 119 NO 8787
New Malden 37 TQ 2166
Newmarket (Isle of Lewis) 131 NB 4235
Newmarket (Suff.) 54 TL 6463
Newmarket Heath 54 TL 6363
New Marske 85 NZ 6220
New Marton 58 SJ 3334
Newmill (Borders) 89 NT 4510
New Mill (Corn.) 18 SW 4534
Newmill (Grampn.) 121 NJ 4352
New Mill (Herts.) 36 SP 9212
New Mill (W Yorks.) 70 SE 1608
Newmill Farm 119 NO 7883
Newmill of Inshewan 109 NO 4260
New Mills (Corn.) 19 SW 8952
New Mills (Derby.) 70 SK 0085
New Mills (Gwent) 45 SO 5107
New Mills (Powys) 57 SJ 0901
Newmiln 108 NO 1230
Newmilns 93 NS 5337
New Milton 26 SZ 2495
New Moat 42 SN 0625
Newnham (Glos.) 46 SO 6911
Newnham (Hants.) 35 SU 7054
Newnham (Herts.) 53 TL 2437
Newnham (Kent) 30 TQ 9557
Newnham (Northants.) 51 SP 5859
Newnham Bridge 49 SO 6469
New Park 26 SU 2904
New Pitsligo 121 NJ 8855
New Polzeath 19 SW 9379
Newport (Devon) 23 SS 5631
Newport (Dyfed) 42 SN 0639
Newport (Essex) 53 TL 5234
Newport (Glos.) 46 ST 7097
Newport (Gwent) 32 ST 3187
Newport (Highld.) 135 ND 1224
Newport (Humbs.) 74 SE 8530
Newport (I. of W.) 27 SZ 4989
Newport (Norf.) 65 TG 5017
Newport (Shrops.) 59 SJ 7419
Newport Bay 42 SN 0340
Newport-on-Tay 109 NO 4228
Newport Pagnell 52 SP 8743
Newpound Common 28 TQ 0627
New Prestwick 93 NS 3424
Newquay (Corn.) 19 SW 8161
New Quay (Dyfed) 43 SN 3859
Newquay Bay 19 SW 8162
New Rackheath 65 TG 2812
New Radnor 48 SO 2161
New River (Cambs.) 53 TL 5869
New River (Lincs.) 63 TF 2518
New River Ancholme 74 SE 9717
New Romney 31 TR 0624
New Rossington 71 SK 6198
New Sauchie 102 NS 8993
New Scone 108 NO 1325
Newseat (Grampn.) 121 NJ 7033
Newseat (Grampn.) 121 NK 0749
Newsham (Northum.) 91 NZ 3079
Newsham (N Yorks.) 84 NZ 1010
Newsholme (Humbs.) 74 SE 7229
Newsholme (Lancs.) 78 SD 8451
New Silksworth 85 NZ 3853
Newstead (Borders) 96 NT 5634
Newstead (Northum.) 97 NU 1526
Newstead (Notts.) 61 SK 5252
New Stevenston 101 NS 7659
Newthorpe 79 SE 4632
Newtimber Place 28 TQ 2613
New Tolsta 131 NB 5348
Newton (Borders) 90 NT 6020
Newton (Cambs.) 63 TF 4314
Newton (Cambs.) 53 TL 4349
Newton (Ches.) 69 SJ 5059
Newton (Ches.) 69 SJ 5274
Newton (Cumbr.) 76 SD 2371
Newton (Dumf. and Galwy.) 89 NY 1194
Newton (Grampn.) 129 NJ 1663
Newton (Hants.) 26 SU 2322
Newton (Here. and Worc.) 45 SO 3433
Newton (Here. and Worc.) 45 SO 5054
Newton (Highld.) 132 NC 2331
Newton (Highld.) 135 ND 3449
Newton (Highld.) 129 NH 7448
Newton (Highld.) 129 NH 7766
Newton (Lancs.) 77 SD 4431
Newton (Lancs.) 77 SD 5974
Newton (Lancs.) 77 SD 6950
Newton (Lincs.) 62 TF 0436
Newton (Lothian) 102 NT 0877
Newton (Mid Glam.) 41 SS 8377
Newton (Norf.) 64 TF 8315
Newton (Northants.) 52 SP 8883
Newton (North Uist) 124 NF 8977
Newton (Northum.) 91 NZ 0364
Newton (Notts.) 61 SK 6841
Newton (S Glam.) 32 ST 2478
Newton (Staffs.) 60 SK 0325
Newton (Strath.) 100 NS 0498
Newton (Strath.) 101 NS 6560
Newton (Strath.) 95 NS 9331
Newton (Suff.) 54 TL 9140
Newton (Warw.) 51 SP 5378
Newton (W Glam.) 40 SS 6088
Newton (W Yorks.) 79 SE 4427
Newton Abbot 21 SX 8671
Newton Arlosh 82 NY 1955
Newton Aycliffe 84 NZ 2824
Newton Bewley 85 NZ 4626
Newton Blossomville 52 SP 9251
Newton Bromswold 52 SP 9966
Newton Burgoland 60 SK 3609
Newton by Toft 72 TF 0487
Newton Dale 80 SE 8191
Newton Ferrers 21 SX 5447
Newtonferry 124 NF 8978
Newton Flotman 65 TM 2198
Newtongarry Croft 121 NJ 5735
Newtongrange 103 NT 3364
Newton Harcourt 61 SP 6397
Newton Heath 26 SZ 0084
Newtonhill 119 NO 9193
Newton House 121 NJ 6629
Newton Kyme 79 SE 4644
Newton-le-Willows (Mers.) 69 SJ 5894
Newton-le-Willows (N Yorks.) 84 SE 2189
Newton Longville 52 SP 8431
Newton Mearns 93 NS 5456
Newtonmill 109 NO 6064
Newtonmore 116 NN 7199
Newton Mountain 42 SM 9807
Newton of Balcanquhal 102 NO 1510
Newton-on-Ouse 79 SE 5059
Newton-on-Rawcliffe 80 SE 8090
Newton-on-the-Moor 91 NU 1605
Newton on Trent 72 SK 8374
Newton or St. Mary's Haven 97 NU 2424
Newton Poppleford 24 SY 0889
Newton Purcell 51 SP 6230
Newton Regis 60 SK 2707
Newton Reigny 83 NY 4731
Newton Solney 60 SK 2825
Newton Stacey 34 SU 4040
Newton St. Cyres 21 SX 8797
Newton Stewart 86 NX 4165
Newton St. Faith 65 TG 2117
Newton St. Loe 33 ST 7064
Newton St. Petrock 22 SS 4112
Newton Toney 34 SU 2140
Newton Tors 97 NT 9026
Newton Tracey 23 SS 5226
Newton under Roseberry 85 NZ 5613
Newton upon Derwent 80 SE 7149
Newton Valence 27 SU 7232
Newtown (Ches.) 59 SJ 6247
Newtown (Ches.) 70 SJ 9784
Newtown (Cumbr.) 89 NY 5062
Newtown (Dorset) 26 SZ 0393
Newtown (Hants.) 26 SU 2710
Newtown (Hants.) 26 SU 3023
Newtown (Hants.) 35 SU 4763
Newtown (Hants.) 27 SU 6013
Newtown (Here. and Worc.) 45 SO 6145
Newtown (Highld.) 115 NH 3504
Newtown (I. of M.) 76 SC 3273
Newtown (I. of W.) 26 SZ 4290
New Town (Lothian 103 NT 4470
Newtown (Northum.) 97 NT 9731
Newtown (Northum.) 91 NU 0300
Newtown (Northum.) 97 NU 0425
Newtown (Powys) 57 SO 1091
Newtown (Shrops.) 59 SJ 4831
Newtown (Staffs.) 69 SJ 9060
Newtown (Wilts.) 25 ST 9128
Newtown Bay 26 SZ 4192
Newtown-in-St. Martin 18 SW 7323
Newtown Linford 61 SK 5110
Newtown St. Boswells 96 NT 5731
New Tredegar 41 SO 1403
New Tupton 71 SK 3966
Newtyle 108 NO 2941
Newtyle Forest 129 NJ 0552
Newtyle Hill 108 NO 0541
New Ulva 99 NR 7080
New Waltham 75 TA 2804
New Wimpole 53 TL 3450
New Winton 103 NT 4271
New Yatt 47 SP 3713
New York (Lincs.) 63 TF 2455
New York (Tyne and Wear) 91 NZ 3270
Neyland 42 SM 9605
Niarbyl Bay 76 SC 2176
Nibley 33 ST 6882
Nibon 142 HU 3073
Nicholashayne 24 ST 1015
Nicholaston 40 SS 5188
Nidd 79 SE 3060
Nidderdale 78 SE 0974
Nigg (Grampn.) 119 NJ 9402
Nigg (Highld.) 129 NH 8071
Nigg Bay (Grampn.) 119 NJ 9604
Nigg Bay (Highld.) 129 NH 7771
Nightcott 23 SS 8925
Nikka Vord (mt.) 143 HP 6210
Nilig 67 SJ 0254
Nine Ashes 38 TL 5902
Ninebanks 83 NY 7853
Nine Barrow Down 26 SZ 0081
Ninemile Bar or Crocketford 88 NX 8272
Ninfield 29 TQ 7012
Ningwood 26 SZ 3989
Nisbet 96 NT 6725
Nithsdale 88 NX 8991
Niton 27 SZ 5076
Nitshill 101 NS 5160
Noak Hill 37 TQ 5493
Nobottle 51 SP 6763
Nocton 72 TF 0564
Noddsdale Water 100 NS 2163
Noke 47 SP 5413
Noltland Castle (ant.) 138 HY 4348
Nolton 42 SM 8718
No Man's Heath (Ches.) 59 SJ 5148
No Man's Heath (Warw.) 60 SK 2709
Nomansland (Devon) 23 SS 8313
Nomansland (Wilts.) 26 SU 2517
Noneley 59 SJ 4727
No Ness 141 HU 4421
Nonington 31 TR 2552
Nook 89 NY 4679
Nookton Fell 84 NY 9148
Noonsbrough 140 HU 2957
Noose, The (sbk.) 46 SO 7107
Noranside Institution (Borstal) 109 NO 4761
Noran Water 109 NO 4860
Norbury (Ches.) 59 SJ 5547
Norbury (Derby.) 60 SK 1242
Norbury (Shrops.) 58 SO 3693
Norbury (Staffs.) 59 SJ 7823
Norbury Camp (ant.) 46 SO 9815
Nordelph 63 TF 5501
Norden (Dorset) 26 SY 9483
Norden (Gtr Mches.) 69 SD 8514
Nordley 59 SO 6998
Norham 97 NT 9047
Norley 69 SJ 5672
Norleywood 26 SZ 3597
Normanby (Humbs.) 74 SE 8716
Normanby (N Yorks.) 80 SE 7381
Normanby-by-Spittal 72 TF 0088
Normanby le Wold 73 TF 1294
Norman Cross 52 TL 1691
Normandy 28 SU 9251
Norman's Green 24 ST 0503
Norman's Law 108 NO 3020
Normanton (Derby.) 60 SK 3433
Normanton (Lincs.) 62 SK 9446
Normanton (Notts.) 61 SK 7054
Normanton (W Yorks.) 79 SE 3822
Normanton le Heath 60 SK 3712
Normanton on Soar 61 SK 5123
Normanton-on-the-Wolds 61 SK 6232
Normanton on Trent 72 SK 7868
Normoss 77 SD 3437
Norrington Common 33 ST 8864
Norris Hill 60 SK 3216
Northallerton 85 SE 3793
Northam (Devon) 22 SS 4429
Northam (Hants.) 26 SU 4312
Northampton 51 SP 7561
Northampton (Sywell) Aerodrome 52 SP 8268
North Ascot 36 SU 9069
North Ashton 69 SD 5600
North Aston 47 SP 4728
Northaw 37 TL 2802
North Baddesley 26 SU 3920
North Ballachulish 106 NN 0560
North Barrow 25 ST 6029
North Barrule (mt.) 76 SC 4491
North Barsham 64 TF 9135
North Bay (Barra) 112 NF 7202
North Bay (Hoy, Orkney) 136 ND 2890
North Bay (Sanday, Orkney) 139 HY 6543
North Benfleet 38 TQ 7590
North Berwick 103 NT 5485
North Berwick Law 103 NT 5584
North Birny Fell 89 NY 4791
North Boarhunt 27 SU 6010
Northborough 62 TF 1508
Northbourne 31 TR 3352
North Bovey 21 SX 7483
North Bradley 33 ST 8554
North Brentor 20 SX 4781
North Buckland 22 SS 4740
North Burlingham 65 TG 3610
North Burnt Hill 100 NS 2665
North Cadbury 25 ST 6327
North Cairn 86 NW 9770
North Carlton 72 SK 9477
North Carr (lightship) 103 NO 6612
North Cave 74 SE 8832
North Cerney 46 SP 0208
Northchapel 28 SU 9529
North Charford 26 SU 1919

O

Pole Hill (Tays.) Reawick

Pole Hill (Tays.) 108 NO 1926
Pole of Itlaw, The 121 NJ 6856
Polesworth 60 SK 2602
Polglass 126 NC 0307
Polgooth 19 SW 9950
Poling 28 TQ 0405
Polkerris 19 SX 0952
Polla 132 NC 3854
Pollachar 112 NF 7414
Pollagach Burn 118 NO 3992
Poll Gainmhich (roadstead) 131 NB 1343
Pollington 71 SE 6119
Polliwilline Bay 92 NR 7409
Poll na h-Ealaidh 122 NG 3759
Polloch 111 NM 7968
Pollokshaws 101 NS 5560
Pollokshields 101 NS 5663
Polmaddie Hill 86 NX 3391
Polmassick 19 SW 9745
Polnessan 93 NS 4111
Polperro 19 SX 2051
Polruan 19 SX 1250
Polsham 33 ST 5142
Polskeoch 88 NS 6802
Polstead 54 TL 9938
Poltalloch 99 NR 8196
Poltimore 21 SX 9696
Polton 103 NT 2964
Polwarth 96 NT 7450
Polyphant 20 SX 2682
Polzeath 19 SW 9378
Pondersbridge 53 TL 2691
Ponders End 37 TQ 3695
Ponsanooth 18 SW 7336
Ponsworthy 21 SX 7073
Pontamman 43 SN 6312
Pontantwn 43 SN 4412
Pontardawe 40 SN 7204
Pontardulais 43 SN 5903
Pontarsais 43 SN 4428
Pont Cwm Pydew 67 SJ 0031
Pont Cyfyng 67 SH 7357
Pontefract 79 SE 4522
Ponteland 91 NZ 1672
Ponterwyd 57 SN 7481
Pontesbury 58 SJ 3905
Pontfadog 58 SJ 2338
Pontfaen (Dyfed) 42 SN 0234
Pont-faen (Powys) 41 SN 9934
Pont-Henri 43 SN 4709
Ponthirwaun 43 SN 2645
Pontllanfraith 41 ST 1895
Pontlliw 40 SN 6101
Pontlottyn 41 SO 1206
Pontlyfni 66 SH 4352
Pont Nêdd Fechan 41 SN 9007
Pont Pentryal 67 SJ 0351
Pont Pen-y-benglog 67 SH 6460
Pontrhydfendigaid 57 SN 7366
Pont Rhyd-y-cyff 41 SS 8788
Pont-rhyd-y-fen 41 SS 7994
Pontrhydygroes 57 SN 7472
Pontrilas 45 SO 3927
Pontrobert 58 SJ 1112
Pont-rug 66 SH 5163
Ponts Green 29 TQ 6717
Pontshaen 43 SN 4346
Pontshill 45 SO 6321
Pontsticill 41 SO 0511
Pontsticill Resr. 41 SO 0513
Pontyates 43 SN 4708
Pontyberem 43 SN 4911
Pontybodkin 68 SJ 2759
Pontyclun 41 ST 0381
Pontycymer 41 SS 9091
Pontymister 32 ST 2490
Pont-y-pant 67 SH 7554
Pontypool 45 SO 2701
Pontypridd 41 ST 0690
Pontywaun 41 ST 2293
Pooksgreen 26 SU 3710
Pool (W Yorks.) 79 SE 2445
Poole (Dorset) 26 SZ 0190
Poole Bay 26 SZ 1089
Poole Harbour 26 SZ 0189
Poole Keynes 46 ST 9995
Poolewe 126 NG 8580
Pooley Bridge 83 NY 4724
Poolhill (Glos.) 46 SO 7329
Pool Hill (Powys) 48 SO 1775
Pool of Virkie 141 HU 3911
Pool o'Muckart 102 NO 0001
Pool Quay 58 SJ 2512
Popham 35 SU 5543
Popham's Eau (ant.) 63 TF 5300
Poplar 37 TQ 3781
Porchfield 27 SZ 4491
Porin 127 NH 3155
Poringland 65 TG 2701
Porkellis 18 SW 6933
Porlock 23 SS 8846
Porlock Bay 23 SS 8848
Port a'Bhata (Colonsay) 98 NR 4195
Port a'Bhata (Ulva) 105 NM 4237
Port a'Bhorrain 92 NR 6635
Port a'Chaisteil An Stuadh 105 NM 8246
Portachoillan 92 NR 7557
Port a' Ghàraidh 123 NG 8017
Port Allen 87 NX 4741
Port Allt a' Mhuilinn 134 NC 8167
Port Alsaig 98 NR 3048
Port a'Mhadaidh 100 NR 9269
Port a' Mhurain 110 NM 1251
Port an Eas 98 NR 2840
Port an Fhearainn 123 NG 6159
Port Ann 100 NR 9086
Port an Obain 98 NR 3994
Port an Righ 129 NH 8573
Port Appin 106 NM 9045
Port Askaig 98 NR 4369
Portavadie 100 NR 9369
Port Bàn 111 NM 5170
Port Bannatyne 100 NS 0867
Port Bharrapol 104 NL 9342
Port Bun a' Ghlinne 131 NB 5244
Portbury 33 ST 4975
Port Cam 123 NG 7731
Port Carlisle 89 NY 2461
Port Castle Bay 86 NX 4136
Port Ceann a'Gharraidh 98 NR 4298
Port Charlotte 98 NR 2558
Portchester 27 SU 6105
Port Cill Maluaig 99 NR 7270
Portclair Forest 115 NH 3815
Port Corbert 92 NR 6528
Port Cornaa 76 SC 4787
Port Dinorwic 66 SH 5267
Port Doir' a'Chrorain 98 NR 5875
Port Driseach 100 NR 9973
Port Ellen 98 NR 3645
Port Elphinstone 119 NJ 7719
Portencross 93 NS 1748
Port Erin 76 SC 1969
Porter or Little Don River, The 71 SK 2399
Port Erradale 126 NG 7381
Portesham 25 SY 6085
Port e Vullen 76 SC 4793
Port-Eynon 40 SS 4685
Port-Eynon Bay 40 SS 4884
Port-Eynon Point 40 SS 4784
Portfield Gate 42 SM 9115
Portgate 20 SX 4185
Portgaverne 19 SX 0080
Port Glasgow 100 NS 3274
Port Gleann na Gaoidh 98 NR 2153
Portgordon 121 NJ 3964
Portgower 135 ND 0013
Port Groudle 76 SC 4278
Porth 41 ST 0291
Porthallow 19 SW 7923
Porthcawl 41 SS 8176
Porth Colmon 66 SH 1934
Porthcothan Bay 19 SW 8572
Porthcurno 18 SW 3822
Porth Dinllaen 66 SH 2741
Port Henderson 123 NG 7573
Porth-gain 42 SM 8132
Porthkerry 41 ST 0866
Porthleven 18 SW 6225
Porthmadog 66 SH 5638
Porth-mawr or Whitesand Bay 42 SM 7227
Porthmeor 18 SW 4337
Porth Navas 18 SW 7428
Porth Neigwl or Hell's Mouth 56 SH 2626
Portholland 19 SW 9541
Porthor 66 SH 1630
Porthoustock 19 SW 8021
Porthpean 19 SX 0350
Porth Resr. 19 SW 8662
Porthtowan 18 SW 6847
Porthyrhyd (Dyfed) 43 SN 5115
Porthyrhyd (Dyfed) 44 SN 7137
Porth Ysglaig 66 SH 2137
Portincaple 100 NS 2393
Portington 74 SE 7830
Portinnisherrich 100 NM 9711
Port Isaac 19 SW 9980
Port Isaac Bay 19 SX 0181
Portishead 33 ST 4676
Port Kemin 86 NX 1231
Portknockie 121 NJ 4868
Portland Grounds (sbk.) 33 ST 4283
Portland Harbour 25 SY 6876
Port Leathan 100 NR 9176
Portlethen 119 NO 9396
Portloe 19 SW 9339
Port Logan 86 NX 0940
Port Logan or Port Nessock Bay 86 NX 0941
Portmahomack 129 NH 9184
Port Mary 87 NX 7545
Port Mean 92 NR 6407
Portmeirion 66 SH 5937
Portmellon 19 SX 0143
Port Mine 110 NM 1254
Port Mooar 76 SC 4890
Port Mór (Gigha Island) 92 NR 6654
Port Mòr (Muck) 111 NM 4279
Port Mór (Strath.) 99 NR 7161
Port Mór (Tiree) 104 NL 9343
Portmore (Hants) 26 SZ 3397
Portmore Loch 95 NT 2650
Port Mór na Carraig 98 NR 2355
Port Mulgrave 85 NZ 7917
Port na Birlinne 98 NR 5265
Port na Croise 105 NM 4326
Portnacroish 106 NM 9247
Port na Cuilce 98 NM 4100
Port na Cullaidh 123 NG 5113
Port na Feannaiche 92 NR 9122
Portnaguran 131 NB 5536
Portnahaven 98 NR 1652
Port na h-Eather 110 NM 2053
Portnalong 122 NG 3434
Port nam Bothaig 131 NB 5446
Port nam Partan 110 NM 3452
Port na Muice Duibhe 105 NM 7023
Portnancon 133 NC 4260
Port nan Crullach 105 NM 7226
Port nan Laogh 99 NR 6792
Portneora 123 NG 7732
Port Nessock or Port Logan Bay 86 NX 0941
Portobello (Dumf. and Galwy.) 86 NW 9666
Portobello (Lothian) 103 NT 3073
Port of Menteith 101 NN 5801
Port of Ness 131 NB 5363
Port of Spittal Bay 86 NX 0152
Porton 26 SU 1836
Portpatrick 86 NX 0054
Portquin 19 SW 9780
Port Quin Bay 19 SW 9480
Port Ramsay 106 NM 8845
Portreath 18 SW 6545
Portree 123 NG 4843
Port Righ 92 NR 8237
Portrye 100 NS 1758
Portscatho 19 SW 8735
Ports Down 27 SU 6406
Portsea 27 SU 6300
Portsea Island 27 SU 6501
Portskerra 134 NC 8765
Portskewett 33 ST 4988
Port Skigersta 131 NB 5562
Portslade 28 TQ 2506
Portslade-by-Sea 28 TQ 2604
Portsmouth 27 SU 6501
Portsmouth Harbour 27 SU 6202
Port Snoig 104 NL 9638
Port Soderick 76 SC 3472
Portsoy 121 NJ 5865
Port St. Mary 76 SC 2067
Port Sunlight 68 SJ 3483
Portswood 26 SU 4314
Port Talbot 41 SS 7690
Portuairk 111 NM 4468
Port Vasgo 133 NC 5865
Portvoller 131 NB 5636
Portvoller Bay 131 NB 5636
Portway (Warw.) 50 SP 0872
Portway, The (Shrops.) (Ant.) 58 SO 4295
Port Wemyss 98 NR 1751
Port William 86 NX 3343
Portwrinkle 20 SX 3553
Portyerrock Bay 87 NX 4839
Poslingford 54 TL 7648
Possingworth Park 29 TQ 5420
Postbridge 21 SX 6579
Postcombe 36 SU 7099
Postling 31 TR 1439
Post Rocks 98 NR 4079
Postwick 65 TG 2907
Potarch 119 NO 6097
Potrail Water 88 NS 9308
Potsgrove 52 SP 9529
Potten End 36 TL 0108
Potterhanworth 72 TF 0566
Potter Heigham 65 TG 4119
Potteries, The 59 SJ 8744
Potterne 34 ST 9958
Potterne Wick 34 ST 9957
Potters Bar 37 TL 2501
Potter's Cross 49 SO 8484
Potterspury 51 SP 7543
Potter Street 37 TL 4608
Potto 85 NZ 4703
Potton 53 TL 2249
Potton Island 38 TQ 9591
Pott Row 64 TF 7021
Pott Shrigley 69 SJ 9479
Poughill (Corn.) 22 SS 2207
Poughill (Devon) 23 SS 8508
Poulshot 34 ST 9659
Poulton 46 SP 1001
Poulton-le-Fylde 77 SD 3439
Pound Bank 49 SO 7373
Pound Hill 29 TQ 2937
Poundon 51 SP 6425
Poundsgate 21 SX 7072
Poundstock 20 SX 2099
Pow Burn (Central) 102 NS 8886
Powburn (Northum.) 91 NU 0616
Powderham 21 SX 9784
Powerstock 25 SY 5196
Powfoot 89 NY 1465
Powick 49 SO 8351
Powis Castle (ant.) 58 SJ 2106
Powmill 102 NT 0197
Pow Water 108 NN 9723
Poxwell 25 SY 7484
Poyle 36 TQ 0376
Poynings 28 TQ 2612
Poyntington 25 ST 6419
Poynton 69 SJ 9283
Poynton Green 59 SJ 5618
Poys Street 55 TM 3570
Poystreet Green 54 TL 9858
Praa Sands 18 SW 5828
Prail Castle 109 NO 6946
Pratt's Bottom 37 TQ 4762
Prawle Point 21 SX 7735
Praze-an-Beeble 18 SW 6336
Precipice Walk (mt.) 57 SH 7321
Predannack Wollas 18 SW 6616
Prees 59 SJ 5533
Preesall 77 SD 3646
Prees Green 59 SJ 5631
Preesgweene 58 SJ 3135
Prees Higher Heath 59 SJ 5636
Prendwick 91 NU 0012
Pren-gwyn 43 SN 4244
Prenteg 66 SH 5841
Prenton 68 SJ 3184
Prescot (Mers.) 68 SJ 4692
Prescott (Shrops.) 58 SJ 4221
Preshaw House 27 SU 5723
Press Castle 97 NT 8765
Pressen 97 NT 8335
Pressendye 118 NJ 4909
Prestatyn 67 SJ 0682
Prestbury (Ches.) 69 SJ 8976
Prestbury (Glos.) 46 SO 9724
Presteigne 48 SO 3164
Presthope 59 SO 5897
Prestleigh 33 ST 6340
Preston (Borders) 97 NT 7957
Preston (Devon) 21 SX 8574
Preston (Dorset) 25 SY 7082
Preston (E Susx) 29 TQ 3107
Preston (Glos.) 46 SO 6734
Preston (Glos.) 46 SP 0400
Preston (Herts.) 37 TL 1724
Preston (Humbs.) 75 TA 1830
Preston (Kent) 31 TR 2561
Preston (Lancs.) 77 SD 5329
Preston (Leic.) 62 SK 8602
Preston (Lothian) 103 NT 5977
Preston (Northum.) 97 NU 1825
Preston (Wilts.) 34 SU 0377
Preston Bagot 50 SP 1766
Preston Bissett 51 SP 6530
Preston Brockhurst 59 SJ 5324
Preston Brook 69 SJ 5680
Preston Candover 35 SU 6041
Preston Capes 51 SP 5754
Preston Gubbals 59 SJ 4819
Preston Hill 97 NT 9223
Preston Law 95 NT 2535
Preston on Stour 50 SP 2049
Preston on Wye 45 SO 3842
Prestonpans 103 NT 3874
Preston St. Mary 54 TL 9450
Preston-under-Scar 84 SE 0791
Preston upon the Weald Moors 59 SJ 6815
Preston Wynne 45 SO 5646
Prestwich 69 SD 8103
Prestwick (Northum.) 91 NZ 1872
Prestwick (Strath.) 93 NS 3525
Prestwick Scotland Airport 93 NS 3626
Prestwood 36 SP 8700
Price Town 41 SS 9392
Prickeny Hill 93 NS 5405
Prickwillow 54 TL 5982
Priddy 33 ST 5250
Priesthope Hill 96 NT 3539
Priest Hutton 77 SD 5273
Priest Island 126 NB 9202
Priestside Bank (sbk.) 89 NY 1164
Priestweston 58 SO 2997
Primethorpe 61 SP 5293
Primrose Green 64 TG 0616
Primrose Hill (Cambs.) 53 TL 3889
Prince Charles's Cave (Island of Skye) 123 NG 5112
Prince Charles's Cave (Island of Skye) 123 NG 5148
Prince Charlie's Cave (Highld.) 107 NN 4968
Prince's Cave 112 NF 8331
Princes Risborough 36 SP 8003
Princethorpe 50 SP 3970
Princetown 21 SX 5873
Prinknash Park (ant.) 46 SO 8713
Prior Muir 103 NO 5213
Prior Park 82 SD 1490
Priors Hardwick 51 SP 4756
Priors Marston 51 SP 4857
Priory, The 27 SZ 6390
Priory Wood 45 SO 2545
Priston 33 ST 6960
Prittlewell 38 TQ 8787
Privett 27 SU 6726
Probus 19 SW 8947
Proncy 129 NH 7792
Prudhoe 91 NZ 0962
Ptarmigan Lodge 100 NN 3500
Puckeridge 37 TL 3823
Puckington 24 ST 3718
Pucklechurch 33 ST 6976
Puckpool Point 27 SZ 6192
Puddington (Ches.) 68 SJ 3273
Puddington (Devon) 23 SS 8310
Puddledock 54 TM 0592
Puddletown 25 SY 7594
Pudleston 45 SO 5659
Pudsey 79 SE 2232
Puffin Island 67 SH 6481
Pulborough 28 TQ 0418
Puldrite Skerry 136 HY 4318
Puleston 59 SJ 7322
Pulford 68 SJ 3758
Pulham 25 ST 7008
Pulham Market 55 TM 1986
Pulham St. Mary 55 TM 2185
Pulloxhill 52 TL 0634
Pulpit Rock 100 NN 3414
Pulverbatch 58 SJ 4202
Pumsaint 43 SN 6540
Puncheston 42 SN 0029
Puncknowle 25 SY 5388
Pund Head 140 HU 1655
Punnett's Town 29 TQ 6220
Purbeck Hills 25 SY 9081
Purbrook 27 SU 6707
Purfleet 37 TQ 5578
Puriton 32 ST 3241
Purleigh 38 TL 8301
Purley (Berks.) 36 SU 6676
Purley (Gtr London) 37 TQ 3161
Purlogue 48 SO 2877
Purls Bridge 53 TL 4787
Purse Caundle 25 ST 6917
Purslow 48 SO 3680
Purston Jaglin 71 SE 4319
Purton (Glos.) 46 SO 6605
Purton (Glos.) 46 SO 6904
Purton (Wilts.) 34 SU 0887
Purton Stoke 34 SU 0890
Purves Hall 96 NT 7644
Pury End 51 SP 7045
Pusey 47 SU 3596
Putley 49 SO 6437
Putney 37 TQ 2274
Puttenham (Herts.) 36 SP 8814
Puttenham (Surrey) 28 SU 9347
Puxton 32 ST 4063
Pwll 40 SN 4801
Pwllcrochan 42 SM 9202
Pwlldefaid 56 SH 1526
Pwlldu Head 40 SS 5786
Pwllheli 66 SH 3735
Pwllmeyric 33 ST 5192
Pwll-y-glaw 41 SS 7993
Pwllygranant 42 SN 1147
Pyecombe 29 TQ 2912
Pye Corner 32 ST 3485
Pykestone Hill 95 NT 1731
Pyle (I. of W.) 27 SZ 4879
Pyle (Mid Glam.) 41 SS 8282
Pylle 33 ST 6038
Pymore 53 TL 4986
Pyrford 36 TQ 0458
Pyrton 36 SU 6895
Pytchley 52 SP 8574
Pyworthy 22 SS 3102

Q

Quabbs 48 SO 2080
Quadring 63 TF 2233
Quainton 36 SP 7419
Quandale 138 HY 3632
Quanter Ness 136 HY 4114
Quantock Forest 24 ST 1736
Quantock Hills 24 ST 1537
Quarff 141 HU 4135
Quarley 34 SU 2743
Quarndon 60 SK 3340
Quarrier's Homes 101 NS 3666
Quarrington 62 TF 0544
Quarrington Hill 84 NZ 3337
Quarrybank (Ches.) 69 SJ 5465
Quarry Bank (W Mids.) 49 SO 9386
Quarry Head 121 NJ 9065
Quarryhill 129 NH 7481
Quarry, The 46 ST 7399
Quarrywood 129 NJ 1864
Quarter 94 NS 7251
Quarter Fell 86 NX 1969
Quatford 49 SO 7390
Quatt 49 SO 7588
Quebec 84 NZ 1743
Quedgeley 46 SO 8114
Queen Adelaide 53 TL 5681
Queenborough 30 TQ 9471
Queen Camel 25 ST 5924
Queen Charlton 33 ST 6366
Queensberry (mt.) 88 NX 9899
Queensbury 78 SE 1030
Queen's Cairn 128 NH 4672
Queensferry (Clwyd) 68 SJ 3168
Queensferry (Lothian) 102 NT 1278
Queen's Forest, The 117 NH 9710
Queen's Ground 64 TL 6793
Queenside Muir 100 NS 2864
Queen's View 108 NN 8560
Queenzieburn 101 NS 6977
Quendale 141 HU 3713
Quendon 53 TL 5130
Queniborough 61 SK 6412
Quenington 47 SP 1404
Quernmore 77 SD 5160
Quethiock 20 SX 3164
Quey Firth 142 HU 3682
Quholm 136 HY 2412
Quidenham 54 TM 0287
Quidhampton (Hants.) 35 SU 5150
Quidhampton (Wilts.) 26 SU 1030
Quien Hill 100 NS 0559
Quies 19 SW 8376
Quilquox 121 NJ 9038
Quilva Taing 140 HU 1757
Quinag (mt.) 132 NC 2028
Quindry 136 ND 4392
Quine's Hill 76 SC 3473
Quinish (Island of Mull) (dist.) 111 NM 4254
Quinish (Pabbay) (is.) 124 NF 8886
Quinish Point 111 NM 4056
Quintin Knowe 88 NS 6508
Quinton 51 SP 7754
Quoditch 20 SX 4097
Quoig 107 NN 8222
Quorndon (Quorn) 61 SK 5616
Quothquan 95 NS 9939
Quoyloo 136 HY 2420
Quoy Ness 139 HY 6236
Quoys 143 HP 6112

R

Raasay House 123 NG 5436
Rabbit Islands 133 NC 6063
Raby 68 SJ 3179
Raby Castle (ant.) 84 NZ 1321
Rachub 67 SH 6268
Rackenford 23 SS 8418
Rackham 28 TQ 0514
Rackheath 65 TG 2814
Racks 89 NY 0374
Rackwick (Hoy, Orkney) 136 ND 1999
Rack Wick (Hoy, Orkney) 136 ND 2098
Rackwick (Westray) 138 HY 4449
Rack Wick (Westray) 138 HY 4450
Rack Wick (Westray) 138 HY 5042
Radcliffe (Gtr Mches) 69 SD 7806
Radcliffe (Northum.) 91 NU 2602
Radcliffe on Trent 61 SK 6439
Radclive 51 SP 6734
Radcot 47 SU 2899
Raddery 129 NH 7159
Radernie 103 NO 4609
Radford Semele 50 SP 3464
Radlett 37 TL 1600
Radley 47 SU 5398
Radnage 36 SU 7897
Radnor Forest 48 SO 1864
Radstock 33 ST 6854
Radstone 51 SP 5840
Radway 50 SP 3648
Radway Green 59 SJ 7754
Radwell 53 TL 2335
Radwinter 54 TL 6037
Radyr 41 ST 1380
Raera 105 NM 8320
Raerinish Point 131 NB 4224
Raes Knowes 89 NY 2882
Rafford 129 NJ 0656
Ragdale 61 SK 6619
Raglan 45 SO 4107
Ragnall 72 SK 8073
Rainberg Mór 98 NR 5687
Rainford 69 SD 4700
Rainham (Gtr London) 37 TQ 5282
Rainham (Kent) 30 TQ 8165
Rainhill 69 SJ 4990
Rainhill Stoops 69 SJ 5090
Rainow 70 SJ 9575
Rainton 79 SE 3775
Rainworth 71 SK 5958
Raisbeck 83 NY 6407
Rait 108 NO 2226
Raithby (Lincs.) 73 TF 3084
Raithby (Lincs.) 73 TF 3767
Raitts Burn 116 NH 7604
Rake 27 SU 8027
Rake Law 88 NS 8717
Ralfland Forest 83 NY 5413
Ramasaig 122 NG 1644
Rame (Corn.) 18 SW 7233
Rame (Corn.) 20 SX 4249
Rame Head 20 SX 4148
Ram Lane 31 TQ 9646
Ramna Stacks 143 HU 3797
Rampisham 25 ST 5502
Rampside 76 SD 2366
Rampton (Cambs.) 53 TL 4268
Rampton (Notts.) 72 SK 7978
Ramsbottom 69 SD 7916
Ramsbury 34 SU 2771
Ramscraigs 135 ND 1427
Ramsdean 27 SU 7021
Ramsdell 35 SU 5957
Ramsden 47 SP 3515
Ramsden Bellhouse 38 TQ 7194
Ramsden Heath 38 TQ 7195
Ramsey (Cambs.) 53 TL 2885
Ramsey (Essex) 55 TM 2130
Ramsey (I. of M.) 76 SC 4594
Ramsey Bay 76 SC 4796
Ramseycleuch 89 NT 2714
Ramsey Forty Foot 53 TL 3187
Ramsey Hollow 53 TL 3186
Ramsey Island (Dyfed) 42 SM 7023
Ramsey Island (Essex) 39 TL 9605
Ramsey Knowe 89 NT 2516
Ramsey Mereside 53 TL 2889
Ramsey Sound 42 SM 7124
Ramsey St. Mary's 53 TL 2588
Ramsgate 31 TR 3865
Ramsgate Municipal Airport 31 TR 3767
Ramsgill 78 SE 1170
Ramshorn 60 SK 0845
Rams Ness 143 HU 6087
Ranachan Hill 92 NR 6825
Ranby 71 SK 6480
Rand 73 TF 1078
Randwick 46 SO 8206
Ranfurly 101 NS 3865
Rangemore 60 SK 1822
Rangeworthy 33 ST 6886
Ranish 131 NB 4024
Rankinston 93 NS 4514
Rannoch Forest 107 NN 4565
Rannoch Moor 107 NN 3852
Rannoch River 105 NM 7046
Rannoch Station 107 NN 4257
Ranskill 71 SK 6587
Ranson Moor 63 TL 3893
Ranton 59 SJ 8524
Ranworth 65 TG 3514
Rapness 138 HY 5141
Rapness Sound 138 HY 5138
Rappach (dist.) 127 NC 2401
Rappach Water 127 NH 3098
Rascarrel 87 NX 7948
Rascarrel Bay 87 NX 8047
Raskelf 79 SE 4971
Rassau 41 SO 1411
Rastrick 78 SE 1321
Ratagan 114 NG 9220
Ratagan Forest 114 NG 8919
Ratby 61 SK 5105
Ratcliffe Culey 60 SP 3299
Ratcliffe on the Wreake 61 SK 6314
Rathen 121 NK 0060
Rathillet 109 NO 3620
Rathmell 78 SD 8059
Ratho 102 NT 1370
Ratho Station 102 NT 1372
Rathven 121 NJ 4465
Rat Island 22 SS 1443
Ratley 50 SP 3847
Ratlinghope 58 SO 4096
Rattar 135 ND 2672
Ratten Row 77 SD 4241
Rattery 21 SX 7361
Rattlesden 54 TL 9758
Rattray 108 NO 1745
Rattray Head 121 NK 1057
Rauceby 62 TF 0146
Rauceby Station 62 TF 0344
Raughton Head 83 NY 3745
Raunds 52 SP 9972
Ravenfield 71 SK 4895
Ravenglass 82 SD 0896
Raveningham 65 TM 3996
Ravenscar 81 NZ 9801
Ravensdale 76 SC 3592
Ravensden 52 TL 0754
Ravenshead 61 SK 5654
Ravens Knowe 90 NT 7806
Ravensmoor 59 SJ 6250
Ravensthorpe (Northants.) 51 SP 6670
Ravensthorpe (W Yorks.) 71 SE 2220
Ravensthorpe Resr. 51 SP 6770
Ravenstone (Bucks.) 52 SP 8450
Ravenstone (Leic.) 60 SK 4013
Ravenstonedale 83 NY 7203
Ravenstonedale Common 83 NY 6900
Ravenstown 77 SD 3574
Ravenstruther 95 NS 9245
Ravensworth 84 NZ 1407
Raw 81 NZ 9305
Rawcliffe (Humbs.) 74 SE 6822
Rawcliffe (N Yorks.) 79 SE 5855
Rawcliffe Bridge 74 SE 6921
Rawmarsh 71 SK 4396
Rawreth 38 TQ 7793
Rawridge 24 ST 2006
Rawtenstall 78 SD 8122
Rayburn Lake 91 NZ 1192
Raydon 54 TM 0438
Raylees 90 NY 9291
Rayleigh 38 TQ 8090
Rayne 38 TL 7222
Ray Sand 39 TM 0500
Rea Brook 49 SO 6586
Reach 53 TL 5666
Read 78 SD 7634
Reading 36 SU 7272
Reading Street 30 TQ 9230
Read's Island 74 SE 9622
Reagill 83 NY 6017
Rearquhar 129 NH 7492
Rearsby 61 SK 6514
Rease Heath 59 SJ 6454
Reaster 135 ND 2565
Reawick 141 HU 3244

River Mease
Rubha Sgorr an t-Snidhe

River Mease 60 SK 2711
River Meden 71 SK 5565
River Medina 27 SZ 5094
River Medway 29 TQ 6446
River Meig 127 NH 3655
River Meoble 111 NM 7986
River Meon 27 SU 5407
River Mersey (Gtr Mches.) 69 SJ 8092
River Mersey (Mers.) 68 SJ 3684
River Misbourne 36 SU 9696
River Mite 82 SD 0998
River Moidart 111 NM 7471
River Mole (Devon) 23 SS 7327
River Mole (Surrey) 37 TQ 1263
River Mole (Surrey) 28 TQ 2347
River Monnow (Afon Mynwy) 45 SO 4716
River Moriston 115 NH 3414
River Mudale 133 NC 5135
River Muick 118 NO 3389
River Nadder 26 SU 0130
River Nairn 129 NH 7947
River Nar 64 TF 6812
River Naver 134 NC 7255
River Neath 41 SN 9013
River Neb 76 SC 2883
River Nene (Cambs.) 63 TL 2398
River Nene (Northants.) 51 SP 5959
River Nene (Northants.) 52 TL 0385
River Nene (Old Course) (Cambs.) 53 TL 3291
River Ness 116 NH 6139
River Nethan 94 NS 7835
River Nethy 117 NJ 0214
River Nevis 106 NN 1370
River Nidd 79 SE 3357
River Nith 88 NS 7012
River Noe 70 SK 1485
River North Esk (Lothian) 103 NT 2158
River North Esk (Tays.) 118 NO 5078
River North Tyne 90 NY 6887
River Ock 47 SU 4095
River Oich 115 NH 3405
River Okement 23 SS 5901
River Orchy 106 NN 2534
River Ore (Fife) 103 NT 2796
River Ore (Suff.) 55 TM 3845
River Orrin 128 NH 4250
River Orwell 55 TM 2138
River Ose 122 NG 3442
River Ossian 107 NN 4172
River Otter 24 SY 0996
River Ottery 20 SX 2788
River Oude 105 NM 8415
River Ouse (E Susx) 29 TQ 4208
River Ouse (Norf.) 64 TF 5903
River Ouse (N Yorks.) 79 SE 4959
River Ouzel or Lovat 52 SP 8831
River Oykel 127 NC 3503
River Pang 36 SU 6173
River Pant 54 TL 6631
River Parrett (Somer.) 32 ST 2842
River Parrett (Somer.) 24 ST 3928
River Pattack 116 NN 5483
River Pean 114 NM 9290
River Penk 59 SJ 8905
River Perry 58 SJ 3828
River Petteril 83 NY 4839
River Piddle or Trent 25 SY 8392
River Plym 21 SX 5464
River Polly 132 NC 0812
River Pont 91 NZ 1676
River Poulter 71 SK 6475
River Quaich 107 NN 7939
River Quin 53 TL 3927
River Ray (Oxon.) 47 SP 5917
River Ray (Wilts.) 34 SU 1191
River Rea 49 SO 6673
River Rede 90 NY 7899
River Rha 123 NG 4065
River Rhee or Cam 53 TL 3647
River Rhiw 58 SJ 1102
River Rib 37 TL 3818
River Ribble 77 SD 6434
River Riccal 79 SE 6382
River Roach 38 TQ 9592
River Roch 69 SD 8712
River Roden 59 SJ 5915
River Roding 37 TQ 4294
River Romesdal 123 NG 4354
River Rother (E Susx) 29 TQ 6125
River Rother (Hants.) 27 SU 7625
River Rother (W Susx) 28 SU 9420
River Roy 115 NN 3088
River Rue 100 NS 0188
River Runie 127 NC 1302
River Rye 79 SE 5784
River Ryton 71 SK 6185
River Sand 126 NG 7779
River Sark 89 NY 3273
River Scaddle 106 NM 9567
River Seaton 20 SX 2959
River Sence (Leic.) 60 SK 3503
River Sence (Leic.) 61 SP 5997
River Seph 85 SE 5691
River Seven 80 SE 7380
River Severn (Avon) 33 ST 5992
River Severn (Here. and Worc.) 49 SO 8448
River Severn (Powys) 58 SJ 2612
River Severn (Powys) 57 SO 0890
River Severn (Shrops.) 59 SJ 6901
River Sgitheach 128 NH 5765
River Sheaf 71 SK 3282
River Shiel 114 NG 9813
River Shin 128 NH 5798
River Shira 106 NN 1518
River Skerne 84 NZ 3026
River Skinsdale 134 NC 7518
River Skirfare 78 SD 8875
River Slea 62 TF 1149
River Sligachan 123 NG 4927
River Snizort 123 NG 4244
River Soar (Leic.) 61 SP 5599
River Soar (Notts.) 61 SK 4925
River Solva 42 SM 8527
River Sorn 98 NR 3563
River South Esk (Lothian) 103 NT 3262
River South Esk (Tays.) 109 NO 3471
River South Tyne 83 NY 6854
River Sow 59 SJ 8628
River Sowe 50 SP 3777
River Spean 115 NN 2481
River Spey (Grampn.) 120 NJ 3050
River Spey (Highld.) 117 NH 9315
River Spey (Highld.) 116 NN 5094
River Sprint 83 NY 4903
River Stiffkey 64 TF 9233
River Stinchar 86 NX 2291
River Stort 53 TL 4829
River Stour (Dorset) 25 ST 7619
River Stour (Dorset) 26 SZ 1096
River Stour (Essex) 54 TL 9233
River Stour (Here. and Worc.) 49 SO 8278
River Stour (Kent) 31 TR 2763
River Stour (Warw.) 50 SP 2249
River Strae 106 NN 1833
River Strathy 134 NC 8051
River Swale 84 SE 2796
River Swere 47 SP 4733
River Swift 51 SP 5283
River Taff 41 ST 1578
River Tale 24 ST 0702
River Tamar 20 SX 3682
River Tame (Gtr Mches.) 69 SJ 9092
River Tame (Staffs.) 60 SK 1807
River Tame (Warw.) 50 SP 2091
River Tarbert 106 NM 9259
River Tarff 115 NH 3805
River Tavy 20 SX 4765
River Taw (Devon) 23 SS 6614
River Tawe (W Glam.) 40 SS 6799
River Tay (Tays.) 108 NO 1138
River Tay (Tays.) 108 NO 1221
River Tees (Cumbr. - Durham) 83 NY 7733
River Tees (Durham - N Yorks.) 84 NZ 2711
River Teign 21 SX 7689
River Teith 101 NN 6306
River Teme (Here. and Worc.) 49 SO 7067
River Teme (Shrops.) 48 SO 3073
River Ter 38 TL 7714
River Tern 59 SJ 7037
River Test 26 SU 3637
River Teviot 96 NT 6424
River Thames (Essex - Kent) 37 TQ 5577
River Thames (Oxon.) 35 SU 5985
River Thames or Isis (Oxon.) 47 SP 4302
River Thames or Isis (Wilts.) 47 SU 1596
River Thet 54 TL 9584
River Thrushel 20 SX 4789
River Thurne 65 TG 4017
River Thurso 135 ND 1055
River Tiddy 20 SX 3064
River Til (Beds.) 52 TL 0268
River Till (Lincs.) 72 SK 9077
River Till (Northum.) 97 NT 9533
River Tillingham 30 TQ 8720
River Tilt 117 NN 9575
River Tirry 133 NC 5318
River Tone 24 ST 3227
River Torne 71 SE 6502
River Torridge 23 SS 5509
River Torridon 126 NG 9255
River Toscaig 123 NG 7438
River Tove 51 SP 7746
River Traligill 132 NC 2720
River Trent (Humbs.) 74 SE 8619
River Trent (Notts.) 61 SK 6239
River Trent (Staffs.) 59 SJ 9231
River Trent or Piddle (Dorset) 25 SY 8392
River Tromie 116 NN 7694
River Truim 116 NN 6485
River Tud 65 TG 0812
River Tummel (Tays.) 107 NN 7459
River Tummel (Tays.) 108 NN 9555
River Turret 115 NN 3394
River Tweed (Borders) 95 NT 0722
River Tweed (Borders) 96 NT 4235
River Tweed (Borders) 96 NT 7737
River Tyne (Lothian) 103 NT 5474
River Tyne (Northum.) 91 NZ 0361
River Ugie 121 NK 0849
River Ure (N Yorks.) 78 SE 2085
River Ure (N Yorks.) 79 SE 4662
River Urie 121 NJ 6629
River Usk 45 SO 2515
River Ver 37 TL 1209
River Waldon 22 SS 3610
River Wampool 82 NY 2454
River Wansbeck 91 NZ 1285
River Washburn 78 SE 1458
River Waveney 55 TM 2381
River Waver 82 NY 1850
River Wear 84 NZ 1134
River Weaver 69 SJ 5877
River Welland (Lincs.) 63 TF 2828
River Welland (Northants.) 62 SP 8894
River Wenning 77 SD 7167
River Wensum 64 TG 0518
River Went 71 SE 5917
River West Allen 83 NY 7854
River Wey (Hants.) 35 SU 7742
River Wey (Surrey) 28 TQ 0557
River Wharfe 78 SE 0262
River Wheelock 69 SJ 7063
River Whitelake 33 ST 5340
River Windrush 47 SP 1817
River Winster 77 SD 4185
River Wiske 85 SE 3497
River Wissey 64 TF 8401
River Witham (Lincs.) 62 SK 9328
River Witham (Lincs.) 72 SK 9463
River Witham (Lincs.) 63 TF 2548
River Wolf 20 SX 4290
River Worfe 59 SO 7698
River Worth 78 SE 0137
River Wreake 61 SK 6616
River Wye (Afon Gwy) (Here. and Worc.) 45 SO 3045
River Wye (Derby.) 70 SK 2069
River Wylye 26 SU 0536
River Wyre 77 SD 4341
River Wyre 77 SD 5553
River Yar 27 SZ 6186
River Yare 65 TG 1108
River Yarrow 69 SD 5117
River Yarty 24 ST 2505
River Yealm 21 SX 6056
River Yeo (Avon) 33 ST 4463
River Yeo (Devon) 23 SS 7306
River Yeo (Devon) 23 SS 7726
River Yeo (Somer.) 25 ST 5223
River Ythan 121 NJ 8636
Rivington 69 SD 6214
Riv, The (sbk.) 139 HY 6847
Rivvalee (pt.) 143 HP 4805
Roade 51 SP 7551
Roadmeetings 95 NS 8649
Roadside 135 ND 1560
Roadside of Kinneff 119 NO 8476
Road, The (chan.) 18 SV 8912
Roadwater 32 ST 0238
Roag 122 NG 2744
Roa Island 76 SD 2364
Roana Bay 137 HY 5905
Roan Fell 89 NY 4592
Roan Head 136 ND 3896
Roath 41 ST 1978
Roberton (Borders) 89 NT 4314
Roberton (Strath.) 95 NS 9428
Roberton Law 95 NS 9129
Robertsbridge 29 TQ 7323
Roberttown 78 SE 1922
Robeston Cross 42 SM 8809
Robeston Wathen 42 SN 0815
Robin Hood's Bay 81 NZ 9505
Roborough 23 SS 5717
Rob Roy's Cave 100 NN 3310
Rob Roy's House 106 NN 1516
Roby Mill 69 SD 5106
Rocester 60 SK 1039
Roch 42 SM 8821
Rochdale 69 SD 8913
Rochdale Canal (Gtr Mches.) 70 SD 9518
Rochdale Canal (W Yorks.) 69 SD 9420
Roche 19 SW 9860
Roche Abbey (ant.) 71 SK 5489
Rochester (Kent) 30 TQ 7467
Rochester (Northum.) 90 NY 8397
Rochester Airport 30 TQ 7464
Rochford (Essex) 38 TQ 8790
Rochford (Here. and Worc.) 49 SO 6268
Rock (Corn.) 19 SW 9475
Rock (Here. and Worc.) 49 SO 7371
Rock (Northum.) 91 NU 2020
Rockbeare 24 SY 0195
Rockbourne 26 SU 1118
Rockbourne Down 26 SU 1020
Rockcliffe (Cumbr.) 89 NY 3561
Rockcliffe (Dumf. and Galwy.) 87 NX 8553
Rocken End 27 SZ 4875
Rock Ferry 68 SJ 3386
Rockfield (Gwent) 45 SO 4814
Rockfield (Highld.) 129 NH 9282
Rockham Bay 22 SS 4546
Rockhampton 46 ST 6593
Rockingham 52 SP 8691
Rockingham Forest 52 SP 9490
Rockland All Saints 64 TL 9896
Rockland St. Mary 65 TG 3104
Rockland St. Peter 64 TL 9897
Rockley 34 SU 1571
Rockwell End 36 SU 7988
Rodbourne 34 ST 9383
Rodd 48 SO 3162
Roddam 91 NU 0220
Rodden 25 SY 6184
Rode 33 ST 8053
Rode Heath (Ches.) 59 SJ 8056
Rodeheath (Ches.) 69 SJ 8766
Rodel 124 NG 0483
Roden 59 SJ 5716
Rodhuish 32 ST 0139
Rodings, The (dist.) 37 TL 5813
Rodington 59 SJ 5814
Rodley 46 SO 7411
Rodmarton 46 ST 9397
Rodmell 29 TQ 4106
Rodmersham 30 TQ 9261
Rodney Stoke 33 ST 4849
Rodono Hotel 95 NT 2321
Rodsley 60 SK 2040
Roecliffe 79 SE 3765
Roehampton 37 TQ 2373
Roe Ness 141 HU 3242
Roer Water 142 HU 3386
Roesound 141 HU 3465
Roewen 67 SH 7571
Roffey 28 TQ 1931
Rogan's Seat (mt.) 84 NY 9203
Rogart 129 NC 7303
Rogart Halt 129 NC 7202
Rogate 27 SU 8023
Roger Sand 63 TF 4841
Rogerstone 32 ST 2688
Rogerton 94 NS 6256
Rogiet 33 ST 4587
Roineabhal (mt.) 124 NG 0486
Roineval (Island of Skye) (mt.) 123 NG 4135
Roineval (Isle of Lewis) (mt.) 131 NB 2321
Roinn a' Bhuic 131 NB 4057
Rois-Bheinn 111 NM 7577
Roker 91 NZ 4059
Rollesby 65 TG 4415
Rolleston (Leic.) 61 SK 7300
Rolleston (Notts.) 61 SK 7452
Rolleston (Staffs.) 60 SK 2327
Rolston 75 TA 2145
Rolvenden 30 TQ 8431
Rolvenden Layne 30 TQ 8530
Romaldkirk 84 NY 9921
Romanby 85 SE 3693
Roman Gold Mines (ant.) 44 SN 6740
Romannobridge 95 NT 1547
Roman Ridge (ant.) 79 SE 4235
Roman River 39 TL 9920
Roman Road (ant.) 45 SO 4137
Romansleigh 23 SS 7220
Roman Steps 67 SH 6530
Rombalds Moor 78 SE 0845
Romford 37 TQ 5188
Romiley 69 SJ 9390
Romney Marsh 31 TR 0430
Romney Sands 31 TR 0823
Romsey 26 SU 3521
Romsley (Here. and Worc.) 50 SO 9679
Romsley (Shrops.) 49 SO 7883
Rona (is.) 130 HW 8132
Ronachan House 92 NR 7455
Ronachan Point 92 NR 7455
Ronague 76 SC 2472
Ronas Hill 142 HU 3083
Ronas Voe 142 HU 2881
Rona, The (chan.) 141 HU 3260
Ronay 124 NF 8955
Roneval (South Uist) (mt.) 112 NF 8114
Rooken Edge 90 NY 7895
Rookhope 84 NY 9342
Rookley 27 SZ 5084
Rooks Bridge 32 ST 3752
Roos 75 TA 2830
Roosebeck 76 SD 2568
Roos Wick 139 HY 6545
Rootpark 95 NS 9554
Ropley 27 SU 6431
Ropley Dean 27 SU 6331
Ropsley 62 SK 9834
Rora 121 NK 0650
Rora Head 136 ND 1799
Rora Moss 121 NK 0451
Rorandle 119 NJ 6518
Rorrington 58 SJ 3000
Rosall Point 77 SD 3147
Rosarie Forest 121 NJ 3548
Rose 18 SW 7754
Roseacre 77 SD 4336
Rose Ash 23 SS 7821
Rosebank 95 NS 8049
Rosebery Resr. 96 NT 3056
Rosebrough 97 NU 1326
Rose Cottage 111 NM 5369
Rosedale 80 SE 7295
Rosedale Abbey 80 SE 7296
Rosedale Moor 80 SE 7199
Roseden 97 NU 0321
Rosefield 129 NH 8552
Rosehaugh House 128 NH 6755
Rosehearty 121 NJ 9367
Rosehill 59 SJ 6630
Roseisle 129 NJ 1367
Roseisle Forest 129 NJ 1266
Rosemarket 42 SM 9508
Rosemarkie 129 NH 7357
Rosemarkie Bay 129 NH 7457
Rosemary Lane 24 ST 1514
Rosemount (Strath.) 93 NS 3729
Rosemount (Tays.) 108 NO 2043
Rosemullion Head 19 SW 7928
Rosenannon 19 SW 9566
Rose Ness 137 ND 5298
Rosewell 103 NT 2862
Roseworthy 18 SW 6139
Rosgill 83 NY 5316
Roshven 111 NM 7078
Rosinish (is.) 112 NL 6187
Roskhill 122 NG 2745
Rosley 82 NY 3245
Roslin 103 NT 2663
Rosliston 60 SK 2416
Rosneath 100 NS 2583
Rosneath Point 100 NS 2780
Ross (Dumf. and Galwy.) 87 NX 6444
Ross (Northum.) 97 NU 1336
Ross (Tays.) 107 NN 7621
Rossdhu House 101 NS 3689
Rossett 68 SJ 3657
Rossie Farm School 109 NO 6653
Rossie Moor 109 NO 6554
Rossie Ochill 102 NO 0812
Rossie Priory 108 NO 2830
Rossington 71 SK 6298
Rossinish 124 NF 8653
Rosskeen 128 NH 6869
Rossland 101 NS 4370
Ross of Mull (dist.) 105 NM 3919
Ross-on-Wye 45 SO 6024
Ross Priory 101 NS 4187
Roster 135 ND 2639
Rostherne 69 SJ 7483
Rosthwaite 82 NY 2514
Roston 60 SK 1241
Rosyth 102 NT 1183
Rothbury 91 NU 0601
Rothbury Forest 91 NU 0600
Rotherby 61 SK 6716
Rotherfield 29 TQ 5529
Rotherfield Greys 36 SU 7282
Rotherfield Peppard 36 SU 7081
Rotherham 71 SK 4492
Rother Levels 30 TQ 8725
Rothersthorpe 51 SP 7156
Rotherwick 35 SU 7156
Rothes 120 NJ 2749
Rothesay 100 NS 0864
Rothesay Bay 100 NS 0865
Rothiebrisbane 121 NJ 7437
Rothiemurchus 117 NH 9206
Rothienorman 121 NJ 7235
Rothiesholm 137 HY 6123
Rothiesholm Head 137 HY 6021
Rothley 61 SK 5812
Rothley Lakes 91 NZ 0490
Rothmaise 121 NJ 6832
Rothwell (Lincs.) 75 TF 1599
Rothwell (Northants.) 52 SP 8181
Rothwell (W Yorks.) 79 SE 3428
Rotsea 81 TA 0651
Rottal 109 NO 3769
Rottingdean 29 TQ 3702
Rottington 82 NX 9613
Roud 27 SZ 5280
Rougham 64 TF 8320
Rougham Green 54 TL 9061
Roughburn 115 NN 3781
Rough Close 59 SJ 9239
Rough Common 31 TR 1359
Rough Hill 93 NS 5445
Rough Island 87 NX 8453
Roughlee 78 SD 8440
Roughley 60 SP 1399
Rough Pike 90 NY 6285
Roughrigg Resr. 101 NS 8164
Roughsike 90 NY 5275
Roughton (Lincs.) 73 TF 2364
Roughton (Norf.) 65 TG 2136
Roughton (Shrops.) 59 SO 7594
Rough Tor (Corn.) 19 SX 1480
Rough Tor (Devon) 21 SX 6079
Rough Tower 55 TM 3928
Round Fell 87 NX 5372
Roundhay 79 SE 3235
Round Hill (Cumbr.) 83 NY 7336
Round Hill (Grampn.) 121 NJ 3427
Round Hill (N Yorks.) 78 SE 1253
Roundhill Resr. 78 SE 1476
Round Island 18 SV 9017
Round Loch of the Dungeon 87 NX 4684
Roundstreet Common 28 TQ 0528
Roundway 34 SU 0163
Roundway Hill 34 SU 0164
Rounton 85 NZ 4103
Rousay 138 HY 4030
Rousay Sound 136 HY 4529
Rousdon 24 SY 2990
Rous Lench 50 SP 0153
Routenburn 100 NS 1961
Routh 74 TA 0842
Row (Corn.) 19 SX 0976
Row (Cumbr.) 83 SD 4589
Rowallan Castle (ant.) 93 NS 4342
Rowanburn 89 NY 4177
Rowardennan Forest 101 NS 3896
Rowardennan Lodge 101 NS 3699
Rowde 34 ST 9762
Rowe Ditch (ant.) 45 SO 3859
Rowfoot 90 NY 6860
Row Head 136 HY 2218
Rowhedge 39 TM 0221
Rowhook 28 TQ 1234
Rowington 50 SP 2069
Rowland 70 SK 2072
Rowland's Castle 27 SU 7310
Rowland's Gill 91 NZ 1658
Rowledge 35 SU 8243
Rowley (Devon) 23 SS 7219
Rowley (Humbs.) 74 SE 9732
Rowley (Shrops.) 58 SJ 3006
Rowley Regis 50 SO 9787
Rowlstone 45 SO 3727
Rowly 28 TQ 0441
Rowney Green 50 SP 0471
Rownhams 26 SU 3816
Rowsham 36 SP 8518
Rowsley 71 SK 2566
Rowston 62 TF 0856
Rowton (Ches.) 68 SJ 4464
Rowton (Shrops.) 59 SJ 6119
Rowton Castle (ant.) 58 SJ 3712
Roxburgh 96 NT 6930
Roxby (Humbs.) 74 SE 9217
Roxby (N Yorks.) 85 NZ 7616
Roxby Beck 85 NZ 7415
Roxby High Moor 85 NZ 7512
Roxton 52 TL 1554
Roxwell 38 TL 6408
Royal British Legion Village 29 TQ 7257
Royal Forest 106 NN 2053
Royal Greenwich Observatory 29 TQ 6410
Royal Leamington Spa 50 SP 3166
Royal Military Canal 31 TR 0133
Royal Sovereign (lightship) 29 TV 7393
Royal Tunbridge Wells 29 TQ 5839
Roybridge 115 NN 2781
Roydon (Essex) 37 TL 4009
Roydon (Norf.) 64 TF 7022
Roydon (Norf.) 55 TM 0980
Royl Field (mt.) 141 HU 3928
Royston (Herts.) 53 TL 3541
Royston (S Yorks.) 71 SE 3611
Royton 69 SD 9207
Ruabon 58 SJ 3043
Ruabon Mountain 58 SJ 2446
Ruadh Sgeir 99 NR 7292
Ruadh-stac Mór 126 NG 9561
Ruaig 104 NM 0647
Ruan Lanihorne 19 SW 8942
Ruan Minor 18 SW 7115
Ruardean 45 SO 6117
Ruardean Woodside 45 SO 6216
Rubers Law 90 NT 5715
Rubery 50 SO 9777
Rubha a Ghraineig 110 NM 1555
Rubha Aird Druimnich 111 NM 5772
Rubha Airigh Bheirg 92 NR 8848
Rubha a'Mhail 98 NR 4872
Rubha a'Mharaiche 92 NR 5812
Rubha an Aird 110 NM 3855
Rubha an Daraich 123 NG 7909
Rubha an Dùine 124 NF 9771
Rubha an Fhasaidh 111 NM 4487
Rubha an Ridire 105 NM 7340
Rubha Ard Slisneach 123 NG 7409
Rubha Ardvule 112 NF 7029
Rubha Beag 126 NG 8997
Rubh' a'Bhacain 99 NR 7096
Rubh' a' Bhaid Bheithe 106 NN 0259
Rubh' a' Bhàigh Uaine 131 NB 4229
Rubh' a' Bhaile Fo Thuath 124 NF 9087
Rubh' a' Bhaird 125 NB 3101
Rubha Bhilidh 112 NF 8632
Rubh' a' Bhinnein 110 NM 2263
Rubh' a' Bhiogair 131 NB 3451
Rubha Bhlanisgaidh 131 NB 3755
Rubha Bhocaig 125 NG 1891
Rubha Bhoisnis 124 NF 8880
Rubha Bholsa 98 NR 3778
Rubha Bhrollum 125 NB 3202
Rubha Bolum 112 NF 8328
Rubha Buidhe 123 NG 7812
Rubha Cam nan Gall 124 NF 8847
Rubha Caol 131 NB 2447
Rubha Carrach 111 NM 4670
Rubh' a'Chàirn Bhàin 92 NR 6653
Rubh' a'Chamais 98 NR 5978
Rubh' a'Chaoil 104 NM 3346
Rubha Charn nan Cearc 111 NG 5503
Rubha Chlachan 92 NR 6106
Rubh' a'Chnaip 105 NM 7810
Rubh' a' Choin 132 NC 0314
Rubha Chràiginis 104 NL 9245
Rubh' a'Chrois-aoinidh 98 NR 5080
Rubha Chuaig 123 NG 6959
Rubha Còigeach 132 NB 9818
Rubha Crago 125 NG 2397
Rubha Creagan Dubha 92 NR 9352
Rubha Dubh (Colonsay) 98 NR 3991
Rubha Dubh (Island of Mull) 105 NM 5621
Rubha Dubh (Tiree) 104 NM 0948
Rubha Dubh Tighary 124 NF 7072
Rubha Dùin Bhàin 92 NR 5914
Rubha Fàsachd 110 NM 1652
Rubha Garbh àird 105 NM 8736
Rubha Garbh-ard 99 NR 7896
Rubh'a'Geodha 98 NR 4399
Rubha Ghlamraidh 98 NR 1758
Rubha Hellisdale 112 NF 8430
Rubha Hogh 110 NM 1759
Rubha Hunish 125 NG 4077
Rubha Iosal 131 NB 4216
Rubh' Aird an Fheidh 111 NM 6375
Rubh' Aird an t-Sionnaich 132 NC 1443
Rubh' Aird-mhicheil 112 NF 7233
Rubh' Aird na Sgitheich 98 NR 4779
Rubha Lamanais 98 NR 2068
Rubha Langanes 110 NG 2406
Rubha Leacach 124 NB 0107
Rubha Leathan 100 NR 9261
Rubha Leathann 131 NB 3654
Rubha Leumair 132 NC 0426
Rubha Màs a' Chnuic 124 NF 9794
Rubha Meall na Hoe 112 NF 8217
Rubh a'Mhail 98 NR 4279
Rubha Mhic Gille-mhicheil 124 NF 9363
Rubh' a' Mhill Dheirg 132 NC 0228
Rubh' a' Mhucard 132 NC 1637
Rubha Mór (Barra) 112 NL 6997
Rubha Mór (Coll, Strath.) 110 NM 2464
Rubha Mór (Highld.) 132 NB 9814
Rubha Mór (Highld.) 126 NG 8696
Rubha Mór (Highld.) 106 NM 9655
Rubha Mór (Island of Mull) 105 NM 5844
Rubha Mór (Islay) 98 NR 2948
Rubha na Brèige 132 NC 0519
Rubha na Crannaig 111 NM 4984
Rubha na Creige Móire (Isle of Lewis) 131 NB 4217
Rubha na Creige Móire (South Uist) 112 NF 8320
Rubha na Faing 98 NR 1553
Rubha na Faing Móire 111 NM 6477
Rubha na Fearn 123 NG 7261
Rubha na Gainmhich 98 NR 4346
Rubha na Greine 131 NB 5633
Rubha na h-Airde 99 NR 7083
Rubha na h-Airde Glaise 123 NG 5145
Rubha na h-Airde Uinnsinn 111 NM 8752
Rubha na h-Aiseig 123 NG 4476
Rubha na h-Easgainne 123 NG 5211
Rubha na h-Ordaig 112 NF 8414
Rubha na h-Uamha 105 NM 4028
Rubha na h-Uamha-sàile 98 NR 6094
Rubha na' Leac 123 NG 5938
Rubha na Leacaig 132 NC 2055
Rubha nam Bàirneach 131 NB 5531
Rubha nam Bàrr 99 NR 7491
Rubha nam Bràithrean 105 NM 4317
Rubha nam Brathairean 123 NG 5262
Rubha na Mèise Bàine 98 NR 3341
Rubha nam Faoilean 105 NM 6704
Rubha nam Maol Móra 104 NM 3316
Rubha nam Meirleach 110 NM 3691
Rubha nam Plèac 124 NF 9467
Rubha nan Cearc 104 NM 3225
Rubha nan Clach 122 NG 3033
Rubha nan Còsan 132 NC 0734
Rubha nan Crann 98 NR 6181
Rubha nan Eun 112 NF 7307
Rubha nan Gall (Island of Mull) 111 NM 5056
Rubha nan Gall (Ulva) 105 NM 4141
Rubha nan Leacan 98 NR 3140
Rubha nan Oirean 110 NM 3551
Rubha nan Sasan 126 NG 8192
Rubha nan Sgarbh (Highld.) 129 NH 7087
Rubha nan Sgarbh (Strath.) 92 NR 8033
Rubha nan Totag 124 NB 0303
Rubha nan Tri Chlach 111 NM 4989
Rubha na Rodagrich 124 NF 8953
Rubha na Roinne 111 NG 4200
Rubha na Seann Charraige 104 NM 0445
Rubha na Stròine 104 NM 3642
Rubha na Tràille 98 NR 5162
Rubh' an Dùnain (Island of Skye) 122 NG 3816
Rubh' an Dùnain (Isle of Lewis) 131 NB 2448
Rubha Nead a' Gheòidh 104 NM 0946
Rubh' an Fhir Léithe 132 NC 1863
Rubh' an Teampuill 124 NF 9791
Rubh' an Tòrra Mhóir 123 NG 5333
Rubh' an t-Sàilein 98 NR 5082
Rubh' an t-Suibhein 104 NM 3645
Rubh 'Aoineadh Mhéinis 105 NM 6521
Rubha Port Bhiosd 104 NL 9648
Rubha Port na Caranean 111 NM 4298
Rubha Port Scolpaig 124 NF 7068
Rubha Quidnish 125 NG 1086
Rubha Raonuill 111 NM 7399
Rubha Raouill 124 NF 7166
Rubh' Ardalanish 104 NM 3516
Rubh' Ard na Bà 126 NG 8584
Rubha Réidh 126 NG 7391
Rubha Righinn 105 NM 7002
Rubh' Arisaig 111 NM 6184
Rubha Rodha 132 NC 0523
Rubha Romagi 124 NG 0396
Rubha Rossel 112 NF 8734
Rubha Ruadh (Highld.) 132 NC 1651
Rubha Ruadh (Highld.) 111 NG 8208
Rubha Seanach 105 NM 8025
Rubha Sgeirigin 124 NF 9998
Rubha Sgorr an t-Snidhe 110 NM 3493

Skegness Stanegate (Northum.) (ant.)

Skegness 73 TF 5663
Skegness (Ingoldmells) Aerodrome 73 TF 5667
Skelberry 141 HU 3916
Skelbo 129 NH 7995
Skelda Ness 141 HU 3041
Skelda Voe 141 HU 3144
Skeldyke 63 TF 3337
Skelfhill Pen 89 NT 4403
Skellingthorpe 72 SK 9272
Skellister 141 HU 4654
Skellow 71 SE 5310
Skelly Rock 119 NJ 9614
Skelmanthorpe 71 SE 2210
Skelmersdale 68 SD 4605
Skelmonae 121 NJ 8839
Skelmorlie 100 NS 1967
Skelmorlie Castle (ant.) 100 NS 1965
Skelmuir 121 NJ 9842
Skelpick 134 NC 7256
Skelpick Burn 134 NC 7355
Skelton (Cleve.) 85 NZ 6518
Skelton (Cumbr.) 83 NY 4335
Skelton (N Yorks.) 84 NZ 0900
Skelton (N Yorks.) 79 SE 3568
Skelton (N Yorks.) 79 SE 5656
Skelwick (Westray) 138 HY 4845
Skel Wick (Westray) 138 HY 4945
Skelwith Bridge 82 NY 3503
Skendleby 73 TF 4369
Skene House 119 NJ 7609
Skenfrith 45 SO 4520
Skerne 81 TA 0455
Skeroblingarry 92 NR 7026
Skerray 133 NC 6563
Skerries, The (is.) 66 SH 2694
Skerry of Eshaness 142 HU 2076
Skervuile Lighthouse 98 NR 6071
Sketty 40 SS 6293
Skewen 40 SS 7297
Skewsby 79 SE 6270
Skeyton 65 TG 2425
Skiag Bridge 132 NC 2324
Skibo Castle 129 NH 7389
Skidbrooke 73 TF 4393
Skidby 74 TA 0133
Skiddaw (mt.) 82 NY 2629
Skiddaw Forest 82 NY 2629
Skigersta 131 NB 5461
Skilgate 23 SS 9827
Skillington 62 SK 8925
Skinburness 82 NY 1255
Skinflats 102 NS 9083
Skinidin 122 NG 2247
Skinningrove 85 NZ 7119
Skipness 92 NR 8957
Skipness Bay 92 NR 9057
Skipness Point 92 NR 9157
Skipsea 81 TA 1655
Skipton 78 SD 9851
Skipton-on-Swale 79 SE 3679
Skipwith 79 SE 6538
Skirling 95 NT 0739
Skirmett 36 SU 7789
Skirpenbeck 80 SE 7457
Skirwith (Cumbr.) 83 NY 6132
Skirwith (N Yorks.) 77 SD 7073
Skirza 135 ND 3868
Skirza Head 135 ND 3968
Skokholm Island 42 SM 7305
Skomer Island 42 SM 7209
Skroo (pt.) 139 HZ 2274
Skuda Sound 143 HU 6099
Skulamus 123 NG 6722
Skullomie 133 NC 6161
Skye of Curr 117 NH 9924
Slack 78 SD 9828
Slackhall 70 SK 0781
Slackhead 121 NJ 4063
Slacks of Cairnbanno (mt.) 121 NJ 8446
Slad 46 SO 8707
Slade 22 SS 5046
Slade Green 37 TQ 5276
Slaggan Bay 126 NG 8394
Slaggyford 83 NY 6752
Slaidburn 77 SD 7152
Slaithwaite 70 SE 0714
Slaley 84 NY 9757
Slamannan 102 NS 8573
Slapton (Bucks.) 36 SP 9320
Slapton (Devon) 21 SX 8244
Slapton (Northants.) 51 SP 6346
Slate, The 92 NR 6316
Slattocks 69 SD 8808
Slaugham 28 TQ 2528
Slawston 61 SP 7794
Sleach Water 135 ND 0145
Sleaford (Hants.) 27 SU 8037
Sleaford (Lincs.) 62 TF 0645
Sleagill 83 NY 5919
Sleapford 59 SJ 6315
Sledge Green 46 SO 8134
Sledmere 81 SE 9364
Sleightholme 84 NY 9510
Sleightholme Moor 84 NY 9208
Sleights 80 NZ 8607
Slepe 25 SY 9293
Sletill Hill 134 NC 9246
Sliabh Gaoil 99 NR 8174
Slickly 135 ND 2966
Sliddery 92 NR 9322
Sliddery Water 92 NR 9525
Slidderywater Foot 92 NR 9321
Slieau Dhoo (mt.) 76 SC 3589
Slieau Ruy (mt.) 76 SC 3282
Sliemore 117 NJ 0320
Sligachan Hotel 123 NG 4829
Slimbridge 46 SO 7303
Slindon (Staffs.) 59 SJ 8232
Slindon (W Susx) 28 SU 9608
Slinfold 28 TQ 1131
Slingsby 80 SE 6974
Slioch (Grampn.) 121 NJ 5638
Slioch (Highld.) (mt.) 126 NH 0069
Slios Garbh 111 NM 8284
Slip End 36 TL 0818
Slipton 52 SP 9479
Slitrig Water 90 NT 5110
Slochd 117 NH 8424
Slockavullin 99 NR 8297
Sloc nam Feàrna 99 NR 8674
Sloley 65 TG 2924
Sloothby 73 TF 4970
Slouchnawen Bay 86 NW 9563
Slough 36 SU 9779
Slugaide Glas 98 NR 2846
Slymaback (mt.) 101 NN 7510
Slyne 77 SD 4765
Sma' Glen 108 NN 9029
Smailholm 96 NT 6436
Smallbridge 69 SD 9114
Smallburgh 65 TG 3324
Smallburn (Grampn.) 121 NK 0141
Smallburn (Strath.) 94 NS 6827
Small Dole 28 TQ 2112
Small Downs, The (roadstead) 31 TR 3957
Smalley 60 SK 4044
Smallfield 29 TQ 3243
Small Hythe 30 TQ 8930
Small Isles 98 NR 5468
Smallridge 24 ST 3001
Smardale 83 NY 7308
Smarden 30 TQ 8842
Smasha Hill 89 NT 4417
Smeatharpe 24 ST 1910
Smeeth 31 TR 0739
Smeeton Westerby 51 SP 6792
Smerclate 112 NF 7415
Smerral 135 ND 1733
Smethwick 50 SP 0288
Smiddy Shaw Resr. 84 NZ 0446
Smigel Burn 134 NC 9057
Smirisary 111 NM 6477
Smisby 60 SK 3419
Smithey Fen 53 TL 4570
Smithfield 89 NY 4465
Smithincott 24 ST 0611
Smith Sound 18 SV 8706
Smithton 129 NH 7145
Snaefell 76 SC 3988
Snaigow House 108 NO 0843
Snailbeach 58 SJ 3702
Snailwell 54 TL 6467
Snainton 81 SE 9182
Snaip Hill 95 NT 0232
Snaith 79 SE 6422
Snape 55 TM 3958
Snape (N Yorks.) 79 SE 2684
Snape (Suff.) 55 TM 3959
Snap, The (pt.) 143 HU 6587
Snarestone 60 SK 3409
Snarford 72 TF 0482
Snargate 31 TQ 9928
Snarravoe 143 HP 5602
Snave 31 TR 0130
Snead 48 SO 3191
Sneaton 81 NZ 8907
Sneatonthorpe 81 NZ 9006
Snelland 72 TF 0780
Snelston 60 SK 1543
Snettisham 64 TF 6834
Sneug, The (mt.) 140 HT 9439
Sneuk Head 136 ND 2095
Snilesworth Moor 85 SE 5396
Snishival 112 NF 7534
Snitter 91 NU 0203
Snitterby 72 SK 9894
Snitterfield 50 SP 2159
Snitton 48 SO 5575
Snodhill 45 SO 3140
Snodland 30 TQ 7061
Snook Point 97 NU 2425
Snowdon (mt.) 66 SH 6054
Snowhope Hill 84 NY 9434
Snowshill 46 SP 0933
Soa (Coll, Strath.) (is.) 110 NM 1551
Soa (Tiree) (is.) 104 NM 0746
Soa Island 104 NM 2419
Soay (Island of Skye) 123 NG 4414
Soay (St. Kilda or Hirta) 124 NA 0601
Soay Mòr 125 NB 0605
Soay Sound 123 NG 4416
Soberton 27 SU 6016
Soberton Heath 27 SU 6014
Socach Burn 100 NR 8899
Socach, The (mt.) 117 NJ 2714
Soham 54 TL 5973
Soham Mere 53 TL 5773
Soldon Cross 22 SS 3210
Soldridge 27 SU 6534
Solent, The (chan.) 27 SZ 4797
Sole Street 30 TQ 6567
Sole Street 31 TR 0949
Solihull 50 SP 1479
Sollas 124 NF 8174
Sollers Dilwyn 45 SO 4255
Sollers Hope 45 SO 6033
Sollom 68 SD 4518
Solva 42 SM 8024
Solway Firth 82 NY 0050
Solway Moss 89 NY 3369
Somerby 61 SK 7710
Somercotes 60 SK 4253
Somerford Keynes 46 SU 0195
Somerley 27 SZ 8198
Somerleyton 65 TM 4897
Somersall Herbert 60 SK 1335
Somersby 73 TF 3472
Somersham (Cambs.) 53 TL 3677
Somersham (Suff.) 55 TM 0848
Somersham High North Fen 53 TL 3581
Somerton (Norf.) 65 TG 4719
Somerton (Oxon.) 47 SP 4928
Somerton (Somer.) 25 ST 4828
Sompting 28 TQ 1605
Sonachan Hotel 111 NN 4566
Sonning 36 SU 7575
Sonning Common 36 SU 7080
Sonnhope Burn 96 NT 5356
Sopley 26 SZ 1596
Sopworth 33 ST 8286
Sorbie 87 NX 4346
Sor Brook 51 SP 4437
Sordale 135 ND 1462
Sorisdale 110 NM 2763
Sorn 93 NS 5526
Sornhill 93 NS 5134
Soroba Hill 105 NM 7905
Sortat 135 ND 2863
Sotby 73 TF 2078
Sots Hole 73 TF 1164
Sotterly 55 TM 4584
Soudley 59 SJ 7228
Soughton (Sychdyn) 68 SJ 2466
Soulbury 52 SP 8827
Soulby 83 NY 7410
Souldern 47 SP 5231
Souldrop 52 SP 9861
Soulseat Loch 86 NX 1058
Sound (Shetld.) 141 HU 3850
Sound (Shetld.) 141 HU 4640
Sound Gruney (is.) 143 HU 5796
Sound of Arisaig 111 NM 6580
Sound of Barra 112 NF 7510
Sound of Berneray (North Uist) 124 NF 9079
Sound of Berneray (W Isles) 112 NL 5581
Sound of Bute 92 NS 0154
Sound of Canna 110 NG 3002
Sound of Eigg 111 NM 4482
Sound of Eriskay 112 NF 7913
Sound of Faray 138 HY 5437
Sound of Fiaray 112 NF 6909
Sound of Fuday 112 NF 7108
Sound of Gigha 92 NR 6747
Sound of Handa 132 NC 1547
Sound of Harris 124 NF 9681
Sound of Hellisay 112 NF 7503
Sound of Hoxa 136 ND 3893
Sound of Insh 105 NM 7318
Sound of Iona 104 NM 2822
Sound of Islay 98 NR 4369
Sound of Jura 99 NR 6480
Sound of Kerrera 105 NM 8328
Sound of Luing 105 NM 7209
Sound of Mingulay 112 NL 5885
Sound of Monach 124 NF 6865
Sound of Mull 105 NM 5945
Sound of Pabbay (North Uist) 124 NF 8984
Sound of Pabbay (W Isles) 112 NL 6289
Sound of Papa 140 HU 1758
Sound of Pladda 92 NS 0220
Sound of Raasay 123 NG 5654
Sound of Rhum 111 NM 4390
Sound of Sandray 112 NL 6393
Sound of Shiant 125 NB 3701
Sound of Shillay 124 NF 8890
Sound of Shuna 106 NM 9248
Sound of Sleat 111 NG 6804
Sound of Spuir 124 NF 8685
Sound of Taransay 124 NB 0500
Sound of Ulva 105 NM 4538
Sound of Vatersay 112 NL 6297
Sound, The 20 SX 4752
Soundwell 33 ST 6574
Source of River Thames 46 ST 9898
Source of River Wye 57 SN 8087
Sourhope 90 NT 8420
Sourin 138 HY 4331
Sourton 21 SX 5390
Soutergate 76 SD 2281
Souter Head 119 NJ 9601
Souterrain (ant) 109 NO 4137
South Achinduin 105 NM 8139
South Acre 64 TF 8014
Southall 37 TQ 1280
South Allington 21 SX 7938
South Alloa 102 NS 8791
Southam (Glos.) 46 SO 9725
Southam (Warw.) 50 SP 4161
South Ambersham 28 SU 9120
Southampton 26 SU 4212
Southampton Airport 27 SU 4516
Southampton Water 27 SU 4506
South Bank 85 NZ 5220
South Barrow 25 ST 6027
South Barrule (mt.) 76 SC 2576
South Bay 139 HY 7552
South Benfleet 38 TQ 7785
Southborough 29 TQ 5842
Southbourne (Dorset) 26 SZ 1491
Southbourne (W Susx) 27 SU 7705
South Brent 21 SX 6960
Southburgh 64 TG 0004
South Burlingham 65 TG 3708
South Burn 136 ND 2299
South Cadbury 25 ST 6325
South Cairn 86 NW 9768
South Carlton 72 SK 9476
South Cave 74 SE 9231
South Cerney 46 SU 0497
South Channel (Humbs.) 74 SE 9521
South Channel (Kent) 31 TR 3272
South Chard 24 ST 3205
South Charlton 97 NU 1620
South Cheek or Old Peak 81 NZ 9802
Southchurch 38 TQ 9186
South Cliffe 74 SE 8736
South Clifton 72 SK 8270
Southcott 21 SX 5495
South Cove 55 TM 5081
South Creake 64 TF 8536
South Croxton 61 SK 6810
South Dalton 74 SE 9645
South Darenth 37 TQ 5669
South Deep 108 NO 2318
South District 63 TL 5298
South Downs 29 TQ 3707
South Drove Drain 62 TF 2013
South Duffield 79 SE 6733
Southease 29 TQ 4205
South Elkington 73 TF 2988
South Elmsall 71 SE 4711
Southend (Berks.) 35 SU 5970
South End (Cumbr.) 76 SD 2063
Southend (Strath.) 92 NR 6908
Southend Municipal Airport 38 TQ 8789
Southend-on-Sea 38 TQ 8885
Southerndown 41 SS 8874
Southerness 82 NX 9754
Southerness Point 82 NX 9754
South Erradale 123 NG 7471
Southery 64 TL 6294
Southery Fens 64 TL 6093
South Fambridge 38 TQ 8694
South Fawley 34 SU 3979
South Ferriby 74 SE 9820
Southfield Reservoir 71 SE 6519
Southfleet 30 TQ 6171
South Foreland 31 TR 3643
South Forty Foot Drain 62 TF 1633
South Galson River 131 NB 4555
South Garth 143 HU 5499
South Garvan 114 NM 9977
Southgate (Gtr London) 37 TQ 3093
Southgate (Norf.) 64 TF 6833
Southgate (Norf.) 65 TG 1324
Southgate (W Glam.) 40 SS 5587
South Goodwin (lightship) 31 TR 4342
South Green 38 TQ 6893
South Hall 100 NS 0672
South Hanningfield 38 TQ 7497
South Harbour 139 HZ 2069
South Harris (dist.) 125 NG 0893
South Harris Forest 125 NG 1098
South Harting 27 SU 7819
South Havra (is.) 141 HU 3627
South Hayling 27 SZ 7299
South Head (Highld.) 135 ND 3749
South Head (Shetld.) 142 HU 2382
South Heath 36 SP 9102
South Heighton 29 TQ 4503
South Hetton 85 NZ 3745
South Hiendley 71 SE 3812
South Hill 20 SX 3272
South Hole 22 SS 2219
South Holland Main Drain 63 TF 3718
South Holms 143 HP 5710
South Holmwood 28 TQ 1745
South Hornchurch 37 TQ 5283
South Hylton 85 NZ 3556
Southill 52 TL 1442
South Isle of Gletness 141 HU 4750
South Kelsey 74 TF 0398
South Kilvington 79 SE 4283
South Kilworth 51 SP 6082
South Kirkby 71 SE 4410
South Kirkton 119 NJ 7405
South Kyme 62 TF 1749
South Kyme Fen 62 TF 1748
South Lancing 28 TQ 1804
South Lee (mt.) 124 NF 9165
Southleigh (Devon) 24 SY 2093
South Leigh (Oxon.) 47 SP 3908
South Leverton 72 SK 7881
South Littleton 50 SP 0746
South Lochboisdale 112 NF 7817
South Lopham 54 TM 0481
South Luffenham 62 SK 9402
South Mains 109 NO 6948
South Malling 29 TQ 4211
South Marston 34 SU 1987
South Medwin 95 NT 0445
South Milford 79 SE 4931
South Milton 21 SX 7042
South Mimms 37 TL 2200
Southminster 38 TQ 9599
South Molton 23 SS 7125
South Moor 84 NZ 1952
South Morar (dist.) 111 NM 7588
South Moreton 35 SU 5688
South Muskham 72 SK 7957
South Ness 140 HT 9636
South Nesting 141 HU 4554
South Nesting Bay 141 HU 4956
South Nevi (pt.) 137 HY 6000
South Newington 47 SP 4033
South Newton 26 SU 0834
South Normanton 61 SK 4456
South Norwood 37 TQ 3468
South Nutfield 29 TQ 3048
South Ockendon 38 TQ 5982
Southoe 52 TL 1864
Southolt 55 TM 1968
South Ormsby 73 TF 3675
Southorpe 62 TF 0803
South Otterington 79 SE 3787
Southowram 78 SE 1123
South Oxhey 37 TQ 1193
South Perrott 25 ST 4706
South Petherton 25 ST 4316
South Petherwin 20 SX 3182
South Pickenham 64 TF 8504
South Pool 21 SX 7740
Southport 68 SD 3316
Southport Birkdale Sands (aerodrome) 68 SD 3116
South Queich 102 NO 0303
South Radworthy 23 SS 7432
South Raynham 64 TF 8723
Southrepps 65 TG 2536
South Reston 73 TF 4082
Southrey 73 TF 1366
South Ronaldsay 136 ND 4590
Southrop 47 SP 1903
Southrope 35 SU 6744
South Runcton 64 TF 6308
South Scarle 72 SK 8463
Southsea 27 SZ 6498
South Shian 106 NM 9042
South Shields 91 NZ 3667
South Shore 77 SD 3033
South Skirlaugh 75 TA 1439
South Somercotes 73 TF 4193
South Sound 143 HU 5390
South Stack (pt.) 66 SH 2082
South Stainley 79 SE 3063
South Stoke (Avon) 33 ST 7461
South Stoke (Oxon.) 35 SU 6083
South Stoke (W Susx) 28 TQ 0210
South Street 29 TQ 3918
South Tawton 21 SX 6594
South Thoresby 73 TF 4077
South Tidworth 34 SU 2347
Southtown (Burray) 136 ND 4895
South Town (Hants.) 35 SU 6536
South Ugie Water 121 NJ 9846
South Uist (is.) 112 NF 7829
South View 141 HU 3842
Southwaite 83 NY 4445
South Walls (is.) 136 ND 3189
South Walsham 65 TG 3613
South Ward (mt.) 141 HU 3264
South Warnborough 35 SU 7247
Southwater 28 TQ 1526
Southway 33 ST 5142
South Weald 37 TQ 5793
Southwell (Dorset) 25 SY 6870
Southwell (Notts.) 61 SK 7053
South Weston 36 SU 7098
South Wheatley 20 SX 2492
Southwick (Hants.) 27 SU 6208
Southwick (Northants.) 52 TL 0192
South Wick (Shetld.) 142 HU 3191
Southwick (Tyne and Wear) 91 NZ 3758
Southwick (Wilts.) 33 ST 8354
Southwick (W Susx) 28 TQ 2405
South Widcombe 33 ST 5756
South Wigston 61 SP 5898
South Willingham 73 TF 1983
South Wingfield 60 SK 3755
South Witham 62 SK 9219
Southwold 55 TM 5076
South Wonston 27 SU 4635
Southwood (Norf.) 65 TG 3905
Southwood (Somer.) 25 ST 5533
South Woodham Ferrers 38 TQ 8097
South Wootton 64 TF 6422
South Wraxall 33 ST 8364
South Zeal 21 SX 6593
Soutra Mains 103 NT 4559
Soval Lodge 131 NB 3424
Sowerby (N Yorks.) 79 SE 4381
Sowerby (W Yorks.) 78 SE 0423
Sowerby Bridge 78 SE 0523
Sowerby Row 83 NY 3940
Sow of Athol, The 116 NN 6274
Sow, The (pt.) 136 HY 1802
Sowton 21 SX 9792
Soyea Island 132 NC 0421
Soyland Moor 78 SD 9819
Spa Common 65 TG 2930
Spadeadam Fm. 90 NY 5870
Spadeadam Forest 90 NY 6272
Spade Mill Resrs. 77 SD 6137
Spalding 63 TF 2422
Spaldington 74 SE 7533
Spaldwick 52 TL 1272
Spalford 72 SK 8369
Spango Hill 88 NS 8118
Spanish Head 76 SC 1865
Sparham 64 TG 0619
Spark Bridge 77 SD 3084
Sparkford 25 ST 6026
Sparkwell 21 SX 5757
Sparrowpit 70 SK 0980
Sparsholt (Hants.) 26 SU 4331
Sparsholt (Oxon.) 34 SU 3487
Spartleton Edge 103 NT 6565
Spaunton 80 SE 7289
Spaunton Moor 80 SE 7194
Spaxton 24 ST 2236
Spean Bridge 115 NN 2281
Spear Head 135 ND 0971
Speen (Berks.) 35 SU 4568
Speen (Bucks.) 36 SU 8499
Speeton 81 TA 1574
Speinne Mòr 111 NM 4949
Speke 68 SJ 4383
Speldhurst 29 TQ 5541
Spellbrook 37 TL 4817
Spelsbury 47 SP 3421
Spencers Wood 35 SU 7166
Spennithorne 84 SE 1489
Spennymoor 84 NZ 2533
Spetchley 49 SO 8953
Spettisbury 25 ST 9002
Spexhall 55 TM 3780
Spey Bay 121 NJ 3866
Speymouth Forest 121 NJ 3657
Spilsby 73 TF 4066
Spindlestone 97 NU 1533
Spinningdale 128 NH 6789
Spirthill 34 ST 9975
Spital Burn 119 NO 6583
Spithead (roadstead) 27 SZ 6396
Spithurst 29 TQ 4217
Spittal (Dyfed) 42 SM 9723
Spittal (Highld.) 135 ND 1654
Spittal (Lothian) 103 NT 4677
Spittal (Northum.) 97 NU 0051
Spittalfield 108 NO 1040
Spittal of Glenmuick 118 NO 3184
Spittal of Glenshee 108 NO 1069
Spixworth 65 TG 2415
Spofforth 79 SE 3650
Spondon 60 SK 3935
Spo Ness (Westray) 138 HY 4846
Spooner Row 65 TM 0997
Spoo Ness (Unst) 143 HP 5607
Sporle 64 TF 8411
Spott 103 NT 6775
Spratton 51 SP 7170
Spreakley 35 SU 8341
Spreyton 21 SX 6996
Spridlington 72 TF 0084
Springburn 101 NS 5968
Springfield (Fife) 103 NO 3411
Springfield (Grampn.) 129 NJ 0459
Springfield (W Mids.) 50 SP 1082
Springfield Resr. 95 NS 9052
Springholm 88 NX 8070
Springkell 89 NY 2575
Spring Mill Resr. 69 SD 8717
Springside 93 NS 3639
Springthorpe 72 SK 8789
Sproatley 75 TA 1934
Sproston Green 69 SJ 7367
Sprotbrough 71 SE 5302
Sproughton 55 TM 1244
Sprouston 96 NT 7535
Sprowston 65 TG 2412
Sproxton (Leic.) 62 SK 8524
Sproxton (N Yorks.) 79 SE 6181
Spuir (is.) 124 NF 8584
Spurn (lightship) 75 TA 4709
Spur Ness 139 HY 6033
Spurness Sound 139 HY 6132
Spurn Head (pt.) 75 TA 3910
Spurstow 59 SJ 5556
Spur, The 135 ND 1669
Spùt Rolla 107 NN 7328
Spynie Palace (ant.) 120 NJ 2365
Srath a'Chràisg 133 NC 5424
Srath Beag 133 NC 3853
Srath Dionard 132 NC 3254
Srath Lungard 126 NG 9165
Srath nan Lòn 127 NC 2300
Srath nan Lùb 100 NS 0691
Srath na Seilge 133 NC 7018
Srianach 131 NB 4010
Sròn Ach' a' Bhacaidh (mt.) 128 NH 6198
Sròn a' Chleirich 116 NN 7877
Sròn a' Choire Ghairbh 115 NN 2294
Sròn a' Gheodha Dhuibh 126 NG 7792
Sròn Bheag (Highld.) 111 NM 4662
Sròn Bheag (Tays.) 107 NN 5262
Sròn Mhòr 107 NN 6526
Sròn na Carra 123 NG 7473
Sròn na Clèite 126 NG 7389
Sròn na h-Iolaire 110 NM 3891
Sronphadruig Lodge 116 NN 7178
Sròn Romul (mt.) 130 NA 9615
Sròn Ruadh 131 NB 4636
Sròn Rubha na Gaoithe 134 NC 9911
Stab Hill 86 NX 1472
Staca Leathann 130 NA 9828
Stac a' Mheadais 122 NG 3325
Stac an Aoineidh 104 NM 2522
Stac an Tuill 122 NG 3521
Stack Clò Kearvaig (pt.) 132 NC 2973
Stackhouse 78 SD 8165
Stack Islands 112 NF 7807
Stack o' da Noup 141 HU 3516
Stack of Billyageo 141 HU 4421
Stack of Birrier 143 HU 6394
Stack of the Brough 141 HU 4015
Stackpole 42 SR 9896
Stackpole Head 42 SR 9994
Stack Rocks 42 SM 8113
Stack Skerry 132 HX 5617
Stacks of Duncansby 135 ND 4071
Stacksteads 78 SD 8421
Stac na Cathaig 116 NH 6430
Stac Pollaidh (mt.) 127 NC 1010
Stac Shuardail 131 NB 4830
Staddiscombe 20 SX 5151
Staddlethorpe 74 SE 8426
Stadhampton 47 SU 6098
Staffa (is.) 104 NM 3235
Staffield 83 NY 5442
Staffin 123 NG 4967
Staffin Bay 123 NG 4869
Staffin Island 123 NG 4969
Stafford 59 SJ 9223
Staffordshire and Worcestershire Canal 49 SO 8689
Stagsden 52 SP 9849
Stainburn 79 SE 2448
Stainby 62 SK 9022
Staincross 71 SE 3210
Stain Dale 80 SE 8690
Staindrop 84 NZ 1220
Staines 36 TQ 0471
Stainfield (Lincs.) 62 TF 0724
Stainfield (Lincs.) 73 TF 1173
Stainforth (N Yorks.) 78 SD 8267
Stainforth (S Yorks.) 71 SE 6411
Stainforth and Keadby Canal 74 SE 7311
Staining 77 SD 3435
Stainland 70 SE 0719
Stainmore Forest 84 NY 9411
Stainsacre 81 NZ 9108
Stainton (Cleve.) 85 NZ 4714
Stainton (Cumbr.) 83 NY 4827
Stainton (Cumbr.) 77 SD 5285
Stainton (Durham) 84 NZ 0718
Stainton (N Yorks.) 84 SE 1096
Stainton (S Yorks.) 71 SK 5593
Stainton by Langworth 72 TF 0577
Staintondale 81 SE 9898
Stainton Fell 82 SD 1594
Stainton le Vale 73 TF 1794
Stainton with Adgarley 76 SD 2472
Stair (Cumbr.) 82 NY 2321
Stair (Strath.) 93 NS 4323
Staithes 85 NZ 7818
Stakeford 91 NZ 2785
Stake Pass 82 NY 2608
Stake Pool 77 SD 4148
Stalbridge 25 ST 7317
Stalbridge Weston 25 ST 7216
Stalham 65 TG 3725
Stalham Green 65 TG 3824
Stalisfield Green 31 TQ 9652
Stallingborough 75 TA 2011
Stalling Busk 78 SD 9185
Stalmine 77 SD 3745
Stalybridge 70 SJ 9698
Stambourne 54 TL 7238
Stamford 62 TF 0207
Stamford Bridge 80 SE 7155
Stamfordham 91 NZ 0772
Stanborough 37 TL 2210
Stanbridge (Beds.) 36 SP 9623
Stanbridge (Dorset) 26 SU 0003
Stand 101 NS 7668
Standard (mt.) 86 NX 3085
Standburn 102 NS 9274
Standeford 59 SJ 9107
Standen 30 TQ 8539
Standford 27 SU 8134
Standish 69 SD 5609
Standlake 47 SP 3902
Standon (Hants.) 26 SU 4227
Standon (Herts.) 37 TL 3922
Standon (Staffs.) 59 SJ 8134
Stane 102 NS 8859
Stanegate (Cumbr.) (ant.) 89 NY 4660
Stanegate (Northum.) (ant.) 90 NY 7868

Stane Street (Essex) (ant.) Sunderland Bank (sbk.)

Stane Street (Essex) (ant.) 37 TL 5421
Stane Street (Surrey) (ant.) 28 TQ 1439
Stanfield 64 TF 9320
Stanford (Beds.) 52 TL 1641
Stanford (Kent) 31 TR 1238
Stanford Bishop 49 SO 6851
Stanford Bridge 49 SO 7165
Stanford Dingley 35 SU 5771
Stanford in the Vale 47 SU 3493
Stanford le Hope 38 TQ 6882
Stanford on Avon 51 SP 5878
Stanford on Soar 61 SK 5422
Stanford on Teme 49 SO 7065
Stanford Rivers 37 TL 5301
Stanger Head 138 HY 5142
Stanghow 85 NZ 6715
Stanhoe 64 TF 8036
Stanhope 95 NT 1229
Stanhope 84 NY 9939
Stanhope Common 84 NY 9642
Stanion 52 SP 9187
Stanley (Derby.) 60 SK 4140
Stanley (Durham) 84 NZ 1953
Stanley (Staffs.) 59 SJ 9252
Stanley (Tays.) 108 NO 1033
Stanley (W Yorks.) 79 SE 3422
Stanley Force 82 SD 1699
Stanmer 29 TQ 3309
Stanmore (Berks.) 35 SU 4778
Stanmore (Gtr London) 37 TQ 1692
Stannery Knowe 93 NS 4912
Stannington (Northum.) 91 NZ 2179
Stannington (S Yorks.) 71 SK 2988
Stansbatch 48 SO 3461
Stansfield 54 TL 7852
Stansore Point 27 SZ 4698
Stanstead 54 TL 8449
Stanstead Abbotts 37 TL 3811
Stansted 30 TQ 6062
Stansted Airport 37 TL 5422
Stansted House 27 SU 7610
Stansted Mountfitchet 37 TL 5124
Stanton (Glos.) 46 SP 0634
Stanton (Northum.) 91 NZ 1390
Stanton (Staffs.) 60 SK 1246
Stanton (Suff.) 54 TL 9673
Stanton by Bridge 60 SK 3627
Stanton by Dale 61 SK 4637
Stanton Drew 33 ST 5963
Stanton Fitzwarren 34 SU 1790
Stanton Harcourt 47 SP 4105
Stanton Hill 71 SK 4860
Stanton in Peak 71 SK 2464
Stanton Lacy 48 SO 4978
Stanton Long 48 SO 5690
Stanton-on-the-Wolds 61 SK 6330
Stanton Prior 33 ST 6762
Stanton St. Bernard 34 SU 0962
Stanton St. John 47 SP 5709
Stanton St. Quintin 34 ST 9079
Stanton Street 54 TL 9566
Stanton under Bardon 61 SK 4610
Stanton upon Hine Heath 59 SJ 5624
Stanton Wick 33 ST 6162
Stanwardine in the Fields 58 SJ 4124
Stanway (Essex) 38 TL 9324
Stanway (Glos.) 46 SP 0532
Stanwell 36 TQ 0574
Stanwell Moor 36 TQ 0474
Stanwick 52 SP 9871
Stanydale 140 HU 2850
Stape 80 SE 7993
Stapehill 26 SU 0500
Stapeley 59 SJ 6749
Staple 31 TR 2756
Staplecross 30 TQ 7822
Staplefield 28 TQ 2728
Staple Fitzpaine 24 ST 2618
Stapleford (Cambs.) 53 TL 4751
Stapleford (Herts.) 37 TL 3117
Stapleford (Leic.) 61 SK 8018
Stapleford (Lincs.) 72 SK 8757
Stapleford (Notts.) 61 SK 4837
Stapleford (Wilts.) 26 SU 0637
Stapleford Abbotts 37 TQ 5095
Stapleford Aerodrome 37 TQ 4996
Stapleford Tawney 37 TQ 5098
Staplegrove 24 ST 2126
Staple Hill 24 ST 2416
Staplehurst 30 TQ 7843
Staplers 27 SZ 5189
Staple Sound 97 NU 2236
Stapleton (Avon) 33 ST 6175
Stapleton (Cumbr.) 89 NY 5071
Stapleton (Here. and Worc.) 48 SO 3265
Stapleton (Leic.) 60 SP 4398
Stapleton (N Yorks.) 84 NZ 2612
Stapleton (Shrops.) 58 SJ 4604
Stapleton (Somer.) 25 ST 4621
Stapley 24 ST 1813
Staploe 52 TL 1460
Star (Dyfed) 43 SN 2435
Star (Fife) 103 NO 3103
Star (Somer.) 33 ST 4358
Starbotton 78 SD 9574
Starcross 21 SX 9781
Stare Dam 108 NO 0438
Starston 55 TM 2384
Start Bay 21 SX 8444
Startforth 84 NZ 0416
Startley 34 ST 9482
Start Point (Corn.) 20 SX 0485
Start Point (Devon) 21 SX 8337
Start Point (Sanday, Orkney) 139 HY 7843
Startup Hill 95 NS 9729
Stathe 24 ST 3728
Stathern 61 SK 7731
Station Town 85 NZ 4036
Stattic Point 126 NG 9796
Staughton Highway 52 TL 1364
Staunton (Glos.) 45 SO 5412
Staunton (Glos.) 46 SO 7929
Staunton Harold Hall 60 SK 3721
Staunton Harold Reservoir 60 SK 3723
Staunton on Arrow 45 SO 3660
Staunton on Wye 45 SO 3645
Stava Ness 141 HU 5060
Staveley (Cumbr.) 83 SD 4698
Staveley (Derby.) 71 SK 4374
Staveley (N Yorks.) 79 SE 3662
Staveley-in-Cartmel 77 SD 3886
Staverton (Devon) 21 SX 7964
Staverton (Glos.) 46 SO 8923
Staverton (Northants.) 51 SP 5461
Staverton (Wilts.) 33 ST 8560
Stawell 32 ST 3638
Staxigoe 135 ND 3852
Staxton 81 TA 0179
Staylittle 57 SN 8892
Staythorpe 61 SK 7554
Stean 78 SE 0873
Stean Moor 78 SE 0770
Stearsby 79 SE 6171
Steart 32 ST 2745
Stebbing 38 TL 6624
Stedham 27 SU 8622
Steele Road 90 NY 5292
Steel's Knowe 102 NN 9607
Steen's Bridge 45 SO 5457
Steep 27 SU 7525
Steep Holm (is.) 32 ST 2260
Steeping River 73 TF 4661
Steeple (Dorset) 25 SY 9080
Steeple (Essex) 38 TL 9303
Steeple Ashton 33 ST 9056
Steeple Aston 47 SP 4725
Steeple Barton 47 SP 4424
Steeple Bumpstead 54 TL 6741
Steeple Claydon 51 SP 7027
Steeple Gidding 52 TL 1381
Steeple Langford 26 SU 0337
Steeple Morden 53 TL 2842
Steer Rig 97 NT 8524
Steeton 78 SE 0344
Steilston Hill 88 NX 8782
Steinacleit (ant.) 131 NB 3954
Steinmanhill 121 NJ 7642
Steisay 124 NF 8544
Stelling Minnis 31 TR 1446
Stemster 135 ND 1862
Stemster Hill 135 ND 1941
Stemster House 135 ND 1860
Stenalees 19 SX 0157
Stenbury Down 27 SZ 5378
Stenhousemuir 102 NS 8682
Stenhouse Resr. 103 NT 2187
Stenness 142 HU 2177
Stenton 103 NT 6274
Stepney 37 TQ 3581
Steppingley 52 TL 0135
Stepps 101 NS 6668
Sternfield 55 TM 3861
Stert 34 SU 0259
Stert Flats (sbk.) 32 ST 2647
Stetchworth 54 TL 6458
Stevenage 53 TL 2325
Stevenston 93 NS 2642
Steventon (Hants.) 35 SU 5547
Steventon (Oxon.) 35 SU 4691
Stevington 52 SP 9853
Stewartby 52 TL 0242
Stewarton 93 NS 4246
Stewkley 52 SP 8525
Stewton 73 TF 3687
Stey Fell 87 NX 5560
Steyning 28 TQ 1711
Steynton 42 SM 9108
Stibb 22 SS 2210
Stibbard 64 TF 9828
Stibb Cross 22 SS 4314
Stibb Green 34 SU 2262
Stibbington 62 TL 0898
Stichill 96 NT 7138
Sticker 19 SW 9750
Stickford 73 TF 3560
Sticklepath 21 SX 6394
Stickle Pike 82 SD 2192
Stickle Tarn 82 NY 2907
Stickney 63 TF 3456
Stiffkey 64 TF 9743
Stifford's Bridge 49 SO 7348
Stilligarry 112 NF 7638
Stillingfleet 79 SE 5940
Stillington (Cleve. - Durham) 85 NZ 3723
Stillington (N Yorks.) 79 SE 5867
Stilton 52 TL 1689
Stinchcombe 46 ST 7298
Stinsford 25 SY 7191
Stiperstones 58 SO 3699
Stirchley 59 SJ 6906
Stirkoke House 135 ND 3150
Stirling 101 NS 7993
Stisted 38 TL 8024
Stithians 18 SW 7336
Stivichall 50 SP 3376
Stixwould 73 TF 1765
Stoak 68 SJ 4273
Stob a'Choin 107 NN 4115
Stob a'Ghrianain 115 NN 0882
Stob an Aonaich Mhóir 107 NN 5469
Stob an Eas 100 NN 1807
Stob an t-Sluichd 117 NJ 1102
Stob Binnein 107 NN 4322
Stob Choire Claurigh 115 NN 2673
Stob Coir' an Albannaich 106 NN 1644
Stob Coire a' Chearcaill 106 NN 0172
Stob Coire Easain (Highld.) 106 NN 2372
Stob Coire Easain (Highld.) 106 NN 3072
Stob Dubh 106 NN 1648
Stob Ghabhar 106 NN 2345
Stobieside 94 NS 6239
Stob Law 95 NT 2333
Stob na Cruaiche 107 NN 3657
Stobo 95 NT 1837
Stoborough 25 SY 9286
Stoborough Green 25 SY 9184
Stock 38 TQ 6998
Stockay 124 NF 6663
Stockbridge 26 SU 3535
Stockbriggs 94 NS 7936
Stockbury 30 TQ 8461
Stockcross 34 SU 4368
Stockdalewath 83 NY 3845
Stockerston 62 SP 8397
Stock Gaylard House 25 ST 7212
Stock Green 50 SO 9859
Stockingford 50 SP 3391
Stocking Pelham 53 TL 4529
Stockinish Island 125 NG 1389
Stockland 24 ST 2404
Stockland Bristol 32 ST 2443
Stockleigh English 23 SS 8406
Stockleigh Pomeroy 23 SS 8703
Stockley 34 SU 0067
Stockport 69 SJ 8989
Stocksbridge 71 SK 2798
Stocksfield 91 NZ 0561
Stocks Resr. 77 SD 7256
Stockton (Here. and Worc.) 48 SO 5161
Stockton (Norf.) 65 TM 3894
Stockton (Shrops.) 59 SO 7299
Stockton (Warw.) 50 SP 4363
Stockton (Wilts.) 34 ST 9738
Stockton Heath 69 SJ 6185
Stockton-on-Tees 85 NZ 4419
Stockton on Teme 49 SO 7167
Stockton on the Forest 79 SE 6556
Stockwith 72 SK 7994
Stock Wood 50 SP 0058
Stodmarsh 31 TR 2160
Stody 64 TG 0535
Stoer 132 NC 0328
Stoford (Somer.) 25 ST 5613
Stoford (Wilts.) 26 SU 0835
Stogumber 24 ST 0937
Stogursey 32 ST 2042
Stoke (Devon) 22 SS 2324
Stoke (Hants.) 34 SU 4051
Stoke (Hants.) 27 SU 7202
Stoke (Kent) 30 TQ 8275
Stoke Abbott 25 ST 4500
Stoke Albany 51 SP 8088
Stoke Ash 55 TM 1170
Stoke Bardolph 61 SK 6441
Stoke Bliss 49 SO 6562
Stoke Bruerne 51 SP 7450
Stoke by Clare 54 TL 7443
Stoke-by-Nayland 54 TL 9836
Stoke Canon 21 SX 9397
Stoke Charity 35 SU 4839
Stoke Climsland 20 SX 3574
Stoke D'Abernon 37 TQ 1259
Stoke Doyle 52 TL 0286
Stoke Dry 62 SP 8597
Stoke Ferry 64 TF 7000
Stoke Fleming 21 SX 8648
Stokeford 25 SY 8787
Stoke Gabriel 21 SX 8457
Stoke Gifford 33 ST 6280
Stoke Golding 60 SP 3997
Stoke Goldington 52 SP 8348
Stokeham 72 SK 7876
Stoke Hammond 52 SP 8829
Stoke Holy Cross 65 TG 2301
Stokeinteignhead 21 SX 9170
Stoke Lacy 45 SO 6149
Stoke Lyne 47 SP 5628
Stoke Mandeville 36 SP 8310
Stokenchurch 36 SU 7596
Stoke Newington 37 TQ 3286
Stokenham 21 SX 8042
Stoke on Tern 59 SJ 6327
Stoke-on-Trent 59 SJ 8745
Stoke Orchard 46 SO 9128
Stoke Poges 36 SU 9884
Stoke Point 21 SX 5645
Stoke Prior (Here. and Worc.) 45 SO 5256
Stoke Prior (Here. and Worc.) 49 SO 9467
Stoke Rivers 23 SS 6335
Stoke Rochford 62 SK 9127
Stoke Row 36 SU 6883
Stokesay 48 SO 4381
Stokes Bay 27 SZ 5897
Stokesby 65 TG 4310
Stokesley 85 NZ 5208
Stoke St. Gregory 24 ST 3426
Stoke St. Mary 24 ST 2622
Stoke St. Michael 33 ST 6646
Stoke St. Milborough 48 SO 5682
Stoke sub Hamdon 25 ST 4717
Stoke Talmage 36 SU 6799
Stoke Trister 25 ST 7328
Stolford 32 ST 2245
Stondon Massey 37 TL 5800
Stone (Bucks.) 36 SP 7812
Stone (Glos.) 46 ST 6895
Stone (Here. and Worc.) 49 SO 8675
Stone (Kent) 37 TQ 5774
Stone (Staffs.) 59 SJ 9034
Stone Allerton 32 ST 3950
Ston Easton 33 ST 6253
Stonebroom 71 SK 4159
Stonechrubie 132 NC 2419
Stone Cross 29 TQ 6104
Stonefield 94 NS 6957
Stonefield Castle Hotel 99 NR 8671
Stonegate 29 TQ 6628
Stonegate Crofts 121 NK 0339
Stonegrave 79 SE 6577
Stonehaugh 90 NY 7976
Stonehaven 119 NO 8685
Stonehenge (ant.) 34 SU 1242
Stone House (Cumbr.) 78 SD 7785
Stonehouse (Glos.) 46 SO 8005
Stonehouse (Northum.) 90 NY 6958
Stonehouse (Strath.) 94 NS 7546
Stone-in-Oxney 30 TQ 9427
Stoneleigh 50 SP 3272
Stonely 52 TL 1067
Stonesby 62 SK 8224
Stonesdale Moor 84 NY 8804
Stonesfield 47 SP 3917
Stones Green 55 TM 1626
Stoneside Hill 82 SD 1489
Stone Street (Kent) (ant.) 31 TR 1350
Stone Street (Suff.) (ant.) 55 TM 3686
Stoneybridge 112 NF 7433
Stoneyburn 102 NS 9762
Stoney Cross 26 SU 2511
Stoneygate 61 SK 6102
Stoneyhills 38 TQ 9497
Stoneykirk 86 NX 0853
Stoney Middleton 71 SK 2275
Stoney Stanton 61 SP 4894
Stoney Stratton 33 ST 6539
Stoney Stretton 58 SJ 3809
Stoneywood 119 NJ 8910
Stonga Banks 142 HU 2985
Stonganess 143 HP 5402
Stonham Aspal 55 TM 1359
Stonnall 60 SK 0603
Stonor 36 SU 7388
Stonton Wyville 61 SP 7395
Stonybreck 139 HZ 2071
Stonyfield 128 NH 6973
Stonyhurst College 77 SD 6838
Stony Stratford 51 SP 7840
Stood Hill 88 NS 8512
Stoodleigh 23 SS 9218
Stoodleigh Beacon 23 SS 8818
Stopham 28 TQ 0219
Stopsley 52 TL 1023
Storeton 68 SJ 3084
Stornoway 131 NB 4233
Stornoway Aerodrome 131 NB 4533
Storridge 49 SO 7448
Storrington 28 TQ 0814
Storrs 83 SD 3994
Storr, The (mt.) 123 NG 4954
Storth 77 SD 4780
Stotfold 52 TL 2136
Stottesdon 49 SO 6782
Stoughton (Leic.) 61 SK 6402
Stoughton (Surrey) 28 SU 9851
Stoughton (W Susx) 27 SU 8011
Stoul 111 NM 7594
Stoulton 49 SO 9049
Stourbridge 49 SO 8984
Stourbrough Hill 140 HU 2152
Stourhead 25 ST 7734
Stourpaine 25 ST 8509
Stourport-on-Severn 49 SO 8171
Stour Provost 25 ST 7921
Stour Row 25 ST 8220
Stourton (Here. and Worc.) 49 SO 8585
Stourton (Warw.) 50 SP 2936
Stourton (Wilts.) 25 ST 7733
Stourton Caundle 25 ST 7114
Stove 139 HY 6035
Stoven 55 TM 4481
Stow (Borders) 96 NT 4644
Stow (Lincs.) 72 SK 8781
Stow Bardolph 64 TF 6205
Stow Bardolph Fen 63 TF 5603
Stow Bedon 64 TL 9596
Stowbridge 64 TF 6007
Stow cum Quy 53 TL 5260
Stowe (Shrops.) 48 SO 3173
Stowe-by-Chartley 60 SK 0027
Stowell 25 ST 6822
Stowe School 51 SP 6737
Stowford 20 SX 4386
Stowlangtoft 54 TL 9568
Stow Longa 52 TL 1171
Stow Maries 38 TQ 8399
Stowmarket 54 TM 0458
Stow-on-the-Wold 47 SP 1925
Stowting 31 TR 1241
Stowupland 54 TM 0659
Straad 100 NS 0462
Strachan 119 NO 6792
Strachur 100 NN 0901
Strachur Bay 100 NN 0801
Stradbroke 55 TM 2373
Stradishall 54 TL 7452
Stradsett 64 TF 6605
Stragglethorpe 62 SK 9152
Strait of Dover 31 TR 3828
Straiton (Lothian) 103 NT 2766
Straiton (Strath.) 93 NS 3804
Straloch (Grampn.) 121 NJ 8621
Straloch (Tays.) 108 NO 0463
Stramshall 60 SK 0735
Strandburgh Ness 143 HU 6793
Strangend Currick 83 NY 8443
Stranraer 86 NX 0660
Strata Florida 57 SN 7465
Stratfield Mortimer 36 SU 6764
Stratfield Saye 36 SU 6961
Stratfield Turgis 36 SU 6959
Stratford St. Andrew 55 TM 3560
Stratford St. Mary 54 TM 0434
Stratford Tony 26 SU 0926
Stratford-upon-Avon 50 SP 2055
Stratford-upon-Avon Canal 50 SP 1764
Strath 126 NG 7978
Strathaird 123 NG 5419
Strathallan 101 NN 8307
Strathallan Castle 108 NN 9115
Strathan (Highld.) 132 NC 0821
Strathan (Highld.) 114 NM 9891
Strath an Lòin 133 NC 4416
Strathaven 94 NS 7044
Strath Avon 117 NJ 1525
Strath Beag 127 NH 1087
Strath Beg 134 NC 8531
Strath Blane (Central) 101 NS 5381
Strathblane (Central) 101 NS 5679
Strathblane Hills 101 NS 5581
Strath Bogie (Grampn.) 121 NJ 5237
Strathbogie (Grampn.) (dist.) 121 NJ 4937
Strathbraan 108 NN 9739
Strath Bran 127 NH 2460
Strath Brora 134 NC 7609
Strath Burn 135 ND 2450
Strathcarron (Highld.) 126 NG 9442
Strathcarron (Highld.) 128 NH 5591
Strathcoil 105 NM 6830
Strathconon 127 NH 4055
Strathconon Forest 127 NH 2347
Strath Cuileannach 128 NH 4393
Strathdearn 116 NH 7724
Strathdon 118 NJ 3513
Strath Dores 116 NH 6137
Strath Eachaig 100 NS 1484
Strath Earn 108 NN 8818
Stratherrick 116 NH 5017
Strath Fillan 107 NN 3628
Strath Finella 119 NO 6879
Strathfinella Hill 119 NO 6978
Strath Fleet 128 NC 6702
Strath Gartney 101 NN 4610
Strathgarve Forest 128 NH 4163
Strathglass 115 NH 3734
Strathgryfe 100 NS 3270
Strath Halladale 134 NC 8953
Strathhardle 108 NO 1153
Strath Isla 121 NJ 4451
Strath Kanaird (Highld.) 127 NC 1400
Strath Kanaird (Highld) 127 NC 1501
Strathkinness 109 NO 4516
Strathlachlan Forest 100 NS 0093
Strath Lungard 126 NG 9264
Strath Mashie 116 NN 5891
Strathmashie House 116 NN 5891
Strath Melness Burn 133 NC 5663
Strathmiglo 103 NO 2109
Strath More (Highld.) 133 NC 4545
Strath More (Highld.) 127 NH 1882
Strathmore (Tays.) (dist.) 109 NO 4353
Strathmore Lodge 135 ND 1047
Strathmore River 133 NC 4546
Strath Mulzie 127 NH 3193
Strathnairn 116 NH 6832
Strathnairn Forest 116 NH 6930
Strath nan Lùb 100 NS 0792
Strath na Sealga 127 NH 0680
Strathnasheallag Forest 127 NH 0483
Strathnaver 134 NC 7148
Strath of Appin 106 NM 9545
Strath of Kildonan or Strath Ullie 134 NC 8923
Strath of Orchy 106 NN 1627
Strathord Forest 108 NO 0631
Strath Oykel 128 NC 4300
Strathpeffer 128 NH 4858
Strath Rannoch (Highld.) 127 NH 3872
Strathrannoch (Highld.) 127 NH 3874
Strath Rory 128 NH 6976
Strath Rusdale 128 NH 5777
Strath Sgitheach 128 NH 5263
Strath Shinary 132 NC 2561
Strath Skinsdale 134 NC 7518
Strathspey 117 NJ 1536
Strath Stack 132 NC 2740
Strath Suardal 123 NG 6221
Strath Tay 108 NO 0043
Strath Tirry 133 NC 5319
Strath Ullie or Strath of Kildonan 134 NC 8923
Strath Vagastie 133 NC 5430
Strath Vaich 127 NH 3572
Strathvaich Forest 127 NH 3276
Strathvaich Lodge 127 NH 3474
Strathwhillan 92 NS 0235
Strathy 134 NC 8465
Strathy Bay 134 NC 8366
Strathy Forest (Highld.) 134 NC 8256
Strathy Forest (Highld.) 134 NC 8262
Strathy Point 134 NC 8269
Strathyre 107 NN 5617
Strathyre Forest 107 NN 5718
Stratton (Corn.) 22 SS 2306
Stratton (Dorset) 25 SY 6593
Stratton (Glos.) 46 SP 0103
Stratton Audley 47 SP 6026
Stratton-on-the-Fosse 33 ST 6550
Stratton St. Margaret 34 SU 1787
Stratton St. Michael 65 TM 2093
Stratton Strawless 65 TG 2220
Stravanan Bay 92 NS 0755
Stravithie 103 NO 5311
Strawarren Fell 86 NX 1679
Streat 29 TQ 3515
Streatham 37 TQ 2972
Streatlam Castle 84 NZ 0819
Streatley (Beds.) 52 TL 0728
Streatley (Berks.) 35 SU 5980
Streens 117 NH 8638
Street (Lancs.) 77 SD 5252
Street (N Yorks.) 80 NZ 7304
Street (Somer.) 25 ST 4836
Street End 27 SZ 8599
Streethay 60 SK 1410
Streetly 60 SP 0898
Strefford 48 SO 4485
Strem Ness 140 HT 9741
Strensall 79 SE 6360
Strensham 49 SO 9040
Stretcholt 32 ST 2943
Strete 21 SX 8447
Stretford 69 SJ 7894
Stretford Court 45 SO 4455
Strethall 53 TL 4939
Stretham 53 TL 5174
Strettington 27 SU 8807
Stretton (Ches.) 58 SJ 4452
Stretton (Ches.) 69 SJ 6182
Stretton (Derby.) 71 SK 3961
Stretton (Leic.) 62 SK 9415
Stretton (Staffs.) 59 SJ 8811
Stretton (Staffs.) 60 SK 2526
Stretton en le Field 60 SK 3012
Stretton Grandison 45 SO 6344
Stretton Heath 58 SJ 3610
Stretton-on-Dunsmore 50 SP 4072
Stretton-on-Fosse 50 SP 2238
Stretton under Fosse 51 SP 4581
Stretton Westwood 59 SO 5998
Strichen 121 NJ 9455
Strines Resr. 71 SK 2290
Stringston 32 ST 1742
String, The 136 HY 4714
Strixton 52 SP 9061
Stroan Loch 88 NX 6470
Stroat 45 ST 5798
Stròc-bheinn 123 NG 4539
Stroin Vuigh (pt.) 76 SC 2174
Stromeferry 123 NG 8634
Stromemore 123 NG 8635
Strom Ness (Muckle Roe) 140 HU 2965
Strom Ness (N. Ronaldsay) 139 HY 7651
Stromness (Orkney) 136 HY 2509
Strom Ness (Vaila) 140 HU 2245
Stromness Taing 136 HY 4425
Stronabo 115 NN 2084
Stronachlachar 101 NN 4010
Stronchreggan 106 NN 0772
Stronchrubie 132 NC 2419
Stronchullin Hill 100 NS 1686
Strond 124 NG 0384
Strone (Highld.) 116 NH 5228
Strone (Highld.) 115 NN 1481
Strone (Strath.) 100 NS 1880
Strone Glen 92 NR 6310
Stronend (mt.) 101 NS 6289
Strone Point (Strath.) 100 NS 0771
Strone Point (Strath.) 100 NS 1980
Strone Water 92 NR 6310
Stronmilchan 106 NN 1528
Stronsay 137 HY 6525
Stronsay Aerodrome 137 HY 6329
Stronsay Firth 137 HY 5722
Strontian 111 NM 8161
Strontian River 111 NM 8363
Stronuich Reservoir 107 NN 5042
Strood 30 TQ 7369
Stroud (Glos.) 46 SO 8504
Stroud (Hants.) 27 SU 7223
Struan 122 NG 3438
Struan Station 107 NN 8065
Strubby 73 TF 4582
Struie (mt.) 128 NH 6584
Strumble Head 42 SM 8941
Strumpshaw 65 TG 3507
Strutherhill 94 NS 7650
Struy 115 NH 4039
Struy Forest 115 NH 3737
Stuartfield 121 NJ 9745
Stubbington 27 SU 5503
Stubbins 69 SD 7918
Stubhampton 25 ST 9113
Stub Place 82 SD 0890
Stubton 62 SK 8748
Stuchd an Lochain 107 NN 4844
Stuckgowan 100 NN 3202
Stuckton 26 SU 1613
Stuc Scardan 100 NN 1114
Studham 36 TL 0215
Studland 26 SZ 0382
Studland Bay 26 SZ 0584
Studley (Warw.) 50 SP 0763
Studley (Wilts.) 34 ST 9671
Studley Roger 79 SE 2970
Stulaval (Isle of Lewis) (mt.) 131 NB 1312
Stulaval (South Uist) (mt.) 112 NF 8024
Stuley 112 NF 8323
Stump Cross 53 TL 5044
Stuntney 53 TL 5578
Sturbridge 59 SJ 8330
Sturdy Hill 119 NO 5977
Sturgate Airport 72 SK 8888
Sturmer 54 TL 6944
Sturminster Common 25 ST 7812
Sturminster Marshall 26 SY 9499
Sturminster Newton 25 ST 7813
Sturry 31 TR 1760
Sturton by Stow 72 SK 8980
Sturton le Steeple 72 SK 7884
Stuston 55 TM 1378
Stutton (N Yorks.) 79 SE 4741
Stutton (Suff.) 55 TM 1434
Styal 69 SJ 8383
Sty Head 82 NY 2109
Sty Wick 139 HY 6838
Suainaval (mt.) 130 NB 0730
Succoth 121 NJ 4235
Suckley 49 SO 7151
Suckley Hills 49 SO 7352
Sudborough 52 SP 9682
Sudbourne 55 TM 4153
Sudbrook 33 ST 5087
Sudbrooke 72 TF 0276
Sudbury (Derby.) 60 SK 1631
Sudbury (Suff.) 54 TL 8741
Suddie 128 NH 6654
Sudeley Castle (ant.) 46 SP 0327
Sudgrove 46 SO 9307
Sueno's Stone (ant.) 129 NJ 0459
Suffield 65 TG 2332
Sugar Loaf 45 SO 2718
Sugnall 59 SJ 7930
Suidh'a'Mhinn 123 NG 4068
Suidhe Ghuirmain (mt.) 115 NH 3826
Suie Hill 121 NJ 5523
Suilven (mt.) 132 NC 1517
Suisgill Burn 134 NC 8925
Suisnish Hill 123 NG 5634
Sula Sgeir (is.) 130 HW 6230
Sulby 76 SC 3994
Sulby Reservoir 51 SP 6581
Sulby River 76 SC 3890
Sule Skerry 132 HX 6224
Sulgrave 51 SP 5545
Sulham 36 SU 6474
Sulhamstead 36 SU 6368
Sullington 28 TQ 0913
Sullom 142 HU 3573
Sullom Voe 143 HU 3773
Sully 41 ST 1568
Sully Island 41 ST 1667
Sulma Water 140 HU 2555
Sumburgh 141 HU 4009
Sumburgh Airport 141 HU 3910
Sumburgh Head 141 HU 4007
Sumburgh Roost (chan.) 141 HU 4006
Summer Bridge 78 SE 1962
Summercourt 19 SW 8856
Summer Down 33 ST 9148
Summer Isles 126 NB 9706
Summerleaze 33 ST 4284
Summerseat 69 SD 7914
Summit 69 SD 9418
Sunadale 92 NR 8145
Sunart (dist.) 111 NM 7966
Sunbury 37 TQ 1069
Sunderland (Cumbr.) 82 NY 1735
Sunderland (Tyne and Wear) 85 NZ 3957
Sunderland Airport 91 NZ 3458
Sunderland Bank (sbk.) 77 SD 3956

Whigstreet Woolfardisworthy (Devon)

Whigstreet	109	NO 4844
Whillan Beck	82	NY 1701
Whilton	51	SP 6364
Whimple	24	SY 0497
Whimpwell Green	65	TG 3829
Whinburgh	64	TG 0009
Whinfell Beacon	83	NY 5700
Whinlatter Pass	82	NY 1924
Whinnyfold	121	NK 0733
Whins Brow	77	SD 6353
Whippingham	27	SZ 5193
Whipsnade	36	TL 0117
Whipsnade Park Zoo	36	TL 0017
Whipton	21	SX 9493
Whissendine	62	SK 8214
Whissonsett	64	TF 9123
Whistley Green	36	SU 7974
Whiston (Mers.)	69	SJ 4791
Whiston (Northants.)	52	SP 8560
Whiston (Staffs.)	59	SJ 8914
Whiston (Staffs.)	60	SK 0347
Whiston (S Yorks.)	71	SK 4489
Whitaloo Point	136	HY 2628
Whitbeck	76	SD 1184
Whitbourne	49	SO 7156
Whitburn (Lothian)	102	NS 9464
Whitburn (Tyne and Wear)	91	NZ 4061
Whitby (Ches.)	68	SJ 4075
Whitby (N Yorks.)	81	NZ 8911
Whitchurch (Avon)	33	ST 6167
Whitchurch (Bucks.)	36	SP 8020
Whitchurch (Devon)	20	SX 4972
Whitchurch (Dyfed)	42	SM 8025
Whitchurch (Hants.)	35	SU 4648
Whitchurch (Here. and Worc.)	45	SO 5417
Whitchurch (Oxon.)	36	SU 6377
Whitchurch (S Glam.)	41	ST 1680
Whitchurch (Shrops.)	59	SJ 5441
Whitchurch Canonicorum	24	SY 3995
Whitchurch Hill	36	SU 6478
Whitcott Keysett	48	SO 2782
Whiteacen	120	NJ 2646
Whiteadder Resr.	103	NT 6563
Whiteadder Water (Borders)	97	NT 8555
Whiteadder Water (Lothian)	103	NT 6267
Whiteash Hill Wood	121	NJ 3657
Whitebrook	45	SO 5306
Whitecairns	119	NJ 9218
White Cart Water	101	NS 5263
White Castle (ant.)	45	SO 3716
White Caterthun (mt.)	109	NO 5465
White Chapel	77	SD 5542
Whitechurch	42	SN 1436
Whitecliff Bay	27	SZ 6485
White Coomb	89	NT 1614
White Coppice	69	SD 6119
Whitecraig (Lothian)	103	NT 3570
Whitecraig (Strath.) (mt.)	95	NT 0753
Whitecroft	45	SO 6106
Whitecross	102	NS 9676
White Esk	89	NY 2499
Whiteface	129	NH 7089
Whitefarland Point	92	NR 8642
Whitefauld Hill	88	NY 0293
White Fen	53	TL 3492
Whitefield (Gtr Mches.)	69	SD 8005
Whitefield (Tays.)	108	NO 1734
Whitefield Loch	86	NX 2355
Whiteford	121	NJ 7126
Whiteford Point	40	SS 4496
Whitehall	137	HY 6528
Whitehaugh Forest	121	NJ 5822
Whitehaven	82	NX 9718
White Hill (Borders)	90	NT 5211
White Hill (Grampn.)	119	NO 5388
Whitehill (Hants.)	27	SU 7934
White Hill (Lancs.)	77	SD 6758
White Hill (Strath.)	93	NS 2656
White Hill (Strath.)	88	NS 8519
White Hill (Tays.)	109	NO 4072
Whitehills	121	NJ 6565
White Hope Edge	89	NY 3397
Whitehope Law	96	NT 3344
Whitehorse Hill	34	SU 2986
Whitehouse (Grampn.)	119	NJ 6214
Whitehouse (Strath.)	99	NR 8161
White Island	18	SV 9217
Whitekirk	103	NT 5981
White Knowes	88	NS 6104
White Lackington	25	SY 7198
White Ladies Aston	49	SO 9252
White Law	97	NT 8526
Whitelaw Hill (Borders)	95	NT 1935
Whitelaw Hill (Lothian)	103	NT 5771
Whitelee Hill	93	NS 5442
Whiteley Village	36	TQ 0962
White Loch	86	NX 1060
White Lyne	90	NY 5373
Whitemans Green	29	TQ 3025
White Meldon	95	NT 2242
Whitemill Bay	139	HY 6946
Whitemill Point	139	HY 7046
Whitemire	129	NH 9754
Whitemoor	19	SW 9757
Whitemoor Reservoir	78	SD 8743
White Mounth	117	NO 2384
White Ness (Kent)	31	TR 4070
White Ness (Shetld.)	141	HU 3844
Whiteness (Shetld.) (dist.)	141	HU 4147
Whiteness Head	129	NH 8058
Whiteness Sands	129	NH 8386
Whiteness Voe	141	HU 3943
Whiten Head or An Ceann Geal	133	NC 4968
White Notley	38	TL 7818
Whiteparish	26	SU 2423
White Preston	90	NY 5977
Whiterashes	121	NJ 8523
White Roding or White Roothing	37	TL 5613
White Roothing or White Roding	37	TL 5613
Whiterow	135	ND 3548
Whitesand Bay (Corn.)	18	SW 3427
Whitesand Bay or Porth-mawr (Dyfed)	42	SM 7227
White Sands	68	SJ 2771
White Shank (mt.)	89	NT 2006
White Sheet Castle (ant.)	25	ST 8034
White Sheet Hill (Wilts.)	25	ST 8034
White Sheet Hill (Wilts.)	26	ST 9424
Whiteshill	46	SO 8307
Whiteshoot Hill	26	SU 2833
Whiteside (Lothian)	102	NS 9667
Whiteside (Northum.)	90	NY 7069
Whitesmith	29	TQ 5214
Whitestaunton	24	ST 2810
Whitestone	21	SX 8694
Whitestone Hill	90	NT 8014
White Top of Culreoch	88	NX 5963
White Waltham	36	SU 8577
Whiteway	46	SO 9110
Whiteway House	21	SX 8783
Whitewell	77	SD 6546
Whiteworks	21	SX 6071
Whitewreath	120	NJ 2356
Whitfell	82	SD 1592
Whitfield (Glos.)	33	ST 6791
Whitfield (Kent)	31	TR 3146
Whitfield (Northants.)	51	SP 6039
Whitfield (Northum.)	90	NY 7758
Whitfield Moor	83	NY 7454
Whitford	68	SJ 1477
Whitgift	74	SE 8022
Whitgreave	59	SJ 8928
Whithorn	87	NX 4440
Whiting Bay (Island of Arran)	92	NS 0425
Whiting Bay (Island of Arran)	92	NS 0526
Whitland	43	SN 1916
Whitletts	93	NS 3622
Whitley (Berks.)	36	SU 7170
Whitley (Ches.)	69	SJ 6178
Whitley (N Yorks.)	79	SE 5521
Whitley Bay	91	NZ 3572
Whitley Chapel	84	NY 9257
Whitley Row	29	TQ 5052
Whitlock's End	50	SP 1076
Whitminster	46	SO 7708
Whit Moor	77	SD 5864
Whitmore	59	SJ 8041
Whitnage	24	ST 0215
Whitnash	50	SP 3263
Whitney	45	SO 2647
Whitrigg (Cumbr.)	82	NY 2038
Whitrigg (Cumbr.)	82	NY 2257
Whitsand Bay	20	SX 3751
Whitsbury	26	SU 1218
Whitsome	97	NT 8650
Whitson	32	ST 3783
Whitstable	31	TR 1166
Whitstone	20	SX 2698
Whittingham	91	NU 0611
Whittingslow	48	SO 4288
Whittington (Derby.)	71	SK 3975
Whittington (Glos.)	46	SP 0120
Whittington (Here. and Worc.)	49	SO 8582
Whittington (Here. and Worc.)	49	SO 8752
Whittington (Lancs.)	77	SD 5976
Whittington (Norf)	64	TL 7199
Whittington (Shrops.)	58	SJ 3230
Whittington (Staffs.)	60	SK 1508
Whittlebury	51	SP 6943
Whittle-le-Woods	77	SD 5822
Whittlesey	63	TL 2797
Whittlesey Mere	53	TL 2290
Whittlesford	53	TL 4748
Whittlewood Forest	51	SP 7243
Whitton (Cleve.)	85	NZ 3822
Whitton (Humbs.)	74	SE 9024
Whitton (Northum.)	91	NU 0501
Whitton (Powys)	48	SO 2667
Whitton (Shrops.)	48	SO 5772
Whitton (Suff.)	55	TM 1447
Whittonditch	34	SU 2872
Whittonstall	84	NZ 0757
Whitwell (Derby.)	71	SK 5276
Whitwell (Herts.)	37	TL 1821
Whitwell (I. of W.)	27	SZ 5277
Whitwell (Leic.)	62	SK 9208
Whitwell (N Yorks.)	84	SE 2899
Whitwell-on-the-Hill	80	SE 7265
Whitwick	60	SK 4316
Whitwood	79	SE 4124
Whitworth	69	SD 8818
Whixall	59	SJ 5034
Whixley	79	SE 4457
Whorlton (Durham)	84	NZ 1014
Whorlton (N Yorks.)	85	NZ 4802
Whorlton Moor	85	SE 4998
Whygate	90	NY 7675
Whyle	45	SO 5560
Whyteleafe	37	TQ 3358
Wiay (Benbecula)	124	NF 8746
Wiay (Island of Skye)	122	NG 2936
Wibdon	45	ST 5797
Wibtoft	51	SP 4787
Wichenford	49	SO 7860
Wichling	30	TQ 9256
Wick (Avon)	33	ST 6972
Wick (Dorset)	26	SZ 1591
Wick (Here. and Worc.)	50	SO 9645
Wick (Highld.)	135	ND 3650
Wick (S Glam.)	41	SS 9272
Wick (Shetld.)	141	HU 4439
Wick (Unst)	143	HP 5603
Wick (Wilts.)	26	SU 1621
Wick (W Susx)	28	TQ 0203
Wick Airport	135	ND 3652
Wick Bay	135	ND 3750
Wick Down	26	SU 1321
Wicken (Cambs.)	53	TL 5770
Wicken (Northants.)	51	SP 7439
Wicken Bonhunt	53	TL 5033
Wickenby	72	TF 0882
Wickenby Airport	73	TF 1081
Wickersley	71	SK 4891
Wickford	38	TQ 7593
Wickham (Berks.)	34	SU 3971
Wickham (Hants.)	27	SU 5711
Wickham Bishops	38	TL 8412
Wickhambreaux	31	TR 2158
Wickhambrook	54	TL 7454
Wickhamford	50	SP 0642
Wickham Market	55	TM 3056
Wickhampton	65	TG 4205
Wickham Skeith	55	TM 0969
Wickham St. Paul	54	TL 8336
Wickham Street (Suff.)	54	TL 7554
Wickham Street (Suff.)	55	TM 0869
Wick Hill	36	SU 8064
Wicklewood	64	TG 0702
Wickmere	65	TG 1633
Wick of Breakon	143	HP 5205
Wick of Gruting	143	HU 6592
Wick of Mucklabrek	140	HT 9438
Wick of Sandsayre	141	HU 4325
Wick of Shunni	141	HU 3515
Wick of Tresta	143	HU 6388
Wick River	135	ND 2953
Wick St. Lawrence	32	ST 3665
Wickwar	33	ST 7288
Widdale Fell	78	SD 8088
Widdington	53	TL 5331
Widdop Resr.	78	SD 9332
Widdrington	91	NZ 2595
Widdrington Station	91	NZ 2494
Widdybank Fell	83	NY 8230
Widecombe In the Moor	21	SX 7176
Wide Firth	136	HY 4316
Wideford Hill	136	HY 4111
Widegates	20	SX 2857
Widemouth Bay	22	SS 2002
Wide Open	91	NZ 2472
Widewall	136	ND 4391
Widewall Bay	136	ND 4292
Widford (Essex)	38	TL 6905
Widford (Herts.)	37	TL 4115
Widmerpool	61	SK 6327
Widnes	69	SJ 5185
Wife Geo	135	ND 3969
Wigan	69	SD 5805
Wiggaton	24	SY 1093
Wiggenhall St. Germans	64	TF 5914
Wiggenhall St. Mary Magdalen	64	TF 5911
Wiggenhall St. Mary the Virgin	63	TF 5814
Wiggington (N Yorks.)	79	SE 5958
Wigginton (Herts.)	36	SP 9410
Wigginton (Oxon.)	47	SP 3833
Wigginton (Staffs.)	60	SK 2106
Wigglesworth	78	SD 8056
Wiggonby	82	NY 2953
Wiggonholt	28	TQ 0616
Wighill	79	SE 4746
Wighton	64	TF 9339
Wigmore (Here. and Worc.)	48	SO 4169
Wigmore (Kent)	30	TQ 8063
Wigsley	72	SK 8570
Wigsthorpe	52	TL 0482
Wigston	61	SP 6099
Wig, The (roadstead)	86	NX 0467
Wigtoft	63	TF 2636
Wigton	82	NY 2548
Wigtown	87	NX 4355
Wigtown Bay	87	NX 5249
Wigtown Sands	87	NX 4556
Wilbarston	52	SP 8188
Wilberfoss	80	SE 7350
Wilburton	53	TL 4875
Wilby (Norf.)	54	TM 0389
Wilby (Northants.)	52	SP 8666
Wilby (Suff.)	55	TM 2472
Wilcot	34	SU 1461
Wildboarclough	70	SJ 9868
Wilden	52	TL 0955
Wildhern	34	SU 3550
Wildmore Fen	63	TF 2551
Wildsworth	72	SK 8097
Wiley Sike	90	NY 6369
Wilford	61	SK 5637
Wilkesley	59	SJ 6241
Wilkhaven	129	NH 9486
Wilkieston	102	NT 1168
Willand	24	ST 0310
Willaston (Ches.)	68	SJ 3277
Willaston (Ches.)	59	SJ 6752
Willen	52	SP 8741
Willenhall (W Mids.)	60	SO 9698
Willenhall (W Mids.)	50	SP 3676
Willerby (Humbs.)	74	TA 0230
Willerby (N Yorks.)	81	TA 0079
Willersey	50	SP 1039
Willersley	45	SO 3147
Willesborough	31	TR 0441
Willesden	37	TQ 2284
Willett	24	ST 1033
Willey (Shrops.)	59	SO 6799
Willey (Warw.)	51	SP 4984
William Law	96	NT 4839
Williamscot	51	SP 4745
Willian	53	TL 2230
Willimontswick	90	NY 7763
Willingale	38	TL 5907
Willingdon	29	TQ 5902
Willingdon Hill	29	TQ 5600
Willingham (Cambs.)	53	TL 4070
Willingham by Stow	72	SK 8784
Willington (Beds.)	52	TL 1150
Willington (Derby.)	60	SK 2928
Willington (Durham)	84	NZ 1935
Willington (Tyne and Wear)	91	NZ 3167
Willington (Warw.)	50	SP 2638
Willington Corner	69	SJ 5367
Willitoft	74	SE 7434
Williton	32	ST 0740
Willoughby (Lincs.)	73	TF 4772
Willoughby (Warw.)	51	SP 5167
Willoughby-on-the-Wolds	61	SK 6325
Willoughby Waterleys	51	SP 5792
Willoughton	72	SK 9293
Willy Howe (ant.)	81	TA 0672
Wilmcote	50	SP 1658
Wilmington (Devon)	24	SY 2199
Wilmington (E Susx)	29	TQ 5404
Wilmington (Kent)	37	TQ 5372
Wilmslow	69	SJ 8480
Wilnecote	60	SK 2201
Wilpshire	77	SD 6832
Wilsden	78	SE 0935
Wilsford (Lincs.)	62	TF 0043
Wilsford (Wilts.)	34	SU 1057
Wilsford (Wilts.)	34	SU 1339
Wilsill	78	SE 1864
Wilson	60	SK 4024
Wilson's Pike	90	NY 5589
Wilstead	52	TL 0643
Wilsthorpe	62	TF 0913
Wilstone	36	SP 9014
Wilstone Reservoir	36	SP 9013
Wilton (Cleve.)	85	NZ 5819
Wilton (N Yorks.)	80	SE 8582
Wilton (Wilts.)	26	SU 0931
Wilton (Wilts.)	34	SU 2661
Wilton Dean	89	NT 4914
Wilton House (ant.)	26	SU 0831
Wimbish	54	TL 5936
Wimbish Green	54	TL 6035
Wimbleball Reservoir	23	SS 9730
Wimbledon	37	TQ 2470
Wimbledon Park	37	TQ 2472
Wimblington	53	TL 4192
Wimblington Fen	53	TL 4589
Wimborne Minster	26	SZ 0199
Wimborne St. Giles	26	SU 0212
Wimbotsham	64	TF 6205
Wimpole Hall (ant.)	53	TL 3351
Wimpstone	50	SP 2148
Wincanton	25	ST 7128
Wincham	69	SJ 6675
Winchburgh	102	NT 0874
Winchcombe	46	SP 0228
Winchelsea	30	TQ 9017
Winchelsea Beach	30	TQ 9115
Winchester	27	SU 4829
Winchfield	35	SU 7654
Winchmore Hill (Bucks.)	36	SU 9394
Winchmore Hill (Gtr London)	37	TQ 3195
Wincle	70	SJ 9565
Windbury Point	22	SS 2926
Windermere (Cumbr.)	83	SD 3995
Windermere (Cumbr.)	83	SD 4198
Winderton	50	SP 3240
Windleden Reservoirs	70	SE 1501
Windlesham	36	SU 9363
Windlestraw Law	96	NT 3743
Windley	60	SK 3045
Windmill Hill (E Susx)	29	TQ 6412
Windmill Hill (Somer.)	24	ST 3116
Windrush	47	SP 1913
Windsor	36	SU 9676
Windsor Forest	36	SU 9373
Windsor Great Park	36	SU 9572
Wind Wick	136	ND 4587
Windy Crag	90	NT 7705
Windygates	103	NO 3400
Windy Gyle	90	NT 8614
Windyheads Hill	121	NJ 8561
Windy Hill	100	NS 0469
Windy Standard (Dumf. and Galwy.) (mt.)	88	NS 6101
Windy Standard (Strath.) (mt.)	93	NS 5204
Wineham	28	TQ 2320
Winestead	75	TA 2924
Winfarthing	55	TM 1085
Winford	33	ST 5364
Winforton	45	SO 2947
Winfrith Newburgh	25	SY 8084
Wing (Bucks.)	36	SP 8822
Wing (Leic.)	62	SK 8903
Wingate (Durham)	85	NZ 4036
Wingates (Gtr Mches.)	69	SD 6507
Wingates (Northum.)	91	NZ 0995
Wingerworth	71	SK 3867
Wingfield (Beds.)	52	SP 9926
Wingfield (Suff.)	55	TM 2276
Wingfield (Wilts.)	33	ST 8256
Wingham	31	TR 2457
Wingrave	36	SP 8719
Win Green	25	ST 9220
Winkburn	72	SK 7158
Winkfield	36	SU 9072
Winkfield Row	36	SU 9071
Winkhill	60	SK 0651
Winklebury (ant.)	26	ST 9521
Winkleigh	23	SS 6308
Winksley	79	SE 2471
Winless	135	ND 3054
Winmarleigh	77	SD 4748
Winna Ness	143	HU 6098
Winnersh	36	SU 7870
Winscales	82	NY 0226
Winscar Resr.	70	SE 1502
Winscombe	32	ST 4157
Winsford (Ches.)	69	SJ 6566
Winsford (Somer.)	23	SS 9034
Winsford Hill	23	SS 8734
Winsham	24	ST 3706
Winshill	60	SK 2623
Winskill	83	NY 5835
Winslade	35	SU 6547
Winsley	33	ST 7960
Winslow	51	SP 7627
Winson	46	SP 0908
Winster (Cumbr.)	83	SD 4193
Winster (Derby.)	71	SK 2460
Winston (Durham)	84	NZ 1416
Winston (Suff.)	55	TM 1861
Winstone	46	SO 9609
Winswell	22	SS 4913
Winterborne Abbas	25	SY 6190
Winterborne Clenston	25	ST 8302
Winterborne Herringston	25	SY 6887
Winterborne Houghton	25	ST 8104
Winterborne Kingston	25	SY 8697
Winterborne Monkton (Dorset)	25	SY 6787
Winterborne Steepleton	25	SY 6289
Winterborne Stickland	25	ST 8304
Winterborne Whitechurch	25	SY 8399
Winterborne Zelston	25	SY 8997
Winterbourne	33	ST 6480
Winterbourne Bassett	34	SU 1074
Winterbourne Dauntsey	26	SU 1734
Winterbourne Earls	26	SU 1633
Winterbourne Gunner	26	SU 1735
Winterbourne Monkton (Wilts.)	34	SU 0972
Winterbourne Stoke	34	SU 0740
Winterburn	78	SD 9358
Winterburn Resr.	78	SD 9460
Wintercleuch Fell	88	NS 9910
Winter Hill	69	SD 6514
Winterhope Reservoir	89	NY 2782
Winteringham	74	SE 9222
Winterley	69	SJ 7457
Wintersett	71	SE 3815
Winterton	74	SE 9218
Winterton-on-Sea	65	TG 4919
Winthorpe (Lincs.)	73	TF 5665
Winthorpe (Notts.)	62	SK 8156
Winton (Cumbr.)	83	NY 7810
Winton (Dorset)	26	SZ 0894
Winton Fell	83	NY 8307
Wintringham	81	SE 8873
Winwick (Cambs.)	52	TL 1080
Winwick (Ches.)	69	SJ 6092
Winwick (Northants.)	51	SP 6273
Wirksworth	60	SK 2854
Wirral	68	SJ 3181
Wirswall	59	SJ 5444
Wisbech	63	TF 4609
Wisbech St. Mary	63	TF 4208
Wisborough Green	28	TQ 0526
Wiseton	72	SK 7189
Wishaw (Strath.)	94	NS 7954
Wishaw (Warw.)	60	SP 1794
Wisp Hill	89	NY 3899
Wispington	73	TF 2071
Wissett	55	TM 3679
Wiss, The (mt.)	89	NT 2620
Wistanstow	48	SO 4385
Wistanswick	59	SJ 6629
Wistaston	59	SJ 6853
Wiston (Dyfed)	42	SN 0218
Wiston (Strath.)	95	NS 9531
Wiston (W Susx)	28	TQ 1512
Wistow (Cambs.)	53	TL 2781
Wistow (N Yorks.)	79	SE 5835
Wiswell	77	SD 7437
Witcham	53	TL 4680
Witchampton	26	ST 9806
Witchford	53	TL 5078
Witham	38	TL 8114
Witham Friary	33	ST 7440
Witham on the Hill	62	TF 0516
Withens Clough Resr.	78	SD 9822
Witherenden Hill	29	TQ 6426
Witheridge	23	SS 8014
Witherley	60	SP 3297
Withern	73	TF 4382
Withernsea	75	TA 3328
Withernwick	75	TA 1940
Withersdale Street	55	TM 2781
Withersfield	54	TL 6547
Witherslack	77	SD 4384
Witherslack Hall	77	SD 4386
Withiel	19	SW 9965
Withiel Florey	23	SS 9832
Withi Gill (mt.)	136	ND 2496
Withington (Ches.)	69	SJ 8170
Withington (Glos.)	46	SP 0315
Withington (Gtr Mches.)	69	SJ 8392
Withington (Here. and Worc.)	45	SO 5643
Withington (Shrops.)	59	SJ 5713
Withington Green	59	SJ 8031
Withleigh	23	SS 9012
Withnell	77	SD 6322
Withybrook	50	SP 4384
Withy Bush Aerodrome	42	SM 9519
Withycombe	32	ST 0141
Withyham	29	TQ 4935
Withypool	23	SS 8435
Withypool Common	23	SS 8135
Witley	28	SU 9439
Witnesham	55	TM 1850
Witney	47	SP 3509
Wittering	62	TF 0502
Wittersham	30	TQ 8927
Witton	65	TG 3331
Witton Gilbert	84	NZ 2345
Witton-le-Wear	84	NZ 1431
Witton Park	84	NZ 1730
Wiveliscombe	24	ST 0827
Wivelsfield	29	TQ 3420
Wivelsfield Green	29	TQ 3519
Wivelsfield Station	29	TQ 3219
Wivenhoe	39	TM 0321
Wivenhoe Cross	39	TM 0423
Wiveton	64	TG 0343
Wix	55	TM 1628
Wixford	50	SP 0854
Wixoe	54	TL 7142
Woburn	52	SP 9433
Woburn Abbey	52	SP 9632
Woburn Sands	52	SP 9235
Woden Law	90	NT 7612
Wokefield Park	36	SU 6765
Woking	36	TQ 0058
Wokingham	36	SU 8068
Wold Fell	78	SD 7885
Woldingham	29	TQ 3755
Wold Newton (Humbs.)	81	TA 0473
Wold Newton (Humbs.)	73	TF 2496
Wolds, The (Humbs.)	81	SE 9762
Wolds, The (Lincs.) (dist.)	64	TF 2585
Wolferlow	49	SO 6661
Wolferton	64	TF 6528
Wolfhill	108	NO 1533
Wolfhole Crag	77	SD 6257
Wolf Rock	18	SW 2612
Wolf's Castle	42	SM 9627
Wolfsdale	42	SM 9321
Woll	96	NT 4622
Wollaston (Northants.)	52	SP 9062
Wollaston (Shrops.)	58	SJ 3212
Wollerton	59	SJ 6229
Wolsingham	84	NZ 0737
Wolsingham Park Moor	84	NZ 0340
Wolston	50	SP 4175
Wolvercote	47	SP 4809
Wolverhampton	59	SO 9198
Wolverley (Here. and Worc.)	49	SO 8279
Wolverley (Shrops.)	58	SJ 4631
Wolverton (Bucks.)	52	SP 8141
Wolverton (Hants.)	35	SU 5557
Wolverton (Warw.)	50	SP 2062
Wolvey	50	SP 4387
Wolviston	85	NZ 4525
Wombleton	79	SE 6683
Wombourne	59	SO 8793
Wombwell	71	SE 3902
Womenswold	31	TR 2250
Womersley	71	SE 5319
Wonastow	45	SO 4811
Wonersh	28	TQ 0145
Wonston	35	SU 4739
Wooburn	36	SU 9187
Wooburn Green	36	SU 9188
Woodale	78	SE 0279
Woodbastwick	65	TG 3315
Woodbeck	72	SK 7777
Woodborough (Notts.)	61	SK 6347
Woodborough (Wilts.)	34	SU 1059
Woodbridge	55	TM 2749
Woodbury	21	SY 0087
Woodbury Hill (ant.)	49	SO 7464
Woodbury Salterton	24	SY 0189
Woodchester	46	SO 8302
Woodchurch	30	TQ 9434
Woodcote (Oxon.)	36	SU 6481
Woodcote (Shrops.)	59	SJ 7715
Woodcroft	45	ST 5495
Wood Dalling	65	TG 0927
Woodditton	54	TL 6559
Woodeaton	47	SP 5311
Woodend (Cumbr.)	82	SD 1696
Wood End (Herts.)	53	TL 3225
Woodend (Northants.)	51	SP 6149
Wood End (Warw.)	50	SP 1071
Wood End (Warw.)	60	SP 2498
Woodend (W Susx)	27	SU 8108
Wood Enderby	73	TF 2764
Woodfalls	26	SU 1920
Woodford (Corn.)	22	SS 2113
Woodford (Devon)	21	SX 7950
Woodford (Gtr London)	37	TQ 4090
Woodford (Gtr Mches.)	69	SJ 8982
Woodford (Northants.)	52	SP 9676
Woodford (Wilts.)	26	SU 1136
Woodford Aerodrome	69	SJ 8982
Woodford Bridge	37	TQ 4291
Woodford Green	37	TQ 4192
Woodford Halse	51	SP 5452
Woodgate (Here. and Worc.)	50	SO 9666
Woodgate (Norf.)	64	TG 0215
Woodgate (W Mids.)	50	SO 9982
Woodgate (W Susx)	28	SU 9304
Wood Green (Gtr London)	37	TQ 3191
Woodgreen (Hants.)	26	SU 1717
Woodhall	84	SD 9790
Woodhall Loch	88	NX 6867
Woodhall Spa	73	TF 1963
Woodham	36	TQ 0261
Woodham Ferrers	38	TQ 7999
Woodham Mortimer	38	TL 8205
Woodham Walter	38	TL 8006
Woodhaven	109	NO 4127
Woodhead (Grampn.)	121	NJ 7938
Woodhead (Grampn.)	121	NJ 9061
Woodhenge (ant.)	34	SU 1543
Woodhill	49	SO 7384
Woodhorn	91	NZ 2988
Woodhouse (Leic.)	61	SK 5315
Woodhouse (S Yorks.)	71	SK 4184
Woodhouse Eaves	61	SK 5214
Woodhouselee	103	NT 2364
Woodhurst	53	TL 3176
Woodingdean	29	TQ 3605
Woodland (Devon)	21	SX 7968
Woodland (Durham)	84	NZ 0726
Woodland Bay	86	NX 1795
Woodland Fell (Cumbr.)	82	SD 2589
Woodland Fell (Durham)	84	NZ 0326
Woodlands	58	SJ 3253
Woodlands (Dorset)	26	SU 0508
Woodlands (Grampn.)	119	NO 7895
Woodlands (Hants.)	26	SU 3111
Woodlands Park	36	SU 8578
Woodleigh	21	SX 7348
Woodlesford	79	SE 3629
Woodley	36	SU 7973
Woodmancote (Glos.)	46	SP 0008
Woodmancote (W Susx)	27	SU 7707
Woodmancott	35	SU 5642
Woodmansey	74	TA 0537
Woodmansterne	37	TQ 2760
Woodminton	26	SU 0122
Woodnesborough	31	TR 3156
Woodnewton	62	TL 0394
Wood Norton	64	TG 0128
Wood of Ordiequish	121	NJ 3555
Woodplumpton	77	SD 4934
Woodrising	64	TF 9803
Woodseaves (Shrops.)	59	SJ 6830
Woodseaves (Staffs.)	59	SJ 7925
Woodsend	34	SU 2275
Woodsetts	71	SK 5483
Woodsford	25	SY 7690
Woodside (Berks.)	36	SU 9371
Woodside (Herts.)	37	TL 2506
Woodside (Tays.)	108	NO 2037
Woodstock	47	SP 4416
Wood Street	28	SU 9551
Woodthorpe (Derby.)	71	SK 4574
Woodthorpe (Leic.)	61	SK 5417
Woodton	65	TM 2894
Woodtown	22	SS 4926
Woodville	60	SK 3119
Woodwalton	52	TL 2180
Wood Wick	136	HY 3923
Woodyates	26	SU 0219
Woody Bay	23	SS 6849
Woofferton	48	SO 5168
Wookey	33	ST 5145
Wookey Hole	33	ST 5347
Wool	25	SY 8486
Woolacombe	22	SS 4543
Woolaston	45	ST 5999
Woolavington	32	ST 3441
Woolbeding	27	SU 8722
Wooler	97	NT 9928
Woolfardisworthy (Devon)	22	SS 3321
Woolfardisworthy (Devon)	23	SS 8208

Key to atlas pages 18-143

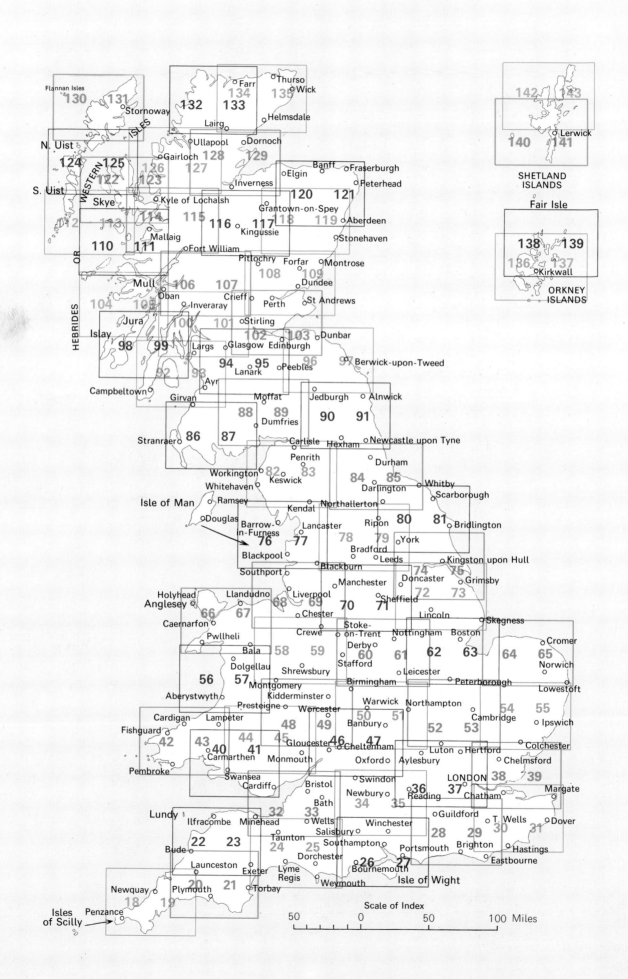

Flannan Isles
130 131 Stornoway
ISLES
N. Uist
124 125 Gairloch 128 129
WESTERN 126
127
122 123
S. Uist
Skye Kyle of Lochalsh
113 114 115 116 117 118 119 Aberdeen
110 111 Mallaig
Fort William
Pitlochry Forfar Montrose
108 109
Mull 106 107 Dundee
104 105 Oban Crieff Perth St Andrews
Inveraray
Stirling
Jura 100 101 102 103 Dunbar
98 99 Largs Glasgow Edinburgh 96
Islay 94 95 97 Berwick-upon-Tweed
92 93 Lanark Peebles
Ayr
Campbeltown Moffat Jedburgh Alnwick
Girvan 88 89 90 91
Dumfries
86 87 Carlisle Hexham Newcastle upon Tyne
Stranraer Penrith Durham
Workington 82 83 84 85
Whitehaven Keswick Darlington Whitby
Isle of Man Ramsey Northallerton Scarborough
Douglas Kendal
Barrow- Lancaster Ripon 80 81 Bridlington
in-Furness 76 77 78 79 York
Blackpool Bradford Leeds Kingston upon Hull
Southport Blackburn 74 75
Manchester Doncaster Grimsby
Holyhead Llandudno Liverpool 72 73
Anglesey 66 67 68 69 70 71 Sheffield
Caernarfon Chester Lincoln Skegness
Pwllheli Stoke- Cromer
Bala 58 59 on-Trent Nottingham Boston
Dolgellau Crewe Derby 60 61 62 63 64 65
56 57 Shrewsbury Stafford Leicester Norwich
Aberystwyth Montgomery Birmingham Peterborough Lowestoft
Kidderminster Warwick Northampton 54 55
Cardigan Lampeter Presteigne Worcester 50 51 Cambridge Ipswich
Fishguard 48 49 52 53
42 Banbury Colchester
43 44 45 Gloucester 46 47 Luton Hertford
40 41 Carmarthen Monmouth Cheltenham Oxford Aylesbury Chelmsford
Pembroke Swindon LONDON 38 39
Swansea Bristol 36 37 Margate
Cardiff Newbury Reading Chatham
Lundy 32 Bath 34 35 Guildford T. Wells Dover
Ilfracombe Minehead 33 Wells Winchester 28 29 30 31
22 23 Taunton Salisbury Southampton Brighton Hastings
Bude 24 25 Dorchester Portsmouth Eastbourne
Launceston Exeter Lyme 26 27 Bournemouth
Newquay 20 21 Regis Weymouth Isle of Wight
18 19 Plymouth Torbay
Isles Penzance
of Scilly

SHETLAND
ISLANDS
142 143
140 141 Lerwick

Fair Isle
138 139
136 137
Kirkwall
ORKNEY
ISLANDS

Scale of Index
50   0   50   100 Miles